STATISTICAL ANALYSIS FOR MANAGERIAL DECISIONS

STATISTICAL ANALYSIS FOR MANAGERIAL DECISIONS

John C. G. Boot
State University of New York at Buffalo

Edwin B. Cox
Arthur D. Little, Inc.

Second Edition

McGraw-Hill Book Company
New York   St. Louis   San Francisco   Düsseldorf   Johannesburg   Kuala Lumpur   London
Mexico   Montreal   New Delhi   Panama   Rio de Janeiro   Singapore   Sydney   Toronto

STATISTICAL ANALYSIS FOR MANAGERIAL DECISIONS

1 2 3 4 5 6 7 8 9 0   KPKP   7 9 8 7 6 5 4 3

This book was set in Bulmer by York Graphic Services, Inc. The editors were Thomas H. Kothman and Annette Hall; the designer was Jo Jones; and the production supervisor was Thomas J. LoPinto.
The printer and binder was Kingsport Press, Inc.

Library of Congress Cataloging in Publication Data

Boot, Johannes Cornelius Gerardus.
  Statistical analysis for managerial decisions.

  Bibliography: p.
  1. Decision-making. 2. Statistical decision.
I. Cox. Edwin Burk, 1930–   joint author.
II. Title.
HD69.D4B56 1974   658.4   73-8916
ISBN 0-07-006518-7

To our wives—Hinke and Myrtle
and to our children—Maren and Mark Boot
and Ned and David Cox

CONTENTS

PREFACE

This book has been written to give you, the reader, an understanding of statistical reasoning and the primary statistical techniques used in solving managerial problems. Throughout the book we have used simple computational procedures to keep attention focused on the principles involved rather than on the arithmetic. Appendix A illustrates the use of computers in solving statistical problems. A good knowledge of high school mathematics (*not* including calculus) and a willingness to think quantitatively are the only requirements for understanding what follows. The book is written for students and practitioners of management, but the principles presented are universally applicable. Each chapter contains numerous examples, and most sections are followed by several exercises, giving you a chance to try out your new knowledge after each section. The solutions are presented at the end of the chapter. Key words and phrases are shown in the margin to help you organize your thoughts, review your reading, and refer back to essential ideas.

The book is organized into three sections. Chapters 1 through 7 present basic concepts of descriptive statistics, probability, and probability distributions important in statistics. Chapter 8 contains a collection of 50 problems based on the material in Chapters 1 through 7 (solutions are not given). Chapters 9 through 13 present the most important concepts and techniques of inferential statistics, including an extensive discussion of *Bayesian* inference in Chapter 12. Chapter 14 contains a set of 50 problems based on the material in Chapters 9 through 13 (again, without solutions). (The solutions to the problems in Chapters 8 and 14 are available in the Instructor's Manual.) Chapters 15 through 19 treat a set of topics important in business and economic research—time series analysis, index numbers, statistical methods for quality assurance, design of sample surveys, and nonparametric statistics. We consider Chapters 1 through 11 essential for even a short course in statistics. The remaining chapters may be used in whatever combination seems appropriate to the length and objectives of the course. (Chapter 15 requires an understanding of Section 13.2; otherwise Chapters 12 through 19 may be taught independently of one another and in any sequence.) The reader who wants to enlarge his knowledge will find suggestions for further study in the annotated bibliography.

In this second edition we have maintained our emphasis on a blend of what we believe are the best of the "classical" and "modern" schools, that is, emphasis on application and interpretation in the classical and the concern for mathematical foundations and decision theory in the modern. In the interest of complete coverage of the topics most preferred by users of the text, we have included a new chapter on nonparametric methods. In addition, we have placed greater emphasis on the t distribution, revised and enhanced the discussion of hypothesis testing, enriched the discussion of decision theory, and introduced a discussion of the hypergeometric distribution and its applications. Tables of the t distribution and the unit normal loss integral have been added to Appendix B. Use of summation notation has been introduced, though the expanded form of summations is retained where we believe it is pedagogically preferable.

We are indebted to the Literary Executor of the late Sir Ronald A. Fisher, F.R.S., Dr. Frank Yates, F.R.S., and Oliver and Boyd Ltd., Edinburgh, for permission to use the tables on pages 621 and 633 adapted from Tables III and IV from their book *Statistical Tables for Biological, Agricultural and Medical Research.*

We are especially grateful for the many helpful comments we have received from friends and users (fortunately, these are still overlapping sets) about the book. In particular, we acknowledge the help of Roger Stanton, Robert T. Riley, James Black, Robert Berner, Kenneth Deal, Ahmed el-Dersh, George Frankfurter, Richard Hoffman, Carl Pegels, Pete Seagle, Harry Sieber, Richard Welke, David Rowe, Joseph Monks, and John Chin.

Photo copying and computer services provided by the Marine Midland Services Corporation of Western New York, Buffalo, and Arthur D. Little, Inc., Cambridge, are gratefully acknowledged.

John C. G. Boot
Edwin B. Cox

STATISTICAL ANALYSIS FOR MANAGERIAL DECISIONS

Chapter 1

INTRODUCTION

1.1 INDUCTION VERSUS DEDUCTION

Have you ever walked through an automobile dealer's showroom opening and slamming the doors of the new cars? Or have you gone to the supermarket and squeezed the tomatoes or the melons before deciding what to buy? Have you leafed through the pages of a magazine or a book trying to decide whether you want to take the time to read it?

You may not think you are a statistician—in fact you may be determined never to become one—but if you answered "yes" to any of the above questions, you behaved like a statistician, albeit an amateur statistician. A professional statistician is a specialist who develops and uses mathematical and logical methods to solve certain types of problems—some fairly simple, some very complex. Even in solving the most complex problem, however, the statistician uses a pattern of reasoning which is essentially the same as the one you use when you pinch a tomato or slam the doors on new cars. If one or two tomatoes feel solid, you figure most of the rest are solid and you buy. If the doors feel and sound well built, you figure the whole car is well built. The statistician takes *samples* and makes statements or decisions about *populations* (the larger group from which the sample is drawn). For the tomato buyer, two tomatoes are a

Samples and populations

1

sample from the population of tomatoes on display. For the car buyer, the door is a sample of the population of all components which combine to make the car. The principal differences between these shoppers and the statistician are the statistician's awareness of when statistical reasoning is being used and his knowledge of how to use it most effectively. We call the effective use of statistical reasoning *statistical analysis*.

Induction

The pattern of reasoning used by the statistician is called *induction*. We reason by induction whenever we use knowledge based on limited experience to reach conclusions which we believe apply outside the realm of our experience. If all the rocks you have ever thrown into water have sunk, you conclude by induction that all rocks will sink when thrown in water. If 5 percent of the pieces produced on a certain machine on Monday were defective, the operator might conclude, by induction, that approximately 5 percent of all parts produced on that machine the rest of the week will be defective (if no change occurs in machine, material, or operator). If, time and again, half an hour after you take an aspirin your headache disappears, you argue by induction that aspirin cures headaches. In all these examples we move from the specific evidence to the general conclusion by induction.

Induction can be misused. More than one boss has said, "You're always late for work," to a punctual secretary who happened to be late once. Such sweeping generalizations are based on induction.

Deduction

The opposite of induction is *deduction*. In deductive reasoning we start with assumptions (or axioms or postulates) and then we deduce conclusions which are implied by the assumptions. Deductive reasoning is the method used in tracing out the implications of a set of assumptions. In the final analysis, however, the worth of the end product of deduction depends on the degree to which the assumptions correspond to reality. A classic example of deductive reasoning is Euclidean geometry.

In deductive reasoning we can reach conclusions which are certain to be true, provided that the assumptions were true. By contrast, nothing can be proved with certainty by induction. Two firm tomatoes do not *prove* that the others will be of good quality as well. Inductive reasoning is somewhat frustrating in that conclusions remain uncertain. The statistician is able to live with this uncertainty because he is an expert in *measuring* it, so that he is aware of the risks he takes.

EXERCISES

1.1   When consumed in large quantities, gin and tonic, gin and orange juice, and gin and vermouth all tend to make one drunk. What might we conclude by induction? Large quantities of bourbon and water, scotch and water, and rye and water tend to make one drunk. What might we conclude by induction?

1.2   How might we argue by deduction that scotch, bourbon, and rye tend to make one drunk?

1.3   On comparing snowfall in Buffalo and Boston, data are presented which show that in 38 out of the last 40 years Buffalo had the heavier snowfall. The Bostonian says that this proves that it snows more in Buffalo than in Boston. The Buffalonian says it does not. Who is right?

1.4   As a result of a poll a paper reports that 61 percent of the population approves of the way the President handles international affairs, while 30 percent disapproves. The remaining 9 percent have no opinion. What type of reasoning is used?

1.5   A businessman states that 2 years from now the price of his raw material will be 8 percent higher. On what evidence and on what type of reasoning might he make such a statement?

1.6   A purchaser tests 25 units from a shipment of 10,000 your firm recently delivered to him, and he refuses to accept the shipment because two units failed the test. What type of reasoning is used? Discuss the merits of the decision.

1.2   STATISTICS AND ITS USES

We define statistics as follows: *Statistics is the body of theory and methodology employed in analyzing and using numerical evidence to choose one among several alternative decisions or actions when not all relevant facts are known.*

Definition of statistics

Three observations regarding the definition are noteworthy. First, we confine ourselves to numerical evidence. Many characteristics are numerical from the start—the value of gross national product, the length of an iron bar, the age of a man, the outcome of a roll of a die. Other characteristics are not in themselves numerical, but can be made so by *counting* them. The sex of a baby (male or female) is not a number, but we can count 1 for a male and zero for a female. The result—that 48 out of 100 babies were boys—*is* numerical evidence. Likewise, a home run is a home run (and not a number), but the number of home runs in a season *is* a number.

Other numerical evidence might take the form of a statement by a salesman that he thinks it is twice as likely that he will sell more rather than less than 100 cans of orange juice today, or the weatherman's stating that there is an 80 percent chance of rain tomorrow.

There are certain characteristics which are not numerical and cannot be counted, for example, intelligence. A great deal of effort is made to quantify such a characteristic. In the case of intelligence, psychologists have tests to measure it on a numerical scale, leading to the well-known intelligence quotient (IQ).

The second element of the definition which we want to emphasize is that statistics is oriented toward making wise decisions in the face of uncertainty. The purpose of analyzing the numerical evidence is to enable us to choose among alternative actions.

Thirdly, we do *not* use statistics in the sense of the man who proudly claims that he knows all baseball statistics by heart. For such, or any other collection of numerical evidence, we use the (plural) word *data*. In our definition, the word *statistics* is singular. The baseball fan uses it in the plural.

Uses of statistics

Statistics is used in many different fields. In agriculture it is widely used to determine the combination of seed strain, fertilizer, and insecticide that maximizes yield or to produce better livestock through controlled feeding and breeding procedures. In medicine it is used to test the effectiveness and possible side effects of drugs and to increase our knowledge about the spread of contagious diseases. In linguistics statistics has been used to determine the authorship of several unsigned *Federalist Papers*. In geology it is used to determine where to drill for oil to increase the chance of "striking it rich."

The use of statistical techniques, polling, to predict who will win an election is very familiar. So are all types of opinion surveys and—in a slightly different field—television rating services. In psychology, sociology, and education statistical techniques have been utilized in a wide variety of research efforts involving the study of individuals and groups. Special statistical techniques have been developed in the area known as psychometrics for the measurement of aspects of individuals' performance in learning situations. The needs of psychologists for special statistical techniques have led to the development of *nonparametric* or distribution-free *statistical methods*.

The physical sciences, including physics and chemistry, have been called the exact sciences, a name which suggests that there are no uncertainties present in the study of the physical world. This was never true, and it would probably be false to say that physical scientists have ever believed it to be true. For one thing, measurement errors create uncertainty. In recent decades, statistical techniques have found increasing application in the physical sciences, where they have influenced the design of experiments, the gathering of evidence, and the testing of theories.

These illustrations are suggestive of the breadth of the areas in which statistical techniques are fruitful. The list could be lengthened by the addition of examples from biology (particularly genetics), food technology, mining, forestry, meteorology, criminology, and so on.

Statistics is also widely and profitably used in business and economics. Its theories, methods, and computations enable one to answer such diverse questions as: What is the average amount of money a baseball fan spends while watching the game? What percentage of customers leaves the department store, having spent over $100? How much more does a basket of goods cost today than it would have cost 5 years ago? If an average of 5 percent of the units produced are defective, what is the probability that a sample of 20 contains no defectives? What is the average waiting time for a customer in a post office, and what, on the other hand, is the average idle time for the clerk? Can we support the claim that bankteller A is faster than bankteller B? Does the manufacturer tell the truth when he claims that a package contains 16 ounces? What are the sales of cans of orange juice next Wednesday morning going to be, or at least within what limits can we be virtually certain they will be? Can a keypunch girl who made 15 mistakes in keypunching 1,000 numbers still maintain that she makes an average of no more than 1 percent of errors? Can we believe a manufacturer who claims that 99 percent of his lightbulbs burn at least 500 hours? What is the probability that someone soliciting for a job answers all 10 true-false questions of the competence test correctly, although the prospective employee is purely guessing each time? How many accounts should an accounting firm check to be 95 percent certain that it can estimate the true percentage of erroneous balances within $\frac{1}{2}$ percent? To what extent and how are consumption and income related? Are possession of a store credit card and the amount a customer spends related?

In all these cases the data will be numerical, and in all these cases one can easily think of someone who would be very interested in the answer if he had certain decisions to make. How many hot dogs should the vendor have in stock when there are 30,000 fans in the ball park? Does teller A deserve a raise? Should we give customers a free radio to induce them to sign up for a credit card in my store?

Uses of
statistics
in business

EXERCISES

1.7   If you see many clouds in the sky in the morning, you may take
       your raincoat with you. How is statistical analysis used to reach
       this decision?

1.8   After a series of interviews and tests, a firm decides to hire a job
       applicant. How is statistical analysis used to reach this decision?

1.3   DATA

It is impossible to overemphasize the importance of knowing the quality
of the data to which a statistical technique is applied in a particular
situation. Data are the raw material to which the statistician applies his
analysis much as wood is the raw material for the cabinet maker or marble
the raw material for the sculptor. Before working with their raw material,
both the cabinet maker and the sculptor take great pains to study its
structure and properties to be sure that it is suited to their purpose. Once
assured that they can produce something of value from the available raw
material, these artisans then plan how they will use it. They will not use
the wood or stone if they find basic structural flaws. Their use of acceptable
raw material takes into consideration the properties of the material so that
they do no less than the best which can be done with it.

**Problems of
definition**
In working with data, there is first the problem of definition. Suppose
we have data on unemployment. What is unemployment? We all agree
that the father of a family of four who badly needs a job but cannot find
one is unemployed. But is the 45-year-old woman who just saw her
youngest offspring off to college and now wants a job unemployed? Is
the student who cannot find a job during the summer unemployed? Is
a man who works 20 hours a week unemployed? To be sure, these are
matters of definition, but it is well to realize that all these issues must
be solved before unemployment (however defined) can be measured.

Similarly, the profit of a company is drastically different depending
upon whether it is pretax or aftertax, upon the method of depreciation,
and upon the policy in forming reserves. To compare the profit figures
given by companies in their annual reports without considering these
differences may give a totally false impression.

**Problems of
measurement**
Measurement poses problems nearly as vexing as those of definition.
It is relatively easy to measure your height up to the nearest inch (even
though morning and evening heights of the same individual are slightly
different, which means that we must define height more precisely). But

to measure the gross national product, or intelligence, or even the wind velocity, is something else again. Whenever possible, the statistician should insist on participating in the defining and measuring process to produce data with the properties needed for the analysis planned. Only in this way can the statistician know the properties of his raw material as the cabinet maker and sculptor do.

When the data used in an analysis are specifically created for that analysis, they are referred to as *primary data.* They are clearly the very best, for the statistician who is aware of the goal sought in the analysis and the statistical techniques to be used is also aware of the precise definitions and techniques of measurement that will yield data perfectly suited to the uses to be made of them. Unfortunately, the high cost of assembling primary data often prevents gathering data specifically for a particular analysis. Assembling primary data usually involves creating new definitions and measuring instruments such as questionnaires or interview forms, and training people to use these specifically designed measuring instruments. When the gathering of primary data is undertaken as part of an analysis, the data collection phase usually absorbs the major part of the allotted time and financial resources.

Primary data

Secondary data are data which were not gathered specifically to meet the needs of the problem at hand. They are often used because they are readily available, usually in company files or government publications. The user of secondary data cannot influence the definitions and means of measurement which produced the data. Yet, if the data he uses are to be satisfactory substitutes for primary data, he must assure himself that the definition and measurement processes which gave rise to the secondary data would be the same or nearly the same as those he would have preferred to use. Making sure that this is so is difficult because the details of the procedures which led to a particular set of secondary data may be unavailable. Data from agencies of the federal government are usually reported with some information about their origins, although the completeness of this supplemental information varies a great deal from agency to agency. Often data which are reported by federal government agencies were not assembled by the agency as the primary source, but were taken from other sources within the government or private organizations. Secondary data are not always *once* removed from their primary source when they appear in published form but may be two, three, or more steps removed. This is important, since each time a body of data comes under new jurisdiction, the possibilities for misinterpretation and changes in the descriptive material accompanying the data increase.

Secondary data

Origins of
inaccurate
data

As a special warning, let us emphasize a number of ways which may give rise to inaccurate data quite apart from poor definitions or erroneous measurements. Whenever the data result from questions being answered by human beings, a host of errors is introduced. Tests have shown that only 76 percent of the people asked for their age give an age exactly 1 higher when asked the same question exactly 1 year later. At least 24 percent must have been in error at least once! On the other hand, 99 percent of the fathers and mothers agreed on the number of children in their family. This is quite high, but one cannot help wondering about the other 1 percent. In cases such as these, the questions are presumably clear and well defined, yet the answers are inconsistent.

When *opinions* are asked rather than facts and when the question cannot be phrased completely neutrally, an unlimited source of error is admitted. The question, "Do you favor the United States' contributing a billion dollars a year to the United Nations?" will have a far more unfavorable response than the question, "Do you favor the United States' supporting a world organization to promote peace?" Moreover, the answers to these questions need not be of the yes-or-no type. They can vary from a long diatribe against communism or the Secretary-General to a heated defense of a world law (notice that both answers evade the question); the answer could also be a reasoned yes-and-no. The pollster must then classify the answer, which introduces inevitable errors. In fact, even the person of the pollster may well introduce distortion, by his (or her) voice, intonation, or age or by being angry, alluring, and so on. However you slice it, polling results should be interpreted with great care, even if they are primary data.

Data which are the result of counting are equally suspect. Even if it is perfectly certain what should be counted and what not (the definition problem), the actual process remains difficult. The decennial census, which counts the people living in the United States at a particular moment of time, clearly will be marred by errors of omission, double counting, false answers, counting dead, and not counting just-born babies, etc.

Another source of error enters when the time dimension becomes relevant. Data which represent the value of some variable at a particular time or over a certain time interval rely for their accuracy on the ability of the observer to associate values of the variable with instants or intervals of time. It is very difficult to say what a company's inventory turnover rate was on a given day or what the profits of a particular branch of a company were during a given month. Such statements are made with great frequency, of course, but according to arbitrary conventions which frequently lead to distortions in the data. Changes over time play an important role in many studies of business phenomena. The factor of time in assessing the accuracy of data is more important in the social sciences than in the natural sciences.

EXERCISES

1.9   In defining the price paid for an automobile, the profit from toasters made by a large appliance manufacturer, or the number of suicides in a year, there is ample room for differences in definition and measurement. Discuss some.

1.4 COMPUTERS

The coming of age of the computer has changed some aspects of statistics. Computers can store massive quantities of data and can perform all sorts of computations on them with little human effort. Computers can be programmed to compute many numbers we discuss here, such as averages, ratios, rates of change, variances, and correlation coefficients. The computer can be programmed to print out the data in tables or even to chart the data in a picture. In Appendix A we have printed out six examples of fairly routine statistical analyses which the computer can perform very efficiently, accurately, and cheaply.

Computers

The computer affects the use of statistical analysis. Its ability to aid in the collection and reporting of masses of data means, in some cases, that it will be possible to get a complete count in situations that were formerly studied through sampling methods. The uncertainty forced on us at one time because we were unable to handle all the data on a particular situation owing to limitations in time or funds then disappears. Other elements of uncertainty will remain, however efficient the computer may be, since the future is intrinsically uncertain. There is, therefore, no danger that the computer will put the statistician out of work. In fact, his work may have increased, since many studies previously impossible because of sheer size can now be handled.

The six examples printed in Appendix A are all routine statistical analyses which were run on time-sharing computer systems. Time-sharing computer systems are often used for problems which have been preprogrammed; one only has to call up the codeword and type in the data. The computer then knows what to do with these data and will give the answer, as in Appendix A. Routine statistical techniques, such as multiple regression analysis or analysis-of-variance techniques, the computations for which are very extensive and laborious if done by hand or desk calculator, are all preprogrammed and easy, although not always cheap, to run.

For less common tests one may need to write the program himself. Such a program is a set of instructions in a language the computer can understand, for example, FORTRAN IV or ALGOL. Different computers understand different languages, although most can be equipped with a translator. The writing of such programs is an art in itself, and not discussed in this book.

EXERCISES

1.10   Before the age of computers, not all individual federal income tax returns were audited. Today they are. Comment on this.

Answers to Exercises

1.1   The first triplet of observations leads to the correct conclusion that gin tends to make one drunk. A completely analogous argument for the second triplet leads to the wrong conclusion that water tends to make one drunk. This shows that induction may lead to false results.

1.2   Assumption: alcohol (C_2H_5OH) tends to make one drunk. Observation: scotch, bourbon, and rye contain alcohol. Ergo, scotch, bourbon, and rye tend to make one drunk.

1.3   It all depends what we mean by "prove." If we think of it as indicating absolute certainty, surely nothing has been proved. All induction is uncertain. If we consider strong evidence as proof of sorts, then the data prove something. A statistician, faced with this evidence would, with his kit of tools, be able to conclude that there is an extremely high probability that it snows more in Buffalo than in Boston.

1.4   Again, this is basically an inductive argument. Apparently, of all the people actually polled, 61 percent were satisfied, 30 percent were dissatisfied, and 9 percent had no opinion. Induction enters when these results, based on a *sample*, are now assumed to hold for the *population* as a whole.

1.5   Apparently the businessman has observed that during the past few years the price of his raw material has increased approximately 4 percent a year. He may reason that the observed experience of the past few years is representative of the behavior of this price in general. Therefore, by induction from the specific to the general, he concludes that the price will continue to rise at the observed rate. Alternatively, he may *assume* that the past trend will continue in the future and deduce his statement from this assumption.

1.6   The purchaser used induction when he generalized from the performance of the test units to the entire shipment. The percentage of test units which failed, 8 percent, was apparently too large. Whether this decision has merit depends on the costs if a good shipment is rejected (the shipment might contain fewer defectives than 8 percent) and the costs if a bad shipment is accepted.

1.7   Subconsciously or deliberately, you realize that there is a large probability of rain when there are many clouds. This assessment will be a consequence of evidence, built up through long experience, that 80 out of 100 times when the sky is cloudy it rains. You now must choose an action (take your coat or do not), and you decide to take it along.

1.8   From long experience the personnel manager can estimate the probability of success on the job for an applicant with a particular combination of personal characteristics (shown in interviews) and test scores. The probability that this applicant will succeed is high enough to justify hiring him; i.e., the risk he will fail is low enough that the personnel manager is willing to take it.

1.9   The price paid for an automobile may or may not include financing charges, allowance for a trade in, taxes, cost of optional equipment, delivery charges, and so on. Each of these must be specifically mentioned in the definition of "price paid." The main problem in determining profit from one product (toasters) arises from the difficulty of allocating fixed costs over the various products made in a plant; for example, what percentage of the night watchman's pay should be charged to toaster production? With suicides the problem is how to report the questionable cases—as accidents or suicides? If a driver slams a car against a bridge post on a clear day with no visible cause, it is recorded as an accident even though studies indicate many such "accidents" are suicides.

1.10   It was too costly to verify all returns by manual labor. Not only can a computer perform the purely mechanical aspects (e.g., additions) much better, but it also has a much better memory so that it can compare consecutive returns for consistency. The weakness of a computer is a lack of ability to interpret exceptional cases. The computer will recognize them and call attention to them for a clerk to review.

Chapter 2

PROBABILITY

2.1 THE CONCEPT OF PROBABILITY

Uncertainty is an established fact of life. It is uncertain how many cars Detroit will produce next year, what the prime interest rate will be next month, whether an expected baby will be a boy or a girl, whether the price of a specific stock will be higher tomorrow than today, or whether a tossed coin will come up heads or tails. All these examples illustrate that the future is uncertain. But uncertainty about the present and past is also prevalent. A member of a jury may be uncertain whether a witness is speaking the truth, and you may be uncertain where your glasses are. It is uncertain in what year Erasmus was born, or how old the earth is.

Uncertainty

While all these matters may be uncertain, they can clearly be more so or less so. For example, in New England it is nearly certain that it will not snow during July, it is not so certain that it will not snow during May, and it is very *un*likely that it will *not* snow during March. Also, the experienced manager of a food store may believe that it is nearly certain that he will sell more than 70 cans of orange juice on a Wednesday, not so certain that he will sell more than 85 cans, and rather unlikely that he will sell more than 100 cans. The terminology in all these cases is suggestive, but not very precise. What does "rather unlikely" mean, and

13

Probability

how does it compare with "very unlikely" or contrast with "nearly certain"? These problems are answered by introducing probabilities. *Probability is a number on a scale, or yardstick, used to measure uncertainty.*

The probability yardstick has a length of 1, and measures from zero to 1. The more unlikely an event, the closer the probability will be to zero. In the extreme case that an event never occurs, its probability equals zero. The probability that a can of orange juice bought at your neighborhood supermarket will be filled with pure gold is zero. So is the probability that the Golden Gate Bridge will evaporate. If an event is certain to occur, it has probability 1. The probability that Easter will fall on a Sunday is 1. So is the probability that it will snow in Vermont during the winter.

The assignment of a numerical value for probabilities between these extreme values is more difficult. It is useful to distinguish three different types of probability assessments.

Subjective probability

The first type of assessment is largely *subjective*. It may differ from person to person, or from time to time for the same person. I may presently believe that the probability that the prime interest rate will be constant for the next 30 days is .80, but someone else may believe it is no more than .40. Should that be the case, we can arrange a bet acceptable to both of us. Frequent betting is a clear indication of different probability assessments made by individuals. Another illustration is provided by trading on the stock market, where people who think stock will appreciate buy millions of shares each day for the same price at which other people sell because they think the shares are going to decline in value. Many probability assessments have at least an element of subjective judgment. Section 12.3 will present more details.

Logical probability

The second type of assessment is *logical* and based on considerations of symmetry. By just looking at a coin, a die, or a deck of cards, we find no reason for believing one outcome to be more likely than another. Thus we conclude that the probability that a roll of a die will produce a 3 is $\frac{1}{6}$, since there are six outcomes, none of which is more or less likely than any other. The probability that a draw from a well-shuffled deck of cards will give the ♠A is $\frac{1}{52}$, since there are 52 cards only one of which is the ♠A. The kind of pure "laboratory" probabilities thus generated by coins, dice, and cards makes them very suitable for illustrative exercises.

As an example, let us ask for the probability of throwing a total of 5 with a pair of dice. The answer is $\frac{4}{36}$, for there are four totals of 5, $(1,4)$, $(2,3)$, $(3,2)$, and $(4,1)$, and a grand total of 36 different outcomes, as exhibited in Table 2.1.

TABLE 2.1   POSSIBLE OUTCOMES IN THROWING TWO DICE

First die shows	Second die shows					
	1	2	3	4	5	6
1	1, 1	1, 2	1, 3	1, 4	1, 5	1, 6
2	2, 1	2, 2	2, 3	2, 4	2, 5	2, 6
3	3, 1	3, 2	3, 3	3, 4	3, 5	3, 6
4	4, 1	4, 2	4, 3	4, 4	4, 5	4, 6
5	5, 1	5, 2	5, 3	5, 4	5, 5	5, 6
6	6, 1	6, 2	6, 3	6, 4	6, 5	6, 6

We can also determine the probability of throwing a total of *at least* 10. By counting, we see that there are six outcomes giving the result of at least 10. In total there are 36 outcomes. By considerations of symmetry all outcomes are equally likely, and thus the correct answer is $\frac{6}{36}$. This simple expedient of counting favorable outcomes and possible outcomes, and determining the probability as their ratio, is only valid *if all outcomes are equally likely.*

The third type of assessment is *experimental.* If we are interested in determining the probability of some event, we can make a large number of trials of an experiment in which the event can result. We then count the number of times that the event does result. We then conclude

$$\text{Probability} = \frac{\text{number of trials in which event did result}}{\text{total number of trials}}$$

For example, let us be interested in the probability that a new baby will be a boy. We may then proceed by collecting data on monthly births in a hospital. These data are given in Table 2.2. From the table we see that during February 295 babies were born, 153 of which were boys. During the year there were a total of 3,774 births, 1,930 of which were boys. We are now tempted to conclude that the probability that a newborn baby is a boy is given—roughly—by $\frac{1,930}{3,774}$, or 51.1 percent. Our confidence in this result is increased when we compare these percentages over a number of years, and find 51.2, 50.0, 50.2, 51.1, 51.2, 50.7, and 51.8

Experimental probability

TABLE 2.2   MONTHLY BIRTHS IN A HOSPITAL, BY SEX (1963)

	Total	Boys	Girls	Boys, percent
January	321	144	177	44.9
February	295	153	142	51.9
March	333	175	158	52.6
April	296	161	135	54.4
May	331	173	158	52.3
June	313	165	148	52.7
July	341	173	168	50.7
August	305	151	154	49.5
September	338	168	170	49.7
October	304	150	154	49.3
November	304	159	145	52.3
December	293	158	135	53.9
Total	3,774	1,930	1,844	51.1

as results for 1960 to 1966. Over all 7 years combined, 27,895 children were born in this hospital, 14,182 of which, or 50.8 percent, were boys. We conclude that, roughly, a newborn baby has a 51 percent probability of being a boy. All further available evidence corroborates this result. At age zero, girls are in short supply. (Fortunately, they are the sturdier type and at marriage age the numbers are about equal.)

Finally, a word of warning. Though the probability that a roll of a die will produce a 3 is $\frac{1}{6}$, this does not mean that out of every six throws, exactly one will result in a 3. There may be zero 3s, or one, . . . , or all six outcomes could be 3. Similarly the fact that the probability that a baby will be a boy is .51 does not imply that every single month the ratio of boys to total births will be precisely .51. It only means that in the long run, on the average, the ratio is .51. On the other hand, as we proceed, we will be able to answer questions such as, "What is the probability that in six throws of a die three 3s show up?" or "What is the probability that 144 out of 321 babies born are boys?"

EXERCISES

2.1   What is the probability of being born on Wednesday?

2.2   What is the probability that the New York Stock Exchange will be open for business on Christmas Day this year?

2.3   What is the probability that the price of premium gasoline will
       be higher next year than this year? How did you arrive at your
       answer?

2.4   What is the probability of throwing exactly 7 with two dice?

2.5   What is the probability that the difference between the numbers
       showing when two dice are rolled is 2?

2.2   THE SAMPLE SPACE OF AN EXPERIMENT

If an act leads to one of several different outcomes, we call it an *experiment*.   Experiment
In the previous sections we discussed several experiments: throwing a die
leads to 1, 2, 3, 4, 5, or 6; the 36 different outcomes presented in Table
2.1 result from throwing two dice.

Our use of the word experiment includes, but is broader than, the
familiar laboratory experiment where conditions are carefully controlled.
In business research, experiments include asking a worker if he belongs
to a union, observing the brand of peanut butter bought by a shopper,
counting the cars passing a toll booth before the first Cadillac appears,
or measuring the temperature in a blast furnace. *The collection of possible*   Sample space
outcomes of an experiment is called its sample space. Furthermore, the
sample space of an experiment is said to have as many points as there
are different outcomes to the experiment. In the throw of one die, the
sample space has 6 points because there are six different outcomes. There
are 36 points in the sample space of the experiment which consists of
throwing two dice. (Notice in particular that (1,4) and (4,1) are considered
different outcomes.) In the toss of a coin, the sample space has 2 points
because there are two different outcomes, head (H) and tail (T). If we
flip two coins, the sample space has 4 points: (H,H), (H,T), (T,H), (T,T).

In questioning the worker about union membership, the sample space
has 2 points—"yes" and "no." In observing the brand of peanut butter
bought, the sample space has as many points as there are brands of peanut
butter. In counting the number of cars passing the toll booth, the sample
space has infinitely many points—0, 1, 2, . . . , 117, 118, . . . because
although the next car may be a Cadillac, it is possible that a Cadillac
will never pass this particular booth. In measuring the temperature in a
blast furnace, the sample space has, in principle, infinitely many points
since there are infinitely many different temperatures.

The union membership example above describes an experiment
leading to two different outcomes. This is a "dichotomous experi-

ment"—yes or no, heads or tails, acceptable or not acceptable. The peanut butter example gives rise to a finite number of specific outcomes, and the Cadillac example to an infinite number of specific outcomes. In the blast furnace example there are an infinite number of outcomes, for example, all outcomes in the range 1000 to 2500°C, which cannot all be specified or enumerated. The outcomes of such an experiment are represented by a "continuous variable"—temperature, time, height.

The determination of the number of points in the sample space is not always easy. For example, how many points are there in the sample space if the experiment consists of throwing three dice? The answer is 216, for there are six outcomes for the first die, which can be combined with each of the six different outcomes for the second die (for a total of $6 \times 6 = 36$ different combinations, all given explicitly in Table 2.1), and finally these can be combined with the six different outcomes on the last die (for a total of $6 \times 6 \times 6 = 216$ different points in the sample space).

The problem of counting points in the sample space is sometimes more complicated still. We will discuss this in detail in Chapter 4, "Combinatorial Analysis."

The expression "the number of points in the sample space" is fully equivalent to "the number of different outcomes to which an experiment can lead," but is somewhat shorter. *Whenever each outcome is equally likely*, the number of points in the sample space is the denominator of the ratio which determines the probability. In Exercises 2.4 and 2.5 the denominator was 36, that is, the number of points in the sample space.

EXERCISES

2.6   How many points are there in the sample space if the experiment consists in drawing a card from a full deck of bridge cards? Hence, what is the probability of drawing ♠Q from a well-shuffled deck?

2.7   How many different outcomes are there in simultaneously tossing a penny, a nickel, and a dime?

2.8   *Stockmarket example:* On any given day, compared with the previous day, a stock can rise, remain unchanged, or decline. How many points has the sample space? Next consider *two* stocks and all possible rise/no change/decline combinations. How many points are there in the sample space?

2.9   *Scheduling example:* A job consists of two tasks—grading (G) and paving (P). Each task can require 1, 2, 3, or 4 days, depending on the weather, terrain, and other factors. Paving cannot begin until grading is finished. The experiment consists of observing the time required for each task. How many points are in the sample space? Suppose the experiment consists of observing the total time required to complete the job. List the points in this sample space.

2.3 THE EVENT SPACE

We may speak of the *event* of "throwing an even number with one die." The outcomes 2, 4, and 6 lead to the occurrence of this event. We may also speak of the event "throwing a total of exactly 5 with two dice." The collection of outcomes leading to the occurrence of this event is (1,4), (2,3), (3,2), and (4,1). If the event is "drawing a diamond from a deck of cards," the collection of outcomes leading to this event consists of 13 outcomes, ♦2, ♦3, . . . , ♦K, ♦A.

In each of these cases, an event occurs when *one* of a collection of outcomes materializes. We refer to this collection of outcomes as the *event space*, and the number of points in the event space is equal to the number of outcomes leading to the event. In the examples above, there are 3, 4, and 13 points in the respective event spaces. The event space is a subset of the sample space; it can never have more points than the sample space.

Event space

In Table 2.3 we present a complete deck of cards, with the 52 possible outcomes of a draw of a card as the 52 points in the sample space. Suppose we now ask for the probability of the event "drawing an honor card," that is, "drawing a 10, J, Q, K, or A." Clearly there are 20 points in the event space, and 52 in the sample space, so the answer is $\frac{20}{52}$. The probability of the event "drawing a spade" is, by an analogous

TABLE 2.3   SAMPLE SPACE OF DRAWING ONE CARD FROM A DECK

	2	3	4	5	6	7	8	9	10	J	Q	K	A
♣	·	·	·	·	·	·	·	·	·	·	·	·	·
♦	·	·	·	·	·	·	·	·	·	·	·	·	·
♥	·	·	·	·	·	·	·	·	·	·	·	·	·
♠	·	·	·	·	·	·	·	·	·	·	·	·	·

TABLE 2.4   STOCKMARKET EXAMPLE

| | Stock II | | |
Stock I	Rises	Unchanged	Declines
Rises	·	·	·
Unchanged	·	·	·
Declines	·	·	·

argument, $\frac{13}{52}$. In both these cases, the denominator is given by the number of points in the sample space and the numerator by the number of points in the event space.

Recall that the correct probability can only be obtained in this way *if all outcomes are equally likely*. Consider, by contrast, the stockmarket example illustrated in Table 2.4. Clearly, there are 9 points in the sample space. Consider the event "neither of the stocks declines." There are 4 points in this event space. Thus, one may be tempted to conclude that the probability of "neither stock declines" is $\frac{4}{9}$. This conclusion, however, is too hasty because in this example the condition that all outcomes are equally likely is not necessarily met. In such cases the simple expedient of counting points in the event space and in the sample space does not suffice. Empirical evidence is called for, as in the example of the babies, where we found that the probability of a boy is .51 rather than .50, which would be the ratio of the number of points in the event space to the number of points in the sample space.

EXERCISES

2.10   What is the probability of drawing a 5 *or* a club?

2.11   If there are 10 winning tickets in a lottery of 1,000 tickets, what is the probability of winning if you hold one ticket?

2.12   If it rains 100 out of 366 days per year, is it true that the probability of rain *tomorrow* is $\frac{100}{366}$?

2.13   For each of the two sample spaces in the *Scheduling example* (Exercise 2.9), list the points comprising the event "job takes exactly 4 days." Do the same for the event "job takes 1 week or more."

2.4 MUTUALLY EXCLUSIVE AND COLLECTIVELY EXHAUSTIVE EVENTS

As is obvious from the name, *events are mutually exclusive if they cannot* *occur together, so that on any one trial of an experiment at most one of the* *events will happen.* Examples of mutually exclusive events are "throwing even" and "throwing odd" with one die; "drawing a spade," "drawing a diamond," and "drawing a club" in drawing one card from a deck; "both stocks rise" and "at least one stock declines" on the stockmarket. In the terminology of the previous section, if events are mutually exclusive, their event spaces have no points in common.

> Mutually exclusive

By contrast, the events "drawing a spade" and "drawing a queen" are not mutually exclusive, for one could draw ♠Q. In throwing one die, the events "an even number" and "at least 3" are not mutually exclusive, for one might throw 4 or 6.

A particularly easy way to obtain two mutually exclusive events is to consider an event and its negation, such as "even" and "*not* even"; "spade" and "*not* a spade"; or in general terms, "A" and "*not*-A."

Events are collectively exhaustive if on any one trial of an experiment *it is certain that at least one of these events will occur.* The events "a red card is drawn" and "a black card is drawn" are collectively exhaustive. So are the events "neither stock declined" and "at least one stock declined." In tossing three coins, the four events "zero head up," "one head up," "two heads up," and "three heads up" are collectively exhaustive, as are the two events "at least one head up" and "at most two heads up."

> Collectively exhaustive

In drawing from a deck of cards, the events "a red card" and "a spade" are not collectively exhaustive, for one might draw a club. Neither are, in rolling three dice, the four events "the total is at least 12," "the total is at most 9," "the total is even," and "the total is divisible by 3" collectively exhaustive, for indeed one could throw a total of 11. (There are 27 different ways to get a total of 11, and a total of 216 different outcomes, so the probability of throwing 11 is $\frac{27}{216}$, or $12\frac{1}{2}$ percent.)

A particularly easy way to produce collectively exhaustive events is to state an event and then its negation. In drawing a card, the events "a diamond" and "*not* a diamond" are collectively exhaustive. In tossing coins the events "exactly one head" and "*not* exactly one head" are also collectively exhaustive. In both cases the latter event is just the negation of the former event.

Events may be mutually exclusive and not collectively exhaustive.

In tossing two coins the events "two heads" and "two tails" fit this description. On the other hand, the events "at least one head" and "at least one tail" illustrate that events may be collectively exhaustive and not mutually exclusive.

As we saw above, if events are mutually exclusive, they cannot occur together, so that *at most one* will materialize. If events are collectively exhaustive, *at least one* of them will occur. Therefore, if events are mutually exclusive *and* collectively exhaustive, *exactly* one of them will occur.

In tossing two coins, the three events "no head," "one head," and "two heads" are collectively exhaustive and mutually exclusive. So are the events "both tails" and "at least one head," or the events "both coins show the same side up" and "the coins show different sides up."

An event plus its negation form a pair of mutually exclusive and collectively exhaustive events. "Both stocks unchanged" and "*not* both stocks unchanged" (or "at least one stock changed") is such a pair. If the probability of an event is given by p, then the probability of its negation is given by $1 - p$. If the probability of throwing a 3 with one die is $\frac{1}{6}$, the probability of *not* throwing a 3 is $1 - \frac{1}{6} = \frac{5}{6}$. If the probability that both stocks remain unchanged is given by .11, the probability that at least one stock changes is given by $1 - .11 = .89$.

Master
example

It is useful to review these concepts with the help of the following master example:

"Stock I rises" and "Stock I declines" are mutually exclusive, but not collectively exhaustive, events.

"Stock I does not rise" and "Stock I does not decline" are collectively exhaustive, but not mutually exclusive, events.

"Stock I rises" and "Stock I does not rise" are mutually exclusive and collectively exhaustive events.

Classifications

In many cases, objects may be grouped in mutually exclusive and collectively exhaustive classes. For example, human beings might be placed in classes according to height: shorter than 5 feet, between 5 feet and 6 feet (including these limits), or over 6 feet. Companies might be grouped according to annual profits: less than $1 million, between $1 million and $10 million (including the lower limit), between $10 million and $100 million (including the lower limit), and $100 million and over. The classification need not be based on numerical evidence. Students may be grouped by field of major, laborers by whether or not they are unionized, or firms by industry. Classification of firms in mutually exclusive and collectively exhaustive industries is obviously difficult and largely arbitrary.

EXERCISES

2.14   In the *Stockmarket example* (Exercise 2.8), are the events "at least one stock remains unchanged" and "stock I rises" mutually exclusive? Are the events "both stocks did the same" and "at least one stock declined" collectively exhaustive?

2.15   Determine one or more reasonable classification schemes for the farms in the United States.

2.16   In classifying the buildings in a city it is proposed to use the following classes: commercial, residential, and institutional. Criticize this classification scheme.

2.5 PROBABILITY NOTATION

At this point, let us introduce some shorthand notation. When A, B, and C are events, then P(A), P(B), and P(C) stand for the *probability of A,* the *probability of B,* and the *probability of C.* These will always be numbers between 0 and 1, including the limits. The expression P(A *or* B) will denote the probability of A *or* B (or both) occurring. In probability theory the "or" is always *inclusive.* If we tell an employee he may have Washington's Birthday *or* Veterans Day as a holiday, he may choose one and only one day. Here the *or* is *exclusive.* On the other hand, if the boss informs you that you will be promoted if you land a contract with firm A *or* with firm B, obviously you will be promoted if you land contracts with both firms. This is the *inclusive or.* We repeat that in probability theory, the *or* is always inclusive: if both A *and* B happen, the condition A *or* B is satisfied.

Probability notation

Inclusive "or"

An example will illustrate more complicated possibilities. Let us throw a die, and let A stand for the event "an even outcome," B for the event "a 3," and C for the event "a 1 *or* 6." Then the following expressions are translated as indicated:

P(A *or* B) = the probability of an even number *or* a 3;
$$\text{hence the probability of a 2, 3, 4, or } 6 = \tfrac{2}{3}$$

P(A *and* C) = the probability of an even number *and* a "1 *or* 6";
$$\text{hence the probability of a } 6 = \tfrac{1}{6}$$

P(A *or* B *or* C) = the probability of an even number *or* a 3 *or* a "1 *or* 6";
hence the probability of 1, 2, 3, 4, or 6 = $\frac{5}{6}$

P(A *and* B *and* C) = the probability of an even number *and* a 3 *and* a
"1 *or* 6," a set of conditions not met by any possible outcome = 0

It is important to recognize that P(A) + P(B) is simply the sum of
two probabilities, and hence whatever A and B may stand for, the value
of P(A) + P(B) will invariably be between 0 and 2, including these limits.
By contrast P(A *and* B) and P(A *or* B) will always be between 0 and
1. Furthermore, P(A *and* B) will never be greater than P(A *or* B), for
(A *or* B) occurs whenever (A *and* B) occurs, but the reverse is not true.

A rule which is valid for the special case where A, B, and C are
three events which are mutually exclusive and collectively exhaustive is

$$P(A) + P(B) + P(C) = 1$$

However, if A, B, and C are mutually exclusive but *not* collectively
exhaustive, we must have

$$P(A) + P(B) + P(C) < 1$$

In the reverse case, if A, B, and C are collectively exhaustive but *not*
mutually exclusive, we will have

$$P(A) + P(B) + P(C) > 1$$

Finally, if A, B, and C are neither mutually exclusive nor collectively
exhaustive, then P(A) + P(B) + P(C) may be smaller than 1, equal to
1, or greater than 1. It can never be greater than 3, or smaller than zero.

If we toss three coins, the sample space consists of 8 points, which
are listed in Table 2.5 in order of the number of heads appearing. All
outcomes are equally likely, so the probability of getting exactly one head

TABLE 2.5 SAMPLE SPACE OF TOSSING THREE COINS

H	H	H	3 heads
H	H	T	
H	T	H	2 heads
T	H	H	
H	T	T	
T	H	T	1 head
T	T	H	
T	T	T	No heads

is $\frac{3}{8}$. The events "no head," "one head," "two heads," and "three heads" are clearly mutually exclusive and collectively exhaustive; indeed, their respective probabilities sum to 1,

$$\tfrac{1}{8} + \tfrac{3}{8} + \tfrac{3}{8} + \tfrac{1}{8} = 1$$

The events "no heads" and "at least two heads" are mutually exclusive but not collectively exhaustive. We find for the sum of their probabilities

$$\tfrac{1}{8} + \tfrac{4}{8} = \tfrac{5}{8} < 1$$

in accordance with the general rule. The events "at least one head" and "at most one head" are collectively exhaustive, but not mutually exclusive. Their probabilities sum to

$$\tfrac{7}{8} + \tfrac{4}{8} = \tfrac{11}{8} > 1$$

Finally, consider the pairs of events:

> "One head" and "an odd number of heads"
> "One head" and "*not* two heads"
> "One head" and "at least one head"

None of these pairs of events is either mutually exclusive or collectively exhaustive. The sum of their probabilities is, respectively, $\frac{7}{8}$, 1, and $\frac{10}{8}$—in turn, smaller than 1, equal to 1, and greater than 1.

In particular, let us consider the events "one head" and "*not* two heads." These events are clearly not mutually exclusive, since if one head shows up, *both* events occur simultaneously. Neither are they collectively exhaustive, for if two heads show up, *neither* event has occurred. We reemphasize that although

$$\text{P(one head)} + \text{P}(not \text{ two heads}) = \tfrac{3}{8} + \tfrac{5}{8} = 1$$

it is not necessarily true that either of the two events specifically mentioned will happen.

EXERCISES

2.17   In drawing from a deck of cards, consider the events:

> A "red card"   D "club"
> B "heart"   E "heart *or* club"
> C "spade"   F "*not* a spade"

(a) Numerically what is:

P(B) + P(C) + P(D)?
P(A) + P(C) + P(D)?
P(A) + P(C) + P(E)?

(b) Determine also:

P(A) + P(B)
P(A) + P(E)
P(A) + P(F)

(c) Relate these results to the above discussion.

2.18   A store manager states that the probability for sales of less than 70 cans of orange juice on a Wednesday is .40, for 70 to 100 cans is .75, and for more than 100 cans is .05. Comment on his assignment of probabilities.

2.19   Let event A be selling more than 8 million cars in a year, and event B selling less than 9 million cars in the same year.
(a) Is P(A *and* B) smaller than, equal to, or greater than 1?
(b) Is P(A) + P(B) smaller than, equal to, or greater than 1?
(c) Is P(A *or* B) smaller than, equal to, or greater than 1?

2.6   CALCULATION OF P(A *OR* B)

In Table 2.3 we gave the complete sample space associated with the experiment of drawing one card from a deck. This sample space is reproduced in Figure 2.1. In the figure we have encircled in red the events "a 5" and "an honor card." These events are mutually exclusive, which is clear from the figure since each point in the sample space is encircled by red *at most once*. The black lines encircle the events "a spade *or* a

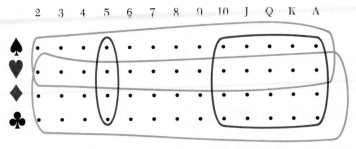

Figure 2.1 Sample space when one card is drawn from a deck.

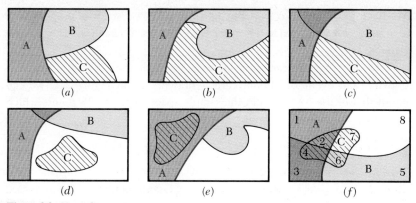

Figure 2.2 Venn diagrams.

heart" and "*not* a spade." These events are collectively exhaustive, for each point in the sample space is encircled by a black line *at least once*. If *some* points are encircled twice and *some* points never, the events are neither mutually exclusive nor collectively exhaustive. This is illustrated in the figure by taking one of the "red" events and combining this with one of the "black" events. If events are mutually exclusive *and* collectively exhaustive, every point is encircled exactly once. This situation is not illustrated in the figure.

We used a specific example here, but we can make similar pictures in more abstract settings. Consider Figure 2.2a to f. These figures are known as *Venn diagrams*. In each Venn diagram all points in the sample space are contained within the rectangle. The events A, B, and C occur when the outcome falls into the event space so labeled and shaded. Clearly, in Figure 2.2a, the events A, B, and C are mutually exclusive, although they are not collectively exhaustive. In b they are both mutually exclusive and collectively exhaustive, but in c they are only collectively exhaustive. In d through f, finally, they are neither mutually exclusive nor collectively exhaustive. When there is an unshaded area, the events are not collectively exhaustive. When some area is shaded more than once, the events are not mutually exclusive.

Venn diagrams are useful in illustrating the calculation of P(A *or* B). In Figure 2.3, events A and B are depicted by full circles, and the total shaded area corresponds to the event (A *or* B). The doubly shaded area corresponds to the event (A *and* B). We infer the *addition rule* from the Venn diagram:

$$P(A \ or \ B) = P(A) + P(B) - P(A \ and \ B)$$

Venn diagrams

The addition rule

We have to deduct P(A *and* B), because otherwise we would count that area twice, once in P(A) and once in P(B). This is an example of a common error known as "double counting."

In drawing one card from a deck, consider the event A, "spade is drawn," and event B, "honor card is drawn." From Figure 2.1, we can count that of the 52 points in the sample space there are 28 points which are either a spade or an honor. Thus,

$$P(\text{spade is drawn } or \text{ honor card is drawn}) = P(A \ or \ B) = \tfrac{28}{52}$$

We will now derive the same result by applying the addition rule. It is clear that P(spade is drawn) = P(A) = $\tfrac{13}{52}$, and similarly, P(honor card is drawn) = P(B) = $\tfrac{20}{52}$. Furthermore, P(A *and* B) = $\tfrac{5}{52}$ because 5 out of the 52 possible outcomes of a draw of a card are both spade and honor. Hence,

$$P(A \ or \ B) = P(A) + P(B) - P(A \ and \ B) = \tfrac{13}{52} + \tfrac{20}{52} - \tfrac{5}{52} = \tfrac{28}{52}$$

If A and B are mutually exclusive, we can use the simpler formula

$$P(A \ or \ B) = P(A) + P(B)$$

This is the same as the addition rule, apart from the fact that there is no deduction for P(A *and* B). However, this expression is always zero whenever A and B are mutually exclusive, so the result is the same.

The general addition rule

$$P(A \ or \ B) = P(A) + P(B) - P(A \ and \ B)$$

deducts P(A *and* B) because one must prevent double counting. (The calculation of P(A *and* B) will be discussed in Section 3.2.) Such double counting is also responsible for the proof that one never works, which goes as follows. Of the 365 days, one works only 8 hours a day (one-third of the time) or 122 days, minus 104 Saturdays and Sundays, leaving 18 days, minus 14 days vacation, leaving 4 days, minus four paid holidays

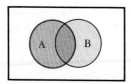

Figure 2.3 Venn diagram illustrating P(A *or* B).

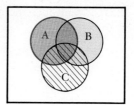

Figure 2.4 Venn diagram illustrating P(A *or* B *or* C).

(Labor Day, etc.) for a net total of zero. The proof that a horse has eight legs (two in front, two behind, two at left, and two at right) falls in the same class of double counting.

The addition rule can be generalized to more than just two events. The general rule, which should be clear from the Venn diagram (Figure 2.4), and the principle of counting every shaded area just once, is

$$P(A \ or \ B \ or \ C) = P(A) + P(B) + P(C) - P(A \ and \ B)$$
$$- P(A \ and \ C) - P(B \ and \ C) + P(A \ and \ B \ and \ C)$$

In Figure 2.4 the whole rectangular area is divided into eight non-overlapping regions, colored white, red, gray, striped, red-gray, red-striped, gray-striped, and red-gray-striped. The striped area corresponds to P(*not*-A *and not*-B *and* C). Other areas can be specified with similar lengthy expressions.

There is a special set notation to simplify the looks of such formulas. In this notation we write ∩ for *and*. The symbol ∩ is called *cap* or *intersection*. We write ∪ for *or*. The symbol ∪ is called *cup* or *union*. For *not*-A we write $\overline{A}$ or, alternatively, ∼A. The expression P($\overline{A}$ ∩ $\overline{B}$ ∩ C) stands for the striped area, and is nicely compact. By looking at Figure 2.4 we can verify that

$$P(\overline{A} \cap \overline{B} \cap \overline{C}) = 1 - P(A \cup B \cup C)$$

Both sides correspond to the white area. With the exception of Exercise 2.26 below, we will not use set notation in this book.

Set notation

EXERCISES

2.20   To what probabilities do the eight numbered areas of Figure 2.2*f* correspond? Express in probability notation *and* in words.

2.21   Consider the *Stockmarket example* (Exercise 2.8) and the events

A = stock I rises
B = stock I is unchanged
C = stock I declines
D = stock II rises
E = stocks I and II react alike

Without knowing the probabilities of these events, we can still make observations on whether or not these events are mutually exclusive or collectively exhaustive or both. What about events A and B? A, B, and C? B, C, and D? D and E? Draw a possible Venn diagram.

2.22   In tossing three coins, what is P(exactly one head *or* at least one head)?

2.23   In throwing two dice, what is P(1st die *3 or* 2d die even)? What is P(1st die *3 or* 1st die even)?

2.24   In throwing three coins, let A be "exactly one head," B "an odd number of heads," and C "*not* all faces the same." Determine P(A *or* B *or* C).

2.25   From a Venn diagram, show that the events "*not*-A *and not*-B" and "A *or* B" are mutually exclusive and collectively exhaustive. Conclude that P(A *or* B) + P(*not*-A *and not*-B) = 1.

2.26   Of 1,000 bank accounts, 400 are in a single name. Furthermore, 700 accounts are less than 5 years old, and half have a balance of less than $200. It is also known that 300 accounts are in a single name and under $200; 200 accounts are in a single name and less than 5 years old; 400 accounts are under 5 years old and have a balance of less than $200. Finally, 100 accounts belong to a single name, have less than $200 in balance, and are less than 5 years old. How many accounts are in multiple names, are at least 5 years old, and have at least $200 in balance?

Answers to Exercises

2.1 $\frac{1}{7}$. This is a logical probability, which assumes that there is no reason that 1 day will have a different probability from the other 6. If this assumption is not valid, for example because births are never induced on weekends, one can only find the answer experimentally.

2.2 0, an experimental probability.

2.3 Any value between 0 and 1 (preferably excluding the end points) is acceptable. The answer depends on where you are, conditions in the gasoline market, and your state of optimism or pessimism. It is, largely, a subjective probability.

2.4 $\frac{6}{36}$ (by reference to Table 2.1), a logical probability.

2.5 $\frac{8}{36}$ (by reference to Table 2.1), a logical probability.

2.6 52, since there are 52 cards in a bridge deck. $\frac{1}{52}$, since there is only one ♠Q in the deck.

2.7 Since each coin can land head or tail, there are $2 \times 2 \times 2 = 8$ points in the sample space.

2.8 Since a price can move in one of three ways, there are 3 points in the sample space. Since each price can move in one of three ways, there are $3 \times 3 = 9$ points in the sample space when both stocks are considered, as shown in Table 2.4 of the text.

2.9 The sample space has 16 points, (1,1), (2,1), . . . , (4,4). For example, the point (2,3) stands for "grading takes 2 days and paving takes 3 days." The sample space for total time required has only 7 points, 2, 3, . . . , 8. The three different points (2,4), (3,3), and (4,2) in the first sample space collapse to 1 point, 6, in the second sample space.

2.10 $\frac{16}{52}$ (for verification refer to Table 2.3).

2.11 $\frac{10}{1,000} = .01$

2.12 No, because it is not true that rain is equally likely each day of the year.

2.13 In the first sample space, there are 3 points, (1,3), (2,2), and (3,1). In the second sample space, there is just 1 point, 4 days. The event "a week or more" has 3 points in the first sample space, (3,4), (4,3), and (4,4), and 2 points in the second sample space, 7 days and 8 days.

2.14   No for both questions. If stock I rises and stock II remains the same, clearly "at least one stock remains unchanged" and "stock I rises" both occurred, but neither "both stocks did the same" nor "at least one stock declined" occurred.

2.15   A conventional way to classify farms is by size. It is easy to make mutually exclusive and collectively exhaustive classes according to this criterion, for example, smaller than 100 acres, from 100 to 1,000 acres, and 1,000 acres or more. Other classification criteria might be major crop (cotton, grain, milk, etc.), number of employees, or state. Such a geographic criterion does not make too much sense here, but is frequently used for other purposes.

2.16   One problem with this classification is that it is obviously not mutually exclusive. Many people run a real estate business from their house, which makes the house both commercial and residential. Nor, obviously, are the classifications collectively exhaustive. Are churches institutions? How are libraries classified? The latter problem always can, and nearly always is, solved by the trick of adding a class "other." By choosing the definitions properly most of these problems can be solved, but without further elaboration the classification is too ambiguous for comfort.

2.17   (a) $\frac{39}{52}$ (which is <1), 1, $\frac{65}{52}$ (which is >1).
        (b) $\frac{39}{52}$ (which is <1), 1, $\frac{65}{52}$ (which is >1).
        (c) Refer to Section 2.5.

2.18   The probabilities add to 1.20! Since the events are mutually exclusive and collectively exhaustive, they should add to 1.00.

2.19   (a) P(A *and* B) is never more than 1 (it is only one probability), and in this case will be less than 1, since it is not certain that between 8 million and 9 million cars will be sold in the year.
        (b) P(A) + P(B) will exceed 1, since A and B are collectively exhaustive but not mutually exclusive.
        (c) P(A *or* B) equals 1. It can never exceed 1. Since A and B are collectively exhaustive, one of them must happen.

2.20   The area labeled 1 is P(A *and not*-B *and not*-C). All eight areas are P(· *and* · *and* ·). On the first dot one fills in "A" or "*not*-A," on the second "B" or "*not*-B," and on the third "C" or "*not*-C," using whichever is appropriate by looking at the shading in the figure.

2.21 A and B are mutually exclusive, as are A, B, and C, which are also collectively exhaustive. B, C, and D are neither, and D and E are neither.

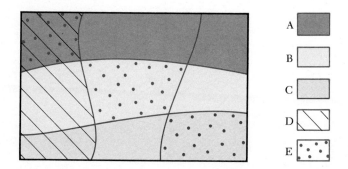

2.22 $\frac{3}{8} + \frac{7}{8} - \frac{3}{8} = \frac{7}{8}$; notice that without subtracting $\frac{3}{8}$ the total probability is greater than 1, which can never be the case.

2.23 $\frac{6}{36} + \frac{18}{36} - \frac{3}{36} = \frac{21}{36}$ answers the first question. For the second question, $\frac{6}{36} + \frac{18}{36} - 0 = \frac{24}{36}$; the events "1st die 3" and "1st die even" are mutually exclusive, and hence P(1st die *3 and* 1st die even) = 0.

2.24 P(A) + P(B) + P(C) − P(A *and* B) − P(A *and* C) − P(B *and* C) + P(A *and* B *and* C) = $\frac{3}{8} + \frac{4}{8} + \frac{6}{8} - \frac{3}{8} - \frac{3}{8} - \frac{3}{8} + \frac{3}{8} = \frac{7}{8}$.

2.25 "Not-A *and* not-B" is all the area that is blank. "A *or* B" is all that is shaded. Hence, they are mutually exclusive, collectively exhaustive, and represent events whose probabilities add to 1.

2.26 Using set notation and obvious symbolism, we are asking for the numerical determination of $P(\overline{S} \cap \overline{<5 \text{ years}} \cap \overline{<\$200})$. This is equal to $1 - P(S \cup <5 \text{ years} \cup <\$200)$. Using the generalized addition rule, we can rewrite this as

$1 - [P(S) + P(<5 \text{ years}) + P(<\$200) - P(S \cap <5 \text{ years}) - P(S \cap <\$200) - P(<5 \text{ years} \cap <\$200) + P(S \cap <5 \text{ years} \cap <\$200)] = 1 - (.4 + .7 + .5 - .2 - .4 - .3 + .1) = 1 - .8 = .2$

Chapter 3

FURTHER PROBABILITY CONCEPTS

3.1 CONTINGENCY TABLES

Suppose that, over a period of 4 years, that is, 1,000 market days, two stocks have been observed to rise, remain unchanged, and decline as in Table 3.1. For somewhat obscure reasons such a table is referred to as a *contingency table*. Notice that the events listed horizontally, as well as those listed vertically, are mutually exclusive and collectively exhaustive. This must always be the case in contingency tables.

Contingency tables

This contingency table tells us that out of the 1,000 days there were 312 days during which both stocks rose. Furthermore, there were 28 days during which stock I declined but stock II rose in price. The reverse occurred about twice as often, on 54 days to be precise.

We can also see that stock I rose for $312 + 34 + 54 = 400$ days in total, that its price remained unchanged for $60 + 110 + 80 = 250$ days, and that it declined during $28 + 56 + 266 = 350$ days. These numbers are given in the column labeled *total*, and they are obtained by simply adding all values in one row. By summing all entries in one column, we get the row labeled *total*, and we see that stock II rose, remained unchanged, and declined 400, 200, and 400 days, respectively.

If on 312 days out of 1,000 both stocks increased, the probability

TABLE 3.1 STOCKMARKET EXAMPLE (DAYS)

Stock I	Stock II			Total
	Rises	Unchanged	Declines	
Rises	312	34	54	400
Unchanged	60	110	80	250
Declines	28	56	266	350
Total	400	200	400	1,000

that both stocks increased during any arbitrarily chosen day is $\frac{312}{1,000} = .312$. Indeed, by systematically dividing all entries in the contingency table by 1,000, we replace the "number of days" by probabilities as in Table 3.2. The entries in Table 3.2 give the *joint probabilities;* for example,

Joint probabilities

P(stock I rises *and* stock II is unchanged) = .034 or 3.4 percent
P(stock I is unchanged *and* stock II rises) = .060 or 6.0 percent

These probabilities are referred to as joint probabilities because they refer to the probability of the joint occurrence of two events.

The entries in the right column and bottom row (both labeled *total*), give the so-called *marginal probabilities.* These probabilities are called marginal probabilities for the simple reason that they are written in the margin. We see, for example,

Marginal probabilities

P(stock II unchanged) = .200 or 20 percent
P(stock I declined)   = .350 or 35 percent

Marginal probabilities give only information concerning the behavior of one stock, either stock I or stock II.

It is clear that the sum of all joint probabilities is exactly 1:

.312 + .034 + .054 + .060 + .110 + .080 + .028
$$+ .056 + .266 = 1$$

TABLE 3.2 STOCKMARKET EXAMPLE (PROBABILITIES)

Stock I	Stock II			Total
	Rises	Unchanged	Declines	
Rises	.312	.034	.054	.400
Unchanged	.060	.110	.080	.250
Declines	.028	.056	.266	.350
Total	.400	.200	.400	1.000

These nine joint probabilities are associated with nine mutually exclusive and collectively exhaustive events, so the sum of these probabilities ought to equal 1. The marginal row and the marginal column (those labeled *total*) both sum to 1, and this again is as it should be, for the events "rises," "is unchanged," and "declines" are mutually exclusive and collectively exhaustive.

As an example of constructing contingency tables, suppose that we are given the following information. On 20 percent of the days rain falls, on 25 percent of the days rain is predicted, and on 18 percent of the days rain is predicted *and* it actually rains. On the basis of this information we can construct the contingency table. First we label the rows and columns, with the mutually exclusive and collectively exhaustive pairs "rain" and "no rain" on the rows, and "rain predicted" and "no rain predicted" on the columns. We complete the table with a row and column marked *total,* and get

	Rain predicted	No rain predicted	Total
Rain			
No rain			
Total			1

Next we fill in the three entries .20, .25, and .18 in appropriate places. The result is

	Rain predicted	No rain predicted	Total
Rain	.18		.20
No rain			
Total	.25		1

Finally, we use the result that the rows and columns must sum to their marginal totals and that the sum of the marginal probabilities is 1. We thus obtain Table 3.3. Observe that only three entries were needed to enable us to complete the entire table.

TABLE 3.3　RAIN AND ITS PREDICTION (PROBABILITIES)

	Rain predicted	No rain predicted	Total
Rain	.18	.02	.20
No rain	.07	.73	.80
Total	.25	.75	1.00

EXERCISES

3.1   Consider the following contingency table. Verify that both weight
        and height are divided into mutually exclusive and collectively ex-
        haustive events, and find P($<$140 pounds *and not* $<$5 feet);
        P($<$140 pounds); P($<$140 pounds *and* $>$6 feet); P($<$140 pounds
        or 5–6 feet); P(*not* $<$140 pounds); and P(160–179 pounds *or* 5–6
        feet).

Weight and Height

Weight, lb	Height, ft			Total
	$<$5	5–6	$>$6	
$<$140	.03	.17	.00	.20
140–159	.02	.23	.01	.26
160–179	.01	.16	.09	.26
$\geq$180	.01	.14	.13	.28
Total	.07	.70	.23	1.00

3.2   Consider the events "A," "*not*-A," "B," and "*not*-B." It is given
        that P(B) $=$ .40, P(A *and not*-B) $=$ .30, and P(*not*-A) $=$ .70. Prove
        that A and B are mutually exclusive.

3.3   Of all males, 70 percent smoke, while of all females, only 40 percent
        smoke. There are as many males as females. Construct a contingency
        table.

3.2   INDEPENDENT AND DEPENDENT EVENTS

*Two events are independent if the occurrence of the one has no effect on the
probability of occurrence of the other.* Standard examples of independent
events are the outcomes on successive rolls of a die or successive tosses of
a coin. In both these examples the result on the second trial is not in the
least influenced by what happened on the first. If two events, A and B, are
independent, the probability that they both occur (the joint probability) is
equal to the product of their separate probabilities:

$$P(A \ and \ B) = P(A)P(B)$$

Independent   provided A and B are independent. Conversely, two events, A and B, are
events   independent if their joint probability equals the product of their marginal

probabilities. Thus, the probability of "a 3 on the first die" *and* "an even number on the second die" equals $\frac{1}{6} \times \frac{1}{2} = \frac{1}{12}$. Indeed, in Table 2.1 we see that 3 out of 36 outcomes satisfy both these events, (3,2), (3,4), and (3,6). Obviously $\frac{3}{36} = \frac{1}{12}$.

Independent events and mutually exclusive events are *totally different.* In fact, it is easy to prove that *independent* events A and B are *never mutually exclusive,* if neither P(A) nor P(B) is zero. For, since A and B are independent, we know that P(A *and* B) = P(A)P(B). This will be greater than zero, since neither P(A) nor P(B) equals 0. If A and B are mutually exclusive, we have P(A *and* B) = 0.

In colloquial terms, events are independent if knowledge about one event does not give you the slightest help in assessing probabilities concerning the other. Suppose you are asked whether it rained June 12, 1893, in Topeka, Kansas. You don't know the answer, so you shrug your shoulders. Next, you are told that *yesterday* it rained in Topeka. This does not help you any, so these events are independent. Now, suppose you are told it rained June 11, 1893, in Topeka, or that it rained June 12, 1893, in Kansas City! Both these will help you in answering, "Oh, well, then it probably rained." These events are *dependent.*

For a more specific example of dependent events, we revisit Table 3.2, where we see that

Dependent events

$$P(\text{stock I rises } \textit{and} \text{ stock II rises}) \neq P(\text{stock I rises}) \, P(\text{stock II rises})$$

for indeed

$$.312 \neq (.400)(.400)$$

Whenever the joint probability of two events is unequal to the product of the marginal probabilities, the events are called *dependent.*

We may contrast this result with Table 3.4, which gives eye color and

TABLE 3.4   EYE COLOR AND HEIGHT (PROBABILITIES)

Eye color	*Height, ft*			
	<5	*5–6*	*>6*	*Total*
Brown eyes	.007	.070	.023	.100
Blue eyes	.014	.140	.046	.200
Green eyes	.021	.210	.069	.300
Other color eyes	.028	.280	.092	.400
Total	.070	.700	.230	1.000

TABLE 3.5   INVESTMENT AND INTEREST (PROBABILITIES)

	Interest $\leq 4\%$	Interest $> 4\%$	Total
Investment $\leq$ \$100 million	.04	.71	.75
Investment $>$ \$100 million	.06	.19	.25
Total	.10	.90	1.00

height. Each joint probability is now equal to the product of the marginal probabilities. For example, we have $.140 = .70 \times .20$, and $.092 = .23 \times .40$. Apparently the characteristics eye color and height are independent. In other words, one is just as likely to have brown eyes if one is smaller than 5 feet as when one is taller than 6 feet.

It is not difficult to think of dependent events. The events "a train passes a grade crossing" and "the gates at the grade crossing are closed" are dependent in the extreme, since the gates are closed if and only if a train passes. In many cases it is obvious whether events are dependent or not. In other cases empirical data are required. Are investment and interest rates dependent? Evidence suggests "yes." An empirical contingency table might resemble Table 3.5, where the probabilities are hypothetical. Apparently, for 75 percent of the years investment was below \$100 million, and for 10 percent of the years the interest rate was below 4 percent. The characteristics are dependent, since $(.75)(.10) \neq .04$, etc.

EXERCISES

3.4   Events A and B are independent, and $P(A) = .40$ and $P(B) = .80$. What is $P(A \ and \ B)$? $P(A \ or \ B)$?

3.5   (a) Are weight and height of one person independent?
(b) Are weight and sex independent?
(c) Are sex and age independent?
(d) Are eye color and age independent?

3.6   A yearly rainfall in Patagonia of less than 20 inches has a probability of .30, while a rainfall of more than 50 inches has a probability of .20. The probability that fewer than 100 sailboats per year overturn on Lake Erie is given by .10, while the probability that more than 200 sailboats do is given by .20. Construct the appropriate contingency table, assuming independence of the characteristics "rainfall in Patagonia" and "overturned sailboats on Lake Erie."

3.7   A salesman has a 60 percent chance of making a sale to each customer. The behavior of successive customers is independent. If two customers A and B enter, what is the probability that the salesman will make a sale to A or B (as always, this is the "inclusive or")?

3.8   A study of the smoking habits and incidence of lung cancer in a group of men showed the following results:

Smoking and Cancer (Probabilities)

	Cancer	*No cancer*	*Total*
Smoker	.030	.720	.750
Nonsmoker	.005	.245	.250
Total	.035	.965	1.000

Would you conclude that smoking and lung cancer are independent events in this group of men? Support your conclusion with calculations.

3.3   CONDITIONAL PROBABILITIES

A conditional probability is the probability that an event will happen given that another event happens. The probability that investment will exceed $100 million *given that* the interest rate is below 4 percent is a conditional probability. In formal notation we ask for

> Conditional probability

    P(investment will exceed $100 million | interest rate < 4 percent)

The vertical bar | is read as "given that." Before the bar, the event is given whose probability we are interested in; and after the bar, the condition is given. Often the formal translation of the formula with "given that" can be improved. The above formula can be read in more proper English as "the probability that investment will exceed $100 million when the interest rate is less than 4 percent." Similarly, P(>6 feet | brown eyes) can be read as "the probability that someone is over 6 feet tall, given that he has brown eyes," or, better, "the probability that someone with brown eyes is over 6 feet tall." The expression P(stock I rises | stock II declines) is formulated in words as "the probability that stock I rises, given that stock II declines" (or ". . . while stock II declines").

    The probability that it will rain if rain is predicted is given by

TABLE 3.6 STOCKMARKET EXAMPLE (DAYS)

Stock I	Stock II			Total
	Rises	Unchanged	Declines	
Rises	312	34	54	400
Unchanged	60	110	80	250
Declines	28	56	266	350
Total	400	200	400	1,000

P(rain | rain predicted), and, conversely, the probability that rain is predicted if it rains is P(rain predicted | rain). The everyday statement "I will go out if it does not rain" can be written in shorthand as

$$P(\text{I'll go out} \mid \text{no rain}) = 1$$

and the statement "The Dodgers are more likely to win than the Giants unless Mighty Muscle pitches" is written as

$$P(\text{Dodgers win} \mid \text{Mighty Muscle does not pitch}) > \tfrac{1}{2}$$

Computation
of conditional
probabilities

The values of conditional probabilities can be found from contingency tables. Let us return to the stockmarket example. Table 3.1 is here reproduced as Table 3.6.

We may want to calculate P(stock II rises | stock I is unchanged). The condition states that "stock I is unchanged," *so that we can confine our attention exclusively to the 250 days that stock I did remain unchanged.* During 60 of these 250 days stock II rose in price; hence the probability equals $\frac{60}{250}$ or .24. Analogously, we find

$$P(\text{stock I is unchanged} \mid \text{stock II rises}) = \tfrac{60}{400} = .15$$

for there are 400 days during which the condition "stock II rises" is met, and 60 of these days Stock I remained unchanged.

Instead of working with the contingency table which gives the number of days, we could just as well use the table which gives the probabilities, which is reproduced as Table 3.7.

Clearly $\frac{60}{250}$ equals $\frac{.060}{.250}$; the only difference is that in the latter ratio both numerator and denominator have been divided by 1,000. Hence

$$P(\text{stock II rises} \mid \text{stock I is unchanged}) = \tfrac{.060}{.250} = .24$$

This gives us the numerical result as before. The *general* result is

P(stock II rises | stock I is unchanged)

$$= \frac{P(\text{stock II rises } and \text{ stock I is unchanged})}{P(\text{stock I is unchanged})}$$

The even more general result, without specific reference to the stockmarket example, is

$$P(A \mid B) = \frac{P(A \ and \ B)}{P(B)}$$

Definitional formula of conditional probabilities

In words: The *conditional probability* that event A will happen given that event B happens equals the *joint* probability of A *and* B divided by the *marginal* probability of B (the condition).

We will end this section with a somewhat subtle point. We found that $P(A \mid B) = P(A \ and \ B)/P(B)$, where we divide by $P(B)$, *which is not allowed* (*not defined*) *if* $P(B) = 0$. This is a freakish case in which P(A *and* B) clearly is also zero and $P(A \mid B)$ can conveniently be defined as zero. The case corresponds to the "I'll give you $1,000 if you can swallow your own nose" type of statement. We have

P(I give $1,000 | you swallow own nose)

$$= \frac{P(\text{I give } \$1,000 \ and \text{ you swallow nose})}{P(\text{you swallow nose})} = \frac{0}{0}$$

Though the last expression is not in general defined, nobody can prevent us from defining it as zero *in the present context*. In words, a conditional probability of which the condition is never satisfied equals zero, by definition.

TABLE 3.7   STOCKMARKET EXAMPLE (PROBABILITIES)

		Stock II		
Stock I	Rises	Unchanged	Declines	Total
Rises	.312	.034	.054	.400
Unchanged	.060	.110	.080	.250
Declines	.028	.056	.266	.350
Total	.400	.200	.400	1.000

EXERCISES

3.9   With reference to Table 3.6 or Table 3.7, what is P(stock I
        unchanged|stock II unchanged)? What is P(stock II un-
        changed|stock I unchanged)? What event has a conditional
        probability of $\frac{266}{350}$, and what event has a conditional probability
        of $\frac{34}{200}$?

3.10   Consider the following contingency table:

	Rain predicted (RP)	No rain predicted (NRP)	Total
Rain (R)	.18	.02	.20
No rain (NR)	.07	.73	.80
Total	.25	.75	1.00

(a) Determine the probability that it will rain if rain is predicted.
(b) Determine the probability that rain was predicted if it rains.
(c) Express in words the conditional probability whose value is
    $\frac{.07}{.25}$.
(d) Verify that $P(R|RP) + P(NR|RP) = 1$.

3.11   Consider the following weight and height contingency table:

	S(hort)	M(edium)	T(all)	Total
L(ight)	.03	.17	.00	.20
ML(medium light)	.02	.23	.01	.26
MH(medium heavy)	.01	.16	.09	.26
H(eavy)	.01	.14	.13	.28
Total	.07	.70	.23	1.00

(a) What is:

   P(ML|T)?
   P(T|ML)?
   P(H|T)?

(b) What is the most likely weight of a person of medium height?
(c) By looking at the table, can you find the *highest* conditional
    probability?
(d) Mention the two conditional probabilities which equal zero.

(*e*) Argue that $P(S|ML) + P(M|ML) + P(T|ML) = 1$.

(*f*) By using the definition formula $P(A|B) = P(A \text{ } and \text{ } B)/P(B)$, solve $P(ML \text{ } or \text{ } MH | not\text{-}M)$; in words, that is, the probability of being medium light *or* medium heavy in weight, given that one is *not* of medium height.

3.4 BAYES' FORMULA

The conditional probability that A will happen, given that B happens is *not* the same as the conditional probability that B will happen given that A happens. We have

$$(1) \qquad P(A|B) = \frac{P(A \text{ } and \text{ } B)}{P(B)}$$

and

$$(2) \qquad P(B|A) = \frac{P(A \text{ } and \text{ } B)}{P(A)}$$

The denominators differ. Yet an easy formula can be derived from these two which expresses $P(A|B)$ in terms of $P(B|A)$, or the other way around. By multiplying (1) through by $P(B)$, we find

$$(3) \qquad P(A \text{ } and \text{ } B) = P(B)P(A|B)$$

This result, known as the *multiplication rule,* gives the joint probability of A *and* B, whether they are independent or not. Recall that in the case where A and B are independent, the formula could be written simply

Multiplication rule

$$P(A \text{ } and \text{ } B) = P(A)P(B)$$

We can express formula (3) in words as follows. For A *and* B to happen together, certainly B must occur, but then—given that B happened—A should also happen. This is the essence of formula (3). For the sun to shine on a Wednesday, certainly the sun must shine; but on top of that, given that the sun shines, it must be Wednesday. Obviously, we can reverse the order. For the sun to shine on a Wednesday, certainly it should be Wednesday; but on top of that, given that it is Wednesday, the sun should shine. This reverse result can be derived from formula (2) by multiplying through by $P(A)$, which gives $P(A \text{ } and \text{ } B) = P(A)P(B|A)$.

Bayes' formula   If we substitute (3) in (2), we find *Bayes' formula*

(4)
$$P(B|A) = \frac{P(A|B)P(B)}{P(A)}$$

In most applications of Bayes' formula the denominator $P(A)$ is rewritten as

(5)
$$P(A) = P(A|B)P(B) + P(A|\textit{not-}B)P(\textit{not-}B)$$

Because B and *not*-B are mutually exclusive and collectively exhaustive, event A can only happen *either* if B happens and then, given B, also A; *or* if B does *not* happen and then, given *not*-B, A. In Exercise 3.12 we will generalize formula (5), and illustrate it with a specific example.

Substitution of (5) in (4) gives us

Alternative   (6)
version of
Bayes' formula
$$P(B|A) = \frac{P(A|B)P(B)}{P(A|B)P(B) + P(A|\textit{not-}B)P(\textit{not-}B)}$$

We will apply the formula to the following problem. Suppose that a bank has a test designed to establish the credit rating of a loan applicant. Of the persons who default (D), 90 percent fail the test (F). Of the persons who will repay the bank (ND), 5 percent fail the test (F). Formally,

$$P(F|D) = .90$$
$$P(F|ND) = .05$$

The test is clearly not ideal; 10 percent of the defaulters slip through and 5 percent of the financially responsible persons are denied a loan. Furthermore, it is given that 4 percent of the population is not worthy of credit, that is, $P(D) = .04$. It is obvious that $P(ND) = .96$.

We may now ask the following: Given that someone failed the test, what is the probability that he actually will default (when given a loan)? Thus, we ask for $P(D|F)$. Applying Bayes' formula gives

$$P(D|F) = \frac{P(F|D)P(D)}{P(F|D)P(D) + P(F|ND)P(ND)}$$
$$= \frac{(.90)(.04)}{(.90)(.04) + (.05)(.96)} = \frac{.036}{.084} = .43$$

We thus find the somewhat surprising result that even though the test is failed, the probability of the applicant's defaulting is less than 50 percent. How come?

To find out, suppose that 1,000 persons are being tested. If they are typical, 40 of these 1,000 persons will default, and 90 percent of these, or 36, will be spotted. Of the 960 financially responsible people only 5 percent or 48 will fail the test. In total, 36 + 48 = 84 persons will fail the test, but only 36 of these (or 43 percent) will in fact default. The unexpected result thus arises because the probability of defaulting in the first place (4 percent) is so small, that 90 percent of this small number is less than 5 percent of the large number (96 percent) of responsible people.

The argument used here can be illustrated with the help of a *tree diagram*. Such a diagram is illustrated in Figure 3.1. A tree diagram consists of *branches* leading outward from *nodes*. A node occurs when alternative events may result from a trial, and the branches from that node portray these alternatives. Each branch carries the probability associated with the events it represents. Since we are given that 4 percent of the applicants are defaulters, we begin with two branches, one labeled "D .04" and the other "ND .96." These are marginal probabilities, in the language of a contingency table. Next, we know that among the 4 percent who are defaulters, 90 percent will fail (F) the test, for a total of (.04)(.90) = .036. The balance of the defaulters, (.04)(.10) = .004, will unfortunately pass (P) the test. The two branches growing out of the node at the end of the D .04 branch are thus F .036 and P .004. We also know that among the 96 percent who repay loans, 5 percent will fail the

Tree diagram

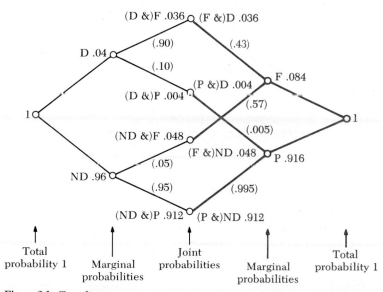

Figure 3.1 Tree diagram.

test, while the remaining 95 percent will pass. These events are represented by the branches F .048 and P .912 extending from the node at the end of the branch marked ND .96. If the tree diagram were a contingency table, these would be shown as joint probabilities associated with the pair of events on the branches needed to reach the final node. To reach the node marked .048, we move along the branches ND and F; so the probability that one will be a nondefaulter *and* fail is .048.

It is possible to round off the tree by combining the branches F and P, as shown by the red lines in Figure 3.1. The sum of the probabilities .036 + .048 = .084 is the probability of failure. The sum of the probabilities .004 + .912 = .916 is the probability of passing. These two sums are marginal probabilities. They sum to 1: every applicant must either pass or fail the test. Combining the end points F .084 and P .916, we reach the final node marked 1. Reading the black lines forward or the red lines backward shows the symmetry of the situation. All conditional probabilities can be derived from the tree. For example, $P(ND|P) = P(P$ *and* $ND)/P(P) = \frac{.912}{.916} = .995$. These conditional probabilities are given in parentheses along the appropriate branches.

In view of the importance of Bayes' formula, we will give another example. It is virtually impossible to design an exam which all good students pass, and all bad students fail. A certain exam is such that 80 percent of the good (G) students pass (P), and only 25 percent of the bad (B) students pass. Furthermore, 70 percent of the students are good students (G). What is the probability that a student who passes is in fact a good student?

We know, in an abbreviated but obvious notation, that $P(P|G) = .80$, $P(P|B) = .25$ and $P(G) = .70$ are therefore $P(B) = .30$. We are asked to determine $P(G|P)$, and we find using Bayes' formula:

$$P(G|P) = \frac{P(P|G)P(G)}{P(P|G)P(G) + P(P|B)P(B)}$$

$$= \frac{.80 \times .70}{.80 \times .70 + .25 \times .30} = \frac{.56}{.635} = .88$$

Before the exam any arbitrarily chosen student had a 70 percent chance of being good. An arbitrarily chosen student who passed the exam had an 88 percent probability of being a good student, and hence a 12 percent chance of being bad. The exam is not foolproof, but has some discriminating power.

We see from these examples that in many practical situations the complicated formula (6) comes naturally, while the much simpler formula (4) cannot be used immediately.

EXERCISES

3.12   Let B_1, B_2, . . . , B_n be n mutually exclusive and collectively exhaustive events. Indicate why $P(A) = P(A|B_1)P(B_1) + P(A|B_2)P(B_2) + \cdots + P(A|B_n)P(B_n)$. Verify from the data in Exercise 3.11 that $P(ML) = P(ML|S)P(S) + P(ML|M)P(M) + P(ML|T)P(T)$.

3.13   Construct a contingency table for the text example on defaulters.

3.14   For the example of students' passing or failing tests, construct a tree diagram and a contingency table.

3.15   One is either a Democrat (D) or a Republican (R), and one either lives in New York City (C) or in the rest of New York State (S). Given $P(D|C) = .60$, $P(D|S) = .45$, and $P(C) = .35$:
(a) Compute $P(C|D)$ by Bayes' formula.
(b) Is it true that $P(C|D) + P(S|D) = 1$?
(c) Is it true that $P(C|D) + P(C|R) = 1$?

3.5 A PRIORI AND A POSTERIORI PROBABILITY

Let us consider the examples in the previous section from a slightly different angle. We found that the probability that someone will default *before* any test is made is .04 or 4 percent. *After* the test is made, his chance either jumps to .43, or 43 percent, if he failed or drops to .005, or $\frac{1}{2}$ percent, if he passed. The probability before the test is known as the *a priori* probability. After the test it is referred to as the *a posteriori* probability. These are just new *words*, not new *concepts*. The a priori probability corresponds to a marginal probability in a contingency table, and the a posteriori probability corresponds to a conditional probability.

According to the data in Table 3.3, before the weather forecast there is a 20 percent probability that it will rain tomorrow. This is the a priori probability, given in the marginal column. After the forecast is heard, there are two possibilities. Rain may be predicted, and then the a posteriori probability of rain is $P(R \mid RP) = \frac{.18}{.25} = .72$. If the forecast says "no rain," the a posteriori probability is $P(R \mid NRP) = \frac{.02}{.75} = .0267$.

The terminology should not hide the very common phenomenon of changing the odds as more information becomes available. Before the first game in the Cincinnati Reds–Oakland Athletics 1972 World Series the bookmaker odds were 9 to 5 in favor of the Reds, which implies that the Reds were given a $\frac{9}{14} = 64.3$ percent chance to win. *After* the Reds lost the first game at home, the odds were reappraised at 7 to 6, but still in favor of the Reds. They were still given a better than even $\frac{7}{13} = 53.8$ percent chance to win. After the Reds lost the second game, again playing at home, the odds changed sharply to 7 to 4 in favor of the Athletics. At that point in the series $P(\text{Reds win}) = \frac{4}{11} = 36.4$ percent. The odds kept changing until after six games, the series tied at three each; they were virtually equal, the Reds perhaps having a slight edge, depending on the bookmaker and timing of the bet. The Reds, however, lost the last game, and after this game was over, $P(\text{Reds win})$ equaled 0. More formally,

At the outset: $P(\text{Reds win}) = 64.3$ percent
After 1 game: $P(\text{Reds win} \mid \text{Reds lost 1st game}) = 53.8$ percent
After 2 games: $P(\text{Reds win} \mid \text{Reds lost 1st two games}) = 36.4$ percent
. . . .
After 6 games: $P(\text{Reds win} \mid \text{Reds won 3 out of 6}) = 51$ percent
After 7 games: $P(\text{Reds win} \mid \text{Reds won 3 out of 7}) = 0$

As a rule, all the *conditional* probabilities are referred to as a posteriori probabilities. From a logical point of view it might be better to consider the 53.8 percent probability (although posterior when compared with 64.3 percent) prior when compared with 36.4 percent. In practice, no terminological confusion is likely to result.

EXERCISES

3.16   A bridge player holding two hearts is equally likely to have the (8,9) or (8,K) or (9,K) of hearts. If he holds (8,9), he will throw either card with equal probability. If he holds (8,K) or (9,K) he will invariably throw the low-value card, never the K. *He throws the 8*. Translate the following a posteriori probabilities into words, and determine them numerically:

$$P[(8,9) \mid 8] \qquad P[(8,K) \mid 8] \qquad P[(9,K) \mid 8]$$

3.17   There is *one* urn which contains *either* 40 *or* 60 percent black balls. These possibilities are considered equally likely. A ball is drawn and found to be black.

(*a*) What is the a posteriori probability that the urn has 60 percent black balls?

(*b*) Next, another ball is drawn, and this one is also black. What is the new a posteriori probability that the urn contains 60 percent black balls?

3.18   A company employs two salesmen, A and B. A is much better than B in that he makes a sale at 70 percent of the houses he calls on, whereas B only makes a sale at 40 percent of the houses he calls on. On a given day the manager gets an urgent message for salesman A. Unfortunately he does not know whether A has the southern or northern route that day; to the best of his knowledge these two alternatives are equally likely. He decides to check the houses along the southern route and finds that both the first and second houses bought the product. What is the a posteriori probability that salesman A had been given the southern route?

Answers to Exercises

3.1   P($<$140 pounds *and not* $<$5 feet) $= .17 + .00 = .17$
P($<$140 pounds) $= .20$
P($<$140 pounds *and* $>$6 feet) $= .00$
P($<$140 pounds *or* 5–6 feet) $= .20 + .70 - .17 = .73$
P(*not* $<$140 pounds) $= 1 - .20 = .80$
P(160–179 pounds *or* 5–6 feet) $= .26 + .70 - .16 = .80$

3.2   The complete contingency table is:

	B	*Not*-B	*Total*
A	.00	.30	.30
Not-A	.40	.30	.70
Total	.40	.60	1.00

Since P(A *and* B) $= 0$, events A and B are mutually exclusive.

3.3   We know 50 percent of the people are male and 70 percent of the males smoke. So $(.50)(.70) = .35$, or 35 percent of all people are male and smoke. Similarly, for females, $(.50)(.40) = .20$. We can now complete the table as follows:

	S	NS	Total
M	.35	.15	.50
F	.20	.30	.50
Total		.55	.45	1.00

3.4 $P(A \text{ and } B) = P(A)P(B) = (.40)(.80) = .32$
$P(A \text{ or } B) = P(A) + P(B) - P(A \text{ and } B)$
$\qquad\qquad = .40 + .80 - .32 = .88$

3.5   (a) No, we expect a taller person to be heavier.
(b) No, men are usually heavier than women.
(c) No! The higher the age bracket, the higher the proportion of females, which starts, as we know, at .49. Life insurance premiums reflect this dependence.
(d) Yes.

3.6   From the data we conclude:

Sailboats overturning	Rainfall in Patagonia, in.			Total
	<20	20–50	>50	
<100				.10
100–200				.70
>200				.20
Total	.30	.50	.20	1.00

The values .70 and .50 are immediately obvious. By independence each entry in the table is equal to the product of the corresponding marginal probabilities, so that the whole table is:

Sailboats overturning	Rainfall in Patagonia, in.			Total
	<20	20–50	>50	
<100	.03	.05	.02	.10
100–200	.21	.35	.14	.70
>200	.06	.10	.04	.20
Total	.30	.50	.20	1.00

3.7   If P(A) is the probability of making a sale to A and P(B) is the probability of making a sale to B, then P(A *or* B) is the probability of making a sale to A or B. P(A *or* B) = P(A) + P(B) − P(A *and* B) = .60 + .60 − .36 = .84. The value P(A *and* B) = (.60)(.60) = .36 follows from the independence of A and B.

3.8   Using self-evident notation, P(C *and* S) ≠ P(C)P(S), .030 ≠ (.035)(.750), and so on, for each of the four joint probabilities. Smoking and the incidence of lung cancer are not independent within this group of men.

3.9
$$P(\text{stock I unchanged}\,|\,\text{stock II unchanged}) = \tfrac{.110}{.200} = .55$$
$$P(\text{stock II unchanged}\,|\,\text{stock I unchanged}) = \tfrac{.110}{.250} = .44$$

The event (stock II declines | stock I declines) has a probability of $\tfrac{.266}{.350}$, and the event (stock I rises | stock II unchanged) has a probability of $\tfrac{.034}{.200}$.

3.10   (*a*) $P(R\,|\,RP) = \tfrac{.18}{.25} = .72$

      (*b*) $P(RP\,|\,R) = \tfrac{.18}{.20} = .90$; hence 90 percent of the time that it rains, it is predicted.

      (*c*) The event whose probability is $\tfrac{.07}{.25}$ is "it did not rain despite the fact that rain was predicted."

      (*d*) $P(R\,|\,RP) + P(NR\,|\,RP) = \tfrac{.18}{.25} + \tfrac{.07}{.25} = 1$. This is obvious, for given that rain is predicted it will either rain or not rain. These "conditional events" are thus mutually exclusive and collectively exhaustive.

3.11   (*a*) $P(ML\,|\,T) = \tfrac{.01}{.23} = .0435,$ $P(T\,|\,ML) = \tfrac{.01}{.26} = .0385,$ $P(H\,|\,T) = \tfrac{.13}{.23} = .565$

      (*b*) To find the most likely weight of a person of medium height we compare P(L | M), P(ML | M), P(MH | M), and P(H | M). These are $\tfrac{.17}{.70}$, $\tfrac{.23}{.70}$, $\tfrac{.16}{.70}$, and $\tfrac{.14}{.70}$, so the answer is medium light.

      (*c*) The *highest* conditional probability is $\tfrac{.23}{.26}$, or P(M | ML).

      (*d*) The conditional probabilities P(L | T) and P(T | L) are zero.

      (*e*) P(S | ML) + P(M | ML) + P(T | ML) = 1 because, given that one is medium light, the three mutually exclusive and collectively exhaustive events are that one is small, medium, or tall.

      (*f*) P(ML *or* MH | *not*-M) = (.02 + .01 + .01 + .09)/(.07 + .23) = .43. In the numerator we have the probability of ML *or* MH *and* *not*-M, in the denominator the probability of *not*-M.

3.12   The formula can be rewritten as $P(A) = P(A \ and \ B_1) + P(A \ and \ B_2) + \cdots + P(A \ and \ B_n)$. The argument is that since B_1, B_2, ..., B_n are mutually exclusive and collectively exhaustive, whenever A happens, it will happen with exactly one and only one of the B's.

In a Venn diagram, this appears as follows:

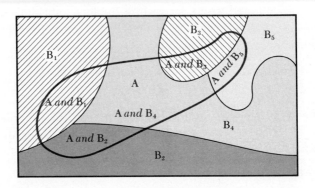

As illustration,

$$P(ML) = 0.26$$
$$= P(ML|S)P(S) + P(ML|M)P(M) + P(ML|T)P(T)$$
$$= (\tfrac{.02}{.07})(.07) + (\tfrac{.23}{.70})(.70) + (\tfrac{.01}{.23})(.23)$$

3.13   We label the rows F and P for fail and pass and the columns D and ND. We know that $P(D) = .04$; hence $P(ND) = .96$. We also know that $P(F|D) = .90$, so

$$P(F|D) = \frac{P(F \ and \ D)}{P(D)} = .90 = \frac{P(F \ and \ D)}{.04}$$

Hence

$$P(F \ and \ D) = (.90)(.04) = .036$$

Similarly, we find from $P(F|ND) = .05$ that $P(F \ and \ ND) = .048$. The table can now be filled in completely by using addition and subtraction to make the marginal probabilities sum to the total of the joint probabilities.

3.14   We are given $P(G) = .70$; hence $P(B) = .30$. These are the first two branches. Next, we know that $P(P|G) = .80$, so $P(F|G) = .20$. These values enable us to branch from the G branch to the branches P and F with probabilities $(.70)(.80) = .56$ and $(.70)(.20) = .14$. Furthermore, $P(P|B) = .25$, so $P(F|B) = .75$. We obtain two branches P and F with probabilities $(.30)(.25) = .075$ and $(.30)(.75) = .225$. The resulting tree is as follows:

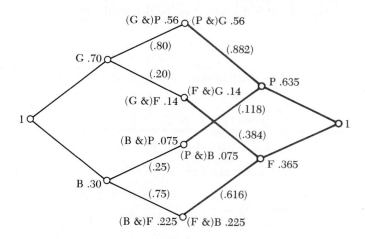

(The examination is apparently a difficult one, since in a class with 30 percent bad students, $36\frac{1}{2}$ percent will fail the test.) The above tree diagram contains all values needed for the following contingency table. It can also be derived as in Exercise 3.13.

	G	B	Total
P	.560	.075	.635
F	.140	.225	.365
Total	.700	.300	1.000

3.15   (a) $P(C|D)$ stands for the probability that a Democrat is a city dweller, and this is

$$P(C|D) = \frac{P(D|C)P(C)}{P(D|C)P(C) + P(D|S)P(S)}$$

$$= \frac{(.60)(.35)}{(.60)(.35) + (.45)(.65)} = 42 \text{ percent}$$

(b) Yes, it is true that $P(C|D) + P(S|D) = 1$, for a Democrat either lives in the city or lives upstate.

(c) No, it is not true that $P(C|D) + P(C|R) = 1$. In fact, $P(C|D) = .42$ and $P(C|R) = .28$, as one can easily verify.

3.16 $P[(8,9)|8]$ is the probability that the player holds $(8,9)$, given that he throws the 8, and so on. Clearly $P[(9,K)|8] = 0$; you cannot discard the 8 if you do not hold it in the first place. Also

$$P[(8,9)|8]$$

$$= \frac{P[8|(8,9)]P(8,9)}{P[8|(8,9)]P(8,9) + P[8|(8,K)]P(8,K) + P[8|(9,K)]P(9,K)}$$

$$= \frac{(\frac{1}{2})(\frac{1}{3})}{(\frac{1}{2})(\frac{1}{3}) + (1)(\frac{1}{3}) + (0)(\frac{1}{3})} = \frac{\frac{1}{6}}{\frac{1}{2}} = \frac{1}{3}$$

One can derive similarly that $P[(8,K)|8] = \frac{2}{3}$.

3.17   (a) A priori, the chances are 50–50. A posteriori we have

$$P(60\%|B) = \frac{P(B|60\%)P(60\%)}{P(B|60\%)P(60\%) + P(B|40\%)P(40\%)}$$

$$= \frac{(.6)(.5)}{(.6)(.5) + (.4)(.5)} = \frac{.3}{.3 + .2} = .6$$

With the present information, the probability is .6 that the balls are predominantly black.

(b) For our next step, $P(60\%) = .6$, and $P(40\%) = .4$. If a black ball is drawn again, we get

$$P(60\%|B) = \frac{P(B|60\%)P(60\%)}{P(B|60\%)P(60\%) + P(B|40\%)P(40\%)}$$

$$= \frac{(.6)(.6)}{(.6)(.6) + (.4)(.4)} = \frac{.36}{.52} = .69$$

If the third ball drawn proves to be black, we have a probability of over 77 percent that we drew from an urn with predominantly black balls, which you should verify.

3.18   After finding that a sale was made at the first house (S1), the manager reappraises the a priori odds as follows:

$$P(A|S1) = \frac{P(S1|A)P(A)}{P(S1|A)P(A) + P(S1|B)P(B)}$$

$$= \frac{(.7)(.5)}{(.7)(.5) + (.4)(.5)} = .64$$

Hence, there is a probability of .64 that A went the southern route. After the second call, using these a posteriori probabilities as the new a priori probabilities, we find

$$P(A \mid S2) = \frac{P(S2 \mid A)P(A)}{P(S2 \mid A)P(A) + P(S2 \mid B)P(B)}$$

$$= \frac{(.7)(.64)}{(.7)(.64) + (.4)(.36)} = .76$$

The probability is now .76 that A went the southern route. Or, we might say the odds are "better than 3 to 1."

Chapter 4

COMBINATORIAL ANALYSIS

4.1 PERMUTATIONS

As we saw in Chapter 2, whenever all outcomes are equally likely, the probability that an event will happen is given by the ratio

$$\frac{\text{Number of points in event space}}{\text{Number of points in sample space}} = \frac{\text{number of ``favorable'' outcomes}}{\text{total number of outcomes}}$$

Importance of counting in determining probabilities

Sometimes the problems are so simple that all possible outcomes can be enumerated, and the counting can be performed by brute force, as was done in Chapter 2. In more elaborate problems, more powerful methods are called for. These will be discussed in this chapter.

A baseball team consists of nine players. Suppose that the batting order is determined by having the players draw slips numbered from 1 through 9. How many different batting orders are possible? The answer, which will be derived below, is

$$9 \times 8 \times 7 \times 6 \times 5 \times 4 \times 3 \times 2 \times 1 = 9!$$
$$9! = 362,880$$

The expression "9!" is read "9 factorial." Therefore, the probability that the players will be in any specific order, for example, alphabetical order, is $\frac{1}{9!}$, which is very small indeed.

Permutations
The number of ways in which n different objects can be ordered is given by $n!$ and is known as the *number of permutations.* Formally, we write

$$P(n,n) = n!$$

where the first n indicates that we have n objects and the second n indicates that all n of them appear in each permutation. If $n = 3$, we have $P(3,3) = 3! = 3 \times 2 \times 1 = 6$. Indeed, the three letters a, b, and c, can be permuted in six ways. Listed in alphabetical order these are abc, acb, bac, bca, cab, cba. The *first* letter can be chosen in three ways, a, b, or c. With each of these first letters, a *second* letter, which can be chosen in two ways, is combined. The *third* letter must be the one that remains—there is no choice left. Thus we have $3 \times 2 \times 1 = 6$ different orders. Graphically:

1st choice	2d choice	3d "choice"	Result

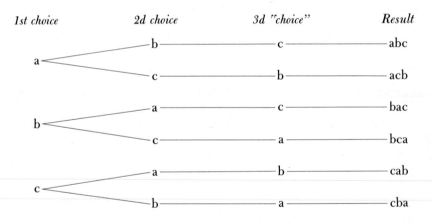

Five men, whose last names start with the letters A, J, N, T, and U, are seeking a name for their new company. They decide to use a permutation of these letters. In how many different ways can the letters A J N T U be permuted? Answer: $P(5,5) = 5! = 120$ different ways. The first letter can be chosen in five ways, and the second in four ways. Therefore, the first two can be chosen in 5×4 different ways, which could be written down without much trouble. The third can be chosen in three ways, the fourth in two ways, the last in only one way, the remaining letter. Only 2 out of these 120 permutations form English words, jaunt and junta. Thus, they found the apt name JUNTA Corporation.

Back to the baseball squad. Each of the nine players can be first in the lineup. With each of these first, there are eight choices left for second, 9×8; with each of these 72 different pairs we can choose the third in the lineup in seven ways, $9 \times 8 \times 7$. The next player is chosen out of six, so that we now have $9 \times 8 \times 7 \times 6$ different starting quartets, and so on, to 9! different starting lineups. The sample space of the experiment, which consists of ordering nine people in random order, has 9! or over 350,000 points. The value of $n!$ increases rapidly as n increases. The value 10! is over 3 million. The value 20! is a 19-digit number. In Table 5 of Appendix B we give the values up to 100! and their logarithms.

Typically, a baseball manager does not actually choose his batting order out of 9 players, but out of a pool of, say, 25 players. The first player chosen is first at bat, . . . , the ninth player chosen is last at bat, and the 16 players not chosen do not make the starting lineup. How many different permutations are there in this case?

The answer is provided by a straightforward extension of the previous line of reasoning. The first batter can be chosen in 25 ways, and the second in 24 ways, so the first two can be chosen in 25×24 different ways. The third batter can be chosen in 23 ways, . . . , the last one in 17 ways, and so the answer is $25 \times 24 \times 23 \times 22 \times 21 \times 20 \times 19 \times 18 \times 17 = 741$ billion. The answer is correct, but somewhat cumbersome notationally. We can, however, multiply through by 1, written as $\frac{16!}{16!}$, which gives

$$\frac{25 \times 24 \times \cdots \times 18 \times 17 \times 16 \times 15 \times \cdots \times 3 \times 2 \times 1}{16 \times 15 \times \cdots \times 3 \times 2 \times 1}$$

$$= \frac{25!}{16!} = \frac{25!}{(25 - 9)!} = P(25,9)$$

As before, the 25 indicates that we have 25 objects—players—and the 9 indicates that 9 players appear in each batting order. In general, there are

$$P(n,k) = \frac{n!}{(n - k)!}$$

ways to choose an *ordered sequence* of k items out of n different items. The expression $P(n,k)$ is read as "the number of permutations of n things taken k at a time." It is necessary that k be smaller than or equal to n.

One cannot choose 26 baseball players out of a pool of 25. If k equals n, we get

$$P(n,n) = \frac{n!}{(n-n)!} = \frac{n!}{0!} = \frac{n!}{1} = n!$$

provided that

$$0! = 1$$

We accept this as a matter of definition.

Suppose that in a company, managers are being selected for stores in Dallas, Detroit, and Denver. Seven qualified candidates are available. The positions can now be filled in

$$P(7,3) = \frac{7!}{(7-3)!} = \frac{7!}{4!} = 210$$

ways.

So far we have discussed permutations *without replacement*. By this we mean that once an item was chosen, it could not be chosen *again*. The number 2 at bat cannot also be chosen to bat as number 7. The same person cannot be manager in both Denver and Dallas. On the other hand, in throwing a die four times, it is possible that the same number will come up *repeatedly*. The number of permutations in this case is $6 \times 6 \times 6 \times 6$. The first result is any one of 6, the second is any one of 6, and so on. If we speak about *permutations with replacement* we write $\bar{P}$, rather than P. The relevant formula is

Permutations with replacement

$$\bar{P}(n,k) = \underbrace{n \times n \times \cdots \times n}_{k \text{ times}} = n^k$$

for k items are being chosen and each choice can be made in n different ways. In choosing k items out of n *with replacement*, k can be larger than n. A die tossed eight times allows for 6^8 different orders.

In Section 2.2 we discussed the number of points in the sample space if we toss three dice. We came to the conclusion that there were $6 \times 6 \times 6 = 216$ points in the sample space. In this section we found the following general result. If each trial can lead to n possible outcomes and one repeats the trial k times, there are $\bar{P}(n,k) = n^k$ points in the sample space. If one tosses 13 coins, there are 2^{13} points in the sample space, of which HHTTTTHTHHHTH is only one.

Whenever we speak about permutations we mean permutations *without* replacement. Permutations *with* replacement will always be so labeled.

EXERCISES

4.1 In how many different ways can one line up six people for an identification lineup of suspects?

4.2 What is the probability that four people riding in an elevator will leave in order of decreasing age?

4.3 In how many orders can a salesman travel to 20 cities, visiting each city once?

4.4 A secretary has typed eight letters and an envelope for each. She puts a letter into each envelope without bothering to check which letter belongs in which envelope. What is the probability that each letter is in the correct envelope? What is the probability that exactly seven are in the correct envelopes?

4.5 Out of 100 persons 10 are chosen to receive 1st to 10th prize in a contest. How many different permutations of winners are there?

4.6 Three out of the four letters A, E, N, P, are chosen. What is the probability that the three letters in the order chosen spell an English word?

4.7 In planning a cruise one can choose 6 cities, in any order, to visit out of a total of 20 cities. How many different cruises are there? How many different cruises are there if one may revisit cities as often as desired?

4.8 In drawing three cards from a deck, what is the probability of drawing ♣5, ♦J, and ♦8 *in that order?*

4.9 How many different permutations are there if one chooses 3 months out of the 12 *with* replacement?

4.2 COMBINATIONS

A baseball player is not very interested in his place in the batting order. For him the important question is whether he plays. A bridge player is not interested in the order in which he received his 13 cards; he is only interested in *which* 13 cards he receives. The question thus becomes, "How many different teams of 9 players can be formed from 25?" or "How many different bridge hands of 13 cards can be formed from 52 cards?" In technical terminology, the question is, "How many *combinations* of 9 can one make out of 25?" and "How many *combinations* of 13 can one make out of 52?"

Combinations

We recall that in a permutation we choose nine players in a *specific order*. If the 25 baseball players are referred to as A through Y, the teams, given in batting order

BQPDAMHTF   and   MHBPFTAQD

are considered different, even though they are composed of the same players. But these *two permutations* clearly are only *one combination*, since the players are the same. In fact, there are 9! permutations giving rise to one and the same combination, because the same nine players (ABDFHMPQT) can be chosen in 9! different orders or permutations—$P(9,9) = 9!$. Therefore, we get the number of combinations, represented by $C(25,9)$, as

$$C(25,9) = \frac{P(25,9)}{P(9,9)} = \frac{25!}{16!9!}$$

or, in general,

$$C(n,k) = \frac{n!}{(n-k)!k!}$$

The expression $C(n,k)$ is read "the number of combinations of n things taken k at a time."

A problem of somewhat smaller dimensions might help in visualizing this important result. Suppose two people are chosen out of five, A, B, C, D, and E. There are $P(5,2) = 5!/(5-2)! = 20$ permutations:

AB   BA   AD   DA   BC   CB   BE   EB   CE   EC

AC   CA   AE   EA   BD   DB   CD   DC   DE   ED

but only

$$C(5,2) = \frac{5!}{(5-2)!2!} = 10$$

combinations. The permutations AB and BA are only one combination; each pair of permutations collapses to one combination.

We can also conclude that there are

$$C(52,13) = \frac{52!}{(52 - 13)!13!} = 635{,}013{,}559{,}600$$

different bridge hands. Only four of these hands are all clubs, all diamonds, all hearts, or all spades, so the probability of getting a hand with all 13 cards in the same suit is very small indeed.

Obviously we cannot choose 13 cards from 52 in the deck without, *at the same time*, choosing the other 39 in the deck. These are the 39 cards that remain in the deck. Therefore, we would expect $C(52,13)$ to equal $C(52,39)$. This, in fact, is true. In general

$$C(n,k) = C(n, n - k)$$

because

$$C(n,k) = \frac{n!}{(n - k)!k!}$$

and

$$C(n, n - k) = \frac{n!}{[n - (n - k)]!(n - k)!} = \frac{n!}{k!(n - k)!}$$

For any value of n, k can vary from zero up to n. There is one and only one way to pick zero people out of n, that is, not to pick any. Thus,

$$C(n,0) = \frac{n!}{(n - 0)!0!} = \frac{n!}{n!} = 1$$

where we used $0! = 1$. There is also one and only one way to get a group of n people out of n, that is, by taking them all. Thus,

$$C(n,n) = \frac{n!}{(n - n)!n!} = 1$$

again using $0! = 1$. There is *no* way to form a group of nine out of seven people, or in general to form a combination of *more than* n out of n people.

If we tabulate the actual values of $C(n,k)$ for various values of n and the appropriate range for k, we get

$n = 0$
$(k = 0)$
$$1$$

$n = 1$
$(k = 0,1)$
$$1 \qquad 1$$

$n = 2$
$(k = 0,1,2)$
$$1 \qquad 2 \qquad 1$$

$n = 3$
$(k = 0,1,2,3)$
$$1 \qquad 3 \qquad 3 \qquad 1$$

$n = 4$
$(k = 0, \ldots, 4)$
$$1 \qquad 4 \qquad 6 \qquad 4 \qquad 1$$

$n = 5$
$(k = 0, \ldots, 5)$
$$1 \qquad 5 \qquad 10 \qquad 10 \qquad 5 \qquad 1$$

$n = 6$
$(k = 0, \ldots, 6)$
$$1 \qquad 6 \qquad 15 \qquad 20 \qquad 15 \qquad 6 \qquad 1$$

Pascal's triangle

This arrangement of numbers is the famous *triangle of Pascal*. The triangle is bordered by 1s, and the other entries can be found by *summing the two diagonally above*. For example, $15 = 5 + 10$. Each line can be found from the one above. In algebra this triangle arises in the following context. Suppose we wish to write out

$$(a + b)^5 = (a + b)(a + b)(a + b)(a + b)(a + b)$$

In the result there will be terms with a^5, a^4b, a^3b^2, a^2b^3, ab^4, and b^5, but *how many* of each? To be specific, how many terms are there of the form a^2b^3? The term a^2b^3 results when a enters from two of the binomial terms $(a + b)$ and b from the other three. Since there are five a's, we can choose two in $C(5,2) = 10$ ways [which is the same as the $C(5,3)$ ways in which we can get the three b's out of the five]. Thus, the coefficient of a^2b^3 is $C(5,2)$ [or, alternatively, $C(5,3)$ if we consider the problem from the b's point of view]. If we number the a's and b's so as to distinguish them

$$(a_1 + b_1)(a_2 + b_2)(a_3 + b_3)(a_4 + b_4)(a_5 + b_5)$$

the 10 terms can be distinguished and written explicitly

$$
\begin{array}{llll}
a_1a_2b_3b_4b_5 & a_2a_3b_1b_4b_5 & a_3a_4b_1b_2b_5 & a_4a_5b_1b_2b_3 \\
a_1a_3b_2b_4b_5 & a_2a_4b_1b_3b_5 & a_3a_5b_1b_2b_4 & \\
a_1a_4b_2b_3b_5 & a_2a_5b_1b_3b_4 & & \\
a_1a_5b_2b_3b_4 & & &
\end{array}
$$

The coefficients of the other terms are derived similarly, and the complete result is

$$(a + b)^5 = C(5,5)a^5b^0 + C(5,4)a^4b^1 + C(5,3)a^3b^2$$
$$+ C(5,2)a^2b^3 + C(5,1)ab^4 + C(5,0)a^0b^5$$

where a^0 and b^0 are fancy ways to write 1. (Any number raised to the power 0 equals 1.) In general,

$$(a + b)^n = C(n,n)a^nb^0 + C(n, n - 1)a^{n-1}b$$
$$+ \cdots + C(n,1)ab^{n-1} + C(n,0)a^0b^n$$

Binomial expansion

This expression is referred to as the *binomial expansion*. Since the terms $C(n,n)$, $C(n, n - 1)$, . . . , $C(n,0)$ appear as coefficients in the binomial expansion, the general term $C(n,k)$ is called a *binomial coefficient*.

Binomial coefficient

So far we have discussed combinations without replacement: one player cannot play two positions on the starting lineup. The ♠ ace, once dealt to a hand, cannot be dealt again. However, sometimes we are concerned with combinations *with* replacement. How many different combinations are there in throwing two dice? If the dice are identical, we have 21 different combinations:

Combinations with replacement

11	12	13	14	15	16
	22	23	24	25	26
		33	34	35	36
			44	45	46
				55	56
					66

Remember, the *two permutations* (1,2) and (2,1) are considered *one combination*. If we speak about combinations with replacement of n objects taken k at a time we write $\overline{C}(n,k)$. Apparently $\overline{C}(6,2) = 21$: the number of combinations *with* replacement in picking two out of six is 21. In general, we have

$$\overline{C}(n,k) = C(n + k - 1, k)$$

so that the number of combinations of n objects taken k at a time *with* replacement is the same as the number of combinations of $(n + k - 1)$ objects taken k at a time *without* replacement. An intuitive argument for this result is that in drawing k items *with* replacement out of n, we put back the first $k - 1$ items drawn, so it amounts to drawing k items *without* replacement out of $n + (k - 1)$. For example, a housewife buying 10 bottles of soft drink, who can choose among gingerale, cola, root beer, and orange soda, has

$$\overline{C}(4,10) = C(13,10) = \tfrac{13!}{10!3!} = 286$$

possible different selections, of which 5 gingerale, 1 cola, 3 root beer, and 1 orange soda is just one. When choosing with replacement, k may be greater than n. Whenever we just say combinations, we mean combinations *without* replacement.

EXERCISES

4.10 (a) How many different five-card poker hands exist?
       (b) How many poker hands contain *no 2 and no 3*?

4.11 In how many ways can a committee of 12 senators be chosen out of 100? If there are 44 Republicans, what is the probability that all 12 will be Republican if the committee is chosen at random?

4.12 (a) Write out $(\tfrac{1}{2} + \tfrac{1}{2})^3$. What is the sum of the terms?
       (b) Write out $(\tfrac{1}{4} + \tfrac{3}{4})^4$.

4.13 A real estate developer has eight different house designs available and six building lots on one street.
       (a) How many different permutations are there *without* replacement, that is, using each design at most once?
       (b) How many permutations are there *with* replacement?
       (c) How many combinations are there *without* replacement?
       (d) How many combinations are there *with* replacement?
       For what persons and in what situations are these different questions relevant?

4.14 In how many ways can 10 lots of 100 shares each be bought out of 80 stocks? Find the answer for both without replacement and with replacement.

4.3 APPLICATIONS OF COMBINATIONS

The main conclusion of the previous section was that there are $C(n,k)$ ways in which a collection of k items can be chosen out of n. There are $C(25,9)$ ways in which the starting team can be formed out of a player pool of 25. Suppose, however, that two baseball teams are to be formed out of the 25, while 7 players are "reserves" (pinch hitter or relief pitcher). We have

$$9 + 9 + 7 = 25$$

and we ask how many different configurations we can distinguish. To find the answer we argue that there are $C(25,9)$ ways to choose the first team. Given the first team, 16 players remain, and $C(16,9)$ different teams can be formed out of these. Seven players remain and there is only $C(7,7) = 1$ way to get a group of 7 out of those. In conclusion, with each of the $C(25,9)$ different first teams, $C(16,9)$ different second teams can be formed and then $C(7,7)$ different groups of reserves, so that we have $C(25,9)C(16,9)C(7,7)$ different configurations. If we write it out, we get

$$C(25,9)C(16,9)C(7,7) = \frac{25!}{16!9!} \times \frac{16!}{7!9!} \times \frac{7!}{0!7!} = \frac{25!}{9!9!7!}$$

Let us go back to bridge. We have already determined that there are $C(52,13)$ different bridge hands. However, even if one player has the same hand on two successive deals, the second complete deal may well be different from the first, for the other players may have been dealt different hands. How many different *deals* are there? We have

$$13 + 13 + 13 + 13 = 52$$

since the 52 cards are going to be split up in four groups of 13 cards. The first hand can be determined in $C(52,13)$ different ways; with each of these possibilities we can combine a second hand, which can be chosen in $C(39,13)$ ways. With the $C(52,13)C(39,13)$ different configurations so far, we can combine $C(26,13)$ different third hands, and finally there is $C(13,13) = 1$ "choice" left for fourth. In total there are $C(52,13)C(39,13)C(26,13)C(13,13) = \frac{52!}{39!13!} \times \frac{39!}{26!13!} \times \frac{26!}{13!13!} \times \frac{13!}{0!13!}$ $= \frac{52!}{13!13!13!13!}$ different *deals*. The numerical answer is of the order of magnitude of 10^{28}, a number with 29 digits. The number of different *bridge hands*, by contrast, is of order 10^{11}. The ratio of these, 10^{17}, may be appreciated if it is realized that the distance between the earth and the sun is of order 10^9 miles.

In general, if

$$k_1 + k_2 + \cdots + k_r = n$$

there are

$$C(n; k_1, k_2, \ldots, k_r) = \frac{n!}{k_1! k_2! \ldots k_r!}$$

Multinomial coefficient

ways to distribute the total of n items in r subgroups of $k_1, k_2, \ldots, k_r$ items respectively. This is known as a *multinomial coefficient*.

Another application of the same formula arises in the following context. A real estate developer can build three early American, four English Tudor, and five Dutch colonial houses on 12 lots on a street. The number of different arrangements is

$$C(12;3,4,5) = \tfrac{12!}{3!4!5!} = 27{,}720$$

Another type of problem which can be solved with combinations is the following. If the Senate consists of 44 Republicans and 56 Democrats, how many different committees can be formed with five Republicans and seven Democrats? The answer is

$$C(44,5)C(56,7) = \frac{44!}{(44-5)!5!} \times \frac{56!}{(56-7)!7!}$$

which is a number with 15 digits!

Along the same lines, to find out how many bridge hands hold exactly three aces, we argue as follows. There are four aces in the deck, of which we must choose three, which can be done in $C(4,3) = 4$ ways. There are 48 other cards, of which we must take 10, which can be done in $C(48,10)$ ways. Each of the $C(4,3)$ ways to get three out of four aces can be combined with each of the $C(48,10)$ ways to get the other 10 cards, so there are $C(4,3)C(48,10)$ different hands holding exactly three aces. The *probability* of getting a hand with three aces is thus

$$\frac{C(4,3)C(48,10)}{C(52,13)} = \frac{(4!/1!3!) \times (48!/38!10!)}{52!/39!13!} = \frac{4!48!13!39!}{52!3!10!38!}$$

$$= \frac{4 \times 13 \times 12 \times 11 \times 39}{52 \times 51 \times 50 \times 49} = .041$$

In a supermarket, because of limited shelf space the manager can stock five brands of pickles from the eight available in the warehouse, three brands of soup from the five available, and two brands of canned peaches from the three available. How many different assortments can be carried? The answer is $C(8,5)C(5,3)C(3,2) = 1{,}680$.

The multinomial coefficient also arises in determining the number of permutations when *not* all items are different. The letters of the word JOKER can be permuted in $5! = 120$ ways, because all its letters are different. The word JOLLY, however, only allows $C(5;2,1,1,1) = \tfrac{5!}{2!1!1!1!} = 60$ permutations, because the two L's are the same and indistinguishable. The word LOLLY only has $\frac{5!}{3!1!1!} = 20$ permutations, and the 10 letters in the words JOLLY JOKER allow

$$C(10;2,2,2,1,1,1,1) = \frac{10!}{2!2!2!1!1!1!1!} = 403,600$$

permutations. There are two J's, two L's, and two O's, and four letters appearing just once, E, K, R, and Y.

The structure of the problems of forming two teams and seven reserves from 25 players, and of permuting the 10 letters of JOLLY JOKER, is apparently the same. This equivalence can be brought out more forcefully by writing, on the one hand,

Players	A B C D E F G H I J K L M N O P Q R S T U V W X Y
Dots	· ·
Team	1 2 1 1 R R 1 2 2 2 R 1 1 R R 1 2 1 2 2 2 2 R 1 R

and on the other hand,

Letters	J O L L Y J O K E R
Dots	· · · · · · · · · ·
Order	L J O Y K L J R O E

In the first instance, we distribute nine 1s (for first team), nine 2s (for second team), and seven R's (for reserves) over 25 dots. We see that players E, F, K, N, O, W, and Y are the bench warmers. In the second example we distribute two J's, two L's, two O's, and the letters E, K, R, Y each once over 10 dots. The two L's end up at places 1 and 6, and so on. Thus we see at a glance that the structure of the problems is equivalent.

EXERCISES

4.15 Four poker hands of 5 cards each are dealt from 52 cards. How many different *deals* exist?

4.16 Of 10 people, A through J, in an elevator, 4 are going to the second floor, 3 to the third, and 3 to the sixth. How many different configurations are there?

4.17 How many permutations do the letters in MISSISSIPPI allow?

4.18 Find a six-letter word which allows 120 permutations.

4.19 In a group of 300 shoppers, 200 are female and 100 are male. Each shopper receives a ticket upon entering the store. Each ticket is numbered, and the numbers run from 1 to 300. At the end of the day 30 numbers are drawn, and the holders of tickets with these numbers win a prize. What is the probability that 19 females and 11 males win a prize?

4.20 At a convention there are 20 people from each of the 50 states. In how many ways can we get 3 people out of each group of 20 to form a 150-member steering committee?

4.4 THE PEDESTRIAN METHOD

Many of the above results can be obtained in a more pedestrian and frequently easier way. In drawing from a deck of cards without replacement, what is the probability of drawing ♣5, ♦J, and ♦8 *in that order?* The answer might be found by the pedestrian method—step by step—as follows. There is a $\frac{1}{52}$ chance of drawing the ♣5 as the first card. Then, 51 cards remain in the deck, only one of which is the ♦J. Thus, there is a $\frac{1}{51}$ probability of getting a ♦J on the second draw. Now a deck of 50 cards remains, one of which is the ♦8, so the probability of drawing this card is $\frac{1}{50}$. The overall probability of drawing ♣5, ♦J, and ♦8 *in that order* is $\frac{1}{52} \times \frac{1}{51} \times \frac{1}{50}$. The answer derived in this way may be compared with the result obtained in Exercise 4.8.

Next, let us ask for the probability of drawing as the first three cards ♣5, ♦8, and ♦J, *without regard to order.* The first card can then be any one of these 3 out of the 52 cards, so the probability is $\frac{3}{52}$. If one of these 3 cards is drawn, 2 of them remain in 51 cards, and the probability of drawing either of them is $\frac{2}{51}$. If we are successful, there is one card remaining out of these, and the probability of drawing this one card is $\frac{1}{50}$, for an overall probability of $\frac{3}{52} \times \frac{2}{51} \times \frac{1}{50}$.

If the problem is to determine the probability that 6 people are born in 6 different months, assuming all months are equally likely, we argue as follows. The first man may state any month; the next has 11 months left if his birth month is to be different from the previous one's. The third man has 10 months left, and the sixth man, if all are to be born in a different month, should name one of the 7 not named by the previous 5 men. The probability of all 6 naming different months is

$$\frac{12}{12} \times \frac{11}{12} \times \frac{10}{12} \times \frac{9}{12} \times \frac{8}{12} \times \frac{7}{12} = .23$$

For example, the probability that the fourth man will name one of the 9 months not already named is $\frac{9}{12}$.

In the next example, we introduce 6 couples, hence 12 people. We choose 4 people by lottery, and ask for the probability that there is *no* couple among them. We call the couples Aa, Bb, Cc, Dd, Ee, and Ff. The first person chosen may be anyone, a choice of 12 out of 12. Say d is chosen. For the next choice 11 people are left (all but d), but only 10 of these may be chosen lest we get a couple (all but D), so the probability of not completing a couple after the second draw is $\frac{10}{11}$. Let us assume A is chosen. Now 10 people remain, a, Bb, Cc, D, Ee, and Ff, of which 8 will not complete a couple, Bb, Cc, Ee, Ff; so the probability of not completing a couple after the third draw is $\frac{8}{10}$. There is a probability of $\frac{6}{9}$ that the last person chosen will not complete a couple; so we have an overall probability $\frac{12}{12} \times \frac{10}{11} \times \frac{8}{10} \times \frac{6}{9} = \frac{48}{99} < 50$ percent.

In many cases, a proper mixture of this step-by-step argument and the formulas will give the correct answer. For example, in Exercise 4.19 we might find the probability of getting 19 female prize winners and 11 male winners by first determining the probability that the prizes are won in a specific order, such as the 19 females first and then the 11 males. This probability, by the pedestrian method, is

$$\frac{200}{300} \times \frac{199}{299} \times \frac{198}{298} \times \cdots \times \frac{182}{282} \times \frac{100}{281} \times \frac{99}{280} \times \cdots \times \frac{90}{271}$$

Any other specific order has the same probability of occurring. By the combinatorial formula there are $C(30,19)$ different orders which can be specified. The probability is therefore obtained by multiplying the above expression by $C(30,19)$. This result corresponds to the answer found for Exercise 4.19.

More complicated exercises can easily be contrived, but the ingredients or cornerstones of the solution techniques have been dealt with. For practical purposes, this will be sufficient.

We will review the accomplishments of this chapter in the final section.

EXERCISES

4.21　Assume that in the Senate there are 44 Republicans and 56 Democrats. What is the probability of getting a committee of 12, chosen in this order: RDDDRRDDRDDR?

4.22　Three salesmen have to visit 18 cities. Each will visit 6. They choose their 6 by picking, in turn, from the cities not previously chosen. The second salesman chooses on the second, fifth, eighth, and so on, turns. How many different permutations are open to him?

4.23   An elevator in a building with 44 floors carries 5 passengers. If the probability of a given passenger's going to a given floor is equal for all floors and all passengers, what is the probability they will all get off the elevator at the same floor? What is the probability that all will get off at the 33d floor? What is the probability they will all get off at different floors?

4.5 SURVEY OF ACCOMPLISHMENTS

To refresh your memory, we shall end the chapter with a brief review.

1. The number of permutations of n different objects taken n at a time is

$$P(n,n) = n! \qquad 0! = 1$$

Typical exercises: In how many ways can a complete deck of cards be arranged? [$52! \approx 10^{68}$.] In how many ways can one permute the letters of the word FATIGUE? [7!; notice that all letters are different.]

2. The number of permutations of n objects taken k at a time *without* replacement is

$$P(n,k) = \frac{n!}{(n-k)!} \qquad k \le n$$

Typical exercises: How many different three-color flags of the form ⬓ can be made with the six colors blue, green, red, yellow, black, and white? [$6!/(6-3)! = 120$; for example, red-white-blue, red-yellow-black, white-blue-red.] How many different ways can a store manager arrange 8 brands of detergent on a shelf if he has 15 brands available in his stock room to choose from? [$15!/(15-8)! =$ approximately 258 million.]

3. The number of permutations of n objects taken k at a time *with* replacement is

$$\overline{P}(n,k) = n^k \qquad k \text{ may exceed } n$$

Typical exercises: How many different flags of the form ☰ can one get out of six colors blue, green, red, yellow, black, and white? [$6^3 = 216$, for now also red-white-red or red-red-red are valid flags. The number would be, unlike 120, sufficient for the world's current needs.]

How many telephone numbers of 7 digits chosen from 0, 1, 2, . . . , 9 exist? [10^7; however, if the number cannot start with 0, the answer is 9×10^6.]

4. The number of combinations of n objects *without* replacement is

$$C(n,k) = \frac{n!}{(n-k)!k!} \qquad k \leq n$$

Typical exercises: In how many ways can one pick a committee of 7 out of 23? [$C(23,7) = \frac{23!}{16!7!}$.] In $(a+b)^{19}$, what is the coefficient of $a^6 b^{13}$? [$C(19,6) = C(19,13) = \frac{19!}{6!13!}$.]

5. The number of combinations of n objects taken k at a time *with* replacement is

$$\overline{C}(n,k) = C(n+k-1, k) = \frac{(n+k-1)!}{k!(n-1)!} \qquad k \text{ may exceed } n$$

Typical exercises: A new car dealer is about to order 20 new cars. There are 6 body styles available. How many different combinations, obviously with replacement, can he order? [$\overline{C}(6,20) = C(25,20) = 25!/20!(25-20)! = 53,130.$] With 4 drill presses available and 10 jobs to be assigned to them, how many different ways (disregarding order) can the jobs be assigned? [$\overline{C}(4,10) = C(13,10) = 13!/10!(13-10)! = 286.$]

6. The number of combinations if n objects are subdivided into r groups of $k_1, k_2, \ldots, k_r$ objects each, with $k_1 + k_2 + \cdots + k_r = n$, is

$$C(n;k_1,k_2,\ldots,k_r) = \frac{n!}{k_1!k_2! \ldots k_r!} \qquad k_1 + k_2 + \cdots + k_r = n$$

This is equal to the number of *permutations* of n objects of which k_1 are alike, k_2 are alike, . . . , k_r are alike.

Typical exercises: How many permutations of the letters in the word TERRITORIAL exist? [$\frac{11!}{3!2!2!1!1!1!1!} \approx 1,663,000.$] A chef receives 10 orders—3 roast beef, 5 steak, and 2 lobster. In how many ways can the orders be filled, one by one, by the chef? [$\frac{10!}{3!5!2!} = 2,520.$]

7. Finally, we introduced the pedestrian method, which was essentially a step-by-step method; hence the name. If k items are drawn, each of which has to satisfy a certain criterion ("it must be the ♣5," "he must be a Democrat," "it must not be a Monday"), we jot down k points . . . and multiply the probabilities of each point's satisfying its criterion, given that the previous ones did.

Typical exercises: Choose one of the digits 0, 1, 2, . . . , 9. Repeat until 4 digits are chosen. What is the probability that all 4 digits will be different? $[\frac{10}{10} \times \frac{9}{10} \times \frac{8}{10} \times \frac{7}{10} = \frac{504}{1,000}$. To derive the answer you might write down four dots . . . . ; the first may be any of the 10 digits; the second must satisfy the criterion of being different from the first, . . . etc.] A man who works a 5-day week is ill for 1 day 15 times a year. Assume he is equally likely to be sick on any of the 7 days in the week. What is the probability that all 15 days are work days? $[\frac{5}{7} \times \frac{5}{7} \times \frac{5}{7} \times \cdots \times \frac{5}{7} = (\frac{5}{7})^{15} \approx .0156.]$

Answers to Exercises

4.1 $P(6,6) = 6! = 720$

4.2 $\frac{1}{24}$, since only 1 out of the $4! = 24$ orders will start with the oldest, then the next oldest, . . . , and finally the youngest.

4.3 $20! \approx 2.433 \times 10^{18}$. He can pick the first in 20 ways, the next in 19, and so on.

4.4   This probability is $\frac{1}{8!}$, since in only one of the 8! possible permutations does each letter match the envelope used. The probability of exactly seven matches is 0, since if seven match, the eighth must also match.

4.5 $P(100,10) = 100!/(100 - 10)! \approx 6 \times 10^{19}$

4.6   There are $P(4,3) = 4!/(4 - 3)! = 24$ different permutations, 5 of which spell an English word (ape, nap, pan, pea, pen), so the probability is $\frac{5}{24}$.

4.7   There are $P(20,6) = 20!/(20 - 6)!$, or about 30 million different cruises, if cruises which visit the same ports in different orders are considered different. If one allows for revisiting cities, the number of possibilities is 20^6, the number of permutations *with* replacement.

4.8   There are $P(52,3) = 52!/(52 - 3)!$ different permutations, and only one of these is ♣5, ♦J, ♦8. Hence, the probability is $1/(52 \times 51 \times 50) = \frac{1}{132,600}$.

4.9 $\overline{P}(12,3) = 12^3$

4.10   (a) $C(52,5) = 52!/(52 - 5)!5! = 2,598,960$

        (b)   We must draw five cards from the $52 - 8 = 44$ cards which are *not* 2 and *not* 3. This can be done in $C(44,5) = 44!/(44 - 5)!5! = 1,086,008$ ways. The *probability* of getting a five-card hand without 2 *and* without 3 is thus $1,086,008/2,598,960 \approx 0.42$.

4.11   There are $C(100,12) \approx 1.053 \times 10^{15}$ ways to get a committee of 12. There are $C(44,12) \approx 2.11 \times 10^{10}$ ways to get only Republicans. The probability of getting only Republicans is given by $C(44,12)/C(100,12) \approx .00002$.

4.12   (a) $(\frac{1}{2})^3 + 3(\frac{1}{2})^2(\frac{1}{2}) + 3(\frac{1}{2})(\frac{1}{2})^2 + (\frac{1}{2})^3$; the sum of the terms is 1 because $(\frac{1}{2} + \frac{1}{2})^3 = 1^3 = 1$.

        (b) $(\frac{1}{4})^4 + 4(\frac{1}{4})^3(\frac{3}{4}) + 6(\frac{1}{4})^2(\frac{3}{4})^2 + 4(\frac{1}{4})(\frac{3}{4})^3 + (\frac{3}{4})^4$

4.13   Call the eight designs A, B, C, D, E, F, G, H.

        (a) $P(8,6) = 8!/(8 - 6)! = 20,160$, for example, C, E, F, A, H, B, or E, B, H, C, A, F.

        (b) $\bar{P}(8,6) = 8^6 = 262,144$, for example, D, F, F, H, D, B.

        (c) $C(8,6) = 8!/(8 - 6)!6! = 28$, for example, C, E, F, A, H, B (but not also E, B, H, C, A, F).

        (d) $\bar{C}(8,6) = C(13,6) = 13!/(13 - 6)!6! = 1,716$, for example, D, F, F, H, D, B (but not also H, D, D, B, F, F).

If limited quantities of certain materials—oval windows, grilled gates, roof shingles—permit the builder to build only one house of any given design, the builder is interested in the number of combinations *without* replacement. If, by contrast, he has enough to build each design six times if so asked, the number of combinations *with* replacement is relevant. Permutations rather than combinations are of interest for a balanced look of the street as a whole, and thus for landscape architects.

4.14   Without replacement the answer is given by $C(80,10) = 80!/(80 - 10)!10!$, or about 4×10^{12}. With replacement the answer is $\bar{C}(80,10) = C(89,10) = 89!/(89 - 10)!10!$, or about 5×10^{12}.

4.15   We have $5 + 5 + 5 + 5 + 32 = 52$, where the 32 stands for the 32 cards remaining in the deck. The answer is $\frac{52!}{5!5!5!5!32!} \approx 1.5 \times 10^{24}$.

4.16 $\frac{10!}{4!3!3!} = 4,200$; one such configuration would be AEHJ to the second, CDF to the third, and BGI to the sixth. By writing down 10 dots under the letters A through J, and distributing four 2s, three 3s, and three 6s over the dots, one can find all other configurations.

4.17 $\frac{11!}{4!4!2!1!} = 34,650$; there are 4 I's and S's, 2 P's, and 1 M.

4.18   If all letters are different, there are $6! = 720$ permutations. To get 120, we must divide by $6 = 3!$ Apparently, the word must have three letters the same, and the other letters all different, e.g., puppet, severe, sneeze, totter, keeper, cannon, bubble, goggle, esteem, armada, bikini, and syzygy, but not banana, which has 60 permutations, because of the two n's.

4.19 $C(200,19)C(100,11)/C(300,30) = .14$. In practice, values such as this are found by computers; before the age of computers approximation formulas were used.

4.20 $[C(20,3)]^{50} = (1,140)^{50}$

4.21 $\frac{44}{100} \times \frac{56}{99} \times \frac{55}{98} \times \frac{54}{97} \times \frac{43}{96} \times \frac{42}{95} \times \frac{53}{94} \times \frac{52}{93} \times \frac{41}{92} \times \frac{51}{91} \times \frac{50}{90} \times \frac{40}{89}$

4.22   The second salesman can choose his first city out of 17 (all but the one chosen already by the first salesman). In the second round he can choose out of 14 cities, in the third out of 11, and so on. In total he has $17 \times 14 \times 11 \times 8 \times 5 \times 2 = 209,440$ choices open to him. These cannot be specified without knowing the choices made by the other salesmen.

4.23   The probability they will all get off at the same floor is $(\frac{1}{44})^4$. The probability that all will get off specifically at the 33d floor is $(\frac{1}{44})^5$. The probability they will all get off at different floors is $\frac{44}{44} \times \frac{43}{44} \times \frac{42}{44} \times \frac{41}{44} \times \frac{40}{44}$.

Chapter 5

MEASURES OF CENTRAL TENDENCY AND DISPERSION

5.1 THE AVERAGE

It is often useful to characterize a series of observations with one or two comprehensive measures. The best-known measure is the *arithmetic average* or, simply, the average. The average is obtained by adding all observations and dividing by the number of observations. The number of pianos sold each week during a 10-week period by a department store was

$$1,2,1,6,2,3,4,4,6,1$$

The average number of pianos sold per week is therefore

$$\frac{1 + 2 + 1 + 6 + 2 + 3 + 4 + 4 + 6 + 1}{10} = \frac{30}{10} = 3$$

If twelve persons are weighed, and the results are, in pounds, 137, 182, 142, 150, 155, 142, 173, 146, 201, 180, 160, 164, the average, obtained by summing these values and dividing by 12, is $\frac{1,932}{12} = 161$ pounds.

The average of n observations $x_1, x_2, \ldots, x_n$ is denoted by $\bar{x}$ and defined as:

Definition of the average $\bar{x}$

$$\bar{x} = \frac{x_1 + x_2 + \cdots + x_n}{n} = \frac{\Sigma x_i}{n}$$

Summation
symbol Σ

The symbol Σ before x_i means that all x_i values, from $i = 1$ to $i = n$, should be added, or summed. This could be written more explicitly as $\sum_{i=1}^{i=n} x_i$, but whenever we use the symbol Σ, it will imply summing over all n values. (In Chapter 18 is the only, clearly labeled, exception.)

The sum of deviations from the average, $(x_1 - \overline{x})$, $(x_2 - \overline{x})$, ..., $(x_n - \overline{x})$, is zero. This is illustrated in Table 5.1. This is, in fact, a useful check on the computations. It is also evident from Table 5.1, by comparing the totals of Columns 1 and 2, that the sum of the observations $(x_1 + x_2 + \cdots + x_n)$ equals the *number* of observations times the average $(n\overline{x})$. The totals of Columns 1 and 2 are thus equal. Algebraically, the result follows by multiplying the definition formula through by n, which leads to $n\overline{x} = x_1 + x_2 + \cdots + x_n$. The left-hand side is the total of Column 2; the right-hand side is the total of Column 1.

Central
tendency

The average is a measure of *central tendency*, in that it gives a value around which the observations tend to cluster. It does not, however, lead a life of its own.

The statement that the average number of children in an American family is 2.8 does not imply that there is even a single family with 2.8

TABLE 5.1   THE SUM OF DEVIATIONS FROM THE AVERAGE IS ZERO

(1)	(2)	(3)
		(1) − (2)
Observations		Deviation
on weight of 12 persons	Average	from average
137	161	−24
182	161	+21
142	161	−19
150	161	−11
155	161	−6
142	161	−19
173	161	+12
146	161	−15
201	161	+40
180	161	+19
160	161	−1
164	161	+3
Total 1,932	1,932	0

Average $= 1,932/12 = 161$

children. Nor was a duck ever killed by the average of two shots, one a yard in front of it, and one a yard behind it. An aspect of central tendency is that the average is always between the extreme values. A man 5 feet tall can drown while standing in a river which *averages* 3 feet in depth if he tries to stand at a point where the river happens to be 6 feet deep.

EXERCISES

5.1   In 12 consecutive months the number of rejected pieces produced by the operator of a lathe was 82, 74, 65, 67, 62, 73, 68, 63, 65, 62, 69, and 66.
(*a*) What was his average number of rejects?
(*b*) Explain the meaning of this result in terms of the problem.
(*c*) What is the sum of the deviations from this average?

5.2   The average daily high temperature in the week from February 5 through February 12 was 4°F below the normal average of 25°F. What might the daily highs have been? What must be true of any set of values you give as your answer to the previous question?

5.3   Ten families have an average of 2.8 children. How many children do they have together?

5.4   The egg consumption per capita in the United States in 1965 was 240. (The "average" person consumed 240 eggs, directly or indirectly, in cakes, etc.) In total, 45.6 billion eggs were consumed. What was the size of the population?

5.5   If Robin Hood's dream came true in the United States, so that all received the same share of the gross national product, how much would each person receive?

5.6   A man claims that his average bank balance during the year was $370. The bank claims he overdrew his account at least 10 times during that year. Can both be right? Why?

5.2 FREQUENCY DISTRIBUTIONS
     AND HISTOGRAMS

Labor can often be saved by grouping like observations together. A simple illustration will bear this out. Suppose that a series of 100 throws of a die leads to the following outcomes:

```
1 3 5 4 .5 4 1 2 5 6 1 1 1 3 5 4 2 2 4 6 1 3 5 2 4
1 4 4 5 6 5 5 1 1 2 2 1 3 3 4 3 4 2 1 6 4 1 6 6 2
6 6 1 3 3 4 1 6 1 2 2 2 3 3 4 5 5 3 1 6 6 6 6 2 1
3 2 4 3 3 4 4 2 2 2 4 1 1 5 6 6 5 1 2 3 6 4 2 6 4
```

Frequency distribution

We count the number of 1s, 2s, . . . , 5s, and 6s, which gives us a *frequency distribution* of these data, shown in Table 5.2 in Columns 1 and 2. The average is computed with the help of Column 3. Instead of 20 times adding 1, and 18 times adding 2, . . . , we simply add 20×1 and 18×2, and so on, to obtain the results faster.

Relative frequency

A slight modification of this scheme provides a useful steppingstone for further results below. We add a column with the *relative frequency* of each outcome. If 20 out of 100 throws lead to the outcome 1, the relative frequency of this outcome is $\frac{20}{100} = .20$. The total of Column 4 of Table 5.3, obtained by multiplying each outcome by its relative frequency, is the average.

We now have three ways to compute the average. If we apply the definition formula, we get

$$\frac{1 + 3 + 5 + 4 + 5 + \cdots + 6 + 4 + 2 + 6 + 4}{100} = \frac{335}{100} = 3.35$$

In Table 5.2 we grouped the data and got

$$\frac{20 \times 1 + 18 \times 2 + 15 \times 3 + 18 \times 4 + 12 \times 5 + 17 \times 6}{100} = \frac{335}{100} = 3.35$$

TABLE 5.2   FREQUENCY DISTRIBUTION OF OUTCOMES OF 100 THROWS OF A DIE AND COMPUTATION OF AVERAGE

(1) Outcome	(2) Frequency	(3) (1) × (2)
1	20	20
2	18	36
3	15	45
4	18	72
5	12	60
6	17	102
Total	100	335

Average $= \frac{335}{100} = 3.35$

TABLE 5.3 FREQUENCY DISTRIBUTION OF OUTCOMES OF 100 THROWS OF A DIE AND COMPUTATION OF AVERAGE VIA RELATIVE FREQUENCIES

(1)	(2)	(3)	(4)
		Relative	
Outcome	Frequency	frequency	(1) × (3)
1	20	.20	.20
2	18	.18	.36
3	15	.15	.45
4	18	.18	.72
5	12	.12	.60
6	17	.17	1.02
Total	100	1.00	Average = 3.35

In Table 5.3 we computed relative frequencies and found

$$\tfrac{20}{100} \times 1 + \tfrac{18}{100} \times 2 + \tfrac{15}{100} \times 3 + \tfrac{18}{100} \times 4 + \tfrac{12}{100} \times 5 + \tfrac{17}{100} \times 6 = \tfrac{335}{100} = 3.35$$

Graphically, the data of the frequency distribution can be shown in a *bar diagram,* as illustrated in Figure 5.1. We have indicated the average in the figure by a red dot.   Bar diagram

An average is a single value used to characterize a set of observations. The observations may be so numerous that it is impractical to work with the individual observations. In such cases the observations may be grouped into classes. Many different numerical outcomes may fall in the same class. Experience has shown that the most convenient number of classes is somewhere between 6 and 12, and that it is unwise to have classes with

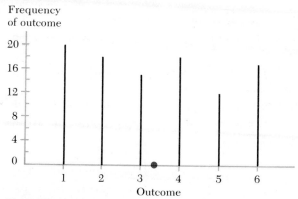

Figure 5.1 Bar diagram.

TABLE 5.4   FREQUENCY DISTRIBUTION OF WEEKLY SALARIES OF SECRETARIES

(1) Weekly salary, dollars	(2) Frequency	(3) Midpoint of interval	(4) (2) × (3)
50 < 60	2	$55	$110
60 < 70	2	65	130
70 < 80	5	75	375
80 < 90	9	85	765
90 < 100	14	95	1,330
100 < 110	19	105	1,995
110 < 120	15	115	1,725
120 < 130	10	125	1,250
130 < 140	3	135	405
140 < 150	1	145	145
Total	80		$8,230

Average = $8,230/80 = $102.88

very few observations. The ideal set of classes will not only conform to these conditions but also have all classes equal in width. This is the case with the frequency distribution presented in Table 5.4. We will determine

Data grouped into classes

the average from these grouped data. Column 1 divides the weekly salary of secretaries into classes, with $80 < $90 standing for "at least $80 but less than $90." Column 2 gives the frequencies; we see that there were nine secretaries with a weekly income of at least $80 but less than $90. Column 3 gives the class midpoint. We now assume that the nine secretaries with incomes between $80 and $90 earned an average of $85, so that their total weekly income is 9 × $85 = $765, as given in Column 4. Proceeding in this way for all income classes, we see that 80 secretaries have a total joint weekly income of $8,230, for an average weekly income per secretary of $8,230/80 = $102.88. *Notice that we made the explicit assumption in these computations that the average income of the girls in any income class coincides with the midpoint of that class.* To the extent that this assumption is not met, the result will only be approximate.

The formula for the computation of the average from data grouped in k classes is

$$\bar{x} = \frac{f_1 \operatorname{mid}_1 + f_2 \operatorname{mid}_2 + \cdots + f_k \operatorname{mid}_k}{n}$$

where f_2 is the frequency of the second class and mid_2 is the midpoint of that class. The number of observations n equals $f_1 + f_2 + \cdots + f_k$.

The data in Table 5.4 can be graphically displayed in a *histogram*.   Histogram
A histogram shows the number of observations in each class. For the histogram of secretaries' salaries we refer to Figure 5.2. The *area* above each class is proportional to the number of secretaries in the class. It is this area, and not the height of the column, that is the key factor. To emphasize this, the vertical axis is labeled *frequency density*, not simply   Frequency
frequency. In the next three paragraphs we will further illustrate the   density
importance of this point.

Usually there is little to be gained by explaining what *not* to do. The following error in connection with histograms is so tempting, however, that a word of caution is in order. Suppose that the data of Table 5.4 were grouped a little differently, as in Table 5.5. As a result of regrouping, the computed average has changed a little, but that is not the point we wish to emphasize here. Rather, the problem here is how to construct a histogram from these data. If we were to proceed without caution and thought, the resulting histogram would look like Figure 5.3. There is something disconcerting about this figure, especially if it is realized that it is based on nearly the same data as in Figure 5.2. The error in the figure is that *the area above each class is no longer proportional to the*

TABLE 5.5   FREQUENCY DISTRIBUTION OF WEEKLY SALARIES OF SECRETARIES

(1) Weekly salary, dollars	(2) Frequency	(3) Midpoint of interval	(4) (2) × (3)
50 < 70	4	$60	$240
70 < 80	5	75	375
80 < 90	9	85	765
90 < 95	6	92.50	555
95 < 100	8	97.50	780
100 < 105	8	102.50	820
105 < 110	11	107.50	1,182.50
110 < 120	15	115	1,725
120 < 130	10	125	1,250
130 < 150	4	140	560
Total	80		$8,252.50

Average = $8,252/80 = $103.15

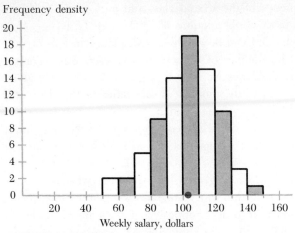

Figure 5.2 Histogram of secretaries' salaries.

number of secretaries in that class. This situation arises because the class intervals have different widths.

The error can be repaired as follows. In drawing a histogram, one should first establish a *standard interval width.* In Figure 5.2 this was 10. The classes all were $10, for example, $80 to $90. Let us agree to use the same standard width here. The intervals from $70 to $80, $80 to $90, $110 to $120, and $120 to $130 are of standard width. What about the four observations in the interval $50 to $70? We don't know where these observations fall, but the most reasonable assumption is that there will be two observations in each of the intervals $50 to $60 and $60 to $70, so the height of the histogram should be 2, not 4! And what about the six observations in the interval $90 to $95? We argue that if

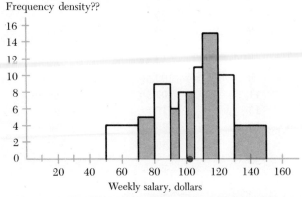

Figure 5.3 Erroneous representation of weekly salaries of secretaries in Table 5.5.

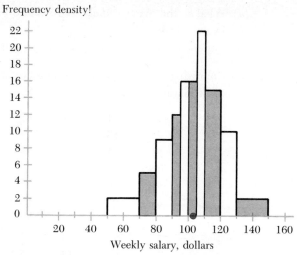

Figure 5.4 Correct representation of weekly salaries of secretaries in Table 5.5.

the interval had been of width 10, which is twice as large, then the observations would have numbered 12, twice as many. If we incorporate these modifications in the histogram, we get Figure 5.4, which is the correct histogram. In the correct histogram, an *area* of given size stands for one observation. If there are four observations between $50 and $70, and eight between $95 and $100, then the latter *area* should be twice as large. To accomplish this the column will be eight times as high. This is true in Figure 5.4, but not in Figure 5.3.

To emphasize that area rather than height is the relevant measure, we label the vertical axis frequency density, because the frequency is spread, more or less densely, depending on the width of the interval.

EXERCISES

5.7   Determine the average of every second throw of the die if the results are as recorded in the beginning of this section. The results begin with 3, 4, 4, 2, 6, 1 and end with 6, 5, 2, 6, 2, 4. There are 50 observations in total. Also, draw a bar diagram.

5.8   A housewife has the following observations on daily out-of-pocket expenses for 1 month (27 days).

< $1	1	$ 5 < $10	10
$1 < $2	0	$10 < $20	7
$2 < $5	4	$20 < $50	5

(a) What is the average daily expenditure for the month?

(b) Draw a histogram.

(c) Comment on the wisdom of grouping these data as shown.

5.9   The following data pertain to the number of flaws found in 100 pieces of fabric of equal size:

24	21	34	13	23
21	15	27	20	25
25	21	20	24	13
18	34	22	32	15
8	29	17	27	22
22	25	23	16	24
22	29	18	22	20
17	17	23	22	31
22	21	30	23	36
26	37	15	18	26
15	41	10	21	20
20	16	39	25	16
23	21	14	34	19
21	11	8	7	19
32	18	48	16	31
21	24	19	16	39
16	24	13	23	23
21	27	25	19	23
18	31	26	21	20
28	14	29	31	32

(a) Group these observations into a reasonable set of classes.

(b) Compute the average from these grouped data.

(c) Draw a histogram.

(d) What is the precise average? If it differs from the result in (b), why?

5.3 OTHER MEASURES OF CENTRAL TENDENCY—THE MEDIAN AND THE MODE

Median   Other measures of central tendency are occasionally used. The *median* is the value of the middle observation when the observations are ranked, that is, listed in order of size. As a result, the number of observations

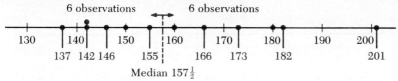

Figure 5.5 Locating the median.

smaller than the median will be the same as the number larger than the median. If there is no unique middle observation—that is, whenever the total number of observations is *even*—the average of the middle two values is taken as median. The 10 weekly sales of pianos were 1, 2, 1, 6, 2, 3, 4, 4, 6, 1. We order them: 1, 1, 1, 2, 2, 3, 4, 4, 6, 6. The two middle values are the fifth and the sixth, 2 and 3. The median is therefore $2\frac{1}{2}$ pianos. The median of the weights 137, 142, 142, 146, 150, 155, 160, 166, 173, 180, 182, 201, is the average of 155 and 160, that is, $157\frac{1}{2}$ pounds. We can rank the observations on an axis, as in Figure 5.5. We see that the median value is such that there are as many observations *lower* as there are *higher*.

The median value of the observations 1, 3, 4, is the same as the median value of the observations 2, 3, 99, or the observations −100, 3, 999, although these three series are rather drastically different. The impression which the median creates in some cases can be very deceptive, because its value is determined strictly by the value of the middle observation(s). The median value of prizes in lotteries is nearly always zero (more than 50 percent of the tickets win no prize), but this does not tell us very much about the matters we are interested in, such as the value of first prize.

We can often determine the median for observations which are not expressed numerically. Consumers may be asked to rank five samples of lemon pudding according to the "trueness" of the flavor—comparing the pudding with real lemon flavor. The pudding ranked third is the median.

We can also determine the median of classed observations. Consider the frequency distribution of secretaries' salaries, Table 5.4. There are 80 secretaries in total, and both the 40th and the 41st are in the class from $100 to $110, so the median is somewhere between $100 and $110. This is all that is certain. To make our result more specific, an assumption must be made. Of the 19 secretaries in this class, the eighth lowest is the 40th, and the ninth lowest the 41st. Hence the median is the "$8\frac{1}{2}$" of the 19 secretaries. We now make the assumption that the 19 salaries are *evenly spaced* between $100 and $110, as in Figure 5.6. Note that

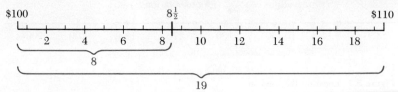

Figure 5.6 Estimating the median of classed observations.

the distance from the first and last secretaries to the endpoints of the interval is $\frac{1}{2}$ as great as the distance between secretaries. The "$8\frac{1}{2}$" secretary is $\frac{8}{19}$ of the distance from \$100 to \$110. The ratio $\frac{8}{19}$ is about .42, and the class width is \$10. We conclude that the median is \$100 + .42 × \$10 = \$104.20. Of course, if we knew the individual salaries, we would find a median that might differ, but chances are, it would not differ much.

We can find the above result algebraically by using the formula for the median of grouped data. In this example, that gives

$$100 + \left(\frac{\frac{80}{2} - 32}{19} \right) 10$$

In this expression \$100 is the lower limit of the interval in which the median must fall, 80 is the number of observations, 32 is the number of secretaries earning less than \$100, 19 is the number of secretaries in the class where the median falls, and \$10 is the width of the class interval.

The formula holds generally:

$$\text{med} = L_{\text{med}} + \left(\frac{n/2 - f_{\text{cum}}}{f_{\text{med}}} \right) i_{\text{med}}$$

where

L_{med} = lower limit of interval containing median
f_{med} = number of observations in interval containing median
i_{med} = width of interval containing median
n = total number of observations
f_{cum} = number of observations smaller than L_{med}

Mode
The *mode* or *modal class* is another measure of central tendency. The mode is the value of the most frequent observation. The mode of the observations 1, 1, 1, 2, 2, 3, 4, 4, 6, 6 is 1, because it is the most prevalent result. This indicates that the mode as a measure of "central tendency" is sometimes deceptive. The mode of the weights recorded above in this section is 142. If one of the two persons of weight 142 had in fact weighed

143, there would have been no mode (or there would have been 12 modes). The mode is most useful if there are many observations which can assume relatively few different values. The mode can be used to express central tendency among observations on qualitative characteristics such as color, sex, or state of birth. The modal color of Volkswagens imported into the United States is red.

In the case of data grouped in classes we speak of the *modal class* rather than the mode. The modal class of secretarial salaries in Table 5.4 is the class $100 to $110. The modal class of Table 5.5 *appears* to be the class from $110 to $120, but more careful consideration of the data, and in particular the different interval widths, shows that the modal class is from $105 to $110, as illustrated in Figure 5.4. In general, the modal class corresponds to the highest column in the histogram. It should be clear that the division of the range between largest and smallest items into class intervals is arbitrary to an extent, and so the modal class is also arbitrary to that extent.

Modal class

EXERCISES

5.10   What is the median of the observations 5, 7, 4, 3, 6, 9, and 11?

5.11   The median of 11 observations is 81, and the smallest observation is 70. What is the largest observation?

5.12   Use the following data to answer the questions below:

Daily output, thousands of tons	No. of days
20 < 25	4
25 < 30	6
30 < 35	9
35 < 40	13
40 < 45	7
45 < 50	6
	45

(a) Calculate the average.
(b) Calculate the median.
(c) Express the meaning of the average and the median in terms of this problem, distinguishing between them.
(d) What is the modal class?

5.13   Using the data from Exercise 5.12, construct a histogram. Show the values of the average and the median.

5.14   Assume the "number of days" values are changed to

6

7

13

9

6

4

(*a*) Is the average different now? Why?

(*b*) Is the median different now? Why?

(*c*) Is the modal class different now? Why?

5.4 INTERESTING PROPERTIES OF THE AVERAGE, MEDIAN, AND MODE

The sum of deviations from the average is zero. The average of the values 6 and 10 is 8. The deviations are -2 and $+2$, and the sum is zero. However, if we sum these deviations, disregarding their sign, the total will always be positive. In our case $2 + 2 = 4$. We refer to this operation as adding the *absolute values* of the deviations. The median has the interesting property that the sum of the absolute values of the deviations from it is never greater than the sum of the absolute values of the deviations from any other value. This is illustrated in Table 5.6. In this table the entries given in red are actually negative deviations, which we treat as positive when we work with absolute values.

Absolute
values

Median
minimizes
absolute
deviations

To prove this statement we use an example of three observations 1, 3, and 7. The median is 3. By moving away from 3 we come closer to 1 point, but we get farther away *by the same distance* from 2 points, so the sum of the absolute deviations from all 3 points increases in the process. This is illustrated in Figure 5.7.

The same general idea is true for any number of observations. If we have 17 points, moving away from the midpoint we come closer to 8 but go farther away from 9 points, for a net deficit. If the number of points is even, any value in between the middle two values (not only the median) leads to the same minimum sum of absolute deviations. If the observations are 2, 5, 11, 12, any point from 5 to 11, in particular also the median 8, leads to a sum of absolute deviations equal to 16.

TABLE 5.6   SUM OF ABSOLUTE VALUES OF DEVIATIONS FROM MEDIAN (157½), AVERAGE (161), AND ARBITRARY VALUE 200 OF WEIGHTS

(1)	(2)	(3)	(4)
	Absolute values of deviations from	*Absolute values of deviations from*	*Absolute values of deviations from*
Weight	*median (157½)*	*average (161)*	*arbitrary value 200*
137	20½	24	63
182	24½	21	18
142	15½	19	58
150	7½	11	50
155	2½	6	45
142	15½	19	58
173	15½	12	27
146	11½	15	54
201	43½	40	1
180	22½	19	20
160	2½	1	40
164	6½	3	36
Total 1,932	188	190	470

A second way to circumvent the difficulty that the sum of deviations from the average is always zero is to *square* these deviations. The average has the interesting property that the sum of the squared deviations from it is less than the sum of squared deviations from any other number. This result is illustrated in Table 5.7 for the example of weekly sales of pianos.

Average minimizes squared deviations

The mode has the property that it minimizes the number of observations different from it and maximizes the number of observations equal to it.

A geographical example may illustrate the difference between average, median, and mode more clearly. Suppose there is a conference with five participants from Buffalo, two from Chicago, and four from Los Angeles. These cities are displayed in Figure 5.8 with their distances in miles from Los Angeles. If we want to select a site for the maximum convenience

Figure 5.7   The median minimizes the total absolute deviations: closer to 1 point (7); farther away *by the same distance* from 2 points (1 and 3).

TABLE 5.7 SUM OF SQUARED DEVIATIONS FROM AVERAGE 3 AND VALUES 2.9 AND 3.1 FOR WEEKLY SALES OF PIANOS

(1) Weekly sales	(2) Squared deviations from average 3	(3) Squared deviations from value 2.9	(4) Squared deviations from value 3.1
1	4	3.61	4.41
2	1	.81	1.21
1	4	3.61	4.41
6	9	9.61	8.41
2	1	.81	1.21
3	0	.01	.01
4	1	1.21	.81
4	1	1.21	.81
6	9	9.61	8.41
1	4	3.61	4.41
Total 30	34	34.10	34.10

of the maximum number of persons, the modal geographic location is appropriate, and the conference will be in Buffalo. If we want to minimize the total of the distance to be traveled, the median is appropriate, and the conference will be held in Chicago. We may want to minimize the sum of the squares of the distances, because we feel that the disutility of travel increases with the square of the distance traveled. We may feel that it is four times as inconvenient to travel 2,000 miles as it is to travel 1,000 miles. We will, according to the computation in Table 5.8, convene 1,564 miles from Los Angeles on the way to Chicago, that is, in Keokuk, Iowa. This location also equalizes the westward travel and the eastward travel. (That the conference will actually be held in Hawaii to maximize the total pleasure of all attending is irrelevant in this context.)

    Another important property of the average can be conveniently

Weighted
average

expressed as follows. A *weighted average* of the averages of separate groups of observations coincides with the average of all observations combined.

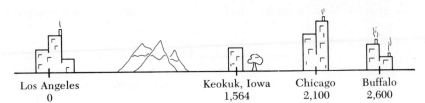

| Los Angeles
0 | | Keokuk, Iowa
1,564 | Chicago
2,100 | Buffalo
2,600 |

Figure 5.8 The average, median, and mode compared.

TABLE 5.8   COMPUTATION OF THE AVERAGE OF THE DISTANCES TO BE TRAVELED

	(1) Distance	(2) Frequency	(3) (1) × (2)
Los Angeles	0	4	0
Chicago	2,100	2	4,200
Buffalo	2,600	5	13,000
Total		11	17,200

Average = 17,200/11 = 1,564

If 10 men in a company have an average salary of $8,420 and 23 women have an average salary of $4,750, the average salary of all employees is

$$\frac{\$8,420 \times 10 + \$4,750 \times 23}{33} = \$5,862$$

where 10 and 23 are weights, which explains the name given this type of average. The median and mode do not share this convenient property. The median salary for men and the median salary for women cannot be combined to give us the median salary for all 33 employees.

The weighted average concept lies at the heart of the construction of an index number. Food, clothing, shelter, and services are four major categories of expenditures in a consumer's budget. Food includes milk and honey, clothing includes shirts and shoes, shelter includes rent and furniture, and services include medical care and education. They might form 20, 15, 25, and 40 percent of a person's budget. Food rises 5 percent in price, clothing rises 2 percent, shelter decreases 1 percent, and services rise 8 percent. What is the average price increase for this person? The answer is given by:

$$\frac{.05 \times .20 + .02 \times .15 + (-.01) \times .25 + .08 \times .40}{.20 + .15 + .25 + .40} = .0425$$

or 4.25 percent.

As we saw, different measures of central tendency have different properties. The question may arise, "Which one is the most appropriate in a given situation?" The guiding principle is that the use to be made of the measure determines which measure to use. A restaurant owner who specializes in one dish only will want to know the modal preference of his potential clientele. If employees receive yearly raises, they might want to know the median raise, so as to be able to know whether they are in the "good" half or the "bad" half. The management, however, is more interested in the average raise, since this is going to determine the total amount of money needed to pay for the raises.

Nevertheless, the choice of the measure to be used involves in many cases some arbitrariness. This leaves room for chicanery. If the higher result is the better, it is tempting to use the measure which gives the highest result. If three light bulbs are tested for length of life, and the results are 100, 110, and 150 hours, an advertising copywriter may use the average 120, rather than the median 110. If the results are 100, 125, and 135 hours, he will be tempted to take the median 125, rather than the average of 120. If the results of testing five bulbs are 100, 115, 125, 130, 130, he might even use the mode of 130 rather than the average 120 or the median 125. Since we can define other measures of central tendency to suit our fancy as well, the possibility of "proving what one sets out to prove" with statistics is large when used unscrupulously or incompetently. Note that the user, not the tool, is at fault here.

EXERCISES

5.15   What will happen to the average, median, and mode if all the frequencies in a frequency distribution are made twice as large as they were to begin with? (Answer for each measure separately.)

5.16   The table below shows the number of skilled and unskilled laborers in two small communities, together with their average hourly wages.

| Labor category | Bosalo | | Buffton | |
	Number	Wage per hr	Number	Wage per hr
Skilled	150	$1.80	350	$1.75
Unskilled	850	1.30	650	1.25

(a) Determine the average hourly wage for each community.

(b) Give the reasons for the result that the average hourly wage in Buffton exceeds the average hourly wage in Bosalo, even though in Buffton the average hourly wage of both categories of worker is lower.

5.17   A manufacturer of hand shovels is deciding what length of handles to use. Studies of user preferences reveal that the average, the median, and the modal preferred length are all different. What are the implications of using each of these values?

5.18 Two brands of tires are tested with the following results:

Life, thousands of miles	Brand X	Brand Y
20 < 25	1	0
25 < 27.5	7	4
27.5 < 30	15	20
30 < 31	10	32
31 < 32	15	30
32 < 33	17	12
33 < 34	13	2
34 < 35	9	0
35 < 37.5	8	0
37.5 < 40	2	0
40 < 45	3	0
	100	100

(a) Draw a histogram for each frequency distribution.
(b) Calculate the average, median, and mode for each distribution.
(c) Which brand of tire would you use on your fleet of trucks?
(d) If the law forbids truck tires to be used for more than 30,000 miles, how does that change your answer, if at all?

5.19 An investor buys $120 worth of stock in a company each month. During the first 5 months he bought the stock at a price of $10, $12, $15, $20, and $24 per share. After 5 months what is the average price paid for the shares in his portfolio?

5.20 In the years 1960–1966 the percentage of boys born was 51.23, 50.01, 50.20, 51.12, 51.19, 50.74, 51.81. Verify that the average of these percentages is 50.90. The actual average over these 7 years was $\frac{14,182}{27,895} = 50.84$, as given in Section 2.1. Explain the difference.

5.5 MEASURES OF DISPERSION

Frequently one is interested in a *stable* level of performance, in a *steady* worker, in a *reliable* product. The words stable, steady, reliable all refer to the idea that fluctuations are limited. A supermarket will try to sell meats and vegetables of *uniformly* high quality. They know that nothing leads to a faster loss of customers than good, fresh corn one day and corn that lingered and languished on the shelf the next day. It is not only high average quality one is after, one also wants little variability in this quality, that is, *dependability*.

If three bags of peanuts contain 3, 4, and 5 grams of salt, and three similar bags from another producer contain 1, 4, and 7 grams of salt, then these triplets have the same average content of salt, but the variability, **Dispersion** or *dispersion,* in the latter case is larger. This statement is intuitive. We will consider two precise measures of dispersion, the range and the variance.

Range   The *range* is determined by the extreme values. The range is strictly defined as the difference between the largest and smallest observations. Thus, the range of 1, 4, and 7 is $(7 - 1) = 6$. It is often convenient to identify these extreme values explicitly, which leads to statements such as, "The median income in our department is \$12,760, and the range is from \$8,640 to \$23,470." In this case the range, in the strict sense, is \$14,830.

The range, despite its ease of computation, is less useful than the **Variance** *variance. The variance is the sum of squared deviations from the average* **var x** *divided by the number of observations.* If there are three observations x_1, x_2, and x_3, with an average $\bar{x} = (x_1 + x_2 + x_3)/3$, the variance equals

$$\text{var } x = \frac{(x_1 - \bar{x})^2 + (x_2 - \bar{x})^2 + (x_3 - \bar{x})^2}{3}$$

In general, for n observations, we have

$$\text{var } x = \frac{(x_1 - \bar{x})^2 + (x_2 - \bar{x})^2 + \cdots + (x_n - \bar{x})^2}{n} = \frac{\Sigma(x_i - \bar{x})^2}{n}$$

For the two short series 3, 4, 5 and 1, 4, 7 the variance is computed in Table 5.9.

By returning to Table 5.7 we see that the variance of the weekly number of pianos sold, 1, 2, 1, 6, 2, 3, 4, 4, 6, and 1, is $\frac{34}{10} = 3.4$. The variance of the 12 weights (in pounds) can also be computed, and is $\frac{4,321}{12} \approx 351$.

Standard   The positive square root of the variance is referred to as the *standard* **deviation** *deviation,* which we will write sd x. We have **sd x**

$$\text{sd } x = \sqrt{\text{var } x}$$

TABLE 5.9   ILLUSTRATIVE VARIANCE COMPUTATIONS

(1) Outcome	(2) Average	(3) (1) − (2)	(4) (3)²
3	4	−1	1
4	4	0	0
5	4	1	1
Total 12	12	0	2

Average = $\frac{12}{3}$ = 4   Variance = $\frac{2}{3}$

(1) Outcome	(2) Average	(3) (1) − (2)	(4) (3)²
1	4	−3	9
4	4	0	0
7	4	3	9
Total 12	12	0	18

Average = $\frac{12}{3}$ = 4   Variance = $\frac{18}{3}$ = 6

The standard deviation is of great importance, as the following will show.

In trying to summarize a large quantity of data, such as the number of automobiles produced each day in an assembly plant or the number of teachers sick each day in a metropolitan school system, one will first use the average as a measure around which the actual values tend to cluster. It is, however, quite possible that no single observation coincides with this average. It may well be that during the past year the average number of sick school teachers was 48, but that this total was never actually recorded on any specific day. Now, if it is also known that the standard deviation of the number of sick teachers is 10, then we have much more information in view of the following *rules of thumb:*

Rules of thumb

1. Practically all actual observations will be within 3 standard deviations of the average (in our example, there will be very few, if any, days during which the actual number of sick teachers was not within the range 48 ± 3 × 10, or from 18 to 78).

2. More than 90 percent of the actual observations will be within 2 standard deviations of the average (in our example, within the range 28 to 68).

3. More than half of the actual observations will be within 1 standard deviation of the average (in our example, although the exact value 48 need never be recorded, more than half the days the actual number of sick teachers will be between 38 and 58).

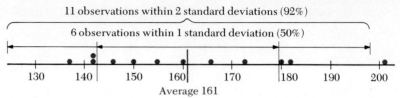

Figure 5.9   The percentage of observations within 1 and 2 standard deviations of the average.

We repeat, these are rules of thumb. It can be *proved mathematically* that at least 75 percent of all observations are within 2 standard deviations of the average, and at least 89 percent are within 3 standard deviations of the average, but usually these percentages will be exceeded.

First, let us check these rules of thumb for the case involving 12 observations on weights. This is done in Figure 5.9. We know that the mean weight is 161 pounds and the standard deviation is $\sqrt{351} = 18.7$ pounds. The interval 161 ± 18.7, or 142.3 to 179.7, should include at least 50 percent, or six, observations. It does. The interval $161 \pm 2\,(18.7)$, or 123.6 to 198.4, should include at least 90 percent, or 11, observations. It does. If we go 3 standard deviations on either side of the average, we easily include all observations.

Let us use these rules the other way around. Can we guess the order of magnitude of the standard deviation from the rules? Consider the following 20 observations, which have an average equal to 51:

5	30	98	61	80
26	42	17	84	32
97	9	21	25	28
94	97	24	68	82

By plotting them graphically, we get Figure 5.10. Could the standard deviation be 20? If it is, only four observations, or 20 percent, will be within 1 standard deviation of the average, and only 14 observations, or 70 percent, within 2 standard deviations. These results are not high enough, so the standard deviation must be larger. If the standard deviation

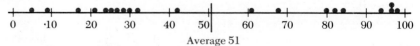

Figure 5.10   Visual estimation of the standard deviation.

is 30, there are 10 or 11 observations within 1 standard deviation, that is, in the range 21 to 81. This is a little over 50 percent. All observations are within 2 standard deviations. The result, 30, seems a reasonable guess. If we try 25, we find that all observations are within 2 standard deviations, but only six or seven, that is, at best 35 percent, are within 1 standard deviation. Our best guess is 30. In fact, the standard deviation is about 32, which is a shade higher than our guess (which is due to the cluster of points around 97). We have 60 percent within 1 standard deviation and 100 percent within 2.

Incidentally, if the observations are not pure numbers, but quantities measured in units such as pounds, dollars, inches, or hours, the standard deviation is also measured in pounds, dollars, inches, or hours. The statement that the height of adult human males has an average of 5 feet 9 inches, with a standard deviation of 6 inches, implies that at least 90 percent of human males have a height of between 4 feet 9 inches and 6 feet 9 inches. This corresponds with the impression obtained from a casual glance at the audience in a stadium.

There are two further issues to be covered. The first concerns a more efficient way to compute the standard deviation. The second concerns the calculation of the variance and standard deviation of grouped data. We will consider them in turn. The definition formula shows exactly what the variance is, but it is not the most convenient for computations. Instead of using

$$\text{var } x = \frac{\Sigma(x_i - \overline{x})^2}{n}$$

we use the mathematically equivalent formula

$$\text{var } x = \frac{1}{n}(x_1^2 + x_2^2 + \cdots + x_n^2) - \overline{x}^2 = \frac{1}{n}\Sigma x_i^2 - \overline{x}^2$$

Efficient computation of var x and sd x

In words, we say that the variance equals the average of the squared observations—that is, $(1/n)(x_1^2 + x_2^2 + \cdots + x_n^2)$—minus the squared average. It can be easily remembered as "the average of the squares minus the square of the average." The derivation of the equivalence is an exercise in algebra.

The advantage of this new formula is that we do not have to deduct the average from each observation. The computations needed to compute the variance are given in Table 5.10. As before, the standard deviation is the square root of the variance, sd $x = \sqrt{\text{var } x}$.

Var x and
sd x from
grouped data

The computations are a little more extensive if a frequency distribution is given. The variance of the secretaries' salaries is given in Table 5.11. Columns 1, 2, 3, and 4 are the same as in Table 5.4. In Column 5 all the midpoints, that is, 55, 65, 75, etc., are squared. In Column 6 these squared midpoints are multiplied by their frequencies and added. The total of Column 6 is the sum of squares of all the observations, assuming that the values in a class are equal to the midpoint. The average of the squared observations is obtained by dividing this sum by 80, and it equals 10,922.5. The square of the average equals $(102.88)^2 =$ 10,584.3, and their difference equals 338.2. This value is var x. The standard deviation sd x is about \$18.40. The average $\bar{x}$ is \$102.88. Between the limits of \$84.48 to \$121.28 are about 55 observations (assuming that 2 of the 10 in the interval \$120 $<$ \$130 are below \$121.28, and 5 of the 9 in the interval \$80 to \$90 are above \$84.48). Thus, about 69 percent are within 1 standard deviation. Only four secretaries are beyond 2 standard deviations, that is, about 5 percent. More than 90 percent are within 2 standard deviations. The formula for the computation of var x from data grouped into k classes is

TABLE 5.10   COMPUTATION OF VARIANCE OF WEEKLY PIANO SALES

(1) Outcome	(2) Squared outcome
1	1
2	4
1	1
6	36
2	4
3	9
4	16
4	16
6	36
1	1
Total 30	124

Average $= 30/10 = 3$

Average of squared outcomes 124/10	$= 12.4$
Squared average	$= 9$
Variance	$= 3.4$
Standard deviation	$\sqrt{3.4} = 1.84$

TABLE 5.11   VARIANCE OF WEEKLY SALARIES OF SECRETARIES

(1) Weekly salary	(2) Frequency	(3) Midpoint of interval	(4) (2) × (3)	(5) Squared midpoints	(6) (5) × (2)
$50 < $60	2	55	110	3,025	6,050
60 < 70	2	65	130	4,225	8,450
70 < 80	5	75	375	5,625	28,125
80 < 90	9	85	765	7,225	65,025
90 < 100	14	95	1,330	9,025	126,350
100 < 110	19	105	1,995	11,025	209,475
110 < 120	15	115	1,725	13,225	198,375
120 < 130	10	125	1,250	15,625	156,250
130 < 140	3	135	405	18,225	54,675
140 < 150	1	145	145	21,025	21,025
Total	80		8,230		873,800

Average = $8,230/80 = $102.88

873,800/80 = 10,922.5

$(102.88)^2 = 10,584.3$

Variance = 338.2

$$\text{var } x = \frac{f_1(\text{mid}_1)^2 + f_2(\text{mid}_2)^2 + \cdots + f_k(\text{mid}_k)^2}{n} - \bar{x}^2$$

where $\bar{x}$ is found by using the formula in Section 5.2.

EXERCISES

5.21   (a) The scores on an exam were 35, 81, 69, 54, 28, 50, 59, 62, 82, 71, 59. Specify the median and the range.

(b) On another exam the scores are 55, 57, 59, 58, 62, 61, 60, 59, 58, 59, 56. Specify the median and the range.

(c) On a third exam the scores were 55, 57, 59, 10, 58, 62, 61, 60, 98, 59, 58, 59, 56. Specify the median and the range.

5.22   The observations are 7, 19, 10, 4. Compute the average. Guess at, and then compute, the standard deviation.

5.23   Determine the variance for the housewife's expenditures, as given in Exercise 5.8.

5.24   Given the data of Exercise 5.9, first make a reasonable guess of the standard deviation, and then compute the standard deviation.

Answers to Exercises

5.1   (a) $\bar{x} = 68$.

         (b) If he had produced 68 rejects each month, the total number of rejects produced during the entire year would have been the same as it actually was.

         (c) 0.

5.2   The series should sum to $7 \times 21°F = 147°F$, so the observations might have been 19, 18, 23, 28, 24, 16, and 19°F.

5.3 $10 \times 2.8 = 28$.

5.4   (45.6 billion eggs)/(240 eggs per person) = 190 million persons.

5.5   If the gross national product is \$1,150 billion (as it was in 1972) and if there are 210 million persons (as there were in 1972), each person would earn \$5,477. The general answer is

$$\frac{\text{Gross national product}}{\text{Population}}$$

5.6   Yes, a positive average balance is compatible with occasional negative balances. A positive balance of \$4,000 for 1 day could be followed by 9 days of a negative balance of \$100, for an average over the 10 days of \$370.

5.7   We find 5 times 1, 11 times 2, 9 times 3, 12 times 4, 3 times 5, and 10 times 6, for an average of $\frac{177}{50} = 3.54$.

5.8   (a) The complete table is:

Daily expenditure	f, days	Mid	f × mid
< \$1	1	.50	.50
\$1 <, 2	0	1.50	0
2 < 5	4	3.50	14.00
5 < 10	10	7.50	75.00
10 < 20	7	15.00	105.00
20 < 50	5	35.00	175.00
			369.50

$$\bar{x} = \$369.50/27 = \$13.69$$

         (b) If we consider 5 the standard length of the base, then we get the following histogram. The four observations in the

Frequency density

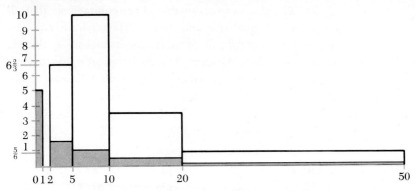

Daily expenses, dollars

interval of length *3* (rather than 5) from \$2 to \$5 are given a height of $\frac{5}{3} \times 4 = 6\frac{2}{3}$. The *area* corresponding to one observation remains unchanged throughout. In the histogram, the area corresponding with one observation in each class is shaded, and this area is the same in all classes.

(*c*) The great variability in the data leads to unequal intervals and small frequencies. It was unwise to group them in the first place.

5.9   (*a*) Tabulation of the data according to size gives the following results:

Flaws	Frequency	Flaws	Frequency
7	1	24	5
8	2	25	5
10	1	26	3
11	1	27	3
13	3	28	1
14	2	29	3
15	4	30	1
16	6	31	4
17	3	32	3
18	5	34	3
19	4	36	1
20	6	37	1
21	10	39	2
22	7	41	1
23	8	48	1

The class intervals 0–9, 10–14, 15–19, 20–24, 25–29, 30–34, 35–39, 40–49 appear reasonable. The requirements that all classes be of equal size and that no classes have very few observations are difficult to meet simultaneously at the extremes, as is often the case. The choice is arbitrary to some extent. Using the suggested classes gives the following result, which incorporates the calculations needed to find $\bar{x}$.

(b)

Flaws	Frequency	Midpoint	$f \times mid$
0–9	3	"5"	15
10–14	7	12	84
15–19	22	17	374
20–24	36	22	792
25–29	15	27	405
30–34	11	32	352
35–39	4	37	148
40–49	2	"45"	90
			2,260

$$\bar{x} = 2{,}260/100 = 22.60 \text{ flaws}$$

The average, as computed from the frequency distribution, is 22.60. The midpoints "5" and "45" are not truly the precise midpoints of the classes 0–9 and 40–49. The precise midpoints are $4\frac{1}{2}$ and $44\frac{1}{2}$. The error introduced by our choice of midpoints is trivial.

(c)

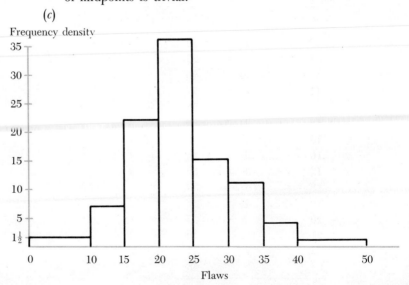

(*d*) The precise average can be computed from the raw data:

$$\bar{x} = \frac{x_1 + x_2 + \cdots + x_n}{n}$$

$$= \frac{24 + 21 + \cdots + 32}{100} = 22.56 \text{ flaws}$$

The very small difference is due to the slight errors introduced by the assumption that the average of the values in each class is the midpoint of the class.

5.10   6; notice again that there are as many values above this value as there are below this value.

5.11   One cannot possibly tell, but it will not be lower than 81; perhaps it will be 82, or more likely something like 100, but possibly 100,000.

5.12   (*a*)

Daily output	Frequency	Midpoint	$f \times mid$
20 < 25	4	22.5	90
25 < 30	6	27.5	165
30 < 35	9	32.5	292.5
35 < 40	13	37.5	487.5
40 < 45	7	42.5	297.5
45 < 50	6	47.5	285
	45		1,617.5

$$\bar{x} = 1{,}617.5/45 = 35.94 = 35{,}944 \text{ tons}$$

(*b*) $\text{med} = 35 + \left(\dfrac{\frac{45}{2} - 19}{13} \right) 5 = 36.35 = 36{,}350 \text{ tons.}$

(*c*) The average means that if output had been 35,944 tons *each day*, the total output would have been the same as it actually was, that is, 1,617,500 tons. The median means that output was at least 36,350 tons on half the days and at most 36,350 on the other half of the days.

(*d*) 35,000 to 40,000 tons.

5.13

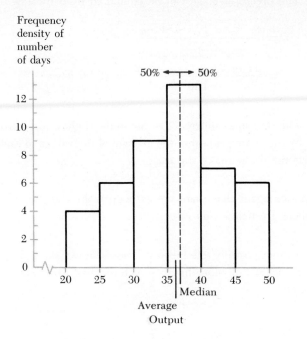

5.14   (a) Yes, it will be as much below 35 as it formerly was above
        35, that is, 34.00, or 34,056 tons.

        (b) The median changes from 36.35 to 33.65. It is now as much
        below 35 as it was above 35 before.

        (c) The modal class will be 30 to 35 in the new frequency
        distribution.

5.15   None of these measures changes. The *relative* frequency of each
        class will be unchanged, so the average will be unchanged (see
        Table 5.3). The median and mode will be unchanged, although
        the number of observations below and above the median will now
        be twice as large and the modal class will have twice as many
        observations.

5.16   (a) The average hourly wage in Bosalo is

$$\frac{\$1.80 \times 150 + \$1.30 \times 850}{150 + 850} = \frac{\$1,375}{1,000} = \$1.375$$

        In Buffton the average hourly wage is

$$\frac{\$1.75 \times 350 + \$1.25 \times 650}{350 + 650} = \frac{\$1,425}{1,000} = \$1.425$$

(b) In Buffton the average hourly wage is higher because skilled workers represent a higher proportion of the labor force than in Bosalo. Therefore, in the calculation for Buffton the higher hourly wage of skilled workers gets more weight, i.e., exerts more influence, on the average for the community.

5.17 If the average is used, the discomfort of those who prefer a shorter handle just offsets the discomfort of those who prefer a longer handle if we assume discomfort is directly proportional to the excess or shortage in the average length when compared with the preferred length. If the median is used, half the users will be uncomfortable because the handle is too short and the other half uncomfortable because it is too long. If the mode is used, the maximum possible number of users will be perfectly satisfied.

5.18 (a)

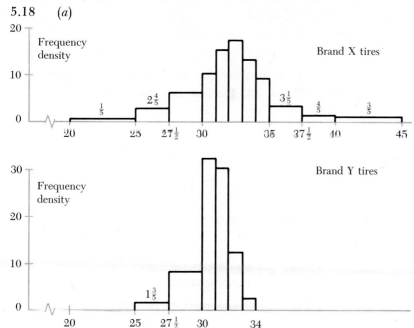

(b) For Brand X,

$$\bar{x} = \frac{f_1 \, \text{mid}_1 + f_2 \, \text{mid}_2 + \cdots + f_k \, \text{mid}_k}{n}$$

$$= \frac{22.50 + 183.75 + \cdots + 127.50}{100}$$

$$= 32.085 = 32{,}085 \text{ miles}$$

$$\text{med} = L_{\text{med}} + \frac{n/2 - f_{\text{cum}}}{f_{\text{med}}} \, i_{\text{med}}$$

$$= 32 + \frac{\frac{100}{2} - 48}{17} \, 1{,}000 = 32.118 = 32{,}118 \text{ miles}$$

The modal class is 32,000 to 33,000 miles.
For Brand Y,

$$\bar{x} = 30{,}580 \text{ miles} \qquad \text{and} \qquad \text{med} = 30{,}812 \text{ miles}$$

The modal class is 30,000 to 31,000 miles.

(c) Brand X has the larger average, median, and mode. However, the performance of Brand Y is more uniform, which may allow a more economical replacement program and reduce loss from flats, blowouts, etc. These two features must be weighed in making the choice.

(d) If no tire can be used for more than 30,000 miles, Brand Y tires will give the greater average and should be used.

5.19   He has 12 shares at a price of $10, 10 at a price of $12, 8 at a price of $15, 6 at a price of $20, and 5 at a price of $24. The average price is

$$\frac{\$10 \times 12 + \$12 \times 10 + \$15 \times 0 + \$20 \times 0 + \$24 \times 5}{12 + 10 + 8 + 6 + 5}$$

$$= \frac{\$600}{41} = \$14.63$$

5.20 $51.23 + 50.01 + 50.20 + 51.12$
$$+ 51.19 + 50.74 + 51.81 = 356.30$$
Also $356.30/7 = 50.90$. From Section 2.1 the true average is $14{,}182/27{,}895 = 50.84$ The difference occurs because there were *relatively many* births in the second, third, or perhaps sixth year, i.e., those years with percentages below the average. For example, if the total births in the years 1960–1966 were, respectively, 3,600, 4,500, 4,500, 3,600, 3,600, 4,495, 3,600 (values which sum to 27,895), then the average would be

$$\frac{3{,}600 \times 51.23 + 4{,}500 \times 50.01 + \cdots + 3{,}600 \times 51.81}{3{,}600 + 4{,}500 + \cdots + 3{,}600}$$

$$= \frac{14{,}182.8}{27{,}895} = 50.84$$

5.21   (a) The median is 59 and the range is 54, from 28 to 82. The
            observations are fairly evenly spread over the range, so the
            median and range give us a fair impression of the situation.
        (b) The median is 59 and the range is 7, from 55 to 62. The
            median and range again give us a fair impression of the
            situation. We see that the exam has little discriminating power.
        (c) The median is 59 and the range is 88, from 10 to 98. The
            impression is created that this is a well-designed exam with
            widely varying scores, when, in fact, there were two extreme
            scores and 11 were closely bunched. The impression created
            is unfair.

5.22   The average is 10. We might guess 5 for the standard deviation,
        so two of the four are within 1 standard deviation of the average
        and all four are within 2 standard deviations. Computation gives
        $\sqrt{\frac{126}{4}} \approx 5.6$.

5.23   The complete table of computations is:

(1) Expenditure	(2) Frequency	(3) Midpoint	(4) (2) × (3)	(5) (3)²	(6) (2) × (5)
< $1	1	.50	.50	.25	.25
$1 < 2	0	1.50	.00	2.25	.00
2 < 5	4	3.50	14.00	12.25	49.00
5 < 10	10	7.50	75.00	56.25	562.50
10 < 20	7	15.00	105.00	225.00	1,575.00
20 < 50	5	35.00	175.00	1225.00	6,125.00
	27		369.50		8,311.75

$$\bar{x} = 369.50/27 = \$13.69$$
$$\text{var } x = 8{,}311.75/27 - (13.69)^2 = 307.84 - 187.42 = 120.42$$
$$\text{sd } x = \sqrt{120.42} = \$10.97$$

As a check, in the range of $2 to $25, we have 22 observations.
This is well above 50 percent. Furthermore, all but about two
observations will be within 2 standard deviations (that is, below
$35) and all will be within 3 standard deviations.

5.24   The average is 22.6. A guess at the standard deviation of 5 gives
        $$22.6 \pm (1)(5) = 17.6 \text{ to } 27.6$$
                                    (includes 56 percent of observations)

$22.6 \pm (2)(5) = 12.6$ to 32.6

(includes 83 percent of observations)

$22.6 \pm (3)(5) = 7.6$ to 37.6

(includes 95 percent of observations)

The last two values are a little lower than we would expect by our rule of thumb. A guess of 7 gives

$22.6 \pm (1)(7) = 15.6$ to 29.6

(includes 69 percent of observations)

$22.6 \pm (2)(7) = 8.6$ to 36.6

(includes 92 percent of observations)

$22.6 \pm (3)(7) = 1.6$ to 43.6

(includes 99 percent of observations)

These results are reasonable, so our guess of 7 seems reasonable. Computing the true value gives

Flaws	f	Mid	Mid^2	$f \times$ mid^2
0–9	3	"5"	25	75
10–14	7	12	144	1,008
15–19	22	17	289	6,358
20–24	36	22	484	17,424
25–29	15	27	729	10,935
30–34	11	32	1,024	11,264
35–39	4	37	1,369	5,476
40–49	2	"45"	2,025	4,050
	100			56,590

$\text{var } x = 56{,}590/100 - (22.6)^2 = 55.1$

$\text{sd } x = \sqrt{55.1} = 7.4 \text{ flaws}$

Chapter 6

RANDOM VARIABLES AND PROBABILITY DISTRIBUTIONS

6.1 INTRODUCTION

In Chapter 2 we introduced a great variety of experiments which led to different outcomes or events with certain associated probabilities. Table 6.1 describes some of these experiments. The outcome or event in each of these examples is a *random variable*. We speak of a random variable whenever an experiment can lead to at least two different numerical values.

    Expressed in this way, the concept of a random variable seems deceptively simple. We will, therefore, elaborate with three further observations and pertinent examples and illustrations. (1) Depending on *how* one collects all the possible outcomes into events, one and the same experiment can give rise to a great many different random variables. (2) If the outcomes or events are not numerical, the experiment does *not* lead to a random variable, but (3) by assigning numbers to nonnumerical outcomes, we can artificially generate random variables. This third comment extends even to the case where the outcomes are numerical originally. We can assign *other* numbers than the original ones and so produce another random variable.

    We return to the experiment of rolling two dice to illustrate (1). In Table 6.2 we have mentioned some events, always mutually exclusive and

Random variable

TABLE 6.1   EXPERIMENTS, OUTCOMES, EVENTS, AND ASSOCIATED PROBABILITIES

Experiment: roll one die		*Experiment: roll two dice*		*Experiment: toss three coins*	
Outcome	Probability	Outcome	Probability	No. of heads	Probability
1	$\frac{1}{6}$	2	$\frac{1}{36}$	0	$\frac{1}{8}$
2	$\frac{1}{6}$	3	$\frac{2}{36}$	1	$\frac{3}{8}$
3	$\frac{1}{6}$	4	$\frac{3}{36}$	2	$\frac{3}{8}$
4	$\frac{1}{6}$	5	$\frac{4}{36}$	3	$\frac{1}{8}$
5	$\frac{1}{6}$	6	$\frac{5}{36}$		$\overline{1}$
6	$\frac{1}{6}$	7	$\frac{6}{36}$		
	$\overline{1}$	8	$\frac{5}{36}$		
		9	$\frac{4}{36}$		
		10	$\frac{3}{36}$		
		11	$\frac{2}{36}$		
		12	$\frac{1}{36}$		
			$\overline{1}$		

TABLE 6.2   RANDOM VARIABLES ASSOCIATED WITH THE EXPERIMENT OF ROLLING TWO DICE

Total value shown	Probability	Highest value shown on single die	Probability	Absolute value of difference between values on die	Probability
2	$\frac{1}{36}$	1	$\frac{1}{36}$	0	$\frac{6}{36}$
3	$\frac{2}{36}$	2	$\frac{3}{36}$	1	$\frac{10}{36}$
4	$\frac{3}{36}$	3	$\frac{5}{36}$	2	$\frac{8}{36}$
5	$\frac{4}{36}$	4	$\frac{7}{36}$	3	$\frac{6}{36}$
6	$\frac{5}{36}$	5	$\frac{9}{36}$	4	$\frac{4}{36}$
7	$\frac{6}{36}$	6	$\frac{11}{36}$	5	$\frac{2}{36}$
8	$\frac{5}{36}$		$\overline{1}$		$\overline{1}$
9	$\frac{4}{36}$				
10	$\frac{3}{36}$				
11	$\frac{2}{36}$				
12	$\frac{1}{36}$				
	$\overline{1}$				

collectively exhaustive, which can be associated with this experiment. These are all random variables associated with the same experiment. Notice that in all cases the probability column adds to 1, a necessary result. The actual numerical values specified for these probabilities can be verified with Table 2.1.

In Table 6.3 we present a number of experiments leading to non-numerical outcomes, as an illustration of (2) and (3). In this form these are *not* random variables. We can, however, assign numerical values to these events, for example, A = 3, B = 2, C = 1, D = 0, F = −1; or boy = 1, girl = 0; or ♠ = 4, ♥ = 3, ♦ = 2, ♣ = 1; or feather = 120, welter = 140, light = 160, middle = 180, heavy = 200. Thus, we have *generated* a random variable in an artificial and somewhat arbitrary way. Journalists do this when they compute the "winner" of the Olympic Games by attaching numerical values to gold, silver, and bronze medals, for example, 3, 2, 1 or 5, 3, 1.

Generated random variable

Assigning different numbers to events can be used even where the outcome is numerical at the outset. In Table 6.4 we reconsider the experiment of rolling one die, and we define a number of random variables associated with this experiment. The *same* set of probabilities—shown in Column 6 of the table—applies to all these random variables, since they are merely functions of the *same* "basic" random variable, shown in Column 1 of the table.

Summarizing these results, we find that with any experiment which leads to different outcomes we can associate—in many ways—mutually exclusive and collectively exhaustive events (Table 6.2). With each of these

TABLE 6.3 EXPERIMENTS LEADING TO NONNUMERICAL OUTCOMES

Grades on test	Hypo-thetical prob-ability	Sex of baby	Prob-ability	Suit in drawing from deck of cards	Prob-ability	Weight of boxer	Hypo-thetical prob-ability
A	.10	Boy	.51	♠	$\frac{1}{4}$	Feather	.1
B	.20	Girl	.49	♥	$\frac{1}{4}$	Welter	.2
C	.40		1	♦	$\frac{1}{4}$	Light	.2
D	.25			♣	$\frac{1}{4}$	Middle	.3
F	.05				1	Heavy	.2
	1						1

events we can associate—in many ways—a numerical value (Table 6.4). The numerical values associated with these events are random variables. Associated with each value of the random variable is a probability. These probabilities sum to 1.

As a matter of notation, we will denote random variables with boldface symbols—**x** or **y**. Boldface symbols therefore stand for variables which can assume different numerical values with certain probabilities. The outcome of a roll of a die is a random variable which can take the values 1, 2, 3, 4, 5, or 6 *as long as* the die has not been actually rolled. After the die has been thrown, and 2 comes up, this value, 2, is no longer a random variable. It is, instead, a known quantity, known to be 2.

If we weigh 10 students out of a class of 30, and compute their average weight, the average $\bar{x}$ will be a specific number, not a random variable. However, before we choose the 10 students, we can ask ourselves, "If we take 10 students out of the 30, what will their average weight be?" and the answer $\bar{\mathbf{x}}$ to this question is a random variable, since it will depend on which 10 students are weighed.

Associated with each random variable is a probability distribution. A *probability distribution* of a random variable shows the probabilities associated with each value which the random variable can take. The name is well chosen. A probability distribution shows us how the total probability, which is 1, is distributed over the possible values of the random variable. To each random variable corresponds a probability distribution, so we can speak of a random variable and *its* probability distribution. This is true even though in practice it may be difficult to specify the probability distribution of a random variable.

We have shown several probability distributions in the tables ex-

Boldface symbols

Probability distributions

TABLE 6.4   POSSIBLE RANDOM VARIABLES ASSOCIATED WITH THE EXPERIMENT OF ROLLING ONE DIE

(1) Outcome	*(2)* Squared outcome	*(3)* Outcome minus $3\frac{1}{2}$	*(4)* (Outcome minus $3\frac{1}{2})^2$	*(5)* Outcome divided by 6	*(6)* Probability
1	1	$-2\frac{1}{2}$	$6\frac{1}{4}$	$\frac{1}{6}$	$\frac{1}{6}$
2	4	$-1\frac{1}{2}$	$2\frac{1}{4}$	$\frac{2}{6}$	$\frac{1}{6}$
3	9	$-\frac{1}{2}$	$\frac{1}{4}$	$\frac{3}{6}$	$\frac{1}{6}$
4	16	$\frac{1}{2}$	$\frac{1}{4}$	$\frac{4}{6}$	$\frac{1}{6}$
5	25	$1\frac{1}{2}$	$2\frac{1}{4}$	$\frac{5}{6}$	$\frac{1}{6}$
6	36	$2\frac{1}{2}$	$6\frac{1}{4}$	1	$\frac{1}{6}$
					1

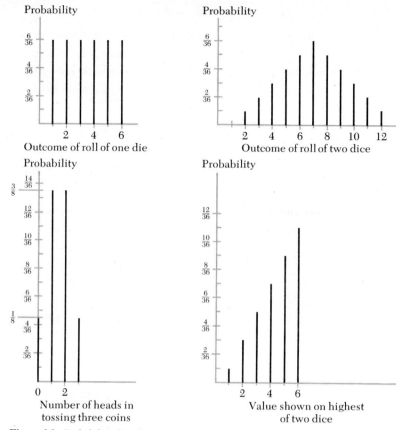

Figure 6.1 Probability distributions.

hibited in the preceding few pages. We can also graph these distributions. Along the horizontal axis we indicate the values which the random variable can assume, and along the vertical axis the associated probabilities. In Figure 6.1 we have illustrated some probability distributions. Notice in particular that the sum of the heights of the bars in each graph is 1.

It is interesting to compare Figures 5.1 and 6.1, that is, the graphical representation of frequency distributions and probability distributions. For a frequency distribution the *observed frequencies* are measured along the vertical axis. The *total frequency* is distributed over the possible outcomes. This total frequency is equal to the number of experiments made, and the sum of the bars therefore equals the total number of experiments—100 in Figure 5.1, since a die was tossed 100 times. For a probability distribution the total probability, which is 1, is distributed over the possible values the random variable can assume.

EXERCISES

6.1   In drawing two cards from a deck, without replacement, consider
       as events the possible combinations of suits, such as "two spades,"
       "a spade and a heart," etc. What are the possible events, and what
       are the associated probabilities? Did we define a random variable?
       Why?

6.2   In the previous example, let a spade count for 4, a heart for 3,
       a diamond for 2, and a club for 1. What are the possible outcomes
       and the associated probabilities? Graph the probability distribu-
       tion.

6.3   Consider the four values 2, 3, 7, 11.
       (a) How many combinations of three can we choose out of these
           four values? List them.
       (b) Compute the average for each of these combinations.
       (c) Is the average a random variable before the three values are
           chosen?
       (d) Assuming all combinations are equally likely, list the possible
           values of the average together with their associated proba-
           bilities.

6.4   Draw 2 cards (without replacement) from a deck of 12 cards
       consisting of four 2s, four 5s, and four 6s. Define at least five
       random variables which can be associated with this experiment,
       and compute the associated probabilities.

6.5   Draw a graph of the probability distribution for the random
       variable in the third and in the fourth columns of Table 6.4.

6.6   What random variable has the probability distribution illustrated
       in the figure below? Can you think of an experiment leading to
       this random variable and the probability distribution shown?

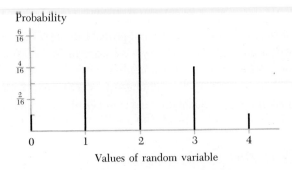

Values of random variable

6.2 EXPECTED VALUE OF A RANDOM VARIABLE

If a random variable $\mathbf{x}$ assumes the values $x_1, x_2, \ldots, x_n$, with probability $p_1, p_2, \ldots, p_n$, the *expected value* of $\mathbf{x}$ is denoted by $E\mathbf{x}$ and defined as

Expected value

$$E\mathbf{x} = p_1x_1 + p_2x_2 + \cdots + p_nx_n = \Sigma\, p_ix_i$$

The expected value of $\mathbf{x}$ is obtained by considering all possible outcomes, multiplying these by their associated probability, and summing the products. The expected value of a roll of a die is

$$\tfrac{1}{6} \times 1 + \tfrac{1}{6} \times 2 + \tfrac{1}{6} \times 3 + \tfrac{1}{6} \times 4 + \tfrac{1}{6} \times 5 + \tfrac{1}{6} \times 6 = 3\tfrac{1}{2}$$

The expected value of a roll of two dice is

$$\tfrac{1}{36} \times 2 + \tfrac{2}{36} \times 3 + \tfrac{3}{36} \times 4 + \tfrac{4}{36} \times 5 + \tfrac{5}{36} \times 6 + \tfrac{6}{36} \times 7$$
$$+ \tfrac{5}{36} \times 8 + \tfrac{4}{36} \times 9 + \tfrac{3}{36} \times 10 + \tfrac{2}{36} \times 11 + \tfrac{1}{36} \times 12 = 7$$

As we see, the expected value itself is *not* a random variable, but a specific number like $3\tfrac{1}{2}$ or 7.

The expected value of a random variable can easily be computed. An example is given in Table 6.5. The first column of the table gives the various possible outcomes of the experiment. In the second column we associate numbers with these outcomes, which gives us the random variable. In the third column we record the probabilities associated with the outcomes. In the fourth column we multiply the corresponding entries in the second and third columns, and we add these products. This sum is the expected value.

In the example represented in Table 6.5 we consider a factory which may burn down. If a fire strikes, the damage is $100,000. Fortunately, the probability of a fire is only 1 percent. The expected value of the damage is $1,000. It should be clear that in any year the damage will be either $0 or $100,000. It will never be $1,000. However, over a period of several centuries setting aside $1,000 a year will be a wise precaution.

TABLE 6.5 EXPECTED VALUE OF DAMAGE DUE TO FIRE

(1) Outcome	*(2)* Damage	*(3)* Probability	*(4)* (2) × (3)
Fire	$100,000	.01	$1,000
No fire	0	.99	0
		Expected value =	$1,000

Losses due to fires can just be met from these reserves if fires occur once a century. Such considerations form the basis of insurance premium calculations.

Expected value and average compared

Intuitively, an average and an expected value have much in common, but there is an important difference. An average is computed from a set of available data. It is a descriptive measure, which tries to summarize in shorthand an important characteristic of the data. On the other hand, the expected value of a roll of a die is defined even though no die has been cast, or for that matter, ever will be cast.

From the computational point of view, expected values and averages are similar. The difference is that in the computation of expected values we work with probabilities, and in the computation of averages we may work with relative frequencies. In this context, we refer back to Table 5.3, where we obtained the average of 100 actual rolls of a die by multiplying the outcomes by the observed relative frequencies:

$$\frac{20}{100} \times 1 + \frac{18}{100} \times 2 + \frac{15}{100} \times 3 + \frac{18}{100} \times 4 + \frac{12}{100} \times 5 + \frac{17}{100} \times 6 = 3.35$$

The *expected value* is, as we just saw, 3.50. The average of the actual throws, 3.35, is a little lower than the expected value anticipated before the actual throws were made and recorded.

It should be clear that we do not "expect" any one roll of a die to correspond to its expected value, $3\frac{1}{2}$. Rather, when we expect something, we look into the future. The future outcomes of an infinitely large number of rolls of a die will average $3\frac{1}{2}$. This is the information conveyed by an expected value.

EXERCISES

6.7   What is the expected value of the number of heads if we toss three coins? Is this expected value a random variable?

6.8   What is the expected value of the random variables in Columns 3 and 4 of Table 6.4?

6.9   A man rolls two dice, and receives as payoff in dollars the value shown on the highest die. What is the expected value of his payoff?

6.10   Assume the following: Fifty percent of all automobile accidents lead to property damage of $100. Forty percent lead to damage of $500. Ten percent lead to total loss, a damage of $1,800. If a car has a 5 percent chance of being in an accident in a year, what is the expected value of the property damage due to that possible accident?

6.3 THE EXPECTED VALUE OF A SUM EQUALS THE SUM OF THE EXPECTED VALUES

In the previous section, we computed the expected value of the outcome of a roll of a die, and found $3\frac{1}{2}$. We also computed the expected value of the outcome of a roll of two dice, and found 7. We will be perceptive enough to notice that $7 = 2 \times 3\frac{1}{2}$. Analogously, if we throw 100 dice, we might guess that the expected value of the total outcome will be $100 \times 3\frac{1}{2} = 350$. This result is, in fact, true. Let us throw 100 dice. The result of the first throw, x_1,† is a random variable. So is x_2, the result of the second throw, . . . , and x_{100}, the result of the last throw. We are interested in knowing

$$E(x_1 + x_2 + \cdots + x_{100})$$

the expected value of the sum of the outcomes. This expected value of the sum equals the sum of the expected values, that is,

$$E(x_1 + x_2 + \cdots + x_{100}) = Ex_1 + Ex_2 + \cdots + Ex_{100}$$
$$= 3\frac{1}{2} + 3\frac{1}{2} + \cdots + 3\frac{1}{2} = 100 \times 3\frac{1}{2}$$
$$= 350$$

$$E(\Sigma\, x_i) = \Sigma(Ex_i)$$

This result is intuitively appealing. The most obvious advantage is that it saves a good deal of work. The computation of the expected value of the outcome of a roll of two dice, 7, was rather cumbersome, but now we see that we need only compute the expected value of the outcome of one die, and multiply the result by 2.

We will illustrate these results. If the probability that a baby is a boy is .51, the expected number of boys if four babies are born on a particular day in a hospital is 2.04 before they are born. (After they are born we *know* whether there were zero, one, two, three, or four boys.)

---

† The difference between x_1 and $\mathbf{x}_1$ is quite important. The symbol x_1 stands for the first value in an actual series of observations, *or* for the lowest value of a series of values which a random variable can take. The symbol $\mathbf{x}_1$ stands for the random variable, the outcome of the first die to be thrown. Therefore, $\mathbf{x}_1$ is unknown (although the probability distribution is known), but x_1 is known.

TABLE 6.6 EXPECTED VALUE OF NUMBER OF BOYS

(1) Outcome	(2) Numerical value	(3) Probability	(4) (2) × (3)
0 Boys	0	$(.49)^4 = .0576$	0
1 Boy	1	$4(.49)^3(.51) = .2401$	.2401
2 Boys	2	$6(.49)^2(.51)^2 = .3747$	.7494
3 Boys	3	$4(.49)(.51)^3 = .2600$	.7800
4 Boys	4	$(.51)^4 = .0677$	.2708
		Expected value $=$	2.0403

We *might* have derived the expected value 2.04, as in Table 6.6. Unfortunately, this approach is cumbersome, and some exactness is lost in rounding errors. The computation of the probabilities associated with each of the possible outcomes will be discussed in Sections 7.1 and 7.2. The basic argument is as follows: The probability of one boy is $4(.49)^3(.51)$, since each of the four possible sequences BGGG, GBGG, GGBG, GGGB has the probability of $(.49)^3(.51)$.

As another example, suppose that the petty cash drawer contains 7 quarters (Q), 4 dimes (D), 9 nickels (N), and 10 pennies (P). We might remove (in the dark) three coins, without replacement; that is, once a coin is drawn, it is not returned. The expected value of the resulting treasure *can* be computed by considering all possible outcomes (QQQ, QQD, QDD, . . . , PPP), their associated values (75, 60, 45, . . . , 3), and their associated probabilities. These probabilities may be computed by the pedestrian method discussed in Section 4.4. The results will enable us to compute the expected value. If we do not make an arithmetical error, this will give us the expected value of the treasure—after an hour of solid work, that is.

A much simpler method is as follows. We determine the expected value of drawing only one coin. We have:

Outcome	Value	Probability	Value × probability
Q	25	$\frac{7}{30}$	$\frac{175}{30}$
D	10	$\frac{4}{30}$	$\frac{40}{30}$
N	5	$\frac{9}{30}$	$\frac{45}{30}$
P	1	$\frac{10}{30}$	$\frac{10}{30}$
		1	Expected value $= \frac{270}{30} = 9$ cents

We conclude that the expected value of three coins is $3 \times 9 = 27$ cents.

As a final example, consider two situations. The first is represented by three houses located at widely separated points. Assume—somewhat unrealistically—that each house has a 10 percent probability of being totally destroyed by fire during the next year. Each house is worth $50,000. The expected damage due to fire for any one house is therefore

$$\$0 \times .90 + \$50,000 \times .10 = \$5,000$$

The expected value of the total fire damage for all three houses is $5,000 + $5,000 + $5,000, by an application of the rule that the sum of the expected values equals the expected value of the sum:

$$E\left(\begin{array}{c}\text{fire damage}\\ \text{to house 1}\end{array} + \begin{array}{c}\text{fire damage}\\ \text{to house 2}\end{array} + \begin{array}{c}\text{fire damage}\\ \text{to house 3}\end{array}\right)$$

$$= E\left(\begin{array}{c}\text{fire damage}\\ \text{to house 1}\end{array}\right) + E\left(\begin{array}{c}\text{fire damage}\\ \text{to house 2}\end{array}\right) + E\left(\begin{array}{c}\text{fire damage}\\ \text{to house 3}\end{array}\right)$$

$$= \$5,000 + \$5,000 + \$5,000 = \$15,000$$

We can find the same result the long way. The possible outcomes are that zero, one, two, or three houses burn down, with corresponding damages of $0, $50,000, $100,000, or $150,000. The probabilities associated with each of these outcomes can be found by using computations similar to those in Table 6.6. They are .729, .243, .027, and .001, respectively. Thus the expected damage is, as before,

$$\$0 \times .729 + \$50,000 \times .243 + \$100,000 \times .027 + \$150,000 \times .001$$
$$= \$12,150 + \$2,700 + \$150$$
$$= \$15,000$$

In the second situation we assume that the three houses are *adjacent*, and that if one burns, they all burn. The possible outcomes are "no house burns" and "all three houses burn." The events "fire in house 1" and "fire in house 2" are no longer independent. The probability that all three will burn is .1. The probability that none will burn is .9. As before, the expected damage to one house is

$$\$0 \times .9 + \$50,000 \times .1 = \$5,000$$

Applying the rule that the expected value of the total damage equals the sum of the expected values of the damages, we conclude that the expected value of the total damage is $15,000. As before, this conclusion is correct. The random variable "fire damage" now has either a value of $0 with a probability of .9 *or* a value of $150,000 with a probability of .1, for an expected value of

$$\$0 \times .9 + \$150,000 \times .1 = \$15,000$$

This illustration demonstrates that the sum rule of expected values is valid whether the random variables are independent or dependent.

EXERCISES

6.11   The probability that a customer makes a purchase is $\frac{1}{3}$. Four customers enter the store. What is the expected value of the number of purchases?

6.12   The probability that the first customer in a group makes a purchase is $\frac{1}{3}$. Other customers who are in the same group are imitators; if the first buys, they all do. If the first does not, none does. If four customers enter the store together, what is the expected value of the number of purchases?

6.13   The ♣A, ♣2, ..., ♣10 are taken from a deck. The 10 cards are shuffled, and then turned face up, one by one. There is a match if the ith card turned up is ♣i. If the sequence is ♣4, ♣A, ♣7, ♣2, ♣5, ♣8, ♣6, ♣3, ♣9, ♣10, there are three *matches* (♣5 was the fifth card, ♣9 the ninth, ♣10 the tenth). What is the expected number of matches?

6.14   On a single trial, the probability of success is $\frac{2}{5}$. What is the expected number of successes in 5, 10, 20, 100, and 1,000 trials?

6.4   VARIANCE OF A RANDOM VARIABLE

The *variance of a random variable* **x**, with its associated probability distribution, is a measure of the dispersion of the distribution. The variance of a random variable **x** is denoted by *V***x** and is defined as

Variance of **x**
$$V\mathbf{x} = p_1(x_1 - E\mathbf{x})^2 + p_2(x_2 - E\mathbf{x})^2 + \cdots + p_n(x_n - E\mathbf{x})^2$$
$$= \Sigma\, p_i(x_i - E\mathbf{x})^2$$

The variance *V***x** is itself an expected value. It is the expected value of the random variable $(\mathbf{x} - E\mathbf{x})^2$. This is the random variable which assumes the values $(x_1 - E\mathbf{x})^2$, $(x_2 - E\mathbf{x})^2$, ..., $(x_n - E\mathbf{x})^2$, each of which is a squared deviation of an outcome from its expected value. In Table 6.4 the random variable $(\mathbf{x} - E\mathbf{x})^2$ is derived from the original random variable $\mathbf{x}$ and displayed in Column 4.

We recall that the variance of a given series of observations x_1, x_2, ..., x_n is defined as

$$\text{var } x = \frac{1}{n} \Sigma(x_i - \overline{x})^2 = \frac{1}{n} \Sigma x_i^2 - \overline{x}^2$$

Table 6.7 summarizes the terminology and notation used in connection with measures of central tendency and dispersion.

Tables 6.8 and 6.9 show the computation of the variance of the outcome of a roll of one die and the outcome of a roll of two dice. Column 1 gives the outcomes of the random variable, Column 2 the associated probabilities, and Column 3 the expected values. In Column

TABLE 6.7   NOTATION, TERMINOLOGY, AND FORMULAS FOR MEASURES OF CENTRAL TENDENCY AND DISPERSION

	Measure of central tendency		
	Name	*Symbol*	*Formula*
Observations $x_1, x_2, \ldots, x_n$	Average	$\overline{N}$	$\dfrac{1}{n} \Sigma N_i$
Random variable **x**, which assumes values $x_1, x_2, \ldots, x_n$ with probabilities $p_1, p_2, \ldots, p_n$	Expected value	$E\mathbf{x}$	$\Sigma p_i x_i$

	Measure of dispersion		
	Name	*Symbol*	*Formula*
Observations $x_1, x_2, \ldots, x_n$	Variance	var x	$\dfrac{1}{n} \Sigma(x_i - \overline{x})^2$
	Standard deviation	sd x	$\sqrt{\text{var } x}$
Random variable **x**, which assumes values $x_1, x_2, \ldots, x_n$ with probabilities $p_1, p_2, \ldots, p_n$	Variance	$V\mathbf{x}$	$\Sigma p_i (x_i - E\mathbf{x})^2$
	Standard deviation	$S\mathbf{x}$	$\sqrt{V\mathbf{x}}$

TABLE 6.8 COMPUTATION OF VARIANCE OF OUTCOME OF ROLL OF ONE DIE

(1)	(2)	(3)	(4)	(5)	(6)
			Outcome		
Outcome	Probability	$(1) \times (2)$	minus $3\frac{1}{2}$	$(4)^2$	$(5) \times (2)$
1	$\frac{1}{6}$	$\frac{1}{6}$	$-2\frac{1}{2}$	$6\frac{1}{4}$	$\frac{25}{24}$
2	$\frac{1}{6}$	$\frac{2}{6}$	$-1\frac{1}{2}$	$2\frac{1}{4}$	$\frac{9}{24}$
3	$\frac{1}{6}$	$\frac{3}{6}$	$-\frac{1}{2}$	$\frac{1}{4}$	$\frac{1}{24}$
4	$\frac{1}{6}$	$\frac{4}{6}$	$\frac{1}{2}$	$\frac{1}{4}$	$\frac{1}{24}$
5	$\frac{1}{6}$	$\frac{5}{6}$	$1\frac{1}{2}$	$2\frac{1}{4}$	$\frac{9}{24}$
6	$\frac{1}{6}$	$\frac{6}{6}$	$2\frac{1}{2}$	$6\frac{1}{4}$	$\frac{25}{24}$
	Expected value $= 3\frac{1}{2}$			Variance $= \frac{70}{24} = 2\frac{11}{12}$	

4 the expected values are deducted from the outcomes, in Column 5 these results are squared, and in Column 6 the variances are computed.

Standard deviation of **x**

The variance of **x** and its square root, which is the *standard deviation* of **x** and is abbreviated *S***x**, are both important. The standard deviation derives its importance from the following rule of thumb. We already know that the random variable **x** *can* assume different values $x_1, x_2, \ldots, x_n$. The expected value of **x**, namely, *E***x**, gives the central location, but it is quite possible that the actual outcome will differ from *E***x**. However,

TABLE 6.9 COMPUTATION OF VARIANCE OF OUTCOME OF ROLL OF TWO DICE

(1)	(2)	(3)	(4)	(5)	(6)
			Outcome		
Outcome	Probability	$(1) \times (2)$	minus 7	$(4)^2$	$(5) \times (2)$
2	$\frac{1}{36}$	$\frac{2}{36}$	-5	25	$\frac{25}{36}$
3	$\frac{2}{36}$	$\frac{6}{36}$	-4	16	$\frac{32}{36}$
4	$\frac{3}{36}$	$\frac{12}{36}$	-3	9	$\frac{27}{36}$
5	$\frac{4}{36}$	$\frac{20}{36}$	-2	4	$\frac{16}{36}$
6	$\frac{5}{36}$	$\frac{30}{36}$	-1	1	$\frac{5}{36}$
7	$\frac{6}{36}$	$\frac{42}{36}$	0	0	0
8	$\frac{5}{36}$	$\frac{40}{36}$	1	1	$\frac{5}{36}$
9	$\frac{4}{36}$	$\frac{36}{36}$	2	4	$\frac{16}{36}$
10	$\frac{3}{36}$	$\frac{30}{36}$	3	9	$\frac{27}{36}$
11	$\frac{2}{36}$	$\frac{22}{36}$	4	16	$\frac{32}{36}$
12	$\frac{1}{36}$	$\frac{12}{36}$	5	25	$\frac{25}{36}$
	Expected value $= \frac{252}{36} = 7$			Variance $= \frac{210}{36} = 5\frac{10}{12}$	

in nearly every situation at least 90 percent of the actual outcomes will be within $E\mathbf{x}$ plus or minus twice $S\mathbf{x}$. In other words, there is at least a 90 percent probability that the *actual* outcome will differ by less than 2 standard deviations from the expected outcome. Similarly, at least 50 percent of the time the actual outcome differs from the expected value by less than 1 standard deviation, and nearly all actual outcomes are within 3 standard deviations of the expected value. These results are valid for nearly all random variables we will meet, and they are a little stronger than the results which are always true as a matter of mathematical necessity. Table 6.10 gives a survey of these rules, plus the mathematically certain percentages.

The standard deviation of the outcome of rolling one die is $\sqrt{2\frac{11}{12}} \approx 1.7$. Since the expected value is $3\frac{1}{2}$, we conclude that at least 50 percent of the time the outcome will be within the range 1.8 to 5.2. In fact, it will be there $\frac{4}{6} = 67$ percent of the time, because 67 percent of the time the outcome is 2, 3, 4, or 5. At least 90 percent of the time the outcome will be within the range .1 to 6.9, and in fact it is within these boundaries 100 percent of the time.

The square root of $5\frac{10}{12}$ is about 2.4. In rolling two dice, the outcome will be within the limits 7 ± 2.4, or 4.6 to 9.4, with a probability of at least 50 percent. In fact, 5, 6, 7, 8, or 9 is thrown with probability $\frac{4}{36} + \frac{5}{36} + \frac{6}{36} + \frac{5}{36} + \frac{4}{36} = \frac{24}{36}$, or 67 percent. The outcome should be between 2.2 and 11.8 with 90 percent probability. In fact, the outcome is within these limits with $\frac{34}{36}$, or about 95 percent, probability.

For computational purposes, we seldom use the definition formula

$$V\mathbf{x} = E(\mathbf{x} - E\mathbf{x})^2 = \Sigma\, p_i(x_i - E\mathbf{x})^2$$

but, rather, the equivalent formula

$$V\mathbf{x} = E\mathbf{x}^2 - (E\mathbf{x})^2 = p_1 x_1^2 + p_2 x_2^2 + \cdots + p_n x_n^2 - (E\mathbf{x})^2$$
$$= \Sigma\, p_i x_i^2 - (E\mathbf{x})^2$$

Efficient computation of $V\mathbf{x}$ and $S\mathbf{x}$

The expression $E\mathbf{x}^2$ is the expected value of $\mathbf{x}^2$, and is thus equal to

TABLE 6.10 PROBABILITY THAT OUTCOMES WILL FALL WITHIN RANGES

Within range	Rule of thumb	Mathematically certain
$E\mathbf{x} \pm S\mathbf{x}$	At least 50%	At least 0%
$E\mathbf{x} \pm 2S\mathbf{x}$	At least 90%	At least 75%
$E\mathbf{x} \pm 3S\mathbf{x}$	Nearly all	At least 89%

$p_1 x_1^2 + p_2 x_2^2 + \cdots + p_n x_n^2$. The expression $(Ex)^2$ is simply the square of the expected value. If $Ex = 7$, then $(Ex)^2 = 7^2 = 49$. It is convenient to remember that Vx is "the expected value of the squares minus the square of the expected value." The proof is an exercise in algebra.

EXERCISES

6.15   What is the variance of the number of heads when three coins are tossed?

6.16   A random variable takes value 1 with probability π, and value 0 with probability $1 - \pi$. What is the expected value? What is the variance? What is the standard deviation?

6.17   What is the standard deviation of the damages in Exercise 6.10?

6.5 PROPERTIES OF THE EXPECTED VALUE AND THE VARIANCE

$E(x + k)$
$= Ex + k$

If a constant value k is added to every value a random variable x can assume, the expected value increases by k:

$$E(x + k) = Ex + k$$

The proof is as follows:

$$E(x + k) = \Sigma\, p_i(x_i + k) = \Sigma\, p_i x_i + \Sigma\, p_i k = Ex + k$$

where we use $\Sigma\, p_i = 1$.

In Section 6.3 we discussed another property of expected values, that is, that the expected value of a sum of random variables is the sum of their expected values

$E \Sigma\, x_i$
$= \Sigma\, Ex_i$

$$E \Sigma\, x_i = \Sigma\, Ex_i$$

A third property of expected values follows directly. The expected value of a constant times a random variable is the constant times the expected value of the random variable

$E(kx) = kEx$

$$E(kx) = kEx$$

The proof is

$$E(kx) = E(\underbrace{x + x + \cdots + x}_{k \text{ times}}) = \underbrace{Ex + Ex + \cdots + Ex}_{k \text{ times}} = kEx$$

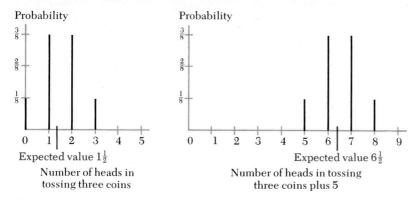

Figure 6.2 Effects on the mean and variance when a constant is added to a random variable.

There are three analogous properties for the variance.

1. If a constant value k is added to every value which a random variable $\mathbf{x}$ can assume, the variance remains the same, although the expected value increases by k. This is illustrated in Figure 6.2. The original variable $\mathbf{x}$ takes the values 0, 1, 2, and 3 with a probability of $\frac{1}{8}$, $\frac{3}{8}$, $\frac{3}{8}$, and $\frac{1}{8}$, respectively. Each of these values is increased by the value $k = 5$; so the new variable, $\mathbf{x} + 5$, assumes the values 5, 6, 7, and 8 with, respectively, the associated probabilities of $\frac{1}{8}$, $\frac{3}{8}$, $\frac{3}{8}$, and $\frac{1}{8}$. It is clear from the picture that the dispersion is unchanged. The fact that the variance remains unchanged can be verified numerically for this, or any other, example. The algebraic argument is that in the formula $V\mathbf{x} = p_1(x_1 - E\mathbf{x})^2 + \cdots + p_n(x_n - E\mathbf{x})^2$ all values $x_1, \ldots, x_n$ increase by k, but so does $E\mathbf{x}$, and therefore $(x_1 - E\mathbf{x}), \ldots, (x_n - E\mathbf{x})$, remain constant.

$V(\mathbf{x} + k) = V\mathbf{x}$

2. If each value which a random variable can assume is *multiplied* by a constant k, the variance is multiplied by a constant k^2 and the standard deviation is multiplied by k. The expected value, we recall, is then multiplied by k also, $E(k\mathbf{x}) = kE\mathbf{x}$. An illustration is given in Figure 6.3. As above, the original random variable $\mathbf{x}$ takes on the values 0, 1, 2, and 3 with respective probability $\frac{1}{8}$, $\frac{3}{8}$, $\frac{3}{8}$, and $\frac{1}{8}$. The variance is $\frac{3}{4}$. The random variable $2\mathbf{x}$ hence assumes the values 0, 2, 4, and 6 with these probabilities. The variance is $2^2 \times \frac{3}{4} = 3$. Thus, the variance becomes four times as large. Since the standard deviation is the square root of the variance, it becomes $\sqrt{4} = 2$ times as large. The algebraic proof is that all values $x_1, \ldots, x_n$, as well as $E\mathbf{x}$, are multiplied by k, and therefore $(x_1 - E\mathbf{x}), \ldots, (x_n - E\mathbf{x})$ are all k times as large, and their squares k^2 times as large.

$V(k\mathbf{x}) = k^2 V\mathbf{x}$

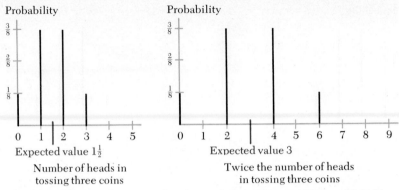

Figure 6.3 Effects on the mean and variance when a random variable is multiplied by a constant.

3. It is the *third* property of the variance which is most important. In Section 6.4, we computed $2\frac{11}{12}$ for the variance of the outcome in throwing one die, and $5\frac{10}{12} = 2 \times 2\frac{11}{12}$ for the variance of the outcome in throwing two dice. Can we generalize this result? Suppose we have 100 dice. The first die leads to x_1, a random variable which can take the values 1 to 6 with equal probability. The second die leads to result x_2. The hundredth die leads to x_{100}, be it 1, 2, 3, 4, 5, or 6. The sum of the results $x_1 + x_2 + \cdots + x_{100}$ *might* be 100 (if all tosses come up 1), or it might be 600 (if all tosses come up 6). The expected value is, as we know, $100 \times 3\frac{1}{2} = 350$. Is the variance, perhaps, $100 \times 2\frac{11}{12} = 291\frac{2}{3}$? Is it true that

$$V(x_1 + x_2 + \cdots + x_{100}) = Vx_1 + Vx_2 + \cdots + Vx_{100}$$
$$= 2\frac{11}{12} + 2\frac{11}{12} + \cdots + 2\frac{11}{12} = 291\frac{2}{3}$$

For independent random variables

$$V \Sigma x_i = \Sigma V x_i$$

The answer is yes, if the variables are independent. *The variance of a sum of independent random variables equals the sum of their variances.* In this example, the successive outcomes of the rolls of the die are independent.

We will illustrate the difference between the variance of random variables which are independent and that of random variables which are dependent with the example of the three houses, which are either far apart or neighbors. In both cases, the probability that a house will burn is .1, and the fire damage if it does burn is $50,000. The variance of the damage to one house can easily be computed, as in Table 6.11, and equals 225 million.

When the houses are far apart, they burn independently of one

TABLE 6.11 COMPUTATION OF VARIANCE OF FIRE DAMAGE TO ONE HOUSE

(1) Outcome	(2) Damage	(3) Probabilities	(4) (2) × (3)	(5) Damage²	(6) (3) × (5)
No Fire	$ 0	.9	0	0	0
Fire	50,000	.1	5,000	2½ billion	250 million
		Expected value = $5,000			250 million

Variance = 250 million − (5,000)² = 225 million

another, and the variance of the total damage will be three times the variance of the damage done to one house, that is, 675 million. The standard deviation is the square root of this number, that is, $25,981. In Table 6.12 we verify this result by making the computations in detail.

The variance will be much larger when the houses are all adjacent. In this situation the random variables "fire damage to house 1" and "fire damage to house 2" are dependent. A fire in one house means a fire in all houses.

As computed in Table 6.13, the variance is now over 2 billion, from which we conclude that the standard deviation has grown to $45,000. The variance computed in Table 6.13 is nine times as large as the variance computed in Table 6.11. This is as it should be because a random variable **x**, which assumes values $0 and $150,000 with probabilities .9 and .1, is exactly three times the random variable which assumes the values $0 and $50,000 with probabilities .9 and .1. Using $V(3\mathbf{x}) = 3^2 V\mathbf{x}$, we conclude that the variance in Table 6.13 must be nine times as large as the variance in Table 6.11.

TABLE 6.12 COMPUTATION OF VARIANCE OF FIRE DAMAGE TO THREE HOUSES, BURNING INDEPENDENTLY

(1) Outcome	(2) Damage	(3) Probability	(4) (2) × (3)	(5) Damage²	(6) (3) × (5)
No Fire	$ 0	.729	0	0	0
1 Fire	50,000	.243	12,150	2½ billion	607½ million
2 Fires	100,000	.027	2,700	10 billion	270 million
3 Fires	150,000	.001	150	22½ billion	22½ million
		Expected value = $15,000			900 million

Variance = 900 million − (15,000)² = 675 million

TABLE 6.13   COMPUTATION OF VARIANCE OF FIRE DAMAGE TO THREE HOUSES, BURNING DEPENDENTLY

(1) Outcome	(2) Damage	(3) Probability	(4) (2) × (3)	(5) Damage^2	(6) (3) × (5)
No Fire	0	.9	0	0	0
Conflagration	150,000	.1	15,000	$22\frac{1}{2}$ billion	$2\frac{1}{4}$ billion

Expected value = $15,000 $2\frac{1}{4}$ billion

Variance = $2\frac{1}{4}$ billion − $(15,000)^2 = 2\frac{1}{40}$ billion

Insurance companies are very reluctant to insure against events which are dependent. They like to insure against independent events, so that bad luck in one place will be offset by good luck elsewhere. No one insurance company will give complete coverage to all structures in a given area.

EXERCISES

6.18   Why should at least 90 percent of the sum total of throws of 100 dice be between 315 and 385?

6.19   The operator of the concession service at the stadium knows from experience that the probability of a customer's preferring a hamburger is 60 percent. The probability of his preferring a hot dog is 40 percent. One stand serves 225 fans.
(a) What is the expected value of the number of hamburgers served?
(b) The variance?
(c) The standard deviation?
(d) Within what limits will the result nearly always be?

6.20   Three husbands have incomes of $4,000, $6,000, and $11,000. Their wives earn, respectively, $2,500, $2,000, and $0. If we pick a husband at random, what is the expected value of his income, and what is the variance of this result? If we pick a family at random, what is the expected value of the family income, and what is the variance of this result? Is this variance equal to the sum of the variance in incomes of husbands and variance in incomes of wives?

6.21   In the above exercise, arbitrarily take any man and any woman, so that each man-woman pair has an equal chance to be chosen. What is the variance of the sum of incomes?

6.6 DISCRETE AND CONTINUOUS VARIABLES

We have met a number of random variables which could take specific values $x_1, x_2, \ldots, x_n$ with associated probability $p_1, p_2, \ldots, p_n$, where $p_1 + p_2 + \cdots + p_n = 1$. All values *other* than $x_1, x_2, \ldots, x_n$ had an associated probability of zero. Such random variables are called *discrete*, because the possible outcomes can only assume discrete, that is, specific or isolated, values.

Many variables, however, are by their nature *continuous*. In Section 2.2 we discussed the example of the temperature in a blast furnace. Other examples include the height of human adults, which varies continuously, or the time that elapses until a light bulb goes dark. Each of these variables can assume all possible values, at least over a certain range. Heights of adults span the range from 50 to 90 inches. It may be countered that although temperature, height, and time *themselves* vary continuously, their *measurement* does not. If we agree to measure height to the nearest inch, we have a discrete variable with the only possible outcomes 50 to 90 inches. If we measure the lifetime of the bulb in hours, lifetime is a discrete variable with possible outcomes 0 to 5,000. But it remains, strictly speaking, discrete even if we measure it to .1 of a second. We must conclude that in practice the distinction between what is discrete and what is continuous is arbitrary. Most practitioners agree that if there are less than 10 possible outcomes, it is nearly always useful to consider the variable as a discrete variable. If there are more than 50 possible outcomes, it is useful to consider the variable as continuous. The possible total scores in throwing 100 dice are 100, 101, . . . , 600, and strictly speaking this random variable is discrete. However, in practice it is, as we will see, treated as a continuous variable. If there are between 10 and 50 possible outcomes, it depends on the individual merits of the case whether it will be more advantageous to consider the variable discrete, as it is, or continuous, as we can pretend it is. For the time being these comments may sound cryptic. This is unfortunate, but help is on the way.

Discrete variable

Continuous variable

EXERCISES

6.22 The percentage of the sky over Logan International Airport that is covered with clouds is recorded daily at noon. Is this a discrete or continuous variable?

6.23 Is the number of employees in a drugstore a discrete or a continuous variable?

6.24   If you look at the second hand of your watch as you read this, the outcome will be a value anywhere between 0 and 60. Is the outcome a discrete or continuous random variable?

6.7 CONTINUOUS PROBABILITY DISTRIBUTIONS

In the graph of a discrete random variable the height of the bar at each possible outcome measures the probability associated with that outcome, and the sum of the heights of all bars must be 1, as in Figure 6.1.

Continuous probability distribution

For a continuous random variable the graph and its interpretation are different, in much the same way as the interpretation of histograms (where *areas* are important) differs from that of bar diagrams (where *heights* are important). In Figure 6.4 we represent a variable which is equally likely to be anywhere between 0 and 60, such as the second hand of your watch if you look at it . . . now! The total area of the rectangle is 1, its base length is 60, and its height is $\frac{1}{60}$. It is often referred to as a *continuous probability distribution*, since the total probability mass of 1 is distributed continuously over the range of the variable, like peanut butter on bread.

Rectangular distribution

In the figure the distribution is equally dense everywhere within the range 0 to 60. The peanut butter has been spread equally densely everywhere on the bread. This density is measured along the vertical axis. The distribution of Figure 6.4 is called a *rectangular probability distribution*.

Probabilities are shown by areas

How should one interpret continuous probability distributions? The basic principle is that *probabilities are shown by areas*. As before, the outcomes are given along the horizontal axis. The scale on the vertical axis is such that the total area will be 1. The value $\frac{1}{60}$ does not, by itself, give a probability. Beware, for this is drastically different from the case of discrete probability distributions. Only areas represent probabilities.

Given the distribution in Figure 6.4, what is the probability of an outcome between 20 and 35? The probability is shown by the area between 20 and 35. This area is $15 \times \frac{1}{60} = \frac{1}{4}$ because the area of a

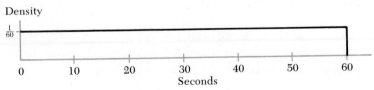

Density

$\frac{1}{60}$

0   10   20   30   40   50   60
                  Seconds

Figure 6.4 Rectangular distribution.

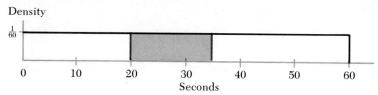

Figure 6.5 Probability under rectangular distribution—I.

rectangle is computed by multiplying the lengths of the base and the height. This is illustrated in Figure 6.5.

We can also conclude that the probability of an outcome between 0 and 60 equals 1. It is, in other words, certain that the outcome will be between 0 and 60. What is the probability of the outcome 25 *exactly?* To find out we consider the *area* above 25. This area is given by the line *AB* in Figure 6.6. It is zero, since a line does not have an area. The probability of 25 is, therefore, zero. This stands to reason, since there are an infinite number of possible outcomes, of which 25, which is shorthand for 25.000000000 . . . and differs from 25.000000100 . . . , is only *one.* If each outcome had a positive probability, however small, the total probability would also be infinite. We conclude that in a continuous probability distribution any *specific* outcome *exactly* has probability zero. Of course, if we interpret 25 as meaning "between $24\frac{1}{2}$ and $25\frac{1}{2}$," the area, and hence the probability, is $1 \times \frac{1}{60} = \frac{1}{60}$, as in Figure 6.7.

In summary, any continuous probability distribution will have an area 1 under its curve. Any specific outcome *exactly* will have probability zero, but any outcome within a certain range will have a probability equal to the area under the curve above that range. The measurement along the vertical axis should always be such that the total area under the curve is 1. That is all there is to it.

In Figure 6.8 we present the *normal distribution.* This is an extraor- Normal dinarily important distribution, which we will meet time and again. It distribution will be discussed in some detail in Section 7.5. In the example illustrated in Figure 6.8 the measurements along the horizontal axis can be thought

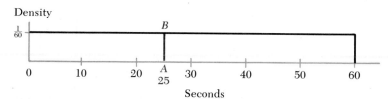

Figure 6.6 Probability under rectangular distribution—II.

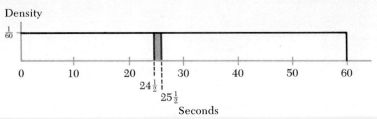

Figure 6.7 Probability under rectangular distribution—III.

of as representing the probability distribution of heights of adult human beings. A distance of 6 inches is considered 1 unit of length along the horizontal axis, and given this unit, a height of close to .4 at the maximum guarantees that the total area will be 1. In the right half of Figure 6.8 we have drawn a rectangle with the same scales along the axes, and we can verify "by eye" that the areas of both figures are the same. The probability that someone will be between 5 and 6 feet is given by the shaded area in Figure 6.9. This probability can be estimated by eye as about 60 to 70 percent. The probability of being smaller than 5 feet 8 inches is exactly 50 percent because the distribution is symmetric. The probability of someone's being *exactly* 5 feet tall is zero.

In this context we make the following comment. Suppose we measure someone very carefully and, lo and behold, he is *exactly* 5 feet tall. Yet, this has probability zero. We conclude that some events which have probability zero may happen. As we have stated in Chapter 2, an outcome which never happens has probability zero. Now we see that the converse is not always true. A tossed coin might come down standing on its edge, although this event has zero probability.

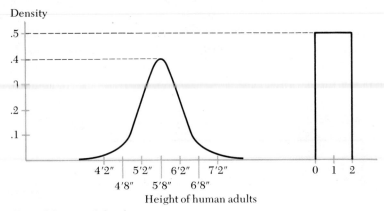

Figure 6.8 Normal distribution.

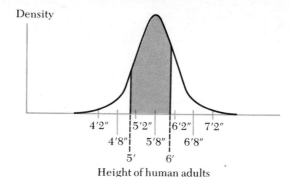

Figure 6.9 Probability under normal distribution.

Figure 6.10 illustrates another distribution. We have measured income along the horizontal axis; the long thin tail represents the small probability of earning high incomes, and the fat steep mountain represents the large probability of earning a low to middle income. Units along the axes are such that the total area under the curve is again 1. Playing it by eye, it is clear that the probability of income between $10,000 and $20,000 is approximately 30 percent. The probability distribution depicted in Figure 6.10 is called a *lognormal distribution;* the logarithm of income is a normally distributed variable. A lognormal distribution is skewed to the right. Any distribution which is not symmetric is *skewed* to either the left or the right depending on the direction toward which the probability is thinly spread, "the tail."

Lognormal distribution Skewness

Figure 6.11 illustrates a distribution which has been called a *reverse J-shaped distribution.* A reverse J-shaped distribution runs downhill all the way, rapidly at first and more slowly later, and tapers off to the horizontal axis. Along the horizontal axis we have measured the length

Reverse J-shaped distribution

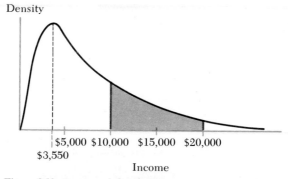

Figure 6.10 Lognormal distribution.

Density

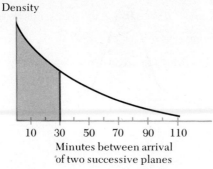

10   30   50   70   90   110
Minutes between arrival
of two successive planes

Figure 6.11   Reverse J distribution.

of time between the arrival of successive airplanes. Such waiting-time distributions are often reverse J-shaped. There are theoretical reasons for this result which are discussed in Section 7.7. The scales along the axes are chosen so that the total area is 1. It looks as if the probability that the next plane will arrive within half an hour is roughly 50 percent.

The J-shaped distribution, like the lognormal distribution, is skewed to the right. A rough-and-ready measure for this skewness will be given at the end of the next section.

EXERCISES

6.25   In the distribution shown below, a sort of reverse J-shaped distribution, estimate the probability of getting an outcome between 0 and 2; between 3 and 7; of exactly 9; of 9, rounded to the nearest integer. Verify your estimates by a geometrical approach, if possible.

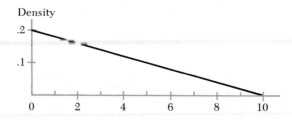

6.26   (*a*) What is the probability of getting an outcome below 8 if the probability density is as follows:

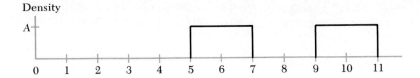

(b) Determine also the probability of an outcome between 5 and 6.

(c) Determine $P(\mathbf{x} > 6 \; or \; \mathbf{x} < 10)$.

(d) What is the value on the vertical scale at A?

6.27   A certain random variable is equally likely to be anywhere between 0 and 1. How does the density look?

6.28   In Exercise 6.25, suppose we were to represent the continuous random variable as a discrete random variable with possible outcomes 0, 1, 2, ..., 10 by rounding to the nearest integer. What would the probabilities associated with each of these values be? Graph the new probability distribution.

6.8   DESCRIPTIVE MEASURES OF CONTINUOUS PROBABILITY DISTRIBUTIONS

We have discussed in Sections 6.2 and 6.4 the expected value and the variance of discrete random variables. In this section we will indicate how we might go about finding the expected value and the variance of a continuous random variable.

Let us look again at the continuous probability distribution which we encountered in Exercise 6.25. The total area under the line is $\frac{1}{2} \times 10 \times .2 = 1$, as it should be. If this were a discrete random variable, its expected value could easily be determined:

$$Ex = p_1 x_1 + p_2 x_2 + \cdots + p_n x_n$$

This formula cannot be used in the continuous case because there are an infinite number of possible outcomes (all numbers between 0 and 10), and each has associated with it a probability zero. On the other hand, it is clear from the picture that an expected value does exist, and is somewhere around 3 or 4.

TABLE 6.14   APPROXIMATION OF EXPECTED VALUE OF
CONTINUOUS PROBABILITY DISTRIBUTION

(1) "Outcome"	(2) Probability	(3) (1) × (2)	(1) "Outcome"	(2) Probability	(3) (1) × (2)
$\frac{1}{2}$	.19	.095	0	.0975	.00
$1\frac{1}{2}$	.17	.255	1	.18	.18
$2\frac{1}{2}$	.15	.375	2	.16	.32
$3\frac{1}{2}$	.13	.455	3	.14	.42
$4\frac{1}{2}$	.11	.495	4	.12	.48
$5\frac{1}{2}$	.09	.495	5	.10	.50
$6\frac{1}{2}$	.07	.455	6	.08	.48
$7\frac{1}{2}$	.05	.375	7	.06	.42
$8\frac{1}{2}$	.03	.255	8	.04	.32
$9\frac{1}{2}$	.01	.095	9	.02	.18
"Expected value" =		3.350	10	.0025	.025
			"Expected value" =		3.325

The road to progress is to consider only discrete outcomes initially. We act as if outcomes were rounded to the nearest integer, or to $\frac{1}{2}$, $1\frac{1}{2}$, ..., $9\frac{1}{2}$. Both these alternatives were dealt with in Exercise 6.28. The results are summarized and the expected values computed in Table 6.14. The outcome is 3.325 or 3.35, depending on whether we round to the nearest integer or the nearest "half-point." Which of these values is the true expected value? The disappointing answer is neither. But both are very good approximations to the true expected value, which is $3\frac{1}{3}$.

The difference is essentially the result of our not taking enough discrete values to represent the continuous variable satisfactorily. We took only about 10 values out of an infinite number of possibilities. It would have been more accurate to take 20, or 50, or 100. But this has a serious disadvantage—it is very laborious. Moreover, even if we take 101 different values, 0, .1, .2, .3, ..., 9.9, 10, we still have a rather meager selection out of an infinite number of possibilities, and some error is likely to remain.

Fortunately, there exists a technique called integration which is both efficient and accurate. The principle is essentially the same as the principle used here: Make the variable discrete, but not in 10, 100, or 1,000 values, but very, very many. The associated probabilities will then become very, very small, but the sum of terms gives exactly the continuous equivalent of $\mathbf{Ex} = \Sigma p_i x_i$.

What has been said for the expected value holds for the variance as well. It can be approximated by making the variable discrete and using the formula for discrete distributions. The variance can be easily determined exactly, however, with integration.

The other measures of central tendency—median and mode—give us no trouble with continuous random variables. The mode is simply the value of the variable corresponding to the highest point of the continuous probability distribution. In Figure 6.10, the mode is clearly $3,550. This does not mean that the probability of an income of exactly $3,550 is more than the probability of any other income exactly. It is not, for the simple reason that the probability of any income exactly is precisely zero. But it is to say that an income between $3,500 and $3,600 is more likely than an income in any other range of equal magnitude.

The mode of the distribution in Figure 6.12 is $3.00. The curve can be thought of as representing the sales in a drugstore. It is worth noting that the figure has two "tops." Such a distribution is usually considered *bimodal,* even though one top is clearly higher than the other, and even though the sales in a narrow range around $3 are higher than those in a similar interval around $11. The second mode is at $11, and we should inquire why. We cannot answer the question in the abstract. The fact may be that sales over $10 are delivered home, or that there is a particularly popular item priced at $11, or even that there is a clerk who reads a roman numeral II as 11. It can be verified from the relevant figures in Section 6.2 that a rectangular distribution has no mode.

The median is the value which partitions the probability distribution into two equal parts, each containing 50 percent of the total probability. In Figure 6.13 some illustrations are presented. The median of a continuous distribution is nearly always unique. An exception is illustrated in the figure of Exercise 6.26.

Just as the median divides the total area into two equal parts, the *quartile points* divide it into four equal parts, each containing 25 percent

Quartile points and quartiles

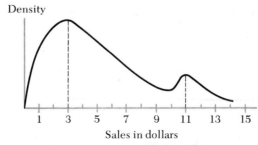

Figure 6.12   The mode of a continuous distribution.

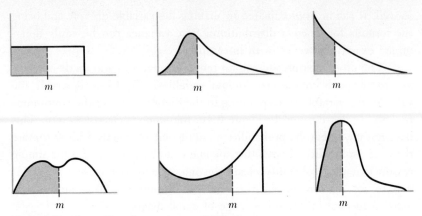

Figure 6.13 The median of a continuous distribution.

of the total probability. There are three quartile points. Figure 6.14 illustrates a number of examples. In each example, the first quartile point is indicated by q_1, the second by m and q_2 since the second quartile point coincides with the median, and the third by q_3. If an observation falls between q_2 and q_3, it is said to be in the *3d quartile*.

Decile points and deciles

Just as the quartile points divide the area into four equal parts, the *decile points* divide it into 10 equal parts, each containing 10 percent of the total probability, and each thus having an area equal to 0.1. There are nine decile points $d_1, d_2, \ldots, d_9$ which divide the area into 10 *deciles*. Analogously, 20 slices of bread are produced by cutting 19 times. If the 9 decile points in grading a test of students are 32, 40, 46, 50, 52, 55,

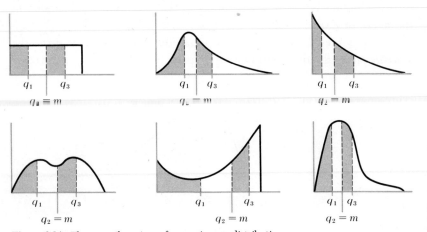

Figure 6.14 The quartile points of a continuous distribution.

59, 66, 80, then 10 percent score below 32, 10 percent score above 80, and 10 percent score between 50 and 52. The students with a score of 56 are in the 7th decile. This implies that 60 percent are strictly worse, and 30 percent strictly better. The remaining 10 percent are in the same decile. This is illustrated in Figure 6.15.

The ultimate refinement is to consider percentiles, and percentile points. There are 99 *percentile points,* which divide a total area into 100 equally large sections, that is, *percentiles,* each containing a probability of .01. This degree of refinement is sometimes useful when there are large masses of data, such as scores on College Board entrance exams. If someone's score is in the 17th percentile, we know that 83 percent scored better and 16 percent scored worse than he did.

Percentile points and percentiles

If a distribution is symmetric, the mean and the median coincide. This is true for the rectangular and the normal distributions. In skewed distributions, it is no longer true. In a right skewed distribution the mean will exceed the median, for the high values in the upper tail contribute greatly to the mean, while the median is wholly unaffected by the precise values taken in the upper half of the distribution. This line of thought somewhat further pursued has led to the following formula as a *measure of skewness*

Measure of skewness

$$\text{Skewness} = \frac{3(\text{mean} - \text{median})}{\text{standard deviation}} = \frac{3(F\mathbf{x} - \text{median})}{S\mathbf{x}}$$

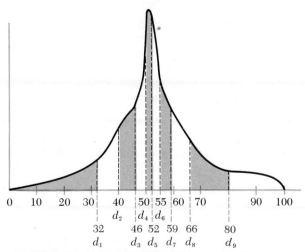

Figure 6.15 The decile points of a continuous distribution.

When this value is positive, the distribution is skewed to the right, the more so the more positive the value. When negative, the distribution is skewed to the left.

The triangular distribution depicted in Exercise 6.25 has a mean of 3.333, a median of 2.929, and a standard deviation of 2.357. These values were computed with integration, but they can be roughly verified by looking at Table 6.14, by looking at the illustration, and by using the rules of thumb, respectively. The measure of skewness of this distribution is

$$\text{Skewness} = \frac{3(3.333 - 2.929)}{2.357} = .515$$

EXERCISES

6.29   What is the expected value of the rectangular distribution of Figure 6.4?

6.30   What is the expected value of the normal distribution in Figure 6.8?

6.31   Someone in the 61st percentile is in what decile? What percentage is strictly better?

6.32   Verify that in the normal distribution the mode and the median coincide. In the lognormal distribution, is the median to the left or to the right of the mode? What about the rectangular and the reverse J-shaped distributions?

6.33   Determine the measure of skewness for the variable "value shown on the highest of two dice" (see Figure 6.1 and Table 6.2).

Answers to Exercises

6.1   The events are ♠♠, ♠♥, ♠♦, ♠♣, ♥♥, ♥♦, ♥♣, ♦♦, ♦♣, ♣♣. There are $\overline{C}(4,2) = C(5,2) = \frac{5!}{2!3!} = 10$ different outcomes possible. The associated probability is (by pedestrian method) $\frac{13}{52} \times \frac{12}{51}$ if the suits are the same, and $2 \times \frac{13}{52} \times \frac{13}{51}$ if the suits are different. (The factor 2 is due to the fact that both ♠♥ and ♥♠ lead to the outcome "a spade and a heart.") There is no random variable, since the outcomes are not numerical.

6.2 8, 7, 6, 5, 4, 3, and 2, with probability $\frac{6}{102}$, $\frac{13}{102}$, $\frac{19}{102}$, $\frac{26}{102}$, $\frac{19}{102}$, $\frac{13}{102}$, and $\frac{6}{102}$, respectively. In this new formulation we do have a random variable.

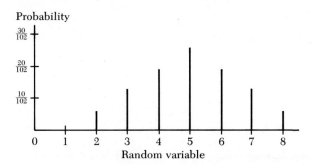

6.3 (a) We can choose $C(4,3) = 4$ combinations of three values out of the four. They are $(2,3,7)$, $(2,3,11)$, $(2,7,11)$, and $(3,7,11)$.

(b)

Combination	Average
2, 3, 7	4
2, 3, 11	$5\frac{1}{3}$
2, 7, 11	$6\frac{2}{3}$
3, 7, 11	7

(c) Before the three values are chosen, the average is a random variable which can take the values 4, $5\frac{1}{3}$, $6\frac{2}{3}$, and 7.

(d) Each average listed in (b) has a probability of $\frac{1}{4}$.

6.4 The sum, the product, the absolute value of the difference, the highest, the lowest, the sum squared, and so on. In a table:

(1)		(2)		(3) Absolute value difference	
Sum	Probability	Product	Probability		Probability
4	$\frac{1}{11}$	4	$\frac{1}{11}$	0	$\frac{3}{11}$
7	$\frac{8}{33}$	10	$\frac{8}{33}$	1	$\frac{8}{33}$
8	$\frac{8}{33}$	12	$\frac{8}{33}$	3	$\frac{8}{33}$
10	$\frac{1}{11}$	25	$\frac{1}{11}$	4	$\frac{8}{33}$
11	$\frac{8}{33}$	30	$\frac{8}{33}$		
12	$\frac{1}{11}$	36	$\frac{1}{11}$		

| (4) | | (5) | | (6)
Sum | |
Highest	Probability	Lowest	Probability	squared	Probability
2	$\frac{1}{11}$	2	$\frac{19}{33}$	16	$\frac{1}{11}$
5	$\frac{1}{3}$	5	$\frac{1}{3}$	49	$\frac{8}{33}$
6	$\frac{19}{33}$	6	$\frac{1}{11}$	64	$\frac{8}{33}$
				100	$\frac{1}{11}$
				121	$\frac{8}{33}$
				144	$\frac{1}{11}$

6.5

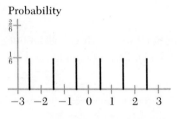

Random variable

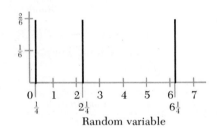

Random variable

6.6   Tossing four coins and counting the number of heads; or the coefficient of a randomly chosen term in the expansion of $(a + b)^4$.

6.7   In view of Table 2.5, page 24, the expected value is $\frac{1}{8} \times 0 + \frac{3}{8} \times 1 + \frac{3}{8} \times 2 + \frac{1}{8} \times 3 = 1\frac{1}{2}$. This is not a random variable, but a constant.

6.8 $\frac{1}{6} \times (-2\frac{1}{2}) + \frac{1}{6} \times (-1\frac{1}{2}) + \frac{1}{6} \times (-\frac{1}{2}) + \frac{1}{6} \times \frac{1}{2} + \frac{1}{6} \times 1\frac{1}{2} + \frac{1}{6} \times 2\frac{1}{2} = 0$, and $\frac{1}{6} \times 6\frac{1}{4} + \frac{1}{6} \times 2\frac{1}{4} + \frac{1}{6} \times \frac{1}{4} + \frac{1}{6} \times \frac{1}{4} + \frac{1}{6} \times 2\frac{1}{4} + \frac{1}{6} \times 6\frac{1}{4} = 2\frac{11}{12}$.

6.9 $\frac{1}{36} \times 1 + \frac{3}{36} \times 2 + \frac{5}{36} \times 3 + \frac{7}{36} \times 4 + \frac{9}{36} \times 5 + \frac{11}{36} \times 6 = 4\frac{17}{36}$; see the fourth column in Table 6.2 for these probabilities.

6.10   The probability of an accident with $100 property damage is .05 × .50 = .025. The probability of an accident with $500 damage is .05 × .40 = .02. The probability of an accident with $1,800 damage is .05 × .10 = .005. The expected value of the damage per year is $0 × .95 + $100 × .025 + $500 × .02 + $1,800 × .005 = $21.50.

6.11   By the rule that the expected value of the sum equals the sum of the expected values, the answer is $\frac{4}{3}$.

E[purchase of customer 1 + purchase of customer 2
+ purchase of customer 3 + purchase of customer 4]
$= E$[purchase of customer 1] + E[purchase of customer 2]
   + E[purchase of customer 3] + E[purchase of customer 4]
$= \frac{1}{3} + \frac{1}{3} + \frac{1}{3} + \frac{1}{3} = \frac{4}{3}$

The detailed solution argues that there is a probability of $\frac{1}{81}$, $\frac{8}{81}$, $\frac{24}{81}$, $\frac{32}{81}$, and $\frac{16}{81}$ of 4, 3, 2, 1, and 0 purchases, respectively, for an expected value of $4 \times \frac{1}{81} + 3 \times \frac{8}{81} + 2 \times \frac{24}{81} + 1 \times \frac{32}{81} + 0 \times \frac{16}{81} = \frac{108}{81} = \frac{4}{3}$.

6.12   By the rule that the expected value of the sum equals the sum of the expected values the answer is, as before, $\frac{4}{3}$. The detailed solution argues that there is a $\frac{1}{3}$ probability of four purchases and a $\frac{2}{3}$ probability of zero purchases, for an expected value of $4 \times \frac{1}{3} + 0 \times \frac{2}{3} = \frac{4}{3}$.

6.13   The probability that one card matches is $\frac{1}{10}$; for example, the probability that the first card is ♣A is $\frac{1}{10}$. The expected number of matches in 10 cards is, therefore, 1. The random variable $\mathbf{x}$ standing for the number of matches takes the values 0, 1, 2, 3, 4, 5, 6, 7, 8, 9, and 10 with probabilities of about .37, .37, .18, .06, .01, .01, .00, .00, .00, 0, and .00; this result, however, is quite difficult to derive. It can be verified that the expected value is $.37 \times 0 + .37 \times 1 + \cdots + .00 \times 10 = 1$.

6.14   2, 4, 8, 40, and 400, respectively.

6.15

(1) Outcome	(2) Probability	(3) (2) × (1)	(4) Outcome − $1\frac{1}{2}$	(5) $(4)^2$	(6) (5) × (2)
0	$\frac{1}{8}$	0	$-1\frac{1}{2}$	$2\frac{1}{4}$	$\frac{9}{32}$
1	$\frac{3}{8}$	$\frac{3}{8}$	$-\frac{1}{2}$	$\frac{1}{4}$	$\frac{3}{32}$
2	$\frac{3}{8}$	$\frac{6}{8}$	$\frac{1}{2}$	$\frac{1}{4}$	$\frac{3}{32}$
3	$\frac{1}{8}$	$\frac{3}{8}$	$1\frac{1}{2}$	$2\frac{1}{4}$	$\frac{9}{32}$
	1	$1\frac{1}{2}$			$\frac{24}{32} = \frac{3}{4} = .75$

The standard deviation is $\sqrt{.75} = .87$, and 75 percent of the outcomes will be between .67 and 2.37, while 100 percent will be within $-.26$ and 3.24.

6.16

(1) Outcome	(2) Probability	(3) (2) × (1)	(4) Outcome − π	(5) (4)^2	(6) (5) × (2)
0	$1 - \pi$	0	$-\pi$	π^2	$(1 - \pi)\pi^2$
1	π	π	$1 - \pi$	$(1 - \pi)^2$	$\pi(1 - \pi)^2$

Expected value = π

$$\text{Variance} = (1 - \pi)\pi^2 + \pi(1 - \pi)^2 = (1 - \pi)\pi[\pi + (1 - \pi)] = (1 - \pi)\pi$$

The variance is $\pi(1 - \pi)$. For example, if $\pi = \frac{1}{2}$, the expected value is $\frac{1}{2}$, the variance is $\frac{1}{2} \times \frac{1}{2} = \frac{1}{4}$, and the standard deviation is $\sqrt{\frac{1}{4}} = \frac{1}{2}$. If $\pi = .1$ and $(1 - \pi) = .9$, the standard deviation is $\sqrt{.09} = .3$.

6.17 The standard deviation is computed in the following table:

Outcome	Damage	Probability	Damage × probability	Damage^2	Damage^2 × probability
No accident	0	.95	0	0	0
Mild accident	$100	.025	$ 2.50	10,000	250
Serious accident	$500	.020	10.00	250,000	5,000
Total loss	$1,800	.005	9.00	3,240,000	16,200
			$21.50		21,450

Variance = $21,450 - (21.50)^2 = 20,987.75$

The standard deviation is $144.80.

6.18 The variance of this sum is $100 \times 2\frac{11}{12} = 291\frac{2}{3}$, so the standard deviation is a shade over 17. More than 90 percent will be within the limits $350 \pm 2 \times 17 = 316$ to 384. To be on the safe side, since the standard deviation is a bit over 17, certainly more than 90 percent will be between the limits 315–385.

6.19 Let us consider the case where there is only one customer, the first. We have

Outcome	Value	Prob- ability	Value × probability	Value²	Value² × probability
Hamburger	1	.6	.6	1	.6
Hot dog	0	.4	.0	0	.0
		Expected value = .6			.6

$$\text{Variance} = .6 - (.6)^2 = .24$$

Hence, the expected value of the number of hamburgers sold to the first customer is .6 and the variance is .24. Then:

(a) The expected number of hamburgers sold to 225 fans is $225 \times .6 = 135$.

(b) In view of the independence of fans' preferences, the variance is $225 \times .24 = 54$.

(c) The standard deviation of the number of hamburgers sold is $\sqrt{54} = 7.35$.

(d) The actual number of hamburgers will almost certainly be within 3 standard deviations, or $3 \times 7.35 = 22$ of the expected value of 135. Hence, the concessionaire will sell within 135 ± 22, or 113 to 157 hamburgers.

6.20 To start with the last question, the answer is presumably no, because one would expect dependence between husbands' and wives' incomes. In this instance the higher the income of the husband, the lower the income of the wife.

Variance Computations for the Husbands

(1) Outcome	(2) Probability	(3) (1) × (2)	(4) (1)²	(5) (2) × (4)
4	$\frac{1}{3}$	$\frac{4}{3}$	16	$5\frac{1}{3}$
6	$\frac{1}{3}$	2	36	12
11	$\frac{1}{3}$	$\frac{11}{3}$	121	$40\frac{1}{3}$
	1	7		$57\frac{2}{3}$

$$Vx = 57\tfrac{2}{3} - (7)^2 = 8\tfrac{2}{3}$$

Variance Computations for the Wives

(1) Outcome	(2) Probability	(3) (1) × (2)	(4) (1)²	(5) (2) × (4)
$2\frac{1}{2}$	$\frac{1}{3}$	$\frac{5}{6}$	$6\frac{1}{4}$	$\frac{25}{12}$
2	$\frac{1}{3}$	$\frac{2}{3}$	4	$\frac{4}{3}$
0	$\frac{1}{3}$	0	0	0
	1	$1\frac{1}{2}$		$\frac{41}{12} = 3\frac{5}{12}$

$$Vx = 3\tfrac{5}{12} - (1\tfrac{1}{2})^2 = 1\tfrac{1}{6}$$

Variance Computations for the Families

(1) Outcome	(2) Probability	(3) (1) × (2)	(4) (1)²	(5) (2) × (4)
$6\frac{1}{2}$	$\frac{1}{3}$	$\frac{13}{6}$	$42\frac{1}{4}$	$14\frac{1}{12}$
8	$\frac{1}{3}$	$\frac{8}{3}$	64	$21\frac{1}{3}$
11	$\frac{1}{3}$	$\frac{11}{3}$	121	$40\frac{1}{3}$
	1	$8\frac{1}{2}$		$75\frac{3}{4}$

$$Vx = 75\tfrac{3}{4} - (8\tfrac{1}{2})^2 = 3\tfrac{1}{2}$$

It is clear that $3\frac{1}{2} \neq 8\frac{2}{3} + 1\frac{1}{6}$. Notice, however, that the expected value of the family income, $8\frac{1}{6}$, equals the sum of the expected values 7 and $1\frac{1}{2}$.

6.21　By independence, we now can use the result that the variance of the sum is the sum of the variances, so the answer will be $8\frac{2}{3} + 1\frac{1}{6} = 9\frac{5}{6}$. The check is:

(1) Outcome	(2) Probability	(3) (1) × (2)	(4) (1)²	(5) (2) × (4)
$4 + 0 = 4$	$\frac{1}{9}$	$\frac{4}{9}$	16	$1\frac{7}{9}$
$6 + 0 = 6$	$\frac{1}{9}$	$\frac{6}{9}$	36	4
$4 + 2 = 6$	$\frac{1}{9}$	$\frac{6}{9}$	36	4
$4 + 2\frac{1}{2} = 6\frac{1}{2}$	$\frac{1}{9}$	$\frac{13}{18}$	$42\frac{1}{4}$	$4\frac{25}{36}$
$6 + 2 = 8$	$\frac{1}{9}$	$\frac{8}{9}$	64	$7\frac{1}{9}$
$6 + 2\frac{1}{2} = 8\frac{1}{2}$	$\frac{1}{9}$	$\frac{17}{18}$	$72\frac{1}{4}$	$8\frac{1}{36}$
$11 + 0 = 11$	$\frac{1}{9}$	$\frac{11}{9}$	121	$13\frac{4}{9}$
$11 + 2 = 13$	$\frac{1}{9}$	$\frac{13}{9}$	169	$18\frac{7}{9}$
$11 + 2\frac{1}{2} = 13\frac{1}{2}$	$\frac{1}{9}$	$\frac{27}{18}$	$182\frac{1}{4}$	$2\frac{9}{36}$
	1	$8\frac{1}{2}$		$82\frac{3}{36}$

$$Vx = 82\tfrac{3}{36} - (8\tfrac{1}{2})^2 = 9\tfrac{5}{6}$$

6.22   It is theoretically continuous because the percentage can have any value, such as 34.315178429 . . . percent. Practically, it is discrete because one considers only values such as 0, 1, 2, . . . , 17, . . . , 100 percent, if only because more accurate measurement is impossible. Yet it is fruitful to consider it as a continuous variable anyway because there are more than 50 different outcomes.

6.23   It is a discrete variable and may range from 0 to perhaps 20 with the high outcomes having exceedingly small probabilities.

6.24   It is clearly continuous, and though rounding to the nearest second may make it discrete, it is expedient to consider it as a continuous variable anyway.

6.25   In area, the answers are given by area A, area B, 0, and area C of the figure. By visual inspection, these are about 30 to 35 percent, 35 to 40 percent, 0 percent, and 2 percent or so. Because of the easy geometrical shape a more precise answer can be computed. First, since the segment OK has length 10, the segment OA is by necessity .2, for the area OAK must be equal to 1. The density (shown on AK) decreases by .02 in equal steps as indicated in the second figure. The area under AC, which represents the probability of an outcome between 0 and 2, equals that of the (dotted) rectangle and hence equals $2 \times .18 = .36$, or 36 percent. (The estimate 30 to 35 percent was a shade low.) The area

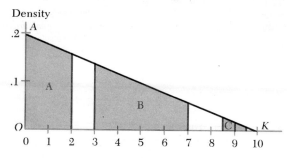

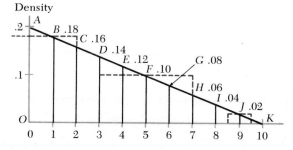

between 3 and 7 equals the area of the corresponding rectangle, and is thus $4 \times .10 = .40$, or 40 percent. The area around 9 has size $1 \times .02 = .02$, or 2 percent. Our estimates were not too bad.

6.26   (a) $P(x < 8) = 50$ percent. In words, the probability that the random variable x will be below 8 is 50 percent.

(b) $P(5 < x < 6) = .25$.

(c) $P(x > 6 \ or \ x < 10) = P(x > 6) + P(x < 10) - P(x > 6 \ and \ x < 10) = .75 + .75 - .50 = 1$.

(d) The value on the vertical scale at A is $\frac{1}{4}$. This makes the total area equal to 1.

6.27   The left figure has the same scale along the axes. This is not necessary for a clear and esthetic figure and is usually ill-advised. In this example there is no harm in it.

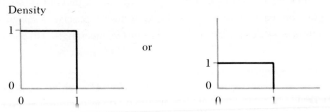

6.28   Continuing our geometric considerations in Exercise 6.25, we find the following table and figures:

Outcomes	Probability	Outcomes	Probability
0	.0975	6	.08
1	.18	7	.06
2	.16	8	.04
3	.14	9	.02
4	.12	10	.0025
5	.10		1

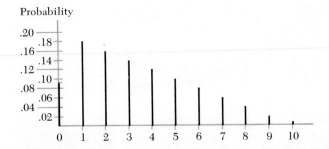

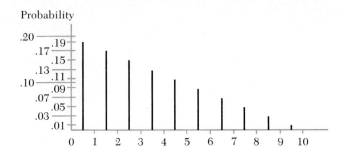

Notice that these bars represent probabilities. Some of the beauty of a triangle has been spoiled by the fact that the result zero is only recorded for an outcome between 0 and $\frac{1}{2}$, but 1 is recorded for an outcome between $\frac{1}{2}$ and $1\frac{1}{2}$, which is a range twice as long. To prevent this, we might make the distribution discrete by rounding to $\frac{1}{2}$, $1\frac{1}{2}$, ..., $9\frac{1}{2}$. An outcome between 6 and 7 is recorded as $6\frac{1}{2}$. These outcomes have associated probabilities .19, .17, .15, ..., .01, as illustrated in the second figure.

6.29 We round the outcomes to $\frac{1}{2}$, $1\frac{1}{2}$, $2\frac{1}{2}$, ..., $59\frac{1}{2}$. An outcome between 37 and 38 is recorded as $37\frac{1}{2}$. All outcomes have a probability of $\frac{1}{60}$. Thus Ex equals $\frac{1}{60} \times \frac{1}{2} + \frac{1}{60} \times 1\frac{1}{2} + \cdots + \frac{1}{60} \times 59\frac{1}{2} = 30$. In this case the answer is exactly correct. We might have anticipated this because of the symmetry of the distribution around the value 30.

6.30 We use symmetry to conclude that the expected value is 5 feet 8 inches.

6.31 He is in the 7th decile, and 39 percent are strictly better.

6.32 In a lognormal distribution the median is to the right of the mode. In a rectangular distribution there is no mode, and the median splits the rectangle up into two equal rectangles. In a reverse J-shaped distribution, the median is to the right of the mode, which is at zero.

6.33 The mean equals $\frac{1}{36} \times 1 + \frac{3}{36} \times 2 + \cdots + \frac{11}{36} \times 6 = \frac{161}{36} = 4\frac{17}{36}$. The median equals 5. The standard deviation equals the square root of $\frac{1}{36}(1 - 4\frac{17}{36})^2 + \frac{3}{36}(2 - 4\frac{17}{36})^2 + \cdots + \frac{11}{36}(6 - 4\frac{17}{36})^2 = \frac{91,950}{46,656}$. This ratio is 1.97, and its square root is 1.40. The measure of skewness is thus $3(4\frac{17}{36} - 5)/1.40 = -1.13$.

Chapter 7

THE BINOMIAL, NORMAL, POISSON, EXPONENTIAL, AND HYPERGEOMETRIC DISTRIBUTIONS

7.1 BINOMIAL TRIALS AND THE BINOMIAL DISTRIBUTION

Frequently an experiment leads to either of two outcomes—such as sale or no sale, accept or reject, red or black, pass or fail—with specified probabilities. One of these outcomes is then referred to as a success (probability π) and the other as a failure (probability $1 - \pi$). The question then is, if such an experiment is repeated n times, what is the probability of obtaining 0, 1, 2, ..., n successes? In concrete terms: If, for each customer, the probability of a purchase is .6, what is the probability that four customers will make 0, 1, 2, 3, or 4 purchases? If red and black both have a 50 percent chance, what is the probability that in 10 spins of the wheel 7 outcomes will be red?

Two outcomes

The answer to these problems is not very difficult, provided that one condition is satisfied. In each and every trial of the experiment there must be the same probability of success π, and the same probability of failure $1 - \pi$. This implies that successive outcomes must be independent. For example, in roulette each single individual spin will lead to red or black with equal probability of $\frac{1}{2}$ (disregarding the outcome zero, which is green). In fact, the casino officials spend a good deal of time and money to

Constant π

Independence

guarantee this, for any systematic tendency to produce red more than black or vice versa could lead to their bankruptcy. As for customers' purchases, the condition spells out that each customer should have a .6 probability of buying. It is not so obvious whether this condition is met in practice. The behavior of one shopper may well influence the actions of others.

Subject to this condition, the probability of k successes in n trials, when the probability of a success on each trial is π, is given by

$$C(n,k)\pi^k(1 - \pi)^{n-k}$$

This is a typical term in the formula for the binomial expansion $(a + b)^n$ (see Section 4.2) with $a = \pi$ and $b = 1 - \pi$. As an illustration, let us take the specific values $n = 6$, $\pi = \frac{1}{4}$, and $k = 2$. We are thus interested in the probability that six trials will produce two successes if each trial results in a success with probability $\frac{1}{4}$. This probability is

$$C(6,2)\left(\frac{1}{4}\right)^2\left(\frac{3}{4}\right)^4 = 15 \times \frac{1}{16} \times \frac{81}{256} = \frac{1,215}{4,096} = 30 \text{ percent}$$

To see why this formula holds, we write down all the different ways in which one can get two successes out of six: SSFFFF, SFSFFF, ..., FFFFSS. *Each* of these sequences has the *same* probability $(\frac{1}{4})^2(\frac{3}{4})^4$ of materializing. For example, the probability of SSFFFF is $\frac{1}{4} \times \frac{1}{4} \times \frac{3}{4} \times \frac{3}{4} \times \frac{3}{4} \times \frac{3}{4}$, and the probability of FFFFSS is $\frac{3}{4} \times \frac{3}{4} \times \frac{3}{4} \times \frac{3}{4} \times \frac{1}{4} \times \frac{1}{4}$. Both expressions are equal to $(\frac{1}{4})^2(\frac{3}{4})^4$, and this will be the case whichever two out of six trials are successful. There are $C(6,2) = 15$ different ways to get two out of six successful. Each of these 15 ways has a probability $(\frac{1}{4})^2(\frac{3}{4})^4$, and all 15 ways are mutually exclusive. The probability of success is therefore $C(6,2)(\frac{1}{4})^2(\frac{3}{4})^4$, as was to be proved.

In Table 7.1 we give the whole distribution for $n = 6$, $\pi = \frac{1}{4}$, and $k = 0, 1, 2, 3, 4, 5,$ and 6. These values are the successive terms in the binomial expansion of $(\frac{1}{4} + \frac{3}{4})^6$. In Appendix A on the uses of the computer the first two examples relate to this problem as well, and their reading now is recommended.

In Table 7.1 we have exhibited the complete probability distribution of the random variable $\mathbf{x}$, the number of successes in six trials if the probability of success is $\frac{1}{4}$ on each. The total probability of 1 is distributed over the possible outcomes. This probability distribution belongs to the class of *binomial* probability distributions. The *bi* in binomial means two, and implies that there are only two possible outcomes, success and failure. Such distributions are fully determined by two parameters—the number of trials n and the probability of success at any one trial π. Given n and

Binomial
distribution
$B(n,\pi)$

TABLE 7.1   BINOMIAL PROBABILITY DISTRIBUTION, $n = 6$, $\pi = \frac{1}{4}$

No. of successes k	Probability
$k = 0$	$\binom{6}{0}\left(\frac{1}{4}\right)^0\left(\frac{3}{4}\right)^6 = \dfrac{729}{4,096} = .1780$
$k = 1$	$\binom{6}{1}\left(\frac{1}{4}\right)^1\left(\frac{3}{4}\right)^5 = \dfrac{1,458}{4,096} = .3560$
$k = 2$	$\binom{6}{2}\left(\frac{1}{4}\right)^2\left(\frac{3}{4}\right)^4 = \dfrac{1,215}{4,096} = .2966$
$k = 3$	$\binom{6}{3}\left(\frac{1}{4}\right)^3\left(\frac{3}{4}\right)^3 = \dfrac{540}{4,096} = .1318$
$k = 4$	$\binom{6}{4}\left(\frac{1}{4}\right)^4\left(\frac{3}{4}\right)^2 = \dfrac{135}{4,096} = .0330$
$k = 5$	$\binom{6}{5}\left(\frac{1}{4}\right)^5\left(\frac{3}{4}\right)^1 = \dfrac{18}{4,096} = .0044$
$k = 6$	$\binom{6}{6}\left(\frac{1}{4}\right)^6\left(\frac{3}{4}\right)^0 = \dfrac{1}{4,096} = .0002$
	Total $= \dfrac{4,096}{4,096} = 1.0000$

n, the probability distribution of the number of successes x is given by the terms

$$C(n,0)\pi^0(1 - \pi)^{n-0}$$
$$C(n,1)\pi^1(1 - \pi)^{n-1}$$
$$\cdots\cdots\cdots\cdots$$
$$C(n,k)\pi^k(1 - \pi)^{n-k}$$
$$\cdots\cdots\cdots\cdots$$
$$C(n,n)\pi^n(1 - \pi)^{n-n}$$

There is a unique binomial distribution for each pair of values (n,π). Once these parameters n and π are specified, the complete distribution is known. For $n = 6$, $\pi = \frac{1}{4}$, this complete distribution is given in Table 7.1. In the general case, we will write $x = B(n,\pi)$ as shorthand for "x is a random variable, representing the number of successes in n trials when the probability of success in any given trial is π," or "x is binomially distributed, with parameters n and π." In Table 7a of Appendix B binomial distributions are specified for a large number of (n,π) combinations, including the combination $n = 6$, $\pi = \frac{1}{4}$.

EXERCISES

7.1   A personal loan may either be repaid to the bank or not repaid. The bank considers repayment as "success." Can the lending officer of the bank safely assume that the probability of success is constant from trial to trial, that is, from loan to loan?

7.2   On Tuesday the probability is .1 that a machine operator will be out sick. On Wednesday the probability is also .1 that he will be out sick. Is the probability that he will be sick on Tuesday or Wednesday (but not both) in the same week $C(2,1)(.1)^1(.9)^1$?

7.3 $x = B(5,\frac{1}{3})$. Specify the distribution numerically. Verify your answer by reference to Table 7a of Appendix B.

7.4   In throwing a die, a 6 is considered a success. What is the probability of getting four successes in five throws?

7.2   THE EXPECTED VALUE AND THE VARIANCE OF THE BINOMIAL DISTRIBUTION

We are interested in Ex, the expected value of the number of successes in a binomial distribution. The answer might be found from the possible outcomes and their associated probabilities. Using the formula $Ex = \Sigma p_i x_i$, we find from the values in Table 7.1, where $x = B(6,\frac{1}{4})$,

$$Ex = \tfrac{729}{4,096} \times 0 + \tfrac{1,458}{4,096} \times 1 + \cdots + \tfrac{1}{4,096} \times 6 = 1\tfrac{1}{2}$$

To be sure, this requires a considerable amount of arithmetic, but the answer is correct.

A much simpler and completely general argument is as follows. For $x = B(1,\pi)$, the expected number of successes is

$$1 \times \pi + 0 \times (1 - \pi) = \pi + 0 = \pi$$

since a success counts for 1 and has probability π, and failure counts for 0—a failure is zero successes—and has probability $(1 - \pi)$. In Section 6.3 we saw that the expected value in n trials is n times the expected value in one trial and, therefore, is $n\pi$. We summarize as follows: If

$$x = B(n,\pi) \qquad \text{then} \qquad Ex = n\pi$$

For $B(n,\pi)$,
$Ex = n\pi$

If $x = B(6,\frac{1}{4})$, then Ex is $6 \times \frac{1}{4} = 1\frac{1}{2}$. We derived the answer without

TABLE 7.2 COMPUTATION OF VARIANCE OF $x = B(1, \pi)$

(1) Outcome	(2) Probability	(3) $(1) \times (2)$	(4) Outcome $- \pi$	(5) $(4)^2$	(6) $(2) \times (5)$
Success $= 1$	π	π	$1 - \pi$	$(1 - \pi)^2$	$\pi(1 - \pi)^2$
Failure $= 0$	$1 - \pi$	0	$-\pi$	$(-\pi)^2$	$(1 - \pi)(-\pi)^2$
		$Ex = \pi$			$Vx = \pi(1 - \pi)$

first having to specify the complete probability distribution, which is laborious.

To compute the variance of the number of successes, we can use a result given in Section 6.5, that is, that the variance of the sum of independent random variables is the sum of their variances. This result is applicable because one of the basic premises of the binomial distribution is that all trials are independent. If we have one trial leading to success 1 with probability π, and failure 0 with probability $(1 - \pi)$, the variance is $\pi(1 - \pi)$, as shown in Table 7.2. Hence, if we have n binomial trials, the variance equals $n\pi(1 - \pi)$, and the standard deviation equals $\sqrt{n\pi(1 - \pi)}$. If $x = B(n,\pi) = B(6,\frac{1}{4})$, then $Ex = 6 \times \frac{1}{4} = 1\frac{1}{2}$, $Vx = n\pi(1 - \pi) = \frac{18}{16}$, and $Sx = \sqrt{\frac{18}{16}}$.

For $B(n,\pi)$, $Vx = n\pi(1 - \pi)$

EXERCISES

7.5   There are 187 flashbulbs, each having a probability of $\frac{1}{11}$ of not working at the proper moment. What is the expected number of failures? After how many shots does the expected number of failures equal 3?

7.6   In tossing 250 coins, what is the expected value of **x**, that is, the number of heads showing? What is the variance of **x**?

7.7   A random variable **x** is binomially distributed with $Ex = 7$ and $Vx = 6$. What are n and π?

7.8   Let $\pi = \frac{1}{10}$. How many trials of a binomial process should there be to guarantee that the standard deviation of a result is equal to 5 percent of the expected value?

7.9   In Table 2.2 the January births for 1963, in a specific hospital, are recorded as 144 males and 177 females. Is this in any way remarkable? In May 1966, 312 children were born in this hospital, 175 of which were boys. Is this unbelievably high?

7.3 THE MEAN AND THE VARIANCE OF PROBABILITY DISTRIBUTIONS

We pause for a moment to make a detour to settle some terminological issues. We already know from Section 6.4 that the concept of an *average* is unbreakably connected with a given series of observations $x_1, x_2, \ldots, x_n$, and is defined by $\bar{x} = (1/n) \Sigma x_i$. The concept of an *expected value* is unbreakably connected with a random variable **x**. If this random variable can assume values $x_1, x_2, \ldots, x_n$ with probabilities $p_1, p_2, \ldots, p_n$, the expected value is defined as $E\mathbf{x} = \Sigma p_i x_i$.

Also unbreakably connected with the concept of a random variable **x** is its probability distribution, which is discussed in Chapter 6. As a matter of fact, we just met the binomial probability distribution, and in the remainder of this chapter we will meet other probability distributions. Instead of speaking of expected values of these distributions, we prefer to speak about their *mean*, which is denoted by the small Greek mu, μ. However, the expected value $E\mathbf{x}$ of a random variable **x** and the mean μ of the probability distribution of **x** are the same:

Mean μ

$$\mu = E\mathbf{x} = p_1 x_1 + p_2 x_2 + \cdots + p_n x_n = \Sigma p_i x_i$$

When we focus attention on the random variable, we speak of its expected value. When we focus attention on the probability distribution we speak about its mean.

In the case of the variance, there is no terminological difference, but there is a notational one. If we want to focus attention on the random variable, we write $V\mathbf{x}$ for its variance and $S\mathbf{x}$ for its standard deviation, as we know. If, however, we want to focus attention on the probability distribution of the random variable, we write σ^2 for the variance and σ for the standard deviation. The symbol σ is the small Greek letter sigma. We have

Variance σ^2

$$\sigma^2 = V\mathbf{x} = p_1(x_1 - \mu)^2 + \cdots + p_n(x_n - \mu)^2 = \Sigma p_i(x_i - \mu)^2$$

The definition is the same, since $\mu = E\mathbf{x}$ and the outcome is the same. In this instance, even the word is the same, but the symbol is different.

We can summarize our accomplishments so far by saying that the binomial distribution $B(n, \pi)$ has a mean $\mu = n\pi$, and a variance $\sigma^2 = n\pi(1 - \pi)$, and a standard deviation $\sigma = \sqrt{n\pi(1 - \pi)}$. In what follows we will be emphasizing distributions rather than random variables, and the terminology of mean μ and standard deviation σ will be used repeatedly. In Table 7.3 we repeat Table 6.7, adding the results of this section.

TABLE 7.3   NOTATION, TERMINOLOGY, AND FORMULAS FOR MEASURES OF CENTRAL TENDENCY AND DISPERSION

	Measure of central tendency		
	Name	*Symbol*	*Formula*
Observations x_1, $x_2, \ldots, x_n$	Average	$\bar{x}$	$\dfrac{1}{n}\Sigma x_i$
Random variable **x**, which assumes values $x_1, x_2, \ldots, x_n$ with probability p_1, $p_2, \ldots, p_n$	Expected value	$E\mathbf{x}$	$\Sigma p_i x_i$
Probability distribution of **x**	Mean	μ	$\Sigma p_i x_i$

	Measure of dispersion		
	Name	*Symbol*	*Formula*
Observations x_1, $x_2, \ldots, x_n$	Variance	var x	$\dfrac{1}{n}\Sigma(x_i - \bar{x})^2$
	Standard deviation	sd x	$\sqrt{\text{var } x}$
Random variable **x**, which assumes values x_1, $x_2, \ldots, x_n$ with probabilities p_1, $p_2, \ldots, p_n$	Variance	$V\mathbf{x}$	$\Sigma p_i (x_i - E\mathbf{x})^2$
	Standard deviation	$S\mathbf{x}$	$\sqrt{V\mathbf{x}}$
Probability distribution of **x**	Variance	σ^2	$\Sigma p_i (x_i - \mu)^2$
	Standard deviation	σ	$\sqrt{\sigma^2}$

7.4   LAW OF LARGE NUMBERS

If we toss 100 coins, the number of heads shown, **x,** will be binomially distributed $B(100,\tfrac{1}{2})$. This implies that the expected value is $100 \times \tfrac{1}{2} = 50$, and the standard deviation is $\sqrt{n\pi(1 - \pi)} = 5$. The actual result will be between $50 \pm (3 \times 5)$, or between 35 and 65 with near certainty. The *proportion* of heads will be between $\frac{35}{100} = .35$ and $\frac{65}{100} = .65$. If we toss 10,000 coins, then $\mathbf{x} = B(10,000, \frac{1}{2})$ and $E\mathbf{x} = 5,000$. The standard deviation is now $\sqrt{n\pi(1 - \pi)} = 50$, so the actual result will almost certainly be between 4,850 and 5,150. The actual *proportion* will be between $\frac{4,850}{10,000} = .485$ and $\frac{5,150}{10,000} = .515$. To be sure, it could be less than .485 or more than .515, but the probability of such an occurrence is extremely small.

If we toss 1 million times, the expected value of the number of heads will be 500,000 and the standard deviation will be 500, so we can reasonably expect that the final outcome will be between 498,500 and 501,500, and the *proportion* of heads will be between .4985 and .5015.

If we continue to take larger and larger values of n, the *proportion* of successes will approach the true probability of success, $\pi = \frac{1}{2}$. This is the famous *law of large numbers*:

Law of large numbers

In n trials, the probability that the relative number of successes deviates numerically from the true proportion of successes in the population by more than any given value (for example, .00001) approaches zero as n becomes larger and larger.

We can express these ideas symbolically as follows. The *number* of successes will nearly always be between

$$n\pi - 3\sqrt{n\pi(1 - \pi)} \quad \text{and} \quad n\pi + 3\sqrt{n\pi(1 - \pi)}$$

We obtain the corresponding statement for the proportion by dividing by n. The *proportion* of successes will nearly always be between

$$\frac{n\pi - 3\sqrt{n\pi(1 - \pi)}}{n} \quad \text{and} \quad \frac{n\pi + 3\sqrt{n\pi(1 - \pi)}}{n}$$

which can be written as

$$\pi - 3\sqrt{\frac{\pi(1 - \pi)}{n}} \quad \text{and} \quad \pi + 3\sqrt{\frac{\pi(1 - \pi)}{n}}$$

With increasing n, the term $3\sqrt{\pi(1 - \pi)/n}$ will decrease, whatever value π may have. For example, if n is made four times as large, the term $3\sqrt{\pi(1 - \pi)/n}$ will be cut in half. The examples at the beginning of this section illustrate that as n becomes 100 times as large, $3\sqrt{\pi(1 - \pi)/n}$ is cut to $\frac{1}{10}$ its former size.

The law of large numbers states that as n increases, the proportion of successes will approach the true probability of success π. Be sure to realize that the law concerns proportions, and not absolute numbers. If we have $\mathbf{x} = B(100, \frac{1}{2})$, the outcome will almost certainly be somewhere in the range of 35 to 65, for example, at 40. The deviation from the expected value is $50 - 40 = 10$. If $\mathbf{x} = B(10,000, \frac{1}{2})$, then the actual outcome will almost certainly be between 4,850 and 5,150, for example, at 4,900. The deviation from the expected value is now $5,000 - 4,900 = 100$. A similar deviation from the mean when $\mathbf{x} = B(100, \frac{1}{2})$ is not possible: There would be -50 heads or $+150$ heads. Finally, if $\mathbf{x} = B(1,000,000, \frac{1}{2})$, a deviation of 1,000 from the expected value 500,000 would not be surprising. As n increases, the difference between k, the actual number of successes, and $n\pi$, the expected number of successes, will tend to increase, but the difference between k/n, the actual proportion of successes, and π, the expected proportion of successes, will decrease.

EXERCISES

7.10   Two players, A and B, have 50 silver dollars each. They play a game in which A has a 50 percent chance of losing a dollar to B and a 50 percent chance of winning a dollar from B. They play again and again, until one is bankrupt. The question is, "Will one of them eventually go bankrupt, or will they play until doomsday?"

7.11   In throwing dice, a "5" or a "6" is considered a success. How many trials are needed to be virtually certain that the actual proportion will be between $32\frac{2}{3}$ and 34 percent?

7.12   A shipment of parts contains 20 percent in overweight pieces. How many pieces must be weighed to be virtually certain that the observed proportion will be between 16 and 24 percent?

7.5   THE NORMAL DISTRIBUTION

The normal distribution is a continuous distribution fully determined by two parameters, its mean μ and standard deviation σ. These parameters uniquely identify a normal distribution just as n and π uniquely identify a binomial distribution. But there are infinitely many normal distributions, one for each combination of values μ and σ, where μ may be any value $(-3, \frac{1}{2}, 0, 100, -100,000)$ and σ may be any positive value.

Occurrence of
normal
distributions

In general, the normal curve will result when there are a large number of independent small factors influencing the final outcome. For example, the time it takes you to get home from the office will be normally distributed. There are a host of factors, all more or less independent, which will influence the total time. The weather, the time you leave the office, the place your car happens to be parked, the innumerable stoplights and stop signs, other drivers, and the number of careless pedestrians will all have a bearing on the total time. Most of the time, a lucky break here will be offset by bad luck elsewhere, so you will end up close to the mean time. Some days "everything goes against you"—all lights are red, you are behind a school bus, and so on. On other days, you are in luck. Such occurrences do happen, however infrequently, and they account for the times represented by the small areas (probabilities) in the tails of the distribution.

Other examples include the results of biological processes, for example, the height of human adult males. This is influenced by many factors—hereditary, food and health, climatic and geographical, and so on. Each factor exerts only a small influence by itself, and most of the time the factors offset one another so that the average height is close to 70 inches. Occasionally there are outlying observations in either tail corresponding to heights below 60 or above 80 inches.

One table of
normal
distribution

Because there are many possible values for the mean μ and the standard deviation σ, there are many possible normal distributions $N(\mu,\sigma)$. Even so, *one* single table is sufficient to determine the probabilities of *all* possible normal distributions, whatever their mean and standard deviation may be. This is due to the following result: The probability that a certain normally distributed variable **x** exceeds a given value depends only on how far that value is from the mean, with the standard deviation as the unit for measuring the distance from the mean.

Use of table
of normal
distribution

This one single table is given here as Table 7.4 and is repeated inside the cover for convenient reference. The table can best be explained in conjunction with Figure 7.1. Table 7.4 gives the area—that is, the probability—that a random variable **x** which is normally distributed will be more than k standard deviations above its expected value. The table gives values of $P(\mathbf{x} > \mu + k\sigma)$ for a large number of values $k = 0, .01, .02, \ldots,$ 3.09. In Figure 7.1 we first give three illustrations of situations in which the tabulated values can be used directly. The shaded areas in these distributions are 1σ, 1.5σ, and 2.35σ above the mean μ of the normal distribution, and contain 15.87, 6.68, and .94 percent of the total area. Concisely,

$$P(x > \mu + \sigma) = .1587$$
$$P(x > \mu + 1\tfrac{1}{2}\sigma) = .0668$$
$$P(x > \mu + 2.35\sigma) = .0094$$

These are the red values in Table 7.4.

Two further applications of the table are an immediate consequence

TABLE 7.4 THE NORMAL DISTRIBUTION: $P(x > \mu + k\sigma)$

Normal deviate k	.00	.01	.02	.03	.04	.05	.06	.07	.08	.09
.0	.5000	.4960	.4920	.4880	.4840	.4801	.4761	.4721	.4681	.4641
.1	.4602	.4562	.4522	.4483	.4443	.4404	.4364	.4325	.4286	.4247
.2	.4207	.4168	.4129	.4090	.4052	.4013	.3974	.3936	.3897	.3859
.3	.3821	.3783	.3745	.3707	.3669	.3632	.3594	.3557	.3520	.3483
.4	.3446	.3409	.3372	.3336	.3300	.3264	.3228	.3192	.3156	.3121
.5	.3085	.3050	.3015	.2981	.2946	.2912	.2877	.2843	.2810	.2776
.6	.2743	.2709	.2676	.2643	.2611	.2578	.2546	.2514	.2483	.2451
.7	.2420	.2389	.2358	.2327	.2296	.2266	.2236	.2206	.2177	.2148
.8	.2119	.2090	.2061	.2033	.2005	.1977	.1949	.1922	.1894	.1867
.9	.1841	.1814	.1788	.1762	.1736	.1711	.1685	.1660	.1635	.1611
1.0	.1587	.1562	.1539	.1515	.1492	.1469	.1446	.1423	.1401	.1379
1.1	.1357	.1335	.1314	.1292	.1271	.1251	.1230	.1210	.1190	.1170
1.2	.1151	.1131	.1112	.1093	.1075	.1056	.1038	.1020	.1003	.0985
1.3	.0968	.0951	.0934	.0918	.0901	.0885	.0869	.0853	.0838	.0823
1.4	.0808	.0793	.0778	.0764	.0749	.0735	.0721	.0708	.0694	.0681
1.5	.0668	.0655	.0643	.0630	.0618	.0606	.0594	.0582	.0571	.0559
1.6	.0548	.0537	.0526	.0516	.0505	.0495	.0485	.0475	.0465	.0455
1.7	.0446	.0436	.0427	.0418	.0409	.0401	.0392	.0384	.0375	.0367
1.8	.0359	.0351	.0344	.0336	.0329	.0322	.0314	.0307	.0301	.0294
1.9	.0287	.0281	.0274	.0268	.0262	.0256	.0250	.0244	.0239	.0233
2.0	.0226	.0222	.0217	.0212	.0207	.0202	.0197	.0192	.0188	.0183
2.1	.0179	.0174	.0170	.0166	.0162	.0158	.0154	.0150	.0146	.0143
2.2	.0139	.0136	.0132	.0129	.0125	.0122	.0119	.0116	.0113	.0110
2.3	.0107	.0104	.0102	.0099	.0096	.0094	.0091	.0089	.0087	.0084
2.4	.0082	.0080	.0078	.0075	.0073	.0071	.0069	.0068	.0066	.0064
2.5	.0062	.0060	.0059	.0057	.0055	.0054	.0052	.0051	.0049	.0048
2.6	.0047	.0045	.0044	.0043	.0041	.0040	.0039	.0038	.0037	.0036
2.7	.0035	.0034	.0033	.0032	.0031	.0030	.0029	.0028	.0027	.0026
2.8	.0026	.0025	.0024	.0023	.0023	.0022	.0021	.0021	.0020	.0019
2.9	.0019	.0018	.0018	.0017	.0016	.0016	.0015	.0015	.0014	.0014
3.0	.0013	.0013	.0013	.0012	.0012	.0011	.0011	.0011	.0010	.0010

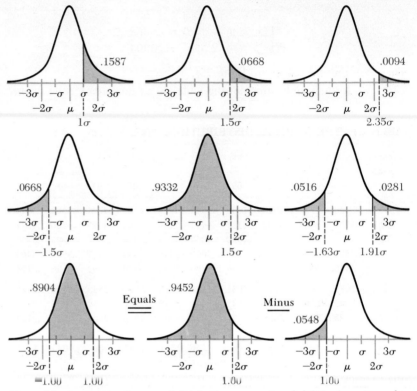

Figure 7.1 Areas under the normal distribution represent probabilities (except μ; values shown are deviations from μ).

of the symmetry of the normal distribution and the fact that the *total area equals 1*. For example, from $P(x > \mu + 1\frac{1}{2}\sigma) = .0668$ we can derive immediately the following two results

$$P(x < \mu - 1\frac{1}{2}\sigma) = .0668$$

$$P(x < \mu + 1\frac{1}{2}\sigma) = 1 - .0668 = .9332$$

These two cases are also illustrated in Figure 7.1. The figure shows that, in fact, all areas or collections of areas can be computed from the table by using only the table and these two rules. We first show the probability that x is more than 1.63σ below the mean *or* more than 1.91σ above the mean, in formula

$$P(x < \mu - 1.63\sigma \qquad or \qquad x > \mu + 1.91\sigma)$$

Since these two events are mutually exclusive, we have

$$P(x < \mu - 1.63\sigma \quad or \quad x > \mu + 1.91\sigma)$$
$$= P(x < \mu - 1.63\sigma) + P(x > \mu + 1.91\sigma)$$
$$= .0516 + .0281 = .0797$$

The figure also illustrates the probability that x is within 1.6σ from the mean, that is,

$$P(\mu - 1.6\sigma < x < \mu + 1.6\sigma)$$

As illustrated in the bottom three graphs, this probability can be rewritten as

$$[1 - P(x > \mu + 1.6\sigma)] - P(x < \mu - 1.6\sigma) = [1 - .0548] - .0548 = .8904$$

In general, we can always make such an illustration and then use the table to find the desired probability. The following results are of particular importance:

$$P(\mu - \sigma < x < \mu + \sigma) = 68.27 \text{ percent}$$
$$P(\mu - 2\sigma < x < \mu + 2\sigma) = 95.45 \text{ percent}$$
$$P(\mu - 3\sigma < x < \mu + 3\sigma) = 99.73 \text{ percent}$$

These probabilities are often put into words, crudely but conveniently, as follows. When a random variable is normally distributed, more than 68 percent is within 1 standard deviation, more than 95 percent is within 2 standard deviations, and nearly everything is within 3 standard deviations.

The table can also be used to find deviations, given probabilities. In this case we read it in reverse. We might want k such that

$$P(x > \mu + k\sigma) = .07$$

In other words, what multiple of σ gives the value on the right tail of a normal distribution exceeded by 7 percent of the area? According to the table, the answer is that k is between 1.47 and 1.48. On a normal distribution 7.08 percent of the area falls more than 1.47 standard deviations above the mean, and 6.94 percent of the area falls more than 1.48 standard deviations above the mean. We can interpolate to find one more place, which gives $k = 1.476$. We would have found $k = -1.476$ if the question had asked for the value of k on the *left* tail, so that 7 percent of the area would have been *to the left of* $k\sigma$. Taken together, these results show that the k values which give points on *both* tails, beyond which 14 percent of the area lies, are -1.476 and $+1.476$.

Using the table in reverse also gives the quartile points of the normal distribution. The first quartile point is $\mu - .674\sigma$; the second is, of course, μ; and the third is $\mu + .674\sigma$.

Illustration of normal distributions

All the normal distributions drawn so far look identical. This may create the impression that there is, really, only *one* normal distribution instead of *many*—one for each (μ,σ) combination. The reason for this apparent uniformity is that all normal distributions can be made to look alike, provided one chooses the unit of measurement along the horizontal axis equal to σ. To clarify this, consider Figure 7.2. At the left, we have drawn three normal distributions with different means and standard deviations, using the same unit of measurement along the horizontal axis for all three graphs. At the right, we have changed the scales of measurement, and all three distributions look the same. Even in their different appearances the basic percentages remain valid: 68.27 percent is within 1 standard deviation of the mean, 95.45 percent is within 2 standard deviations of the mean, and 99.73 percent is within 3 standard deviations of the mean.

As we saw, a most frustrating aspect of the binomial distribution

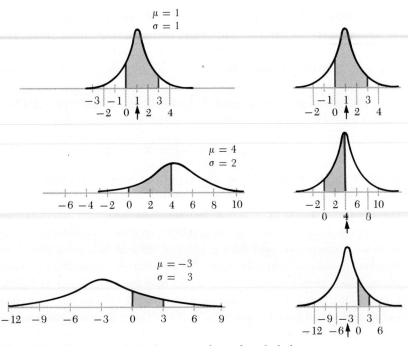

Figure 7.2 Different normal distributions can be made to look the same.

is the immense computational problem in computing values such as $C(81,38)(\frac{1}{2})^{38}(\frac{1}{2})^{43}$. This particular expression arises, for example, if one wishes to know the probability that 38 out of 81 throws of a die give even numbers.

Normal approximation to binomial

It is, therefore, fortunate indeed that the binomial distribution can be approximated by the normal distribution:

If $\mathbf{x} = B(n,\pi)$, and $n\pi > 5$ and $n(1 - \pi) > 5$, then $B(n,\pi)$ is closely approximated by a normal distribution with mean $n\pi$ and standard deviation $\sqrt{n\pi(1 - \pi)}$, that is, $\mathbf{x} = N[n\pi, \sqrt{n\pi(1 - \pi)}]$.

This means that if $\mathbf{x}$ has a binomial probability distribution with parameters n and π, provided that $n\pi$ and $n(1 - \pi)$ are both at least 5, it can be considered to correspond for practical purposes to a normal probability distribution with mean $\mu = n\pi$ and standard deviation $\sigma = \sqrt{n\pi(1 - \pi)}$. This assertion is illustrated in Figure 7.3. The bar diagram becomes nicely symmetric provided $n\pi$ and $n(1 - \pi)$ are both greater than 5.

Let us now compute the probability that 81 throws with one die produce exactly 38 even results. Since the necessary conditions are complied with, we can approximate $\mathbf{x} = B(81,\frac{1}{2})$ by $\mathbf{x} = N(40\frac{1}{2},4\frac{1}{2})$. In other words, $\mathbf{x}$ can be considered normally distributed with mean $\mu = 81 \times \frac{1}{2} = 40\frac{1}{2}$ and standard deviation $\sigma = \sqrt{81 \times \frac{1}{2} \times \frac{1}{2}} = 4\frac{1}{2}$.

As we know, a binomial distribution is discrete, and a normal distribution is continuous. Thus, in a normal distribution the probability of an outcome *exactly* 38 is zero. We now argue that a result of 38 in the discrete (binomial) case corresponds to a result of between $37\frac{1}{2}$ and $38\frac{1}{2}$ in the continuous (normal) case. This step is the *continuity correction*. It is easy to compute that $37\frac{1}{2}$ is $\frac{2}{3}$ standard deviation below the mean $40\frac{1}{2}$ (since $3 = \frac{2}{3} \times 4\frac{1}{2}$) and $38\frac{1}{2}$ is $\frac{4}{9}$ standard deviation below the mean. We conclude from the table that

Continuity correction

$$P(\mu - \tfrac{2}{3}\sigma < \mathbf{x} < \mu - \tfrac{4}{9}\sigma) = P(\mathbf{x} < \mu - \tfrac{4}{9}\sigma) - P(\mathbf{x} < \mu - \tfrac{2}{3}\sigma)$$
$$= .3286 - .2524$$
$$= .0762$$

Figure 7.4 shows this relationship graphically.

There is no difference between the normal distribution which arises spontaneously and the one that we use as an approximation to a binomial distribution. There *is* a difference in the use made of it, in that we must remember that a binomial distribution is, by its nature, discrete. We must,

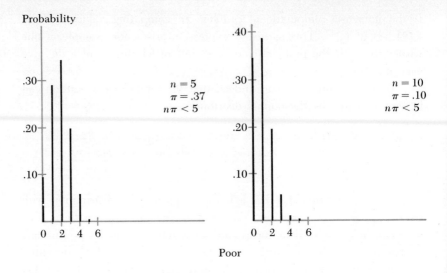

Poor

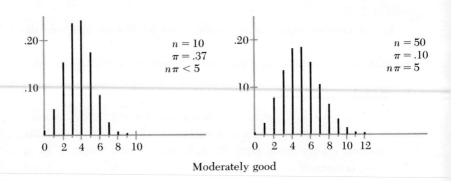

Moderately good

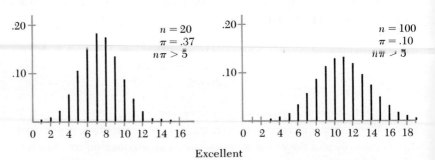

Excellent

Figure 7.3 The normal distribution as an approximation for the binomial.

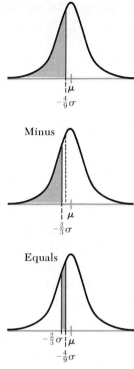

Figure 7.4 Using the normal distribution to approximate the binomial requires a continuity correction.

therefore, be careful on two counts. If we ask for the probability of an outcome 34, 35, or 36 (three outcomes) we should ask for the area over the range $33\frac{1}{2}$ to $36\frac{1}{2}$ (a length of 3). This is the continuity correction we met earlier. Conversely, there will be some positive area between the values 34.1 and 34.9, although we know that a binomial experiment will never lead to outcomes in this range. If we approximate the binomial by the normal, we should be careful to ask the proper questions lest we get nonsensical answers.

In concluding this long section, we want to make one further observation. The normal distribution arises when there are many, individually small, independent factors contributing to the final result. These conditions are met when we compute the average from a fairly large sample: we will have many observations, each will contribute only a small amount to the average, and the observations are independent when drawn by random sampling techniques. Hence, if we were to draw many samples of size n from a population, we could compute many averages, and these averages would tend to be normally distributed. This important result is known as the *Central Limit Theorem*:

Sampling
distribution
of $\bar{x}$ and the
Central Limit
Theorem

> If we take all possible groups of size n from the given set and find the average for each group, this average $\bar{x}$ will be a random variable, assuming different values with specified probabilities (see Exercise 6.3). The distribution of these $\bar{x}$ values is *the sampling distribution of $\bar{x}$.* The *Central Limit Theorem* states that the sampling distribution of $\bar{x}$ will be approximately normal regardless of the shape of the population sampled.

This is true because an average is influenced by a large number of small and independent factors—the n observations in the sample. The larger n is, the closer the approximation to the normal.

As an illustration, consider a rectangular distribution over the range from 1 to 60. Let us now draw 50 observations from this distribution. They could all be below 1, or all above 59, but more likely there will be some large, some small, and some in the middle, and the average of the observations will tend to be around 30, which is the mean of the rectangular distribution. If we compute many such averages, they will be normally distributed, for there are many (50) small, independent factors contributing to the average. The same argument would hold if the original distribution were not rectangular, but reverse J-shaped, normal, binomial, Poisson, or anything else. This is the essence of the Central Limit Theorem: the sampling distribution of $\bar{x}$ is normal. In Chapter 9 we will come back to this theorem, but it may be useful to have a glance at Figure 9.3 now.

EXERCISES

7.13   What are the decile points of a normal distribution?

7.14   The height of adults is normally distributed with mean 70 inches and a standard deviation of 6 inches. What proportion of the population measures between 60 and 80 inches?

7.15   What area symmetric around the mean of a normal distribution contains 50 percent of the observations?

7.16   A coin is tossed 64 times. What is the probability of obtaining:
        (a) Exactly 32 heads?
        (b) Fewer than 25 heads?
        (c) Between 30 and 35 heads, inclusive?

7.17   A company packages a mixture of salted nuts. The label on the can guarantees the weight of the contents is 1 pound. In fact, the process by which the cans are filled gives normally distributed weights with $\mu = 1.05$ pounds and $\sigma = .02$ pound. What is the probability that a can will not contain the guaranteed weight?

7.18   A machine is supposed to drill holes with a diameter of 1 inch. In fact, the diameters are normally distributed with a mean of 1.01 inches and a standard deviation of .02 inch. If there is a tolerance of .02 inch, the holes should be between .98 and 1.02 inches. What percentage of the holes drilled are within tolerance?

7.6 THE POISSON DISTRIBUTION

The approximation of the discrete binomial distribution by the continuous normal distribution is satisfactory only when $n\pi \geq 5$ and $n(1 - \pi) \geq 5$. In general, the approximation is better the larger these values are. When π is $\frac{1}{2}$, n should be at least 10; when π is close to $\frac{1}{10}$ or $\frac{9}{10}$, n ought to be at least 50. The smaller the value of π, the larger n must be for the approximation to be satisfactory.

   If π is very small, and n not sufficiently large, the normal distribution cannot be used. For this case, there exists another distribution which provides an easy and accurate approximation, called the *Poisson distribution:*

If **x** is Poisson distributed with mean λ, then the probability of obtaining exactly k successes is given by

Poisson distribution

$$P(\mathbf{x} = k) = \frac{(\lambda)^k}{k!}\, e^{-\lambda}$$

This looks more complex than it is. The symbol e is another way of writing the number $2.72\ldots$, which shows up repeatedly in mathematics. If λ is known, $e^{-\lambda}$ is also known. For various values of λ, this value $e^{-\lambda}$ is tabulated in Table 7.5. A more detailed table of $e^{-\lambda}$ appears in Appendix B, Table 4.

TABLE 7.5   VALUES OF $e^{-\lambda}$

λ	$e^{-\lambda}$	λ	$e^{-\lambda}$	λ	$e^{-\lambda}$
.00	1.00000	2.30	.10026	4.60	.01005
.10	.90484	2.40	.09072	4.70	.00910
.20	.81873	2.50	.08208	4.80	.00823
.30	.74082	2.60	.07427	4.90	.00745
.40	.67032	2.70	.06721	5.00	.00674
.50	.60653	2.80	.06081	5.10	.00610
.60	.54881	2.90	.05502	5.20	.00552
.70	.49659	3.00	.04979	5.30	.00499
.80	.44933	3.10	.04505	5.40	.00452
.90	.40657	3.20	.04076	5.50	.00409
1.00	.36788	3.30	.03688	5.60	.00370
1.10	.33287	3.40	.03337	5.70	.00335
1.20	.30119	3.50	.03020	5.80	.00303
1.30	.27253	3.60	.02732	5.90	.00274
1.40	.24660	3.70	.02472	6.00	.00248
1.50	.22313	3.80	.02237	6.50	.00150
1.60	.20190	3.90	.02024	7.00	.00091
1.70	.18268	4.00	.01832	7.50	.00055
1.80	.16530	4.10	.01657	8.00	.00034
1.90	.14957	4.20	.01500	8.50	.00020
2.00	.13534	4.30	.01357	9.00	.00012
2.10	.12246	4.40	.01227	9.50	.00007
2.20	.11080	4.50	.01111	10.00	.00005

Like the binomial the Poisson is discrete. Furthermore, it is fully characterized by only one parameter, the mean λ. The following result holds: If $x = B(n,\pi)$ and π is small, $B(n,\pi)$ is closely approximated by a Poisson distribution with parameter $\lambda = n\pi$, that is, Poisson $(n\pi)$.

To illustrate the approximation of the binomial by the Poisson, we consider the case where $x = B(200,\frac{1}{100})$. The parameter λ of the Poisson distribution is then $n\pi = 2$, and the exact binomial values are compared with the results from the corresponding Poisson in Table 7.6. The correspondence is quite close, and using the Poisson requires only a fraction of the time required by the binomial. In cases such as these, the normal distribution would have given unsatisfactory results. The parameters of the approximating normal distribution would be $\mu = 2$ and $\sigma = \sqrt{200(.01)(.99)} = 1.407$. If we consider $x = N(2,1.407)$, the probabilities for $k = 0, 1, 2, 3, 4, 5, 6,$ and 7 are, respectively, .105, .218,

.279, .218, .105, .031, .006, and 0. Moreover, there is a probability of .031 of getting the result -1 successes, and a probability of .006 of getting -2 successes. Clearly the fit is bad.

The Poisson, on the other hand, performs rather well. In general, the smaller π is and the larger n is, the closer the fit will be. In Table 8 of Appendix B the Poisson distribution has been given for a large number of parameter values λ.

Although we introduced the Poisson distribution as a good approximation for the binomial distribution when π is small and n sufficiently large, the Poisson has other claims to fame. Consider the following questions. A book of 400 pages has a total of 80 misprints. How many pages will have 0, 1, 2, ..., misprints? During a whole year there were 73 fatal accidents in Erie County. How many days had 0, 1, 2, ..., fatal accidents? During an hour 420 calls were registered at the local switchboard. How many minutes had 0, 1, 2, ..., calls registered?

In all these cases we have a total number n of occurrences (80 misprints, 73 accidents, 420 calls) and a total span of exposure (a book, a year, an hour). We divide the total span of exposure in t tiny parts or intervals, so that t will be rather large (400 pages, 365 days, 60 minutes). What is the probability distribution of the number of "occurrences" (misprints, accidents, calls) during such a tiny interval? Under the condition that the occurrences are equally likely to occur anywhere or anytime, and that the occurrences are independent, this probability distribution is

TABLE 7.6 COMPARISON OF EXACT BINOMIAL AND APPROXIMATE POISSON FOR x = $B(200,\frac{1}{100})$

	$\mathbf{x} = B(200,\frac{1}{100})$ $\mathbf{x} = k$ *with probability* $\binom{200}{k}(\frac{1}{100})^k(\frac{99}{100})^{200-k}$	$\mathbf{x}$ *is Poisson,* $\lambda = 2$ $\mathbf{x} = k$ *with probability* $\frac{2^k}{k!} \times .1353$
$k = 0$	.1343	.1353
1	.2713	.2707
2	.2726	.2707
3	.1818	.1804
4	.0904	.0902
5	.0358	.0361
6	.0118	.0120
7	.0033	.0034

**TABLE 7.7   THE POISSON DISTRIBUTION FOR MISPRINTS
[POISSON (.2)] AND TELEPHONE CALLS [POISSON (7)]**

80 *misprints*, 400 *pages* $n/t = \frac{80}{400} = .2$			420 *calls*, 60 *min* $n/t = \frac{420}{60} = 7$		
(1)	*(2)*	*(3)*	*(1)*	*(2)*	*(3)*
	Probability of k misprints	*Number of pages with k misprints*		*Probability of k calls*	*Number of min with k calls*
k	*per page*	*(2) × 400*	k	*per min*	*(2) × 60*
0	.81873	328	0	.0009	0
1	.16375	66	1	.0064	0
2	.01637	6	2	.0223	1
3	.00109	0	3	.0521	3
4	.00005	0	4	.0912	5
5	.00001	0	5	.1277	8
		400	6	.1490	9
			7	.1490	9
			8	.1304	8
			9	.1014	6
			10	.0710	4
			11	.0452	3
			12	.0264	2
			13	.0142	1
			14	.0071	
			15	.0033	1
			16	.0014	
			>16	.0009	
					60

a Poisson distribution with parameter $\lambda = n/t$. For two of our examples, the probability distributions are displayed in Table 7.7.

   To be sure these are the theoretical distributions. Even if the underlying assumptions are fully correct, the actual distribution may be somewhat different. In much the same way, if we toss three coins eight times, the distribution of the number of heads, which assumes the values 0, 1, 2, or 3 with probability $\frac{1}{8}$, $\frac{3}{8}$, $\frac{3}{8}$, $\frac{1}{8}$, and which, therefore, should be 1, 3, 3, 1, may not be realized in that one particular instance.

Occurrence
of Poisson
distribution

   The Poisson distribution arises, in colloquial terms, whenever the events occur independently and are randomly spaced over an interval of time, or surface, or book pages, and so forth. A further assumption is that the probability that an event will occur in a certain interval is proportional to the length of that interval. For example, the probability that a machine will break down during the next minute should be half as large as the probability that it will break down during the next 2 minutes. It is clear that the intervals taken should not be too large. Suppose, for example, that there is a 10 percent chance that the machine will break down during the next minute; then there would be a 150 percent "chance" (i.e., certainty with some to spare) that the machine will break down during the next quarter of an hour.

In practice, random variables such as the number of people entering a store, the number of airplanes landing, the number of machines breaking down, the number of units demanded, the number of radioactive particles emitted—all per unit of time—may well be Poisson distributed. Let us take the number of people entering the store as an example. The assumptions are that customers arrive independently, and at random moments of time. Furthermore, it is reasonable to assume that when the probability is 1 percent that someone will enter during the next 10 seconds, the probability is 2 percent that someone will enter during the next 20 seconds.

Clearly, not all these assumptions will be perfectly satisfied. Two ladies may have the habit of going shopping together. These ladies do not arrive independently, and they do arrive at the same time. In practice, the Poisson distribution is often very closely conformed to, despite the fact that some assumptions may not be fully realistic.

An important conceptual difference between the Poisson and the binomial distribution should be noted. In the examples just given the Poisson distribution is used even though the total number of trials is unspecified and often undefined. In a binomial distribution, we can distinguish a total number of trials n, of which a specific number were successes and all others failures. In a Poisson process we can still count the number of successes (customers arriving at the store, radioactive particles emitted), but we can no longer count the number of failures (customers not arriving, radioactive particles not emitted). So the idea of a "total number of trials" becomes meaningless in cases such as these.

EXERCISES

7.19   For $n = 10$, $\pi = \frac{1}{10}$, compute the probability of exactly one success, using the binomial distribution, as well as the Poisson and normal approximations. Which approach do you recommend?

7.20   Consider a Poisson process with $\lambda = 3$. Determine the probability distribution of $k = 0, 1, 2, \ldots$ successes. Verify that $E\mathbf{x}$, where $\mathbf{x}$ is the number of successes, is 3. Verify that $V\mathbf{x} = 3$ also.

7.21   In 200 baseball games 1,200 runs were scored. What is the number of games with 0, 1, 2, ... runs if the number of runs per game is Poisson distributed? Are there reasons to presume they will be?

7.22   In an office, records are kept on the number of secretaries late for work each day. In a period of 200 days, 800 instances of late arrival were recorded. Assuming the number of late arrivals per day follows the Poisson distribution, on how many days will there be five or more late arrivals? With the information given here, could you find the answer using the binomial distribution?

7.7   THE EXPONENTIAL DISTRIBUTION

We have discussed two discrete distributions, the binomial and the Poisson, and one continuous distribution, the normal. One more distribution of the continuous variety will be introduced here, the *exponential distribution*. As we proceed, three more classes of continuous distributions will be met, known as the *t distribution*, *F distribution*, and χ^2 (*chi square*) *distribution*. One more discrete distribution, the *hypergeometric distribution*, will be discussed in Section 7.8.

Exponential distribution

The exponential distribution arises from the same process which gives rise to a Poisson distribution. A typical Poisson problem is the following. Suppose that 30 customers enter during 1 hour. What then is the probability that there will be $k(k = 0, 1, 2, \ldots)$ customers entering during 1 minute? The answer is given by $[(\frac{1}{2})^k/k!]e^{-\frac{1}{2}}$, where the parameter λ is $\frac{30}{60} = \frac{1}{2}$, or, in general terms, n/t, which is the number of occurrences divided by the number of tiny intervals.

The exponential distribution arises when we ask, "If 30 customers arrive during an hour, what is the distribution of the interarrival times $\mathbf{x}$?" (The interarrival time is the time span which elapses between two successive arrivals.) The answer is provided by the exponential distribution, whose parameter $1/\lambda$ is the reciprocal of the Poisson parameter associated with the same process. This reciprocity property is understandable, since 30 customers per 60 minutes is $\frac{1}{2}$ customer per minute (the Poisson parameter λ) and, therefore, one customer every 2 minutes (the exponential parameter $1/\lambda$). Similarly, 80 misprints in 400 pages

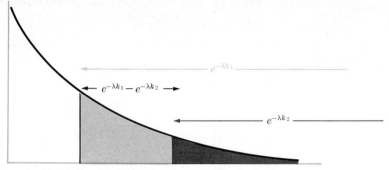

Figure 7.5 Illustration of formula $P(k_1 < \mathbf{x} < k_2) = e^{-\lambda k_1} - e^{-\lambda k_2}$.

is an average of $\frac{1}{5}$ per page (the Poisson parameter λ), or one every 5 pages (the exponential parameter $1/\lambda$).

The basic result for a variable $\mathbf{x}$ which is exponentially distributed with parameter $1/\lambda$ is

$$P(\mathbf{x} > k) = e^{-\lambda k}$$

In words, the probability that we shall have to wait *at least* k units (whether bookpages, hours, or seconds) for the next occurrence is given by $e^{-\lambda k}$

From this basic result we derive that the probability of the next occurrence's being between k_1 and k_2 units away is given by

$$P(k_1 < \mathbf{x} < k_2) = e^{-\lambda k_1} - e^{-\lambda k_2}$$

$k_2 > k_1$, of course, because $\mathbf{x}$ should be larger than k_1 but *not* larger than k_2, see Figure 7.5. With λ known, we can immediately derive the probability that $\mathbf{x}$ will be between two values k_1 and k_2. The probability that the variable $\mathbf{x}$ will be exactly equal to some specific value k is, of course, zero. The exponential is a continuous distribution which looks like a reverse J-shaped distribution.

In the example of 30 customers' entering a store during an hour, the question, "What is the probability that the next customer will enter between 2 and 3 minutes later?" is then answered by

$$e^{-\frac{2}{2}} - e^{-\frac{3}{2}} = e^{-1} - e^{-1\frac{1}{2}} = .368 - .223 = .145$$

More detailed results for this example are shown in Table 7.8. From this distribution we see that although the mean interarrival time is 2 minutes, there is a nearly 40 percent probability that the next customer

TABLE 7.8 PROBABILITIES OF THE EXPONENTIAL DISTRIBUTION

$$P(t_1 < x < t_2) = e^{-\frac{1}{2}k_1} - e^{-\frac{1}{2}k_2}$$

Interarrival time

t_1-t_2	$\frac{1}{2}t_1$	$\frac{1}{2}t_2$	*Probability*
0–1 minute	0	$\frac{1}{2}$	$e^{-0} - e^{-\frac{1}{2}} = 1.000 - .607 = .393$
1–2 minutes	$\frac{1}{2}$	1	$e^{-\frac{1}{2}} - e^{-1} = .607 - .368 = .239$
2–3 minutes	1	$1\frac{1}{2}$	$e^{-1} - e^{-1\frac{1}{2}} = .368 - .223 = .145$
3–4 minutes	$1\frac{1}{2}$	2	$e^{-1\frac{1}{2}} - e^{-2} = .223 - .135 = .088$
4–5 minutes	2	$2\frac{1}{2}$	$e^{-2} - e^{-2\frac{1}{2}} = .135 - .082 = .053$
5–6 minutes	$2\frac{1}{2}$	3	$e^{-2\frac{1}{2}} - e^{-3} = .082 - .050 = .032$
6–7 minutes	3	$3\frac{1}{2}$	$e^{-3} - e^{-3\frac{1}{2}} = .050 - .030 = .020$
7–8 minutes	$3\frac{1}{2}$	4	$e^{-3\frac{1}{2}} - e^{-4} = .030 - .018 = .012$
8–9 minutes	4	$4\frac{1}{2}$	$e^{-4} - e^{-4\frac{1}{2}} = .018 - .011 = .007$
9–10 minutes	$4\frac{1}{2}$	5	$e^{-4\frac{1}{2}} - e^{-5} = .011 - .007 = .004$

will enter within 1 minute and a probability of over 20 percent that the shop will have to wait more than 3 minutes before the next customer comes in.

The mean interarrival time associated with this distribution is indeed 2 minutes. This can be verified with the help of Table 7.8. As an approximation, we have for the mean interarrival time

$$.393 \times \tfrac{1}{2} + .239 \times 1\tfrac{1}{2} + .145 \times 2\tfrac{1}{2} + \cdots + .004 \times 9\tfrac{1}{2} + \cdots$$
$$= 1.96 +$$

where the answer deviates from 2 because we did not extend the table far enough and because we make some error when we round "between 0 and 1 minute" to "$\frac{1}{2}$ a minute," etc. However, the order of magnitude is clearly correct, and more accurate computations will lead to the exactly correct answer of 2 minutes.

The exponential distribution arises rather frequently in queuing problems, "How long does a customer have to wait in line?" "What percentage of the time is the clerk behind the counter idle?" "What is the probability that three planes will want to land within 2 minutes?" The shape of the distribution (see Figure 7.5) is such that short interarrival times are quite likely, but long interarrival times are by no means impossible. This often will tend to generate the impression of clustered events, for example three in quick succession and then nothing for a long time.

The barber's observation, "it never rains but it pours," meaning there are either a lot of customers or none at all, but seldom a nicely spaced arrival of customers, is correct. It is, however, not a result of customers' conspiring against the barber, but a result of statistical laws, in particular the exponential distribution.

EXERCISES

7.23   There are 73 accidents per year. What is the interarrival time of accidents, in days?

7.24   In an hour, 420 telephone calls were recorded. What is the probability that the next call will be made within 10 seconds?

7.8   THE HYPERGEOMETRIC DISTRIBUTION

If an appliance store receives 10 washers from a factory, it can ask for the probability that 0, 1, 2, . . . , 10 of these will be substandard. A substandard washer looks the same as the others, and performs just as well as the others—the first and second time around. However, it breaks down soon and often, ages fast, and is unreliable. It is, in short, a "lemon," but the only way to find out is to buy and use it.

   If we know that the percentage of substandards the factory produces is 15 percent, and if we assume our shipment to be a random sample out of the factory's total output, the probability of receiving 0, 1, 2, . . . substandards is given by the binomial distribution $B(10,.15)$. From Table 7a in Appendix B we then find, looking under $n = 10$, $\pi = .15$, that the probability of 0, 1, 2, 3, . . . defectives is .197, .347, .276, .123, ... Specifically, the probability of receiving three substandards is a shade over 12 percent, or nearly one chance in eight. Let us suppose that this shipment indeed contained exactly three substandards.

   The store now has three out of ten, or 30 percent, substandard washers on the floor. A laundromat operator enters and wants to buy four washers. We can now inquire for the probability that these four will include 0, 1, 2, 3, or 4 substandards. If we were to answer this by looking at the binomial distribution for $n = 4$, $\pi = .3$, we should find from Table 7a answers of 24, 41, 26, 8, and 1 percent, respectively. But this *cannot* be right, because there are only three defectives on the floor, and so the probability of getting four substandards is zero, not 1 percent.

   The reason for the error is not hard to see. When the total number in the population is small and one draws without replacement, *the proba-bilities change in the process;* that is, they are not constant from pick to pick. If the first washer chosen is good, which it is with a probability of $\frac{7}{10}$, the second will be good with a probability of only $\frac{6}{9}$, and so forth.

Hypergeometric distribution

For such cases the *hypergeometric distribution* gives the answer: The probability that n draws without replacement out of a population of N will give x successes when there are X in the population is given by

$$\frac{C(X,x)C(N - X, n - x)}{C(N,n)}$$

In our example we have $n = 4$ draws out of a population of $N = 10$. The probability of obtaining $x = 1$ substandard ("success") when there are $X = 3$ in the population is

$$\frac{C(3,1)C(7,3)}{C(10,4)} = \frac{3 \times 35}{210} = .5$$

By the same formula, the probability of obtaining 0, 1, 2, 3, 4 substandards is equal to 17, 50, 30, 3, and 0 percent. The 0 percent comes about because $C(3,4)$, standing for the number of ways in which one can draw 4 items out of 3 without replacement, is clearly zero. Section 4.3 and Exercise 4.19 in particular can be profitably reread at this juncture.

The hypergeometric distribution generalizes rather easily. An auto-mobile manufacturer wants to see what happens with his cars during their lifetimes. He decides to follow the life of 22 cars in detail. Of these 22 cars, 9 happen to be red, 7 are blue, and 6 are green. Five years later 8 cars are out of circulation because of wear and tear or accidents. If one assumes that these 8 cars are a random selection out of the 22, the probability that of the defunct cars 4 are red, 3 blue, and 1 green is equal to

$$\frac{C(9,4)C(7,3)C(6,1)}{C(22,8)} = \frac{126 \times 35 \times 6}{319,770} = \frac{26,460}{319,770} = 8 \text{ percent}$$

In formulas of the hypergeometric distribution the sum of the first numbers inside the parentheses above the line equals the first number in parentheses below the line, $9 + 7 + 6 = 22$. The same result holds for the last numbers, $4 + 3 + 1 = 8$.

EXERCISES

7.25   In a population of 50 customers who tried a certain new tooth-
        paste, 30 are satisfied that it is an improvement over their currently
        used paste, but 20 do not think so. What is the probability that
        a random sample of size 10, obviously drawn without replacement,
        includes only 4 satisfied customers?

7.26   What is the probability of getting a bridge hand with five ♠, five
        ♥, three ♦, and no ♣?

Answers to Exercises

7.1   Much of the screening of loan applicants is designed to ensure
        that all those to whom loans are given have a high probability
        of repaying. The screening is not perfect, but as long as the bank's
        policies remain the same, the probability of repayment will be
        virtually constant from trial to trial.

7.2   No, since the formula given would lead to the correct answer only
        if being sick on Tuesday and being sick Wednesday of the same
        week are independent events, that is, if P(sick Wednesday)
        = P(sick Wednesday | sick Tuesday). These events are not inde-
        pendent, so the binomial cannot be used.

7.3   The number of successes can be 0, 1, 2, 3, 4, or 5, with proba-
        bility of $\frac{32}{243}$, $\frac{80}{243}$, $\frac{80}{243}$, $\frac{40}{243}$, $\frac{10}{243}$, and $\frac{1}{243}$, respectively. These
        probabilities sum to 1. The value $\frac{40}{243}$ is computed as
        $C(5,3)(\frac{1}{3})^3(\frac{2}{3})^2$. In decimal notation this equals .1646, as given in
        Table 7a of Appendix B.

7.4 $C(5,4)(\frac{1}{6})^4(\frac{5}{6})^1 = 5 \times \frac{1}{1,296} \times \frac{5}{6} = \frac{25}{7,776}$, just over .3 percent.

7.5 $Ex = 187 \times \frac{1}{11} = 17$. Notice that we have this result without
        computing the probability distribution. That would be very
        cumbersome. For example, the probability of 23 failures equals
        $C(187,23)(\frac{1}{11})^{23}(\frac{10}{11})^{164}$. This is difficult to compute. After 33 shots,
        the expected number of failures is 3, for $33 \times \frac{1}{11} = 3$.

7.6   Clearly, $n = 250$, $\pi = \frac{1}{2}$; hence $Ex = 125$, $Vx = 62\frac{1}{2}$, and Sx
        is about 7.9.

7.7   Apparently, $n\pi = 7$, and $n\pi(1 - \pi) = 6$. Therefore $n\pi - n\pi^2 = 6$ or $n\pi^2 = n\pi - 6$, or $n\pi^2 = 7 - 6 = 1$. Thus, $n\pi^2/n\pi = \frac{1}{7}$, or $\pi = \frac{1}{7}$. Since $n\pi = 7$, we have $n = 7 \times 7 = 49$. So $\mathbf{x} = B(49,\frac{1}{7})$. In general, given that a variable is binomially distributed, any two of the following four enable us to determine the other two: the number of trials n, the probability of success π, the expected value $E\mathbf{x}$, and the variance $V\mathbf{x}$.

7.8   3,600; we derive this result as follows. The standard deviation is $\sqrt{n\pi(1 - \pi)}$, and we want to choose n so that $\sqrt{n\pi(1 - \pi)} = 0.05n\pi$, given that $\pi = \frac{1}{10}$. What remains is algebra.

$$\sqrt{n \times \tfrac{1}{10} \times \tfrac{9}{10}} = \tfrac{3}{10}\sqrt{n} = .05 \times \tfrac{1}{10}n$$

or $3\sqrt{n} = .05n$, or $9n = .0025n^2$; hence $n = 3,600$. As a check, let $\mathbf{x} = B(3,600, \frac{1}{10})$; then $E\mathbf{x} = 360$, and $V\mathbf{x} = 324$, so $S\mathbf{x} = 18$. Indeed, 18 is 5 percent of the expected value 360.

7.9   In January 1963, a total of 321 children were born. We have $E\mathbf{x} = n \times .51 = 163.7$ and $S\mathbf{x} = \sqrt{n \times .51 \times .49} \approx 9$. The value 144 is outside 2 standard deviations, but within 3 standard deviations, and is not very remarkable. In May 1966, we have $E\mathbf{x} = 312 \times .51 = 159.1$, and $S\mathbf{x} = \sqrt{312 \times .51 \times .49} \approx 8.9$. The value 175 is within 2 standard deviations. Of the 89 months recorded, January 1963 and July and August 1965 (167 boys and 127 girls, 176 boys and 132 girls) had outcomes outside 2 standard deviations. Out of a total of 89 (1960 through May 1967), *three* outcomes outside 2 standard deviations is quite reasonable.

7.10   One of the players will go bankrupt, eventually. If they play 10,000 games, a quite possible result is that A wins 4,975 games, and loses 5,025 games. That is, he lost 50 games more than he won, and forfeited his initial capital. In fact, the game would be over sooner or later, or much later, but eventually one or the other will go bankrupt. You may be interested to know that the expected length of the game is $50 \times 50 = 2,500$ games. Had

A and B started with $4 and $6, respectively, then **x,** the number of games played before one or the other was bankrupt, would have an expected value $Ex = 4 \times 6 = 24$. The actual number of games is, of course, at least four.

7.11   In this case, $\pi = \frac{1}{3}$, and $3\sqrt{\pi(1-\pi)/n}$ should be at most $\frac{2}{3}$ percent, since the deviations from $33\frac{1}{3}$ percent are $\frac{2}{3}$ percent $= \frac{2}{300}$. As an exercise in arithmetic we have $3\sqrt{\frac{1}{3} \times \frac{2}{3}}/\sqrt{n} = \frac{2}{300}$ or $\sqrt{2}/\sqrt{n} = \frac{2}{300}$. Hence $2/n = 4/90,000$, and $n = 45,000$. As a check, for $\mathbf{x} = B(45,000, \frac{1}{3})$, we have $Ex = 15,000$, and $Vx = 10,000$, so $Sx = 100$. The actual outcome will be between $15,000 \pm (3 \times 100)$, or between 14,700 and 15,300. The proportion will be between $\frac{14,700}{45,000}$ and $\frac{15,300}{45,000}$, which is between $32\frac{2}{3}$ and 34 percent.

7.12   In this case the true proportion is $\pi = .2$, and the standard deviation of this proportion is $\sqrt{\pi(1-\pi)/n} = \sqrt{.2 \times .8/n} = .4/\sqrt{n}$. Three times this value should be at most 4 percent or .04. Algebra gives $n = 900$. As a check, for $\mathbf{x} = B(900,.2)$ we have $Ex = 180$, $Vx = 900(.8)(.2) = 144$, and $Sx = 12$. The actual outcome will be between $180 \pm 3(12) = 144$ and 216 parts. The proportion will be between $\frac{144}{900} = 16$ and $\frac{216}{900} = 24$ percent.

7.13   The decile points, in order from 1st to 9th, are: $\mu - 1.282\sigma$, $\mu - .842\sigma$, $\mu - .524\sigma$, $\mu - .253\sigma$, μ, $\mu + .253\sigma$, $\mu + .524\sigma$, $\mu + .842\sigma$, and $\mu + 1.282\sigma$.

7.14   For $N(70,6)$, $P(\mu - 1.667\sigma < \mathbf{x} < \mu + 1.667\sigma) = .9044$. The value 1.667 is used because 10 inches is 1.667 times 6 inches, where 6 inches is the standard deviation.

7.15   According to the table, $P(\mathbf{x} > \mu + .6745\sigma)$ is .25, and $P(\mathbf{x} < \mu - .6745\sigma)$ is .25. Hence, by taking just a little more than $\frac{2}{3}\sigma$ on both sides of the mean, we include the middle 50 percent of all observations. For a normally distributed random variable there is a 50–50 chance for an outcome to be more than .6745 standard deviation from the mean, as illustrated in the figure.

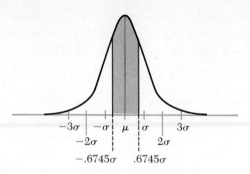

7.16   (a) To find $P(x = 32)$, we must use the continuity correction. To find $P(x = 32)$ for the binomial requires that we find $P(31\frac{1}{2} < x < 32\frac{1}{2})$ for the normal used as an approximation. So x should be between $\mu - \frac{1}{8}\sigma$ and $\mu + \frac{1}{8}\sigma$. From our table, .45 is the area below $\mu - \frac{1}{8}\sigma$ or above $\mu + \frac{1}{8}\sigma$. Therefore, $1 - 2(.45) = .10$ or 10 percent of the area lies between $\mu - \frac{1}{8}\sigma$ and $\mu + \frac{1}{8}\sigma$.

(b) By the same reasoning $P(x < 25)$ for the binomial is given by $P(x < 24\frac{1}{2})$ for the normal. $P(x < 24\frac{1}{2}) = P(x < \mu - 1\frac{7}{8}\sigma) = $ slightly over 3 percent.

(c) Similarly, $P(30 \leq x \leq 35)$ for the binomial is given by $P(29\frac{1}{2} < x < 35\frac{1}{2})$ for the normal. $P(29\frac{1}{2} < x < 35\frac{1}{2}) = P(\mu - \frac{5}{8}\sigma < x < \mu + \frac{7}{8}\sigma) = .234 + .309 = .543$ or 54.3 percent.

To check these results it will be helpful to draw a normal distribution and shade the areas corresponding to your numerical results.

7.17   The weight 1 pound is $2\frac{1}{2}$ standard deviations below the mean weight $[1.05 - 2\frac{1}{2}(.02) = 1]$. The area in the tail beyond $2\frac{1}{2}$ standard deviations is .0062. The probability that a can will be under the guaranteed weight is .62 percent.

7.18   .98 inch is $1\frac{1}{2}$ standard deviations below the mean of 1.01 inches. This area, illustrated in the picture, is .4332. 1.02 inches is $\frac{1}{2}$ standard deviation above the mean of 1.01 inches. This area, also illustrated, is .1915. Thus, $.4332 + .1915 = 62.47$ percent of the holes are within the tolerance.

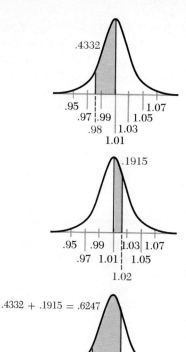

.95 | .97 | .99 | 1.05 | 1.07
.98 | 1.03
1.01

.1915

.95 | .99 | 1.03 | 1.07
.97 | 1.01 | 1.05
1.02

.4332 + .1915 = .6247

.05 | .00 | 1.03 | 1.07
.97 | 1.01 | 1.05

7.19   The binomial! The normal is not applicable, since $n\pi < 5$, and π is not really small enough for the Poisson distribution to be used. The answers given by the exact binomial and the Poisson approximation, respectively, are $C(10,1)(\frac{1}{10})^1(\frac{9}{10})^9 = (\frac{9}{10})^9 = .387$ and $[(1)/1!]e^{-1} = .368$. Using the normal distribution with mean 1 and standard deviation of just less than .95 leads to the question,

k	Binomial $(10,\frac{1}{10})$	Poisson $(\lambda = 1)$
0	.349	.368
1	.387	.368
2	.194	.184
3	.057	.061
4	.011	.015
5	.0015	.003
6	.0001	.0005

"What percentage of the area is between $\frac{1}{2}$ and $1\frac{1}{2}$, or within $.53\sigma$ of the mean μ?" The answer is .404. Neither the Poisson nor the normal approximation is very good. The binomial distribution for $n = 10$, $\pi = \frac{1}{10}$, and the corresponding Poisson with parameter $\lambda = 10 \times \frac{1}{10} = 1$ are compared below. These distributions can be found in Tables 7a and 8 of Appendix B.

7.20   Using Table 8 of Appendix B:

(1) Outcome	(2) Probability	(3) (1) × (2)	(4) Outcome² × (2)
0	.050	.000	.000
1	.149	.149	.149
2	.224	.448	.896
3	.224	.672	2.016
4	.168	.672	2.688
5	.101	.505	2.525
6	.050	.300	1.800
7	.022	.154	1.078
8	.008	.064	.512
9	.003	.027	.243
10	.001	.010	.100
	1.000	2.999	12.007

Rounding gives $Ex = 3$
$Vx = 12 - (3)^2 = 3$

7.21 $P(k \text{ runs}) = e^{-6}(6^k/k!)$, since the Poisson parameter is $\dfrac{1,200}{200}$

$= 6$.
Numerically we have:

k	P(k runs)	k	P(k runs)	k	P(k runs)
0	.002	6	.161	12	.011
1	.015	7	.138	13	.005
2	.045	8	.103	14	.002
3	.089	9	.069	15	.001
4	.134	10	.041	16	.000
5	.161	11	.023	17	.000

There is, of course, no reason to assume that the actual observations will be in accordance with the Poisson model. In different games there is a different probability of scoring by different teams, and runs are not independently scored but are often scored in bunches.

7.22   From Table 8 of Appendix B:

(1) Outcome	(2) Probability
0	.018
1	.073
2	.146
3	.195
4	.195
5	.156
6	.104
7	.060
8	.030
9	.013
10	.005
11	.002
12	.001
	.999

The probability that there will be five or more late arrivals is $1 - P(0, 1, 2, 3,$ *or* 4 late arrivals$) = 1 - (.018 + .073 + .146 + .195 + .195) = .373$. This answer cannot be found by using the binomial distribution since we do not know the total number of secretaries. We have used the Poisson, $\lambda = 4$.

7.23   There are 365 days, and 73 accidents. The Poisson parameter is $\frac{1}{5}$. The exponential parameter is $1/\frac{1}{5} = 5$. We can now make the following table, using Table 4 of Appendix B, or Table 7.5 of the text:

Interarrival time	$\frac{1}{5}t_1$	$\frac{1}{5}t_2$	Probability $e^{-t_1/5} - e^{-t_2/5}$
0–1	0	$\frac{1}{5}$	$1.000 - .819 = .181$
1–2	$\frac{1}{5}$	$\frac{2}{5}$	$.819 - .670 = .149$
2–3	$\frac{2}{5}$	$\frac{3}{5}$	$.670 - .549 = .121$
3–4	$\frac{3}{5}$	$\frac{4}{5}$	$.549 - .449 = .100$
4–5	$\frac{4}{5}$	1	$.449 - .368 = .081$
5–6	1	$1\frac{1}{5}$	$.368 - .301 = .067$
6–7	$1\frac{1}{5}$	$1\frac{2}{5}$	$.301 - .247 = .054$
7–8	$1\frac{2}{5}$	$1\frac{3}{5}$	$.247 - .202 = .045$
8–9	$1\frac{3}{5}$	$1\frac{4}{5}$	$.202 - .165 = .037$
9–10	$1\frac{4}{5}$	2	$.165 - .135 = .030$
10–15	2	3	$.135 - .050 = .085$
15–20	3	4	$.050 - .018 = .032$
>20		>4	$.018 \qquad = .018$

For example, there is a 45 percent probability that the next accident will be within 3 days. If we graph the results as a discrete distribution, assuming that between 0 and 1 day means after $\frac{1}{2}$ day, we get:

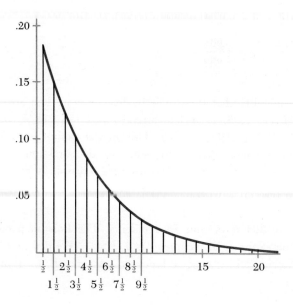

Little imagination is required to see that the distribution could be approximated by a continuous reverse J-shaped distribution.

7.24 If the Poisson condition is satisfied that a call is equally likely to be made anytime, we have an average interarrival time of about $8\frac{1}{2}$ seconds. Hence the answer is

$$e^{-0/8\frac{1}{2}} - e^{-10/8\frac{1}{2}} = e^{-0} - e^{-1.15} = 1.000 - .317 = .683$$

The value for $e^{-1.15}$ is found in Table 4 of Appendix B.

7.25 The probability of finding $x = 4$ customers satisfied in a sample of size $n = 10$, when there are $X = 30$ satisfied persons in a population of size $N = 50$ equals

$$\frac{C(30,4)C(20,6)}{C(50,10)} = \frac{(27,405)(38,760)}{10,272,278,170} = .10$$

7.26 This probability is given by

$$\frac{C(13,5)C(13,5)C(13,3)C(13,0)}{C(52,13)}$$

$$= \frac{1,287 \times 1,287 \times 286 \times 13}{635,013,559,600}$$

and equals about 1 in 10,000.

Chapter 8

PROBLEMS FOR REVIEW-I

1 The manager of an exclusive restaurant in a summer resort plans 4 choices for an appetizer, 10 choices for the main course, 5 choices for dessert, and 6 choices for beverages.

(a) How many different complete dinners are possible?

(b) Suppose that each customer represents an independent trial. What is the probability that three customers will all ask for the same complete dinner? For three different dinners? That at least two will ask for the same dinner?

2 A bus from Los Angeles to New York travels 2,000 miles at an average of 60 miles per hour, 800 miles at an average of 50 miles per hour, and 200 miles at an average of 36 miles per hour. What is the average speed for the total distance of 3,000 miles?

3 The officers' suite in a bank has six doors in a row, which for variety's sake can be painted in five colors. If each officer can choose his door color freely, how many different variations are there? How many different combinations? Next, suppose that one can only choose the colors such that no two adjacent doors have the same color. How many different variations will there be in this case?

4   Mr. Green and Mr. Brown are employees of a mail-order house. Mr. Green is faster than Mr. Brown: he fills 60 percent of the orders. Unfortunately, he makes more errors: he errs in 1 of 50 orders, while Mr. Brown errs only once in 100 orders. A customer writes a letter to the company that his order was erroneously processed. What is the probability that Mr. Brown is to blame?

5   How many different sets of 10 families can an interviewer choose on a street on which 100 families live? If 50 of these families live in apartments and the other 50 in single homes, and he needs 6 out of the home-living families and 4 out of the apartment dwellers, how many different combinations are there?

6   A bank can construct its computer facility in any of six available locations and its new main office in any of three other locations. How many different selections of a computer location and an office location can be made?

7   A survey of a large number of investors showed the following results: 10 percent of the respondents were under 50 years of age and owned preferred stock, 60 percent were under 50 years old, and 75 percent did not own any preferred stock. What is the probability that an investor who is selected at random from among those interviewed:
(a) Will own preferred stock?
(b) Will own preferred stock *and* be 50 years old or older?
(c) Will not own preferred stock *and* be 50 years old or older?
(d) Will own preferred stock *if* he is under 50 years old?

8   Salesman A is successful in 60 percent of his housecalls, while salesman B is successful at only 30 percent of his housecalls. The sales manager completely forgot whether A or B had been assigned Rainbow Road for the morning. On checking Rainbow Road, he found that the first two households had bought the product. What is the probability that salesman A had been at work on Rainbow Road?

9   Two salesmen each have a 50–50 chance to make a sale on a call. On one day, both made six calls. What is the probability that they each made the same number of sales?

10   A contractor has 10 projects on his list. Three of them give a profit of $1,000, and five give a profit of $400, while two give

a loss of $100. Determine the average profit. What is the standard deviation?

11   An electric utility has found that the weekly number of occurrences of lightning's striking transformers on its system is Poisson distributed with $\lambda = .5$.

(a) What is the probability no transformer will be struck in a given week?

(b) What is the probability none will be struck in any 2-week period?

(c) What is the probability the next transformer will be struck by lightning between 1 and 2 weeks from now?

12   If a shipment of 12 electronic tubes contains 1 defective tube, what is the probability that if one chooses 3 of these tubes, the defective one will be included?

13   An investor owns three stocks. He has $1,200 invested in stock X, which pays a 4 percent dividend; $2,000 in stock Y, paying 5 percent; and $3,000 in stock Z, paying 6 percent. What is the average yield on his portfolio? What is the variance in the yield on his portfolio?

14   An assembly consists of two pieces of metal tubing A and B, which are clamped together, end to end. The population from which the A piece is drawn is normally distributed with $\mu = 6$ inches and $\sigma = .01$ inch. Part B is drawn from a normal population with $\mu = 10$ inches and $\sigma = .02$ inch. If the length of the assembly l is the sum of the lengths of piece A and piece B, so that $l = l_A + l_B$, what are El and Vl?

15   You are given the information in the following contingency table.

	Sales of used car U	Sales of new car N
Sales with money M	.60	.25
Sales with credit C	.05	.10

What are $P(U|M)$ and $P(M|U)$? What is $P(M|N) + P(C|N)$? Why?

16   A survey of dentists' waiting rooms indicates that the dentists
      subscribe, for the benefit of waiting patients, to *Time* (T) and/or
      Newsweek (N) and/or *U.S. News and World Report* (US) as
      follows:

None of three	10	Only T and N	20
Only T	25	Only T and US	10
Only N	15	Only US and N	10
Only US	5	All three	5

What is the probability of finding *Time* on a dentist's table? Of
finding *Newsweek?* Of finding *Newsweek given that Time* is there?
Are the events "finding *Time*" and "finding *Newsweek*" dependent?

17   Of all boards of directors, 60 percent have a lawyer on the board,
      and 50 percent have a banker, while 20 percent have a professor.
      Is it possible to have a board without banker, lawyer, or professor?
      Determine which of the following statements could conceivably
      be true:

$$P(B \text{ or } L) = 1.10 \quad P(B \text{ and } L) = .6 \quad P(B \text{ or } P \text{ or } L) = 1$$
$$P(B \text{ or } L) = 1 \quad\quad P(B \text{ and } L) = .5 \quad P(B \text{ or } P \text{ or } L) = .6$$
$$P(B \text{ or } L) = .9 \quad\quad P(B \text{ and } L) = .4$$
$$P(B \text{ or } L) = .5 \quad\quad P(B \text{ and } L) = .05$$

If all characteristics are independent, what is $P(P \text{ and } L)$, $P(B \text{ and } L)$, $P(P \text{ or } L)$, $P(B \text{ or } P \text{ or } L)$?

18   A secretary reads novels 20 percent of the time. The boss at
      random times spotchecks her activity, and in four checks finds her
      busily engaged in work. What is the probability of the secretary's
      being so lucky?

19   Three tasks are needed to build a home: the foundation must
      be laid, the structure must be built, and the finishing touches
      (painting, plumbing, etc.) must be performed. These tasks must
      be done in order. We are given:

$$P(\text{foundation takes 3 weeks}) = .4$$
$$P(\text{foundation takes 4 weeks}) = .6$$
$$P(\text{building takes 8 weeks}) = .2$$
$$P(\text{building takes 9 weeks}) = .3$$
$$P(\text{building takes 10 weeks}) = .5$$
$$P(\text{finishing takes 3 weeks}) = .2$$
$$P(\text{finishing takes 4 weeks}) = .5$$
$$P(\text{finishing takes 5 weeks}) = .3$$

Assuming that the times needed for laying the foundation, building, and finishing are independent, what is the probability that the house will be ready in 13, 14, 15, 16, 17, 18, 19, 20 weeks?

20 The following is the historical pattern of the size of orders received daily in the small-order department of a mail-order house:

Size of orders, dollars	Percent of orders
5.00–9.99	10
10.00–14.99	15
15.00–19.99	20
20.00–24.99	25
25.00–29.99	15
30.00–34.99	10
35.00–39.99	5
	100

(Orders for over $40.00 are handled in a separate department.) The pattern is stable, so we may view order size as a random variable x.

(a) Find Ex and Vx.

(b) If $z = x_1 + x_2$, the size of the first two orders in the morning, what is Ez and Vz? What assumption must be made to answer this question?

21 A group of 10,000 persons contains 80 percent males and 20 percent females. A random sample of 100 is chosen.

(a) What is the probability that this sample contains between 85 and 88 males?

(b) What is the probability that this sample contains 75 or more males?

(c) What is the probability that this sample contains fewer than 72 males?

22   The following table shows wages paid to production workers by the Fizzle Rocket Company during a recent week:

Weekly wage	Number of production workers
$140 and less than $160	60
160 and less than 180	70
180 and less than 200	85
200 and less than 220	110
220 and less than 240	95
240 and less than 260	80
	500

(a) Compute the average of these wages.

(b) Compute the standard deviation of these wages.

(c) The average weekly wage of production workers at Zoom Aircraft Company during the same week was $250 with a standard deviation of $40. In which company were weekly wages of production workers more uniform this week? Explain.

23   A process produces steel wheels with diameters which are normally distributed with mean $\mu = 16$ inches and standard deviation $\sigma = .1$ inch.

(a) What is the probability that two wheels will both be wider than 16.1 inches?

(b) What is the probability that the diameter of a wheel will differ from 16 inches by more than .115 inch?

(c) What is the probability that at least one out of four wheels will be less than 15.8 inches in diameter?

(d) Calculate the median and q_z for the distribution of diameters.

24   The following frequency distribution shows the price of the dinners eaten by the customers patronizing a particular restaurant on a particular evening:

Price	Dinners
$0 and under $1	50
1 and under 2	230
2 and under 3	350
3 and under 4	190
4 and under 5	110
5 and under 6	60
6 and under 7	10
	1,000

(a) Calculate the average and the standard deviation for these dinner prices.

(b) Find the median. Find the 1st and 3d quartile points, using the median formula with appropriate modifications.

25   A wholesaler has 110 accounts receivable. The accounts are classified according to their age in days:

50 accounts are class A (age < 30)
20 accounts are class B (30 < age < 60)
10 accounts are class C (60 < age < 90)
30 accounts are class D (90 < age)
110

(a) If a sample of 11 accounts is taken without replacement, what is the probability it contains 5A, 2B, 1C, 3D accounts?

(b) What is the answer to (a) if sampling is done with replacement?

(c) If a sample of 11 accounts is taken without replacement, what is the probability it contains no class D accounts?

26   An automatic drilling machine produces good pieces 91 percent of the time. Faulty parts are drilled either off-center or at an incorrect angle. Of the parts 5 percent are drilled off-center, and 2 percent are drilled both off-center and at an incorrect angle.

(a) What percentage is drilled at an incorrect angle?

(b) Is off-center drilling independent of off-angle drilling?

(c) What is the conditional probability of a part's being drilled off-angle, given that it is drilled off-center?

27   Over a very long succession of trading days, the changes in the
price per share of two stocks A and B were observed to have
the following relative frequency:

| | Relative frequency | |
Price change	A	B
-2	.05	.12
$-1\frac{1}{2}$	.07	.10
-1	.10	.09
$-\frac{1}{2}$	.12	.10
0	.15	.12
$+\frac{1}{2}$	.20	.14
$+1$	.15	.10
$+1\frac{1}{2}$	.10	.11
$+2$	.06	.12

(a) If the change in the price of A, namely **a,** and the change
in the price of B, namely **b,** are random variables with probability distributions given by these relative frequencies, find
Ea, Va, Eb, and **Vb.**

(b) It is widely believed that the price changes in a stock on
successive trading days are independent. Assuming this is so,
find the expected value and the variance of the change in
the price of A between today and 100 trading days from now.

(c) If price changes in A and B are independent, find the expected
value and variance of the change from one trading day to the
next in the value of a portfolio consisting of 100 shares of
A and 200 shares of B.

28   An automobile dealer has ordered eight cars of a particular model
delivered from the factory to his showroom. There are three red,
three green, and two blue in the group. He receives word that
three are delayed because of a strike. Assume that one color is
as likely to be delayed as another.

(a) What is the probability that the delayed cars are of the same
color?

(b) What is the probability that the delayed cars are of three
different colors?

(c) What is the probability that two delayed cars are of the same
color and the third of a different color?

29   In a certain forest, 40 percent of the trees are oak and the rest
      are maples. Among the oaks, 25 percent are diseased. Of all the
      trees in the forest, 80 percent are not diseased.
      (*a*) What is the probability that the tree selected at random will
           be a diseased oak?
      (*b*) What is the probability that a maple tree selected at random
           will be healthy?
      (*c*) What is the probability that a diseased tree selected at random
           will be an oak?

30   A sample of four is selected *with* replacement from employees
      in a factory in which 30 percent are nonunion and 70 percent
      are union members. Find the probabilities that the sample con-
      tains:
      (*a*) All union members.
      (*b*) Exactly one union member.
      (*c*) At least two union members.
      (*d*) No union members.

31 · Suppose surgical cases arrive in the accident ward of a hospital
      according to a Poisson distribution with a mean $\lambda = 2$ per 6-hour
      period. Find the probability that:
      (*a*) No surgical case will arrive in the next 6-hour period.
      (*b*) More than three surgical cases will arrive in the next 6-hour
           period.
      (*c*) The next surgical case will arrive within the next hour.

32   Among a group of 100 men, 7 are blue-eyed, tall, and left-handed;
      21 are blue-eyed and tall; 17 are tall and left-handed; 16 are
      blue-eyed and left-handed; 57 are blue-eyed; 42 are tall; 28 are
      left-handed.
      (*a*) Depict these data in a Venn diagram.
      (*b*) How many men are blue-eyed and left-handed but not tall?
      (*c*) How many men are neither blue-eyed, nor tall, nor left-
           handed?
      (*d*) What is the probability that a man selected at random from
           the group is left-handed but neither tall nor blue-eyed?

33   The production from a certain manufacturing operation includes
      7 percent defective parts. In a subsequent inspection of each part

produced by this operation, all parts which are not defective pass and 15 percent of those which are defective pass. What is the probability that a part which has passed inspection is defective?

34   There are 100 blue disks in box B of which 40 bear the letter D (for correct decision) and 60 bear the letter D′ (for incorrect decision). In box W there are 100 white disks of which 25 bear the letter D and 75 bear the letter D′. One disk is drawn from each box. What is the probability that:
(a) Both disks bear the letter D?
(b) The white disk is D and the blue disk is D′?
(c) At least one disk bears a D?
(d) Neither disk bears a D?
(e) At most one disk bears a D?

35   For a selected ball club, 25 percent of their wins are followed by losses and 20 percent of their losses are followed by wins. The probability that they will win today's game is .7. What is the probability that they will win tomorrow's game?

36   In a carton of 50 electric shavers, 5 items are defective. Compute the probability that you will find exactly 2 defective shavers by taking a random sample of 4 from the carton.

37   In the following table, the random variable x represents the number of available parking spaces in a lot at exactly 9 A.M., and p gives the associated probabilities:

x	0	2	4	6	8	10
p	.05	.10	.40	.25	.12	.08

Determine from the data in this table:
(a) $Ex = \mu$
(b) $Vx = \sigma^2$
(c) $Sx = \sigma$

38   Assume there are two groups of people and one person leaves one group and becomes a member of the other.
(a) As a result of his act is it possible that the average height in *each* group is now greater than before? Explain the reasons for your answer.
(b) Assuming the same situation, is it possible that the median height in *each* group is now greater than before? Explain.

39   The ABC Company has a clerical staff of 100 persons. The average annual salary for all women is $3,000. The average annual salary for all men is $4,000. The annual payroll for the entire clerical staff is $370,000. How many women are on the clerical staff?

40   A firm plans a 60 percent increase in production of a fabric which contains wool, rayon, and nylon. It is claimed that since the fabric is only 10 percent wool, the firm will only have to increase its purchases of wool 6 percent over the present amount. Comment.

41   The Longview Company has a special purpose machine essential to the manufacture of a particular made-to-order part. The number of orders per week follows a Poisson distribution with $\lambda = 5$. Find the probability that:
(a) Exactly two orders will arrive in the next week.
(b) More than five orders will arrive in the next week.
(c) The next order will arrive within the next 3 days.

42   Observe the following table showing the current annual yield (ratio of dividends to market price) for 75 stocks in the portfolio of Mr. I. M. Rich:

Yield, percent	Number of stocks
0 and under 1	4
1 and under 2	6
2 and under 3	8
3 and under 4	12
4 and under 5	17
5 and under 6	14
6 and under 7	9
7 and under 8	5
Total	75

(a) Find the average yield per issue on the stocks in Mr. Rich's portfolio, to the nearest $\frac{1}{10}$ of a percent.
(b) Find the standard deviation of the yields on the stocks in Mr. Rich's portfolio, to the nearest $\frac{1}{10}$ of a percent.
(c) The yields on the stocks in Mr. Wealthy's portfolio have an average of 6 percent and a standard deviation of 2 percent. Which man's portfolio shows the greater variance in yields?

43   In a machine shop, the product from machines A, B, C, and D
       was separated into three grades. These grades were G, "good";
       L, "large"; S, "small." The small parts had to be scrapped. The
       large parts could be turned to size (i.e., reworked), and the good
       parts could be packaged for shipment.

       (a) Are the two variables (machine and grade) statistically inde-
           pendent in the table below?

Grade	Machine				Total product
	A	B	C	D	
G	2,800	1,000	2,200	1,500	7,500
L	600	250	300	350	1,500
S	600	250	0	150	1,000
	4,000	1,500	2,500	2,000	10,000

       (b) What is the symbolic notation for the probability that a part
           selected at random:
           (1) Is good?
           (2) Was produced by machine D?
           (3) Was produced by machine C and is large?
           (4) Should be scrapped if we know that it was produced by
               machine B?

       (c) Find the following probabilities from the table:
           (1) P(G *and* C)   (3) P(G *and* S)   (5) P(L *and* B)
           (2) P(L *or* C)   (4) P(B *or* C)   (6) P(G *or* S)

44   The ages of XYZ refrigerators turned in for new models in a recent
       survey are:

Years	*No. of refrigerators*
0 and under 1	10
1 and under 2	19
2 and under 3	26
3 and under 4	18
4 and under 5	13
5 and under 6	8
6 and under 7	3
7 and over	3†
Total	100

† Note: the average age of these three refrigerators is $10\frac{1}{2}$ years.

(a) What is the average of the ages of these 100 refrigerators?

(b) Estimate the median age of these refrigerators to the nearest year.

(c) Estimate the mode.

(d) Explain the reasons that your answers to (a), (b), and (c) differ.

45   Suppose that if a person with tuberculosis is given a chest x-ray, the probability that his condition will be detected is .95, and that if a person without tuberculosis is given a chest x-ray, the probability that he will be diagnosed incorrectly as having the disease is .002. Suppose further that .1 percent of the adult residents of a certain city have tuberculosis. If one of these persons (selected at random) is diagnosed as having tuberculosis on the basis of a chest x-ray, what is the probability that he actually has it?

46   On a piecework operation, the Jackson and Sons Company pays a bonus if an employee processes 320 or more acceptable pieces in a day. The daily number of acceptable pieces processed by Wilbur White and Lawrence Halverson, two employees in the department, is normally distributed with the following characteristics:

Employee	Average	Standard deviation
White	290 pieces	20 pieces
Halverson	300 pieces	10 pieces

(a) On what percentage of the days will White get the bonus?

(b) On what percentage of the days will Halverson get the bonus?

(c) Is the bonus plan a "fair" one for White and Halverson? In answering this question, consider the total number of acceptable pieces processed over a period of time and the advantages and disadvantages of uniform production rates. Assume, for this discussion, that the percentage of all pieces processed that are acceptable is the same for both employees.

(d) What proportion of the time does Halverson's daily output of acceptable pieces exceed White's?

47   A restaurant offers its patrons a choice of steak, chicken, and ham; if so desired, red wine or white wine may be ordered with the main course. It is known from experience that the probabilities that a customer will order steak, chicken, or ham are, respectively, .60, .30, and .10. Also, the probability that a customer will order

red wine, white wine, or no wine after he has selected steak is .40, .10, and .50; and the corresponding probabilities are for chicken .05, .25, and .70; and for ham .15, .20, and .65. Finally, the probability that a customer leaves a good tip is .80 if he had steak and red wine, .30 if he had steak and white wine, .60 if he had steak and no wine, .40 if he had chicken and red wine, .80 if he had chicken and white wine, .70 if he had chicken and no wine, .70 if he had ham and red wine, .70 if he had ham and white wine, and .50 if he had ham and no wine. What is the probability that a customer will leave a good tip?

48   A company has four machines used in the manufacture of a certain product. The number of pieces produced by these machines each day is 1,000, 1,200, 1,800, and 2,000, respectively. Furthermore, the first machine is known to produce an average of 1 percent defective, the second $\frac{1}{2}$ percent defective, the third $\frac{1}{2}$ percent defective, and the fourth 1 percent defective. If one piece is selected at random from a day's production and found to be defective, what is the probability that this piece came from the fourth machine?

49   The probability that an airplane accident which is due to structural failure is diagnosed correctly is .05, and the probability that an airplane accident which is not due to structural failure is diagnosed incorrectly as being due to structural failure is .35. If 30 percent of all airplane accidents are due to structural failures, find the probability that an airplane accident is due to structural failure, given that it has been diagnosed as due to structural failure.

50   An automobile dealership receives 12 cars from the manufacturer. Three of these twelve are not yet properly adjusted, and another four have only been roughly adjusted, because of the mad rush of business just before Christmas. Seven cars are sold without the salesmen's being aware of any adjustment problems in any of the cars. What is the probability that none of the unadjusted cars is sold? What is the probability that no fully adjusted car is sold? What is the probability that two unadjusted, three roughly adjusted, and two fully adjusted cars are sold?

Chapter 9

SAMPLING AND ESTIMATION

0.1 POPULATIONS AND SAMPLES

If an economist is interested in the average yearly expenditures on sugar by families with two children, he could conceivably ask all such families how much money they spend for sugar during a year, and then compute the average. The problem is that in practice it is very difficult, time consuming, and expensive to find all such families. Even if he does, the economist may well get guesses instead of accurate answers.

If a manufacturer is interested in the average lifetime of a batch of 10,000 bulbs produced on a certain machine on a given day, he could proceed by burning them all until they burn out. The average burning time for this batch could then be easily determined. However, it would have cost a small fortune in electricity; all the bulbs would have burned out, and they would be worthless in the market place. Yet it is of importance to the producer to know the quality of his product.

If a prospective buyer is interested in the amount of sugar he can produce from a given shipment of sugar beets, he could buy the shipment and find out the answer precisely by processing the beets to sugar. However in making a bid, he would like to know in advance the quality of the beets. He dislikes the risk of paying dearly for a shipment of bad quality.

If an agronomist wants to trace the effect of a certain type of fertilizer on the productivity of the soil in producing a specific type of wheat, he can plant some wheat on fertilized soil and some on otherwise identical but unfertilized soil, and determine the difference in the amount of wheat produced. Unfortunately, this would only tell him what happened in this specific instance, whereas he is interested in what will happen *in general,* even including cases in which the wheat has not yet been planted.

In cases such as those described above, progress is made by drawing a sample from the population. In the first example the population consists of all families composed of two parents and two children. If there are 6 million such families, a sample can be taken by choosing 1,000 families and then inquiring about their annual expenditures for sugar. This will save money and time. Moreover, it will be possible for the pollsters to obtain more accurate answers by verifying the records of these one thousand families in some detail. To the extent that the information obtained in the sample enables us to make inferences about the population and, in particular, the mean expenditure on sugar in the population, we have made progress.

In the second example the population consists of the 10,000 bulbs produced on that machine that day. A sample can be taken by picking 100 of these bulbs, and then determining their lifetime. If the average observed lifetime is 779 hours, one might conclude—by an argument which we explain below—that the other 9,900 bulbs can be guaranteed to burn at least 750 hours. The sampling saves money on electricity, and leaves the large majority of bulbs available for sale.

In the third example the population may consist of 100,000 sugar beets. The sugar content per beet may differ from beet to beet, just as the lifetime of bulbs will differ from bulb to bulb. In other words, the sugar content per beet is a random variable. We are essentially interested in the mean sugar content per beet. If it turns out to be 8.8 ounces, the whole batch will be known to contain 55,000 pounds of sugar. A sample can be obtained by choosing 100 beets, and then analyzing them in a laboratory for sugar content. If proper inference is used, the sample can give the prospective buyer an idea about the mean sugar content of the beets in the population, so that he can make a reasonable bid.

In the fertilizer example the population is composed of acres available for cultivation. This population is infinitely large, not only because there are infinitely many different acres but also because each acre can be used over and over again. The agronomist can sample 100 observations out of the (in principle) infinitely large population, and, by fertilizing 50 acres and leaving 50 acres unfertilized, he can obtain the data needed to compare yield on fertilized acres with yield on unfertilized acres. In this case the agronomist samples from pure necessity, since an infinite number of observations can never be obtained. It remains true, however, that the sample is not of interest for its own sake. We are interested in the results of the sample only to the extent that it gives us knowledge about the population.

We can summarize these results as follows. For a specific problem, the population consists of the set on which measurements are to be made. In these examples we have the sets of *all* American families of father, mother, and two children, *all* bulbs produced on a given day on a given machine, *all* beets in a certain shipment, and *all* available acres of soil. The measurements to be made are amount spent on sugar per year, hours of lifetime of a bulb, sugar content per beet, and wheat output.

A sample from a population is drawn by choosing some of its members—some families, some bulbs, some beets, some acres of soil. We then measure the pertinent characteristic of these items—their expenditures on sugar, their lifetime, etc. Sampling, as opposed to a complete investigation of the whole population, is used in practice for any of a variety of reasons. These include:

Reasons for sampling

1. The population may contain infinitely many members (fertilizer example).
2. It may save time and money (all examples).
3. It may enable more accurate measurements (sugar expenditure example).
4. Measuring the characteristic may destroy the item (bulbs example).

Sampling is a means to an end. The end is to obtain information concerning some characteristic of the population.

EXERCISES

9.1   Consider the outcomes of 10 tosses of a coin as a sample from a population. What might the measured characteristic be? What is the population?

9.2   A dairy manager is interested in the proportion of milk bottles, filled on a specific day by a specific bottling machine, which contain less than the specified content of 1 quart. What population is he interested in?

9.3   A metropolitan newspaper decides to conduct an interview survey to predict the results of the upcoming election for mayor. What is the population appropriate to this survey?

9.2 RANDOM SAMPLING

"Simple"
random
sample

When sampling is guided purely by chance, we have *random sampling*. During most of our discussion we shall deal with the type of random sample easiest to understand, the *simple* random sample. For simplicity, the word "simple" will be understood until Chapter 18, where we meet other types of random samples.

There are at least three alternative but roughly equivalent ways of defining a simple random sample. If there are N items in a population and if a sample of size n is drawn, the sample is a simple random sample if one or all of the following are true:

1. At each draw all the remaining items in the population have the same chance of being drawn.
2. Each of the $C(N,n) = N!/n!(N - n)!$ possible ways to choose n out of N items is equally likely and, therefore, has a probability of $1/C(N,n)$ to occur.
3. All items have the same chance to be included in the sample, and all choices are independent of one another.

For example, one can easily draw a random sample of 5 different letters from the 26 letters of the alphabet. Some experiments along this line led to:

WIUMF   EMZOH   FICKA   ATZMX   VBJGR

These combinations were obtained by putting 26 Scrabble blocks with letters A to Z into a sack, and drawing, one-by-one, 5 of the letters from the sack. These 5 were returned and the process was repeated. In this way conditions (1), (2), and (3) above are complied with. Essentially, these definitions are equivalent, but if the population is infinite, definition (2) is inapplicable.

On the other hand, one cannot draw a random sample of five letters by going to a dictionary and picking a five-letter word with all different letters. This is not a random sample of five letters because not all letters have an equal chance of being chosen. Vowels are more prevalent than consonants, and r is more popular than q. Moreover, not all letters chosen are independent, since after a q we invariably get a u, and after an x we *never* get a k. It is easy to verify that all three definitions are violated.

One remark concerning definition (3) is in order. It is *not* sufficient for randomness that all items have the same chance to be included in the sample. This would be the case if, in drawing 10 numbers from the first 100, we pick items 1 through 10, *or* 11 through 20, . . . , *or* 91 through 100, all with probability .10. All numbers now have the same chance of being included in the sample, but the sampling is *not* random. Indeed, definitions (1) and (2) are grossly violated. Definition (1) is violated because once number 17 is drawn, number 26, for example, has no chance of being drawn next. Definition (2) is violated because not all $\frac{100!}{10!90!}$ combinations of numbers are equally likely, but only 10 combinations are equally likely, and all others are impossible. To remedy this, the additional clause *"and all choices are independent of one another"* must be added to definition (3).

It is one thing to define what a random sample is, and it is another thing to draw one. How would we go about drawing a simple random sample of size 100 from a batch of 10,000 bulbs? Conceptually, as in the Scrabble example, we put the 10,000 bulbs in a big bowl, shuffle well and draw a bulb, shuffle again and draw a second bulb, etc. In practice, we will turn to a book of *random digits* of which a small part may look like Table 9.1. If one number is, by chance, chosen twice (which could occur, since these tables are constructed in such a way that every next digit has a .10 chance of being 0, 1, 2, . . . , 8, or 9), we will simply disregard it and go to the next. According to this table, the bulb numbered 576 (that is, coming out of the machine as the 576th bulb produced that day), the one numbered 6,332, and so forth, are taken in the sample. Number 0001 is considered bulb 1, and number 0000 would stand for

Random digits

TABLE 9.1 RANDOM DIGITS

0576	6332	4785	0906	4838	0501	0126	8372	6234	7905
2243	2844	9646	9876	1052	5506	8162	7426	9218	9954
2337	5717	6113	2283	1941	7716	5659	4843	7576	0230
9073	8274	6232	5341	1093	7977	6624	5549	2292	6923
8228	6900	3992	5183	1636	2146	1464	1229	5511	5950
5850	9601	1395	8572	2023	9724	9115	1888	3742	7441
1878	9203	1100	6156	4494	8441	6009	2668	7027	9370
6997	0927	0391	5185	1981	1479	8991	6882	6077	0791
1750	9228	8752	9690	4130	0841	2732	0242	9662	2478
0814	2961	0944	0898	0212	1368	4636	7905	8855	1664

bulb 10,000, but, as so happens, this number was not drawn in this particular sample.

A widely used source of random digits is the Rand Corporation's "A Million Random Digits with 10,000 Normal Deviates." Even with a book of random digits, random sampling is easier said than done because all items in the population must be numbered as well. To draw a random sample of 1,000 families out of 6 million families is possible by the random digit method only if the 6 million families can be listed and numbered. Rereading Table 9.1 for this case would imply that family 0576633, family 2478509, family 0648380, and so forth, are in the sample. The fifth family chosen would be family 8372623, which would not exist in a population of only 6 million families. Such observations are disregarded, and we proceed to the next family, 4790522. However, such a list does not always exist. If it does not exist, other methods to guarantee randomness are called for. For example, highly detailed maps of cities and towns are often used for the purpose.

A sample is made random by the process used to select it. If a sample is random, we refer not to the composition of the particular items in it but to the process by which it was obtained. Whether a poker hand AAAAJ is random does not depend on the cards in this particular hand but only on the process by which the cards were shuffled and dealt.

EXERCISES

9.4   A magazine polls its subscribers concerning their choice for President in the forthcoming election. Can this sample of opinions be considered a random sample out of the population of opinions of all voters?

9.5   Can telephone numbers be considered random digits?

9.6   Is the mail a congressman receives on a controversial topic a random sample of the opinions of all his constituents?

9.7   Could one get the word "quote" by drawing a simple random sample of 5 different letters from the 26 letters of the English alphabet?

9.3   ESTIMATING THE MEAN

At this point we are prepared to discuss a typical statistical problem, the problem of estimation. Consider the shipment of sugar beets again—100,000 of them in a shipload. Some beets will be larger, some smaller. Some will be "sweeter" than others. It all depends on a host of factors: the soil they were in, the sunshine they got, the water they received, the proximity of other beets, and so on. The amount of sugar per beet will thus vary from beet to beet; it will be a random variable. What is the distribution of this random variable? For reasons explained in Section 7.5—many individually small factors acting independently—it seems natural to assume that it will be a normal distribution, but its mean μ and standard deviation σ are unknown. Does "the mean beet" contain 8.9 ounces of sugar, or 9.1, or 7.8? And is the standard deviation .4 ounce, .9 ounce, or 1.3 ounces?

This is a typical estimation problem. We know, or we assume that we know, the type of distribution of a certain variable, but the parameters of this distribution (usually the mean and the standard deviation) are unknown and have to be estimated. In this case, we know we have a normal distribution, but the mean μ and standard deviation σ are unknown.

Estimation

We will first indicate how a random sample of beets may give us an idea about the mean μ under the assumption that the standard deviation σ is known. We will assume that the standard deviation is .7 ounce, and omit the units when we refer to it. Hence

$$\sigma = .7$$

We start to estimate μ by drawing one beet from the shipment at random. The sugar content $\mathbf{x}_1$ of this first beet is a random variable—hence the boldface symbol—since it will vary depending on the beet we actually come up with. By our random choice, however, we know that $\mathbf{x}_1$ is a random drawing out of a normal distribution with mean μ and standard deviation σ. The expected value of $\mathbf{x}_1$ equals μ ounces,

Sample of size 1

$$E\mathbf{x}_1 = \mu \qquad \mu \text{ is unknown}$$

and the standard deviation equals $\sigma = .7$ ounce,

$$S\mathbf{x}_1 = \sigma = .7 \qquad \sigma \text{ is known by assumption}$$

If instead of a random beet we had picked a beet from the top of the heap, it might very well be true that $E\mathbf{x}_{\text{top}} > \mu$. The sugar content of the beets on top may be larger, for example, because the seller made it a point to display the best beets on the top. The random selection is quite important.

If we now actually draw a beet, it is reasonable to consider its sugar content x_1 an estimate of μ. The sugar content of the first beet drawn was found to be

$$x_1 = 7.8 \text{ ounces}$$

and so we state that, on this evidence, the *estimated mean* is 7.8 ounces. This is called a *point estimate*. We know, however, that x_1 has a standard deviation of .7 ounce and is normally distributed, so we can be 95.45 percent confident that the true mean μ will be between

Point versus
interval
estimate

$$7.8 \pm 2 \times .7 = 6.4 \text{ to } 9.2 \text{ ounces}$$

This is called an *interval estimate with a confidence level of 95.45 percent*, since 95.45 percent of all estimates made in this way (with $k = 2$) will include μ.

An illustration will help to bring this point home more forcefully. In Figure 9.1 we assume first that we know μ as well as σ. We have assumed $\mu = 8.3$ and $\sigma = .7$. Since we have a normal distribution, we do know that 95.45 percent of the observations will be within $8.3 \pm 2 \times .7$, or between 6.9 and 9.7. We thus have a probability of 95.45 percent that a random draw out of this distribution of sugar contents will be between 6.9 and 9.7; whenever the observation actually drawn is between these limits, a range of twice the standard deviation .7 around the observation will include the true mean μ. If we draw $x_1 = 7.8$, the range $7.8 \pm 2 \times .7$ includes the value $\mu = 8.3$. If we draw any other value within the range 6.9 to 9.7, for example 7.0, 9.0, or 9.6, the same thing is true.

$$7.0 \pm 2 \times .7, \text{ or } 5.6 \text{ to } 8.4, \text{ includes } 8.3$$
$$9.0 \pm 2 \times .7, \text{ or } 7.6 \text{ to } 10.4, \text{ includes } 8.3$$
$$9.6 \pm 2 \times .7, \text{ or } 8.2 \text{ to } 11.0, \text{ includes } 8.3$$

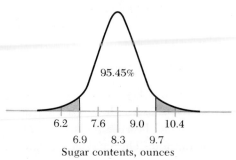

Figure 9.1 Normally distributed sugar contents of beets, $N(8.3, .7)$.

We will draw a beet with a sugar content outside the range of 6.9 to 9.7 in less than 5 percent of the cases (see Figure 9.1 again). If we happen to be unfortunate enough to draw a beet with a sugar content of 6.7, we will conclude that the true mean μ is within the range of 5.3 to 8.1. There is a 4.55 percent chance of such an erroneous conclusion. By playing it safer, and taking 3 standard deviations around the value x_1 which we find in the sample, our interval will include μ with 99.7 percent confidence, but the interval will be rather wide. Whatever we do, some uncertainty will always remain. However, the level of uncertainty we are able to live with is up to us.

A sample of size 1 leaves a lot to be desired. Let us see what we can do by increasing the size of the sample to 25. Before we actually draw the sample, we have 25 random variables $\mathbf{x}_1, \mathbf{x}_2, \ldots, \mathbf{x}_{25}$, where $\mathbf{x}_2$ stands for the sugar content of the second beet we shall draw. Clearly we have

Larger samples

$$E\mathbf{x}_1 = E\mathbf{x}_2 = \cdots = E\mathbf{x}_{25} = \mu$$

provided we draw a random sample. But we know more. The expected value of the sum of these 25 random variables is

$$
\begin{aligned}
E(\mathbf{x}_1 + \mathbf{x}_2 + \cdots + \mathbf{x}_{25}) &= E\mathbf{x}_1 + E\mathbf{x}_2 + \cdots + E\mathbf{x}_{25} \\
&= \mu + \mu + \cdots + \mu \\
&= 25\mu
\end{aligned}
$$

since the expected value of a sum is the sum of the expected values (recall Section 6.3). Hence

$$
\begin{aligned}
E\overline{\mathbf{x}} &= E\left(\frac{\mathbf{x}_1 + \mathbf{x}_2 + \cdots + \mathbf{x}_{25}}{25}\right) \\
&= \tfrac{1}{25}E\mathbf{x}_1 + \tfrac{1}{25}E\mathbf{x}_2 + \cdots + \tfrac{1}{25}E\mathbf{x}_{25} \\
&= \tfrac{1}{25}25\mu = \mu
\end{aligned}
$$

In words, the expected value of the sample average $\overline{\mathbf{x}}$ is μ. For this reason, if we draw a sample and find as the result $x_1, x_2, \ldots, x_{25}$, we use the sample average

$\overline{x}$ estimates μ

$$\overline{x} = \frac{x_1 + x_2 + \cdots + x_{25}}{25} = \frac{\Sigma x_i}{25}$$

as an estimate for μ. We now have a point estimate $\overline{x}$. We prefer to have an interval estimate. It is here that the advantages of a larger sample size will become evident since the standard deviation of $\bar{\mathbf{x}}$ will be much less than .7.

Because we have a random sample, which in particular implies that all outcomes are independent, we can use the result in Section 6.5. Using the relationship $V\mathbf{x} = (S\mathbf{x})^2$, we have

$$V(\mathbf{x}_1 + \mathbf{x}_2 + \cdots + \mathbf{x}_{25}) = V\mathbf{x}_1 + V\mathbf{x}_2 + \cdots + V\mathbf{x}_{25}$$
$$= .49 + .49 + \cdots + .49$$
$$= 25 \times .49$$

In the same section we found that if a random variable has a variance $V\mathbf{x}$, or its distribution a variance σ^2, then k times that random variable has a variance equal to $k^2 V\mathbf{x} = k^2\sigma^2$. Hence

$$V\bar{\mathbf{x}} = \sigma_{\bar{\mathbf{x}}}^2 = V\left(\frac{\mathbf{x}_1 + \mathbf{x}_2 + \cdots + \mathbf{x}_{25}}{25}\right)$$

$$= V\tfrac{1}{25}\mathbf{x}_1 + V\tfrac{1}{25}\mathbf{x}_2 + \cdots + V\tfrac{1}{25}\mathbf{x}_{25}$$
$$= \tfrac{1}{625}V\mathbf{x}_1 + \tfrac{1}{625}V\mathbf{x}_2 + \cdots + \tfrac{1}{625}V\mathbf{x}_{25}$$
$$= \tfrac{1}{625} \times 25 \times .49 = \tfrac{.49}{25}$$

Standard deviation of $\bar{\mathbf{x}}$ We conclude that $\sigma_{\bar{\mathbf{x}}}$, the standard deviation of $\bar{\mathbf{x}}$, equals $\sqrt{\tfrac{49}{25}} = \tfrac{7}{5} = .14$. In general, if the sample size is n, the standard deviation of the sampling distribution of $\bar{\mathbf{x}}$ is

$$\sigma_{\bar{\mathbf{x}}} = \frac{\sigma}{\sqrt{n}}$$

where σ is the standard deviation in the population.

Now we see that we have made progress. If we draw a sample of size 25, and determine the sugar content in the 25 beets, we may find

7.8	7.2	8.3	8.5	7.9
9.0	6.8	7.3	8.2	8.2
7.6	9.5	8.9	8.7	8.1
8.0	7.5	8.7	9.0	8.6
7.5	7.7	8.9	7.4	7.2

so that $\bar{x} = 8.1$; hence our point estimate of μ is 8.1. The standard deviation of the sample average is only .14, which implies that the true mean μ will be within the interval

$$8.1 \pm 2 \times .14 = 7.82 \text{ to } 8.38$$

with 95.45 percent confidence. The estimate is much "sharper"; that is, the interval is narrower.

Let us illustrate this conclusion. We assume that we know the sugar contents are normally distributed with $\mu = 8.3$, $\sigma = .7$. This is illustrated at the top of Figure 9.2. Then we know that the average sugar content $\bar{x}$ based on a sample of size 25 will have an expected value of

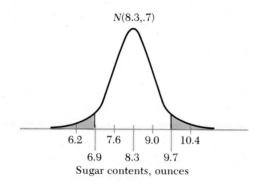

$N(8.3, .7)$

| 6.2 | 7.6 | 9.0 | 10.4 |

6.9   8.3   9.7

Sugar contents, ounces

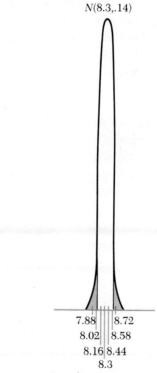

$N(8.3, .14)$

7.88   8.72
8.02   8.58
8.16 8.44
8.3

Sample mean x, ounces

Figure 9.2 Sampling distribution of $\bar{x}$ is $N\left(\mu, \dfrac{\sigma}{\sqrt{n}}\right)$.

μ and a standard deviation of $\sigma_{\bar{x}} = \sigma/\sqrt{n} = \frac{.7}{5} = .14$. According to the Central Limit Theorem (discussed in Section 7.5) the distribution of $\bar{x}$ will also be a normal distribution, as shown at the bottom of Figure 9.2. In shorthand,

$$\bar{x} = N\left(\mu, \frac{\sigma}{\sqrt{n}}\right) = N\left(8.3, \frac{.7}{\sqrt{25}}\right)$$

Thus, in 95.45 percent of the cases, the average of the sample which we draw will be within $8.3 \pm 2 \times .14$, or between 8.02 and 8.58. And whenever it *is* between these limits, a range of two times $\sigma/\sqrt{n}$ around it will include the true mean $\mu = 8.3$. In our example we found $\bar{x} = 8.1$, and the range $8.1 \pm 2 \times .14$ does include the true mean $\mu = 8.3$. In only 4.55 percent of the cases will the sample average $\bar{x}$ be outside the range 8.02 to 8.58. If we happen to find $\bar{x} = 8.0$, then we erroneously conclude that the true mean will be in the range 7.72 to 8.28; however, such errors happen less than once in 20 times. We have illustrated the Central Limit Theorem in Figure 9.3 by showing the distribution of $\bar{x}$ in samples of 50 from three radically different populations. In each, the distribution of $\bar{x}$ is close to the normal distribution and would become even closer for larger n.

Review

We will review the results of this section. Suppose we know the general form of a distribution—normal, exponential, Poisson, or any other distribution—but we do not know its parameters, in particular the mean μ and the standard deviation σ. Suppose, next, that an angel whispers the true standard deviation σ in our ear, but the devil prevents the angel from also communicating the true value μ. Then we estimate μ by drawing a sample of size n and considering the sample average $\bar{x}$ an estimate for the population mean μ. The sample average $\bar{x}$ is a random variable as long as we do not know the sample items actually drawn, but we know that

$$E\bar{x} = \mu \qquad \text{and} \qquad \sigma_{\bar{x}} = \frac{\sigma}{\sqrt{n}}$$

Furthermore, the distribution of $\bar{x}$ is a normal distribution. This all leads us to conclude that if we now draw a sample and find $\bar{x}$, the interval

$$\bar{x} \pm \frac{2\sigma}{\sqrt{n}}$$

will include the true mean μ with 95.45 percent confidence. More gener-

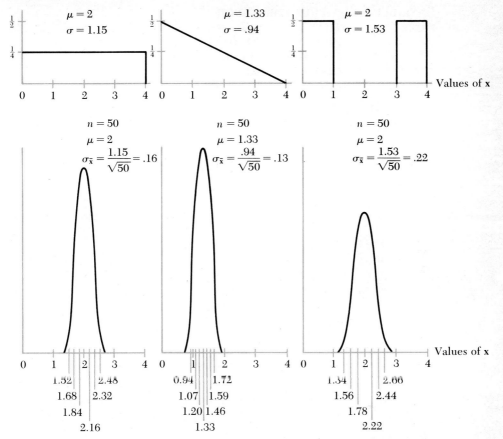

Figure 9.3   The Central Limit Theorem.

ally, the interval

$$\bar{x} \pm k\frac{\sigma}{\sqrt{n}}$$

will include the true mean μ with a confidence level which can be determined from Table 9.2. The entries in Table 9.2 are derived from Table 7.4.

In closing this long section, a word of warning. It is imperative to keep the difference between sd, σ, and $\sigma_{\bar{x}}$ clearly in focus. The abbreviation sd is associated with observed values. It is computed by adding the squared deviations from the average of these observed values, dividing by n, and taking the square root. At the very beginning of the next section we will meet yet another numerical example of this computation. The σ is the

sd, σ, and $\sigma_{\bar{x}}$ compared

TABLE 9.2   VALUES FOR k SUCH THAT $\bar{x} \pm k\ \sigma/\sqrt{n}$ INCLUDES μ WITH CONFIDENCE LEVEL GIVEN IN FIRST COLUMN

(1) Confidence level, percent	(2) k
50	.674
68.27	1.000
75	1.152
90	1.645
95	1.960
95.45	2.000
98	2.326
99	2.576
99.73	3.000

standard deviation in the population (or of the distribution); for example, the population of sugar contents in beets, or the distribution of heights of human beings. More than 00 percent of all actual population values will be within 2σ of the population mean. The symbol $\sigma_{\bar{x}}$ is the standard deviation of the sampling distribution of $\bar{x}$. It equals $\sigma/\sqrt{n}$ if the samples are of size n, and can be "imagined" as the value derived when we draw *many* samples of size n from the population, compute for each of these samples the sample average $\bar{x}_1, \bar{x}_2, \ldots,$ and then compute the standard deviation, sd, of these actual observations $\bar{x}_1, \bar{x}_2, \ldots.$ Provided we take enough samples of size n, this computed sd will equal $\sigma/\sqrt{n}$. Even so, this result can only be imagined, because we never draw that many samples of size n.

EXERCISES

9.8   Estimate the expected value of the outcome of the roll of a die on the basis of a sample of size 10. Make use of the fact that $\sigma = \sqrt{2\frac{11}{12}}$ to determine a 90 percent confidence interval.

9.9   Let us assume that the lifetime of lightbulbs is normally distributed with an unknown mean and a standard deviation of 100 hours.

The average in a random sample of size 100 is 1,022.

(a) Determine a 90, a 95, and a 99 percent confidence interval for μ.

(b) How would your answers change if the lifetimes were rectangularly distributed?

(c) How large would the sample size have to be to guarantee that the total length of a 90 percent confidence interval will be 20 hours?

(d) How much larger would the sample size have to be to guarantee that the total length of a 99 percent confidence interval will be 20 hours?

9.10   The time a clerk in a supermarket takes to check out customers is normally distributed with a standard deviation of $\frac{3}{4}$ minute. A random sample of 225 customers shows an average time of $2\frac{1}{2}$ minutes. Determine an 80 percent confidence interval for the true mean time this clerk takes to check out customers.

9.4   ESTIMATING THE VARIANCE; THE t DISTRIBUTION

In the previous section we showed that increasing the sample size has the great virtue of diminishing the width of the interval

$$\bar{x} \pm k \frac{\sigma}{\sqrt{n}}$$

This is an important result. But there is a further advantage in increased sample sizes. So far, we have assumed that the standard deviation σ was known. In practice, it will be unknown. Then we must use the information from the sample to estimate the standard deviation σ. A sample of size 1 cannot be of any help here, since there is no variability in the outcomes. But a sample of size 25 is quite useful.

To see this, let us return to the sample of the sugar contents of 25 beets. These were:

7.8	7.2	8.3	8.5	7.9
9.0	6.8	7.3	8.2	8.2
7.6	9.5	8.9	8.7	8.1
8.0	7.5	8.7	9.0	8.6
7.5	7.7	8.9	7.4	7.2

There is considerable variability in the results, and we can easily compute the sample variance, var x, and standard deviation, sd x. We already know that the average $\bar{x}$ is equal to 8.1, and hence

$$\text{var } x = \frac{(7.8 - 8.1)^2 + \cdots + (7.2 - 8.1)^2}{25} = \frac{11.76}{25} = .47$$

and

$$\text{sd } x = \sqrt{.47} = .686$$

We are now tempted to consider this value .47 as an estimate of σ^2, the unknown population variance.

It is better, however, to make a small amendment. We must realize that the true mean μ is unknown. Instead, we use the sample average $\bar{x} = 8.1$. But what if the true mean is 8.3? Then the sum of the squared deviations from 8.3 is

$$(7.8 - 8.3)^2 + (7.2 - 8.3)^2 + \cdots + (7.2 - 8.3)^2 = 12.76$$

which is larger than 11.76. In fact, the sum of the squared deviations of the sample values from the sample average 8.1 will *always* be less than the sum of the squared deviations from any other value, as we saw in Section 5.4. The consequence is that we tend to *underestimate* the variance by using the sample average $\bar{x}$ rather than the true mean μ in our computations. However, we cannot use μ, since we do not know it. The solution to this problem of underestimation is given by multiplying var x by $n/(n - 1)$, or, equivalently, by dividing the sum of squared deviations from $\bar{x}$ by $n - 1$, rather than by n. Then the denominator is also smaller (underestimated), and the *ratio* turns out to be, on the average, just right. If we do this, we find the following for the estimate of σ^2, which we will denote by s^2:

s^2 estimates σ^2
$$s^2 = \text{var } x \frac{n}{n - 1} = \frac{11.76}{25} \times \frac{25}{24} = \frac{11.76}{24} = .49$$

We use var x, found by dividing the sum of squared deviations by n, if we want a descriptive measure of the dispersion in the sample. We use s^2, found by dividing the sum of squared deviations by $n - 1$, if we want an estimate of σ^2, the population variance. Of course, when n is 100 or more, the difference between s^2 and var x becomes trivial and can be ignored.

Once the sample values $x_1, x_2, \ldots, x_n$ are known, s^2 is a specific number

$$s^2 = \frac{(x_1 - \bar{x})^2 + (x_2 - \bar{x})^2 + \cdots + (x_n - \bar{x})^2}{n-1} = \frac{\Sigma(x_i - \bar{x})^2}{n-1}$$

Before the sample values are known, $\mathbf{s}^2$ is a random variable

$$\mathbf{s}^2 = \frac{(\mathbf{x}_1 - \bar{\mathbf{x}})^2 + (\mathbf{x}_2 - \bar{\mathbf{x}})^2 + \cdots + (\mathbf{x}_n - \bar{\mathbf{x}})^2}{n-1}$$

The random variable $\mathbf{s}^2$ has the desirable property that its expected value is the population variance σ^2, that is,

$$E\mathbf{s}^2 = \sigma^2$$

When the expected value of an estimate is the parameter, the estimator is said to be *unbiased*. The average of a sample, $\bar{\mathbf{x}}$, is an unbiased estimate of the population mean μ, since $E\bar{\mathbf{x}} = \mu$.

Unbiased estimate

  We can summarize the discussion up to this point as follows: Assume we know that we are sampling from a specific distribution with unknown mean μ and unknown standard deviation σ. We draw a random sample of size n, which leads to observations $x_1, x_2, \ldots, x_n$. We then compute $\bar{x}$, and use this as our estimate for μ,

$$\bar{x} = \frac{x_1 + x_2 + \cdots + x_n}{n}$$

We also compute the sum of squared deviations from $\bar{x}$ and divide by $n-1$, which gives us an estimate s^2 of σ^2,

$$s^2 = \frac{(x_1 - \bar{x})^2 + (x_2 - \bar{x})^2 + \cdots + (x_n - \bar{x})^2}{n-1}$$

We finally conclude that 95.45 percent of all intervals

$$\bar{x} \pm 2\frac{s}{\sqrt{n}}$$

computed in this way will include the true mean μ. In general

$$\bar{x} \pm k\frac{s}{\sqrt{n}}$$

will include the true mean μ at a confidence level determined by k, as in Table 9.2.

The beauty of all this is that one sample gives $\overline{x}$, an estimate of μ, and also, through s^2 as an estimate of σ^2, an interval within which μ will be with a confidence level of our choice. Quite often one takes twice $s/\sqrt{n}$ on either side of $\overline{x}$, so that the interval has a length of $4s/\sqrt{n}$ and a 95.45 percent probability of including the true μ. Greater confidence can be obtained only at the expense of lengthening the interval.

t distribution

Degrees of freedom

To all this there is one amendment. If σ is unknown, and therefore estimated by s, the value of k which gives the required confidence level ought to be derived from a *t* distribution. A *t* distribution is characterized by one parameter, which is nearly always referred to as its number of "degrees of freedom." We should use the *t* distribution with the number of degrees of freedom 1 less than the number of observations in the sample from which σ was estimated. In our beet example, we would therefore be interested in the *t* distribution with 24 degrees of freedom.

Whether we have a *t* distribution with 1, 2, ..., 24, ..., or 169 degrees of freedom, it will always look roughly like a normal distribution, symmetric and with a peak at the center. It will, however, be flatter at the top and thicker at the tails (see Figure 9.4). In Table 9.3 we give the appropriate k value for many *t* distributions and for four specific levels of confidence, 90, 95, 98, and 99 percent. For large numbers of degrees of freedom, these k values do not differ much from those of the normal distribution given in red in Table 9.2. For low numbers of degrees of freedom, that is, small sample sizes, the k values are substantially larger. In our case, with 24 degrees of freedom, we should use $k = 2.06$, rather than $k = 1.96$, to get a 95 percent confidence interval. In Table 10 of Appendix B a more detailed table of *t* distributions is recorded.

For a sample of size 5, and therefore 4 degrees of freedom, a 95 percent confidence interval requires a k value of 2.78, so that the range is $\overline{x} \pm 2.78 \, s/\sqrt{5}$. For a sample size of 10, the k value is 2.26. For sample sizes of 20 and 30, the k value declines to 2.09 and 2.04; and for even larger sample sizes, it gradually converges to 1.96, the value for the normal distribution. In many business problems n is large enough to use the

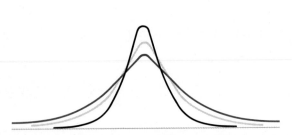

Figure 9.4 The *t* distribution with 1, 5, and s degrees of freedom.

TABLE 9.3 t-DISTRIBUTION VALUES FOR k SUCH THAT $\bar{x} \pm ks/\sqrt{n}$ INCLUDES μ WITH STATED CONFIDENCE LEVEL

Sample size n	Degrees of freedom	Confidence level 90%	95%	98%	99%
2	1	6.31	12.71	31.82	63.66
3	2	2.92	4.30	6.96	9.92
4	3	2.35	3.18	4.54	5.84
5	4	2.13	2.78	3.75	4.60
6	5	2.02	2.57	3.36	4.03
7	6	1.94	2.45	3.14	3.71
8	7	1.90	2.36	3.00	3.50
9	8	1.86	2.31	2.90	3.36
10	9	1.83	2.26	2.82	3.25
11	10	1.81	2.23	2.76	3.17
12	11	1.80	2.20	2.72	3.11
13	12	1.78	2.18	2.68	3.06
14	13	1.77	2.16	2.65	3.01
15	14	1.76	2.14	2.62	2.98
16	15	1.75	2.13	2.60	2.95
17	16	1.75	2.12	2.58	2.92
18	17	1.74	2.11	2.57	2.90
19	18	1.73	2.10	2.55	2.88
20	19	1.73	2.09	2.54	2.86
21	20	1.72	2.09	2.53	2.84
22	21	1.72	2.08	2.52	2.83
23	22	1.72	2.07	2.51	2.82
24	23	1.71	2.07	2.50	2.81
25	24	1.71	2.06	2.49	2.80
26	25	1.71	2.06	2.48	2.79
27	26	1.71	2.06	2.48	2.78
28	27	1.70	2.05	2.47	2.77
29	28	1.70	2.05	2.47	2.76
30	29	1.70	2.04	2.46	2.76
31	30	1.70	2.04	2.46	2.75
41	40	1.68	2.02	2.42	2.71
51	50	1.68	2.01	2.40	2.68
61	60	1.67	2.00	2.39	2.66
71	70	1.67	2.00	2.38	2.65
81	80	1.66	1.99	2.38	2.64
91	90	1.66	1.99	2.37	2.63
101	100	1.66	1.98	2.36	2.63
1,001	1,000	1.65	1.96	2.33	2.58

normal distribution as an approximation to the appropriate t distribution. Whenever n is less than 30, however, it is advisable to refer to the table of t distributions.

It is intuitively appealing that when σ is unknown and must be estimated, the range becomes wider. We can have greater confidence in a range based on knowledge that $\sigma = .7$ than in a range of the same size based on an estimate of σ, $s = .7$.

EXERCISES

9.11   How would you make a confidence interval estimate of the mean value of common stock holdings by individual investors in the United States?

9.12   A sample of size 51 has $\bar{x} = 67$, and the sum of the squared deviations from $\bar{x}$ is 1,250. Determine a 98 percent confidence interval for the population mean μ, using both the normal and the appropriate t distribution.

9.13   A forest contains 10,000 trees. A sample of 150 trees yields an average of 480 board feet per tree and an $s^2 = 19,500$. Make a 95.45 percent confidence interval estimate of the total board feet in the forest.

9.5   TOLERANCE INTERVALS

In the previous section we found confidence intervals for the population mean μ. These intervals are of the form

$$\bar{x} \pm k \frac{s}{\sqrt{n}}$$

where $\bar{x}$ and s are both determined as functions of the n sample observations. In this section we deal with a slightly different problem. On the basis of the sample information, we want to construct an interval within which 95 (or 99, or . . .) percent of *all* actual observations will lie. This may be useful for a bulb manufacturer who wants to guarantee a minimum lifetime. Suppose he could state that 95 percent of all bulbs will burn between 780 and 1,150 hours, with $2\frac{1}{2}$ percent lasting less than 780 and $2\frac{1}{2}$ percent more than 1,150. A guaranteed lifetime of 780 hours will fail to be met by only $2\frac{1}{2}$ percent of the bulbs, or about 25 out of 1,000.

If that is not considered safe enough, the manufacturer would want to find an interval containing the burning times of 99 percent of all bulbs.

Unfortunately, such intervals cannot be found. The best we can do is to determine a tolerance interval. A *tolerance interval* is an interval such that there is a predetermined probability (90, or 95, or 99, or ... percent) that a specific percentage (90, or 95, or 99, or ... percent) of the actual observations will fall within that interval.

Tolerance interval

At this point we will take time out for a short diversion. The purpose of this diversion is to indicate why we cannot find tolerance intervals which are *certain* to contain 90, or 95, or 99 percent of all observations, given only sample information. If we happen to know the true μ and σ, there is no problem on this score. For example, in a normal distribution we know that 68.27 percent of all observations are within the interval $\mu \pm \sigma$, 95.45 percent lie within the interval $\mu \pm 2\sigma$, and 99.73 percent lie within the interval $\mu \pm 3\sigma$. Note, however, that no finite interval will have 100 percent of the observations within its range with certainty.

The situation changes drastically if we do not know μ. We can then estimate μ by the sample average $\bar{x}$. If we assume optimistically that we still know σ, we can state that the interval $\bar{x} \pm 2\sigma/\sqrt{n}$ will contain μ at a confidence level of 95.45 percent. We should be surprised if μ were less than the lower limit or more than the upper limit, *but we cannot be certain that it will not be.* So one probability statement is necessary because the mean is unknown and no finite range is certain to include it, and a second percentage statement is necessary because, even if the mean is known, no finite range contains all observations. Therefore, at best, we can specify ranges which contain with a given probability a given percentage of the observations. These ranges will be wider, the higher the probability and the higher the percentage of observations to be included.

After this slightly philosophical digression, we return to the main topic. In Table 9.4 we give the *tolerance factors f* for a number of combinations of probability h and percentage j for various sample sizes. These tolerance factors can be used for variables which are normally distributed. Their use is as follows. Let us consider the case of the lifetime of the bulbs and suppose that we have 100 sample observations. The average lifetime in the sample is

Tolerance factors

$$\bar{x} = 1{,}022 \text{ hours}$$

and s is 100.

If we now want to know the tolerance interval such that there is a 99 percent probability that 95 percent of the burning times will fall

TABLE 9.4   TOLERANCE FACTOR f IF THERE IS h PERCENT
PROBABILITY THAT THE RANGE $m \pm fs$ INCLUDES
j PERCENT OF THE OBSERVATIONS†

	$h = 90\%$		$h = 95\%$		$h = 99\%$	
Sample size n	$j = 95\%$	$j = 99\%$	$j = 95\%$	$j = 99\%$	$j = 95\%$	$j = 99\%$
10	3.018	3.959	3.379	4.433	4.265	5.594
15	2.713	3.562	2.954	3.878	3.507	4.605
20	2.564	3.368	2.752	3.615	3.168	4.161
25	2.474	3.251	2.631	3.457	2.972	3.904
30	2.413	3.170	2.549	3.350	2.841	3.733
35	2.368	3.112	2.490	3.272	2.748	3.611
40	2.334	3.066	2.445	3.213	2.677	3.518
45	2.306	3.030	2.408	3.165	2.621	3.444
50	2.284	3.001	2.379	3.126	2.576	3.385
60	2.248	2.995	2.333	3.066	2.506	3.293
70	2.222	2.920	2.299	3.021	2.454	3.225
80	2.202	2.894	2.272	2.986	2.414	3.173
90	2.185	2.872	2.251	2.958	2.382	3.130
100	2.172	2.854	2.233	2.934	2.355	3.096
150	2.127	2.795	2.175	2.859	2.270	2.983
200	2.102	2.762	2.143	2.816	2.222	2.921
300	2.073	2.725	2.106	2.767	2.169	2.850
400	2.057	2.703	2.084	2.739	2.138	2.809
500	2.046	2.689	2.070	2.721	2.117	2.783
1,000	2.019	2.654	2.036	2.676	2.068	2.718

† Adapted by permission from C. Eisenhart, M. W. Hastay, and W. A. Wallis, "Techniques of Statistical Analysis," McGraw-Hill Book Company, New York, 1947.

within that interval we look under $n = 100$, $h = 99$ percent, $j = 95$ percent, and find 2.355. The interval

$$1,022 \pm 2.355 \times 100 = 786.5 \text{ to } 1,257.5$$

will—with 99 percent probability—include 95 percent of the observations. We are 99 percent sure that no more than $2\frac{1}{2}$ percent of the observations will fall below 786.5, and the producer feels safe in guaranteeing a lifetime of 775 hours.

Observe that the value 2.355 exceeds the value 1.96, which spans 95 percent of the observations in the normal distribution with known μ and σ. If the sample size gets very large, f approaches 1.96 but never reaches it, due to the uncertainty in the estimates $\bar{x}$ and s.

EXERCISES

9.14   Consider the sample of sugar contents of 25 beets as given in Section 9.4. Determine a tolerance interval such that 99 percent of the beets will have a sugar content within that interval, with 95 percent probability.

9.15   Use the information in Exercise 9.13 to determine a tolerance interval such that 95 percent of the trees will have a number of board feet within that interval, with 90 percent probability.

9.16   The time required for the Times Square–Grand Central shuttle to make a one-way trip is a normally distributed variable with $\mu = 3$ and $\sigma = .1$ minute. Within what limits could you be 99 percent sure of finding the durations of 95 percent of all one-way trips?

9.6   ESTIMATING PROPORTIONS

We began Chapter 7 by introducing the binomial distribution. This distribution arises whenever an experiment leads to an "either/or" outcome: Either a housewife prefers Dot toothpaste or she prefers Freckles toothpaste. One of the outcomes is considered a success, the other a failure. Two parameters characterize the binomial distribution, the probability of success at each trial π, and the number of trials n. We recall that, given π and n, the probability that we will have exactly k successes is given by

$$C(n,k)\pi^k(1 - \pi)^{n-k} \qquad k = 0, 1, 2, \ldots, n$$

The expected number of successes will be $n\pi$, and the standard deviation of this result will be $\sqrt{n\pi(1 - \pi)}$. Furthermore, provided $n\pi > 5$ and $n(1 - \pi) > 5$, we know that the binomial distribution with parameters π and n can be approximated rather well by the normal distribution with parameters $\mu = n\pi$ and $\sigma = \sqrt{n\pi(1 - \pi)}$; that is,

$$B(n,\pi) \approx N[n\pi, \sqrt{n\pi(1 - \pi)}]$$

Sadly, the true proportion of successes in the population is generally unknown. This is precisely the plight of the marketing executive who wants to know whether package design X or package design Y is preferred by shopping housewives. What can our marketing man do? He selects at random a sample of housewives and asks them, "Do you prefer X or

Y?" Suppose he asks the question of 225 housewives, 153 of whom prefer design X (which is considered a success). He can then estimate the true p estimates π percentage π by the sample proportion p,

$$p = \tfrac{153}{225} = .68$$

This is, in fact, an unbiased estimate of π. If we draw many samples, the proportion **p** will fluctuate from sample to sample (i.e., it will be a random variable), but the expected value of **p** will equal π, $E\mathbf{p} = \pi$. The proof is similar to the proof of $E\overline{\mathbf{x}} = \mu$ in Section 9.3.

So far, so good, but the sample actually drawn may well produce a specific value p different from π. Suppose that there are 100,000 housewives whose opinions form the relevant population, and that 65,000 of them would profess, when asked, to prefer design X. The true percentage is then .65. A sample of size 225 might, however, contain zero housewives who prefer design X, so that our estimate would be $p = \tfrac{0}{225} = 0$. On the other hand, we might find only housewives preferring design X, which would lead to the erroneous conclusion that $p = \tfrac{225}{225} = 1$. Both results would be rather dramatically at odds with the true value $\pi = .65$.

Such sample outcomes, however, while theoretically possible, seldom occur in practice. As we saw in Section 7.4, the expected value of the proportion of successes is

$$E\mathbf{p} = \frac{n\pi}{n} = \pi$$

and the standard deviation of this proportion is

$$\sigma_{\mathbf{p}} = \sqrt{\frac{\pi(1-\pi)}{n}}$$

These last two results are immediately relevant here. Suppose we know that $\pi = .65$. In our sample of size 225 the expected proportion of successes is .65 and the standard deviation of this proportion is .032.

Interval   The sample proportion will be between $.65 \pm 2 \times .032$, with a estimate for π probability of 95.45 percent, since the distribution will be nearly normal as long as n is not too small and π not too far from $\tfrac{1}{2}$.

Now back to the real problem. We do not know $\pi = .65$. Therefore, we cannot use the formula $\sqrt{\pi(1-\pi)/n}$ for the standard deviation. Instead, we know only that a sample of size 225 gave as a result $p = .68$. This is the point estimate. We make an interval estimate by using the sample proportion p as a proxy for π, which gives in this case

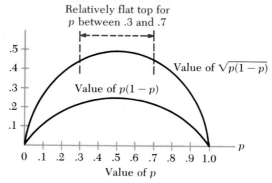

Figure 9.5   Effect of p on $\sqrt{p(1-p)}$.

$$p \pm k \sqrt{\frac{p(1-p)}{n}} = .68 \pm k \sqrt{\frac{.68(1-.68)}{225}} = .68 \pm k(.031)$$

The value of k will depend on the confidence level used, and can be read from Table 9.2.

The use of p in place of π is not very dangerous because the value of $\sqrt{p(1-p)}$ does not change very much if p is within the range .3 to .7. This is illustrated in Figure 9.5. From this figure we see that $\sqrt{p(1-p)}$ is greatest when $p = .5$, and slopes downward very gently as p moves away from .5. If we want to be very cautious, we can assume $p = .5$. This will guarantee that we never underestimate the size of σ_p.

The problem of determining confidence intervals for proportions is made easy for us by *confidence belts*. There is one set of belts for every specified confidence level. The set for a confidence level of 95 percent is given in Figure 9.6. We see that a 95 percent confidence interval for π when the sample proportion $p = .3$ and the sample size $n = 50$ runs from about .175 to about .45. These confidence belts can be used even when the approximation of the binomial by the normal is unwarranted, because np or $n(1-p)$ is less than 5. For $n = 15$ and $p = .2$, the interval estimate for π at the 95 percent confidence level is from about .04 to about .48.

Confidence belts

EXERCISES

9.17   One of the most frustrating events in mechanized living is the failure of a vending machine either to produce the product or to return the coin(s). In 121 tries a particular machine fails 22

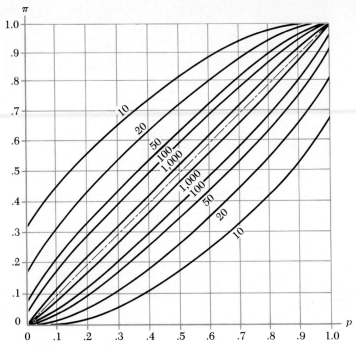

Figure 9.6 Confidence belts showing confidence intervals for π at the .95 confidence level. (*Adapted from C. J. Clopper and E. S. Pearson, "The Use of Confidence or Fiducial Limits Illustrated in the Case of the Binomial," Biometrika, vol. 26, p. 404, 1934. Reproduced by permission of Professor E. S. Pearson.*)

times. Within what range will the true proportion of "hoarding" be with 90 percent confidence?

9.18   A department store wants to determine the percentage of shoppers who leave only after having actually bought at least one item. A random sample of 900 shoppers leaving the store showed that 750 had bought something, ranging from a candy bar to a complete bedroom furniture set. What is a 90 percent confidence interval for the true percentage of buyers?

9.19   A preliminary survey of 100 opinions indicates a close to 50–50 split between two candidates for political office. In fact, Mr. Donkey scored 51 and Mr. Elephant 49 preferences. How large should the sample size n be to limit the standard deviation to .001?

9.20   A preliminary survey of 100 opinions 1 week before an election shows an exactly 50–50 split between two candidates for political office, but when the returns are counted a week later, one candidate gets twice as many votes as the other. How do you account for this surprising outcome?

9.7   THE CHOICE OF SAMPLE SIZE FOR ESTIMATION

In each example we have assumed the sample size n is known. This conveniently avoided the fact that n must be chosen by some logical process *before* the sample is taken. How should we choose n? The sample size should be just large enough to give us a confidence interval of the desired width and acceptable confidence level.

We may want to estimate the mean sugar content of a shipload of beets within .1 ounce of the true mean with 95 percent confidence. Table 9.2 shows that $k = 1.96$ for a 95 percent confidence level. Since our sample mean is to be within .1 ounce of the true mean, we say that the *acceptable* error $e = .1$.

We know a confidence interval for μ is given by

$$\bar{x} \pm k \frac{\sigma}{\sqrt{n}}$$

If the difference $\mu - \bar{x} = e$ is to be kept to .1 with 95 percent confidence, we must make

$$1.96 \frac{\sigma}{\sqrt{n}} = .1$$

Thus,

$$n = \frac{(1.96)^2(\sigma)^2}{(.1)^2}$$

The value of σ must be estimated from past experience or a trial sample. The rules of thumb given in Section 5.5 can be helpful. If we have reason to believe $\sigma = .7$, then

$$n = \frac{(1.96)^2(.7)^2}{(.1)^2} = 188$$

More generally, if we want to estimate μ in a population with standard deviation σ with an error no greater than e by calculating a confidence interval with confidence corresponding to k, the necessary sample size is

$$n = \frac{k^2\sigma^2}{e^2}$$

If we are estimating a proportion, the reasoning is similar. An airline wants to estimate the proportion of its passengers willing to pay extra fare for expedited baggage delivery. The estimated proportion must be within .02 of the true value with 90 percent confidence. Thus, $e = .02$ and $k = 1.645$.

We know a confidence interval for π is given by

$$p \pm k \sqrt{\frac{\pi(1 - \pi)}{n}}$$

If the difference $\pi - p = e$ is to be kept to .02, we must make 1.645 $\sqrt{\pi(1 - \pi)/n} = .02$. We do not know π and must estimate it, again, from past experience or a trial sample. As we saw in the previous section, $\pi(1 - \pi)$ is largest when $\pi = .5$ and gets smaller as π moves away from .5. Thus, a conservative estimate is one close to .5. We will assume $\pi = .5$ in this example. This gives

$$1.645 \sqrt{\frac{.5(1 - .5)}{n}} = .02$$

or

$$n = \frac{(1.645)^2(.5)(1 - .5)}{(.02)^2} = 1,691$$

In general, if we want to estimate π with an error no greater than e by calculating a confidence interval with confidence corresponding to k, the necessary sample size is

$$n = \frac{k^2(\pi)(1 - \pi)}{e^2}$$

EXERCISES

9.21   A sample of fuses is to be randomly selected from a large shipment. An estimate of the mean blowing time is desired with maximum error of .07 second. The standard deviation of blowing times is known from past experience to be .52 second. A 99 percent confidence interval for the true mean μ will be needed. Determine the necessary sample size.

9.22   A bank manager wants to be 90 percent certain that his estimate of a particular transaction time is within $\frac{1}{2}$ minute of the true mean transaction time. He assumes that the standard deviation σ is 2 minutes.

(a) How large should the sample size be?

(b) A sample of the recommended size is drawn, and s is found to be 1.5 minutes. What effect will this have on the interval estimate?

(c) A sample of the recommended size is drawn, and s is found to be 3 minutes. What effect will this have on the interval estimate? Comment.

9.23   The proportion of "bouncing checks" presented to banks in Suffolk County is to be estimated within .002. The confidence level is to be 95 percent. Evidence from a similar study 3 years ago showed this percentage to be in the range of 4 to 6 percent with confidence level of 99 percent. How many checks must be included in the sample?

Answers to Exercises

9.1   The measured characteristic is, for example, the proportion of heads. The population has infinitely many members, obtained by tossing the coin over and over and over again.

9.2   All bottles filled that day on that machine constitute the population. Accurate measurements for content on a random sample of bottles will provide him with relevant information.

9.3   The population appropriate to the survey is everyone who will actually vote in the election for mayor. It is very difficult to locate the members of this population prior to the election.

9.4   Definitely not. Presumably, if the magazine is *Fortune*, the Republican candidate will be more popular in the sample than in the population. If it is the *Nation*, the reverse will hold. Generally, political inclinations are not independent of subscriptions to certain periodicals.

9.5   No, not as such. But it may well be that the sixth digit, reading down, will form an approximation. In the second column of page 1247 of the 1966–1967 Buffalo telephone book we find

1094	3886	1341	3752	9344	7560	4680	6930
5518	0317	3709	9452	3744	0748	4518	3868
0507	0893	3234	2653	3977	1407	8701	3629

Some tests for randomness are complied with. There are about as many even as odd numbers, and about as many four-digit numbers with at least two digits the same as with all four digits different (for $\frac{10}{10} \times \frac{9}{10} \times \frac{8}{10} \times \frac{7}{10} \approx \frac{1}{2}$). The frequency of all digits is within 9.6 (their expected value, since there are 96 digits) plus or minus 2×3 (the approximate value of the standard deviation).

9.6   No. In general people who disagree or are against something are far more likely to write than those who agree. There are also organized efforts by pressure groups to flood congressmen's offices with mail giving the organization's view on a particular issue.

9.7   Yes, not only is that possible, but we can even give the probability of such an occurrence, which is $\frac{1}{26} \times \frac{1}{25} \times \frac{1}{24} \times \frac{1}{23} \times \frac{1}{22} = \frac{1}{7,000,000}$.

9.8   To find a point estimate, we roll the die 10 times and compute the average $\bar{x}$. To find the interval estimate, we should add and deduct $1.645(\sigma/\sqrt{n}) = 1.645\sqrt{2\frac{11}{12}}/\sqrt{n}$ to and from $\bar{x}$. An actual 10 rolls produced the outcomes 6, 2, 2, 3, 2, 3, 6, 5, 5, 3; $\bar{x} = 3.7$. The interval estimate is $3.7 \pm 1.645(\sqrt{2\frac{11}{12}}/\sqrt{10}) = 2.81$ to 4.59

9.9   (a) The answers are

$$1{,}022 \pm 1.645 \frac{100}{\sqrt{100}} = 1{,}022 \pm 16.45$$

$$= 1{,}005.55 \text{ to } 1{,}038.45$$

$$1{,}022 \pm 1.96 \frac{100}{\sqrt{100}} = 1{,}022 \pm 19.60$$

$$= 1{,}002.40 \text{ to } 1{,}041.60$$

$$1{,}022 \pm 2.576 \frac{100}{\sqrt{100}} = 1{,}022 \pm 25.76$$

$$= 996.24 \text{ to } 1{,}047.76$$

(b) Not at all, since the sampling distribution would still be normal, according to the Central Limit Theorem.

(c) The total length of a 90 percent confidence interval is $2(1.645)(100/\sqrt{n})$. The 2 represents the fact that the range is found by adding *and* deducting $1.645(100/\sqrt{n})$ to and from $\bar{x}$. The total length must be 20, so

$$2(1.645)\frac{100}{\sqrt{n}} = 20$$

$$\sqrt{n} = 10(1.645) = 16.45$$

$$n = (16.45)^2 = 270$$

(d) We now must have

$$2(2.576)\frac{100}{\sqrt{n}} = 20$$

$$\sqrt{n} = 10(2.576) = 25.76$$

$$n = (25.76)^2 = 663$$

Thus, the sample must be larger by 393 bulbs, or 145 percent larger.

9.10   The interval is $2\frac{1}{2} \pm 1.282 \, (\frac{3}{4}/\sqrt{225})$ or between 146.154 and 153.846 seconds, or (slightly rounded), between 146 and 154 seconds.

9.11   The New York Stock Exchange makes this estimate every 3 or 4 years for the Census of Shareowners by obtaining a random sample of names of owners of listed and unlisted issues from company and brokers' records and by conducting personal interviews with the individuals in this sample.

9.12   We first estimate σ^2 by finding s^2, namely, $s^2 = \frac{1,250}{50} = 25$. The interval estimate therefore is, by using the value $k = 2.326$ from the normal distribution, $67 \pm 2.326(5/\sqrt{51}) = 67 \pm 1.63 = 65.37$ to 68.63. Using the t distribution with 50 degrees of freedom at the 98 percent confidence level gives us a k value of 2.40, whence

$$67 \pm 2.40 \frac{5}{\sqrt{51}} = 67 \pm 1.70 = 65.30 \text{ to } 68.70$$

9.13   The interval estimate of the mean is

$$\bar{x} \pm 2 \frac{s}{\sqrt{n}} = 480 \pm 2 \frac{\sqrt{19,500}}{\sqrt{150}}$$

$$= 480 \pm 22.8 = 457.2 \text{ to } 502.8$$

Therefore, the 95.45 percent confidence interval estimate of the total is 10,000(457.2) to 10,000(502.8) = 4,572,000 to 5,028,000 board feet.

9.14   We have $\bar{x} = 8.1$ ounces, and $s^2 = .49$; so $s = .7$. Looking under $n = 25$, $h = 95$ percent, and $j = 99$ percent, we find the tolerance interval

$$8.1 \pm 3.457 \times .7 = 8.1 \pm 2.42 = 5.68 \text{ to } 10.52$$

9.15   From Exercise 9.13 we know $\bar{x} = 480$, $s = 139.6$, and $n = 150$. The tolerance interval with 90 percent probability of including 95 percent of the trees is (in board feet)

$$\bar{x} \pm 2.127s = 480 \pm (2.127)(139.6)$$

$$= 480 \pm 297 = 183 \text{ to } 777$$

9.16   We can do better than be only 99 percent sure; we can be certain that 95 percent of all trips take $\mu \pm 1.96\sigma$ minutes or $3 \pm 1.96(.1) = 3 \pm .196 = 2.804$ to 3.196 minutes. This is because we *know* μ and σ.

9.17   The proportion in the sample is $\frac{22}{121}$, or $.18$. Using

$$\sqrt{.18 \times .82/121} = .035$$

for the standard deviation, we conclude that the true proportion is within the range $.18 \pm 1.645 \times .035$, or $.1225$ to $.2375$ with a probability of 90 percent.

9.18 $p = \frac{750}{900} = .833$, and the standard deviation is

$$\sqrt{.833 \times .167/900} = .0124$$

A 95 percent confidence interval is $.833 \pm 1.96 \times .0124 = .833 \pm .0243 = .8087$ to $.8573$.

9.19   Clearly, we will do well to use the value $p = .5$ for our computation. Then the standard deviation of **p** is $\sqrt{.5(1 - .5)}/\sqrt{n}$, which must be .001. Hence,

$$\frac{\sqrt{.5(1-.5)}}{\sqrt{n}} = .001$$

$$.5 = .001\sqrt{n}$$
$$500 = \sqrt{n}$$
$$250,000 = n$$

This is a very large sample!

9.20   A sample of size 100 has a maximum standard deviation of $\sqrt{.5(1-.5)}/\sqrt{100} = .05$. So with 95.45 percent confidence the true proportion will be between .40 and .60, and with 99.7 percent confidence the true proportion will be between .35 and .65. In fact, the election results showed the true value to be .667. (1) Though vastly unlikely, our sample result could occur due to the vagaries of sampling; a fair die might produce a total of 50 fives and sixes in 100 rolls. (2) More likely, the sample was biased, either because the sample of persons was biased, or because the question was wrongly phrased, or because the sample did not cover those who actually voted, etc. (3) It is also possible that in the intervening week opinions changed drastically in favor of one of the candidates, in which case some cause can usually be pinpointed.

9.21   We can apply the formula routinely and find

$$n = \frac{k^2\sigma^2}{e^2} = \frac{(2.576)^2(.52)^2}{(.07)^2} = 366$$

9.22   (a) Using the formula, we find

$$n = \frac{k^2\sigma^2}{e^2} = \frac{(1.645)^2(2)^2}{(.5)^2} = 43$$

(b) The interval will be narrower than 1 minute, which will give an estimate with greater precision than required. If σ is actually 1.5, a smaller sample would have sufficed.

(c) The interval will be wider than 1 minute and the desired precision has not been attained. If σ is actually 3 minutes, the required sample size would be 97. We must enlarge our sample by adding 54 observations.

9.23   Use the upper limit of the interval estimate of π in the old study, that is, 6 percent. The formula then gives

$$n = \frac{k^2 \pi (1 - \pi)}{e^2} = \frac{(2.576)^2 (.06)(.94)}{(.002)^2} = 93{,}564$$

Chapter 10

HYPOTHESIS TESTING: PROPORTION, MEAN, AND DIFFERENCE

10.1 BASIC CONCEPTS

If a student answers all 10 true-false questions on an examination correctly, the teacher will be convinced that the student is knowledgeable. Convinced, perhaps, but not certain. After all, someone who purely guesses may *by chance* be right all 10 times. Indeed, if we hypothesize that the student is only guessing, his chance of being right all 10 times is given by

$$C(n,k)\pi^k(1 - \pi)^{n-k} = C(10,10)\tfrac{1}{2}^k(1 - \tfrac{1}{2})^{n-k} = \tfrac{1}{1,024}$$

This is the binomial formula for the probability of $k = 10$ successes in $n = 10$ trials, when the probability of success at each trial is $\pi = \tfrac{1}{2}$. This value $\tfrac{1}{2}$ is a result of our hypothesis that the student purely guesses. Another way of looking at the value $\tfrac{1}{1,024}$ is that if 1,024 monkeys were to answer 10 true-false questions, we would expect one monkey to be right throughout purely by chance. That particular monkey would not be any smarter than another monkey who might be wrong throughout purely by chance.

Both teacher and students are quite aware of this element of guessing, but even so the teacher gives the student an A without serious misgivings.

Null
hypothesis
H_0

Alternative
hypothesis
H_1

If he were a statistician, the teacher would formally argue as follows: He would begin by formulating a *null hypothesis*. The null hypothesis is denoted by H_0 in shorthand, and the null serves to distinguish it from the *alternative hypothesis,* which is denoted by H_1. In our example the null hypothesis is

H_0:   The student purely guesses

The consequence of this H_0 is that, if true, the probability of answering a question, *any* question, correctly is $\pi = \frac{1}{2}$. The alternative hypothesis H_1 is, rather more vaguely, that the student does not purely guess, but gives somewhat knowledgeable answers. So far, the statistician has really added nothing but fancy terminology.

The teacher is then faced with the observed evidence that the student answers correctly 10 times out of 10. He is now on the horns of a dilemma:

Either the teacher sticks with H_0 (that the student purely guesses), but then he has to admit that something exceedingly unlikely happened—to be precise, something which has a probability of only $\frac{1}{1,024}$—*or* he rejects H_0, but then he must assume, in contrast, that the student is not purely guessing but knowledgeable.

At this point a second concept, *significance level, or level of signifi-cance,* enters the scene. The level of significance is always a percentage, usually 5 percent, but it can be set at 1, 10, 20 percent, or whatever, and it should be chosen with care, thought, and reason, as we will indicate below. Let us assume that the teacher sets the significance level at 5 percent. This implies *that H_0 will be rejected when the observed evidence has a less than 5 percent probability of occurring if H_0 is true.* In our example, since $\frac{1}{1,024}$ is much less than 5 percent, we reject the null hypothesis of purely guessing, and accept the idea that the student knows what he is doing.

By adopting a 5 percent significance level, we know that 5 percent of the time someone who purely guesses (perhaps one of the monkeys) will be considered knowledgeable. Thus by using a 5 percent level of significance the teacher is willing *to take as much as a 5 percent risk of concluding that a student is knowledgeable when he is not.*

We will give another example to illustrate the terminology and concepts. Suppose a pharmaceutical company wants to test the effectiveness of an anti-poison-ivy medicated cream. They send the cream to a doctor who specializes in poison ivy; they tell him they *believe* it is a very helpful medicine, but they want to be *sure*. The doctor answers that he will design a test in which the risk is no more than 1 percent that he will conclude that the cream is helpful when in fact it is not.

To do this, the doctor begins by formulating, as his null hypothesis,

H_0:   The cream is ineffective; it does not help

He will test this hypothesis at the 1 percent level of significance. This limits to 1 percent his chance of rejecting H_0 (and thus concluding that the cream is helpful) while H_0 in fact is true (the cream does not help).

To test this hypothesis, the doctor is fortunate in being located on Cape Cod, where during the summer, he sees 200 patients a week with the skin affliction. In the past, he used to give his patients a cream of inert and ineffective ingredients which he knew had no medical value, although it may have had some psychological value and helped control the itching. On the average, 70 percent of the patients so "treated" recovered in 3 days, by the mere passage of time. Now he gives his patients the new cream, and he tells them to come back 3 days later.

The empirical evidence obtained from his returning patients is that 160 out of the 200 patients are cured 3 days later. His past experience enables him to argue that if "H_0: the cream is ineffective" is true, the probability that an arbitrary patient will recover in 3 days is .70. He actually observes that 160 out of 200 patients treated with the medicated cream recover in 3 days. If each patient has a .70 probability of being cured, the probability that 160 out of 200 will be cured can be easily determined. We use the normal distribution to approximate the binomial, that is,

$$B(n = 200, \pi = .70) \approx N[\mu = n\pi = 140, \sigma = \sqrt{n\pi(1 - \pi)}$$
$$= \sqrt{200(.70)(.30)} = 6\tfrac{1}{2}]$$

The value 160 is 20 above the mean of 140, but when we take the continuity correction into account, it is only $19\tfrac{1}{2}$. The value $19\tfrac{1}{2}$ is precisely 3 standard deviations, $\sigma = 6\tfrac{1}{2}$, above the mean. Such values do not occur more than .13 percent of the time by the vagaries of chance.

To clinch the argument, the value .13 percent is less than the significance level of 1 percent, and so the doctor rejects the null hypothesis that the cream is ineffective, and instead accepts the company's claim that the cream is helpful. Incidentally, if the doctor had found only 120 patients recovered in 3 days, he would have been tempted to conclude that the medication is not only ineffective, but actually harmful. However, there is a little more to this seemingly innocuous conclusion than meets the eye, and we will therefore come back to this issue in the next section.

Choice of
significance
level

As for the appropriate *choice* of the level of significance, it should be noted that this level acts as a two-edged sword: On the one hand, it determines (limits) the risk you are willing to run of rejecting H_0 while it is in fact true (of concluding that a guessing student is knowledgeable or an ineffective cream is helpful). On the other hand, it automatically also influences the risk (probability) of accepting H_0, including the probability of accepting H_0 while it is false (of concluding that a knowledgeable student is guessing, or a helpful cream is ineffective). In Table 10.1 we illustrate these two possible errors, first in general terms, and then in the specific student application.

From Table 10.1 it should be clear that the problem arises in the first place because the state of nature is unknown. Is the student guessing? Or is he not? That is the problem. To find out, we give him 10 questions. It stands to reason that the more questions he answers correctly, the more inclined we will be to conclude that he is knowledgeable.

We can make two types of errors. We can conclude that he is not guessing when in fact he is. This is equivalent to rejecting H_0 while it is true. It is referred to as an *Error of Type I*, and is indicated in red throughout Table 10.1. *When we set the level of significance at 5 percent, we thereby limit the risk of an Error of Type I to 5 percent* (see Table 10.1*a*). At the 5 percent level of significance we accept that the student is knowledgeable when in truth he is purely guessing only if he is lucky enough to guess right 9 or 10 times out of 10.

By contrast, we can make the error of concluding that the student is purely guessing while in fact he is, at least somewhat, knowledgeable. This happens when we accept H_0 while it is false. It is referred to as an *Error of Type II*, and these errors are displayed in pink throughout Table 10.1. At the 5 percent level of significance we make an Error of Type II *if* the student is knowledgeable but, even so, not able to answer more than 8 out of the 10 questions correctly.

Review

In review, we have:

Error of Type I = reject H_0 when true (= conclude guessing student is knowledgeable)

Error of Type II = accept H_0 when false (= conclude knowledgeable student is guessing)

The level of significance determines the probability of making an Error of Type I.

At a 20 percent significance level we run a vastly *greater* risk of committing an Error of Type I. Omitting mathematical details, we should

**TABLE 10.1   TYPES OF ERRORS AND SIGNIFICANCE
LEVELS ILLUSTRATED**

(a)		Evidence indicates: Accept H_0	Evidence indicates: Reject H_0
Unknown state of nature	Null hypothesis, *True*	Correct!	Error of Type I Risk equal to significance level
	Null hypothesis, *False*	Error of Type II	Correct!

(b) Level of significance, 5 percent		Evidence indicates: Accept H_0	Evidence indicates: Reject H_0
Unknown state of nature	Null hypothesis, *True*	Correct!	Error! When student *by chance* answers 9 or 10 questions correctly
	Null hypothesis, *False*	Error! When student, though knowledgeable, answers 8 or fewer questions correctly	Correct!

(c) Level of significance, 20 percent		Evidence indicates: Accept H_0	Evidence indicates: Reject H_0
Unknown state of nature	Null hypothesis, *True*	Correct!	Error! When student *by chance* answers 7 or more questions correctly
	Null hypothesis, *False*	Error! When student, though knowledgeable, answers only 6 or fewer questions correctly	Correct!

conclude that a student is knowledgeable when in fact he is purely guessing if he is lucky enough to be right 7 times or more out of 10. (The probability is $\frac{120}{1,024} + \frac{45}{1,024} + \frac{10}{1,024} + \frac{1}{1,024} = \frac{176}{1,024} < 20$ percent.) As the other side of this coin we have a much *smaller* probability of concluding that the student is purely guessing while in fact he is somewhat knowledgeable: he only needs 7 or more correct answers, rather than 9 or more.

What, then, is the "correct" level of significance? One cannot tell, either in the abstract or even in many concrete situations. It is a balancing act between limiting, on the one hand, the probability of rejecting H_0 while true and on the other hand accepting H_0 while false. However, the following concrete suggestions can be made. If we have a great confidence in the null hypothesis, *or* if the consequences of rejecting H_0 while in fact it is true are very serious, we should use a very stringent significance level, such as 1 percent or even .1 percent. Such levels somewhat para-
High
significance
level
doxically are commonly called *high significance* levels, although the word *stringent* makes more sense. A judge, whose null hypothesis *must* be that the defendant is not guilty, should use a most stringent significance level to test this H_0, for the consequences of rejecting H_0 (concluding therefore that the defendant is guilty) when H_0 is true (the defendant is in fact not guilty) are very serious: an innocent victim would be jailed. Thus we say that the evidence must be convincing "beyond reasonable doubt," implying a very stringent significance level.

Low
significance
level
By contrast, if we have no great a priori faith in the null hypothesis, a lax, lenient, or low significance level can be used, such as 10 or 20 percent. A teacher who has had a student in his course will use a low level of significance when testing the hypothesis that the student is purely guessing, for this is unlikely to be true inasmuch as the student sat in on the course and therefore very likely picked up something from it. On the other hand, a student asking for a waiver of a calculus course because he knows calculus already will be given a test and judged at a much higher level of significance, for the teacher will be most unwilling to conclude that the student is knowledgeable when in fact he is bluffing his way through.

EXERCISES

10.1   Construct a table displaying the two types of error the doctor can make in testing H_0: The cream is ineffective, it does not help. How does this table change when the level of significance changes from 1 to 10 percent?

10.2   Mr. A comes in and claims that he can read your mind; that is,
        if you are thinking either "red" or "black," he can tell what you
        are thinking of. Mr. B comes in and states that he can taste the
        difference between cigarette X and cigarette Y by puffing without
        looking. Mr. C comes in and states that he can taste the difference
        between a cigar and a cigarette by puffing without looking. If
        you want to test these claims, which levels of significance seem
        appropriate?

10.2 TESTING HYPOTHESES—MEANS AND PROPORTIONS

The specific question we will test in this section is whether a stipulated   Testing
mean can indeed be believed to be the true mean. In the process of testing   means
this we will automatically review some of the highlights of the previous
section. Moreover, we will be somewhat more specific with respect to the
alternative hypothesis and its importance, and with respect to some
mathematical points. The concept of a critical region will be introduced.

  Quite often a claim is made concerning a product or a performance.
A manufacturer may claim, "These packages contain on the average 16
ounces." It is important for him that this be so, for it would be costly
to him if it were more, and quite unfortunate if it were less, because the
consumer would be displeased, *Consumer Report* would be on his back,
and the government would levy fines. How can the manufacturer's claim
be tested?

  The *first* step is to formulate a null hypothesis,   Four steps

  H_0:   The mean content of the packages is 16 ounces, neither
           more, nor less

It is, and always should be, a specific hypothesis. It says 16 ounces, not
about or approximately 16 ounces. Also, the alternative is twofold; it
should be neither more nor less. Thus we can formulate as the alternative
hypothesis H_1,

  H_1:   The mean content of the packages is not 16 ounces, but
           more or less

  The *second* step is to establish a level of significance. This ought
to be a matter for careful consideration. By asking, "What are the consequences of rejecting the null hypothesis if in fact it is true?" we can decide
to be very strict, that is, to use a 1 percent significance level if he is very

serious, and we can decide to be somewhat lenient, that is, to use a 10 or even a 25 percent level of significance if he is not so serious. In our example, rejection of the null hypothesis will have as a consequence summoning an engineer or maintenance man to have a look at the packaging machine. This will cost money, particularly if the machine has to be stopped to be serviced. This cost must be compared with the possible loss if the machine is permitted to continue systematically putting too little or too much in the container. After some soul searching, a 10 percent level of significance is set. This implies that one in ten times we will judge the mean to be different from 16 ounces when in fact it is not (Error of Type I), so that an engineer comes for nought and machine time is wasted.

The *third* step is to draw a sample and thus obtain empirical evidence. Suppose that the average content in a sample of size 49 is 15.82 ounces and that the estimate for the population variance σ^2, given by s^2, is

$$s^2 = \frac{(x_1 - \overline{x})^2 + (x_2 - \overline{x})^2 + \cdots + (x_n - \overline{x})^2}{n - 1} = .49$$

Then the variance of the sampling distribution of the average is estimated as

$$s_{\overline{x}}^2 = \frac{s^2}{n} = \frac{.49}{49} = .01$$

and hence the estimated standard deviation of the average $s_{\overline{x}}$ is .1.

In the *fourth* step we ask ourselves the following question, "If the true mean is 16 ounces (from the null hypothesis) and the estimated standard deviation of the sample average is .1 (from the sample result), within what symmetric interval around 16 ounces will 90 percent of the sampling distribution of the average be?" Figure 10.1 illustrates this question, and Table 10.2 summarizes the result in the columns marked "two tails." The values in this table have been found from the table of the normal distribution because we know from Section 9.3 that the sampling distribution of sample averages is normal, even if the original distribution is not, provided n is not too small. (For values of n less than 30 one should use the relevant values from the appropriate t distribution.)

From the table and the figure we see that 10 percent of the sample averages fall beyond 1.645 standard deviations above and below the hypothesized true mean of 16 ounces. We note that the actually observed average is 15.82, which is outside the interval $16 \pm 1.645 \times .1$. A result

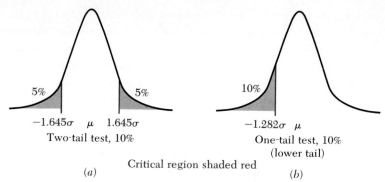

−1.645σ μ 1.645σ
Two-tail test, 10%

10%

−1.282σ μ
One-tail test, 10%
(lower tail)

Critical region shaded red
(a)   (b)

Figure 10.1 Comparison of two-tail and one-tail hypothesis test.

this far from the true mean will be found less than 10 percent of the time *if indeed the null hypothesis is true.* Such results fall in *the critical region.* We conclude that we *reject* the null hypothesis at the 10 percent *level of significance.* The size of the critical region equals the level of significance. If we had taken a 5 percent significance level, we would *not* have rejected the null hypothesis, since 15.82 is *not* in the critical region; it is *inside* the interval 16 ± 1.960 × .1.

    Three further observations on this example are in order. The first of these is that we took a *two-tail test* because the manufacturer does not like to give either too much or too little. When a two-tail test is used, the critical region is in two parts, one on each end of the sampling distribution. On the other hand, detectives from *Consumer Report* do not care about too *much;* they care about too *little.* They might want to test the hypothesis that the true mean is 16 ounces against the one-sided alternative that it is, in fact, less. If they were to test the null hypothesis at the 5 percent level of significance, they would use a *one-tail test,* as

Critical region

Two-tail test versus one-tail test

TABLE 10.2 **AREA UNDER *TWO TAILS* AND *SINGLE TAIL* OF NORMAL DISTRIBUTION FALLING MORE THAN *k* STANDARD DEVIATIONS FROM THE MEAN**

k	Area, percent Two tails	Single tail	k	Area, percent Two tails	Single tail
0	100	50	1.645	10	5
.675	50	25	1.960	5	2.5
1.150	25	12.5	2.326	2	1
1.282	20	10	2.576	1	.5

illustrated in Figure 10.1, for a 10 percent level of significance. In a one-tail test, the critical region is entirely on one end of the sampling distribution. Which end depends on the nature of the test. In this example it is the lower tail. In Figure 10.1 the lower tail is shaded because we only fear "too little." The argument in this case is that if the true mean is 16 ounces and the estimated standard deviation of the average of a sample of size 49 is .1, a result as low as 15.82 is more than 1.645 standard deviations below the mean, and a result so low or lower occurs less than 5 percent of the time owing to sampling variability. Therefore, at the 5 percent significance level the detectives reject the manufacturer's claim, in preference for the alternative assumption that the true mean is less than 16 ounces.

The second point is that the choice of the level of significance, as well as the choice between a one-tail and a two-tail test, depends on the purpose of the investigation. *These factors are inputs for the design, and they should be determined before the sample is drawn.* In other words, one should not *first* observe the 15.82 as sample average, and .1 as estimate for the standard deviation, and *then* decide on the significance level and the type of test. As we saw above, we could get the desired result, whether rejecting or accepting the null hypothesis, by taking a two-tail test and using either the 10 or the 5 percent significance level. To prevent such juggling to get results to suit our fancy, we specify the type of test and the significance level in advance, as we did in steps 1 and 2.

The third observation is that, once again, there are two possible errors. It is possible that we reject the null hypothesis while it is, in fact, true. This is an Error of Type I. The probability of such an error has been specified before as the level of significance. The other possible error is to accept the null hypothesis when in fact the mean weight is not 16 ounces. This is an Error of Type II.

Reviewing these four steps, we begin with a claim which we formulate as a null hypothesis. The formulation of the hypothesis will indicate whether we should use a one-tail or a two-tail test. Next, we specify a level of significance. Then we determine a sample size and draw a sample to furnish the empirical data. If the sample result is in the critical region, we reject the null hypothesis, and thereby run a risk of at most the level of significance of committing an Error of Type I. If it is not in the critical region, we accept the null hypothesis, and thereby run some risk of committing an Error of Type II. The size of this risk cannot be specified as long as the alternative hypothesis is vague rather than specific. In this section, we tested the null hypothesis that the true package content was

16 ounces against the alternatives "it is different, whether greater or smaller" (a two-tail test) and "it is smaller" (a one-tail test). Clearly, these are not specific alternatives. A specific alternative would be, "The true mean is 15.7 ounces." Such specific alternatives will be taken up in Section 10.4.

Even when vague and unspecified, the formulation of the alternative hypothesis is no trivial matter: It determines whether a one-tail or a two-tail test is appropriate. Once formulated, one should stick with it. It is incorrect, perhaps one should say fraudulent, to view the evidence first and then formulate the alternative. We return to the doctor on Cape Cod to bring home this point more forcefully.

Since the pharmaceutical company claimed that the cream was helpful, the doctor tested

H_0:   The cream is ineffective; it does not help

The specification, "it does not help," implies that he tests one-sidedly. A two-sided test would be called for by "it neither helps nor hurts." Given his formulation, rejection of H_0 implies that the cream *does* help. A 1 percent significance level was specified, so in this case a 1 percent upper-tail test is called for. With $N(140, 6\frac{1}{2})$ any value above $140 + 2.920 \times 6\frac{1}{2} = 155.1$ is in the upper 1 percent tail. Therefore, if 156 or more persons recover, the doctor will reject H_0, and accept the alternative that the cream is helpful.

But what if only 120 people recover? The answer is that 120 is not in the critical region, and so we do not reject H_0. Yet, we feel uncomfortable, because the evidence leads us to suspect that the cream is actually harmful. The way to find out is to test

H_0:   The cream is ineffective; it does not harm

with a *new* sample of 200 patients coming in the next week. It is very tempting, but quite incorrect, to formulate the hypothesis or hypotheses after the evidence is in. The temptation should be resisted, since such behavior undermines all the probabilistic measurements. It *is* permissible to hold a small pilot study or trial sample to guide in the formulation of the alternative hypothesis (and even the null hypothesis), but then new samples should be drawn to test these hypotheses.

To test

H_0:   The true proportion is π_0; it is neither more nor less

Testing
proportions

at the 1 percent significance level, a sample of size n is drawn and the sample proportion p is determined. If p is *in* the critical region, that is *outside* the range $\pi_0 \pm 2.576\sqrt{\pi_0(1 - \pi_0)/n}$, the hypothesis is rejected. The value 2.576 is read from Table 10.2. To test

H_0:   The true proportion is π_0; it is not more

at the 1 percent significance level, one determines whether the sample proportion p is in the critical region, that is, beyond

$$\pi_0 + 2.326\sqrt{\pi_0(1 - \pi_0)/n}$$

This is a one-tail test.

EXERCISES

10.3   If a sample of size 170 gives observations $x_1, x_2, \ldots, x_{170}$ whose average is $\bar{x} = 119$ and whose sum of squared deviations from the average $(x_1 - \bar{x})^2 + (x_2 - \bar{x})^2 + \cdots + (x_{170} - \bar{x})^2 = 229,840$, test the hypothesis that the true mean in the population is 115 against the alternative hypothesis that the true mean is more than 115, at the 5 percent significance level. (These requirements were specified before the sample was drawn.) Do we accept the hypothesis?

10.4   The null hypothesis is that the population mean μ equals 58. The standard deviation σ of the population is known to be 7. Can we accept the hypothesis that $\mu = 58$, when tested against the hypothesis that μ is different from 58, at the 1 percent level of significance, if a sample of size 98 has an average of 63?

10.5   An airline must allocate available seating space between first-class passengers and economy-class passengers. The null hypothesis is that 20 percent of the passengers fly first-class, but management recognizes the possibility that the percentage could be more or less. A random sample of 400 passengers includes 70 passengers holding first-class tickets. Can the null hypothesis be rejected at the 10 percent level of significance?

10.6   A claim is made that a batch of bulbs has a mean lifetime of 2,000 hours. From past experience it is known that the standard deviation of the lifetimes is $\sigma = 100$ hours. A buyer specifies that he wants to test the claim against the alternative hypothesis that the mean burning time is, in fact, *below* 2,000 hours at the 2 percent significance level. A sample of size 25 is drawn, and the sample average is found to be 2,210 hours. Should the buyer accept the hypothesis that the mean lifetime of all bulbs in the population is 2,000 hours?

10.3 TESTING HYPOTHESES—DIFFERENCES

Consider the claim made by a manufacturer that nylon cord is stronger than cotton cord. He bases this claim on 200 tests—100 with the nylon and 100 with the cotton cord. The nylon cord breaks with weights averaging 102 pounds. The estimated standard deviation s, as computed from the sample, is 40. The standard deviation of the average $\sigma_{\bar{x}}$ is estimated by $s_{\bar{x}} = 40/\sqrt{100} = 4$ pounds. The cotton cord breaks with weights averaging 93 pounds. The estimated standard deviation s is 60, so the standard deviation of the average is estimated by $s_{\bar{x}} = 60/\sqrt{100} = 6$ pounds.

Difference in averages $\bar{x}_1 - \bar{x}_2$

To test this claim, let us agree to use a 10 percent level of significance and a one-tail test. We use a one-tail test because of the specific claim that the nylon cord is stronger, rather than simply *different* in strength, that is, stronger *or* weaker. In that case we would have used a two-tail test. In a case like this we assume as null hypothesis that there is *no difference* between the mean strength of nylon and that of cotton cord. Hence, we assume that the claim is *not* true; only if we *reject* the null hypothesis will we *accept* the claim made by the manufacturer.

It is helpful to compare this with the null hypotheses tested in the previous section. There we hypothesized that a mean or proportion had a specific value. Here we hypothesize that two means or proportions are *equal*, without the necessity of specifying what their value is.

The observed difference in the average breaking strengths is $102 - 93 = 9$ pounds. We must realize that this is a difference in sample averages and if we make 200 new tests the results will vary. The difference between another pair of sample averages could be, for example, 6 pounds, or even -3 pounds, which would happen if the cotton cord had the higher average breaking strength in the sample. The relevant question is, "What is the standard deviation of the *difference* between these sample averages?" The answer is that the standard deviation of the difference σ_d must be estimated by finding the square root of the sum of the estimated variances of the sample averages. In our example

$$\text{Estimated } \sigma_{\mathbf{d}} = s_{\mathbf{d}} = \sqrt{4^2 + 6^2} = \sqrt{52} = 7.2 \text{ pounds}$$

The values 4 and 6 are the estimated standard deviations of the average of nylon cords and cotton cords, respectively, as given above.

With this result we are in business. We use the sampling distribution of the difference $\mathbf{d}$ to test the hypothesis. The observed difference is 9, and under the null hypothesis that there is in fact no difference in strength between the cords, the expected value of $\mathbf{d}$ is zero. The value 9 is 1.25 standard deviations above zero ($9 = 1.25 \times 7.2$). With a 10 percent level of significance and a one-tail test, a difference is not significant unless the observed value exceeds the expected value by 1.282 standard deviations. At the 10 percent significance level, therefore, the result is not significant. We accept the null hypothesis that there is no difference, and we reject the manufacturer's claim on the basis of this evidence.

The formula for $s_{\mathbf{d}}$ can be derived by using the results shown in Section 6.5.

$$
\begin{aligned}
V\mathbf{d} &= V(\bar{\mathbf{x}}_1 - \bar{\mathbf{x}}_2) \\
&= V[\bar{\mathbf{x}}_1 + (-1)\bar{\mathbf{x}}_2] && \text{(write differently)} \\
&= V\bar{\mathbf{x}}_1 + V[(-1)\bar{\mathbf{x}}_2] && [\text{use } V(\mathbf{x}_1 + \mathbf{x}_2) = V\mathbf{x}_1 + V\mathbf{x}_2] \\
&= V\bar{\mathbf{x}}_1 + (-1)^2 V\bar{\mathbf{x}}_2 && (\text{use } Vk\mathbf{x} = k^2 V\mathbf{x}) \\
&= V\bar{\mathbf{x}}_1 + V\bar{\mathbf{x}}_2 && \text{(rewrite)} \\
&= \sigma_{\bar{\mathbf{x}}_1}^2 + \sigma_{\bar{\mathbf{x}}_2}^2
\end{aligned}
$$

We use the sample variance $s_{\bar{\mathbf{x}}_1}^2$ and $s_{\bar{\mathbf{x}}_2}^2$ to estimate $\sigma_{\bar{\mathbf{x}}_1}^2$ and $\sigma_{\bar{\mathbf{x}}_2}^2$, and find

$$s_{\mathbf{d}} = \sqrt{s_{\bar{\mathbf{x}}_1}^2 + s_{\bar{\mathbf{x}}_2}^2}$$

The formula is only valid if the observations on the cotton and the nylon cords are *independent,* a requirement which was also needed for the result in Section 6.5 that the variance of a sum of random variables is the sum of their variances.

Difference in proportions $p_1 - p_2$

Our second example, as far as the argument is concerned, is identical with the previous example. The mathematics, however, is a little different because we will make a claim concerning proportions. Let the claim be made that upstate New York contains a greater proportion of Republicans than New York City. To test this claim, we assume as null hypothesis that there is *no difference* in the proportion of Republicans between upstate and city residents. We will test this hypothesis at the 10 percent level of significance, and will obviously use a one-tail test, since the claim is specifically that upstate is *more* Republican.

Suppose we take random samples of size 225 in the city, and of size 100 upstate. We observe that 81 of the 225 city residents are Republicans, for a sample percentage $p_1 = 36$ percent. We find that 43 of the 100 upstaters are Republicans, for a percentage $p_2 = 43$ percent. Is this difference of 7 percentage points significant? To determine this, we need the standard deviation of the difference in proportions. This is our next task.

One way to proceed is to argue that the variance of the proportion $p_1 = .36$, based on a sample of size 225, equals $.36 \times .64/225 = .2304/225$. Similarly the variance of the proportion $p_2 = .43$, based on a sample of size 100, equals $.43 \times .57/100 = .2451/100$. The estimate of the standard deviation of the difference is then, by using the same result as in the previous example,

$$s_d = \sqrt{\frac{.2304}{225} + \frac{.2451}{100}} = \sqrt{.003475} = .059$$

There is one objection against this procedure: it is somewhat illogical. The null hypothesis is that there is no difference between the proportions. If that is true, the best estimate of the overall proportion is

$$\frac{81 + 43}{225 + 100} = \frac{124}{325} = .382 \text{ or } 38.2 \text{ percent}$$

Hence, we do best by estimating the variances of the two proportions p_1 and p_2 by $.382 \times .618/225$ and $.382 \times .618/100$, respectively. Numerically, this does not make much difference, but philosophically it is much more appealing. We then get

$$s_d = \sqrt{\frac{.382 \times .618}{225} + \frac{.382 \times .618}{100}} = \sqrt{.00341} = .0584$$

Armed with this value, we close the discussion by observing that .07 is about 1.2 standard deviations ($.07 = 1.2 \times .0584$) from the hypothesized value of zero, and such a deviation is just less than the 1.28 standard deviations needed for significance at the 10 percent level. We accept the null hypothesis of no difference, and reject the claim.

In general, if a sample of size n_1 has a proportion of successes p_1 and a second sample of size n_2 has a proportion of successes p_2, the best estimate of the true proportion in the population under the null hypothesis

that the samples have been drawn from populations with the same proportion of successes is

$$p = \frac{n_1 p_1 + n_2 p_2}{n_1 + n_2}$$

The estimated standard deviation of the difference, $\mathbf{d} = (\mathbf{p_1} - \mathbf{p_2})$, is given by

$$s_\mathbf{d} = \sqrt{\frac{p(1 - p)(n_1 + n_2)}{n_1 n_2}}$$

These formulas are equivalent to the ones used in the preceding example.

Paired observations

In the two examples we have just seen, the members of the two samples were completely different—different pieces of cord in the first example and different voters in the second. There was no matching or pairing of members in the two samples. On the other hand, suppose we select a sample of accounts in a savings and loan association to study the change in balances during a year. Management may want to test its suspicion that balances have been declining during the year. We sample 100 accounts and record the balance in each account at the beginning of the year and at the end of the year.

We must recognize that, while we have 100 beginning-of-the-year balances and 100 end-of-the-year balances, we have only *one sample* of 100 accounts. If we are interested in testing the null hypothesis that the mean change in balance during the year was \$0, we must work with the 100 changes that are found by subtracting the beginning-of-the-year balance from the end-of-the-year balance for each account. We will represent change by a random variable $\mathbf{c}$, and the particular changes found for these accounts by $c_1, c_2, \ldots, c_{100}$. The average change is

$$\bar{c} = \frac{c_1 + c_2 + \cdots + c_{100}}{100}$$

and the estimated variance is

$$s_c^2 = \frac{(c_1 - \bar{c})^2 + (c_2 - \bar{c})^2 + \cdots + (c_{100} - \bar{c})^2}{100 - 1}$$

We proceed as usual to test the hypothesis that the mean change $\mu_\mathbf{c}$ is \$0 by finding

$$s_{\bar{c}} = \frac{s_c}{\sqrt{n}}$$

and verifying whether $\bar{c}$ lies in the critical region for the given level of significance.

In our example, let $\bar{c} = -\$50$ and $s_c = \$200$. Using a 99 percent significance level gives as critical region the region to the left of

$$\$0 - 2.326 \frac{200}{\sqrt{100}} = -\$46.52$$

since we are concerned about the possibility that balances have declined. Our $\bar{c} = -\$50$ is less than $-\$46.52$, that is, farther to the left on the left tail of the sampling distribution of $\bar{c}$; therefore we conclude the mean change per account was not $\$0$, but a minus value.

The use of *paired observations,* where possible, affords valuable savings in sampling costs. When separate samples are used there is great variability *within* each sample. This tends to overshadow the variability *between* the samples. The variability between cotton and nylon cords was swamped by the variability among the cotton cords themselves and nylon cords themselves.

EXERCISES

10 7   A man claims that he can distinguish the difference between Pepsi and Coca Cola. He is given six glasses, and he correctly identifies them all. Is this result significant at the 5 percent level?

10.8   A supervisor claims that employee A is faster than employee B. The average time A needs for a transaction is 60 seconds. This average has a standard deviation of 3 seconds. The average time B needs for a transaction is 65 seconds. This average has a standard deviation of 2 seconds. Is the supervisor right?

10.9   The proportion of defectives in a sample of size 400 from a product delivered by Company A is .14. The proportion of defectives of an identical product delivered by Company B is .10. The latter value is based on a sample of size 600. Can we make any claim concerning different qualities?

10.10   To verify whether a course in accounting improved performance, a similar test was given to 12 participants both before and after the course. The original grades—recorded in alphabetical order of the participants—were 44, 40, 61, 52, 32, 44, 70, 41, 67, 72, 53, and 72. After the course, the grades were, in the same order, 53, 38, 69, 57, 46, 39, 73, 48, 73, 74, 60, and 78.

(a) Was the course useful, as measured by performance on the test? Consider these 12 participants as a sample from a population.

(b) Would the same conclusion be reached if the tests were not considered paired?

10.4 STATISTICAL DECISION RULES

In this section and the following ones we will discuss some further complications which arise when the alternative hypothesis is as specific as the null hypothesis. The example may appear somewhat artificial, but it is easy to understand and helps illustrate the important features very nicely. The same example will be tackled differently in Chapter 12.

A computer manufacturer is offered a batch of transistors for sale. He would like to accept the batch, provided its quality is not too bad. In Table 10.3 the value of the transistors to the manufacturer over and above the price he has to pay is given. This value depends on the percentage of defectives in the batch. If it is .05 or less, the manufacturer should accept the batch. If it is .06 or more, he should not use the transistors. Since the true percentage of defectives is unknown, the manufacturer is faced with a difficult dilemma.

To find his way out of this dilemma, he decides to take a sample from the batch. He samples 225 items, and finds 9 of them defective.

TABLE 10.3 VALUE OF BATCH TO MANUFACTURER, GIVEN A PARTICULAR PERCENTAGE OF DEFECTIVES

Defectives in batch, percent	Value of batch to manufacturer
1	$10,000
2	8,000
3	6,000
4	4,000
5	2,000
6	−$ 500
7	−$ 3,500

The sample proportion of defectives is

$$p = \tfrac{9}{225} = .04$$

According to Section 9.6, an interval estimate for the true percentage of defectives in the batch π with a confidence level of 95.45 percent is given by

$$p \pm 2\sqrt{\frac{p(1-p)}{n}} = .04 \pm 2\sqrt{\frac{.04 \times .96}{225}} = .04 \pm 2(.013)$$

or from .014 to .066. The most relevant point to observe is that the interval extends on either side of .05. If the manufacturer decides to accept, he cannot be sure that he will not regret this decision later. By the same token, if he rejects the batch he may regret the decision later, since there may actually be only .03 defectives. The sample has not really helped the manufacturer solve his dilemma.

Progress can be made if we request him to be more specific. In particular, four further items of information are needed. The first is a percentage of defectives *so low* that he would be "extremely reluctant" to reject the batch. This percentage will be denoted by π_0, and we will assume π_0 is .03. The second is a percentage of defectives *so high* that he would "really hate" to accept the batch. This percentage will be denoted by π_1. In our numerical illustration we will assume π_1 is .07. In more statistical terminology, we have "H_0: The true percentage of defectives is $\pi_0 = 3$ percent" and "H_1: The true percentage of defectives is $\pi_1 = 7$ percent." These are both quite specific hypotheses.

The third and fourth items will require the manufacturer to define more carefully what he means by "extremely reluctant" and "really hate." If π_0, the true percentage of defectives, is .03, he would be extremely reluctant to reject the batch. However, he must recognize that certainty, if it can be had at all, is expensive. It may require a complete testing of every single transistor. Hence, we request him to specify a level of risk he is willing to run. We will denote this level by r_0. In our illustration we will take $r_0 = 10$ percent. This risk level implies that *if* π_0 is .03, he wants to have a probability of at most 10 percent of rejecting the batch, which is the decision he is extremely reluctant to make.

Analogously, the knowledge that the manufacturer really hates to buy if $\pi_1 = .07$ should be made more specific by giving a risk level. We will denote this risk level by r_1. In our illustration we will assume that $r_1 = 10$ percent. This means that if $\pi_1 = .07$, he is willing to run a risk of at most 10 percent of accepting the batch, the decision he really hates. In more statistical terminology, the Error of Type I (rejecting H_0 while true), as well as the Error of Type II (accepting H_0 while false, *or*, what amounts to the same thing, rejecting H_1 while true), is set at 10 percent.

In summary, our manufacturer states, "If the shipment contains $\pi_0 = .03$ defectives, I want to have a probability of rejecting the batch at most equal to $r_0 = 10$ percent. If the shipment contains $\pi_1 = .07$ defectives, I want to have a probability of accepting the batch of at most $r_1 = 10$ percent."

It is only the *form* of this statement which is relevant here. He might have said, "If $\pi_0 = .04$, I want to reject with at most $r_0 = 5$ percent probability, while if $\pi_1 = .06$ I want to accept with at most $r_1 = 1$ percent probability." In fact, this seems much better, and the question may well be asked why he does not say that. The answer is that the size of the sample needed to guarantee such strict criteria may be excessively large, and the sampling, therefore, prohibitively expensive.

With the information now provided, the next step on the road to progress is to compute the probabilities that a sample of size 225 will contain 0, 1, 2, . . . defectives *if indeed* the true proportion of defectives $\pi_0 = .03$. Similarly, we compute the probabilities that there will be 0, 1, 2, . . . defectives in a sample of size 225 *if indeed* the true proportion of defectives is $\pi_1 = .07$. This is the familiar routine used in Sections 7.2, 7.5, and 7.6. We repeat the highlights here.

If $\pi = .03$, the probability that a sample of 225 will contain exactly k defectives is given by

$$C(225,k)(.03)^k(.97)^{225-k}$$

according to the binomial distribution. If π and n are not too small, we can approximate this binomial distribution with the normal distribution, with mean $\mu = n\pi = 6.75$ and standard deviation $\sigma = \sqrt{n\pi(1 - \pi)} = \sqrt{225(.03)(.97)} = 2.56$. In this case, π is rather small, and, although $n\pi$ is just over 5, the Poisson approximation is a little more accurate. According to the Poisson formula, the probability of exactly k successes when $n = 225$ and $\pi = .03$, and therefore $n\pi = 6.75$, equals

$$e^{-6.75}\frac{(6.75)^k}{k!}$$

Whichever version is used, the results will be approximately the same. Using the exact binomial, the results are as recorded in Table 10.4.

**TABLE 10.4   PROBABILITY THAT
A SAMPLE OF SIZE
225 LEADS TO
k DEFECTIVES FOR
$\pi_0 = .03$ AND $\pi_1 = .07$**

k	$\pi_0 = .03$	$\pi_1 = .07$
0	.1	
1	.7	
2	2.5	
3	5.8	
4	10.0	
5	13.7	.1
6	15.6	.2
7	15.1	.6
8	12.7	1.2
9	9.5	2.2
10	6.3	3.5
11	3.8	5.2
12	2.1	7.0
13	1.1	8.6
14	.5	9.8
15	.2	10.4
16	.1	10.3
17		9.5
18		8.3
19		6.8
20		5.3
21		3.9
22		2.7
23		1.8
24		1.1
25		.7
26		.4
27		.2
28		.1
29		.1
30		
	1	1

Statistical
decision rule
and critical
value

These results are quite instructive. We see that we should *accept* the batch if there are 10 or fewer defectives in the sample of 225 and *reject* the batch if there are more than 10 defectives, as illustrated in the table. Such a rule is known as a *statistical decision rule*. The value 10 is known as the *critical value*. A statistical decision rule specifies the appropriate decision to take for each possible sample outcome. In our case the decision rule is: Accept with 10 or fewer defectives in a random sample of size 225; reject otherwise. Under this rule we *reject* a batch when $\pi_0 = .03$ with a probability of

$$3.8 + 2.1 + 1.1 + .5 + .2 + .1 = 7.8 \text{ percent}$$

and we *accept* a batch when $\pi_1 = .07$ with a probability of

$$3.5 + 2.2 + 1.2 + .6 + .2 + .1 = 7.8 \text{ percent}$$

Both percentages—which by pure coincidence happen to be equal—are well below 10 percent, and we have met the manufacturer's requirement. Any other critical value would violate one of the requirements. For example, if the critical value is 9, we accept with 9 or fewer defectives, and reject with 10 or more. We then reject 14.1 percent of the good batches. However, we would only accept 4.3 percent of the bad batches, which is an improvement.

A number of questions and problems remain. As an illustration, suppose the buyer wished to limit his risk to 5 percent rather than 10 percent in both cases. The evidence in Table 10.4 indicates that this is too ambitious a requirement. It can only be met when we increase the sample size. We will come back to that question in the next section.

EXERCISES

10.11   If a manufacturer decides to accept when 11 or fewer items are defective in a sample of 225, what is the probability of accepting a batch with .07 defectives?

10.12   A market research company wants to test whether a new package design is preferred by customers. The question is whether old design X or new design Y is preferred. The decision is either to keep X, or change to Y. The company states that if the new design Y is in fact preferred by $\pi = .60$ of the population, we ought to accept the new design with a probability of at least 95 percent. On the other hand, if the new design is preferred by only .50, it ought to be rejected (in view of the substantial cost of making the change) with 85 percent probability. A sample of size 100 is to be drawn. Determine the critical value which provides the desired probability of making the correct decision, if that is possible.

10.13 Review your results in Exercise 10.12. Try a sample of size 196. Find the appropriate critical value in this case.

10.5 DETERMINATION OF SAMPLE SIZE AND CRITICAL VALUE

As we saw in the previous section, the decision criterion is expressed in terms of two specific alternative values of the parameter, for example, $\pi_0 = .03$ and $\pi_1 = .07$, or $\pi_0 = .50$ and $\pi_1 = .60$, and the maximum acceptable risk of reaching the wrong conclusion if one or the other of the alternatives is true, for example, $r_0 = 10$ percent and $r_1 = 10$ percent, or $r_0 = 5$ percent and $r_1 = 15$ percent. *The choice of these values π_0 and π_1 and their associated risks r_0 and r_1 is the task of the decision maker.* Once they are specified, the statistician takes over for the more technical aspects of the problem.

The first problem is to determine the *minimum* sample size n needed to meet the specifications. This is a problem which can best be explained with the help of a picture such as the one shown in Figure 10.2. In this figure we assume that n is known already, as well as two alternatives π_0 and π_1, and their associated risks. We can always assume that π_0 is *smaller* than π_1, and in the figure we furthermore assume that r_0 is 10 percent and r_1 is 5 percent. The critical value should then be such that 10 percent

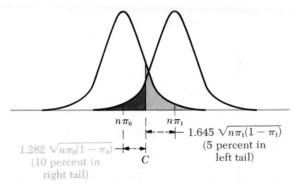

Figure 10.2 Relationship between sample size and critical value.

of the area is in the right tail of the sampling distribution for π_0, and 5 percent of the area is in the left tail of the sampling distribution for π_1.

We will interpret Figure 10.2 in more detail. If we draw a sample of size n from a population with a parameter π_0, the number of successes in the sample will be approximately normally distributed with mean $n\pi_0$ and standard deviation $\sqrt{n\pi_0(1 - \pi_0)}$. This is the normal curve on the left side in Figure 10.2. Similarly, the distribution of the number of successes in the sample if the parameter is π_1 is approximately normal, with mean $n\pi_1$ and standard deviation $\sqrt{n\pi_1(1 - \pi_1)}$. This is the normal curve on the right side in Figure 10.2.

Because π_0 is smaller than π_1, it stands to reason that *if* the number of successes in the sample is *below* a certain critical value, we will conclude that the true proportion is π_0; otherwise, we will conclude that it is π_1, and act accordingly. However, it is possible that, although π_0 is true, the sample number of successes will exceed this critical value, and we will erroneously conclude that π_1 is true. The *risk* of this occurrence, however, must be limited to 10 percent, and thus the pink shaded area in the upper tail to the right of the critical value should be 10 percent.

From our table of the normal distribution, Table 7.4, we know that the 10 percent of the area under the normal curve in the upper tail corresponds to values at least 1.282 standard deviations above the mean. For the sake of convenience we give in Table 10.5 the relevant values

Table 10.5   **AREA UNDER**
             ***SINGLE* TAIL OF**
             NORMAL
             DISTRIBUTION
             FALLING MORE
             THAN k STANDARD
             DEVIATIONS FROM
             THE MEAN

Area, percent	k
1	2.326
2	2.054
$2\frac{1}{2}$	1.960
5	1.645
10	1.282
20	.892
25	.675

for the specified risks. If we specify a risk of 2 percent, this corresponds to values at least 2.054 standard deviations above the mean.

In our example $r_0 = 10$ percent, and so we know that when the sample value falls *above*

$$n\pi_0 + 1.282 \sqrt{n\pi_0(1 - \pi_0)}$$

or in general,

$$n\pi_0 + k_0 \sqrt{n\pi_0(1 - \pi_0)}$$

we take a risk of at most 10 percent of being wrong when we conclude that π_1 is true. Also, $r_1 = 5$ percent, and so we know that when the sample value falls *below*

$$n\pi_1 - 1.645 \sqrt{n\pi_1(1 - \pi_1)}$$

or in general,

$$n\pi_1 - k_1 \sqrt{n\pi_1(1 - \pi_1)}$$

we take a risk of at most 5 percent of being wrong when we conclude that π_0 is true. The minus sign arises because if π_1 is true, the sample values which may lead us to the wrong conclusions are *less* than π_1; that is, the *lower* tail represents the danger, shown by red shading in Figure 10.2. Since these expressions define the same number, the critical value, the minimum value of the sample size n which allows us to satisfy both criteria is obtained when they are equal, as in the figure. Thus we have

$$n\pi_0 + 1.282 \sqrt{n\pi_0(1 - \pi_0)} = n\pi_1 - 1.645 \sqrt{n\pi_1(1 - \pi_1)}$$

After a little algebra we find as the general expression for n

$$n = \left(\frac{k_0 \sqrt{\pi_0(1 - \pi_0)} + k_1 \sqrt{\pi_1(1 - \pi_1)}}{\pi_1 - \pi_0} \right)^2$$

Sample size for decision rule for proportion

The factors k in this formula can be read from Table 10.5 once the acceptable risks have been given.

In the previous section we had a situation where $\pi_0 = .03, \pi_1 = .07$, $r_0 = 10$ percent, and $r_1 = 10$ percent, so that $k_0 = k_1 = 1.282$. Substitution and computation give

$$n = \left(\frac{1.282 \sqrt{.03 \times .97} + 1.282 \sqrt{.07 \times .93}}{.07 - .03} \right)^2 = 185$$

So *theoretically* a sample of size 185 would have been sufficient. In fact, n was 225, and the extra margin allowed us to limit the risks r_0 and r_1 to 7.8 percent and 7.8 percent, rather than exactly 10 percent.

The word theoretically is emphasized because as a practical matter n ought to be a little larger than the strict minimum. The main reason for this is that the number of successes is, by necessity, an integer value, while in the picture and the analysis, everything is continuous.

Once the sample size has been determined, the only matter that remains is to determine the critical value. Sample results below or at the critical value lead us to conclude that π_0 is true, while sample results above it lead us to conclude that π_1 is true. The critical value should be at or above

$$n\pi_0 + k_0\sqrt{n\pi_0(1 - \pi_0)}$$

The critical value should be at or below

$$n\pi_1 - k_1\sqrt{n\pi_1(1 - \pi_1)}$$

These last two expressions are equal if n is chosen exactly equal to the minimum sample size needed to meet the requirements. If, however, we use a somewhat bigger value of n in view of the continuity problem, there will be a margin between them.

As an example, consider again the case where $\pi_0 = .03$, $\pi_1 = .07$, $r_0 = r_1 = 10$ percent, and $n = 225$. Then all values *above*

$$225 \times .03 + 1.282\sqrt{225 \times .03 \times .97} = 10.02$$

and all values *below*

$$225 \times .07 - 1.282\sqrt{225 \times .07 \times .93} = 10.83$$

will do. Luckily the value 10.50 is above 10.02 and below 10.83. Since only integer values are possible, all integer values up to 10 will lead to acceptance of π_0, and all integer values of 11 or more will lead to acceptance of π_1. This is indeed the result we found above. In general the value of n should be large enough that the range between

$$n\pi_0 + k_0\sqrt{n\pi_0(1 - \pi_0)} \quad \text{and} \quad n\pi_1 - k_1\sqrt{n\pi_1(1 - \pi_1)}$$

includes a "$\frac{1}{2}$ value," for example, $10\frac{1}{2}$ or $14\frac{1}{2}$. The critical value—the highest value for which we accept π_0—will be the largest integer smaller than this $\frac{1}{2}$ value.

The last two sections have introduced relatively many new concepts.

In the closing paragraphs of this section we give the parallel argument for a continuous normally distributed variable. We want to test whether this variable has a mean μ_0 against the alternative that it has a mean μ_1. An automobile manufacturer considers buying car windows made from a new type of safety glass. The glass is alleged to be able to withstand, on the average, a pressure of 500 pounds per square inch (psi). In short, the mean breaking strength is claimed to be 500 psi. The breaking strength is normally distributed with a standard deviation of 50 psi.

Currently, the automobile manufacturer uses windows with an average breaking strength of 470 psi. He decides to test the new windows, with $\mu_0 = 500$ psi, $\mu_1 = 470$ psi, $r_0 = 10$ percent, and $r_1 = 5$ percent. In words, this means that *if* the true mean breaking strength is indeed 500 psi, the manufacturer is willing to run a risk of 10 percent of not recognizing this—and thereby continuing to use the inferior glass presently used. On the other hand, if the true mean breaking strength of the new windows is 470 psi—just like the windows in current use—he is willing to take at most a 5 percent risk of changing.

In view of the destructive character of the testing, the sample size is limited to 25. The standard deviation of the average of this sample equals $\sigma_{\bar{x}} = \sigma/\sqrt{n} = 50/\sqrt{25} = 10$ psi. In this example μ_1 is smaller than μ_0. A high sample average will tend to confirm μ_0, and a low sample average to confirm μ_1. Since $r_0 = 10$ percent, there should be at most 10 percent of the area of the sampling distribution of $\bar{x}$, that is, a normal curve with mean μ_0 and standard deviation 10, in the lower tail. A value of

$$\mu_0 - k_0\sigma_{\bar{x}} = 500 - 1.282(10) = 487.18 \text{ psi}$$

leaves 10 percent in the lower tail. Similarly, a value of

$$\mu_1 + k_1\sigma_{\bar{x}} = 470 + 1.645(10) = 486.45 \text{ psi}$$

leaves 5 percent in the upper tail of the sampling distribution of $\bar{x}$, a normal curve with mean μ_1 and standard deviation 10. Therefore, any value between 486.45 and 487.18 can serve as critical value. We choose 487 as critical value. If the sample average of breaking strength of 25 new windows is less than 487 psi, the manufacturer should stay with the windows currently in use. If the sample average is more, he should switch to the new windows. This is his decision rule.

You might think that the manufacturer was lucky that all his requirements could be met by a sample of size 25. Indeed, we suggested in the above paragraph that the value $n = 25$ was chosen more or less arbitrarily.

Sample size and critical value for decision rule for mean

However, there was solid reasoning behind the choice. The manufacturer reasoned that the critical value should be such that

$$\mu_1 + k_1 \frac{\sigma}{\sqrt{n}} = \mu_0 - k_0 \frac{\sigma}{\sqrt{n}}$$

from which we can derive n explicitly as

$$n = \frac{\sigma^2 (k_0 + k_1)^2}{(\mu_1 - \mu_0)^2}$$

This is the general formula for the sample size needed when a decision rule involves a mean. It is valid whether μ_0 is smaller or larger than μ_1. By using the numerical values given in our example, this gives

$$n = \frac{(50)^2 (1.282 + 1.645)^2}{(470 - 500)^2} = \frac{2,500 \times 8.57}{900} = 23.8$$

so that a sample size of 25 is ample. In the continuous case there is no need for a continuity correction, of course. The critical value can be found from

$$\mu_0 \pm k_0 \frac{\sigma}{\sqrt{n}} \qquad \text{and} \qquad \mu_1 \pm k_1 \frac{\sigma}{\sqrt{n}}$$

where the appropriate signs depend on whether $\mu_0 < \mu_1$ or $\mu_0 > \mu_1$.

EXERCISES

10.14   A consumer decides to switch from cigarette A to cigarette B if the mean content of tobacco in a package of cigarette B is higher. He knows that the mean weight of a package of cigarette A is .80 ounce. If the true mean weight of a package of cigarette B is .82 ounce, he wants to switch with a probability of 95 percent. If the true mean per package is only .80 ounce, he wants to stay with cigarette A with a probability of 75 percent. He buys 25 packages, and finds an average of .808 ounce. What does he do if it is known that the weight of cigarette packages has a standard deviation of .06 ounce?

10.15   An existing drug cures 40 percent of those who use it. A new drug is said to be better. Find the n and critical value to use in a trial designed to give a 10 percent risk of recommending the new drug when in fact it is no better, and a 5 percent risk of rejecting the new drug when in fact it cures 45 percent of those who use it.

10.16   In the example of the manufacturer who is offered transistors for sale, assume $\pi_0 = .04$, $\pi_1 = .06$, $r_0 = .05$, and $r_1 = .01$. How large should the sample size be?

10.17   A new feed mixture is advertised to increase chicken weights an average of .6 pound per week. Find the n and critical value for a decision rule to meet the following conditions: $\mu_0 = .60$, $\mu_1 = .55$, $r_0 = .05$, and $r_1 = .10$. Assume $\sigma = .1$.

10.18   The manufacturer of a grass seed mixture advertises that the mixture contains 20 percent bluegrass seed. Periodically, a sample of 144 seeds is taken and the composition studied, including counting bluegrass seeds. The decision rule used gives a 10 percent risk of saying the percentage of bluegrass is 30 when it is actually 20. What is the risk of concluding it is 20 when it is actually 30?

10.6   THE OPERATING CHARACTERISTIC CURVE

In the previous two sections one hypothesis, for example, $\pi_0 = .03$ or $\mu_0 = 500$ psi, is tested against another hypothesis, for example, $\pi_1 = .07$ or $\mu_1 = 470$ psi. In general, neither hypothesis will be precisely true, but that is not relevant for the process of decision making. What is relevant for decision making is that we want to decide on a decision rule, expressed in terms of n and a critical value, so that *if* $\pi_0 = .03$, we will reject the batch with at most 10 percent probability, and, *if* $\pi_1 = .07$, we will accept the batch with at most 10 percent probability. These requirements lead to the conclusion that if a sample of 225 contains 10 or fewer defectives, we should accept the batch, and if it contains more than 10 defectives, we should reject the batch. In fact, as we saw, the sample size could even be a little smaller.

Once this decision rule, that is, $n = 225$ and accept with 10 or fewer defectives, has been formulated, we can answer other questions, such as, "What is the probability of accepting the batch if the true percentage is 2 or 4 or 6 or 8 percent?" To find out, all we have to do is to determine the probability that a sample of size 225 contains 10 or fewer defectives *if* the true percentage of defectives is 2, 4, 6, or 8 percent. These results can be computed just as they were in Section 10.4 for the levels of 3 and 7 percent. They are given in Table 10.6. The red entries in this table are illustrated in Figure 10.3. From the four small illustrations in this figure we see that the critical value remains constant but that the area to the left of it gradually diminishes from 100 to practically 0 percent as the value of the true proportion of defectives moves from 0 to 10 percent. In particular, when $\pi_0 = .04$, then 70.7 percent of the area under the sampling distribution is to the left of the critical value, and so the probability of rejecting the batch is 29.3 percent. The probability of wrong decisions has been shaded in the figure. It will be clear that *really* good quality batches are nearly always accepted, while *truly* poor batches are nearly always rejected. If, however, the true percentage is between 4 and 6 percent, the probability of a wrong decision is rather high. However, it is important to recognize that the consequences of the decision, even when it is wrong, will not be terribly serious because the profits and losses are rather small in that range.

The first two columns of Table 10.6 are illustrated in Figure 10.4. The curve in Figure 10.4 is called an *operating characteristic curve*, and is referred to in the trade as an "OC curve." In an ideally discriminating test, if π is .055, the OC curve would look as in Figure 10.5. In general, the "steeper" the curve, the better the test. By increasing the sample size,

OC curve

TABLE 10.6

True π equals, percent	Probability of accepting, percent	Probability of rejecting, percent
0	100	0
1	100	0
2	99.7	.3
3	92.3	7.8
4	70.7	29.3
5	41	59
6	19.9	80.1
7	7.8	92.3
8	3.3	96.7
9	1.1	98.9
10	.1	99.9

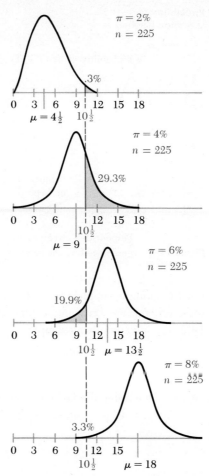

Figure 10.3 Probability of rejecting the lot as a function of π.

the curve can be made steeper, but only at a cost in time and money, that is, the cost of sampling. We will meet OC curves again in Chapter 17 on quality control.

The OC curve in Figure 10.4 also enables one to specify *both* the probability of making an Error of Type I associated with the null hypothesis $\pi_0 = .03$ (that is, rejecting the null hypothesis while true) *and* the probability of making an Error of Type II associated with the alternative hypothesis $\pi_1 = .7$ (that is, rejecting this alternative hypothesis while true). In our example both types of error had to be limited to 10 percent,

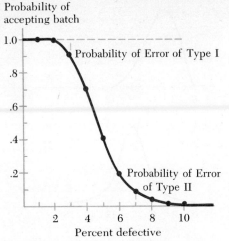

Figure 10.4 Typical operating characteristic curve.

but by taking a sample size of 225 rather than the 185 required to meet these criteria, we were able to limit the errors to 7.8 percent. In Exercise 10.21 we give another example.

EXERCISES

10.19 Determine the OC curve for the case where $\pi_0 = .50$, $\pi_1 = .60$, $r_0 = 10$ percent, and $r_1 = 5$ percent. Use $n = 225$ as the sample size.

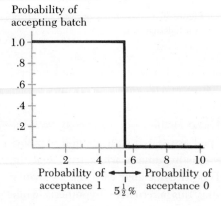

Figure 10.5 Ideal operating characteristic curve.

10.20 Determine the OC curve for the case where $\mu_0 = 500$ psi, $\mu_1 = 470$ psi, $r_0 = 10$ percent, $r_1 = 5$ percent, $n = 25$, and the critical value is 487. Assume $\sigma = 50$ psi; hence $\sigma_{\bar{x}} = 50/\sqrt{25} = 10$.

10.21 The null hypothesis that the true mean $\mu_0 = 16$ ounces is tested against the alternative hypothesis that the true mean $\mu_1 = 15.7$ ounces. The standard deviation of the average of a sample of size 49 is .1. What is the critical region if the risk of an Error of Type I (rejecting $\mu_0 = 16$ when it is true) is 5 percent? What is the risk of an Error of Type II (rejecting the alternative hypothesis $\mu_1 = 15.7$ when it is true)?

Answers to Exercises

10.1

		Evidence indicates: Accept H_0	Evidence indicates: Reject H_0
Unknown state of nature	Null hypothesis: cream ineffective, *True*	Correct!	Error of Type I, Prob. = significant level, ineffective cream judged helpful
	Null hypothesis, *False*	Error of Type II, helpful cream judged ineffective	Correct!

When the level of significance changes from 1 to 10 percent, it will be easier to make an Error of Type I, and more difficult to make an Error of Type II. If the cream in fact is ineffective, $140 + 2.326 \times 6\frac{1}{2}$, or 156 or more, out of 200 patients must recover in 3 days to conclude that the cream is helpful at the 1 percent level of significance. At the 10 percent level we would conclude this when $140 + 1.282 \times 6\frac{1}{2}$ or 149 or more recover. These computations will be further clarified in the next section.

10.2 For Mr. A a very stringent level is required, since such claims of extrasensory perception should not be taken jocularly, and since the a priori likelihood of such ability is small indeed. Thus, we use a 1 percent significance level, or better yet, .5 or .1 percent to test "H_0: Mr. A cannot read my mind." As for Mr. B, it is by no means impossible that he can, and not very important whether he can, so we rather gladly give him the benefit of the doubt and set the significance level at 10 percent or so. If, however, a heavy bet is made dependent on the result, the level should be higher, perhaps 5 percent. As for Mr. C, we think his claim is very likely true, and we can be content with a significance level of perhaps 20 percent. If we are, we would accept his claim if he is right three times out of three.

10.3 The variance in the population σ^2 is estimated by s^2, where

$$s^2 = \frac{(x_1 - \bar{x})^2 + (x_2 - \bar{x})^2 + \cdots + (x_n - \bar{x})^2}{n - 1}$$

$$= \frac{229,840}{169} = 1,360$$

The variance of the average of a sample of size 170 is then estimated as $s_{\bar{x}}^2 = s^2/n$, or $\frac{1,360}{170} = 8$, and the standard deviation of this average $s_{\bar{x}} = \sqrt{8} = 2.83$. If the true mean is 115 and the standard deviation of the average of a sample of size 170 is 2.83, the result 119 is not significant at the 5 percent level; that is, we accept the hypothesis $\mu = 115$ at the 5 percent level of significance. Only values higher than $115 + 1.645 \times 2.83 = 119.66$ would be significant at the 5 percent level.

10.4 The standard deviation of the population is 7, so the standard deviation of the average is $7/\sqrt{98} = .71$. Using the value 2.576 for a two-tail test at the 1 percent level of significance, we see that 63 is well outside the range $58 \pm 2.576 \times .71$. The null hypothesis $\mu = 58$ is rejected.

10.5 The critical region is any *outside*

$$\pi_0 \pm k\sqrt{\frac{\pi_0(1 - \pi_0)}{n}} = .20 \pm 1.645\sqrt{\frac{(.20)(.80)}{400}}$$

$$= .20 \pm .0329$$

The observed proportion of $\frac{70}{400} = .175$ is *not* outside this range. The null hypothesis cannot be rejected.

10.6 Yes. The critical region is given by all values at or below

$$\mu_0 - k\frac{\sigma}{\sqrt{n}} = 2{,}000 - 2.054\frac{100}{\sqrt{25}} = 1{,}959$$

The null hypothesis is *not* rejected. (The value 2,210 is in the wrong tail, so to speak—it is very probably true that the actual mean lifetime *exceeds* 2,000 hours.)

10.7 As null hypothesis we assume that our man *cannot* tell the difference, and that he purely guesses. The probability that he will be right on any one guess is $\frac{1}{2}$. If the null hypothesis is true, then a result where six out of six glasses are correctly identified has a probability of $(\frac{1}{2})^6$, or $\frac{1}{64}$. Hence such a result, when only due to chance, will happen but once in 64 times. This is well below 5 percent, and we reject the null hypothesis that he guesses, and accept his claim.

10.8 We cannot tell whether he is right, but we can say the following at the 5 percent (one-tail) significance level. The difference in the average time is 5 seconds, and the standard deviation of the difference is $s_d = \sqrt{3^2 + 2^2} = \sqrt{13} = 3.6$ seconds. The value 5 is nearly 1.4 standard deviations above zero; this is less than 1.645 needed for significance at the 5 percent level. So at the 5 percent level the observed difference is *not* significant. There is *more* than a 5 percent chance that such a result would occur from sampling fluctuations. At the 10 percent level of significance the result would be judged significant, and this once again shows the importance of specifying the significance level explicitly in advance, which the supervisor failed to do.

10.9 Let us assume that the qualities (i.e., the percentage of defectives) are the same, and let us test this against the alternative that they are different at the 5 percent level of significance. We therefore use a two-tail test. The observed difference is .04. If there is no difference, the best we can do is to estimate the true percentage of defectives at

$$\frac{400 \times .14 + 600 \times .10}{1{,}000} = 11.6 \text{ percent}$$

The standard deviation of the difference is therefore

$$s_d = \sqrt{\frac{.116 \times .884}{400} + \frac{.116 \times .884}{600}}$$

$$= \sqrt{.00042727} = .0207$$

The two-tail test at a 5 percent level of significance requires a difference of *more* than 1.960 standard deviations. We can compute that $1.960 \times .0207 = .0405$, which is just above the 4 percent difference observed; hence, at the 5 percent level of significance we cannot reject the null hypothesis that the percentage of defectives is the same, when tested against the alternative that the percentage of defectives from Company A and Company B are different.

10.10   (a) We clearly have a set of paired observations, with observed changes equal to

$$53 - 44 = 9$$
$$38 - 40 = -2$$
$$69 - 61 = 8$$
$$57 - 52 = 5$$
$$46 - 32 = 14$$
$$39 - 44 = -5$$
$$73 - 70 = 3$$
$$48 - 41 = 7$$
$$73 - 67 = 6$$
$$74 - 72 = 2$$
$$60 - 53 = 7$$
$$78 - 72 = 6$$

The null hypothesis that these changes are drawn from a normal distribution with mean 0 will be tested with a one-tail test at the 5 percent level of significance. We have $\bar{c} = \frac{60}{12} = 5$. Also

$$s_c^2 = \frac{(9 - 5)^2 + \cdots + (6 - 5)^2}{11} = \frac{278}{11} = 25.3$$

Thus $$s_{\bar{c}} = \frac{\sqrt{25.3}}{\sqrt{12}} = 1.45$$

We found $\bar{c} = 5$. This is more than $1.645 \times 1.45 = 2.39$. The result is significant, and we reject the null hypothesis of no difference and conclude that the mean difference in test scores in the population is positive; i.e., the course has a beneficial effect.

(b) If we do not recognize the paired sample and erroneously assume that the observations are independent, we have a first sample of 12 observations with an average score of

$$\frac{44 + 40 + \cdots + 72}{12} = 54$$

The variance s_1^2 estimated from this first sample is

$$s_1^2 = \frac{(44 - 54)^2 + (40 - 54)^2 + \cdots + (72 - 54)^2}{11}$$

$$= \frac{2,176}{11} = 198$$

The variance of the average is estimated as

$$s_{\bar{x}_1}^2 = \tfrac{198}{12} = 16.5$$

The second sample has an average of

$$\frac{53 + 38 + \cdots + 78}{12} = 59$$

The variance is estimated to be

$$s_2^2 = \frac{(53 - 59)^2 + (38 - 59)^2 + \cdots + (78 - 59)^2}{11}$$

$$= \frac{2,250}{11} = 205$$

The variance of the average is estimated from the second sample as

$$s_{\bar{x}_2}^2 = \tfrac{205}{12} = 17$$

The hypothesis that the true difference in means is zero can now be tested with a one-tail test at the 5 percent level of significance. The observed difference in the averages is $59 - 54 = 5$. We have

$$s_d = \sqrt{s_{\bar{x}_1}^2 + s_{\bar{x}_2}^2} = \sqrt{16.5 + 17} = \sqrt{33.5} = 5.8$$

Clearly 1.645×5.8 is greater than the observed difference of 5, so we accept the hypothesis and conclude that the means are equal and, therefore, that the course has no beneficial effect. Testing the inappropriate hypothesis of differences in the mean rather than the mean difference has led to the wrong conclusion. The variability *within* the exam results swamped the variability *between* the exam scores.

10.11   Looking back at Table 10.4 we find $5.2 + 3.5 + 2.2 + 1.2 + .6 + .2 + .1 = 13.0$ percent.

10.12   Consider $\pi_0 = .50, \pi_1 = .60$. Then $r_0 = 15$ percent and $r_1 = 5$ percent. In words, if in truth the new design is preferred by

PROBABILITY OF k SUCCESSES IN 100 TRIALS

k	$\pi_0 = .50$ (keep X)	$\pi_1 = .60$ (change to Y)
<42	6.7	
43	3.0	
44	3.9	
45	4.8	.1
46	5.8	.1
47	6.7	.3
48	7.4	.4
49	7.8	.7
50	8.0	1.0
51	7.8	1.5
52	7.4	2.1
53	6.7	2.9
54	5.8	3.8
55	4.8	4.8
56	3.9	5.8
57	3.0	6.7
58	2.2	7.4
59	1.6	7.9
60	1.1	8.1
61	.7	8.0
62	.4	7.5
63	.3	6.8
>64	.3	23.8

$\pi_0 = .50$ of the population, it ought to be accepted with a probability at most equal to 15 percent; whereas if in truth $\pi_1 = .60$, we ought to reject it with a probability of at most 5 percent. Consider the accompanying table, which has been derived from the data and the binomial distribution. The requirements can clearly not be met. The decision to accept $\pi_0 = .50$ (keep X) when 54 or fewer prefer Y, and $\pi_1 = .60$ (change to Y) when there are 55 or more results in risks of 18.3 and 12.9 percent, respectively, which are far higher than the stipulated risks of 15 and 5 percent. The decision rule which meets the 15 percent requirement would lead to accepting the $\pi_0 = 50$ percent hypothesis when the sample has 55 or fewer who prefer Y, but this would lead to a whopping 17.7 percent probability of accepting $\pi_0 = .5$ when in fact $\pi_1 = .6$.

10.13 **PROBABILITY OF k SUCCESSES IN 196 TRIALS**

k	$\pi_0 = .50$ (*keep* X)	$\pi_1 = .60$ (*change to* Y)
<97	47.2	.1
98	5.7	.1
99	5.6	.2
100	5.5	.2
101	5.2	.3
102	4.8	.4
103	4.4	.6
104	3.9	.8
105	3.5	1.1
106	3.0	1.4
107	2.5	1.8
108	2.1	2.2
109	1.7	2.6
110	1.3	3.1
111	1.0	3.6
112	.8	4.1
113	.6	4.6
114	.4	5.0
115	.3	5.3
116	.2	5.6
117	.1	5.8
118	.1	5.8
>119	.1	45.0

The sample size of 196 is less frustrating. If one decides to accept $\pi_0 = .5$ when there are 105 or fewer expressed preferences for Y, and to accept $\pi_1 = .6$ when there are 106 or more preferences for Y, the risks of being wrong are 14.2 and 3.8 percent, respectively. The accompanying table gives the detailed results.

10.14   In this exercise we can take $\mu_0 = .80$ ounce, $\mu_1 = .82$ ounce, $r_0 = 25$ percent, $r_1 = 5$ percent. The critical value should be above $\mu_0 + k_0(\sigma/\sqrt{n})$, or $.80 + .675(.06/\sqrt{25}) = .808$ and below $\mu_1 - k_1(\sigma/\sqrt{n})$, or $.82 - 1.645(.06/\sqrt{25}) = .80026$. There is no value satisfying both criteria, and the consumer should therefore either relax his criteria, in particular his risk level(s) r_0 and/or r_1, or increase his sample size to

$$n = \frac{\sigma^2(k_0 + k_1)^2}{(\mu_1 - \mu_0)^2} = \frac{(.06)^2(.675 + 1.645)^2}{(.02)^2} = 49$$

Then the critical value is above $.80 + .675\frac{.06}{7} = .80579$ and below $.82 - 1.645\frac{.06}{7} = .80590$, for example, $.8058$. If the average weight of 49 packs of cigarette B is below .8058 ounce, he should stick to A; otherwise, he should switch to B.

10.15   We have $\pi_0 = .40$, $\pi_1 = .45$, $r_0 = 10$ percent, $r_1 = 5$ percent. Using the formula for n, with $k_0 = 1.282$ and $k_1 = 1.645$, we get

$$n = \left(\frac{1.282\sqrt{.40 \times .60} + 1.645\sqrt{.45 \times .55}}{.45 - .40}\right)^2$$

$$= \left(\frac{.628 + .818}{.05}\right)^2 = 837$$

Rounding upward to 841, a complete square, we get critical values *above* $841 \times .40 + 1.282\sqrt{841(.40)(.60)} = 336.4 + 18.2 = 354.6$ and *below* $841 \times .45 - 1.645\sqrt{841(.45)(.55)} = 378.4 - 23.7 = 354.7$. The range does not quite include a $\frac{1}{2}$ value, but unless we increase the sample size, we do best by keeping the old drug if 354 or fewer patients recover in a sample of 841. Otherwise, switch to the new drug. A decision rule which nearly fulfills all requirements is $n = 841$, $c = 354$.

10.16
$$n = \left(\frac{1.645 \sqrt{.04 \times .96} + 2.326 \sqrt{.06 \times .94}}{.02} \right)^2$$
$$= \left(\frac{.321 + .552}{.02} \right)^2 = 43.65^2 = 1{,}906$$

One may compare this answer with the value 185 found in the text (Section 10.5) for less stringent requirements.

10.17 By the formula,

$$n = \frac{(.1)^2(1.645 + 1.282)^2}{.05^2} = \frac{(.01)(8.57)}{.0025} = 35$$

The critical value should be above

$$\mu_1 + k_1 \frac{\sigma}{\sqrt{n}} = .55 + 1.282 \frac{.1}{\sqrt{35}} = .55 + .0217 = .5717$$

and below

$$\mu_0 - k_0 \frac{\sigma}{\sqrt{n}} = .60 - 1.645 \frac{.1}{\sqrt{35}} = .60 - .0278 = .5722$$

or at .572.

10.18 In this case we know $n = 144$. Consider $\pi_0 = .20$; then $r_0 = 10$ percent. Also, $\pi_1 = .30$. We can now determine r_1, using

$$n = \left(\frac{k_0 \sqrt{\pi_0(1 - \pi_0)} + k_1 \sqrt{\pi_1(1 - \pi_1)}}{(\pi_1 - \pi_0)} \right)^2$$

Taking square roots on both sides of the equation and substituting known values gives

$$12 = \frac{1.282 \sqrt{(.2)(.8)} + k_1 \sqrt{(.3)(.7)}}{.1}$$

Then $1.2 = .5128 + k_1(.458)$; and $.6872 = k_1(.458)$, or $k_1 = 1.500$. From the table of the normal distribution, Table 7.4, we see that 6.68 percent of the area is in the tail beyond 1.5σ. Hence, $r_1 = 6.68$ percent.

10.19 First, we can determine the critical value at 122. Hence, we will accept $\pi_0 = .50$ if a sample of 225 has 122 or fewer defectives, and $\pi_1 = .60$ if a sample of size 225 has 123 or more defectives.

We next compute the following values:

If true π equals	Probability that sample will contain 122 or fewer defectives, that is, probability of accepting $\pi_0 = .50$
.40	100
.45	99.8
.50	91.88
.55	45.35
.60	4.79
.65	0

The values in red indicate that the criteria are met: if indeed $\pi_0 = .50$, there is only a $1 - .9188 = 8.12$ percent probability of accepting $\pi_1 = .60$. However, if $\pi_1 = .60$, there is a 4.79 percent probability of accepting $\pi_0 = .50$. The operating characteristic curve looks as follows:

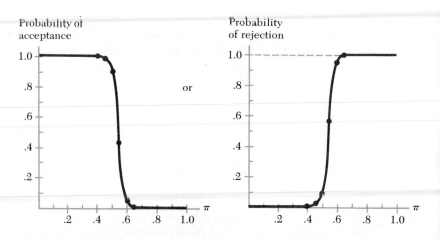

10.20   For various values of μ we compute the probability that the sample average has a value *above* 487 psi, which leads us to accept μ_0 as true. These values are all derived from Table 7.4. For example, if $\mu = 480$, a value of 487 for the average is $.7\sigma_{\bar{x}}$ above the mean,

If true mean μ equals	Probability of sample average above 487, that is, probability of accepting μ_0
460	.0035
470	.0446
480	.2420
485	.4207
490	.6179
500	.9032
510	.9893

and a value as high or higher has a probability of .2420. The red entries show that the stipulated risk levels are complied with.

10.21   We wish to limit the risk of an Error of Type I to 5 percent. Since the alternative hypothesis is that the mean is lower than 16 ounces (15.7 ounces to be specific), we use a one-tail test, at the 5 percent level, so that the appropriate number of standard deviations is 1.645. The critical value is $16 - 1.645 \times .1 = 15.8355$. If the sample of size 49 gives an average of 15.8355 or over, we accept $\mu_0 = 16$. Otherwise, we accept $\mu_1 = 15.7$. To determine the risk of an Error of Type II, we assume that the true mean is indeed $\mu_1 = 15.7$. An average of over 15.8355 (which would lead to the erroneous decision to accept $\mu_0 = 16$) is 1.355 standard deviations above the mean, and such a result only occurs with a probability of 8.8 percent (see the table of the normal distribution). The risk of an Error of Type II is 8.8 percent.

Chapter 11

HYPOTHESIS TESTING: GOODNESS OF FIT, INDEPENDENCE, AND ANALYSIS OF VARIANCE

11.1 DEGREES OF FREEDOM AND THE CHI-SQUARE DISTRIBUTION

In this chapter our concern will continue to be hypothesis testing. As before, we proceed in four steps. First, we state a null hypothesis. Next, we select a level of significance and specify the type of test, one-tail or two-tail. Third, we choose a sample and view the evidence. Finally, we reject the null hypothesis if the result observed falls into the critical region.

In the previous chapter we discussed some tests concerning proportions and means and the differences in means and proportions. In this chapter we will discuss tests to determine whether observed data come from a given theoretical distribution, whether attributes in a contingency table are independent, and whether the mean values in several populations are the same. As an added bonus, we will establish a confidence interval for the true population variance σ^2, just as in Section 9.3 we derived a confidence interval for μ, of the form $\bar{x} \pm k(s/\sqrt{n})$.

In most of the tests the chi-square, or χ^2, distribution (pronounce ki-square, rhymes with hi-there) plays a role of vital importance. The χ^2 distribution typically looks like a normal distribution which is skewed to the right—with a long tail to the right. It is a continuous distribution

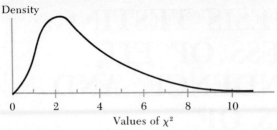

Figure 11.1 χ^2 distribution.

which assumes only positive values; Figure 11.1 illustrates a prototype.

Degrees of freedom

An important concept connected with the χ^2 distribution is that of *degrees of freedom*, that is, *the number of values one can freely choose.* For example, suppose that 10 observations have a given total t. Then only 9 observations can be chosen freely; the 10th must be

$$x_{10} = t - x_1 - x_2 - \cdots - x_9$$

so as to conform with the given total, and cannot be freely chosen. There are only 9 degrees of freedom. As another example, consider a 2×2 contingency table with given totals, as in Table 11.1. Now when any *one* value in the table is specified, the other three are uniquely determined. There is only 1 degree of freedom. More generally, a contingency table with r rows and c columns has $(r - 1)(c - 1)$ degrees of freedom. Further hurdles concerning degrees of freedom will be cleared as we reach them.

Table of χ^2 distributions

Table 11.2 gives some numerical values associated with χ^2 distributions. There is a different χ^2 distribution for each number of degrees of freedom. As we see, the χ^2 distribution with 7 degrees of freedom has the value 2.833 in the column headed $\chi^2_{.90}$. This means that 90 percent of the area under the χ^2 curve is to the *right* of the value 2.833, when there are 7 degrees of freedom. Figure 11.2 illustrates the location of several values in the χ^2 distribution for 5 degrees of freedom. The table is versatile

TABLE 11.1   TWO-BY-TWO CONTINGENCY TABLE WITH GIVEN TOTALS

	B	*Not*-B	*Total*
A	·	·	t_1
Not-A	·	·	t_2
Total	t_3	t_4	T

TABLE 11.2   SOME PERCENTAGE POINTS OF SOME χ^2 DISTRIBUTIONS

Degrees of freedom	$\chi^2_{.99}$	$\chi^2_{.95}$	$\chi^2_{.90}$	$\chi^2_{.50}$	$\chi^2_{.10}$	$\chi^2_{.05}$	$\chi^2_{.01}$
1	.000	.004	.016	.455	2.706	3.841	6.635
2	.020	.103	.211	1.386	4.605	5.991	9.210
3	.115	.352	.584	2.366	6.251	7.815	11.345
4	.297	.711	1.064	3.357	7.779	9.488	13.277
5	.554	1.145	1.610	4.351	9.236	11.070	15.086
6	.872	1.635	2.204	5.348	10.645	12.592	16.812
7	1.239	2.167	2.833	6.346	12.017	14.067	18.475
8	1.646	2.733	3.490	7.344	13.362	15.507	20.090
9	2.088	3.325	4.168	8.343	14.684	16.919	21.666
10	2.558	3.940	4.865	9.342	15.987	18.307	23.209
20	8.260	10.851	12.443	19.337	28.412	31.410	37.566
30	14.953	18.493	20.599	29.336	40.256	43.773	50.892

in its use. It gives, for example, the medians of the χ^2 distributions. These medians, $\chi^2_{.50}$, are always close to the number of degrees of freedom. We can also read off values such that 90 percent of the area is between these values, with 5 percent in either tail. These are the values $\chi^2_{.95}$ and $\chi^2_{.05}$. For the χ^2 distribution with 9 degrees of freedom, these values are 3.325 and 16.919. Table 6 of Appendix B gives more detailed χ^2 values.

When the number of degrees of freedom m exceeds 30, the random variable $\mathbf{u}$ which is χ^2 distributed can be transformed to a variable $\mathbf{x} = \mathcal{N}(0,1)$, where $\mathbf{x} = \sqrt{2\mathbf{u}} - \sqrt{2m-1}$. For example, if $\mathbf{u}$ is χ^2 distributed with 85 degrees of freedom, is the value $u = 98$ in the extreme

Degrees of freedom more than 30

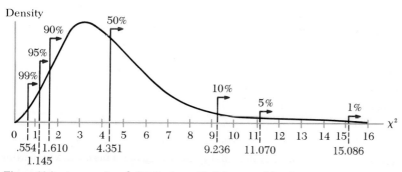

Figure 11.2   Areas under χ^2 distribution with 5 degrees of freedom.

5 percent of the area under the upper tail of the distribution? The answer is no, for we have $x = \sqrt{2 \times 98} - \sqrt{(2 \times 85)} - 1 = 14 - 13 = 1$. Since x is normally distributed with mean 0 and standard deviation 1, a value of 1 is not in the extreme 5 percent of the upper tail; values over 1.645 are.

In the argument in the next sections the χ^2 distribution will be used as follows: A comparison will be made between hypothesized reality and the observed random variable u with a distribution approximated by a particular χ^2 distribution. For example, the random variable might have the value 10.2 for the χ^2 distribution with 4 degrees of freedom. Such a high value has less than a 5 percent chance of occurring according to Table 11.2, for 10.2 exceeds 9.488. At the 5 percent significance level our hypothesis about reality will be rejected.

EXERCISES

11.1   How large should the random variable u be before we reject a null hypothesis at the 10 percent significance level, when there are 7 degrees of freedom?

11.2   If there are 8 degrees of freedom, what is the median of the distribution of the random variable u? What are the values within which 80, 90, and 98 percent of the area lies if the remaining area is equally divided between the two tails of the distribution?

11.3   A random variable u is χ^2 distributed with 113 degrees of freedom. In an experiment we find $u = 162$. Is this significant at the 1 percent level?

11.2   AN ILLUSTRATION OF THE TEST FOR GOODNESS OF FIT

Suppose that, under some null hypothesis, we expect to observe values $e_1, e_2, \ldots, e_n$. For example, in throwing a die 30 times we expect to observe, under the null hypothesis that the die is fair, five 1s, five 2s, $\ldots$, and five 6s. Thus, $e_1, e_2, \ldots, e_6$ are each equal to 5. Next suppose that we are about to throw the die 30 times, to generate observations $o_1, o_2, \ldots, o_6$, the number of 1s, 2s, $\ldots$, 6s. These observed values will differ from experiment to experiment, and are thus random variables.

The basic result can now be stated. The derived random variable **u**

$$\mathbf{u} = \frac{(\mathbf{0}_1 + e_1)^2}{e_1} + \frac{(\mathbf{0}_2 - e_2)^2}{e_2} + \cdots + \frac{(\mathbf{0}_6 - e_6)^2}{e_6}$$

has a distribution closely approximated by the χ^2 distribution. In this example the distribution will have 5 degrees of freedom. We know the total number of throws. There are six different outcomes, and the frequencies with which each occurs must add to this known total. Given any five of these frequencies, the sixth is determined. We now throw the die, and find as results $o_1, o_2, \ldots, o_6$. We compute

$$u = \frac{(o_1 - e_1)^2}{e_1} + \frac{(o_2 - e_2)^2}{e_2} + \cdots + \frac{(o_6 - e_6)^2}{e_6}$$

Turning to Table 11.2, we see that, for 5 degrees of freedom, χ^2 exceeds 11.07 with a probability of 5 percent. If the value of u just computed is above 11.07, we reject the hypothesis that the die is fair at the 5 percent level of significance.

The 30 throws give the following results:

	k, outcome	Actual number of times	Expected number of times
4, 3, 6, 5, 6	1	6	5
5, 1, 5, 3, 2	2	5	5
3, 3, 1, 1, 1	3	7	5
3, 3, 6, 5, 1	4	2	5
6, 5, 3, 2, 4	5	5	5
2, 2, 6, 1, 2	6	5	5

or

for a total of six 1s, five 2s, seven 3s, two 4s, five 5s, and five 6s. So we compute

$$u = \frac{(6-5)^2}{5} + \frac{(5-5)^2}{5} + \frac{(7-5)^2}{5}$$
$$+ \frac{(2-5)^2}{5} + \frac{(5-5)^2}{5} + \frac{(5-5)^2}{5} = 2.8$$

The result is not significant, and we accept the hypothesis that the die is fair.

As a second experiment, we throw a die which we know to be biased.

The bias is such that the outcomes 1, 2, 3, and 4 have a .2 probability, while a 5 or a 6 only have a .1 probability. *Pretending we do not know this,* we throw 30 times to test the null hypothesis that the die is fair. We obtain the following results:

		$k,$ outcome	Actual number of times	Expected number of times
4, 1, 6, 4, 4		1	4	5
4, 3, 1, 6, 3	or	2	2	5
5, 3, 3, 6, 2		3	8	5
6, 4, 4, 6, 1		4	9	5
1, 4, 2, 3, 6		5	1	5
3, 3, 3, 4, 4		6	6	5

There are four 1s, two 2s, eight 3s, nine 4s, one 5, and (somewhat surprisingly) six 6s. Under the hypothesis that the die is fair, the value of $\mathbf{u}$ is approximately χ^2 distributed with 5 degrees of freedom. In our experiment we find

$$u = \frac{(4-5)^2}{5} + \frac{(2-5)^2}{5} + \frac{(8-5)^2}{5}$$

$$+ \frac{(9-5)^2}{5} + \frac{(1-5)^2}{5} + \frac{(6-5)^2}{5} = 10.4$$

This is not significant at the 5 percent level. Hence, a value of $\mathbf{u}$ exceeding 10.4 occurs more than 5 percent of the time if a true, unbiased die is tossed 30 times. We *incorrectly* accept the null hypothesis and maintain that the die is unbiased. In doing so we make an Error of Type II because we have rejected the alternative hypothesis—the die is biased—which we know to be true. The test did not reveal the bias, but that may be due to the fact that the sample size was limited to 30 throws. So we throw the die another 30 times and we get:

		$k,$ outcome	Actual number of times	Expected number of times
1, 4, 3, 4, 3		1	6	5
3, 6, 1, 4, 4		2	6	5
1, 4, 2, 4, 6		3	4	5
2, 2, 1, 2, 6	or	4	9	5
3, 4, 4, 2, 5		5	2	5
5, 1, 2, 1, 4		6	3	5

In all 60 throws combined we have ten 1s, eight 2s, twelve 3s, eighteen 4s, three 5s, and nine 6s. In 60 throws with a fair die we expect to get 10 of each, so we have

$$u = \frac{(10 - 10)^2}{10} + \frac{(8 - 10)^2}{10} + \frac{(12 - 10)^2}{10} + \frac{(18 - 10)^2}{10}$$
$$+ \frac{(3 - 10)^2}{10} + \frac{(9 - 10)^2}{10} = 12.2$$

This result is significant at the 5 percent level, and we reject the null hypothesis that the die is fair.

In this experiment, we know how wise this decision is. We will now test the null hypothesis that the outcomes 1, 2, 3, and 4 have a .2 probability of occurring and 5 and 6 have a .1 probability of occurring. Under this hypothesis the expected outcomes are twelve 1s, twelve 2s, twelve 3s, and twelve 4s, but only six 5s and six 6s. We find

$$u = \frac{(10 - 12)^2}{12} + \frac{(8 - 12)^2}{12} + \frac{(12 - 12)^2}{12} + \frac{(18 - 12)^2}{12}$$
$$+ \frac{(3 - 6)^2}{6} + \frac{(9 - 6)^2}{6} = 7\tfrac{2}{3}$$

which is not significant at the 5 percent level. We accept the null hypothesis, and are correct in doing so.

While the general philosophy should be clear from these examples, we have glossed over a rather large number of details, some of which we will now discuss.

First, one should be leery of using the χ^2 distribution unless *all* e_1, $e_2, \ldots, e_n$ values are *at least* equal to 5. In our first experiments this requirement was just barely met. If, in some group, the expected value is smaller than 5, we should combine this group with others, so as to satisfy this minimum requirement. We will meet examples as we proceed.

Theoretical cell frequencies all at least 5

Second, suppose that in our first experiment, where we threw a fair die 30 times, exactly five 1s, five 2s, . . . , five 6s were obtained. All observed values would exactly coincide with their expected values. The value of u would be zero, and an outcome as low as zero with 5 degrees of freedom is in the 1 percent *left* tail (since $0 < .554$). If the null hypothesis of a fair die is true, this result is as remarkable as a result of $u > 15.086$. Yet it would seem preposterous to reject the hypothesis that we have a fair die if it does precisely what we "expect" it to do. The critical region in our tests will always fall in the higher tail, where

Values of u near zero

a value of **u** indicates an exceptionally large deviation from expectations. However, we will be alert to values of **u** near zero, since they indicate a remarkable correspondence with expectations. *They give us some reason to believe that the observations themselves are not honest, but made up or fabricated.*

Choice of
null
hypothesis

Third, suppose we have a given set of observations. There will always be many null hypotheses which will be accepted, at a given level of significance, if tested with these observations. In other words, the observations will be consistent with many different hypotheses. Therefore, the choice of a null hypothesis should be rooted in common sense. It should be a logical choice, and it should be expressed before the data are observed.

No specific
alternative
hypothesis

Fourth, if the null hypothesis is rejected, we are in real trouble because we have no specific alternative hypothesis. After 60 throws we rejected the hypothesis of a fair die. Normally this would leave us with no idea regarding the nature of the bias—only the fact that bias is present. In this particular example we were fortunate in knowing the true bias of the die.

Increasing
sample size

Fifth, we are more likely to reject false null hypotheses at a given level of significance when we have larger samples. We have already showed this by increasing an original 30 throws with a biased die to 60. We will give another example here. A marksman states that 60 percent of his shots are on target. We will test his claim at the 5 percent level of significance. He shoots 20 times and has 9 hits and 11 misses, rather than the 12 hits and 8 misses we would expect if his claim is true. There is 1 degree of freedom, since the number of hits fully determines the number of misses, given the total of 20. We find

$$u = \frac{(9-12)^2}{12} + \frac{(11-8)^2}{8} = 1\frac{7}{8}$$

This is not significant at the 5 percent level. We watch the next group of 20 shots. His score this time is 8 hits out of 20, so

$$u = \frac{(8-12)^2}{12} + \frac{(12-8)^2}{8} = 3\frac{1}{3}$$

This result is also not significant at the 5 percent level. Yet by now we really doubt the claim. We have good reason. If we combine the evidence from the two groups he should make 24 hits out of 40 shots, while he only scored 17. The value of u is

$$u = \frac{(17 - 24)^2}{24} + \frac{(23 - 16)^2}{16} = 5\frac{5}{48}$$

which is significant at the 5 percent level.

Sixth, in cases with only 1 degree of freedom, subtracting $\frac{1}{2}$ from each numerator *before* squaring gives a **u** value whose distribution is more closely approximated by χ^2. With this *continuity correction,* instead of Continuity correction

$$u = \frac{(17 - 24)^2}{24} + \frac{(23 - 16)^2}{16} = \frac{7^2}{24} + \frac{7^2}{16} = 5\frac{5}{48}$$

we get

$$u = \frac{(6\frac{1}{2})^2}{24} + \frac{(6\frac{1}{2})^2}{16} = 4\frac{77}{192}$$

The u value is lower but still significant at the 5 percent level. We repeat that this correction is used when there is only *1* degree of freedom.

EXERCISES

11.4   In Section 5.2, we obtained twenty 1s, eighteen 2s, fifteen 3s, eighteen 4s, twelve 5s, and seventeen 6s in 100 rolls of a die. Are these results consistent with the hypothesis that the die is fair at the 5 percent level of significance?

11.5   Out of 27,895 children born, 14,182 are boys. Is this consistent with the hypothesis that the probability of a boy is .50? Use a 5 percent level of significance.

11.6   Test the null hypothesis that 60 percent of a marksman's shots hit the target if 17 out of 40 shots do, using methods explained in Chapter 10. Use a 5 percent significance level.

11.7   The division manager of a retail chain believes the average number of customers entering each of the five stores in his division weekly is the same. In a given week the managers report the following numbers of customers in their stores: 3,000, 2,960, 3,100, 2,780, 3,160. Test the division manager's belief at the 10 percent level of significance.

11.3   TESTS FOR GOODNESS OF FIT— POISSON AND NORMAL

Testing the fit of the Poisson

A large industrial company keeps records on the occurrence of accidents among its production workers. We want to test, at a 1 percent significance level, whether these accidents are Poisson distributed. In 1,095 days 1,295 accidents were reported. As shown in the first two columns of Table 11.3, there were 364 days with no accident, 376 days with one accident, 218 days with two accidents, and so on. The management believes the accidents occur independently, so a Poisson distribution with mean $\frac{1,295}{1,095} = 1.18$ is used to find the expected number of days with 0, 1, 2, . . . accidents. These numbers are given in the third column of Table 11.3. We note that the last two classes have expected number of days smaller than 5, so we combine them with the previous class, which gives us $k = 0$, 1, 2, 3, 4, and "5 or more," as our six classes. To determine the degrees of freedom, we argue as follows: It may appear as though there are 6 degrees of freedom, since there are six classes. However, since we are given $n = 1,095$ and since the Poisson parameter was computed from the data, we lose 2 degrees of freedom and are left with $6 - 2 = 4$ degrees of freedom.

From Columns 2 and 3 in Table 11.3, we compute

$$u = \frac{(364 - 337)^2}{337} + \frac{(376 - 397)^2}{397} + \cdots + \frac{(33 - 27)^2}{27}$$
$$+ \frac{(16 - 8)^2}{8} = 13.8$$

which is significant at the 1 percent level. We conclude that the actual data cannot be adequately described by a Poisson distribution and, therefore, are not likely to occur independently.

Testing the fit of the normal

As a next example, consider the data presented in Table 11.4. We assume that the lifetime of bulbs is normally distributed. If they are, and if a sample of size 100 is all we have available, we can do no better than to estimate the mean μ by $\bar{x} = 1,022$ and the standard deviation σ by $s = 110$. Is the evidence consistent with the null hypothesis of normality at the 10 percent level of significance?

To find out, we must establish some theoretical frequencies with which to compare the observations. One way is to derive the 10 deciles from a table of the normal distribution. There ought to be 10 percent of the observations within each of the deciles, as shown in Table 11.4.

TABLE 11.3   COMPARISON OF ACTUAL AND THEORETICAL NUMBER OF DAYS WITH k ACCIDENTS

k, number of accidents	Actual number of days with k accidents	Expected number of days with k accidents, according to Poisson (1,295/1,095)
0	364	337
1	376	397
2	218	234
3	89	92
4	33	27
5 ⎫	13 ⎫	7 ⎫
6 ⎬ 5 or more	2 ⎬ 16	1 ⎬ 8
7 ⎭	1 ⎭	0 ⎭
	1,095	1,095

We refer back to Exercise 7.13 for the determination of the decile points. By considering the sample evidence, we can count the number of observations in each of the 10 deciles. We lose 3 degrees of freedom, since the number of observations n, the average $\bar{x}$, and the standard deviation s are all determined from the sample data. So there are $10 - 3 = 7$ degrees

TABLE 11.4   COMPARISON OF ACTUAL AND THEORETICAL NUMBER OF OBSERVATIONS IN 10 DECILES

Decile interval ($\bar{x} = 1,022$, $s = 110$)	Actually observed	Theoretical number of observations in each decile
<881	10	10
881–929	8	10
930–964	7	10
965–994	8	10
995–1,022	16	10
1,023–1,050	13	10
1,051–1,080	11	10
1,081–1,115	7	10
1,116–1,164	12	10
>1164	8	10

of freedom. We must compute

$$u = \frac{(10-10)^2}{10} + \frac{(8-10)^2}{10} + \frac{(7-10)^2}{10} + \cdots + \frac{(12-10)^2}{10}$$

$$+ \frac{(8-10)^2}{10} = 8$$

which is not significant at the 10 percent level. We accept the hypothesis that the burning time of the bulbs is normally distributed.

Interestingly enough, in this example the 100 observations were generated from a normal distribution with mean $\mu = 1,000$ and standard deviation $\sigma = 100$. Using these values, we can derive from a table of the normal distribution that 10 percent of the observations ought to be within each of the 10 deciles given in Table 11.5. In fact, these deciles contained 8, 8, 8, 4, 7, 16, 11, 11, 17, and 10 observations. The value of u equals

$$u = \frac{(8-10)^2}{10} + \frac{(8-10)^2}{10} + \cdots + \frac{(10-10)^2}{10} = 14.4$$

This value is significant at the 10 percent level if there are 7 degrees of freedom. However, in this case $\mu = 1,000$ and $\sigma = 100$ were determined *outside* of the sample evidence, and so we have, not 7, but 9 degrees

TABLE 11.5   COMPARISON OF ACTUAL AND
THEORETICAL NUMBER OF OBSERVATIONS
IN 10 DECILES

Decile interval ($\mu = 1,000$, $\sigma = 100$)	Actually observed	Theoretical number of observations in each decile
<860	8	10
860–919	8	10
920–947	8	10
948–974	4	10
975–1,000	7	10
1,001–1,025	16	10
1,026–1,052	11	10
1,053–1,080	11	10
1,081–1,140	17	10
>1,140	10	10

of freedom. The value 14.4 is not significant at the 10 percent level, when there are 9 degrees of freedom. This illustrates the importance of determining the number of degrees of freedom correctly.

EXERCISES

11.8 Given the accompanying set of 100 observations, with average $\bar{x} = 2$, determine the number of outcomes with value 4 and the number of outcomes with value 5. How many degrees of freedom are there?

Outcome	No. of observations
0	12
1	15
2	44
3	20
4	?
5	?

11.9 A book has 748 pages. The number of pages with various numbers of misprints is recorded below. At the 5 percent significance level, are the misprints Poisson distributed?

No. of misprints k	No. of pages with k misprints
0	665
1	71
2	10
3	2
4	0
	748

11.10 A teacher claims to grade so the grades follow a normal curve with standard deviation 10 and a mean of $69\frac{1}{2}$. The following grades are recorded:

Grade	Frequency	Grade	Frequency
38	1	72	5
45	1	73	3
47	2	75	3
48	1	76	4
50	1	77	2
53	3	78	1
54	1	79	1
56	1	80	2
57	4	81	1
58	4	82	7
59	1	83	3
60	1	84	1
62	5	86	2
64	3	88	1
65	1	90	1
66	7	91	1
68	7	99	2
69	3	100	1
70	5		100
71	7		

(a) Do we accept the teacher's claim? Use a 5 percent level of significance.

(b) What is the probability of finding a value of **u** larger than the one found in part (a) if the null hypothesis is true?

11.4   TEST FOR INDEPENDENCE IN CONTINGENCY TABLES

The χ^2 distribution is used to test the independence of characteristics for classifying sample observations in a contingency table. Table 11.6 shows 100 cars purchased in a recent week from a dealer, classified according to terms of purchase (cash, C, or installment, I) and age of car (new, N, or used, U). If we consider the observations in the table a random sample of all cars sold by this dealer, are the characteristics age of car and terms of purchase independent in the population? If they are, then, by the general formula P(A *and* B) = P(A)P(B) and the given totals, the entries are expected to be as given in Table 11.7. So we have to compare 15, 5, 45, and 35 with 12, 8, 48, and 32. Are the deviations of the

TABLE 11.6   TWO-BY-TWO
CONTINGENCY TABLE,
ACTUAL NUMBERS OF
OBSERVATIONS

Terms of purchase	Type of car		Total
	New	Used	
Cash	15	5	20
Installment	45	35	80
Total	60	40	100

observed values (Table 11.6) from the expected values (Table 11.7) significant at the 5 percent level?

At the outset we observe that we have only 1 degree of freedom. For example, in Table 11.7 the totals *and* the value 12 completely determine the three other values. We refer back to Section 11.1. Next, we compute

$$u = \frac{(15 - 12)^2}{12} + \frac{(5 - 8)^2}{8} + \frac{(45 - 48)^2}{48} + \frac{(35 - 32)^2}{32}$$

But since there is only 1 degree of freedom, we must use the continuity correction. The numerator in each term is $(2\frac{1}{2})^2$, rather than $(3)^2$. The resulting value of u is

$$u = \frac{(2\frac{1}{2})^2}{12} + \frac{(2\frac{1}{2})^2}{8} + \frac{(2\frac{1}{2})^2}{48} + \frac{(2\frac{1}{2})^2}{32} = 1.63$$

TABLE 11.7   TWO-BY-TWO
CONTINGENCY TABLE,
THEORETICAL NUMBER
OF OBSERVATIONS
UNDER INDEPENDENCE

Terms of purchase	Type of car		Total
	New	Used	
Cash	12	8	20
Installment	48	32	80
Total	60	40	100

TABLE 11.8   COMPARISON OF ACTUAL AND THEORETICAL NUMBER OF OBSERVATIONS IN TWO-BY-TWO CONTINGENCY TABLES, 200 OBSERVATIONS

	Actual				*Theoretical, under independence*		
	N	U	*Total*		N	U	*Total*
C	30	10	40	C	24	16	40
I	90	70	160	I	96	64	160
Total	120	80	200	Total	120	80	200

We accept the null hypothesis and conclude that the age of car and terms of purchase are independent.

Suppose that the percentages remain the same throughout, but that we have 200 observations. The actual and theoretical outcomes—under the assumption of independence—are recorded in Table 11.8. We compute, remembering to deduct $\frac{1}{2}$ from the numerators before squaring,

$$u = \frac{(5\frac{1}{2})^2}{24} + \frac{(5\frac{1}{2})^2}{16} + \frac{(5\frac{1}{2})^2}{96} + \frac{(5\frac{1}{2})^2}{64} = 3.94$$

The outcome exceeds 3.84 and is thus significant at the 5 percent level. We now reject the hypothesis of independence between age of car and terms of purchase. This is another illustration of point five in Section 11.2. As evidence accumulates in the test of a hypothesis which should be rejected, results may become significant. Let us look at it this way. If age of car and terms of purchase are independent, the result shown in Table 11.6, or one leading to an even larger value for **u,** occurs about 20 percent of the time according to the χ^2 table in the back of the book. Precisely the same statement can be made about a *new* set of observations on 100 cars, which are also described in Table 11.6. However, obtaining such a result *twice in a row* has a probability of .20 $\times$ .20 or about 4 percent, and is thus significant at the 5 percent level.

In Exhibit 3 of Appendix A on the use of computers we have displayed an example of a χ^2 test for independence of characteristics in a two-by-two contingency table.

Converting percentages to numbers

Clearly, in using the χ^2 test the *actual numbers* and not the percentages are relevant in determining significance. The observed percentages in Tables 11.6 and 11.8 are the same. The absolute magnitude of the numbers makes the difference. If we have only observed percentages, u cannot be found. If we know the absolute total on which the percentages are based, we can express all values as absolute numbers and proceed.

TABLE 11.9   COMPARISON OF ACTUAL AND THEORETICAL NUMBER OF OBSERVATIONS IN THREE-BY-THREE CONTINGENCY TABLES, 1,000 OBSERVATIONS

	Actual				*Theoretical, under independence*			
	Stock 2					Stock 2		
Stock 1	R	NC	D	*Total*	*Stock 1*	R	NC	D	*Total*
R	312	34	54	400	R	160	80	160	400
NC	60	110	80	250	NC	100	50	100	250
D	28	56	266	350	D	140	70	140	350
Total	400	200	400	1,000	Total	400	200	400	1,000

We can test independence in the movement of prices of two stocks. The actual observations in a sample of 1,000 days are given in Table 11.9, next to the theoretical outcomes under the null hypothesis of independence (R = rise, NC = no change, D = decline). Since the table has $r = 3$ rows and $c = 3$ columns, the table has $(3 - 1) \times (3 - 1) = 4$ degrees of freedom, as we saw in Section 11.1. This can be verified by noting that once the marginal totals have been given, the four upper left-hand entries completely determine the other five. The value of u is

$$u = \frac{(312 - 160)^2}{160} + \cdots + \frac{(266 - 140)^2}{140} = 538.9$$

The value is very high indeed, and significant at just about any level of significance, however small we might have specified it.

A problem of slightly different form is the following: Let three samples of 100 lightbulbs be chosen from the output of three different machines. The lifetime of these bulbs is recorded in Table 11.10. The question is,

TABLE 11.10   LIFETIME OF BULBS, THREE SAMPLES OF SIZE 100

Lifetime, hours	*Sample I*	*Sample II*	*Sample III*	*Total*
<900	20	15	25	60
900–1,000	25	20	33	78
1,000–1,100	35	35	26	96
>1,100	20	30	16	66
Total	100	100	100	

TABLE 11.11   LIFETIME OF BULBS, THEORETICAL EXPECTATIONS

Lifetime, hours	Sample I	Sample II	Sample III	Total
<900	20	20	20	60
900–1,000	26	26	26	78
1,000–1,100	32	32	32	96
>1,100	22	22	22	66
Total	100	100	100	

"Can we accept the null hypothesis that these samples come from three populations with the same characteristics?" We will use a 5 percent level of significance. We argue as follows: If they do come from populations with the same characteristics, we would expect the given totals to be spread evenly over the various classes, as in Table 11.11. There are $(4 - 1)(3 - 1) = 6$ degrees of freedom. We find

$$u = \frac{(20 - 20)^2}{20} + \cdots + \frac{(16 - 22)^2}{22} = 12.2$$

which is significant at the 5 percent level. We reject the null hypothesis that all samples were drawn from populations with the same characteristics.

EXERCISES

11.11   Derive in detail the value 12 found as the upper left-hand entry in Table 11.7.

11.12   On the basis of the following sample evidence, can sex and smoking be considered independent in the population at the 10 percent level of significance? How would you proceed if the numbers in the table were percentages, rather than actual numbers of people?

	Smoker	Nonsmoker	Total
Male	40	20	60
Female	20	20	40
Total	60	40	100

11.13 The following sample data are available on income and age. Are these characteristics independent in the population? Use a 5 percent level of significance.

Age	Income				Total
	<5,000	5,000 < 10,000	10,000 < 15,000	15,000 < 20,000	
20 < 30	150	80	15	5	250
30 < 40	120	95	25	10	250
40 < 50	90	110	35	15	250
50 < 60	60	125	45	20	250
Total	420	410	120	50	1,000

11.5 THE CONFIDENCE INTERVAL FOR THE VARIANCE OF A NORMAL DISTRIBUTION

In this section we will show how the χ^2 distribution is used to determine confidence intervals for the variance of a normal distribution. In Chapter 9 we found an interval estimate for the mean as follows: If a sample of size n led to observations $x_1, x_2, \ldots, x_n$ we took $\bar{x} = \sum x_i / n$ as a point estimate for μ. Clearly, the value $\bar{x}$ will differ from sample to sample, but the expected value of $\bar{x}$ equals μ. We continued to argue that this is small comfort as long as some particular $\bar{x}$ found in some particular sample could differ drastically from μ. However, we also found confidence limits for μ. We have 95.45 percent confidence that the interval

$$\bar{x} \pm 2 \frac{\sigma}{\sqrt{n}} \quad \text{or} \quad \bar{x} \pm 2 \sqrt{\frac{\sigma^2}{n}}$$

will include μ. Unfortunately, we do not know σ^2, but we agreed to use its unbiased estimate

$$s^2 = \frac{(x_1 - \bar{x})^2 + \cdots + (x_n - \bar{x})^2}{n - 1}$$

as a proxy. Clearly, s^2 will also differ from sample to sample, but its expected value can be shown to coincide with σ^2. (We recall in passing that when σ^2 is unknown and therefore has to be estimated by s^2 from a sample of size n, the confidence interval should be estimated by using the relevant k value from the t distribution with $n - 1$ degrees of freedom.)

Again we can continue to argue that this is small comfort, as long as in any individual sample s^2 can differ drastically from σ^2. The purpose of this section is to give a confidence interval for σ^2. This problem is discussed here because the approach involves the χ^2 distribution, through the following result: For samples of size n from a normal population with variance σ^2, the random variable

$$\mathbf{u} = \frac{\Sigma(x_i - \bar{x})^2}{\sigma^2}$$

has a χ^2 distribution with $n - 1$ degrees of freedom.

The entries in Table 11.2 can be used to determine the values between which 90 (or 80 or 98) percent of the area of the relevant χ^2 distribution lies. For example, the values in the columns $\chi^2_{.95}$ and $\chi^2_{.05}$ are such that $\mathbf{u}$ will have a 90 percent probability of falling between these limits. Therefore

$$\chi^2_{.95} < \frac{\Sigma(x_i - \bar{x})^2}{\sigma^2} < \chi^2_{.05}$$

with 90 percent probability. When there are 10 observations in the sample, there are 9 degrees of freedom, and the values $\chi^2_{.95}$ and $\chi^2_{.05}$ are then 3.325 and 16.919 as illustrated in Figure 11.3. Thus

$$3.325 < \frac{(\mathbf{x}_1 - \bar{\mathbf{x}})^2 + (\mathbf{x}_2 - \bar{\mathbf{x}})^2 + \cdots + (\mathbf{x}_{10} - \bar{\mathbf{x}})^2}{\sigma^2} < 16.919$$

A little reordering gives

$$\frac{(\mathbf{x}_1 - \bar{\mathbf{x}})^2 + (\mathbf{x}_2 - \bar{\mathbf{x}})^2 + \cdots + (\mathbf{x}_{10} - \bar{\mathbf{x}})^2}{16.919}$$

$$< \sigma^2 < \frac{(\mathbf{x}_1 - \bar{\mathbf{x}})^2 + (\mathbf{x}_2 - \bar{\mathbf{x}})^2 + \cdots + (\mathbf{x}_{10} - \bar{\mathbf{x}})^2}{3.325}$$

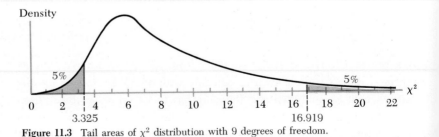

Figure 11.3 Tail areas of χ^2 distribution with 9 degrees of freedom.

with 90 percent probability. We conclude that if a sample of size 10 gives the observations $x_1, x_2, \ldots, x_{10}$, the range

$$\frac{(x_1 - \bar{x})^2 + (x_2 - \bar{x})^2 + \cdots + (x_{10} - \bar{x})^2}{16.919}$$

to

$$\frac{(x_1 - \bar{x})^2 + (x_2 - \bar{x})^2 + \cdots + (x_{10} - \bar{x})^2}{3.325}$$

is a 90 percent confidence interval for σ^2. In general, a 90 percent confidence interval for σ^2 is given by

$$\frac{\Sigma(x_i - \bar{x})^2}{\chi^2_{.05}} \quad \text{to} \quad \frac{\Sigma(x_i - \bar{x})^2}{\chi^2_{.95}} \quad (n - 1 \text{ degrees of freedom})$$

90 percent confidence interval for σ^2

A 98 percent confidence interval is obtained by using the entries in the columns $\chi^2_{.01}$ and $\chi^2_{.99}$, and in the row with the appropriate number of degrees of freedom, $n - 1$.

Incidentally, the point estimate for σ^2 in a sample of size 10,

$$s^2 = \frac{(x_1 - \bar{x})^2 + \cdots + (x_{10} - \bar{x})^2}{9}$$

falls near the middle of the confidence interval, but the confidence interval is not precisely symmetric around this value, unlike the confidence interval for μ which is symmetric around $\bar{x}$.

Though this result is, strictly speaking, only valid for an estimate of the variance of a normal distribution, we will illustrate it by throwing a die. The probability distribution for this experiment is not normal, but is the discrete version of a rectangular distribution defined for the values 1, 2, 3, 4, 5, 6, with probability $= \frac{1}{6}$ for each. We throw 10 times and obtain

$$6 \; 2 \; 2 \; 3 \; 2 \; 3 \; 6 \; 5 \; 5 \; 3$$

for which $\bar{x} = 3.7$, and

$$(x_1 - \bar{x})^2 + \cdots + (x_{10} - \bar{x})^2 = 24.1$$

The 90 percent confidence interval $\frac{24.1}{16.9}$ to $\frac{24.1}{3.3}$, or 1.4 to 7.3, includes the true σ^2, which, as we know, is $2\frac{11}{12} = 2.92$.

In fact, we throw 50 samples of 10 throws each. The 32d sample contains the outcomes

$$5\ 5\ 6\ 4\ 5\ 5\ 6\ 3\ 5\ 5$$

We find $\overline{x} = 4.9$ and

$$(x_1 - \overline{x})^2 + \cdots + (x_{10} - \overline{x})^2 = 6.9$$

The interval $\frac{6.9}{16.9}$ to $\frac{6.9}{3.3}$, or .41 to 2.1, does not include 2.92, but lies entirely below the value 2.92. At the other extreme, sample 21 gives as results

$$1\ 4\ 1\ 6\ 6\ 1\ 6\ 6\ 5\ 1$$

We find $\overline{x} = 3.7$ and

$$(x_1 - \overline{x})^2 + \cdots + (x_{10} - \overline{x})^2 = 52.1$$

The interval $\frac{52.1}{16.9}$ to $\frac{52.1}{3.3}$, or 3.1 to 15.8, does not include 2.92, but lies entirely above the value 2.92. These exceptions need not surprise us, however, since σ^2 will be outside a 90 percent confidence interval 10 percent of the time in the long run.

EXERCISES

11.14   A sample of 21 weights of beef cattle (in pounds), drawn from a normal distribution of weights, leads to a point estimate s^2 of σ^2 equal to 110. Which interval will include σ^2 for these weights with 90 percent confidence?

11.15   A random sample of size 170 has a sum of squared deviations from the average = 229,840. Determine the 95 percent confidence interval for σ^2.

11.16   A random sample of 11 segments of telephone cable showed $s^2 = .07$ for the thicknesses of insulation. The production process is supposed to maintain $\sigma^2 = .04$. Test the hypothesis that the process is operating satisfactorily. Use a 10 percent level of significance.

11.6   INTRODUCTION TO ANALYSIS
   OF VARIANCE

A significance test of special importance is used in the technique known as *analysis of variance*. It arises in a context where the basic question

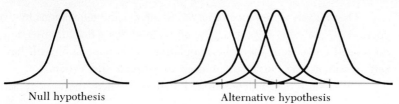

Null hypothesis   Alternative hypothesis
Figure 11.4 Hypotheses tested in analysis of variance.

is, "Can we accept the hypothesis that these samples were drawn from populations described by the same normal distribution?" As alternative, there is the possibility that the samples were drawn from populations described by different normal distributions. Strictly speaking, the version of the analysis of variance which we will discuss is only applicable when the normal distributions differ in mean but *not* in variance. In Figure 11.4 we have illustrated the null hypothesis, that is, all samples are drawn from the same normal distribution, and the alternative, that is, the samples are drawn from normal distributions with the same variance but different means. Fortunately, analysis of variance is a "robust" test. This means that it gives usable results even if the distributions of the populations are not quite normal and if the variances differ somewhat from population to population.

Null
hypothesis:
equal means

Are there differences among the mean salaries paid to banktellers in various cities? Samples of six banktellers in each of four cities—Pittsburgh, Richmond, Spokane, and Topeka—gave results which are recorded in Table 11.12. Are these samples drawn from the same population, so that the differences among the observations are due entirely to sampling fluctuations from sample to sample? Or are the samples drawn from different populations, so that the differences among the observations are due to differences among the mean salaries in the cities, as well as sampling fluctuations?

**TABLE 11.12   WEEKLY SALARIES, IN DOLLARS, OF
BANKTELLERS IN FOUR CITIES**

Pittsburgh	Richmond	Spokane	Topeka
143	159	154	165
187	152	164	188
156	172	162	157
167	177	200	145
213	145	179	167
202	161	155	114

The analysis of variance proceeds to answer these questions by—you guessed it—analyzing variances. The null hypothesis is that all observations do indeed come from the same population. This population will have a certain variance σ^2, so let us proceed to estimate this variance.

Given only the evidence from Pittsburgh, where the average salary is

$$\bar{x}_P = \frac{143 + 187 + \cdots + 202}{6} = 178$$

we can estimate the population variance σ^2 by s_P^2 as

$$s_P^2 = \frac{(143 - 178)^2 + (187 - 178)^2 + \cdots + (202 - 178)^2}{5} = 742.4$$

The subscript P implies that we base the estimate on sample information from Pittsburgh.

Clearly we can do better, for we have four samples, which we hypothesize to be from the same population. We compute the average salaries in Richmond, Spokane, and Topeka, $\bar{x}_R$, $\bar{x}_S$, and $\bar{x}_T$ and the sample variances s_R^2, s_S^2, and s_T^2 as estimates of the population variance σ^2. The results of these computations, which are analogous to those for Pittsburgh, are recorded in Table 11.13. The estimates s_P^2, s_R^2, s_S^2, and s_T^2 differ from city to city, but they are all *unbiased* estimates of σ^2. If we take their average, we have the best estimate we can find on the basis of these four samples. We then obtain

s_w^2
$$s_w^2 = \frac{742.4 + 143.6 + 311.2 + 622.4}{4} = 454.9$$

The subscript w stands for within. The only information used in obtaining this estimate is information contained *within* the separate samples. Only variability within the cities affects s_w^2. This variability is the same whether or not the hypothesis is true (see Figure 11.4).

TABLE 11.13   AVERAGE AND VARIANCE OF
WEEKLY SALARY IN FOUR CITIES

Cities	Average weekly salary	Variance
Pittsburgh	$\bar{x}_P = 178$	$s_P^2 = 742.4$
Richmond	$\bar{x}_R = 161$	$s_R^2 = 143.6$
Spokane	$\bar{x}_S = 169$	$s_S^2 = 311.2$
Topeka	$\bar{x}_T = 156$	$s_T^2 = 622.4$

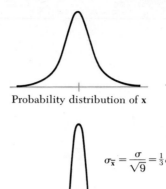

$$\sigma_{\bar{x}} = \frac{\sigma}{\sqrt{9}} = \tfrac{1}{3}\sigma$$

Probability distribution
of $\bar{x}$ based on samples
of nine observations

Figure 11.5 Within sample variance
based on population variability.

If the null hypothesis is true, we can estimate σ^2 by a different approach. For a proper understanding of this approach we reproduce in Figure 11.5 a result we met first in Section .7.5, and later in Section 9.3. In the upper portion of the figure is drawn the distribution of a normal variable **x**, and in the lower part is the corresponding distribution of $\bar{x}$, as obtained from samples of size n. We know that $E\bar{x} = Ex$; that is, the means of the two distributions are the same. We also know that $\sigma_{\bar{x}}^2 = \sigma^2/n$; that is, the variance of $\bar{x}$ is $1/n$ times the variance of **x**. In our previous use of this formula, we took σ^2 as given, and derived $\sigma_{\bar{x}}^2$. This gave us an interval estimate for the mean (see Section 9.3). In what follows, we work the other way around.

Figure 11.6 is based on the data in Table 11.12. In total, we have

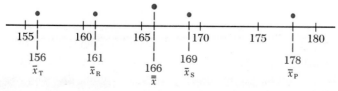

Figure 11.6 Among sample variance based on differences among sample means.

24 observations, and the overall average of these values is

$$\bar{\bar{x}} = \frac{143 + 187 + \cdots + 114}{24} = 166$$

This is the best estimate we have of the true mean μ. Since the sample sizes are equal, this estimate can also be found by taking the average of the sample averages recorded in Table 11.13:

$$\bar{\bar{x}} = \frac{178 + 161 + 169 + 156}{4} = 166$$

The "double bar" above the x symbolizes the fact that we have taken an average of averages. The sample averages shown in Figure 11.6 enable us to compute an estimate of the variance of $\bar{\mathbf{x}}$. Numerically, we find

$$s_{\bar{\mathbf{x}}}^2 = \frac{(178 - 166)^2 + (161 - 166)^2 + (169 - 166)^2 + (156 - 166)^2}{3}$$

$$= \frac{278}{3} = 92\tfrac{2}{3}$$

We divide by 3 rather than 4 because the value 166 does not necessarily coincide with the true mean μ. An estimate of σ^2, the population variance, is obtained by multiplying this value by 6, since $s_{\bar{\mathbf{x}}}^2 = \sigma^2/n$, where n is the number of observations on which the average is based, six in this example. Thus

s_a^2

$$s_a^2 = 6 \times s_{\bar{\mathbf{x}}}^2 = 6 \times 92\tfrac{2}{3} = 556$$

is another estimate of σ^2. The subscript a stands for among, because it is based on comparing averages *among* the various samples.

Since s_a^2 and s_w^2 are estimates of the same value σ^2 *if the null hypothesis is true,* we would expect them to be close together. We would expect their ratio F

The F ratio

$$F = \frac{s_a^2}{s_w^2}$$

to be close to 1. If it is much *greater* than 1, doubt is cast on the null hypothesis. Instead, it is likely that the distributions of salaries in the four cities have different means. If we examine Figure 11.4, this can be easily explained. Suppose that the means actually do differ from city to city. In computing s_a^2, we use the averages among the samples; and if these differ not only because of inevitable sampling fluctuations but also because the means of the populations are in fact different, the value will be inflated. The next question is, "How large a value of F is significant at the 5 percent level?" We take this matter up in the next section.

EXERCISES

11.17 Four machines produce ball bearings. A sample of five observations is drawn from the output of each machine, and the diameter is recorded. The following results are obtained:

Machine 1	Machine 2	Machine 3	Machine 4
8.16	8.27	8.32	8.06
8.28	8.27	8.30	8.28
8.23	8.32	8.32	8.29
8.13	8.32	8.20	8.20
8.35	8.12	8.26	8.12

Find s_a^2 and s_w^2. If the analysis of variance is applied to these observations, what hypothesis is being tested?

11.18 Using only the observations in the samples from the output of machines 3 and 4, find s_a^2 and s_w^2.

11.19 The accompanying table shows the average and variance of annual expenditures on transportation by families of various sizes. A sample of five families was selected in each size group. Find s_a^2 and s_w^2.

	Family size			
	3	4	5	6
Average expenditure	200	260	216	240
Variance	100	160	200	100

11.7 THE F DISTRIBUTION

As we saw in Section 11.5, in samples from a normal population the distributions of s_a^2/σ^2 and s_w^2/σ^2 are χ^2 distributions with the appropriate number of degrees of freedom. The distribution of

$$F = \frac{s_a^2}{s_w^2}$$

is therefore the ratio of these two χ^2 distributions. It is characterized by two numbers of degrees of freedom, one associated with the numerator, and one with the denominator. In Table 11.14 we give values of F significant at the 5 percent level. Values equal to or larger than those shown are significant at the 5 percent level. The value of F at the 1 percent significance level, which is not recorded in Table 11.7, is in most cases between $1\frac{1}{2}$ and 2 times as large as the value at the 5 percent significance level. This can be verified from Table 9 in Appendix B.

The general shape of the F distribution is shown in Figure 11.7. In the figure, the value 2.96 is indicated. When there are 5 degrees of

TABLE 11.14 *F* DISTRIBUTION

df of s_w^2 (denominator)	df of s_a^2 (numerator)									
	1	2	3	4	5	6	7	8	9	10
5	6.61	5.79	5.41	5.19	5.05	4.95	4.88	4.82	4.78	4.74
10	4.96	4.10	3.71	3.48	3.33	3.22	3.14	3.07	3.02	2.97
11	4.84	3.98	3.59	3.36	3.20	3.09	3.01	2.95	2.90	2.86
12	4.75	3.88	3.49	3.26	3.11	3.00	2.92	2.85	2.80	2.76
13	4.67	3.80	3.41	3.18	3.02	2.92	2.84	2.77	2.72	2.67
14	4.60	3.74	3.34	3.11	2.96	2.85	2.77	2.70	2.65	2.60
15	4.54	3.68	3.29	3.06	2.90	2.79	2.70	2.64	2.59	2.55
16	4.49	3.63	3.24	3.01	2.85	2.74	2.66	2.59	2.54	2.49
17	4.45	3.59	3.20	2.96	2.81	2.70	2.62	2.55	2.50	2.45
18	4.41	3.55	3.16	2.93	2.77	2.66	2.58	2.51	2.46	2.41
19	4.38	3.52	3.13	2.90	2.74	2.63	2.55	2.48	2.43	2.38
20	4.35	3.49	3.10	2.87	2.71	2.60	2.52	2.45	2.40	2.35
21	4.32	3.47	3.07	2.84	2.68	2.57	2.49	2.42	2.37	2.32
22	4.30	3.44	3.05	2.82	2.66	2.55	2.47	2.40	2.35	2.30
23	4.28	3.42	3.03	2.80	2.64	2.53	2.45	2.38	2.32	2.28
24	4.26	3.40	3.01	2.78	2.62	2.51	2.43	2.36	2.30	2.26
25	4.24	3.38	2.99	2.76	2.60	2.49	2.41	2.34	2.28	2.24
30	4.17	3.32	2.92	2.69	2.53	2.42	2.34	2.27	2.21	2.16
40	4.08	3.23	2.84	2.61	2.45	2.34	2.25	2.18	2.12	2.07
50	4.03	3.18	2.79	2.56	2.40	2.29	2.20	2.13	2.07	2.02
60	4.00	3.15	2.76	2.52	2.37	2.25	2.17	2.10	2.04	1.99
80	3.96	3.11	2.72	2.48	2.33	2.21	2.12	2.05	1.99	1.95
100	3.94	3.09	2.70	2.46	2.30	2.19	2.10	2.03	1.97	1.92

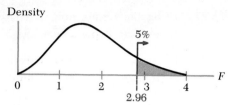

Figure 11.7 *F* distribution, 5 and 14 degrees of freedom.

freedom in the numerator and 14 in the denominator, this value or larger values are significant at the 5 percent level. This implies that if the null hypothesis is true so that s_a^2 and s_w^2 are both estimates of the variance σ^2 in the same population, a value of F equal to or larger than 2.96 occurs only 5 percent of the time owing to sampling fluctuations. Of the area under the F distribution with 5 and 14 degrees of freedom, 5 percent is to the right of 2.96.

In the previous section we found that four samples of size six gave an F value of

$$\frac{s_a^2}{s_w^2} = \frac{556}{455} = 1.22$$

The appropriate number of degrees of freedom is determined as follows. There are four samples, and s_a^2 is based on the four sample averages. We lost 1 degree of freedom in using $\bar{x}$ and are left with 3 degrees of freedom for the numerator. There are 24 observations on which s_w^2 is based. We lost 4 degrees of freedom in using the four sample averages and are left with 20 degrees of freedom in the denominator. In the next section we will make these results more general. From Table 11.14 we see that a value of 3.10 or higher is significant at the 5 percent level for 3 and 20 degrees of freedom. A value of 1.22 is not significant. We accept the hypothesis that all four samples came from the same population. As a matter of fact, they did. The samples were drawn from a population with a mean of 160 and a standard deviation of 20.

Determination of degrees of freedom

EXERCISES

11.20   Using the results from Exercise 11.17, test the hypothesis that the mean diameter produced on all four machines is the same. Use a 5 percent level of significance.

11.21   Using the results from Exercise 11.18, formulate and test the appropriate hypothesis at the 5 percent level of significance.

11.22   Using the results from Exercise 11.19, formulate and test the appropriate hypothesis at the 5 percent level of significance.

11.8 MORE COMPLICATED ANALYSIS OF VARIANCE

In the previous sections we explained the basic philosophy and method of the analysis of variance. This section will be devoted to two extensions of those ideas: (1) from equal to unequal sample sizes, and (2) from one source of variation—different cities or different family sizes—to more than one.

Unequal sample sizes

When not all sample sizes are equal, the calculations are a little different because results of samples which have more observations ought to carry more weight in the calculation of variance estimates. A standard layout for the computations is presented in Table 11.15. There are k samples, and sample 1 has n_1 observations, sample 2 has $n_2, \ldots,$ and sample k has n_k observations. If the first sample has observations $x_1, x_2, \ldots, x_{n_1},$ the average is

$$\bar{x}_1 = \frac{x_1 + x_2 + \cdots + x_{n_1}}{n_1}$$

and the variance is

$$s_1^2 = \frac{(x_1 - \bar{x}_1)^2 + (x_2 + \bar{x}_1)^2 + \cdots + (x_{n_1} - \bar{x}_1)^2}{n_1 - 1}$$

The average and variance for the other samples are found in the same way. The value s_w^2 is now a weighted average of the values $s_1^2, s_2^2, \ldots, s_k^2,$ with weights equal to the sample size minus 1. The value s_w^2 so computed has $n_1 + n_2 + \cdots + n_k - k$ degrees of freedom, since there are $n_1 + n_2 + \cdots + n_k$ observations in total, but k averages $\bar{x}_1, \bar{x}_2, \ldots, \bar{x}_k$ were used in computing $s_w^2.$

The overall average $\bar{\bar{x}}$ is a weighted average of the averages of the k samples, with weights equal to the sample sizes. The value s_a^2 in the previous section was equal to $6 \times s_{\bar{x}}^2,$ which can be written out as

$$s_a^2 = \frac{6(178 - 166)^2 + 6(161 - 166)^2 + 6(169 - 166)^2 + 6(156 - 166)^2}{4 - 1} = 556$$

TABLE 11.15 COMPUTATIONS TO DETERMINE F RATIO IN k SAMPLES OF DIFFERENT SIZES

Sample	1	2	3	...	k
	1	1	1	...	1
	2	2	2	...	2
	. . . .				
Average	n_1	n_2	n_3	...	n_k
Estimated	$\overline{x}_1$	$\overline{x}_2$	$\overline{x}_3$	...	$\overline{x}_k$
variance	s_1^2	s_2^2	s_3^2	...	s_k^2

$$s_w^2 = \frac{(n_1 - 1)s_1^2 + (n_2 - 1)s_2^2 + \cdots + (n_k - 1)s_k^2}{n_1 + n_2 + \cdots + n_k - k} = \frac{\Sigma(n_i - 1)s_i^2}{\Sigma n_i - k}$$

$$\overline{\overline{x}} = \frac{n_1\overline{x}_1 + n_2\overline{x}_2 + \cdots + n_k\overline{x}_k}{n_1 + n_2 + \cdots + n_k} = \frac{\Sigma n_i \overline{x}_i}{\Sigma n_i}$$

$$s_a^2 = \frac{n_1(\overline{x}_1 - \overline{\overline{x}})^2 + n_2(\overline{x}_2 - \overline{\overline{x}})^2 + \cdots + n_k(\overline{x}_k - \overline{\overline{x}})^2}{k - 1} = \frac{\Sigma n_i(\overline{x} - \overline{\overline{x}})^2}{k - 1}$$

$$F = \frac{s_a^2}{s_w^2} \text{ (numerator } k - 1 \text{ } df\text{; denominator } \Sigma n_i - k \text{ } df\text{)}$$

The formula in the table is the same, aside from the fact that the weights of the squared differences of the sample averages from the overall average are equal to the sample sizes n_1, n_2, . . . , n_k. The value s_a^2 is based on k sample averages, from which one overall average $\overline{\overline{x}}$ is computed, so there are a total of $k - 1$ degrees of freedom for s_a^2, which equals the value of the denominator. A numerical example is given in Table 11.16.

In Table 11.16 we find $F = 2.14$, with 4 degrees of freedom for s_a^2 (since there are five samples) and $21 - 5 = 16$ degrees of freedom for s_w^2. A value of 3.01 or higher would have been significant. Again, we accept the hypothesis that all samples are drawn from the same population. In fact, the true means were 50, 55, 60, 50, and 40, and the standard deviation was 25. The means differed, but we did not have sufficiently large samples to obtain significant results in view of the high standard deviation.

You may be surprised by this lack of significance. In looking at the data in Table 11.16, we might decide to test whether samples 3 and 5

TABLE 11.16   NUMERICAL EXAMPLE OF COMPUTATION OF
F RATIO

1	2	3	4	5
91	90	64	52	53
14	94	78	73	39
68	36	86	41	6
27	44		34	24
45				33
$n_1 = 5$	$n_2 = 4$	$n_3 = 3$	$n_4 = 4$	$n_5 = 5$
$\bar{x}_1 = 49$	$\bar{x}_2 = 66$	$\bar{x}_3 = 76$	$\bar{x}_4 = 50$	$\bar{x}_5 = 31$
$s_1^2 = 962\frac{1}{2}$	$s_2^2 = 914\frac{2}{3}$	$s_3^2 = 124$	$s_4^2 = 290$	$s_5^2 = 306\frac{1}{2}$

$$s_w^2 = \frac{4 \times 962\frac{1}{2} + 3 \times 914\frac{2}{3} + 2 \times 124 + 3 \times 290 + 4 \times 306\frac{1}{2}}{5 + 4 + 3 + 4 + 5 - 5}$$

$$= \frac{8{,}938}{16} = 559 \ (16 \ df)$$

$$\bar{\bar{x}} = \frac{5 \times 49 + 4 \times 66 + 3 \times 76 + 4 \times 50 + 5 \times 31}{5 + 4 + 3 + 4 + 5} = \frac{1{,}092}{21} = 52$$

$$s_a^2 = \frac{5(49-52)^2 + 4(66-52)^2 + 3(76-52)^2 + 4(50-52)^2 + 5(31-52)^2}{5-1}$$

$$= \frac{4{,}778}{4} = 1{,}194 \ (1 \ df)$$

$$F = \frac{s_a^2}{s_w^2} = \frac{1{,}194}{559} = 2.14$$

came from the same population at the 5 percent level of significance. If we consider only these two samples, s_a^2 is over 2,300, with 1 degree of freedom, and s_w^2 is close to 245, with 6 degrees of freedom. Their ratio is more than 9, which is significant at the 5 percent level. If we consider all five samples, we accept the hypothesis that they are all from the same population. If we consider only samples 3 and 5, we reject the hypothesis that they come from the same population. The fallacy of comparing only samples 3 and 5 is that we compare not two randomly chosen samples, but rather the samples with the lowest and highest average. It can be shown that the probability that the largest differences among the averages in five samples drawn from the same population will exceed 2 standard deviations of the average is about 20 percent. This is far more than 5 percent, so we should not be surprised at finding such a pair. The temptation to look at the data and then formulate the hypothesis to be tested is appealing. However, it must be resisted.

The second extension of our basic discussion of the analysis of variance will deal with the complications that arise when there is more than one possible source of variability in the observations in addition to chance. In the example dealing with the salaries of bank clerks in four cities, we tested the hypothesis that the mean wage in each city was the same. The only possible source of variation in the data, apart from chance or sampling variability, was variability among these city means. We refer to this as a *single-factor* analysis of variance since only one possible source of variation, other than chance, is present.

Multifactor analysis of variance

We might be told that in each sample the first three salaries shown are for women and the last three for men. This sets the stage for a *two-factor* analysis of variance. In place of four means, one for each city, there are now eight means, one for each sex in each city. Our null hypothesis says these are all equal; that is, neither sex nor city is a source of difference in mean salary among these eight populations of bank clerks.

Using formulas not introduced here, we could make four independent estimates of the variance σ^2, which we assume is equal in all eight populations.

s_c^2: based on the differences among the averages in the samples from each city

s_s^2: based on the differences among the averages in the samples from each sex

s_{cs}^2: based on the differences among the averages in the samples from each sex in each city

s_w^2: based on the differences within the samples from each sex in each city

We test the major hypothesis in stages, by forming several F ratios. The s_{cs}^2 estimate includes the effect of variability due to an *interaction* between city and sex. If

Interaction effect

$$F = \frac{s_{cs}^2}{s_w^2}$$

is significant, we say the interaction between city and sex is significant. This may happen if men earn more than women in some cities, but in other cities the reverse is true. If the interaction is not significant, we proceed to test the *main effects*, city and sex. If

Main effects

$$F = \frac{s_c^2}{s_w^2}$$

is significant, we conclude that there are differences among the city means. That is, we reject the null hypothesis that the mean salary of bank clerks is the same in the four cities. Finally, if

$$F = \frac{s_s^2}{s_w^2}$$

is significant, we conclude that there is a difference between the mean salaries of men and women. It is entirely possible that only one main effect will be significant, or that both main effects will be significant, but the interaction will not be.

The analysis can be generalized to more than two factors.

EXERCISES

11.23   As computed from nine samples with a total of 69 observations, $s_a^2 = 843$ and $s_w^2 = 440$. Do we reject the null hypothesis that all nine samples come from the same population?

11.24   Three different employees in a gas station were observed as they changed tires on cars. The times taken by employee A to do four tires, one on each of four cars, were (in minutes) 10, 11, 11, and 12. Employee B switched five tires in 10, 10, 14, 14, and 12 minutes. Employee C did six tires in 11, 11, 9, 7, 9, and 7 minutes. Use analysis of variance to test the relevant hypothesis. What is the hypothesis? What is F? What is your conclusion?

11.25   A sample of six senior professors in a technical institute gives ages 45, 46, 48, 51, 39, and 47. In a liberal arts college the ages in a sample of seven senior professors are 62, 51, 49, 71, 49, 50, 46. What hypothesis do we test? Do we accept it?

11.26   In Exercise 11.19, each sample of five families contained two with an income below $10,000 and three with an income of $10,000 or more. If a two-factor analysis of variance is made, what would a significant interaction effect imply?

Answers to Exercises

11.1   The random variable **u** should be at least 12.017.

11.2   The median is 7.344. There is 80 percent of the area between the values 3.490 and 13.362. For 90 percent these values are 2.733 and 15.507, and for 99 percent they are 1.646 and 20.090.

11.3   We know the random variable $\mathbf{x} = \sqrt{2\mathbf{u}} - \sqrt{2m-1}$ has the distribution $N(0,1)$. For $u = 162$ we find $x = \sqrt{2 \times 162} - \sqrt{(2 \times 113) - 1} = \sqrt{324} - \sqrt{225} = 18 - 15 = 3$.   In $N(0,1)$, the value 3 is outside the interval $\mu \pm 2.58\sigma$; therefore, $u = 162$ is significant at the 1 percent level.

11.4   The expected number is $16\frac{2}{3}$ of each; hence

$$u = \frac{(20 - 16\frac{2}{3})^2}{16\frac{2}{3}} + \cdots + \frac{(17 - 16\frac{2}{3})^2}{16\frac{2}{3}} = 2.36$$

This is not significant at the 5 percent level, when there are 5 degrees of freedom.

11.5   We compute

$$u = \frac{(14{,}182 - 13{,}942\frac{1}{2})^2}{13{,}942\frac{1}{2}} + \frac{(13{,}713 - 13{,}942\frac{1}{2})^2}{13{,}942\frac{1}{2}}$$

$$\approx \frac{(293)^2}{13{,}942\frac{1}{2}} + \frac{(293)^2}{13{,}942\frac{1}{2}} = 6.1$$

We square 293 rather than $293\frac{1}{2}$ since there is but 1 degree of freedom. The value of 6.1 is significant at the 5 percent level. Note that we have no alternative hypothesis, although many, for example, P(boy) = .505 or P(boy) = .51, would not be rejected, given the evidence.

11.6   We have $\pi_0 = .60$. If the alternative is that the marksman in fact hits less than 60 percent of his shots, all values below $40(.60) - 1.645\sqrt{40(.60)(.40)} = 18.9$ are in the critical region. A result of 18 or fewer hits leads to rejection of the null hypothesis at the 5 percent level of significance. This result corresponds to the conclusion reached by the χ^2 test in the text.

11.7   We expect, under the manager's null hypothesis, 3,000 customers in each store. We find

$$u = \frac{(3{,}000 - 3{,}000)^2}{3{,}000} + \frac{(2{,}960 - 3{,}000)^2}{3{,}000}$$

$$+ \frac{(3{,}100 - 3{,}000)^2}{3{,}000} + \frac{(2{,}780 - 3{,}000)^2}{3{,}000}$$

$$+ \frac{(3{,}160 - 3{,}000)^2}{3{,}000} = 28\frac{1}{2}$$

With 4 degrees of freedom, any value over 7,779 is significant at the 10 percent level. We reject the manager's null hypothesis. Some stores have a larger patronage than others.

11.8 The total number of observations is 100; hence there are $100 - (12 + 15 + 44 + 20) = 9$ observations either 4 or 5. The average is 2, so the 100 observations add up to 200. The 91 observations add to 163, so the nine remaining observations must add to 37. Clearly there will be eight observations 4, and one observation 5. We have shown that, given n and $\bar{x}$, we lose 2 degrees of freedom.

11.9 From the data we derive that there are 97 misprints in total. The Poisson parameter is $\frac{97}{748} = .13$, the average number of misprints per page. The theoretical probability of k mistakes is $e^{-.13}(.13)^k/k!$ For $k = 0, 1, 2, 3$, these values are 87.8, 11.4, .7, and .1 percent. If we multiply these probabilities by 748, the number of pages, we obtain the expected number of pages with 0, 1, 2, 3 misprints as 657, 85, 5, 1 for a total of $657 \times 0 + 85 \times 1 + 5 \times 2 + 1 \times 3 = 98$ misprints. (The difference between 97 and 98 is due to rounding.) So we have to compare 665, 71, 10, and 2 with 657, 85, 5, and 1. We must combine the last two classes, and are left with 1 degree of freedom only. (There are three classes, but n and the parameter take care of two of these.) We consider

$$u = \frac{(665 - 657)^2}{657} + \frac{(71 - 85)^2}{85} + \frac{(12 - 6)^2}{6}$$

And, because there is only 1 degree of freedom, we compute

$$\frac{(7\frac{1}{2})^2}{657} + \frac{(13\frac{1}{2})^2}{85} + \frac{(5\frac{1}{2})^2}{6} \approx 6.5$$

This is significant at the 5 percent level. We reject the hypothesis of a Poisson distribution.

11.10 (a) As already observed in Exercise 7.13, the decile points of the normal distribution are

$$\mu \pm 1.28\sigma \qquad \mu \pm .842\sigma \qquad \mu \pm .524\sigma \qquad \mu \pm .254\sigma \qquad \mu$$

In this case, 10 percent of the grades should be in each of

the intervals 56 or below, 57–61, 62–64, 65–67, 68–69, 70–71, 72–74, 75–77, 78–82, 83 or over. In fact, these intervals contain 11, 10, 8, 8, 10, 12, 8, 9, 12, 12 observations. The value

$$u = \frac{(11 - 10)^2}{10} + \cdots + \frac{(12 - 10)^2}{10} = 2.6$$

is not significant at the 5 percent level when there are 9 degrees of freedom. There are 9 degrees of freedom, since μ and σ were *not* determined from the sample information. Only the number of observations n was.

(*b*) More than 95 percent, since 2.6 *is* in the 5 percent area in the *lower* tail. The fit is remarkably close. The teacher may be manipulating grades to get the desired normal distribution.

11.11 We have $P(C) = \frac{20}{100} = .20$, $P(N) = \frac{60}{100} = .60$; hence, under independence, $P(C \ and \ N) = P(C)P(N) = (.20)(.60) = .12$. There are 100 observations, so $.12 \times 100 = 12$ should be the number of customers who pay for a new car with cash.

11.12 Under independence we would *expect* to have 36, 24, 24, and 16 rather than 40, 20, 20, and 20. All differences between expectations and reality are 4, but we decrease this to $3\frac{1}{2}$, since there is but 1 degree of freedom. The value

$$u = \frac{(3\frac{1}{2})^2}{36} + \frac{(3\frac{1}{2})^2}{24} + \frac{(3\frac{1}{2})^2}{24} + \frac{(3\frac{1}{2})^2}{16} = 2.13$$

is not significant at the 10 percent level. (One may check that without the continuity correction the answer would have been significant at the 10 percent level.) If the numbers were percentages, we would have to know the number of observations on which the percentages are based. With this information we could find the actual frequencies and test for independence.

11.13 Under independence, the entries would have been

105	$102\frac{1}{2}$	30	$12\frac{1}{2}$
105	$102\frac{1}{2}$	30	$12\frac{1}{2}$
105	$102\frac{1}{2}$	30	$12\frac{1}{2}$
105	$102\frac{1}{2}$	30	$12\frac{1}{2}$

There are 9 degrees of freedom, and

$$u = \frac{(45)^2}{105} + \frac{(22\frac{1}{2})^2}{102\frac{1}{2}} + \cdots + \frac{(7\frac{1}{2})^2}{12\frac{1}{2}} = 80.5$$

which is, as simple inspection of the table would already indicate, significant.

11.14   We have

$$s^2 = \frac{(x_1 - \bar{x})^2 + \cdots + (x_{21} - \bar{x})^2}{20} = 110$$

so $(x_1 - \bar{x})^2 + \cdots + (x_{21} - \bar{x})^2 = 110 \times 20 = 2,200$. We now look in the χ^2 table in Appendix B, for the values $\chi^2_{.95}$ and $\chi^2_{.05}$ in the row of $n - 1 = 20$ degrees of freedom, and find the values 31.41 amd 10.85. Hence the range is $\frac{2,200}{31.41}$ to $\frac{2,200}{10.85}$, or roughly 70 to 200.

11.15   The 95 percent confidence interval runs from

$$\frac{229,840}{\chi^2_{.025}} \quad \text{to} \quad \frac{229,840}{\chi^2_{.975}}$$

where the χ^2 distribution has 169 degrees of freedom. We know that if $\mathbf{u}$ is χ^2 with 169 degrees of freedom then $\mathbf{x} = \sqrt{2u} - \sqrt{2m - 1}$ is $N(0,1)$. Values of $\mathbf{x}$ outside the interval $0 \pm 1.960(1)$ are in the extreme $2\frac{1}{2}$ percent of the tails. The values -1.960 and $+1.960$ of x correspond to the u values as follows:

$$-1.960 = \sqrt{2u} - \sqrt{2(169) - 1} \qquad +1.960 = \sqrt{2u} - \sqrt{2(169) - 1}$$
$$= \sqrt{2u} - 18.41 \qquad\qquad = \sqrt{2u} - 18.41$$
$$16.45 = \sqrt{2u} \qquad\qquad\qquad 20.37 = \sqrt{2u}$$
$$270.6 = 2u \qquad\qquad\qquad\quad 414.9 = 2u$$
$$135.3 = u \; (= \chi^2_{.975}) \qquad\qquad 207.5 = u \; (= \chi^2_{.025})$$

The point estimate for σ^2 is $\frac{229,840}{169} = 1,360$. The 95 percent interval estimate is from $\frac{229,840}{207.5}$ to $\frac{229,840}{135.3}$, or 1,107 to 1,699.

11.16   The null hypothesis is that $\sigma^2 = .04$. The value $s^2 = .07$, based on a sample of size 11, implies that $(x_1 - \bar{x})^2 + \cdots + (x_{11} - \bar{x})^2 = 10(.07) = .7$. Under the null hypothesis there is 90 percent probability that

$$3.940 < \frac{(x_1 - \bar{x})^2 + \cdots + (x_{11} - \bar{x})^2}{.04} < 18.307$$

Therefore, if the sample observations are such that

$$3.940 < \frac{(x_1 - \bar{x})^2 + \cdots + (x_{11} - \bar{x})^2}{.04} < 18.307$$

we will accept the hypothesis that $\sigma^2 = .04$. In the sample we have observed

$$\frac{(x_1 - \bar{x})^2 + \cdots + (x_{11} - \bar{x})^2}{.04} = \frac{.7}{.04} = 17.5$$

Therefore the inequalities are satisfied and we accept the hypothesis.

11.17   We find $\bar{x}_1 = 8.23$, $\bar{x}_2 = 8.26$, $\bar{x}_3 = 8.28$, $\bar{x}_4 = 8.19$, and $\bar{\bar{x}} = 8.24$. Also, $s_1^2 = .00795$, $s_2^2 = .00675$, $s_3^2 = .00260$, $s_4^2 = .01000$. Hence

$$s_w^2 = \frac{.00795 + .00675 + .00260 + .01000}{4} = .006825$$

$$s_a^2 = \frac{5(8.23 - 8.24)^2 + 5(8.26 - 8.24)^2 + 5(8.28 - 8.24)^2 + 5(8.19 - 8.24)^2}{3} = .007665$$

Analysis of variance is used to test whether the mean diameters of all the ball bearings made on each of these four machines are equal.

11.18 $$s_w^2 = \frac{.00260 + .01000}{2} = .00630$$

$$s_a^2 = \frac{5(8.28 - 8.235)^2 + 5(8.19 - 8.235)^2}{1} = .02025$$

11.19 $$s_w^2 = \frac{100 + 160 + 200 + 100}{.4} = 140$$

$$\bar{\bar{x}} = 229$$

$$s_a^2 = \frac{5(200 - 229)^2 + 5(260 - 229)^2 + 5(216 - 229)^2 + 5(240 - 229)^2}{3} = 3,485$$

11.20 $F = \frac{.007665}{.006825} = 1.15$. Hypothesis is accepted. For 3 degrees of freedom in the numerator and 16 in the denominator, values of F above 3.24 lead to rejection.

11.21 $F = \frac{.02025}{.00630} = 3.20$. The hypothesis that the mean diameters of bearings produced on machines 3 and 4 are the same is accepted. For 1 degree of freedom in the numerator and 8 in the denominator, values of F above 5.32 lead to rejection.

11.22 $F = \frac{3,485}{140} = 24.9$. There are 3 degrees of freedom in the numerator, 16 in the denominator. Any value of F above 3.24 is significant at the 5 percent level. We reject the hypothesis that mean annual expenditures on transportation for families of different sizes are the same.

11.23 $F = \frac{843}{440} = 1.92$. There are 8 degrees of freedom in s_a^2, and 60 in s_w^2, and any value over 2.10 is significant at the 5 percent level. No, we do not reject the null hypothesis.

11.24

$$n_1 = 4 \qquad n_2 = 5 \qquad n_3 = 6$$
$$\bar{x}_1 = 11 \qquad \bar{x}_2 = 12 \qquad \bar{x}_3 = 9$$
$$s_1^2 = \tfrac{2}{3} \qquad s_2^2 = 4 \qquad s_3^2 = 3\tfrac{1}{5}$$

$$s_w^2 = \frac{3 \times \tfrac{2}{3} + 4 \times 4 + 5 \times 3\tfrac{1}{5}}{4 + 5 + 6 - 3} = \frac{34}{12} = 2\tfrac{5}{6}$$

$$\bar{\bar{x}} = \frac{4 \times 11 + 5 \times 12 + 6 \times 9}{15} = \frac{158}{15} \approx 10\tfrac{1}{2}$$

$$s_a^2 = \frac{4(11 - 10\tfrac{1}{2})^2 + 5(12 - 10\tfrac{1}{2})^2 + 6(9 - 10\tfrac{1}{2})^2}{3 - 1}$$

$$= \frac{25\tfrac{3}{4}}{2} = 12\tfrac{7}{8}$$

$$F = \frac{12\tfrac{7}{8}}{2\tfrac{5}{8}} \approx 4.9$$

We test the hypothesis that the mean time to change a tire is the same for all three employees. We reject the null hypothesis. With 2 degrees of freedom in the numerator and 12 in the denominator, values of F greater than 3.88 occur with probability less than 5 percent. The conclusion is that the three employees do not require the same mean time to change a tire.

11.25

$$n_1 = 6 \qquad n_2 = 7$$
$$\bar{x}_1 = 46 \qquad \bar{x}_2 = 54$$
$$s_1^2 = 16 \qquad s_2^2 = 82$$

$$s_w^2 = \frac{5 \times 16 + 6 \times 82}{11} = \frac{572}{11} = 52$$

$$\bar{\bar{x}} = \frac{6 \times 46 + 7 \times 54}{13} = \frac{654}{13} \approx 50$$

$$s_a^2 = \frac{6(46 - 50)^2 + 7(54 - 50)^2}{1}$$

$$= 6 \times 16 + 7 \times 16 = 208$$

$$F = \frac{208}{52} = 4$$

We test the hypothesis that the mean age of senior professors in the technical institute and the mean age of senior professors in the liberal arts college are equal. With 1 degree of freedom in the numerator and 11 in the denominator, values of F greater than 4.84 occur with probability less than 5 percent. We accept the hypothesis.

11.26 A significant interaction effect would show that we cannot accept the hypothesis that mean expenditures on transportation are the same in all eight combinations of family size and income group. Income and family size apparently do not influence expenditures on transportation independently. Some combinations of income and family size produce a higher mean expenditure on transportation than others.

Chapter 12

PAYOFF TABLES, THE VALUE OF INFORMATION, AND BAYESIAN INFERENCE

12.1 INTRODUCTION

Our takeoff point in this chapter is the example discussed in Sections 10.4 to 10.6. A manufacturer is offered a shipment of transistors for sale, which he wants to buy if the percentage that is defective is .05 or less, but not otherwise. Since the true percentage of defectives is unknown, he faces a difficult problem, and calls a statistician for help. The statistician proceeds by looking the manager firmly in the eye and saying, "I realize that you'd like to buy if there are not more than .05 defectives, and that you'd rather not buy otherwise. But I'm sure that if the true percentage of defectives is .045 or .055 you will not be greatly concerned, since the loss or profit involved is bound to be small. There must be a quality *so* good that you would definitely want to accept it, and a quality *so* rotten that you would rather not touch it with a 10-foot pole. What are these qualities?" The manufacturer thinks for a while, and somehow comes up with the answer that when there are .03 defectives he would *really* like to buy, while if there are .07 defectives he would *much rather not* buy. The statistician promises the manufacturer that he will be able to tell him what to do, provided the manufacturer is willing to run a 10 percent risk of buying a shipment with .07 defectives, and a 10 percent risk of not

327

buying a shipment with .03 defectives. The manufacturer reluctantly approves these risks, and the statistician now has a routine task. The manufacturer has established for him the null hypothesis $\pi_0 = .03$, the alternative hypothesis $\pi_1 = .07$, and the risks of errors of Type I and Type II $r_0 = r_1 = 10$ percent. He establishes the sample size n by the formula

$$n = \left(\frac{1.282 \sqrt{.03 \times .97} + 1.282 \sqrt{.07 \times .93}}{.07 - .03} \right)^2 = 13.62^2 \approx 185$$

To play it safe—because of continuity problems—the statistician decides to sample 225 items. He then determines the critical value, which in this case is any value *above*

$$.03 \times 225 + 1.282 \sqrt{.03 \times .97 \times 225} = 10.02$$

and *below*

$$.07 \times 225 - 1.282 \sqrt{.07 \times .93 \times 225} = 10.83$$

The value 10.5 nicely satisfies both conditions. The value 10.5 in the continuous normal distribution implies for our discrete case that if the sample of size 225 has 10 or fewer defectives, the statistician will advise to buy, whereas if there are 11 or more he will advise not to buy. In this way the risks of errors of Type I and Type II are both slightly less than 10 percent, which will please the manufacturer. The statistician now draws a sample, observes the result, and recommends to management in accordance with his findings.

Explicit use of profit and loss

     Several features of this procedure deserve a closer look. For one, how did the manufacturer arrive at the values .03 and .07? If the statistician asks him, the manufacturer will no doubt reply that they are based on considerations of profit and loss, which he implicitly took into account. If they enter into the manufacturer's computations *im*plicitly, however, they may just as well and perhaps better figure *explicitly* in the computations. With this observation the statistician scores one point.

Use of a priori information

     As the next observation, it is perfectly possible that the manufacturer will have some a priori idea about the quality of the shipment. He may have traded before with the same supplier, he may be aware of the technical difficulties in the production process, he may have received similar batches from elsewhere, and so on. The manufacturer will be prone to deny this, and remark that, if he knew the quality of the shipment, he would have no use for the statistician. The statistician might challenge him by asking,

"I'll give you \$10 if a sample of size 50 has 2 or fewer defectives, and you give me \$10 if it has 3 or more. Will you accept the bet?" If the manufacturer says that he will, the statistician suggests that they *reverse the bet:* The manufacturer will give the statistician \$10 if a sample of 50 has 2 or fewer defectives, and receive \$10 otherwise. The manufacturer says *no*. The statistician has established that the manufacturer thinks it more likely that the shipment will have *fewer* than .05 defectives rather than *more*. He has scored again.

Finally, a third shortcoming can be observed in the procedure. The sample size is more or less automatically determined at 225, but the *cost* of sampling and the *value* of the sample information have not entered the discussion at all. The point is well taken. The score is 3 to 0:

Compare cost and value of sample

1. The profit and loss data did not enter explicitly.
2. The a priori ideas of the manufacturer had no role in the analysis.
3. The sample size was determined without comparing sampling costs

with the value of sample information.

It is time to do something about these omissions. In this chapter we will tackle them in order.

12.2 PAYOFF TABLES

The most convenient way to display and analyze profit and loss figures for decision making is the *payoff table.* Such a table shows the possible states of nature, the possible decisions, and the gain or loss which results from a particular decision, given a state of nature. We will give some examples.

Payoff tables

In Table 12.1 we present the plight of a jury. The states of nature, innocent or guilty, and the possible decisions, acquit or condemn, lead to payoffs which each person must evaluate for himself. The following

TABLE 12.1 PAYOFF (IN SOCIAL UTILITY) FOR JURY'S DECISION

State of nature	Decision	
	Acquit	*Condemn*
Innocent	0	−5 (?)
Guilty	−1	0

argument explains the values shown in the table. They are measured on the authors' personal scale of "social utility." We feel no particular utility or disutility attached to convicting a guilty person or to acquitting an innocent person. These correct decisions have a payoff of 0 on our social utility scale. It is bad to acquit a guilty person, and by way of fixing the unit of measurement the payoff for this is −1 unit of social utility. It is terrible to condemn an innocent person (after all, he could be one of us)—perhaps five times as serious as acquitting a guilty person. Some readers may consider this only twice as serious as acquitting a guilty man, while others might think it 10 times as serious. We will not argue with any of you on such personal, subjective feelings.

In the business world we are fortunate to have a much more objective yardstick, that is, *money!* Suppose a manager has to decide on an investment that will increase capacity by either 1,000 or 2,000 units. If future demand—the unknown state of nature—is going to be brisk, it is advisable to increase capacity by 2,000 units, but if demand is going to be slack, it is better to decide on 1,000 units. The payoffs are given in Table 12.2. We see that if demand is brisk, expansion by 2,000 units leads to a profit of $7,000, compared with only $2,000 if demand is slack. Obviously, if the prevailing state of nature were known, the best decision would follow immediately. The problem arises only because the true state of nature is unknown.

In Table 12.3 we summarize the data of the next example. It illustrates the problem faced by a manager about to make up his mind on fire insurance. If he insures, the premium of $4,000 will be lost, whether there is a fire or not. If he does not insure, the loss will be $90,000 in case of fire, but nothing if all goes well.

Let us summarize the three essential components of a *statistical decision problem* shown in a payoff table. The *first* requirement is that

Three components of a statistical decision problem

TABLE 12.2   PAYOFF FOR DECISION ON EXPANSION

State of nature	Decision	
	Expand 2,000	*Expand 1,000*
Brisk demand	$7,000	$3,500
Slack demand	$2,000	$4,000

TABLE 12.3 PAYOFF FOR DECISION ON INSURANCE

| State of nature | Decision | |
	Insure	Do not insure
Fire	− $4,000	− $90,000
No fire	− $4,000	0

there must be various possible actions that one can take. A man with two broken legs on a ski slope has a serious problem, but no decision problem, since he has no alternative but to wait till help arrives. The *second* requirement is that there must be several possible states of nature. It is known that a newborn baby wets diapers. The parents have to decide on paper diapers, diaper service, or washing the diapers at home, but this is not truly a *statistical* decision problem. There is no uncertainty about the state of nature. The *third* requirement is that there should be a definite numerical payoff associated with each possible combination of state of nature and decision.

Hidden in the entries of a payoff table are the *opportunity losses*. They can be illustrated with the following example. A newspaperboy can sell papers at a profit of 3 cents per paper. He loses 2 cents on any paper left unsold at the end of the day. He knows from experience that he will sell between 10 and 20 papers each day. He must decide how many papers to order from the press. This is his decision problem. The payoff table (see Table 12.4) is determined as follows: The unknown state of nature is the number of copies, 10, 11, . . . , 20, he will sell today. The alternative acts available to him are to order 10, 11, . . . , 20 papers, or possibly more or less. The actual numerical entries, which give the profit, are easy to compute. For example, if he orders 16 copies and sells 13 copies, he has a profit of $13 \times 3 - 3 \times 2 = 33$ cents, because he gains 3 cents on each of the 13 copies sold, and loses 2 cents on each of the $16 - 13 = 3$ copies left unsold. If he orders 16 copies and "sells" 19—that is, if he had had them, he *could* have sold 19 papers that day—his profit is $16 \times 3 = 48$ cents. He also has an opportunity loss of 9 cents, since he could have sold 3 papers more if they had been available. This 9 cents is the difference between the profit he actually made and the profit he would have had if he had made the best decision, given demand for 19 papers. This decision would have been to buy 19 papers from the press. *Opportunity losses are found by subtracting the highest value in each*

Opportunity losses

TABLE 12.4   PAYOFF TABLE AND OPPORTUNITY LOSS TABLE FOR PAPERBOY

Payoff Table

State of nature (sales)	(9)	10	11	12	13	14	15	16	17	18	19	20	(21)
10	27	30	28	26	24	22	20	18	16	14	12	10	8
11	27	30	33	31	29	27	25	23	21	19	17	15	13
12	27	30	33	36	34	32	30	28	26	24	22	20	18
13	27	30	33	36	39	37	35	33	31	29	27	25	23
14	27	30	33	36	39	42	40	38	36	34	32	30	28
15	27	30	33	36	39	42	45	43	41	39	37	35	33
16	27	30	33	36	39	42	45	48	46	44	42	40	38
17	27	30	33	36	39	42	45	48	51	49	47	45	43
18	27	30	33	36	39	42	45	48	51	54	52	50	48
19	27	30	33	36	39	42	45	48	51	54	57	55	53
20	27	30	33	36	39	42	45	48	51	54	57	60	58

Opportunity Loss Table

State of nature (sales)	(9)	10	11	12	13	14	15	16	17	18	19	20	(21)
10	3	0	2	4	6	8	10	12	14	16	18	20	22
11	6	3	0	2	4	6	8	10	12	14	16	18	20
12	9	6	3	0	2	4	6	8	10	12	14	16	18
13	12	9	6	3	0	2	4	6	8	10	12	14	16
14	15	12	9	6	3	0	2	4	6	8	10	12	14
15	18	15	12	9	6	3	0	2	4	6	8	10	12
16	21	18	15	12	9	6	3	0	2	4	6	8	10
17	24	21	18	15	12	9	6	3	0	2	4	6	8
18	27	24	21	18	15	12	9	6	3	0	2	4	6
19	30	27	24	21	18	15	12	9	6	3	0	2	4
20	33	30	27	24	21	18	15	12	9	6	3	0	2

row from each of the other values in that row. These differences are shown as positive values in the opportunity loss table. The payoff table and the opportunity loss table are shown together in Table 12.4.

From the payoff table we see that the paperboy should never order 9 papers; by ordering 10 his profit is 3 cents more, whatever the state of nature may be. He should never order 21 papers; by ordering only

20 his profit is 2 cents more, whatever the state of nature may be. Furthermore, we observe that the diagonal elements are invariably the largest element in each row. Profit is greatest when he orders exactly the amount he will sell. In each column the values below the diagonal are the same. This similarity, however, is deceptive.

To see this, we turn to the opportunity loss table. The two red 36s in the payoff table correspond to the red entries 9 and 21 in the opportunity loss table. One 36 corresponds to the case in which 12 papers were ordered on a day when demand was for 15 papers. He could have sold 3 more papers for an opportunity loss of $3 \times 3 = 9$ cents. The other 36 corresponds to the case in which 12 papers were ordered on a day when demand was for 19 papers. His opportunity loss on such a day is $7 \times 3 = 21$ cents.

The diagonal elements in the opportunity loss table are all zero, indicating that he could do no better, given the prevailing state of nature. The losses below the diagonal result from not having ordered enough. The losses above the diagonal result from having ordered too many.

Three omissions in the manufacturer's original approach to decision making were cited at the end of the first section. We have now dealt with the first; that is, a correct analysis of payoff tables will enable us to take profit and loss data into account explicitly.

EXERCISES

12.1   Construct a payoff table for the decision whether to take an umbrella or not, since it may rain—or not.

12.2   A pig breeder can either produce 10 or 20 pigs. The total production of his competitors can be either 10,000 or 20,000 pigs. If they produce 10,000 pigs, his profit per pig is $70; if they produce 20,000 pigs his profit per pig is only $15. Construct a payoff table. What should he decide?

12.3   A prisoner can try to escape, or stay where he is. If he successfully escapes he is free; if he is unsuccessful in his bid for freedom he will receive solitary confinement for a month—and he will still have to be in jail for the 13 remaining years of his term. Construct a payoff table.

12.4   The President and Vice President can fly in the same plane or they can fly in different planes, so that one crash won't kill them both. Construct a payoff table.

12.5   Determine opportunity loss tables from Tables 12.2 and 12.3 in the text.

12.6   *Whimsical machine problem.* Depending upon its "whim of the day" a machine produces 2 or 10 or 25 percent defectives. It costs $1,000 to check the machine each morning to guarantee that it will produce 2 percent defectives for that day. If the machine is not checked, the extra cost created by a batch containing 10 percent defectives is $500, and by a batch containing 25 percent defectives, $3,000. Determine the payoff table.

12.3   SUBJECTIVE PROBABILITIES AND DECISION CRITERIA

Personal probability assessments on states of nature

We introduced various *possible* states of nature in the previous section, but we did not speak at all about how *probable* they were. Yet this information is quite relevant. The manager who is virtually certain that demand will be brisk will expand by the full 2,000 units, whereas the manager who gloomily foresees a slack demand will do best if he expands by only 1,000 units. The payoff tables must be completed by adding a probability assessment of the states of nature. In Table 12.5 we give probability assessments for the expansion and fire insurance examples. The probability assessment concerning the level of demand may be based on

TABLE 12.5   PAYOFF TABLES ON EXPANSION AND INSURANCE, PROBABILITIES ADDED

State of nature	Decision	
	Expand 2,000	Expand 1,000
Brisk demand, 40%	$7,000	$3,500
Slack demand, 60%	$2,000	$4,000

State of nature	Decision	
	Insure	Do not insure
Fire, 1%	−$4,000	−$90,000
No fire, 99%	−$4,000	0

information given by the marketing department or by *Business Week,* or it may be based on "feeling." The probability estimate for fire could be based on the fire history of the factory, fire histories of similar factories, the precautions against fire, or other data. Assessments in both examples are largely subjective.

Imaginary bets are a convenient method for constructing such subjective probabilities. In assessing the probability of brisk demand versus slack demand you may argue as follows: You are quite willing to make a bet such that you lose $1 if there is brisk demand, and win $1 if there is slack demand. Apparently you believe that demand will be slack rather than brisk. On the other hand, you may not be willing to lose $2 if there is brisk demand, and win $1 in case of slack demand. Apparently, while you believe that demand will be slack, you do not think it is twice as likely to be slack as it is to be brisk. After further thought you may feel just willing to lose $1.50 if there is brisk demand, provided you win $1 if there is slack demand. In fact, you would also be just willing to reverse the bet; that is, you win $1.50 if there is brisk demand and lose $1 in case of slack demand.

Once you have gone through this mental torment you may need a psychiatrist to straighten you out again, but you have established that your subjective probability of brisk demand is 40 percent versus 60 percent for slack demand. For these are the only probabilities consistent with the fact that you are willing to bet on either alternative:

> Lose $1.50 if brisk demand; win $1 if slack demand
> Win $1.50 if brisk demand; lose $1 if slack demand

With probabilities as given, the *first* bet has an expected value

$$(.4)(-\$1.50) + (.6)(\$1) = \$0$$

and the *second* has an expected value

$$(.4)(\$1.50) + (.6)(-\$1) = \$0$$

Any other probabilities would lead to a positive expected value for one alternative and a negative expected value for the reverse. In that case you would be willing to accept the one bet, but not the reverse.

In general, the problem is to determine dollar values x and y, such that you are willing to bet either way

> Lose x if A; win y if *not*-A
> Win x if A; lose y if *not*-A

Then we must have $P(A) = y/(x + y)$, and $P(not\text{-}A) = x/(x + y)$. We have $P(A) + P(not\text{-}A) = 1$, and an expected value for the first bet equal to

$$\frac{y}{x + y}(-x) + \frac{x}{x + y}y = 0$$

and for the second bet equal to

$$\frac{y}{x + y}x + \frac{x}{x + y}(-y) = 0$$

All this does not preclude the possibility that someone else has different subjective probabilities. Suppose your assistant believes that the probability of brisk demand is 60 percent, rather than 40 percent as you believe, and for slack demand it is 40 percent, instead of 60 percent. Then you can make a *real* bet instead of an *imaginary* one. For example: You lose $1 to your assistant in case of brisk demand, but win $1 from your assistant in case of slack demand. In *your mind*, this is a good bet. The expected value is

$$(.4)(-\$1) + (.6)(\$1) = \$.20$$

In your *assistant's mind* this is also a good bet. The assistant will use his own subjective probabilities and find an expected value of

$$(.6)(\$1) + (.4)(-\$1) = \$.20$$

Both you and your assistant have a positive expected value because your probability assessments differ. The fact that frequent betting occurs around us suggests that subjective probability assessments are often different.

A rough check of someone else's subjective probability against the standards of betting odds is useful, since otherwise anyone can state whatever odds he wishes without there being any way to check his honesty or seriousness. When someone states that he considers it very likely that IBM will split its stock before the end of the year, but is not willing to accept a bet such that he loses $1 if the stock does not split and wins $1 otherwise, we may doubt his seriousness. Similarly, the research professor who is sure that he can invent a new plastic if only management will give him a research grant of $1,000,000, but who is unwilling to accept a side bet in which he gains $1,000 if he succeeds and loses $1,000 if he fails, may be less sure than he professes.

In addition to the subjective probabilities, one further element is needed for a decision. This is the *decision criterion*. A widely used decision criterion is the *expected value* criterion. Under the expected value criterion, one sets out to maximize the expected profit *or* to minimize the expected loss. If the manager applies this criterion to the data presented in Table 12.5, he will decide to expand by the full 2,000 units because

$$.4 \times \$7,000 + .6 \times \$2,000 = \$4,000$$

exceeds

$$.4 \times \$3,500 + .6 \times \$4,000 = \$3,800$$

The expected profit from expanding by 2,000 units is therefore \$4,000, while it is only \$3,800 from expanding by 1,000 units. Using the same criterion, this manager would decide *not* to insure because

$$(.01)(-\$4,000) + (.99)(-\$4,000) = -\$4,000$$

and

$$(.01)(-\$90,000) + (.99)(\$0) = -\$900$$

The expected loss is \$4,000 by insuring, but only \$900 by not insuring. It is imperative to realize that if he does insure, his *expected* loss of \$4,000 will be his *actual* loss, whatever may happen. This \$4,000 is the premium he forfeits. By contrast, an *expected* loss of \$900 if he does not insure is a sort of proxy for an *actual* loss of either \$90,000 or nothing at all. This may give the uninsured manager something to ponder about as he tries to fall asleep.

In fact, of course, most people do insure, which leads us to reconsider the problem. The first possibility is that the probability assessment is wrong. For example, suppose that the probability of a fire is 5 percent. The expected loss without insurance would be

$$(.05)(-\$90,000) + (.95)(\$0) = -\$4,500$$

which is more than the loss due to the insurance premium, that is, \$4,000. Such a situation could, admittedly, be true in an individual instance, but it could not be systematically true. After all, insurance companies usually make a profit after all their costs are paid, so clearly their inflow of premiums exceeds their outgo for claims.

Two alternative arguments may serve to explain the observed behavior that people do in fact insure when faced with evidence as presented in Table 12.5. Both explanations have some intrinsic interest, and they are worth a short detour.

Expected value as a decision criterion

The payoffs in Table 12.5 are the purely monetary losses incurred. However, it may well be that these monetary values do not properly reflect the relative seriousness of the four possible outcomes. A loss of $90,000 may be considered more than $22\frac{1}{2}$ times as serious as a loss of $4,000. A loss of $4,000, though serious, is presumably within the range of normal business risks, but a loss of $90,000 may spell bankruptcy. According to this argument we should not measure the losses in dollars, but in utilities—the manager's subjective evaluation of the seriousness of the four possible outcomes.

Utility of money

There is evidence that many persons do not consider a profit of $50,000 ten times as joyous as a profit of $5,000. By contrast, they consider a loss of $50,000 more than 10 times as serious as a loss of $5,000. Typically, a person feels that successive increments in his assets produce smaller and smaller increments in utility, while successive decrements in his assets produce larger and larger increments in *dis*utility. These feelings can be shown graphically by a *utility curve,* as shown in Figure 12.1.

In this figure, for illustrative purpose only, the loss of $4,000 has

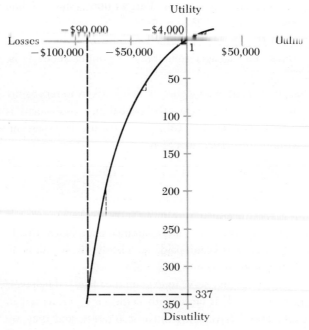

Figure 12.1 Utility curve.

a disutility of 1; the loss of $90,000 has a disutility of 337. The appropriate decision criterion when payoffs are measured in utility is to maximize expected utility rather than expected profits, or to minimize expected disutility rather than expected losses. Using this criterion, the appropriate decision is to insure because

$$.01 \times 337 + .99 \times 0 = 3.37 \qquad \text{exceeds} \qquad .01 \times 1 + .99 \times 1 = 1$$

The disutility if the manager insures is 1, and the expected disutility if he does not insure is 3.37. This explanation leaves the decision criterion *as such* unchanged; he still maximizes expected profits or minimizes expected losses, even though profits and losses are no longer measured by the objective yardstick of money but by the subjective yardstick of the utility attached to the money.

An alternative explanation of the decision to insure is based on the use of a different decision criterion from that of expected values. The weakness of the expected value approach was pointed out above. An expected loss of $4,000 which is *in fact* a loss of $4,000, and an expected loss of $900 which is *in fact* either a loss of nothing at all or a loss of $90,000, are altogether different. To compare them is an offense against common sense.

The alternative decision criterion is the *minimax* criterion. The minimax criterion minimizes (the "*min*" of minimax) the maximum possible loss (the "*max*" of minimax) that can prevail. The maximum possible loss results from a fire without insurance. Since it is impossible to be sure that there will be no fire, the manager can only defend against the maximum possible loss by insuring. The minimax argument is colloquially expressed by "We have to prevent this at all costs." Such an approach is often warranted when there is a vast difference between the possible values of the various payoffs. The misery of an inoculation against polio is small compared with the misery of getting polio; thus one takes the inoculation. The cost of condemning an innocent victim is large compared with the cost of acquitting a criminal, so the jury acquits unless the guilt is proved "beyond reasonable doubt."

The opposite of minimax is *maximax*. The maximaxer is someone who maximizes (the "*max* . . ." of maximax) the maximum possible gain (the ". . . *max*" of maximax). This may explain why people buy lottery tickets despite their negative expected value. In such a case there is a vast difference between the possible values of the various payoffs. The cost of a ticket is small compared with the value of the first prize. A prisoner will try to escape even though success is highly doubtful. The

Minimax and maximax

cost (a month in solitary confinement) is small compared with the possible result (freedom). A trailing football team will take to the air with a passing attack. The cost (of really being clobbered) is small compared with the possible gain (winning the game). A nearly bankrupt company may go for a highly risky, but potentially immensely profitable, investment. The cost (of going bankrupt or being taken over a little sooner) is small compared with the possible profit (a viable, profitable company).

Notice that both the minimaxer and the maximaxer have no use for probability assessments based on the states of nature. They only look at the worst, or best, possible payoffs, and prevent the worst, or "attract" the best by the appropriate decision. In the answer given to Exercise 12.3, the maximaxing prisoner would try to escape; in Exercise 12.4, the minimaxer recommends flying in different planes.

Three omissions in the manufacturer's original approach to decision making were stated at the end of the first section. In this section we have introduced subjective probabilities which are the a priori beliefs of the decision maker. They enter the analysis when we use the expected value criterion.

EXERCISES

12.7   Reconsider Exercise 12.1, and the payoff matrix constructed in the answer. Suppose the probability of rain is given as 20 percent by the weatherman. Would you take your umbrella? If the probability of rain is 25 percent, what would you do?

12.8   Consider the following payoff table. What would the expected value criterion lead to? The minimax criterion? The maximax criterion?

State of nature	Probability, %	Choose urn 1	Choose urn 2
I	10	$ 100	$100,000
II	90	10,000	1,000

12.9   Consider the following payoff table. What would the expected value criterion lead to? The minimax criterion? The maximax criterion?

State of nature	Probability, %	Don't expand	Expand 1,000 units	Expand 2,000 units
Great demand	40	$2,500	$3,500	$5,000
Some demand	40	2,500	3,500	2,500
Small demand	20	2,500	1,500	−1,000

12.10 Show that if the utility curve for an individual is shaped as in Figure 12.1, any fair bet he makes (expected payoff = 0) will decrease his utility.

12.11 *Whimsical machine problem, continued.* The probability that the machine will be in a state producing a percentage of defectives of 2, 10, or 25 percent is .7, .2, and .1, respectively. What should the manager decide if his objective is to minimize the expected costs?

12.4 THE EXPECTED VALUE OF PERFECT INFORMATION

In Section 12.1 we reviewed the problem of the manufacturer who was offered a batch of transistors of unknown quality. We discussed one approach to this problem in Chapter 10, but we then recognized opportunities for improving the methods used there. The cost data were not used explicitly, the a priori information was disregarded, and the cost of the sample and the value of the sample information were not considered. In the previous two sections we organized the data so that we could use the cost data and a priori information. The determination of the value of sample information is the problem that remains. We will first solve the easier problem of determining the value of perfect information: *The expected value of perfect information is the difference between the maximum expected payoff when perfect information is available and the maximum expected payoff when only a priori information is available.*

Expected value of perfect information

We will determine the value of perfect information for the paperboy. What would it be worth to him to know each day, before he orders his papers, how many he can sell that day? He has a priori probabilities for the number of papers he can sell. Based on experience he believes that the probability of selling 10, 11, 19, or 20 papers is only 5 percent. The probability of selling 12, 13, 14, 17, or 18 papers is 10 percent, and the probability of selling 15 or 16 papers is 15 percent. These are his ideas, and he proceeds by considering the complete payoff table and the associated probabilities as given in Table 12.6.

From Table 12.6 the expected value of his profit when he orders 14 papers is

$$.05 \times 22 + .05 \times 27 + .10 \times 32 + \cdots + .05 \times 42 = 38\tfrac{3}{4} \text{ cents}$$

This value is obtained by multiplying the payoffs in the column headed "14" with their associated probabilities, and summing these products. The other expected values are similarly obtained. Our paperboy would order 16 papers if he sets out to maximize his expected value. The maximum expected value of the profit is 40 cents.

Even so, the situation is frustrating. If he orders 16 papers, his expected profit is 40 cents, but he may have to be satisfied with only 18 cents. On the other hand, he might get as much as 48 cents, but even that will leave a bad aftertaste if he *could*, on that day, have sold 18 papers for a total profit of 54 cents.

None of this frustration remains when he has perfect information. If he knows in advance how many papers he can sell, he will order that many papers. If he is informed that he can sell 13 papers, he will order

TABLE 12.6　PAYOFF TABLE FOR PAPERBOY, PROBABILITIES ADDED

State of nature (sales)	Probability	Decision (order quantity)										
		10	11	12	13	14	15	16	17	18	19	20
10	(.05)	30	28	26	24	22	20	18	16	14	12	10
11	(.05)	30	33	31	29	27	25	23	21	19	17	15
12	(.10)	30	33	36	34	32	30	28	26	24	22	20
13	(.10)	30	33	36	39	37	35	33	31	29	27	25
14	(.10)	30	33	36	39	42	40	38	36	34	32	30
15	(.15)	30	33	36	39	42	45	43	41	39	37	35
16	(.15)	30	33	36	39	42	45	48	46	44	42	40
17	(.10)	30	33	36	39	42	45	48	51	49	47	45
18	(.10)	30	33	36	39	42	45	48	51	54	52	50
19	(.05)	30	33	36	39	42	45	48	51	54	57	55
20	(.05)	30	33	36	39	42	45	48	51	54	57	60
Expected payoff		30	$32\tfrac{3}{4}$	$35\tfrac{1}{4}$	$37\tfrac{1}{4}$	$38\tfrac{3}{4}$	$39\tfrac{3}{4}$	40	$39\tfrac{1}{2}$	$38\tfrac{1}{2}$	37	$35\tfrac{1}{4}$

13 papers, and make a profit of 39 cents. This value 39 is greater than any other value in the *row* labeled 13 of Table 12.6. A similar argument holds throughout: If he knows the row he will be in, he makes the decision that maximizes the profit *in that row*. These are the red values on the diagonal in Table 12.6. The maximum expected payoff with perfect information is therefore

$$.05 \times 30 + .05 \times 33 + .10 \times 36 + \cdots + .05 \times 60 = 45.15 \text{ cents}$$

Without perfect information the maximum expected payoff is 40 cents. With perfect information the maximum expected payoff is 45.15 cents. Therefore, the expected value of perfect information is 5.15 cents.

There are three possible situations. In the *first,* the paperboy has his a priori notions concerning the true state of nature. In this situation he will do best by ordering 16 papers each day for an expected profit of 40 cents.

In the *second* situation, perfect information is available. With perfect information, the paperboy's expected profit is 45.15 cents. Thus, as we have seen, the expected value of perfect information is $45.15 - 40 = 5.15$ cents. In other words, if the paperboy could bribe an angel for 10 cents to provide him with perfect information, he would be wrong to do so—but for 5 cents it would just be profitable.

In the *third* situation the paperboy has been told what the sales of the day will be. The profit is then certain. It is one of the red entries in Table 12.6; which one depends on what he was told. If he was told sales will be 14, the boy will order 14 papers and the profit will be 42 cents. This is 4 cents more than the 38 cents he would have collected if he had bought 16 papers, as he would have done without the perfect information. Had he been told that he would sell 10 papers, the profit with perfect information (30 cents) is 12 cents more than the profit without perfect information (18 cents). Had he been informed that he would sell 16 papers, there would be no gain over the situation with no information, since he would have ordered 16 papers anyway. The *actual* increase in profit thus depends on the *actual* information he will receive. The *expected* increase in profit before the actual information is received is 5.15 cents, as we saw above. The expected value of perfect information is the upper limit the paperboy is willing to pay for the information.

As another example, consider the manager faced with the situation summarized in Table 12.7. The problem is similar to the one discussed in Section 12.1. If the manager buys a shipment with 2 percent defectives, his profit will be $2,500. If he does *not* buy this shipment, he will have

TABLE 12.7   PAYOFF TABLE FOR MANAGER, WITH A PRIORI
PROBABILITIES

State of nature, %	A priori (subjective) probability	Decision	
		Buy	Don't buy
2	.10	$2,500	0
3	.30	1,700	0
4	.20	900	0
5	.15	0	0
6	.10	− 200	0
7	.10	− 700	0
8	.05	−1,300	0

no profit at all, and therefore, he will have an opportunity loss of $2,500.
The question is, "What is the expected value of perfect information?"

Without any further information the manager should decide to buy.
Given his a priori probabilities, this decision leads to an expected profit
of

$$.10 \times \$2,500 + .30 \times \$1,700 + \cdots + .05 \times (-\$1,300) = \$785$$

If he does not buy, his expected profit is obviously zero. Now assume
that he could obtain perfect information. He will obviously buy the
shipment if the information is that less than 5 percent is defective, and
he will not buy the shipment if the information is that more than 5 percent
is defective. The expected profit is found by using the payoffs shown in
red:

$$.10 \times \$2,500 + .30 \times \$1,700 + .20 \times \$900 + .15 \times \$0$$
$$+ .10 \times \$0 + .10 \times \$0 + .05 \times \$0 = \$940$$

The difference ($940 − $785) is $155, the expected value of perfect
information. This is the maximum amount the manager should pay for
the privilege of being able to obtain perfect information.

EXERCISES

12.12   *Whimsical machine problem, continued.* What is the expected value
of perfect information concerning the true state of nature (2, 10,
or 25 percent)? (See Exercise 12.11.)

12.13   *Oil drilling example.* What is the expected value of perfect
information for the oil man faced with the following payoff table:

State of nature	Probability	Drill	Don't drill
Oil	.2	$400,000	0
No oil	.8	−100,000	0

12.14 Using Table 12.4, show that the expected value of the opportunity losses in the column headed "16" (with use of the a priori probabilities in Table 12.6) equals the expected value of perfect information for the paperboy. Comment on this result.

12.5 THE VALUE OF INFORMATION IN A SAMPLE WITH KNOWN OUTCOME

In the previous section we discussed the very special case where perfect information could be obtained. We determined how much a decision maker should be willing to pay for knowing the true state of nature before the decision has to be made. He should be willing to pay at most the expected value of perfect information. In reality the information which can be obtained will usually not give complete certainty of what will happen—it will only change the a priori probabilities.

The basic technique in reevaluating the a priori probabilities to obtain a posteriori probabilities by incorporating new information is the use of Bayes' formula. It may be worthwhile to reread Section 3.4. Here we will use an artificial example to give a short review and a convenient layout for the necessary computations.

Conversion of prior to posterior probabilities

A man draws a ball from an urn which contains 80 percent green balls *or* 60 percent green balls *or* 20 percent green balls, the remainder being red. To the best of his knowledge, there is a .5 probability that the urn contains 80 percent green balls, a .1 probability that the urn contains 60 percent green balls, and a .4 probability that the urn contains 20 percent green balls. These are his a priori probabilities. The information is summarized in the first two columns of Table 12.8.

Now a sample of size three is drawn, and it is observed that two out of the three balls are green. The relevant question is how this information influences our assessment of the probabilities attached to each state of nature. For example, what is the a posteriori probability that the urn contains 80 percent green balls, given that a sample of size three contains two green balls? In shorthand, what is $P(80\% | 2 \text{ green}, 1 \text{ red})$? Similarly, we want to know $P(60\% | 2 \text{ green}, 1 \text{ red})$ and $P(20\% | 2 \text{ green}, 1 \text{ red})$.

TABLE 12.8 COMPUTATION OF A POSTERIORI FROM A PRIORI
PROBABILITIES, ARTIFICIAL EXAMPLE

(1) State of nature, % green	(2) A priori probability	(3) Conditional probability	(4) (2) × (3)	(5) A posteriori probability
80	.5	.384	.1920	$\frac{.1920}{.2736} = .702$
60	.1	.432	.0432	$\frac{.0432}{.2736} = .158$
20	.4	.096	.0384	$\frac{.0384}{.2736} = .140$
			.2736	

While the values of these conditional probabilities are not immediately evident, the reverse conditional probabilities can easily be computed. What is P(2 green, 1 red|80%)? That is, what is the probability of drawing a sample of two green balls and one red ball out of an urn which contains 80 percent green balls and 20 percent red balls? Using the binomial distribution $B(3,.8)$, we find

$$P(2 \text{ green}, 1 \text{ red}|80\%) = 3(.8)^2(.2) = .384$$

Using $B(3,.6)$, we find

$$P(2 \text{ green}, 1 \text{ red}|60\%) = 3(.6)^2(.4) = .432$$

Using $B(3,.2)$, we find

$$P(2 \text{ green}, 1 \text{ red}|20\%) = 3(.2)^2(.8) = .096$$

These conditional probabilities are given in Column 3 of Table 12.8. To obtain the a posteriori probabilities we use Bayes' formula. For example,

P(80%|2 green, 1 red)

$$= \frac{P(2 \text{ green}, 1 \text{ red}|80\%)P(80\%)}{P(2g, 1r|80\%)P(80\%) + P(2g, 1r|60\%)P(60\%) + P(2g, 1r|20\%)P(20\%)}$$

$$= \frac{.384 \times .50}{.384 \times .50 + .432 \times .10 + .096 \times .40} = \frac{.1920}{.2736} = .702$$

In the denominator each conditional probability is multiplied by the corresponding a priori probability. In Table 12.8 these products are shown in the fourth column. The a posteriori probabilities are obtained by dividing the individual entries in Column 4 by the total of Column 4, as is evident from Bayes' formula. The computations are shown in Column 5. After incorporating the sample information, the a posteriori probabilities are .702, .158, and .140. The probability that the contents are preponderantly green has gone up (from 50 to 70.2 percent and from 10 to 15.8 percent), while the probability that the contents are largely red has decreased from 40 to 14 percent. These results confirm intuition, since the sample was preponderantly green.

In summary, we start in Column 2 with the a priori probability. We then get sample results, and we show in Column 3 how likely these observed sample results are, given the various states of nature. We get Column 4 by multiplying the a priori probabilities of Column 2 with the conditional probabilities of Column 3, and sum these products. The a posteriori probabilities are now found by dividing the entries in Column 4 by the total of Column 4.

So much for the review. We return to the example of the manager who has an option to buy a shipment with an unknown percentage of defectives. His a priori probabilities are given above in Table 12.7. They are repeated in Column 2 of Table 12.9. Now he draws a sample of size 25, and finds 1 defective. The probability that such a sample will be drawn from a shipment with 2 percent defectives is equal to

$$C(25,1)(.98)^{24}(.02) = .3079$$

Similarly, if in truth the shipment contains 3 percent defectives, the probability that a sample of size 25 contains 1 defective equals

$$C(25,1)(.97)^{24}(.03) = .3611$$

TABLE 12.9 CONVERSION OF A PRIORI TO A POSTERIORI PROBABILITIES IN PROBLEM OF MANAGER, CASE 1

Payoff if batch is accepted	(1) State of nature, %	(2) A priori probability	(3) Conditional probability	(4) (2) × (3)	(5) A posteriori probability
($2,500)	2	.10	.3079	.03079	.088
(1,700)	3	.30	.3611	.10833	.312
(900)	4	.20	.3754	.07508	.216
(0)	5	.15	.3650	.05475	.158
(−200)	6	.10	.3398	.03398	.098
(−700)	7	.10	.3066	.03066	.088
(−1,300)	8	.05	.2744	.01372	.039
				.34731	

We also compute the conditional probabilities for 4, 5, 6, 7, and 8 percent defectives:

State of nature, %	Conditional probabilities
4	$C(25,1)(.96)^{24}(.04) = .3754$
5	$C(25,1)(.95)^{24}(.05) = .3650$
6	$C(25,1)(.94)^{24}(.06) = .3398$
7	$C(25,1)(.93)^{24}(.07) = .3066$
8	$C(25,1)(.92)^{24}(.08) = .2744$

These conditional probabilities are given in Column 3 of Table 12.9. Columns 4 and 5 can now be computed. The expected profit after the sample, if the manager decides to buy, is

$$.088 \times \$2,500 + .312 \times \$1,700 + .216 \times \$900 + .158 \times \$0$$
$$+ .098 \times (-\$200) + .088 \times (-\$700) + .039 \times (-\$1,300)$$
$$= \$812.90$$

The expected profit is $0 if he decides not to buy, since, regardless of the state of nature, the profit is $0 if he does not buy. The manager will stick to his original decision to buy. The expected profit has increased from $785 to $812.90.

What value should the manager attach to this sample of size 25 containing 1 defective? As we saw before, the expected value of perfect information *before* the sample is $155. As we will see below, the expected value of perfect information *after* the sample is $944.80 − $812.90 = $131.90. The expected value of perfect information has declined from $155.00 to $131.90. The difference, $23.10, is the value of a sample of 25 containing 1 defective.

Value of sample with specific outcome   In general, *the value of a sample with a specific outcome is the difference between the expected value of perfect information before the sample and the expected value of perfect information after the sample.*

We will verify that the expected value of perfect information after the sample is $131.90. After the sample we work with the a posteriori probabilities given in Column 5 of Table 12.9. Given these probabilities the expected payoff when we buy the batch is $812.90. With perfect information we would buy the batch only if less than 5 percent of the batch is defective, and not buy otherwise. The expected value of the payoff is

$$.088 \times \$2,500 + .312 \times \$1,700 + .216 \times \$900 + .158 \times \$0$$
$$+ .098 \times \$0 + .088 \times \$0 + .039 \times \$0 = \$944.80$$

The value of perfect information after the sample is therefore computed in exactly the same way as the value of perfect information before the sample, with the understanding that we use a posteriori probabilities rather than a priori probabilities. In this example it equals $\$944.80 - \$812.90 = \$131.90$, as stated above.

By way of recapitulation, we will list the eight steps used to find the expected value of a sample with a specific outcome.

1. Use a priori probabilities to compute the expected payoff for each possible decision. Take the highest of these values.

2. Use a priori probabilities to compute the expected value of the largest payoff in each row.

3. The difference between the results in steps 2 and 1 is the expected value of perfect information before sampling.

4. Draw a sample, observe the outcome, and compute the a posteriori probabilities.

5. Repeat step 1 using a posteriori probabilities.

6. Repeat step 2 using a posteriori probabilities.

7. The difference between the results in steps 6 and 5 is the expected value of perfect information after sampling.

8. The value of the sample drawn in step 4 is the expected value of perfect information before sampling (found in step 3) minus the expected value of perfect information after sampling (found in step 7).

Incidentally, not all sample outcomes reduce the expected value of sample information. We will show this by considering a sample of 25 that contains 2 defectives.

1. We find $785, as before.
2. We find $940, as before.
3. We find $155, as before.
4. We find the a posteriori probabilities in Column 5 of Table 12.10.
5. We find

$$.040 \times \$2,500 + .214 \times \$1,700 + .200 \times \$900 + .184 \times \$0$$
$$+ .139 \times (-\$200) + .148 \times (-\$700) + .075 \times (-\$1,300)$$
$$= \$414.90$$

TABLE 12.10 CONVERSION OF A PRIORI TO A POSTERIORI PROBABILITIES IN PROBLEM OF MANAGER, CASE 2

Payoff if batch is accepted	(1) State of nature, %	(2) A priori probability	(3) Conditional probability	(4) (2) × (3)	(5) A posteriori probability
($2,500)	2	.10	.0754	.00754	.040
(1,700)	3	.30	.1340	.04020	.214
(900)	4	.20	.1877	.03754	.200
(0)	5	.15	.2305	.03458	.184
(−200)	6	.10	.2602	.02602	.139
(−700)	7	.10	.2770	.02770	.148
(−1,300)	8	.05	.2821	.01411	.075
				.18769	1

6. We find

$$.040 \times \$2,500 + .214 \times \$1,700 + .200 \times \$900 + .184 \times \$0$$
$$+ .139 \times \$0 + .148 \times \$0 + .075 \times \$0 = \$643.80$$

7. We find

$$\$643.80 - \$414.90 = \$228.90$$

8. We find

$$\$155 - \$228.90 = -\$73.90$$

In other words, this particular sample outcome is such that we would now be willing to pay $228.90 instead of only $155 for perfect information. The "value" of this sample of 25 with 2 defectives is −$73.90.

The following example will help to understand this paradoxical result. In a forthcoming game between the Red Sox and the White Sox, there are two possible states of nature (Red Sox win or Red Sox lose), and two possible decisions (bet or do not bet $10 on the Red Sox to win). However, you can make your decision on betting after three innings are played.

Before the game starts, you consider the probability of the Red Sox winning to be 80 percent. The payoff table is therefore:

	Bet	Do not bet
Red Sox win (.80)	$10	$0
Red Sox lose (.20)	−$10	$0

Samples with negative "values"

It is easy to verify that the best decision is to bet, which gives an expected payoff of $6. With perfect information the expected payoff is $8. The expected value of perfect information is $2.

Consider now three different situations after three innings. In the first, the Red Sox are ahead 6 to 0. The a posteriori probability of their winning is now, in your mind, 99 percent. The best decision is to bet, and the expected value of perfect information is $9.90 − $9.80 = 10 cents. The value of this rather conclusive sample is $2 − $.10 = $1.90.

In the second situation the score after three innings is 0 to 6. The Red Sox trail badly. You now assess their a posteriori probability of winning at only 10 percent. The best decision is not to bet (payoff $0). The expected payoff with perfect information is $.80. The value of this conclusive sample is $2 − $.80 = $1.20.

In the third situation the Red Sox trail by only 0 to 1 after three innings. The a posteriori probability of the Red Sox winning is now assessed at .65. The best decision is to bet, giving an expected payoff of $6.50 − $3.50 = $3. With complete information the expected payoff is $6.50. Perfect information is worth $6.50 − $3 = $3.50. The "value" of this very inconclusive sample is $2 − $3.50 = −$1.50. The interpretation is that after this sample you feel less certain, less secure, of making the correct decision.

In general, samples with extreme outcomes—very few or very many defectives, very high scores either way—have a positive value. Samples with "in between" outcomes may have a negative "value," in particular when the sample size is small.

EXERCISES

12.15   *Oil drilling example, continued.* Our oil man (see Exercise 12.13) can decide to drill to 50 feet at a cost of only $10,000. If there is oil to be found, the probability of finding stone formation A is 60 percent, while if there is no oil, the probability of finding stone formation A is only 20 percent. The man decides to drill, and he *does* find stone formation A.

(a) What are the a posteriori probabilities?

(b) What should he decide if he wants to maximize expected profits?

(c) What is the value of the oil drilling that showed stone formation A at a 50-foot depth?

12.16 *Whimsical machine example, continued.* The story continues with the drawing of a sample of size 10, which contains 1 defective.

(*a*) Determine the a posteriori probabilities of the various states of nature.

(*b*) Should the machine be checked?

(*c*) What is the value of a sample of size 10 containing 1 defective? (See Exercise 12.12.)

12.17 In the baseball example in the text, the score after three innings is 3 to 0 in favor of the White Sox. Your a posteriori probability that the Red Sox will win has declined to .40. What is the value of this "sample"?

12.6 THE EXPECTED VALUE OF SAMPLE INFORMATION

In the previous section we saw that the value of a sample of size 25 containing 1 defective is $23.10. The "value" of a sample of size 25 containing 2 defectives is − $73.90. However, before we draw a sample of size 25 we do not know how many defectives it will contain.

The question therefore is, "What is the expected value of the information in a sample of size 25?" The answer obviously is

Probability of 0 defectives × value of sample with 0 defectives +
Probability of 1 defective × value of sample with 1 defective +
. . . .
Probability of 25 defectives × value of sample with 25 defectives

The difficulty is to find these probabilities and values. Table 12.11 shows the probabilities of getting a sample of 25 with 0, 1, 2, . . ., defectives if the percentage of defectives in the batch is 2, 3, . . ., 8 percent. The columns of this table give conditional probabilities. Columns 1 and 2 are the same as Column 3 of Tables 12.9 and 12.10. The rows of the table give complete binomial distributions. For example, the row labeled "4 percent" is $B(25,.04)$. Each row sums to 1.

From Table 12.11 the probability that a sample of 25 will contain 0, 1, 2, . . . defectives can be determined. For example, the probability of getting a sample with zero defectives is

.10 × .6035 + .30 × .4670 + .20 × .3604 + .15 × .2774
    + .10 × .2129 + .10 × .1630 + .05 × .1244 = 35.8 percent

**TABLE 12.11 PROBABILITY OF OBTAINING SAMPLE OF 25
WITH k DEFECTIVES**

State of nature, %	A priori probability	$k=0$	$k=1$	$k=2$	$k=3$	$k=4$	$k=5$	$k=6$	$k=7$	$k=8$	$k=9$
2	.10	.6035	.3079	.0754	.0118	.0013	.0001	.0	.0	.0	.0
3	.30	.4670	.3611	.1340	.0318	.0054	.0007	.0001	.0	.0	.0
4	.20	.3604	.3754	.1877	.0600	.0137	.0024	.0003	.0	.0	.0
5	.15	.2774	.3650	.2305	.0930	.0269	.0060	.0010	.0001	.0	.0
6	.10	.2129	.3398	.2602	.1273	.0447	.0120	.0026	.0004	.0001	.0
7	.10	.1630	.3066	.2770	.1598	.0662	.0209	.0052	.0011	.0002	.0
8	.05	.1244	.2704	.2821	.1881	.0899	.0324	.0095	.0022	.0004	.0001

The argument for this result is as follows: *If* the true state of nature is 2 percent defective with a probability of .10, there is a probability of .6035 of getting a sample with 0 defectives; *if* the true state of nature is 3 percent defective with a probability of .30, there is a probability of .4670 of getting a sample with 0 defectives; . . . ; finally *if* the true state of nature is 8 percent defective with a probability of .05, there is a probability of .1244 of getting a sample with 0 defectives. The overall probability of a sample with zero defectives is, therefore, .10 × .6035 + .30 × .4670 + · · · + .05 × .1244 = 35.8 percent. Similarly, the probability of a sample which has one defective is .10 × .3079 + .30 × .3611 + · · · + .05 × .2704 = 34.7 percent.

In Table 12.12 we have given the probability of obtaining a sample with 0, 1, 2, . . . , defectives in Column 2 and the value of these samples in Column 3 (computed as in Section 12.5). It is worth noting that the value of samples with few or many defectives is substantial. Samples with two, three, four defectives make perfect information more valuable after the sample than it was before. The expected value of the information in a sample of size 25, found by multiplying the probabilities by the values, is given in Column 4. The result is that the expected value of the sample is $9.96, or about $10. We conclude that if it costs *less* than 40 cents to sample one item, and there are no overhead costs of sampling, a sample of size 25 is worth the cost.

This, of course, is not the end of the story. The next step in the analysis would be to see what the expected value of the information in a sample of size 50 is. It may turn out to be $25. This would mean that a sample of size 50 is better than one of size 25, since $25 is more than twice $10. Clearly, such a series of computations is tedious, but, since

TABLE 12.12 COMPUTATION OF EXPECTED VALUE OF SAMPLING
              25 ITEMS

(1) No. of defectives in sample of size 25	(2) Probability, %	(3) Value	(4) (2) × (3)
0	35.8	$ 88.90	$31.83
1	34.7	23.10	8.02
2	18.8	−73.90	−13.89
3	7.5	−192.60	−14.44
4	2.4	−74.00	−1.78
5	.7	19.40	.14
6	.1	85.00	.08
7	0	155.00	0
8	0	155.00	0
	100		Expected value = $9.96

all computations are routine and repetitive in structure, computers help make the theory of practical value.

We have come to the end of our story. The cost data are used explicitly, the a priori information plays a vital role throughout, and the cost and value of sample information have been incorporated into the analysis.

EXERCISES

12.18   In the problem in the text, why is the value of a sample of size 25 which contains 4 defectives −$74?

12.19   *Whimsical machine problem, concluded.* What is the expected value of the information in a sample of size 10?

12.20   In the baseball example the probability that the Red Sox will lead by 10, 9, 8, 7, . . . , 1, 0, −1, −2, , −10 runs after three innings is computed as .01, .02, .03, .03, .04, .05, .08, .12, .20, .15, .10, .08, .05, .02, .01, .01, .00, .00, .00, .00, and .00. The value of a score with difference 10, 9, 8, . . . , −10 after three innings is $2, $2, $2, $1.95, $1.90, $1.80, $1.50, $1.20, $.90, $.50, −$.10, −$1.50, −$2.20, −$2.00, −$1.00, $.00, $.30, $.90, $1.20, $1.80, and $2.00.

(*a*) Explain why the value of the "sample information" is never more than $2.

(b) What a posteriori probabilities make $1.20 the value of knowing that the Red Sox lead by three runs at the end of the third inning?

(c) What is the value of the privilege of delaying your decision to bet until the end of the third inning?

12.7 THE ANALYSIS FOR CONTINUOUS VARIABLES

In our example of the manager faced with the decision whether to buy the shipment of transistors, you may have sensed that the list of states of nature represented an oversimplification of reality. After all, the percentage of defectives in the shipment need not be exactly 2, or 3, . . . , or 8. It could be 3.479, 5.641 percent, etc. In large shipments, the percentage of defectives is virtually a continuous variable. Similarly, the payoffs associated with each decision—buy and not buy—are continuous variables, since the economic consequences, that is, the profits or losses, of either decision are different for each possible percentage defective.

Seen in this light, the problem calls for a continuous distribution to describe the manager's subjective a priori probabilities for the possible states of nature and continuous distributions to describe the payoffs in each column of the payoff table. The methods of computation used in this chapter, which work perfectly for states, probabilities, and payoffs stated in discrete form cannot be used when continuous distributions replace the discrete values. Fortunately, the continuous case has been studied thoroughly, and analytical techniques have been developed to deal with it.

When certain reasonable assumptions about these distributions are made, the calculations reduce to several relatively simple formulas. These assumptions are that the a priori probabilities follow a normal distribution with known mean and standard deviation and that the payoffs are a linear function of the value of the state of nature. In our example, these assumptions would be met if

1. The manager's a priori probabilities for the possible percentage of defectives are normally distributed.

2. Each increase of 1 in the percentage of defectives increases the loss by the same amount.

We will use another example as an illustration of these formulas. It will turn out that the mathematics are much simpler and less laborious, but the derivation of the formulas themselves is much more difficult. They are not given in what follows.

In Section 10.5 we sketched the problem faced by an automobile manufacturer who is currently using windows with a mean breaking strength of 470 pounds per square inch (psi). He is offered a new quality glass, which the producer claims has a mean breaking strength of 500 psi and a standard deviation of 50 psi. These figures imply that 99.73 percent of all windows have a breaking strength within the range 350 to 650 psi.

In Section 10.5 we formulated a null hypothesis $\mu_0 = 500$ psi, an alternative hypothesis $\mu_1 = 470$ psi, a risk level $r_0 = 10$ percent of *not* using the new glass if its mean breaking strength is indeed 500 psi, as well as a risk level $r_1 = 5$ percent of *switching* to the new glass if it is no better than the old. From these data and figures it was determined that, *if* in a sample of size $n = 25$ the average breaking strength is 487 psi or less, the manufacturer should stick with his present glass, but if more, he should switch.

In a Bayesian analysis of the same problem we also use the subscripts zero and one (μ_0, σ_0; μ_1, σ_1), but to differentiate not between null and alternative hypotheses, but between a priori and a posteriori distribution parameters. First, we need the manager's a priori probability distribution of the mean breaking strength—that is, where does he believe the mean strength really is, and how certain is he of his assessment? After soul-searching introspection the manager states that his best guess is that the true mean $\mu_0 = 490$ psi. However, he is rather unsure about this: In his mind he views the true mean more or less as a random drawing from a normal distribution with mean $\mu_0 = 490$ psi and standard deviation $\sigma_0 = 40$ psi. This implies, among other things, that there is a nearly 20 percent probability that the true mean is below 470 psi, in which case a switch to the new glass is certainly bad.

The manager next computes that any 1-psi increase in mean breaking strength, given the price of the new glass, the price of the old glass, the number of cars he will equip with it, the marketing value of the superior glass, etc., is valued by him at $1,300. We will write $u = \$1,300$, for *unit profit*. This is a linear function, for *every* 1-psi increase is valued at $1,300 whether the mean increases from 470 to 471 psi, or from 536 to 537 psi, or from 320 to 321 psi. (We refer to Section 13.1 for more on straight lines and linear functions.) The manager also states that his *break-even point bp* is 475 psi. At 475 psi he is indifferent to whether he keeps the old, slightly inferior windows of 470 psi or goes through the trouble of switching to the slightly superior glass of 475 psi.

Unit profit

Points 1 and 2 noted above have now been complied with. The manager's a priori notion of the mean breaking strength is normally distributed $N(\mu_0 = 490$ psi, $\sigma_0 = 40$ psi$)$, and the payoff is a linear function of the mean breaking strength, $+\$1,300$ for every psi over 475 psi, and $-\$1,300$ for every psi below 475 psi.

Our first problem now is to blend, as if it were Scotch whisky, the a priori distribution with sample information to get an a posteriori distribution. (For a discrete variable, this was done in Tables 12.8 to 12.10.) Suppose, then, that the manager draws a sample of size $n = 50$ and finds breaking strength $x_1, x_2, \ldots, x_{50}$ such that $\bar{x} = 478$ psi and $s^2 = \Sigma(x_i - 478)^2/49 = 1,800$. This value s^2 is an estimate of the population variance σ^2. We conclude that $s^2_{\bar{x}} = s^2/n = \frac{1,800}{50} = 36$, and hence $s_{\bar{x}} = 6$ psi. The sampling distribution of the average is normally distributed with a mean estimated at 478 psi, and a standard deviation at 6 psi.

The following results then hold—in words, in formulas, and when applied to our numerical example: The *a posteriori mean* μ_1 is equal to a weighted average of the a priori mean μ_0 and the sample average $\bar{x}$, with weights equal to the reciprocal of the variances of these respective distributions,

A posteriori mean

$$\mu_1 = \frac{(1/\sigma_0^2)\mu_0 + (1/s_{\bar{x}}^2)\bar{x}}{1/\sigma_0^2 + 1/s_{\bar{x}}^2} = \frac{\frac{1}{1,600} \times 490 + \frac{1}{36} \times 478}{\frac{1}{1,600} + \frac{1}{36}} = 478.28$$

The numerical answer is rather close to the sample average, 478 psi, for the sample evidence relating to the mean is rather specific (its standard error is only 6 psi) and the a priori estimate is rather diffuse (its standard deviation is 40 psi).

The *a posteriori variance* σ_1^2 is equal to the *product* of the variance of the prior distribution σ_0^2 and the variance of the sampling distribution of the average ($\sigma_{\bar{x}}^2$ as estimated by $s_{\bar{x}}^2$), divided by the *sum* of these variances,

A posteriori variance

$$\sigma_1^2 = \frac{\sigma_0^2 \times s_{\bar{x}}^2}{\sigma_0^2 + s_{\bar{x}}^2} = \frac{1,600 \times 36}{1,600 + 36} = 35.21 \qquad \sigma_1 = \sqrt{35.21} = 5.93$$

We now turn to our second and more important problem, "How large a sample should be drawn?" The answer is that one should choose a sample size which maximizes *the expected value of sample information* minus the *sampling costs*. The difficulty is to determine the expected value of sample information before one has actually drawn a sample, let alone

Determination of optimum sample size

observed its outcome. (For a discrete variable, this was done in Table 12.12.)

To make progress, we need as input some idea about the variance (or the standard deviation) of the breaking strengths in the population σ_p^2. Such a rough idea will often be available. In the present example, the glass manufacturer himself stated that the standard deviation of the breaking strengths was 50 psi, and we may believe him, especially if that figure is in line with previous experiences, such as the experience with the glass currently being used. If we know the population variance σ_p^2 *without* having drawn a sample (but not, of course, the population *mean*, on which we only have very diffuse a priori ideas), then we also know the a posteriori variance σ_1^2 *without* drawing a sample, *as a function of n*,

$$\sigma_1^2 = \frac{\sigma_0^2 \times \sigma_{\bar{x}}^2}{\sigma_0^2 + \sigma_{\bar{x}}^2} = \frac{\sigma_0^2 \times \sigma_p^2/n}{\sigma_0^2 + \sigma_p^2/n} = \frac{1{,}600 \times 2{,}500/n}{1{,}600 + 2{,}500/n}$$

The value of D, which measures how many times $\sqrt{\sigma_0^2 - \sigma_1^2}$ goes into the difference between the a priori mean and the break-even point, can also be determined as a function of n,

$$D = \frac{\mu_0 - bp}{\sqrt{\sigma_0^2 - \sigma_1^2}} = \frac{490 - 475}{\sqrt{\sigma_0^2 - \sigma_1^2}} = \frac{490 - 475}{\sqrt{1{,}600 - \dfrac{1{,}600 \times 2{,}500/n}{1{,}600 + 2{,}500/n}}}$$

This value of D plays an important role in the determination of the expected value of sample information (EVSI) because this is given by

$$\text{EVSI} = u\sqrt{\sigma_0^2 - \sigma_1^2}\, f(D)$$

In this example, u is \$1,300 as given above; $\sigma_0^2 = 40^2 = 1{,}600$; and σ_1^2 and D are given above as functions of n. The value of the function $f(D)$ is given in Table 12.13 and, in a more elaborate version, Table 11 of Appendix B. For $n = 25$ we have $\sigma_1^2 = \frac{160{,}000}{1{,}700} = 94.1$ and $D = \frac{15}{38.8} = .387$, since $\sqrt{\sigma_0^2 - \sigma_1^2} = 38.8$. Table 12.13 now tells us that $f(D)$ is between .2374 and .2339. If we interpolate, we find .2349. Therefore, a sample of size 25 has an expected value of sample information equal to \$1,300 $\times$ 38.8 $\times$ .2349 = \$11,848. If it costs \$200 to sample one item—the window must be broken in the process, so it is not cheap—the expected value of sample information minus the sampling costs (SC) is \$6,848.

In Table 12.14 we have made similar computations for a number

TABLE 12.13 $f(D)$ **AS A FUNCTION OF** D

D	$f(D)$	D	$f(D)$	D	$f(D)$	D	$f(D)$	D	$f(D)$	D	$f(D)$
.00	.3989	.20	.3069	.40	.2304	.70	.1429	1.10	.0680	1.50	.0293
.01	.3940	.21	.3027	.41	.2270	.72	.1381	1.12	.0660	1.55	.0261
.02	.3890	.22	.2986	.42	.2236	.74	.1334	1.14	.0634	1.60	.0232
.03	.3841	.23	.2944	.43	.2203	.76	.1289	1.16	.0609	1.65	.0206
.04	.3793	.24	.2904	.44	.2169	.78	.1245	1.18	.0584	1.70	.0183
.05	.3744	.25	.2863	.45	.2137	.80	.1202	1.20	.0561	1.75	.0162
.06	.3697	.26	.2824	.46	.2104	.82	.1160	1.22	.0538	1.80	.0143
.07	.3649	.27	.2784	.47	.2072	.84	.1120	1.24	.0517	1.85	.0126
.08	.3602	.28	.2745	.48	.2040	.86	.1080	1.26	.0495	1.90	.0111
.09	.3556	.29	.2706	.49	.2009	.88	.1042	1.28	.0475	1.95	.0097
.10	.3509	.30	.2668	.50	.1978	.90	.1004	1.30	.0455	2.00	.0085
.11	.3464	.31	.2630	.52	.1917	.92	.0968	1.32	.0436	2.10	.0065
.12	.3418	.32	.2592	.54	.1857	.94	.0933	1.34	.0418	2.20	.0049
.13	.3373	.33	.2555	.56	.1799	.96	.0899	1.36	.0400	2.30	.0037
.14	.3328	.34	.2518	.58	.1742	.98	.0865	1.38	.0383	2.40	.0027
.15	.3284	.35	.2481	.60	.1687	1.00	.0833	1.40	.0367	2.50	.0020
.16	.3240	.36	.2445	.62	.1633	1.02	.0802	1.42	.0351	2.60	.0015
.17	.3197	.37	.2409	.64	.1580	1.04	.0772	1.44	.0336	2.70	.0011
.18	.3154	.38	.2374	.66	.1528	1.06	.0742	1.46	.0321	2.80	.0008
.19	.3111	.39	.2339	.68	.1478	1.08	.0714	1.48	.0307	2.90	.0005

of different sample sizes n. We conclude that our manager should draw a sample of size 7 to maximize the net expected value of his sample information. If this sample results in an average above the value of the break-even point $bp = 475$ psi, he will switch; otherwise, he will stick

TABLE 12.14   DETERMINATION OF OPTIMAL SAMPLE SIZE

(1) n	(2) $\sqrt{(\sigma_0^2 - \sigma_1^2)}$	(3) D	(4) $f(D)$	(5) EVSI	(6) EVSI − SC
5	34.9	.430	.2203	$ 9,995	$8,995
6	35.6	.421	.2232	10,329	9,129
7	36.2	.414	.2255	10,612	9,212
8	36.6	.410	.2270	10,801	9,201
9	36.9	.406	.2282	10,947	9,146
10	37.2	.403	.2293	11,089	9,089
15	38.1	.394	.2325	11,515	8,515
25	38.8	.387	.2349	11,848	6,848

to the glass he currently uses. A sample of size 25 is, as is observed, much too large in view of the high sampling costs.

EXERCISES

12.21   What would happen to the optimal sample size if the value $u = \$1,300$ were to be much larger, let us say $u = \$5,000$?

12.22   A buyer believes that the shipment offered for sale has a percentage of defectives which, to the best of his ability to judge, is normally distributed with a mean $\mu_0 = 20$ percent and a standard deviation of 2 percent. He draws a sample of size 100 and finds 17 defectives. What are the mean and variance of his a posteriori distribution?

12.23   A person believes that the mean number of hamburgers to be sold in each of his many, at present exclusively, hot-dog joints is 200 a day, but he is not sure about it. In his mind this mean number is normally distributed with a mean of 200 and a standard deviation of 10. If he sells 190 on the average, he breaks even. Every unit increase in the average above 190 brings him a profit of $575; every unit decrease below 190 brings a loss of $575. Finally, the standard deviation in the population of hamburger outlets he operates is known to him to be 40. If it costs $20 + 5n$ dollars to sample n of his outlets, how large a sample should he draw, and what should he do?

Answers to Exercises

12.1   The states of nature are "rain" or "no rain," the decisions are "take umbrella" or "leave umbrella home," and the payoffs, measured in utilities, could be as stated below. We have given a zero to the worst possibility (rain without umbrella) and a 10 to the best (no rain and no umbrella to carry). Rain with an umbrella is noted as 6, and no rain with an umbrella as 8. This is less than 10, since there is a certain disutility in carrying an umbrella, and if the clouds disappear, you may even look foolish. Different people may feel differently, however, and the values 6 and 8 are only the authors' subjective opinion.

State of nature	Umbrella	No umbrella
Rain	6	0
No rain	8	10

12.2 The construction of the payoff table, with payoffs measured in dollars, is straightforward. The farmer should conclude that whatever the competitors do, he is better off producing 20 pigs, since $1,400 is more than $700 and $300 exceeds $150.

State of nature	Produce 10 pigs	Produce 20 pigs
Competitors jointly produce 10,000 pigs	$700	$1,400
Competitors jointly produce 20,000 pigs	$150	$300

12.3 The exact values of the utilities here are again subjective and somewhat arbitrary. The following values appear reasonable: There is no payoff for no try; a successful try is rated at 100; and the disutility in case of failure is 1.

State of nature	Try escape	Don't try escape
Success	100	0
No success	−1	0

12.4 Our result is:

State of nature	Flying in same plane	Flying in separate plane
No plane crashes	10	9
One plane crashes	0	5
Both planes crash		1

The *best* situation is one plane and no crash. This is slightly better than using two planes if only because it is less costly. The *worst* situation is one plane which crashes. Two planes (of which one crashes) saves at least one of the two top executives. There is no possibility that two planes crash if only one plane flies, and if both of the two planes crash, we can at least feel some consolation in that we tried our best to prevent such a situation.

12.5 The highest entry in each row of a payoff table is replaced by a zero in the opportunity loss table. The other cells in the row show the difference between the corresponding entry in the payoff table and the highest entry in the same row in the payoff table. We get the following table:

	Expand				Decision	
State of nature	2,000	1,000	State of nature	Insure	No insurance	
Brisk	$ 0	$3,500	Fire	$ 0	$86,000	
Slack	2,000	0	No fire	4,000	0	

12.6 The following table summarizes the data in the exercise:

State of nature, %	Check	Don't check
2	$1,000	$ 0
10	1,000	500
25	1,000	3,000

Notice that the values are *costs,* and that a decision maker will strive to *minimize* costs.

12.7 According to the criterion of maximizing expected utilities, you should not. The expected utility is $.2 \times 6 + .8 \times 8 = 7.6$ if you do take an umbrella, and the expected utility is $.2 \times 0 + .8 \times 10 = 8$ if you don't. However, if there is a 25 percent probability of rain, both expected utilities are 7.5, and either action is correct. For rain probabilities higher than 25 percent, you should take an umbrella.

12.8 The expected value criterion points to choosing urn II, since $.1 \times \$100,000 + .9 \times \$1,000$ exceeds $.1 \times \$100 + .9 \times \$10,000$. The minimax criterion looks at the worst possible situation ($100), which can be prevented by choosing urn II. The maximax criterion looks at the best possible situation ($100,000), which can be realized only by choosing urn II. All three decision criteria point to urn II (although personally you might well prefer urn I with its high probability of getting $10,000, and we would not blame you if you did). The exercise is meant to preach care and moderation in the use of any fixed criterion—in particular those completely neglecting variability in outcomes, like expected value criteria; or minimax or maximax, which completely neglect associated probabilities.

12.9   The expected value criterion leads to expanding by 1,000 units, for an expected value of $3,100, which is more than $2,500 or $2,800. A decision maker using minimax would certainly not expand by 2,000 units for fear of losing $1,000, and in the choice of expanding by 1,000 or not at all he would choose not at all. This leads to a return of $2,500, while expanding by 1,000 could lead to a return of only $1,500. Using maximax he would expand by 2,000, and hope for Lady Luck to bring him $5,000 as a reward. [In the previous exercise all three criteria pointed to a decision which many decent, honest citizens would not make; in this example the three decision criteria lead to three different decisions. Some skepticism regarding these (and, for that matter, any) decision criteria is warranted; but the *concept* of a decision criterion is quite important.]

12.10   In the figure we start at point A, corresponding to assets OA' and a utility $U(A)$. Any bet will lead to a new position on the utility curve, to the left of A if you lose (point B, for example), or to

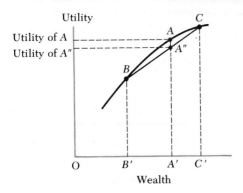

the right of A if you win (point C, for example). The fact that the bet is fair means that the expected payoff is zero, so the *expected* assets after the bet are still OA'. The *actual* assets will be either OB' or OC', depending on whether you lose (probability p) or win (probability $1 - p$). The expected utility will be $p \times U(B) + (1 - p) \times U(C)$, that is, the point on the straight line connecting B and C corresponding to assets OA'. This is A'' in the figure. $U(A'')$ is less than $U(A)$. In general, if we connect any point to the left of A with any point to the right of A on the utility curve with a straight line, the point corresponding to the same assets as point A on this straight line will be *below* A, implying a smaller utility.

12.11   The payoff table is:

State of nature, %	Probability	Check	Don't check
2	.7	$1,000	$ 0
10	.2	1,000	500
25	.1	1,000	3,000

The expected costs will be $1,000 if he does check, and $.7 \times \$0 + .2 \times \$500 + .1 \times \$3,000 = \$400$ if he does not check. Since $400 is less than $1,000, the manager should not check.

12.12   As we saw in Exercise 12.11, without perfect information the manager has minimum expected costs of $400 (by not checking). *With* perfect information, he will pay nothing if he is informed that the true state of nature is 2 percent (probability .7), he will pay $500 if he is informed that the true state is 10 percent (probability .2), and he will pay $1,000 for checking if he is told that the true state is 25 percent (probability .1). The expected costs are now $.7 \times \$0 + .2 \times \$500 + .1 \times \$1,000 = \$200$. This is $200 less than the expected profit under the best decision without perfect information, and, therefore, the expected value of perfect information is $400 - \$200 = \$200$.

12.13   Without any information his (maximum) expected profit is $0, whichever decision is made. With perfect information he gains $400,000 if this information states that there is oil (probability

.2). If the information received states that there is no oil (probability .8), he will not drill and not get anything. The expected profit under perfect information is, therefore, .2 × $400,000 + .8 × $0 = $80,000. The expected profit without information is $0, and so the expected value of perfect information is $80,000 − $0 = $80,000.

12.14 We find

$$.05 \times 12 + .05 \times 10 + .10 \times 8 + .10 \times 6 + .10 \times 4$$
$$+ .15 \times 2 + .15 \times 0 + .10 \times 3 + .10 \times 6 + .05 \times 9$$
$$+ .05 \times 12 = 5.15$$

The values 12, 10, 8, . . . are by definition equal to 30 − 18, 33 − 23, 36 − 28, . . . , that is, the highest value in each row minus the value under column "16". We can rewrite the formula as

$$.05(30 - 18) + .05(33 - 23) + .10(36 - 28) + \cdots$$

and observe that this is precisely the expected profit under perfect information minus the expected profit of the best decision "16" when there is only a priori information. In general, the expected value of perfect information can be found by determining the expected value of the opportunity losses in the column corresponding to the best decision, with the use of the a priori probabilities. This expected value is referred to as the *expected opportunity loss*.

12.15 (*a*) The following table contains the relevant computations and the answers:

(1) State of nature	(2) A priori probability	(3) Conditional probability	(4) (2) × (3)	(5) A posteriori probability
Oil ($400,000)	.2	.6	.12	$\frac{.12}{.28} = .429$
No oil (−100,000)	.8	.2	.16	$\frac{.16}{.28} = .571$
			.28	

In Column 5 we have the a posteriori probabilities of oil and no oil.

(*b*) The expected profit of drilling is now .429 × $400,000 +

$.571(-\$100,000) = \$114,500$. As before, the expected profit of not drilling is still $0. (Both these figures disregard the sunk costs, rather literally sunk in this case, of the $10,000 needed for drilling 50 feet.) The decision is to go ahead and drill.

(c) The expected value of perfect information without drilling is $80,000, as found in Exercise 12.13. The expected value of perfect information by using a posteriori probabilities is determined as follows. Step 5: *Without* perfect information, the best decision is to drill, which leads to an expected profit of $114,500. Step 6: *With* perfect information, we drill when we hear that there is oil (probability .429, profit $400,000), and we don't when there is no oil (probability .571, no costs). Therefore, the expected profit is $.429 \times \$400,000 + .571 \times \$0 = \$171,600$. Step 7: The difference is $57,100. Step 8: The value of the sample is therefore $\$80,000 - \$57,100 = \$22,900$, which is much more than the $10,000 sample cost. The oil man is delighted with his investment.

12.16 (a) If the true state of nature is 2 percent defectives, the probability of finding 1 defective in a sample of size 10 is $10(.02)(.98)^9 = .1667$. If there are 10 percent defectives, it is $10(.10)(.90)^9 = .3874$. If there are 25 percent defectives, it is $10(.25)(.75)^9 = .1877$. Hence:

(1) State of nature, %	(2) A priori probability	(3) Conditional probability	(4) (2) × (3)	(5) A posteriori probability
2 ($ 0)	.7	.1667	.1167	$\frac{.1167}{.2130} = .548$
10 (500)	.2	.3874	.0775	$\frac{.0775}{.2130} = .364$
25 (3,000)	.1	.1877	.0188	$\frac{.0188}{.2130} = .088$
			.2130	

(b) The cost of checking the machine is still $1,000, and the expected cost of not checking is $.548 \times \$0 + .364 \times \$500 + .088 \times \$3,000 = \$446$. The machine should *not* be checked.

(c) Before the sample was taken, the expected value of perfect information was $200, as computed in Exercise 12.12. After the sample, the probabilities changed from .7, .2, and .1 to

.548, .364, and .088. Step 5: Therefore, after the sample the expected costs of not checking are .548 × $0 + .364 × $500 + .088 × $3,000 = $446. Step 6: Under perfect information they would be .548 × $0 + .364 × $500 + .088 × $1,000 = $270. Step 7: The expected value of perfect information is $446 − $270 = $176, after the sample. Step 8: Evidently, the value of this sample is $200 − $176 = $24.

12.17   In the text we found that the expected value of perfect information is $2 before this game begins. Step 5: The best decision is *not* to bet; expected payoff $0. Step 6: With perfect information the expected payoff is .4 × $10 + .6 × $0 = $4. Step 7: The value of perfect information is $4 − $0 = $4. Step 8: The "value" of this outcome is $2 − $4 = − $2. This does not mean that the information is worthless, but that it lowered the degree of assurance in your mind about the outcome and made perfect information even more desirable; that is, there is more uncertainty to be removed from your mind now than before.

12.18   Before any sample, the value of complete information is $155. Step 4: After a sample of 25 with 4 defectives, the a priori probabilities are converted to a posteriori probabilities, with the results recorded below (we use the data of Table 12.11, under "4" in Column 3).

(1) State of nature, %	(2) A priori probability	(3) Conditional probability	(4) (2) × (3)	(5) A posteriori probability
2 ($2,500)	.10	.0013	.00013	.005
3 (1,700)	.30	.0054	.00162	.067
4 (900)	.20	.0137	.00274	.114
5 (0)	.15	.0269	.00403	.168
6 (−200)	.10	.0447	.00447	.186
7 (−700)	.10	.0662	.00662	.275
8 (−1,300)	.05	.0889	.00444	.185
			.02405	1

Step 5: Given these a posteriori probabilities, the best decision is *not* to buy (for a profit of $0), since buying leads to an expected profit of .005 × $2,500 + .067 × $1,700 + ⋯ +

.275 × (−$700) + .185 × (−$1,300) = −$239. Without further information we do *not* buy, and have a profit of $0. Step 6: If we get perfect information, then we will buy if the information is that less than 5 percent is defective, for an expected profit of .005 × $2,500 + .067 × $1,700 + .114 × $900 + .168 × $0 + .186 × $0 + .275 × $0 + .185 × $0 = $229. Step 7: Hence, the expected value of perfect information is $229 − $0 = $229. Step 8: The expected value of perfect information *was* $155, and the difference $155 − $229 = −$74 is the value of a sample of size 25 with 4 defectives.

12.19   It all depends on the outcome of the sample. The expected value of the information in a sample of size 10 is

P(0 defectives) × value of sample with 0 defectives +
P(1 defective) × value of sample with 1 defective +
. . . .
P(10 defectives) × value of sample with 10 defectives

The computations to obtain these probabilities and values require the following *basic data:*

Probability of Obtaining Sample of 10 with *k* Defectives

State of nature, %	A priori probability	k=0	k=1	k=2	k=3	k=4	k=5	k=6	k=7	Total
2	.7	.818	.167	.015	0	0	0	0	0	1
10	.2	.349	.387	.194	.057	.011	.001	0	0	1
25	.1	.056	.188	.282	.251	.146	.058	.016	.003	1

From this table, compute the a posteriori probabilities, given that a sample contains *k* (*k* = 0, 1, 2, . . .) defectives. For *k* = 0, the a posteriori probability is computed as follows:

(1) State of nature, %	(2) A priori probability	(3) Conditional probability	(4) (2) × (3)	(5) A posteriori probability
2	.7	.818	.5726	$\frac{.5726}{.6480} = .884$
10	.2	.349	.0698	$\frac{.0698}{.6480} = .108$
25	.1	.056	.0056	$\frac{.0056}{.6480} = .008$
			.6480	

The other a posteriori probabilities are:

A Posteriori Probability if Sample Contains *k* Defectives

State of nature, %	k=0	k=1	k=2	k=3	k=4	k=5	k=6	k=7
2	.884	.548	.135	0	0	0	0	0
10	.108	.364	.501	.312	.131	.017	0	0
25	.008	.088	.364	.688	.869	.983	1	1

(Notice that the higher the number of defectives in the sample, the higher the probability that there are 25 percent defectives.) From the last table above, determine the best action (check or not check) given the objective to minimize expected costs. The expected cost of *not* checking the machine is, dependent upon the sample outcome of zero, one, two, three, four, five, six, or seven defectives, equal to $78, $446, $1,342, $2,220, $2,672, $2,957, $3,000, and $3,000. (For example, with two defectives .135 × $0 + .501 × $500 + .364 × $3,000 = $1,342.) Check whenever there are 2 or more defectives in a sample of size 10, for a cost of $1,000. Otherwise, don't check, for an expected cost of $78 or $446, depending on whether there are zero or one defectives.

Next compare these costs with those under perfect information, which are

Number of defectives k	Cost With perfect information		With sample information
0	.884 × $0 + .108 × $500 + .008 × $1,000 = $	62	$ 78
1	.584 × 0 + .364 × 500 + .088 × 1,000 =	270	446
2	.135 × 0 + .501 × 500 + .364 × 1,000 =	614	1,000
3	.312 × 500 + .688 × 1,000 −	844	1,000
4	.131 × 500 + .869 × 1,000 =	934	1,000
5	.017 × 500 + .983 × 1,000 =	991	1,000
6	1 × 1,000 = 1,000		1,000
7	1 × 1,000 = 1,000		1,000

By comparing the costs under perfect information with those under sample information, we see that the value of the perfect information is $78 − $62 = $16, $446 − $270 = $176, $386, $156, $66,

$9, $0, and $0. Before the sample, the value of perfect information was $200, and so the sample information—depending on the sample results—is worth $184, $24, −$186, $44, $134, $191, $200, or $200, respectively. The probabilities of getting a sample with zero, one, two, three, four, five, six, or seven defectives are (using our *basic data*)

$$.7 \times .818 + .2 \times .349 + .1 \times .056 = .6480$$
$$.7 \times .167 + .2 \times .387 + .1 \times .188 = .2131$$
$$.7 \times .015 + .2 \times .194 + .1 \times .282 = .0775$$
$$.2 \times .057 + .1 \times .251 = .0365$$
$$.2 \times .011 + .1 \times .146 = .0168$$
$$.2 \times .001 + .1 \times .058 = .0060$$
$$.1 \times .016 = .0016$$
$$.1 \times .003 = .0003$$

The expected value of a sample of size 10 equals $.6480 \times \$184 + .2131 \times \$24 + .0775 \times (-\$186) + .0365 \times \$44 + .0168 \times \$134 + .0060 \times \$191 + .0016 \times \$200 + .0003 \times \$200 = \$115$. A sample of size 10 should be drawn if the cost is less than $115.

12.20 (a) No sample information can be better than perfect information. If after the sample the value of perfect information is $0, then the sample is worth the expected value of perfect information, $2. This happens only with very conclusive samples, such as 10 to 0 or 0 to 10.

(b) The expected value of perfect information must be $.80 after the Red Sox three-run lead after the third inning is known. The payoff table is:

State of nature	Probability	Bet	Don't bet
Red Sox win	p	$10	$0
Red Sox lose	$1 - p$	−$10	$0

The values of p and $1 - p$ are unknown. Without further information the best alternative will be to bet, expected payoff $p \times \$10 + (1 - p)(-\$10) = 2p \times \$10 - \$10$. With perfect information the expected payoff is $p \times \$10 + (1 - p)(\$0)$. We must have $p \times \$10 - (2p \times \$10 - \$10) = \$.80$. Hence $p \times \$10 = \$9.20$ and $p = \frac{9.20}{10.00} = .92$.

(c) The value is $.01 \times \$2 + .02 \times \$2 + \cdots + .00 \times \$2 = 57.35$ cents.

12.21 The entries in Column 5 of Table 12.14 will then all be four times as large, and the entries in Column 6 will be changed accordingly. We then find

n	(5)	(6)
5	$39,980	$38,980
6	41,316	40,116
7	42,448	41,048
8	43,204	41,604
9	43,788	41,988
10	44,356	42,356
15	46,060	43,060
25	47,392	43,392

The value is largest for $n = 15$ (although it might be larger still for $n = 14$ or $n = 16$), and so the sample size is much larger than before. It stands to reason that one wants more information if the consequences of wrong decisions can be expensive and of correct decisions very profitable.

12.22 We have $\mu_0 = .20$ and $\sigma_0 = .02$, $\sigma_0^2 = .0004$. We also have $\bar{x} = .17$, and the standard deviation of this proportion is $\sqrt{.17 \times .83/100} = .0376$, the variance $.0014$. Therefore

$$\mu_1 = \frac{\frac{1}{.0004} \times .20 + \frac{1}{.0014} \times .17}{\frac{1}{.0004} + \frac{1}{.0014}} = .1933$$

In this case the answer is closer to .20 than .17, because the a priori notion concerning the true proportion of defectives was more accurate than the sample information. Also

$$\sigma_1^2 = \sqrt{\left(\frac{.0004 \times .0014}{.0004 + .0014}\right)} = \sqrt{(.0003111)} = .0176$$

12.23 We have $\mu_0 = 200$, $\sigma_0 = 10$, $u = \$575$, $bp = 190$, and $\sigma_p^2 = 40^2 = 1,600$. Furthermore, we can compute (as functions of the sample size n) $\sigma_1^2 = (100 \times 1,600/n)/(100 + 1,600/n)$ and therefore $\sigma_0^2 - \sigma_1^2 = 100 - \sigma_1^2$, which can be written as $100 \times 100/(100 + 1,600/n)$ after a little algebra, and finally

$D = (200 - 190)/\sqrt{\sigma_0^2 - \sigma_1^2}$. Thus we can make the following table:

(1)	(2)	(3)	(4)	(5)	(6)
n	$\sqrt{\sigma_0^2 - \sigma_1^2}$	D	$f(D)$	EVSI	EVSI − SC
10	6.20	1.61	.0227	$ 80.92	$10.92
20	7.45	1.34	.0418	179.06	59.06
25	7.81	1.28	.0475	213.31	68.31
28	7.98	1.25	.0503	230.80	70.80
30	8.08	1.24	.0517	240.20	70.20
40	8.45	1.18	.0584	283.75	63.75

We should draw a sample of size 28 and market our hamburgers if the average in this sample exceeds the break-even number of 190.

Chapter 13

RELATIONS BETWEEN VARIABLES: REGRESSION AND CORRELATION

13.1 THE SCATTER DIAGRAM AND THE REGRESSION LINE

When we say that two variables are independent, we have said all there is to say about the relationship between them; that is, they are not related in any way. When two variables are dependent, the problems just begin. What is the nature of the relationship between the variables? In some cases, this question is not difficult to answer. For example, there is a definite relationship between the weight of a first-class airmail letter sent within the United States and the required postage. Anyone who wants specifics on this relationship can phone the post office.

Let us now consider a more interesting case. Economic theory, as well as a casual glance around, tells us that family income and consumption are related. In general, an above-average income will go together with above-average consumption. This, however, is a rather vague statement. We will proceed to describe the relationship more precisely.

The first problem is to consider whether a causal relationship exists. In this example, it is clear that a causal relationship does exist. The level of income will influence the level of consumption. There also is a causal relationship between hours of sunshine and the rate of growth of tulips.

Causal relationships

373

Hours of sunshine will influence the rate of growth of tulips. Conversely, higher consumption will seldom cause a higher income, nor will we make the sun shine more by forcing tulips to grow faster. In these examples, the variable whose value is influenced (consumption, growth) is called the *dependent variable* and is written *y*; the variable which exerts the influence (income, sunshine) is called the *independent variable* and is written *x*. The value of the independent variable "explains" the value of the dependent variable. For this reason the independent variable is often called the *explanatory variable*.

Dependent and independent, or explanatory, variables

In other cases variables will be related without the existence of a causal relationship. Stock prices of Ford and Chrysler will usually go up and down together, but it is incorrect to say that one price change causes the other. Both stocks, however, react similarly to the same type of news (strong demand for cars, for example), and tend to move in the same direction. The vocabularies and shoe sizes of children in the elementary grades are related, but they are not causally related. Changes in age bring changes in vocabulary size *and* foot size. In such cases it may still be interesting to establish the nature of the statistical relationship, but no causal relationship follows. When a statistical relationship is established, we say there is *correlation* between the variables. A loud word of warning in this context is called for: Although a causal relationship usually implies correlation, a correlation does not in and of itself prove causality. The fact that during the 1960s hemlines of skirts and wages of ministers were correlated (both went higher and higher) does not imply a causal relationship in either direction.

Correlation

While we are looking for a relationship between consumption and income, we must recognize at the outset that consumption is related to other factors such as the number of dependents, personal tastes, and state of health. Growth of tulips depends on factors such as rainfall, soil, type of bulb, and quality of bulb, in addition to amount of sunshine. Thus we see that there can be many explanatory variables for one dependent variable. We will get back to this issue later, but for the time being we will devote our attention to the case where we consider but one explanatory variable.

More than one explanatory variable

Clearly the relationship between consumption and income cannot be found without data. We need to have, for many families, data on their consumption expenditures and their income. We depict the available data graphically in a *scatter diagram*. Suppose that we have data on consumption *y* and income *x*, as in Table 13.1. These data are expressed in dollars per day. For convenience, we will usually omit the units. In Figure 13.1

Scatter diagram

TABLE 13.1 SEVEN OBSERVATIONS ON INCOME x AND CONSUMPTION y IN DOLLARS PER DAY

(1) Observation	(2) Income x	(3) Consumption y
1	30	27
2	35	30
3	19	18
4	39	32
5	26	19
6	29	29
7	32	20

the data are plotted with the dependent variable (consumption) along the vertical axis, and the explanatory variable (income) along the horizontal axis. Point 1 in Figure 13.1 corresponds to a family with an income of 30 and a consumption of 27. The data for other families are similarly plotted. The overall impression is one of points scattered in a plane, which accounts for the name.

Such a scatter diagram may be very suggestive. The points may all be clustered as in Figure 13.2a. The impression is created of points around an upward sloping straight line. In such a case we speak of a *positive* relationship, meaning that increases in the dependent variable tend to go

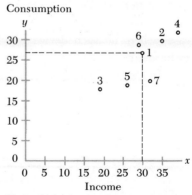

Figure 13.1 Scatter diagram of income and consumption for seven families, in dollars per day.

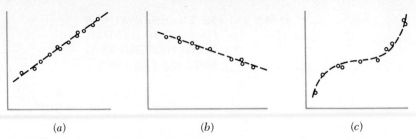

(a)   (b)   (c)

Figure 13.2 Positive, negative, and curvilinear relationships between two variables.

together with increases in the independent variable. Another possibility is that the points in the scatter diagram may cluster around a downward sloping straight line, as in Figure 13.2*b*. This is an illustration of a *negative* relationship. *De*creases in the dependent variable are associated with *in*creases in the independent variable.

In Figure 13.2*c* the impression is created of a curved-line relationship. Such *curvilinear relationships* may be detected on a scatter diagram, but they are mathematically less convenient than straight-line relationships. There are great mathematical advantages when the relationship can be represented by a straight line, and we will limit our attention to such relationships.

This is not so restrictive as it sounds. For one thing, many curves can be approximated by straight lines, *over limited ranges,* as seen in Figure 13.3. For another, it may well be that, while there is no good straight-line relationship between dependent variable y and independent variable x, there *is* a good linear fit between y and x^2, or y and $\log x$, or $\log y$ and x. A scatter diagram may point out such a relationship. (In Chapter 15 we discuss an example of this.) Obviously, however, there will remain cases where no such device will help us, and curvilinear fits will have to be used.

In the scatter diagram plotting the relationship between consumption and income (Figure 13.1), we will assume that the relationship can be

Figure 13.3 Straight lines approximate segments of curves.

represented by a straight line, although the scatter of the 7 points themselves is somewhat inconclusive. A straight line is symbolically written as

$$y = a + bx$$

where y is the dependent variable and x the independent variable. The a is the *intercept* and b is the *slope*. A straight line is fully determined by its intercept and its slope. The three lines in Figure 13.4 illustrate this. The intercept measures the value where the line crosses the vertical axis. The slope measures the increase in y associated with a *unit* increase in x. In our example a slope of $b = .8$ means that a \$1 increase in income leads to a $.8 \times \$1 = \$.80$ increase in consumption. We can now translate the straight-line assumption in more concrete terms. It implies that \$1 more income will typically lead to \$.80 more consumption—and this will be true whether income rises from \$19 to \$20 or from \$30 to \$31.

Which line—which value for a and which value for b—among the infinite number of straight lines shall we pick? In Figure 13.5, we have shown a number of possible alternatives. Lines 1 and 2 appear quite reasonable; line 3 is not very appealing. There are many reasonable lines, and we must establish some criterion on which to base the choice. The

Straight line, intercept, and slope

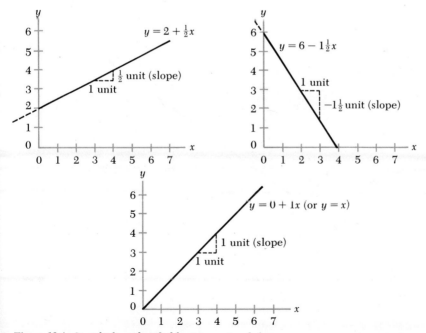

Figure 13.4 Straight line identified by intercept and slope.

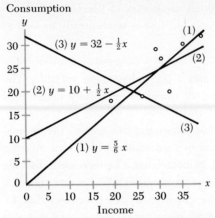

Figure 13.5   Several possible regression lines.

criterion universally used is the *least-squares* criterion: The sum of the *squares* of the deviations of the points from the line should be minimized (or made *least*). This gives us the *regression line,* showing the relationship, or *regression* of consumption y on income x. In Figure 13.6 we have drawn the regression line and the deviation d_1, d_2, . . . , d_n from this

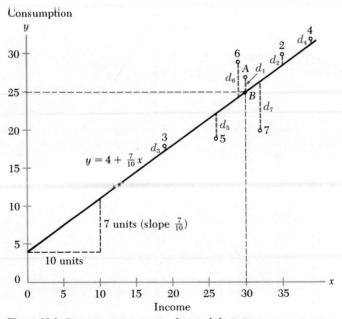

Figure 13.6   Least-squares regression line and deviations.

line. As can be seen, the deviations are measured in a vertical direction. The reason for this is as follows: According to the line in Figure 13.6, consumption should be 25 for a family whose income is 30. In fact, we observed a family whose consumption is 27. The difference is given by the length of the *vertical* line *AB*.

One may wonder why there is any deviation at all. These deviations are easy to understand when it is remembered that there are other factors besides income which influence consumption. We hope that these influences from other factors are relatively small, but it would be too much to expect that there would be no deviations at all. A consequence of the least-squares criterion is that the sum of the positive and negative deviations is zero. We will see this in the next section after we have introduced the technique for finding the values a and b which identify the regression line. In the example illustrated in Figure 13.6 it implies that $d_3 + d_6 + d_1 + d_2 + d_4$, .that is, the positive deviations *above* the regression line, equal $d_5 + d_7$, that is, the negative deviations *below* the line.

EXERCISES

13.1   The price of tea, together with the quantities bought in five periods, was as follows:

Price	9	11	12	13	15
Quantity	16	15	15	14	10

Draw a scatter diagram and fit a reasonable line by hand.

13.2   Consider the following 35 pairs of numbers. Draw a scatter diagram and a reasonable line.

22, 14	29, 18	4, 17	2, 2
30, 4	2, 15	19, 19	4, 5
13, 4	24, 9	5, 18	10, 20
16, 28	7, 8	18, 24	30, 12
28, 4	23, 8	20, 13	8, 26
11, 23	23, 1	29, 6	14, 28
15, 8	12, 15	27, 6	29, 22
5, 24	29, 31	15, 8	27, 22
9, 4	27, 23	28, 3	

One will notice that there appears to be little regularity in the scatter; this is no surprise. The pairs represent the dates of birth and death of 35 American Presidents, from Washington to Johnson (August 27, 1908 to January 22, 1973).

13.3   What is the equation of the line:
    (*a*) With slope 3 and intercept -3?
    (*b*) With slope 2 and passing through the point (4,7)?
    (*c*) With slope -1 and intercept 4?
    (*d*) Passing through the points (4,1) and (7,3)?
    (*e*) Passing through the origin and (2,2)?
    (*f*) With slope 0 and intercept 4?

13.4   (*a*) Draw the lines $y = 3 + 2x$ and $y = 11 - x$. Determine the point where these lines intersect graphically.
    (*b*) Consider the two equations in two unknowns

$$-2x + y = 3$$
$$x + y = 11$$

and solve for x and y. Does the answer surprise you?

13.2 THE INTERCEPT AND SLOPE OF THE REGRESSION LINE

In this chapter we will quite frequently use the summation symbol Σ. In each case we sum over n observations, so that we have, for example,

$$\Sigma y_i = y_1 + y_2 + \cdots + y_n$$

$$\Sigma x_i y_i = x_1 y_1 + x_2 y_2 + \cdots + x_n y_n$$

$$\Sigma x_i^2 = x_1^2 + x_2^2 + \cdots + x_n^2$$

$$\Sigma d_i^2 = d_1^2 + d_2^2 + \cdots + d_n^2$$

As we saw in the previous section, the problem is to determine those values for a and b which minimize the sum of squared deviations of the points (x_i, y_i) from the line $y = a + bx$. In this context, one useful result was found in Section 5.4: The sum of the squared deviations of the observations from the *average* is less than the sum of the squared deviations from any other value. We will use this result here, but turned around. We want to minimize the sum of the squared deviations of points from a line, and therefore the line ought to pass through the average of the points.

In Figure 13.7 we have again plotted the 7 points in Table 13.1. The average income $\bar{x}$ is

$$\bar{x} = \frac{30 + 35 + 19 + 39 + 26 + 29 + 32}{7} = 30$$

The average consumption $\bar{y}$ is

$$\bar{y} = \frac{27 + 30 + 18 + 32 + 19 + 29 + 20}{7} = 25$$

The regression line passes through the point (30,25). More generally, the regression line will pass through the point $(\bar{x},\bar{y})$. So we must have

$$\bar{y} = a + b\bar{x}$$

Regression line passes through $\bar{x}, \bar{y}$

This point $(\bar{x},\bar{y})$ is referred to as the *center of gravity*.

The slope coefficient b is given by

$$b = \frac{\Sigma x_i y_i - n\bar{x}\bar{y}}{\Sigma x_i^2 - n\bar{x}^2}$$

We will not derive this result, but note that its value is fully determined by the n pairs of actual observations (x_i, y_i) and the value of n itself. These values specify $\bar{x}$ and $\bar{y}$, and by substitution in the above formula, the value

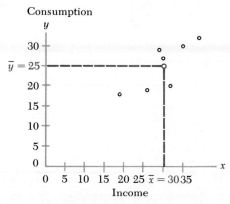

Figure 13.7 Center of gravity $(\bar{x},\bar{y})$.

for b. In our example of the regression of consumption on income, we have

$$b = \frac{\begin{array}{c} 30 \times 27 + 35 \times 30 + 19 \times 18 + 39 \times 32 \\ + 26 \times 19 + 29 \times 29 + 32 \times 20 - 7 \times 30 \times 25 \end{array}}{30^2 + 35^2 + 19^2 + 39^2 + 26^2 + 29^2 + 32^2 - 7 \times 30^2} \approx .7$$

Now that we have computed the slope b from the data $x_1, x_2, \ldots, x_n$ and $y_1, y_2, \ldots, y_n$, we use $\bar{y} = a + b\bar{x}$; hence

$$a = \bar{y} - b\bar{x}$$

This determines the intercept once the slope b is known. In our example

$$a = 25 - .7 \times 30 = 4$$

We conclude that the regression line is $y = 4 + .7x$. This is the line drawn in Figure 13.6.

EXERCISES

13.5   Determine the regression line for the data in Exercise 13.1.

13.6   Determine the regression line for the data in Exercise 13.2.

13.7   Determine the regression line in each of the following cases:

(a) x	y	(b) x	y	(c) x	y
1	2	1	1	1	0
2	3	2	4	2	7
3	4	3	5	3	4
4	5	4	4	4	1
5	6	5	6	5	8

13.8   Prove that the average of all deviations from the regression line is zero.

13.3 THE COEFFICIENT OF DETERMINATION

In Exercise 13.7 we have derived the regression lines for three different sets of data, which are illustrated in Figure 13.8. It will be observed that in all three cases the regression line has the equation

$$y = 1 + x$$

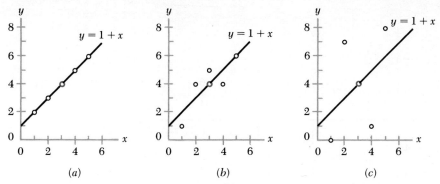

Figure 13.8 Regression lines vary in goodness of fit.

Yet all three sets of data are rather different as far as the goodness of fit is concerned. In the first case, the fit is perfect. All the points are exactly on the straight line. The second fit is not perfect, since not all points fall on the line. The third fit is much worse than the second, since the deviations of the points from the line are much greater. The purpose of this section is to introduce a precise and reasonable measure of the goodness of fit of a regression line.

The *coefficient of determination* R^2 is the most frequently used measure of goodness of fit. It is defined as

$$R^2 = 1 - \frac{\text{var } d}{\text{var } y} = 1 - \frac{\Sigma d_i^2 - n\bar{d}^2}{\Sigma y_i^2 - n\bar{y}^2}$$

Coefficient of determination R^2

where we use the formula for the computation of the variance given in Section 5.5. The numerator of the last ratio is n var d; the denominator is n var y. The average deviation $\bar{d}$ is always zero, and is written only for the sake of symmetry.

The properties of R^2 will prove its merits. The value R^2 will be 1 only if all deviations $d_1, d_2, \ldots, d_n$ are zero, so that all points are exactly on a straight line. This is the maximum possible value of R^2. It is illustrated in Figure 13.8a. The fit is perfect.

The R^2 value is never less than zero. The value of R^2 *equals* zero when var $d = $ var y. In Figure 13.9 we have illustrated together the case where var $d = $ var y and the case where var d is less than var y. In general, var $d = $ var y if and only if *the regression line is horizontal through $\bar{y}$*.

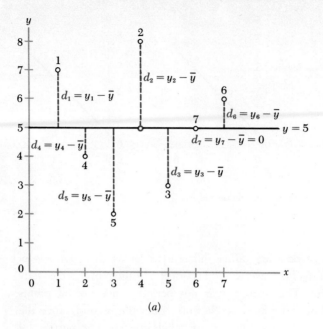

(a)

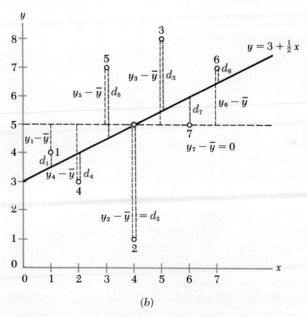

(b)

Figure 13.9 Coefficient of determination shows relationship between var d and var y.

Then

$$d_1 = y_1 - \bar{y}$$
$$d_2 = y_2 - \bar{y}$$
$$\cdots\cdots\cdots$$
$$d_n = y_n - \bar{y}$$

and hence

$$\frac{\Sigma d_i^2}{n} = \frac{\Sigma(y_i - \bar{y})^2}{n}$$

so that var d = var y. This is illustrated in Figure 13.9a. The points (1,7), (4,8), (5,3), (2,4), (3,2), (7,6), and (6,5) lead to the regression line $y = 5$, that is, $y = \bar{y}$. The R^2 is zero.

If the regression line is *not* horizontal, var d will be *less* than var y, so that R^2 will be between 0 and 1. The proof that var d will be less than var y can be given in three short, though somewhat subtle, steps. First, we determine the regression line by *minimizing* $d_1^2 + d_2^2 + \cdots + d_n^2 = n$ var d, and thereby minimizing var d. Second, as we saw above, we can always draw a horizontal line through $\bar{y}$ and thus guarantee var d = var y. Third, var d will, therefore, when minimized, never exceed var y. This is illustrated in Figure 13.9b. The points (1,4), (4,1), (5,8), (2,3), (3,7), (7,7), and (6,5) lead to the regression line $y = 3 + \frac{1}{2}x$, and an R^2 between 0 and 1.

In our income-consumption example, we observe a variation in consumption between families. We wonder how this comes about. We then are told by economists that variation in consumption may well be due to different incomes. We regress consumption y on income x, and find $y = 4 + .7x$. The observed values for consumption still vary around this regression line, *but they vary much less* around the regression line than around the line of average consumption $\bar{y}$. This decrease in variance is a measure of the goodness of fit: The smaller var d (the variation around the regression line) compared with var y (the variation around $\bar{y}$), the higher R^2.

In Figure 13.10 we have illustrated two sets of data side by side. The data—the regression line, the computed y values y_c, as well as the deviations d—are given in Table 13.2. *The values y_c are the values of y on the regression line for given x.* For example, in the regression line $y = 1 + x$, a value of 3 for x implies $y_c = 1 + 3 = 4$. In fact, we

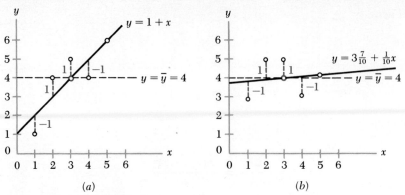

Figure 13.10 Effect of different var y on R^2.

observed $y = 5$ where $x = 3$, so the deviation between the observed value 5 and the computed value 4 is $d = y - y_c = 5 - 4 = 1$.

The graphs (a) and (b) in Figure 13.10 show deviations d, point by point, the same. They are -1, 1, 1, -1, and 0. The coefficient of determination is much higher in graph (a), however. The variability around the steeply sloping regression line is relatively much less than the variability around $y = \bar{y}\ (=4)$. In graph (b) of Figure 13.10, the variability around the ever-so-gently sloping line $y = 3.7 + .1x$ is relatively not much less than the variability around $y = \bar{y}\ (=4)$. In fact,

$$R^2 = 1 - \frac{(-1)^2 + 1^2 + 1^2 + (-1)^2 + 0^2}{1^2 + 4^2 + 5^2 + 4^2 + 6^2 - 5 \times 4^2} = 1 - \frac{4}{14} = \frac{10}{14}$$

in graph (a) and

$$R^2 = 1 - \frac{(-1)^2 + 1^2 + 1^2 + (-1)^2 + 0^2}{(2.8)^2 + (4.9)^2 + (5.0)^2 + (3.1)^2 + (4.2)^2 - 5 \times 4^2}$$

$$= 1 - \frac{4}{4.1} = \frac{1}{41}$$

TABLE 13.2   TWO SETS OF OBSERVATIONS ON x AND y

	Set 1				Set 2		
x	y	$y_c = 1 + x$	d	x	y	$y_c = 3.7 + .1x$	d
1	1	2	-1	1	2.8	3.8	-1
2	4	3	1	2	4.9	3.9	1
3	5	4	1	3	5.0	4	1
4	4	5	-1	4	3.1	4.1	-1
5	6	6	0	5	4.2	4.2	0

in graph (*b*). One should be careful not to conclude from this illustration that if one regression line has a steeper slope than another, it has a higher R^2. This is true when var d is the same, as illustrated in Figure 13.10, but it is not necessarily true otherwise. For example, if all points in Figure 13.10*b* happened to be *on* the gently sloping line, its R^2 would be 1, which is higher than the $R^2 = \frac{10}{14}$ of the steeply sloping line. We must always remember that the definition of R^2 includes *both* var d *and* var y. Looking only at var d or only at var y will not give an indication of the value of R^2.

A somewhat subtle case is the following. We saw that when all points are exactly on a straight line, we have $R^2 = 1$. Further, if the regression line is horizontal, $R^2 = 0$. What happens when all points are exactly on a straight horizontal line? We would expect $R^2 = 1$, since they are all on a straight line. However, we would also expect $R^2 = 0$, since the regression line is horizontal. The mathematics is

$$R^2 = 1 - \frac{\text{var } d}{\text{var } y} = 1 - \frac{0}{0} \qquad \text{undefined}$$

In Figure 13.11 we have correlated the height of the Empire State Building on 6 successive days with the average of the authors' calorie intake during those 6 days. The graph is a straight line, since the height of the Empire State Building is the same whether we fast or feast. Such cases should not occur at all. The purpose of regression analysis is to explain observed variation in some variable *y*. If no variability is observed, there is nothing to explain.

Conventionally, R^2 is computed by using the formula

$$R^2 = \frac{(\Sigma x_i y_i - n\bar{x}\bar{y})^2}{(\Sigma x_i^2 - n\bar{x}^2)(\Sigma y_i^2 - n\bar{y}^2)}$$

Computation of R^2

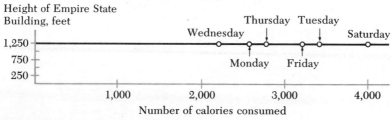

Figure 13.11 R^2 not defined when var $y = 0$.

This is mathematically identical with the definition formula, but is easier because it uses only the data and their averages. We do not need to compute the deviations. The numerator of R^2 is equal to the square of the numerator of the slope coefficient b determined in the previous section. So we can verify that R^2 is 0 if the slope $b = 0$, that is, if the regression line is horizontal.

Coefficient of
correlation R

The square root of the coefficient of determination, R^2, is called the *correlation coefficient* R. The sign of R is by convention positive if b is positive, and negative if b is negative. Thus

$$R = \pm\sqrt{R^2}$$

the sign depending on the sign of $\Sigma x_i y_i - n\bar{x}\bar{y}$.

EXERCISES

13.9   Using the computational formula for R^2, show that the data in Table 13.2 lead to R^2 of $\frac{10}{14}$ and $\frac{1}{41}$, respectively.

13.10   Determine R^2 and R for the three cases given in Exercise 13.7.

13.11   Determine R^2 and R for the data in Exercise 13.1.

13.12   Determine R^2 and R for the data in Exercise 13.2.

13.13   Using the fact that

$$1 - \frac{n \text{ var } d}{n \text{ var } y} = \frac{(\Sigma x_i y_i - n\bar{x}\bar{y})^2}{(\Sigma x_i^2 - n\bar{x}^2)(\Sigma y_i^2 - n\bar{y}^2)}$$

since both are equal to R^2, show that

$$n \text{ var } d = \Sigma d_i^2 = \Sigma y_i^2 - n\bar{y}^2 - \frac{(\Sigma x_i y_i - n\bar{x}\bar{y})^2}{\Sigma x_i^2 - n\bar{x}^2}$$

13.4 CONFIDENCE INTERVALS FOR INTERCEPT AND SLOPE OF THE REGRESSION LINE

In the previous sections we have derived the straight line which gives the best fit, according to the least-squares criterion, to a given scatter of points. We have *adapted* a straight line to a scatter of points. The least-squares criterion gives a regression line which *is the way it is*. Barring errors in arithmetic, the same set of points gives exactly the same line, whether computed by an Eskimo on the North Pole or an Indian in Bombay, in 1800 or in 2412.

We must realize that the line was determined from one particular set of observations. It describes the relationship between the variables for this set of observations only. However, we are more interested in the relationship between consumption and income for the population as a whole—all families, not just the seven in the sample.

Consider the first family, whose income is $30 and whose consumption is $27. Surely this family is not the only family in the nation earning $30 a day. In fact, there will be many more families with an income of $30—but *not* all these families will have consumption expenditures of $27 a day. Some will spend less, some more. A few will spend much less, and a few much more. We can assume that with all families who earn $30, consumption expenditures will be normally distributed (because there are a host of small factors influencing the final result), but the mean and the variance of this distribution will be unknown.

What we have just said for the first family is true for all seven families. Of all families earning $35 we happened to pick one who consumed $30, but we might have come across one whose consumption was $25, or $35. Figure 13.12 illustrates this; it shows the actual points of the sample with dots. If we had picked other families, we would have found other consumption levels, for example, those indicated by the crosses, and the least-squares line would have been different. Further comments about Figure 13.12 will be made as we proceed.

If we look at the problem in this way, the objective is no longer to *adapt* a line to a given scatter of points. The objective, instead, is to use sample information to estimate the parameters of the line which describes the relationship in the population, just as, in Chapter 9, we used sample information and tried to estimate the true mean in the population. In this section we will show the similarities between the methods used to solve these estimation problems. We will compare the estimation of

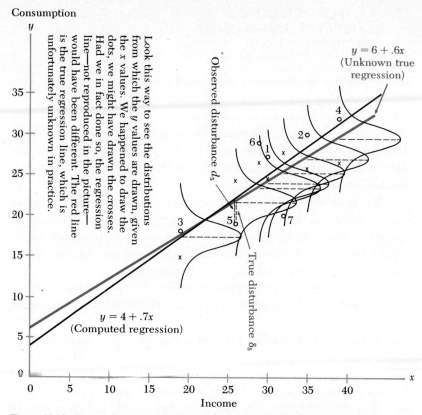

Figure 13.12 True regression, computed regression, and distributions of y.

the mean sugar content of beets (see Chapter 9) with the estimation of the slope and intercept of the line describing the relationship between consumption and income.

Estimating μ	*Estimating* α *and* β
1 Hypothesis: sugar contents are normally distributed with unknown mean μ.	1 Hypothesis: Consumption y and income x are linearly related; $y = \alpha + \beta x$, where α and β are unknown.
2 Draw random sample of beets; determine average sugar content $\overline{x}$; use $\overline{x}$ as estimate of μ.	2 For *specified* incomes, draw random samples of families; determine regression line $y = a + bx$; use a and b as estimates of α and β.

3 $\bar{x}$ is a normally distributed random variable which will differ from sample to sample.	3 **a** and **b** are normally distributed random variables, which will differ from sample to sample.
4 $\bar{x}$ is an unbiased estimate of μ.	4 **a** and **b** are unbiased estimates of α and β.
5 Even so, $\bar{x}$ found in a specific sample may differ greatly from μ.	5 Even so, a and b found in a specific sample may differ greatly from α and β.
6 Assume variance of sugar contents is σ^2, but not known.	6 Assume variance in consumption for families with specified income x is σ_δ^2. Assume σ_δ^2 is the same for all values of x, but not known.
7 Standard deviation of $\bar{x}$ is $\sigma_{\bar{x}} = \sigma/\sqrt{n}$.	7 Standard deviation of **b** is $\sigma_b = \sigma_\delta/\sqrt{n \operatorname{var} x}$ and standard deviation of **a** is $\sigma_a = \sqrt{(\sigma_\delta^2/n) + \bar{x}^2\sigma_b^2}$.
8 Since σ is unknown, it must be estimated. It is estimated by $$s = \sqrt{\frac{\Sigma(x_i - x)^2}{n - 1}}$$	8 Since σ_δ is unknown, it must be estimated. It is estimated by $$s_d = \sqrt{\frac{\Sigma d_i^2}{n - 2}}$$
9 An interval estimate (confidence interval) for μ is given by $\bar{x} \pm k(s/\sqrt{n})$, where the level of confidence depends on our choice of k.	9 Interval estimates (confidence intervals) for α and β are given by $a \pm ks_a$ and $b \pm ks_b$, where the level of confidence depends on k.
10 When n is small, the relevant k value from the appropriate t distribution should be used.	10 When n is small, the relevant k value from the appropriate t distribution should be used.

We enumerated these 10 points rather rapidly, so as not to lose sight of our main train of thought. In the next section, we shall repeat the 10 points, adding clarifying comments where appropriate.

13.5 ESTIMATING α AND β

Step 1 The assumption is that there is a true straight-line relation between consumption y and income x,

$$y = \alpha + \beta x$$

This is the red line in Figure 13.12, with regression equation $y = 6 + .6x$. We will not observe this relationship in reality because there are *other factors* influencing consumption—number of dependents, tastes, wealth, and so on. These create *disturbances*. If x_i is the income of the ith family, y_i equals $\alpha + \beta x_i$ *apart from* a disturbance term δ_i. Hence we have

$$y_i = \alpha + \beta x_i + \delta i$$

These disturbance terms are assumed to be normally distributed with mean 0 and variance σ_δ^2.

Step 2 For a *given* set of incomes $x_1, x_2, \ldots, x_n$, we draw a sample of associated consumption levels $\mathbf{y}_1, \mathbf{y}_2, \ldots, \mathbf{y}_n$. These consumption levels are random variables. They will equal $\alpha + \beta x_1 + \boldsymbol{\delta}_1$, $\alpha + \beta x_2 + \boldsymbol{\delta}_2, \ldots, \alpha + \beta x_n + \boldsymbol{\delta}_n$, where $\boldsymbol{\delta}_1, \boldsymbol{\delta}_2, \ldots, \boldsymbol{\delta}_n$ are random drawings from a normal distribution with mean 0 and variance σ_δ^2. However, after the sample has been drawn, we observe $y_1, y_2, \ldots, y_n$, and *they are the way they are*—even though they would have been different in a different sample.

Step 3 We compute

$$b = \frac{x_1 y_1 + x_2 y_2 + \cdots + x_n y_n - n\bar{x}\bar{y}}{x_1^2 + x_2^2 + \cdots + x_n^2 - n\bar{x}^2} \qquad \text{and} \qquad a = \bar{y} - b\bar{x}$$

After the sample has been drawn, these are the way they are. Before the sample is drawn, these are random variables, and

$$\mathbf{b} = \frac{x_1 \mathbf{y}_1 + x_2 \mathbf{y}_2 + \cdots + x_n \mathbf{y}_n - n\bar{x}\bar{\mathbf{y}}}{x_1^2 + x_2^2 + \cdots + x_n^2 - n\bar{x}^2}$$

The incomes x_i are not random, since we work with a *given* set of incomes (see step 2). The associated values for consumption are random variables with *expected* value

$$E\mathbf{y}_i = \alpha + \beta x_i$$

but actual value

$$y_i = \alpha + \beta x_i + \delta_i$$

Step 4 **a** and **b** are unbiased estimators of α and β. We will prove that $E\mathbf{b} = \beta$. Using the results under step 3, we have

Point estimates for α and β

$$E\mathbf{b} = E\frac{x_1 y_1 + x_2 y_2 + \cdots + x_n y_n - n\overline{x}\,\overline{y}}{x_1^2 + x_2^2 + \cdots + x_n^2 - n\overline{x}^2} \qquad \text{definition of } \mathbf{b}$$

$$= \frac{x_1 E y_1 + x_2 E y_2 + \cdots + x_n E y_n - n\overline{x} E\overline{y}}{x_1^2 + x_2^2 + \cdots + x_n^2 - n\overline{x}^2} \qquad Ek\mathbf{x} = kE\mathbf{x}$$

$$= \frac{\Sigma x_i(\alpha + \beta x_i) - n\overline{x}(\alpha + \beta\overline{x})}{\Sigma x_i^2 - n\overline{x}^2} \qquad E y_i = \alpha + \beta x_i$$

$$= \frac{\alpha(\Sigma x_i - n\overline{x}) + \beta(\Sigma x_i^2 - n\overline{x}^2)}{\Sigma x_i^2 - n\overline{x}^2} \qquad \Sigma x_i - n\overline{x} = 0$$

$$= \beta$$

In a similar way, it can be shown that $E\mathbf{a} = \alpha$.

Step 5 We would like interval estimates (confidence intervals) for α and β, rather than the point estimates a and b.

Step 6 We already stated above, and repeat here, that the disturbance terms $\delta_1, \delta_2, \ldots, \delta_n$ all come from the *same* distribution with mean 0 and variance σ_δ^2. In Figure 13.12 the seven distributions are all *centered* above the red line $\alpha + \beta x$—which implies that the *expected* value of the disturbance is zero, whatever the income x_i may be—and they all have the same shape, and, in particular, the same *variance*. This is referred to as the *homoscedasticity* assumption.

Homo-scedasticity

Step 7 We have the result

$$\sigma_\mathbf{b}^2 = \frac{\sigma_\delta^2}{x_1^2 + x_2^2 + \cdots + x_n^2 - n\overline{x}^2} = \frac{\sigma_\delta^2}{n \text{ var } x}$$

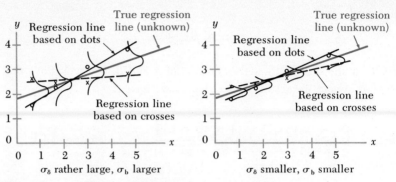

Figure 13.13 Sampling variability of **b** varies directly with σ_δ.

The smaller the variance of the disturbances, σ_δ^2, the larger the number of observations, n; and the larger the variance of x, var x, the smaller the variance of **b**, σ_b^2. These points will not be proved, but Figures 13.13 to 13.15 illustrate their intuitive appeal. Also

$$\sigma_a^2 = \frac{\sigma_\delta^2}{n} + \bar{x}^2\sigma_b^2$$

The intercept **a** will vary more if σ_δ^2 is larger, if $\bar{x}$ is larger (see Figure 13.10), and if σ_b^2 is larger (see Figures 13.13 to 13.15) and will vary less if n is larger.

Step 8 Unfortunately, we do not know σ_δ^2. In fact, we do not even know the true disturbances δ_i because we do not know α and β. We do,

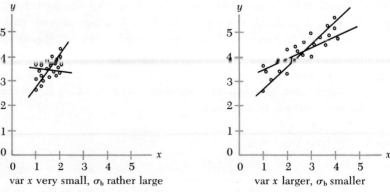

Figure 13.14 Sampling variability of **b** varies inversely with var x.

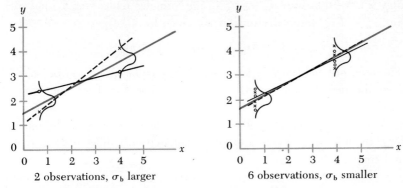

Figure 13.15 Sampling variability of **b** varies inversely with n.

however, know the deviations d_i from $y_i = a + bx_i + d_i$. We estimate σ_δ^2 by

$$s_d^2 = \frac{d_1^2 + \cdots + d_n^2}{n - 2} = \frac{n \text{ var } d}{n - 2}$$

where we divide by $n - 2$, since the sum of squared deviations Σd_i^2 is *minimized* by our choice of *a and b*. This will bias the estimate for the variance of the true disturbances downward, and to offset this bias we divide not by n but by $n - 2$. [We use 2 instead of 1 because we adapt two values (*a and b*) so as to minimize the sum of squares.]

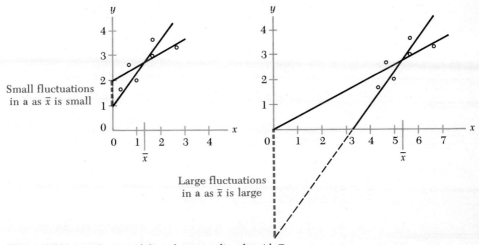

Figure 13.16. Sampling variability of **a** varies directly with $\bar{x}$.

Interval
estimates for
α and β

Step 9 We substitute s_d^2 for σ_δ^2 in the formulas under step 7, and then find s_b^2 and s_a^2. Interval estimates are given by

$$b \pm ks_b \quad \text{and} \quad a \pm ks_a$$

The level of confidence depends on the choice of k, and can be read off from the table of the normal distribution. For $k = 1.96$, the level of confidence is 95 percent; for $k = 1.645$, it is 90 percent. If we use $k = 2$, we have an approximately 95 percent confidence interval. If the interval for β includes zero, b is said to be "not significantly different from zero," and similarly for a.

Step 10 In step 9 we used k values read from the normal distribution, which is acceptable when the sample size n is large. For n below 30, we ought to use the t distribution with $n - 2$ degrees of freedom. [Generally, when there are m explanatory variables, there will be $n - (m + 1)$ degrees of freedom.] For $n = 7$, a 95 percent confidence interval is given by $b \pm 2.57s_b$, rather than $b \pm 1.96s_b$.

EXERCISES

13.14   Using the result of Exercise 13.13, determine s_a and s_b for the data in Table 13.1 on income and consumption. Are they significantly different from zero?

13.15   For the two cases in Exercise 13.9, which lead to the regressions

$$y = 1 + x \qquad R^2 = \tfrac{10}{14}$$

and

$$y = 3.7 + \tfrac{1}{10}x \qquad R^2 = \tfrac{1}{41}$$

determine the standard deviations of the coefficients. Are they significantly different from zero?

13.16   For the three cases in Exercise 13.7, all leading to the regression equation $y = 1 + x$, determine the standard deviations of the coefficients and the 95.45 percent confidence interval. Which coefficients are significant?

13.6   AN EXAMPLE AND THE PROBLEM OF FORECASTING

As before, we will consider the regression of consumption on income, but this time we will use actual data. For a number of years ranging from

TABLE 13.3 REGRESSION OF AGGREGATE CONSUMPTION ON AGGREGATE INCOME

Year	Income x	Consumption y
1950	208	195
1955	274	257
1959	337	314
1960	350	328
1961	364	336
1962	385	357
1963	403	375
1964	431	398
1969	634	580
1970	690	617
1971	744	665
1972	783	713

Basic data

$$\bar{x} = \frac{5{,}603}{12} = 467$$

$$\bar{y} = \frac{5{,}135}{12} = 428$$

$$\Sigma x_i y_i - 12\bar{x}\bar{y} = 2{,}760{,}497 - 2{,}398{,}512$$
$$= 361{,}985$$

$$\Sigma x_i^2 - 12\bar{x}^2 = 3{,}027{,}981 - 2{,}617{,}068$$
$$= 410{,}913$$

$$\Sigma y_i^2 - 12\bar{y}^2 = 2{,}517{,}311 = 2{,}198{,}208$$
$$= 319{,}103$$

Regression results

$$b = \frac{361{,}985}{410{,}913} = .881$$

$$a = 428 - (.881)(467) = 16.57$$

Regression line is $y = 16.57 + .881x$

$$R^2 = (361{,}985)^2/(410{,}913 \times 319{,}103) = .99931$$

Standard error results

n var $d = 319{,}103 - (361{,}985)^2/410{,}913 = 319{,}103 - 319{,}003 = 220$

$s_d^2 = 220/(12 - 2) = \frac{220}{10} = 22$

$s_b^2 = \frac{22}{410{,}913} = .00005354$; therefore the standard error $s_b = .00732$.

$s_a^2 = \frac{22}{12} + (467)^2(.00005354) = 13.509$; therefore we have $s_a = 3.67$.

Result of regression of consumption y on income x

$$y = 16.57 + .881x \qquad R^2 = .99931$$
$$(3.67) \quad (.00732)$$

Forecasting results

var $(y_{t+1} - y_{actual}) = 22(1 + \frac{1}{12}) + .00005354(x_{t+1} - 467)^2$

For $x_{t+1} = 800$, this gives $23.833 + 5.937 = 29.77$; also $\sqrt{29.77} = 5.45$.

Interval estimate of y_{t+1} when $x_{t+1} = 800$ is $16.57 + .881(800) \pm k(5.45)$.

A 95 percent confidence interval, by using the t distribution with 10 degrees of freedom and thus a k value of 2.23, is $721.37 \pm (2.23)(5.45)$, or from 709.22 to 733.52.

1950 to 1972 the total aggregate personal disposable income (roughly all that remains after taxes have been paid and transfer payments, such as social security, received) and the total consumption expenditures (roughly everything that is not saved) are given in Table 13.3. By the standard procedures explained in Section 13.2, we compute the regression line $y = 16.57 + .881x$. The coefficient of determination is $R^2 = .99931$, and the standard deviations of the coefficients **a** and **b** are 3.67 and .00732, respectively. It is possible for us to reproduce all these results compactly

$$y = 16.57 + .881x \qquad R^2 = .99931$$
$$(3.67) \quad (.00732)$$

The conclusion is that we are 95 percent confident that the true β is between $.881 \pm (2.23)(.00732)$, where the value 2.23 is read from the t distribution with $n - 2 = 10$ degrees of freedom in the 5 percent column. These limits are from .865 to .897, which implies that we can be 95 percent confident that of an extra dollar, between 86.5 and 89.7 cents will be spent.

At the bottom of Table 13.3 we use the regression for the purpose of making forecasts. For example, suppose that next year's disposable income x_{t+1} will be \$800 billion. Then we *forecast* that the total consumption y_{t+1} will be close to $16.57 + .881(800) = \$721.37$ billion. Thus relationships of this nature, once established, can be used to forecast future values of the dependent variable, given information on the independent variable.

The estimate $y_{t+1} = 721.37$ when $x_{t+1} = 800$ is a point estimate. The actual y_{t+1} which will be observed in year $t + 1$ need not coincide with it, even if x_{t+1} were to be exactly 800. The reason for this is that we do not know the true α and β (but only a and b), and even if we did, there would be a disturbance δ_{t+1}. The variance of the difference between predicted y_{t+1} and actual y_{t+1} is given by

$$\text{var}\left[y_{t+1}(\text{predicted}) - y_{t+1}(\text{actual})\right] = \sigma_\delta^2\left(1 + \frac{1}{n}\right) + \sigma_b^2(x_{t+1} - \bar{x})^2$$

and estimated by

$$\text{var}\left[y_{t+1}(\text{predicted}) - y_{t+1}(\text{actual})\right] = s_d^2\left(1 + \frac{1}{n}\right) + s_b^2(x_{t+1} - \bar{x})^2$$

In general, the larger s_d^2, the larger s_b^2, and the farther away x_{t+1} is from $\bar{x}$, the larger is this variance. In Figure 13.17 we have illustrated the

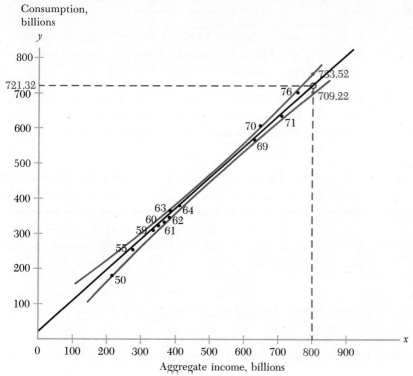

Figure 13.17 Point and interval estimate of y.

regression in Table 13.3, and we have indicated in red the point estimate and the interval estimate, using $k = 2.23$ as in Table 13.3. The general shape of the interval predictions is more clearly discernible from Figure 13.18—the farther away from $\bar{x}$, the wider the range.

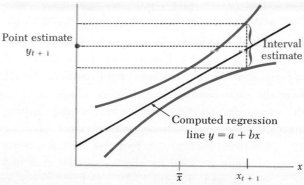

Figure 13.18 Width of interval estimate of y depends on distance from $\bar{x}$.

EXERCISES

13.17 In the example in Section 13.6, let income next year be given by 0, 467, and 1,000, respectively. Determine interval estimates at 95 percent confidence.

13.18 Let the five observations on x and y be (10,1), (8,4), (6,6), (4,7), and (2,7). Determine the regression line, the R^2, the standard deviations of the coefficients, and a 95 percent interval estimate for y when $x = 7$.

13.19 The number of books sold during the first week after publication, x, and the total number of books sold in a year, y, are correlated. We are given $\bar{x} = 10$, $\bar{y} = 220$, $x_1^2 + \cdots + x_{17}^2 = 1,720$, $x_1 y_1 + \cdots + x_{17} y_{17} = 37,800$, and $y_1^2 + \cdots + y_{17}^2 = 831,000$. If for a book, $x = 17$, what is a 95 percent interval estimate of total sales y?

13.7 ANALYSIS OF VARIANCE APPLIED TO REGRESSION

There are three ways to measure the significance of a relationship. The first measurement is simply the size of the coefficient of determination, R^2. The closer R^2 is to 1, the closer the relationship. In our example of the previous section it was *very* high; in problems in the social sciences an $R^2 = .8$ is respectable. The second method is to determine the value of b *and* the standard deviation s_b and then to determine whether it differs significantly from zero. The level of significance is nearly always taken at 5 percent, so that *if* the interval $b \pm 2s_b$ includes zero, the correlation is not considered significant. Recall that if β is zero, the true regression line is horizontal, which implies no correlation.

A third measure used to assess the significance of a relationship is the value of F obtained by analysis of variance (previously discussed in Sections 11.6 to 11.8). This analysis can be applied nicely in the context of regression. We test, as it were, the hypothesis that all y values are drawn from the *same* distribution, whatever x may be (Figure 13.19), against the alternative that the values are drawn from distributions with different means but the same variance, as in Figure 13.20.

In deriving the necessary formulas, let us first consider the very special example where we have six observations for each of four specific values x_1, x_2, x_3, x_4, as in Figures 13.19 and 13.20. This approach will enable

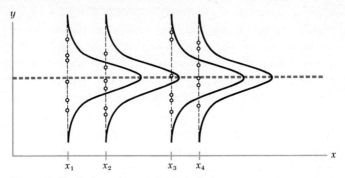

Figure 13.19 Horizontal regression line, $\beta = 0$.

us to employ an argument similar to the discussion in Section 11.6. If the slope of the regression line is *in fact* zero (a horizontal line), we can estimate the variance σ_δ^2 of the disturbances by estimating the variances in each of the four distributions, s_1^2, s_2^2, s_3^2, and s_4^2. Since each of these values is based on the same number of observations, their arithmetic average is our best estimate of σ_δ^2. We could also estimate σ_δ^2 by first determining the overall average of all observations ($\bar{y}$ in the present notation), then the average in each of the four classes, $\bar{y}_1$, $\bar{y}_2$, $\bar{y}_3$, and $\bar{y}_4$, and then the expression

$$\frac{6[(\bar{y} - \bar{y}_1)^2 + (\bar{y} - \bar{y}_2)^2 + (\bar{y} - \bar{y}_3)^2 + (\bar{y} - \bar{y}_4)^2]}{4 - 1}$$

where the 6 appears because there are six observations in each class. In this context, however, it *is* done a little differently. Instead of taking the

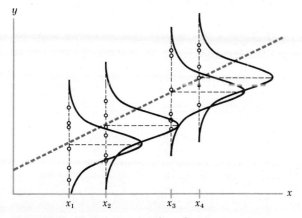

Figure 13.20 Sloping regression line, $\beta \neq 0$.

squared deviations of the averages in each group ($\bar{y}_1, \bar{y}_2, \bar{y}_3, \bar{y}_4$) from the overall average $\bar{y}$, we take the squared deviations of the averages *as computed by the regression line*, that is, $a + bx_1$, $a + bx_2$, $a + bx_3$, $a + bx_4$ from the overall average $\bar{y}$. This is the logical conclusion from the regression philosophy; that is, to the best of our knowledge, the distribution of y values corresponding to the x value x_1 is a normal distribution with mean $a + bx_1$. To see what the further implications of this change are, let us now turn our attention to the more realistic example where there are n, in principle all different, values $x_1, x_2, \ldots, x_n$, and n associated y_i values.

There is no problem in determining our best estimate for σ_δ^2 from the n deviations $d_1, d_2, \ldots, d_n$. As before, we get

$$s_d^2 = \frac{d_1^2 + \cdots + d_n^2}{n - 2}$$

This value is equivalent to what was referred to in Section 11.6 as s_w^2. We divide by $n - 2$, since there are $n - 2$ degrees of freedom, for there are n observations from which a and b have been determined. Alternatively, to determine σ_δ^2 we consider the following expression (which is the analog of s_a^2 of Section 11.6) denoted by $s_{\bar{y}-y_c}^2$,

$$[\bar{y} - (a + bx_1)]^2 + [\bar{y} - (a + bx_2)]^2 + \cdots + [\bar{y} - (a + bx_n)]^2$$

In this case there is no factor 6 because all "groups" have but one observation, the averages in each "group" (of one observation) are replaced by the averages as computed by the regression line, and instead of dividing by the number of degrees of freedom, which was $4 - 1$ above, we divide by 1, since there is but 1 degree of freedom. This is true because all averages $a + bx_1, \ldots, a + bx_n$ are on the regression line, and this will always pass through $(\bar{x}, \bar{y})$. Since a line is fully determined by 2 points, only 1 degree of freedom remains (whatever the number of observations n may be).

To summarize, we have an s_d^2 that is analogous to the s_w^2 of Section 11.6; that is,

$$s_d^2 = \frac{\Sigma d_i^2}{n - 2} \qquad n - 2 \text{ degrees of freedom}$$

We have an $s_{\bar{y}-y_c}^2$ that is analogous to s_a^2 of Section 11.6; that is,

$$s_{\bar{y}-y_c}^2 = \Sigma[\bar{y} - (a + bx_i)]^2 \qquad 1 \text{ degree of freedom}$$

When we apply the analysis of variance to linear regressions with *one* explanatory variable, the number of degrees of freedom in the numerator is 1, and in the denominator it is $n - 2$, where n stands for the number of observations. When there are two explanatory variables, the numerator $s^2_{\bar{y}-y_c}$ has 2 degrees of freedom, and the denominator s^2_d has $n - 3$ degrees of freedom. For k explanatory variables, the numerator has k degrees of freedom, and the denominator has $n - (k + 1)$ degrees of freedom. For the sake of convenience, we have reproduced in Table 13.4 values of F which are significant at the 5 percent level, for both one explanatory variable and two explanatory variables (which are discussed in the next section).

In Exhibit 6 of Appendix A we have given a computer run of a single linear regression. The printout gives us the standard error and the F ratio automatically.

F test in regression

TABLE 13.4   VALUES FOR SIGNIFICANT *F* RATIOS AT 5 PERCENT LEVEL

Sample size	One explanatory variable	Two explanatory variables
5	10.13	19.00
6	7.71	9.55
7	6.61	6.94
8	5.99	5.79
9	5.59	5.14
10	5.32	4.74
12	4.96	4.26
14	4.75	3.98
16	4.60	3.80
18	4.49	3.68
20	4.41	3.59
25	4.28	3.44
30	4.20	3.35
40	4.10	3.26
60	4.01	3.16
80	3.96	3.12
100	3.94	3.10

EXERCISES

13.20   Determine the F value for the data in Exercise 13.18.

13.21   Determine the F value for the data in Table 13.3.

13.22   Determine the F value for the three sets of data in Exercise 13.7.

13.8   MORE THAN ONE EXPLANATORY VARIABLE

Multiple regression theory

When there is more than one explanatory variable in regression theory, we speak of *multiple regression theory*. The relation with only one explanatory variable is called a *simple regression*.

Suppose that "the amount on the expense accounts submitted by traveling executives" is the dependent variable y. This amount y varies from account to account, and the variation is to be explained. It stands to reason that "the number of days on the road" is a reasonable explanatory variable x, since trips of longer duration will in general cost more. From the many expense accounts in the archives, a sample of 400 accounts is drawn, their amounts y are noted, and the number of days x is recorded. A simple linear regression is run, and the result is

$$y = 85 + 45x \qquad R^2 = .83$$
$$\quad (20) \quad (5)$$

A trip of 7 days can be expected to cost around $\$85 + \$45 \times 7 = \$400$. An extra day on the road costs, on the average, $\$45$. The R^2 is not extremely high, and the high positive constant begs further explanation. Apparently traveling executives have fairly substantial costs ($\$85$) apart from those due to hotels, meals, etc., needed for subsistence ($\$45$ a day). These are the travel costs, for example, the cost of a plane ticket or automobile expenses. Since travel costs will be closely correlated with the distance traveled, this distance is added as a second explanatory variable. We will denote this variable, measured in miles, by z. We now use multiple regression theory. We will first give the result and then add explanatory comments as we proceed. The result is

$$y = 20 + 40x + .13z \qquad R^2 = .98$$
$$\quad (12) \quad (6) \quad (.01)$$

The coefficient of determination is now much higher. If an executive travels a distance of 650 miles and stays away for 6 days, we expect the amount of his expense account to be around

$$\$20 + \$40 \times 6 + \$.13/\text{mile} \times 650 \text{ miles} = \$344.50$$

It may well be a little more or less—the R^2 is not precisely 1—but an amount of \$560 clearly would be in need of some check. It may then be found that a dinner for customers was hosted, but it can also be found that the executive took his wife along on the trip. In the multiple regression the constant term is not significantly—at the 5 percent level—different from zero, since $20 + 1.96 \times 12$ includes the value zero.

In *multiple* regression we still prefer to use a linear relationship. Analytically, this means that we consider a relation of the type $y = a + bx + cz$, where a, b, and c are to be determined. Geometrically, this means that we adapt a plane to a scatter of points in three dimensions. In Figure 13.21 we have drawn the plane represented by $y = 20 + 40x + .13z$, and a few of the 400 points. The center of gravity $(\overline{x}, \overline{z}, \overline{y})$ is in the *regression plane*. The scales on the axes should be carefully chosen lest the resulting graph is too flat or too steep for easy interpretation. The intercept of the plane with the y axis is 20. *If* z remains constant, a unit increase in x (a trip lasting 1 day longer) will increase the y_c value (the y value in the plane) by \$40. *If* x remains the same, a 100-unit increase in z will increase the y_c value by \$13. All these points are illustrated in Figure 13.21.

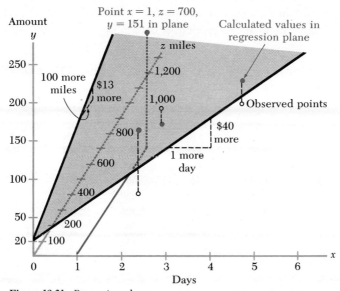

Figure 13.21 Regression plane.

In this example, the linearity assumption is quite reasonable: the cost of travel increases roughly in proportion to the distance, and the hotel bill will increase in proportion to the duration of the stay.

The *formulas* for finding the coefficients a, b, and c from the data on y, x, and z are substantially more complicated than in simple regression. If we have n observations on the dependent variable, $y_1, y_2, \ldots, y_n$, and the associated n observations on the independent variables $x_1, x_2, \ldots, x_n$ and $z_1, z_2, \ldots, z_n$, then the coefficients b and c are found by solving the following two equations in two unknowns, which are known as the *normal equations*:

$$(\Sigma x_i y_i - n\bar{x}\bar{y}) = b(\Sigma x_i^2 - n\bar{x}^2) + c(\Sigma x_i z_i - n\bar{x}\bar{z})$$
$$(\Sigma z_i y_i - n\bar{z}\bar{y}) = b(\Sigma x_i z_i - n\bar{x}\bar{z}) + c(\Sigma z_i^2 - n\bar{z}^2)$$

The terms in parentheses all follow from the raw data. The solution of this system of equations gives us b and c. The coefficient a then follows from

$$a = \bar{y} - b\bar{x} - c\bar{z}$$

The formulas for the standard errors are also rather complex, although luckily they are easy for computers to digest. Table 13.5 gives an example of the computations needed to determine a, b, and c.

TABLE 13.5   LAYOUT FOR COMPUTATIONS TO DETERMINE THE COEFFICIENTS IN A REGRESSION WITH TWO EXPLANATORY VARIABLES

y	x	z	y^2	yx	yz	x^2	xz	z^2
31	6	16	961	186	496	36	96	256
48	9	12	2,304	432	576	81	108	144
22	5	18	484	110	396	25	90	324
40	8	14	1,600	320	560	64	112	196
19	2	20	361	38	380	4	40	400
160	30	80	5,710	1,086	2,408	210	446	1,320
$\bar{y}=32$	$\bar{x}=6$	$\bar{z}=16$	$n\bar{y}^2=5,120$	$n\bar{x}\bar{y}=960$	$n\bar{z}\bar{y}=2,560$	$n\bar{x}^2=180$	$n\bar{x}\bar{z}=480$	$n\bar{z}^2=1,280$
			590	126	-152	30	-34	40

$126 = b(30) + c(-34);\ -152 = b(-34) + c(40)$; hence $b = -2\frac{10}{11}$ and $c = -6\frac{3}{11}$
$a = 32 - (-2\frac{10}{11})6 - (-6\frac{3}{11})16 = 149\frac{9}{11}$

Multicollinearity is a problem which does not arise in simple regression, but one which nearly always arises in multiple regression. If we go back to our expense account regressions, we observe a slight inconsistency. If duration of the trip x is the *only* explanatory variable, the regression equation is $y = 85 + 45x$, implying that an extra day costs $45. If duration *and* distance, x *and* z, are explanatory variables, we find a regression $y = 20 + 40x + .13z$, implying that—*provided* the distance z remains the same—an extra day costs $40. How do we explain this? The explanation is that the distance and duration of the trip are themselves correlated. If we consider the regression of z on x, the R^2 will not be zero. Let us assume that their correlation is such that the longer the trip the more, by and large, the distance. The statement "*provided* the distance z remains the same" is therefore somewhat deceptive, since an extra day will by and large mean a greater distance. Thus, roughly speaking, we might explain the divergence between $40 and $45 as follows: In the multiple regression example an increase in duration of one day will lead *directly* to an increase in expenses of $40. Moreover, there is an *indirect* effect since a *longer* trip will more often than not mean a *further* trip. The extra distance will cost $5 in daily expenses.

Three different types of multicollinearity can be distinguished. If the explanatory variables x and z are *not at all correlated*, there is *no* multicollinearity. In that case R^2 and hence $x_1 z_1 + x_2 z_2 + \cdots + x_n z_n - n\bar{x}\bar{z}$ will be zero. The two equations in two unknowns needed to find b and c then become simply

$$\Sigma x_i y_i - n\bar{x}\bar{y} = b(\Sigma x_i^2 - n\bar{x}^2)$$

and

$$\Sigma z_i y_i - n\bar{z}\bar{y} = c(\Sigma z_i^2 - n\bar{z}^2)$$

The first gives us b, and is exactly the same as it would be in a simple linear regression of y on x. The second gives us c, and this coefficient is the same as the one obtained in a simple linear regression of y on z. In other words, if the explanatory variables are not at all correlated, we can determine the slope coefficients one by one by regressing y in turn on each of the explanatory variables.

The other extreme is that the explanatory variables x and z are perfectly correlated, $R^2 = 1$. In that case the two equations in two unknowns *cannot be solved at all*. As an example, consider the data in

Multi-collinearity

Table 13.6. Here x and z are perfectly correlated; we have

$$z = 1 + 2x \qquad \text{or} \qquad x = \tfrac{1}{2}z - \tfrac{1}{2}$$

If someone somehow were to state that the true regression is

$$y = 2.1 + 2.3x + 0z$$

we can *with exactly the same deviations* write

$$y = 2.1 + 1.3x + (\tfrac{1}{2}z - \tfrac{1}{2}) = 1.6 + 1.3x + .5z$$

or any other equation we want by replacing each unit of x by $\tfrac{1}{2}z - \tfrac{1}{2}$, or each unit of z by $1 + 2x$. The normal equations here are

$$23 = 10b + 20c \qquad \text{and} \qquad 46 = 20b + 40c$$

The second equation is just twice the first, and thus superfluous. The first equation can be solved in arbitrarily many ways by giving b any desired value and then choosing c so as to satisfy the equation. Where $R^2 = 1$ there is perfect multicollinearity. This type is as scarce as the first with no multicollinearity at all. Neither variant ever happens in practice.

In practice, the situation will always be between these extremes. In the expense account example, the degree of multicollinearity was rather limited. The b coefficients ($40 and $45) were rather close together. If we take account of the standard deviations of these coefficients, the results are not contradictory. In general, high multicollinearity will lead to high standard deviations.

Multicollinearity is a nuisance. It makes results hard to interpret. The

TABLE 13.6   EXAMPLE OF EXTREME MULTICOLLINEARITY

y	x	z	y^2	yx	yz	x^2	xz	z^2
5	1	3	25	5	15	1	3	9
7	2	5	49	14	35	4	10	25
8	3	7	64	24	56	9	21	49
10	4	9	100	40	90	16	36	81
15	5	11	225	75	165	25	55	121
45	15	35	463	158	361	55	125	285
$\bar{y}=9$	$\bar{x}=3$	$\bar{z}=7$	$n\bar{y}^2=405$	$n\bar{x}\bar{y}=135$	$n\bar{z}\bar{y}=315$	$n\bar{x}^2=45$	$n\bar{x}\bar{z}=105$	$n\bar{z}^2=245$
			58	23	46	10	20	40

Regression of z on x: $b = \tfrac{20}{10} = 2$, $a = \bar{z} - b\bar{x} = 7 - 2 \times 3 = 1$, and $z = 1 + 2x$.
Normal equations: $23 = 10b + 20c$, and $46 = 20b + 40c$. There is no unique solution.

statement, "if the distance remains the same, an extra day in duration of the trip costs \$40," is meaningless when we *know* that the distance will *not* remain the same since distance and duration are correlated. In a study purporting to explain profits by banks, the "number of bank offices" is featured as one of the explanatory variables with a *negative* coefficient. "Other things being equal" the profit of a bank declines when it adds a new office. However, other things will not be equal—the new office will generate new deposits and new loans, and so on. These will tend to lead to an increase in profit, and on balance bank offices are definitely profitable. A new shopping plaza without a branch office is a rare occurrence. In Table 13.6 we have illustrated an example of serious multicollinearity. It is clear that x and y tend to go up and down together; the coefficient of x ought to be positive. In fact, the z variable confuses the picture. It is highly correlated with x, and the resulting coefficient is negative, although not significant when standard errors are considered.

The last two problems—determining the coefficients and the multi-collinearity—become more complicated the more explanatory variables there are. In practice, one proceeds *stepwise*, as follows: A certain variable y is to be explained. There are theoretical considerations which lead us to conclude that $x_1, x_2, \ldots, x_k$ may qualify as explanatory variables. These variables must all be carefully defined, and it must be possible to measure them. Let us then assume that we have a set of n observations on the dependent variable y and each of the independent variables $x_1, x_2, \ldots, x_k$. These observations are then entered in a computer. The computer runs k simple regressions in turn, of y on x_1, y on x_2, $\ldots$, up to y on x_k. It then takes as the first explanatory variable the one which explains most of the variability in y, as determined by some criterion, usually R^2 or the F ratio. In the next round each of the $k-1$ not-yet-chosen explanatory variables is paired with the one already chosen. This gives $k-1$ regressions with two explanatory variables. Again, the variable which explains most of the variability that remained after the first explanatory variable had done its work is chosen. R^2 or the F ratio is used as criterion. So one continues until each new variable gives no further "significant" improvement or has an F ratio below 2, for example. Variables which are highly correlated with others previously entered will not be entered if we proceed in this pragmatic way.

Computers are quick-working busy bees, and it is obviously easy to regress just about anything on everything else—rainfall in Patagonia on sailboats overturning in Lake Erie, for example. If many people make many attempts, once in a while a high R^2 will be obtained by pure chance.

More than two independent variables

Such procedures, though prevalent and tempting, ought to be discouraged. A good, solid theory and careful measurements, rather than computer experimentation in search of high R^2, are the cornerstones of an honest regression.

EXERCISES

13.23 We are given

y	x	z
1	10	1
4	8	1
6	6	2
7	4	3
7	2	3

Regress y on x, y on z, and y on x *and* z. Discuss the results.

13.24 The precision of the diameter of a hole varies. Management wishes to explain the variations insofar as they are the result of systematic causes rather than purely random fluctuation. The age of the 20 machines on which the hole is made differs, as does the experience of employees measured by their years of service. Which of the following plans is best for getting data necessary for running a multiple regression, with machine age and years of service as explanatory variables, and deviation from standard as dependent variable?

(*a*) The newer workers get the older machines.

(*b*) The older workers have the older machines.

(*c*) The employee's surname determines the machine he works on; that is, A gets the first machine, etc.

Answers to Exercises

13.1 Since, for most consumers, the price is given and the quantity is chosen with price clearly in mind, we plot the price horizontally.

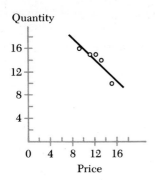

Quantity

13.2   We have drawn the picture, but no line, since there is no visible
        pattern that stands out. Given the source of the data, this stands
        to reason. The point (15,8) is specially emphasized, since it occurs
        twice. There is no special reason for plotting birth dates hori-
        zontally and death dates vertically.

Death dates

31
30 ∘33   ∘17
        ∘4
   32
25 ∘8   ∘6   ∘22   18∘ ∘34
                      35°
20   ∘30   ∘20   ∘10
   19∘∘21
15 ∘11   ∘16   ∘1   ∘31
           23∘
10   26   ∘12
   ∘13   8   14∘
        7   25∘ ∘24
5 ∘29   ∘9 ∘3   5∘ ∘2
   ∘28   27
0   15∘
   0   5   10   15   20   25   30

Birth dates

13.3   (a) $y = -3 + 3x$
        (b) $b = 2$; furthermore, since $x = 4$, $y = 7$ is on the line,
             $7 = a + 2 \times 4$ or $a = -1$. The equation is $y = -1 + 2x$.
        (c) $y = 4 - x$
        (d) We have $1 = a + 4b$ and $3 = a + 7b$. Deducting the first
             from the second equation gives $2 = 3b$, or $b = \frac{2}{3}$. Substi-

tution gives $1 = a + 4 \times \frac{2}{3}$, or $a = -1\frac{2}{3}$. The equation is $y = -1\frac{2}{3} + \frac{2}{3}x$.

(e) $y = 0 + bx$, and $2 = 0 + b2$, or $b = 1$. The equation is $y = x$.

(f) $y = 4 + 0x$, or $y = 4$.

13.4 (a)

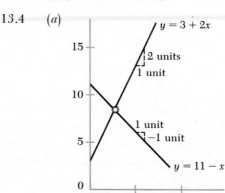

$y = 3 + 2x$

15

2 units
1 unit

10

1 unit
-1 unit

5

$y = 11 - x$

0

0   5   10

(b) Deducting the first from the second gives $3x = 8$, or $x = 2\frac{2}{3}$. Hence $y = 8\frac{1}{3}$. The point $x = 2\frac{2}{3}$, $y = 8\frac{1}{3}$ is the point of intersection in the figure.

13.5 We consider the following data:

x	y	xy	x^2	
9	16	144	81	$\bar{x} = \frac{60}{5} = 12$
11	15	165	121	$\bar{y} = \frac{70}{5} = 14$
12	15	180	144	$n\bar{x}\bar{y} = 5 \times 12 \times 14 = 840$
13	14	182	169	$n\bar{x}^2 = 5 \times 12^2 = 720$
15	10	150	225	
60	70	821	740	

The line passes through $x = 12$, $y = 14$, and has a slope

$$b = \frac{821 - 840}{740 - 720} = -\frac{19}{20}$$

Hence $a = 14 - (-\frac{19}{20}) \times 12 = 25\frac{2}{5}$, and $y = 25\frac{2}{5} - \frac{19}{20}x$ is the regression line.

13.6 We easily compute $\bar{x} = 17\frac{19}{35}$ and $\bar{y} = 14\frac{2}{35}$. Furthermore, $n\bar{x}\bar{y} = 35 \times 17\frac{19}{35} \times 14\frac{2}{35} = 8,631$ and $n\bar{x}^2 = 35 \times 17\frac{19}{35} = 10,771$.

We also compute $\Sigma x_i y_i = 8,467$ and $\Sigma x_i^2 = 13,842$. Hence $b = (8,467 - 8,631)/(13,842 - 10,771) = (-164)/3,071 = -.053$ and $a = 14\frac{2}{35} - (-.053)(17\frac{19}{35}) = 14.99$. The regression line is $y = 14.99 - .053x$.

13.7　(a)

x	y	xy	x²	
1	2	2	1	$\bar{x} = \frac{15}{5} = 3$
2	3	6	4	$\bar{y} = \frac{20}{5} = 4$
3	4	12	9	$n\bar{x}\bar{y} = 5 \times 3 \times 4 = 60$
4	5	20	16	$n\bar{x}^2 = 5 \times 3^2 = 45$
5	6	30	25	
15	20	70	55	

The slope is $b = (70 - 60)/(55 - 45) = 1; a = 4 - 1 \times 3 = 1$, and $y = 1 + x$ is the regression line.

(b)

x	y	xy	x²	
1	1	1	1	$\bar{x} = \frac{15}{5} = 3$
2	4	8	4	$\bar{y} = \frac{20}{5} = 4$
3	5	15	9	$n\bar{x}\bar{y} = 5 \times 3 \times 4 = 60$
4	4	16	16	$n\bar{x}^2 = 5 \times 3^2 = 45$
5	6	30	25	
15	20	70	55	

The slope is $b = (70 - 60)/(55 - 45) = 1; a = 4 - 1 \times 3 = 1$, and the regression line is $y = 1 + x$.

(c)

x	y	xy	x²	
1	0	0	1	$\bar{x} = \frac{15}{5} = 3$
2	7	14	4	$\bar{y} = \frac{20}{5} = 4$
3	4	12	9	$n\bar{x}\bar{y} = 5 \times 3 \times 4 = 60$
4	1	4	16	$n\bar{x}^2 = 5 \times 3^2 = 45$
5	8	40	25	
15	20	70	55	

The slope is $b = (70 - 60)/(55 - 45) = 1; a = 4 - 1 \times 3 = 1$, and the regression line is $y = 1 + x$.

13.8 The deviations $d_1, d_2, \ldots, d_n$ are given by $y_1 - (a + bx_1)$, $y_2 - (a + bx_2), \ldots, y_n - (a + bx_n)$. For example, in Figure 13.6 the deviation d_7 equals $y_7 - (a + bx_7)$. The $y_7 = 20$, for the seventh family has a consumption of 20. It has an income of 32, and people with an income of 32 consume, according to the regression line $y = 4 + .7x$, an amount $4 + .7 \times 32 = 26.4$. The difference $20 - 26.4 = -6.4$ is the deviation. If we sum all deviations we get $y_1 + y_2 + \cdots + y_n - (a + bx_1) - (a + bx_2) - \cdots -(a + bx_n) = n\bar{y} - na - bn\bar{x} = 0$ because $\bar{y} = a + b\bar{x}$.

13.9

x	y	xy	x^2	y^2
1	1	1	1	1
2	4	8	4	16
3	5	15	9	25
4	4	16	16	16
5	6	30	25	36
15	20	70	55	94

$$\bar{x} = \tfrac{15}{5} = 3$$
$$\bar{y} = \tfrac{20}{5} = 4$$

$$\Sigma x_i y_i - n\bar{x}\bar{y}$$
$$= 70 - 60 = 10$$
$$\Sigma x_i^2 - n\bar{x}^2$$
$$= 55 - 45 = 10$$
$$\Sigma y_i^2 - n\bar{y}^2$$
$$= 94 - 80 = 14$$
$$R^2 = 10^2/(10 \times 14) = \tfrac{10}{14}$$

x	y	xy	x^2	y^2
1	2.8	2.8	1	7.84
2	4.9	9.8	4	24.01
3	5.0	15.0	9	25.00
4	3.1	12.4	16	9.61
5	4.2	21.0	25	17.64
15	20.0	61.0	55	84.10

$$\bar{x} = \tfrac{15}{5} = 3$$
$$\bar{y} = \tfrac{20}{5} = 4$$

$$\Sigma x_i y_i - n\bar{x}\bar{y}$$
$$= 61 - 60 = 1$$
$$\Sigma x_i^2 - n\bar{x}^2$$
$$= 55 - 45 = 10$$
$$\Sigma y_i^2 - n\bar{y}^2$$
$$= 84.1 - 80 = 4.1$$
$$R^2 = 1^2/(10 \times 4.1) = \tfrac{1}{41}$$

13.10 In the answer to Exercise 13.7 we have already available all relevant information apart from $y_1^2 + \cdots + y_n^2 - n\bar{y}^2$. In the first case we find $2^2 + 3^2 + 4^2 + 5^2 + 6^2 - 5 \times \bar{y}^2 = 90 - 80 = 10$; hence $R^2 = 10^2/(10 \times 10) = 1$, $R = +1$. In the second case we have $1^2 + 4^2 + 5^2 + 4^2 + 6^2 - 5 \times \bar{y}^2 = 94 - 80 = 14$; hence $R^2 = 10^2/(10 \times 14) = \frac{10}{14} = .714$, $R = +.845$. This answer was also found in Exercise 13.9 above. In the third case we have $0^2 + 7^2 + 4^2 + 1^2 + 8^2 - 5 \times \bar{y}^2 = 130 - 80 = 50$, and hence $R^2 = 10^2/(10 \times 50) = \frac{1}{5} = .2$; $R = +.447$.

13.11   In the answer to Exercise 13.5 we found all relevant information apart from $y_1^2 + \cdots + y_n^2 - n\bar{y}^2$. We have $16^2 + 15^2 + 15^2 + 14^2 + 10^2 - 5 \times 14^2 = 1,002 - 5 \times 196 = 1,002 - 980 = 22$. Hence $R^2 = (-19)^2/(20 \times 22) = \frac{361}{440} = .82$. The correlation coefficient R equals $-\sqrt{.82} = -.906$. The minus sign indicates a negatively sloping line.

13.12   In the answer to Exercise 13.6 we found all relevant information apart from Σy_i^2 and $n\bar{y}^2$. These are equal to 9,552 and 6,916, respectively. Their difference is 2,636. We find $R^2 = (-164)^2/(3,071 \times 2,636) = .003325$, and therefore $R = -.058$. There is no correlation to speak of between the birth and death dates of American Presidents.

13.13   Since $n \operatorname{var} y = \Sigma y_i^2 - n\bar{y}^2$, the answer follows immediately by algebraic manipulations

$$1 - \frac{n \operatorname{var} d}{n \operatorname{var} y} = R^2$$

hence

$$n \operatorname{var} d = n \operatorname{var} y - n \operatorname{var} y(R^2)$$

$$= \Sigma y_i^2 - n\bar{y}^2 - (\Sigma y_i^2 - n\bar{y}^2) \frac{(\Sigma x_i y_i - n\bar{x}\bar{y})^2}{(\Sigma x_i^2 - n\bar{x}^2)(\Sigma y_i^2 - n\bar{y}^2)}$$

In the last expression we cancel $\Sigma y_i^2 - n\bar{y}^2$ from numerator and denominator to obtain the desired expression. Notice that $n \operatorname{var} d$ can be determined from exactly the same data as R^2.

13.14

x	y	xy	x^2	y^2
30	27	810	900	729
35	30	1,050	1,225	900
19	18	342	361	324
39	32	1,248	1,521	1,024
26	19	494	676	361
29	29	841	841	841
32	20	640	1,024	400
210	175	5,425	6,548	4,579

$$\bar{x} = \tfrac{210}{7} = 30$$
$$\bar{y} = \tfrac{175}{7} = 25$$

$$\Sigma x_i y_i - 7\bar{x}\bar{y}$$
$$= 5,425 - 5,250 = 175$$

$$\Sigma x_i^2 - 7\bar{x}^2$$
$$= 6,548 - 6,300 = 248$$

$$\Sigma y_i^2 - 7\bar{y}^2$$

$$b = \tfrac{175}{248} = .7$$

$$a = 25 - .7(30) = 4$$

$$R^2 = (175)^2/(248 \times 204)$$
$$= \tfrac{30,625}{50,592} = .6$$

We have $n \operatorname{var} d = 204 - (175)^2/248 = 204 - 123 = 81 = (d_1^2 + \cdots + d_7^2)$. Hence

$$s_d^2 = \frac{d_1^2 + \cdots + d_7^2}{5} = \frac{81}{5} = 16.2$$

Furthermore, $n \operatorname{var} x = x_1^2 + \cdots + x_7^2 - 7\bar{x}^2 = 248$, as above. Hence

$$s_b^2 = \tfrac{16.2}{248} = .065 \qquad\qquad s_b = .255$$
$$s_a^2 = \tfrac{16.2}{7} + 30^2 \times .065 = 60.8 \qquad s_a = 7.8$$

The result may be recorded as

$$y = 4 + .7x \qquad R^2 = .6$$
$$(7.8)\ (.255)$$

The coefficient a is not significantly different from zero.

13.15   For the first case $n \operatorname{var} d = d_1^2 + \cdots + d_7^2 = 14 - (10)^2/10 = 4$. Hence

$$s_d^2 = \tfrac{4}{3} = 1\tfrac{1}{3}$$

$$s_b^2 = \frac{1\tfrac{1}{3}}{10} = \frac{4}{30} = .133 \qquad\qquad s_b = .365$$

$$s_a^2 = \frac{1\tfrac{1}{3}}{5} + 3^2 \times .133 = 1.46 \qquad s_a = 1.21$$

The *a* is not significantly different from zero, but the *b* is!

For the second case, n var $d_1^2 + \cdots + d_7^2 = 4.1 - (1)^2/10 = 4$. Hence

$$s_d^2 = \tfrac{4}{3} = 1\tfrac{1}{3}$$

$$s_b^2 = \frac{1\tfrac{1}{3}}{10} = \frac{4}{30} = .133 \qquad\qquad s_b = .365$$

$$s_a^2 = \frac{1\tfrac{1}{3}}{5} + 3^2 \times .133 = 1.46 \qquad s_a = 1.21$$

The standard deviations of the estimates are the same, which is no surprise since n var x, n var d, and $\bar{x}$ are all the same. In this case, however, the *b* coefficient is not significant and the *a* is.

13.16 Using the information in the answers to Exercises 13.7 and 13.10, we find:

Case 1: n var $d = 10 - (10)^2/10 = 0$. The standard deviations are zero.

Case 2: n var $d = 14 - (10)^2/10 = 4$; $s_d^2 = \tfrac{4}{3}$. Hence $s_b^2 = \tfrac{4}{3}/10 = \tfrac{4}{30} = .133$, $s_a^2 = (1\tfrac{1}{3}/5) + 3^2 \times .133 = 1.46$, $s_b = .365$, and $s_a = 1.21$. With 95.45 percent confidence, the true β will be between $1 \pm 2 \times .365 = .27$ to 1.73, and the true α will be between $1 \pm 2 \times 1.21 = -1.42$ to 3.42.

Case 3: n var $d = 50 - (10)^2/10 = 40$, $s_d^2 = \tfrac{40}{3}$. Hence $s_b^2 = \tfrac{40}{3}/10 = 1.33$, $s_a^2 = \tfrac{40}{3}/5 + 3^2 \times 1.33 = 14.64$, $s_b = 1.15$, and $s_a = 3.83$. With 95.45 percent confidence, the true β will be between $1 \pm 2 \times 1.15 = -1.30$ to 3.30, and the true α will be between $1 \pm 2 \times 3.83$, or -6.66 to 8.66. Neither is significant.

Note: The 95.45 percent confidence interval suggests that we take $k = 2$ from the normal distribution, as indeed we did. It is better to use $k = 3.18$ from the t distribution with $3(n - 2 = 5 - 2 = 3)$ degrees of freedom at the 95 percent level. If we do, no *a* or *b* value in either case 2 or case 3 is significantly different from zero.

13.17 In general, it makes little sense to extrapolate linear regressions so far away from the range over which observations are available as 0 or 1,000. One way in which this becomes evident is in the large ranges of the interval estimates. Using the results of Table 13.3 and the formula

$$s_d^2\left(1 + \frac{1}{n}\right) + s_b^2(x_{t+1} - \bar{x})^2$$

we get the following results:

For $x_{t+1} = 0$: $22(1 + \frac{1}{12}) + .00005354(467)^2 = 35.515$. A 95 percent confidence interval is given by 16.57 ± 2.23 $\sqrt{35.515}$, or from 3.28 to 29.86.

For $x_{t+1} = 467$: $22(1 + \frac{1}{12}) + .00005354(0)^2 = 23.833$. A 95 percent confidence interval is given by $427.00 \pm 2.23 \sqrt{23.833}$, or from 416.12 to 437.88.

For $x_{t+1} = 1,000$: $22(1 + \frac{1}{12}) + .00005354(533)^2 = 39.043$. A 95 percent confidence interval is given by $897.57 \pm 2.23\sqrt{39.043}$, or from 883.64 to 911.50.

The value 2.23 is read from the t distribution with 10 degrees of freedom at the column marked 5 percent. Note that the interval is least when x_{t+1} equals $\bar{x}$.

13.18

x	y	xy	x^2	y^2
10	1	10	100	1
8	4	32	64	16
6	6	36	36	36
4	7	28	16	49
2	7	14	4	49
30	25	120	220	151

$\bar{x} = \frac{30}{5} = 6$

$\bar{y} = \frac{25}{5} = 5$

$\Sigma x_i y_i - 5\bar{x}\bar{y}$
$\quad = 120 - 150 = -30$
$\Sigma x_i^2 - 5\bar{x}^2$
$\quad = 220 - 180 = 40$
$\Sigma y_i^2 - 5\bar{y}^2$
$\quad = 151 - 125 = 26$

Thus we have $b = (-30)/40$, $a = 5 - (-\frac{3}{4})(6) = 9.5$, and $R^2 = (-30)^2/(40 \times 26) = \frac{900}{1,040} = .86$. Then n var $d = 26 - (-30)^2/40 = 3.5$, $s_d^2 = \frac{3.5}{3} = 1.17$, $s_b^2 = \frac{1.17}{40} = 0.29$, $s_b = .17$, $s_a^2 = \frac{1.17}{5} + .029(6^2) = 1.27$, and $s_a = 1.13$. Hence

$$y = 9.5 - .75x \qquad R^2 = .86$$
$$(1.13) \quad (.17)$$

Furthermore,

$$s_d^2\left(1 + \frac{1}{n}\right) + s_b^2(x_{t+1} - \bar{x})^2$$

$$= 1.17(1 + \tfrac{1}{5}) + .029(x_{t+1} - 6)^2$$

For $x_{t+1} = 7$, we find $1.4 + .029 = 1.429$. The 95 percent interval estimate is $4.25 \pm 3.18\sqrt{1.429} = 4.25 \pm 3.18(1.195)$, or from .45 to 8.05. The value 3.18 is read from a t distribution with 3 degrees of freedom.

13.19 $$b = \frac{37,800 - 37,400}{1,720 - 1,700} = \frac{400}{20} = 20$$

$$a = 220 - 20 \times 10 = 20$$

$$R^2 = \frac{400^2}{20 \times (831,800 - 822,800)} = \frac{160,000}{20 \times 9,000} = \frac{16}{18}$$

n var $d = 9,000 - \frac{160,000}{20} = 1,000 \qquad s_d^2 = \frac{1,000}{16} = 62.5$

$s_d = 7.9 \qquad s_b^2 = \frac{62.5}{20} = 3\frac{1}{8} \qquad s_b = 1.77$

$s_a^2 = \frac{62.5}{17} + 3\frac{1}{8} \times 10^2 = 316.2 \qquad s_a = 17.8$

If $x_{t+1} = 17$, then

$$s_d^2\left(1 + \frac{1}{n}\right) + s_b^2(x_{t+1} - \bar{x}) = 62\tfrac{1}{2}(1 + \tfrac{1}{17}) + 3\tfrac{1}{8}(7)^2$$

$$= 66.17 + 153.12 = 219$$

A 95 percent confidence interval estimate is $(20 + 20 \times 17) \pm 2.13\sqrt{219} = 360 \pm 2.13(14.8)$, or roughly from 329 to 391. We used a t distribution with 15 degrees of freedom.

13.20   We found in the answer to Exercise 13.18 that $s_d^2 = 1.17$. Furthermore, $\bar{y} = 5$ and the regression line is $y = 9\frac{1}{2} - \frac{3}{4}x$; hence

x	$y_c = 9\frac{1}{2} - \frac{3}{4}x$
10	2
8	3½
6	5
4	6½
2	8

Hence $s_{y-y_c}^2 = (5 - 2)^2 + (5 - 3\frac{1}{2})^2 + (5 - 5)^2 + (5 - 6\frac{1}{2})^2 + (5 - 8)^2 = 22\frac{1}{2}$. The ratio $(s_{y-y_c}^2)/s_d^2 = \frac{22.5}{1.17} = 19.2$. This value exceeds 10.13 in Table 13.4, and is significant.

13.21   We find in Table 13.3 that $s_d^2 = 2.76$. Furthermore, $\bar{y} = 320$ and the regression line is $6.48 + .9114x$; hence

x	$y_c = 6.48 + .9114x$
208	196.05
274	256.20
337	313.62
350	325.47
364	338.23
385	357.37
403	373.77
431	399.29

Hence $s_{\bar{y}-y_c}^2 = (320 - 196.05)^2 + \cdots + (320 - 399.29)^2 = 30,289$. The ratio $\frac{30,289}{2.76} = 10,974$, which is much higher than the 5.99 needed for significance.

13.22   In all cases, $\bar{y} = 4$, $y = 1 + x$ is the regression equation and x takes on the values 1, 2, 3, 4, and 5, so y_c has values 2, 3, 4, 5, and 6. Therefore $s_{\bar{y}-y_c}^2 = (2 - 4)^2 + (3 - 4)^2 + (4 - 4)^2 + (5 - 4)^2 + (6 - 4)^2 = 10$ in all three cases. By the result of Exercise 13.16, the value s_d^2 equals 0, 1.33, and 13.3, respectively. The F ratios are $\frac{10}{0}$, $\frac{10}{1.33} = 7.5$, and $\frac{10}{13.3} = .75$. The first F ratio, $\frac{10}{0}$, can be taken to be quite large and is significant. The second is not quite significant ($7.5 < 10.13$), and the third is not remotely significant.

13.23

y	x	z	y^2	yx	yz	x^2	xz	z^2	
1	10	1	1	10	1	100	10	1	$\bar{y} = \frac{25}{5} = 5$
4	8	1	16	32	4	64	8	1	$\bar{x} = \frac{30}{6} = 6$
6	6	2	36	36	12	36	12	4	
7	4	3	49	28	21	16	12	9	$\bar{z} = \frac{10}{5} = 2$
7	2	3	49	14	21	4	6	9	
25	30	10	151	120	59	220	48	24	

Hence, for the regression of y on x:

$$\text{Slope } b = \frac{120 - 150}{220 - 180} = -\frac{30}{40}$$

$$\text{Intercept } a = 5 - (-\tfrac{3}{4}) \times 6 = 9\tfrac{1}{2}$$

regression equation $\quad y = \quad 9\frac{1}{2} \quad - \quad \frac{3}{4}x$

$\qquad\qquad\qquad\qquad (1.13) \quad (0.29)$

For the regression of y on z:

Slope $b = \dfrac{59 - 50}{24 - 20} = \dfrac{9}{4}$ $\qquad$ Intercept $a = 5 - \frac{9}{4} \times 2 = \frac{1}{2}$

regression equation $\quad y = \quad \frac{1}{2} \quad + \quad \frac{9}{4}x$

$\qquad\qquad\qquad\qquad (1.5) \quad (.73)$

For the regression of y on x *and* z we consider the regression equation $y = a + bx + cz$. The values b and c are determined by solving the normal equations, which are $-30 = 40b - 12c$, and $9 = -12b + 4c$. Hence $b = -\frac{3}{4}$, $c = 0$, and $a = 5 - (-\frac{3}{4})(6) - (0)(2) = 9\frac{1}{2}$. The regression equation is

$$y = \quad 9\frac{1}{2} \quad - \quad \frac{3}{4}x \quad + \quad 0z$$
$$\quad\;\; (8.1) \quad\;\; (.66) \quad\;\; (2.1)$$

The standard deviations have been added; their derivation is omitted. In view of the severe multicollinearity ($z = 3.8 + .3x$, $R^2 = .9$), the interpretation is awkward. When each variable was used singly as an explanatory variable, the slope was significant. When used together, the multicollinearity prevents either coefficient from being significant.

13.24 Alternative c is much the best *for the purpose of the regression* (not necessarily for employee morale or for other purposes), since it means that there will be no systematic correlation between years of service and machine age.

Chapter 14

PROBLEMS FOR REVIEW-II

1   A sample is going to be taken from a very large batch of parts. Each part is either effective or defective. The batch is to be accepted or rejected on the sample evidence. The following conditions must be met: (1) the risk of rejecting the batch if 5 percent are defective should be 1 percent; and (2) the risk of accepting the batch if 20 percent are defective should be 5 percent.
(a) Find the appropriate sample size and critical value.
(b) State the decision rule.
(c) Find the probability that a batch with 10 percent defective is accepted, using the decision rule stated in part (b).

2   A simple random sample of 400 families in a large city showed the average expenditures on clothes equal to $175 per year and the standard deviation equal to $25.
(a) Draw a sketch of the sampling distribution applicable in this problem. Label the axis carefully.
(b) Find an 85 percent confidence interval estimate of the true mean for all families in the city.
(c) Explain exactly what your answer to part (b) means for this problem.

(d) Suppose later information reveals that the true standard deviation in the population is $40. How does this information affect your answer in part (c)?

3   Two bank tellers are observed helping 100 customers. The null hypothesis that they are equally efficient is tested against the alternative that A, with 7 years of service, is faster than B, with 3 years of service. For A, the average service time was 48 seconds. The standard deviation in service time was 11 seconds. For B, the average was 53 seconds. The standard deviation was 12 seconds. Should the null hypothesis be rejected at the 10 percent level of significance? Suppose that A and B were being observed helping the *same* 100 customers with the *same* transactions. Would this influence the test to be applied? If so, how?

4   In a regression of investment on the interest rate, the following results were observed during 10 years:

Average interest rate x	Yearly investment y
4.4	1,060,000
4.7	940,000
5.0	920,000
4.8	1,110,000
4.2	1,590,000
3.5	2,050,000
3.7	2,070,000
3.9	2,030,000
4.7	1,780,000
5.5	1,420,000

(a) Find $y = a + bx$, R^2, s_a, and s_b.
(b) Include a trend as a second explanatory variable.
(c) Use your equation to estimate yearly investment if the average interest rate 5 years from now is 4.0 percent.

5   A simple random sample of 100 housewives reveals that 60 percent prefer electric stoves to gas stoves.
(a) Within what limits is the true percentage of housewives who prefer electric stoves to gas? Use a confidence coefficient of 90 percent.

(b) Suppose you learn later that the population proportion you are estimating does not lie within the interval you constructed in part (a). What would this imply?

6 The extensive records of a certain achievement test show a mean score of 60 with a standard deviation of 10. How large a group of students should be tested to assure that its average differs from the mean by not more than 2, at a 98 percent confidence level?

7 A simple random sample of 400 persons shows that 30 percent of them never heard of a consumer product your company manufactures. You have decided that unless at least 75 percent of the population knows of this product, your advertising agency should be replaced.

(a) Using a 1 percent level of significance, decide on the basis of this sample whether to retain your present agency. Explain your answer and support it statistically.

(b) What is the probability of obtaining two independent simple random samples of 400 persons in which 30 percent had never heard of your product if actually 75 percent of the population knows of this product? Explain how you arrive at your answer.

8 In a regression of monthly piano sales against average family income (in \$100s) for 45 randomly chosen communities of comparable size, we have the following results:

$$n = 45 \qquad x_1 y_1 + \cdots + x_{45} y_{45} = 1{,}221{,}095$$
$$\bar{x} = 127 \qquad x_1^2 + \cdots + x_{45}^2 = 728{,}805$$
$$\bar{y} = 213 \qquad y_1^2 + \cdots + y_{45}^2 = 2{,}046{,}605$$

Determine a, b, s_a, s_b, and R^2. Interpret each value you find in terms of the problem.

9 There are two possible states of nature: a man asking for a charge account will default or will not. In general 5 percent of the customers default. If the application is accepted, the damage is \$1,000 if the customer defaults and the profit is \$100 if he does not. Determine a payoff matrix and the best decision under minimax, maximax, and the expected value criterion.

10 See Problem 9. Applicants are asked if they have either a black telephone or a color telephone. Among applicants with a black

telephone—of which there are 40 percent in the population—only 2 percent will default, while of those with a color telephone—of which there are 60 percent in the population—7 percent will default. Verify that these data are consistent with a 5 percent overall rate of default, and determine the best decision if our man states that he has a color telephone.

11   The following are results obtained in a random sample of size 20 for the weekly income of barbers. Determine an interval estimate for μ at the 95 percent confidence level, and for σ at the 90 percent level, using the appropriate t distribution.

155	170	150	180
135	130	140	210
140	140	135	150
125	160	130	170
175	160	110	135

12   A man who claims telepathic sight states that he can guess the digit 0, 1, ..., 9 a person writes down and thinks about. We test his claim by having him perform, and two out of two times he is right. Do we accept the null hypothesis that the man has no telepathic qualities at the 2 percent level of significance? Why? Do we accept it at the $\frac{1}{2}$ percent level of significance?

13   In a random sample of 2,025 voters, 1,050 persons prefer candidate A and 975 prefer B. Can the null hypothesis that the two are equally "preferred" be rejected at the 5 percent level? Why? (Before answering, state the alternative hypothesis you will use.)

14   A plant manager wants to estimate for each individual employee the percentage of working time spent away from his regular place of work, i.e., getting materials, talking to others, in rest room, etc. He is going to do this by observing each worker at random moments to see if he is away from his place of work.

(a) Assuming that no worker spends over 10 percent of his time away from his work place, how many observations should be made on each worker to estimate his percentage of time absent within 2 percentage points with 95 percent confidence?

(b) Suppose the budget restricts the manager to 200 observations on each employee. Again assuming that π is not more than .10, what confidence can he have that p is within 2 percentage points of π? Explain.

15   Observe the following decision rule: Take a simple random sample of 100 pieces of a particular product. If $\bar{x} < 20$ pounds, conclude that the process is operating satisfactorily. If $\bar{x} \geq 20$ pounds, conclude that the process is faulty and stop it for complete investigation. Assume the population standard deviation equals 2 pounds.

   (a) Determine the ordinates on the operating characteristic curve of this decision rule for the following values (in pounds):

   19.5   19.7   19.9   20   20.2   20.4   20.6

   (b) Plot the curve carefully, labeling both axes.
   (c) What does the curve show?

16   A section manager wishes to estimate the mean number of seconds required by a worker to do a particular task. He observed this worker on 25 randomly selected occasions. The average number of seconds required in the 25 observations was 100 seconds and the standard deviation was 10 seconds. Use the normal or t distribution.

   (a) Using an 80 percent confidence coefficient, construct an interval estimate of the true mean number of seconds required by this worker to perform this task

   (b) If the true mean time for this worker is 105 seconds, what is the probability of a sample result as much or more below the true mean as the one obtained by the plant manager? Would you accept the null hypothesis that the true mean is 105?

   (c) What size sample (i.e., how many observations) would be necessary to estimate the true mean within .5 second with a 90 percent confidence coefficient? (Use the standard deviation of the sample as the best available estimate of the standard deviation of the population.)

17   Some states require a minimum bodily injury liability coverage on automobiles licensed in their state. Many automobile owners, however, decide to carry as much as 10 times the amount of minimum insurance. Discuss the nature of the reasoning that results in the decisions of these individuals to carry large amounts of insurance. Your answer must state specifically in terms of this problem the relevant (a) alternatives, (b) states of nature, (c) uncertainty, (d) consequences, and (e) numerical information.

18   A bank wished to learn certain facts about the total group of persons who had checking accounts there. The information was not available in the bank's records, so management hired a research organization to interview a random sample of 500 persons having checking accounts with the bank.

(*a*) Why was the decision made to use sampling to obtain the information?

(*b*) Why was the decision made to use random sampling to obtain the information?

(*c*) Exactly how would you select a simple random sample of 500 persons having checking accounts with the bank?

19   Consider the following payoff table:

State of nature	A priori probability	Decision I	Decision II
A	.6	4	7
B	.4	9	2

What is the value of a sample which leads to a result that *if* A is true, the result has a probability of .25, while *if* B is true, it has a probability of only .10?

20   In Problem 19, the possible sample outcomes 1, 2, 3, and 4 have the following probabilities:

State of nature	1	2	3	4
A	.10	.25	.25	.40
B	.25	.60	.10	.05

What is the value of taking a sample?

21   Test the hypothesis that the following interarrival times—rounded to the nearest minute—are exponentially distributed: 5, 9, 0, 4, 2, 0, 0, 3, 1, 1, 7, 0, 4, 13, 2, 4, 4, 3, 0, 0, 1, 1, 5, 6, 10, 6, 0, 2, 2, 1, 4, 0, 5, 7, 2, 0, 3, 1, 4, 8, 1, 2, 0, 4, 3, 2, 2, 1, 1, 5.

22   In the first round, 11 marksmen of team A have 12, 14, 14, 17, 19, 12, 15, 20, 16, and 15 hits out of 20. In the second

round, 11 marksmen of team B have 11, 13, 16, 13, 18, 11, 15, 19, 14, and 13 hits. Can we accept the hypothesis that round 1 was better at a 10 percent level of significance?

23 In the first round, 11 marksmen of team A score 12, 14, 14, 17, 19, 12, 15, 20, 16, and 15 hits out of 20. In the second round, their scores are 11, 13, 16, 13, 18, 11, 15, 19, 14, and 13, respectively. Can we accept the hypothesis that round 1 was better at the 10 percent level of significance?

24 In a regression we have 20 observations on x: 18, 36, 34, 20, 23, 36, 14, 28, 35, 35, 14, 14, 25, 20, 17, 17, 37, 18, 26, 33. Clearly, $\bar{x} = 25$ and $x_1^2 + x_2^2 + \cdots + x_{20}^2 = 13,884$. Furthermore,

$$\bar{y} = 40$$
$$x_1 y_1 + \cdots + x_{20} y_{20} = 22,768$$
$$y_1^2 + \cdots + y_{20}^2 = 38,000$$

Determine the F ratio. Interpret it in terms of this problem.

25 Fifty cans randomly chosen from production of three canneries are carefully weighed, with the following results:

Weight, ounces	Number of cans		
	Cannery 1	Cannery 2	Cannery 3
< 10	5	7	9
$10 \ < 10.1$	15	24	21
$10.1 < 10.2$	20	17	14
$10.2 < 10.3$	10	2	6

Should we accept the hypothesis that all come from the same population? Why? Use a 5 percent level of significance.

26 An airline wishes to estimate the mean weight of the hand baggage carried on board its planes by passengers. A simple random sample of 400 passengers is chosen, and the weight of their hand baggage is found to have an average of 6 pounds and a standard deviation of 2 pounds.

(a) Construct an interval estimate of the population mean with a confidence coefficient of 80 percent. State exactly what this interval tells you.

(*b*) What would be your best single-valued estimate of the percentage of passengers whose hand baggage weighs more than 8 pounds? Assume that the distribution of the weight of passengers' hand baggage is normal.

27   An investigator believes that the percentage of output deviating from standards in producing plastic molds *y* is due to length of employment of the employee producing the mold *x*. He collects data, using simple random sampling, and finds:

y	*x, years*
7	10
17	2
5	4
4	6
10	8
7	6
16	4
11	1
17	5
8	3

Another investigator believes that the age of the machine is a better explanatory variable. He draws a sample and finds observations *y* and age of machine on which the mold was produced *x*:

y	*x, years*
6	11
8	8
10	5
8	8
9	6
9	7
13	1
8	8
12	2
10	5

Using these observations, determine which investigator is right. If a determination is not possible, explain why.

28   In a large city the Board of Assessors wishes to estimate the percentage of homes in the city which have central air conditioning. They have no evidence suggesting what this percentage might be. They would like to estimate the true figure within 3 percentage points with a confidence coefficient of 90 percent.

(a) How many homes should be chosen at random from the homes in the city to provide the estimate with the desired accuracy?

(b) How would your answer to part (a) be affected if the Board of Assessors felt sure that the percentage of homes in the city with central air conditioning did not exceed 20? Calculate the sample size that would be needed, and say why it differs from your answer to (a).

29   A supermarket chain must decide which of two available sites to select for the construction of a new supermarket. Formulate this problem in terms of (a) states of the world, (b) courses of action, and (c) consequences. What uncertainty is present in this situation? What decision criteria would you use? Why?

30   In each of the following instances describe how you would select the required sample:

(a) A random sample of 50 from invoices for a given month that are numbered from 2463 to 3981 consecutively.

(b) Samples of apples from trees to compare the effectiveness of different sprays on the weight of the apples.

(c) A random sample of entries in an accounts receivable ledger. The ledger contains 150 accounts with varying numbers of debit and credit entries and is to be checked for accuracy.

31   A retail store is testing a new system of delivering items from a warehouse to the pickup counter in the main store. The new system may be installed to replace the old one if the new provides faster delivery. The old has a mean delivery time of 5 minutes. During the test period 100 items were delivered in such a manner that the average delivery time was $\bar{x} = 4.7$ minutes, and the standard deviation of these delivery times was 1 minute. Management is willing to take a 1 percent risk of continuing with the old system if the new one has a mean time of 4.5 minutes.

(a) What action should be taken? Why?

(b) What is the probability that the action taken was wrong?

32   Comment on the following procedure for collecting data. Your
        answer should be precise, constructive, and thorough. To study
        attitudes of the public toward rent control in New York City,
        every 500th name was selected from the Manhattan phone book
        and if anyone answered the phone when the number was called,
        he was asked, "Do you favor regulations to curb excessive rents?"
        Calls were made between 9 A.M. and 5 P.M., Monday through
        Friday, and only one attempt was made to reach a selected
        number.

33   In a study of the factors associated with fires in homes, a simple
        random sample of 10,000 insured homes was chosen. For a 3-year
        period, fires occurred in 60 homes, 14 of which had fireplaces
        in them. In all, 1,000 of the sampled homes had fireplaces in
        them.
        (a) Organize these data into a contingency table.
        (b) Test the hypothesis that the occurrence of a fire and the
            presence of a fireplace are independent characteristics in all
            insured homes. Use a 5 percent level of significance.
        (c) Relate your conclusion in part (b) to the insurance company's
            rate structure.

34   In a simple random sample of 400 individual stockholders of the
        A.O.K. Satellite Corporation the average income was $12,500,
        and the standard deviation was $2,000.
        (a) Make an interval estimate of the mean income of all individual
            stockholders of the corporation, using a 96 percent confidence
            coefficient.
        (b) Explain the meaning of your answer in part (a).
        (c) Suppose it is learned later, from a complete census of the
            individual stockholders, that their mean income was actually
            $14,000 when the sample of 400 on which you based your
            answer in part (a) was taken. Would this information contra-
            dict what you said in part (b)? Why?

35   Suppose you are a statistician for a manufacturer of razor blades.
        How would you utilize a table of random numbers in selecting
        a simple random sample of:
        (a) Employees of the company?
        (b) Razor blades coming from the production line on 1 specific
            day?
        (c) Persons buying blades in retail stores on 1 specific day?

36 A manufacturer of home freezers must decide between two types of hinge for the door of a new model freezer. Type A is more expensive, but is a better-wearing hinge than type B. The manufacturer knows that the choice should be based on the habits of freezer buyers. If the mean number of times users will open the freezer door each week is 20 or more, A should be used. A counting device is to be attached to the freezers in a random sample of homes to find how often users actually open the door of their freezer. The manufacturer is willing to take only a .05 risk of using B when A should be used.

(a) In a simple random sample of 100 homes, the average number of openings per week is 19.3, and the standard deviation is 5. Set up the appropriate decision rule.

(b) Which hinge should be used? Why?

(c) In using the decision rule you set up in part (a), what risk did you take of concluding that the type A hinge should be used when the true mean equals 18 openings per week?

(d) If the manufacturer feels your answer in part (c) represents a larger risk than he is willing to tolerate, what can be done about it?

37 A quality control engineer takes a daily sample of 20 electronic components, checking them for slight imperfections. Working thus for 100 days, on 23 days he obtained zero defectives, on 51 days he obtained one defective, on 23 days he obtained two defectives, and on 3 days he obtained three defectives. Using a level of significance of .01, test the null hypothesis that these data may be looked upon as samples from a binomial population with a probability of a defective equal to .05.

38 The following are three different weeks' earnings (in dollars) of five salesmen employed by a certain company:

Jones	Smith	Brown	Miller	Black
126	148	204	119	156
152	171	182	125	184
139	176	172	155	161

Consider the assumptions of the analysis of variance met. Test at a level of significance of .05 whether the differences among the average earnings of these salesmen over the given time period may be attributed to chance.

39   A manufacturer assigns the following prior probability values to
          the percentage of defectives in a production process considered
          a binomial process:

Event	p(event)
.03	.60
.05	.20
.10	.10
.15	.10
	1.00

The rework cost of a defective is $.50, and the length of a run
is 400 pieces. Alternatively, a mechanic can be hired at a cost
of $8.00 to readjust the machine to produce a run with 3 percent
defective.

(a) What should the manager do before a sample is taken?

(b) A sample of size 50 contains one defective. The probability
    of this result under the four possible states of nature is .337,
    .202, .029, and .003, respectively. What should he do now?
    What is the value of this sample outcome?

40   It has been claimed that at least 30 percent of all students entering
          college drop out before the beginning of the second year.

(a) Test this claim against the alternative that the proportion is
    less than 30 percent, if a random sample of 100 students,
    who entered college in 1972, contains 24 who dropped out
    before the second year. Use a level of significance of .05.

(b) Draw an OC curve by computing the probability of accepting
    the null hypothesis with values of π equal to .15, .20, .25,
    .30, .35, and .40 (π = true proportion of students who drop
    out). Use the decision rule implied by the test under part (a).

(c) Under what conditions would you be committing an error
    of Type II? What is the probability of committing an error
    of Type II if the alternative hypothesis is $\pi_1 = .20$?

41   On a certain day the Gutter Corporation produced 100 bowling
          balls which had a mean weight of 14 pounds and a standard
          deviation of 2 pounds. Suppose that many simple random samples

of size nine are taken. Create an interval about the mean such that 97 percent of the sample averages will fall in this interval.

42   The product made on four machines is inspected and classified P (premium), C (common), or R (reject). A simple random sample of 1,000 units from these machines contained the following:

Product	Machine			
class	A	B	C	D
P	280	100	220	150
C	60	25	30	35
R	60	25	0	15

Using a 5 percent level of significance, test the hypothesis that in the population of all products produced on these machines, machine and product class are independent. Explain your conclusion in terms of the problem.

43   The planning commission in a city containing 31,800 dwelling places wished to estimate the mean number of inhabitants per dwelling place in the city. It selected a simple random sample of 600 dwelling places, and the sample results were as follows:

$$x_i = \text{number of inhabitants in } i\text{th dwelling sampled}$$
$$n = \text{sample size} = 600$$
$$x_1 + x_2 + \cdots + x_n = 3{,}124$$
$$(x_1 - \bar{x})^2 + (x_2 - \bar{x})^2 + \cdots + (x_n - \bar{x})^2 = 20{,}419$$

(a) What is the point estimate of the mean number of inhabitants per dwelling place in the city?

(b) Construct an interval estimate, with a 99 percent confidence coefficient, of the mean number of inhabitants per dwelling place in the city.

(c) In another simple random sample of 500 dwelling places would the same 99 percent confidence limits have been obtained?

44   The balances of 5, 7, and 8 randomly drawn clients of the three major banks in town are:

	Bank	
A	B	C
100	150	60
120	50	90
180	140	210
30	460	110
320	500	70
	230	620
	190	20
		130

Can we accept the hypothesis that the mean balance of all customers in each bank is the same, at the 5 percent level of significance?

45   What explanatory variables seem reasonable in explaining the total yearly sale of butter? The yearly net investment of a large company? Is there danger of multicollinearity in either or both cases? Explain why.

46   The standard IBM card has 80 columns in which one character per column is punched by a keypunch operator. After the operator has punched a card, it is verified by another operator. Assume that 100 cards randomly chosen from a week's work by one keypunch operator show the following distribution of number of errors per card when verified:

Number of errors	Number of cards
0	27
1	35
2	18
3	9
4	5
5	2
6	0
7	2
8	0
9	1
10	1

Using the 5 percent level of significance, test the hypothesis that in the long run, the distribution of errors per card for this keypunch operator follows the Poisson distribution.

47   Price x and advertising expenditures z are possible explanatory variables for sales y. The following data are available from six test market areas.

Sales y, units	Price x, dollars	Expense z, dollars
1,000	10	100
1,080	9	120
1,200	9	200
1,020	10	50
910	11	0
850	12	50

Determine the regression equation. Interpret the constants in terms of this problem.

48   What is the value of a sample which gives 7 out of 10 preferences for A if one is faced with the decision problem summarized in the payoff table below?

		Payoff	
State of nature†	Probability	Action I	Action II
.40	.1	$200	$ 20
.45	.2	150	50
.50	.3	100	80
.55	.2	50	120
.60	.2	0	160

† Proportion of customers preferring A.

49   Structure as a decision problem the dilemma at the bridge table of whether or not to double a bid of four spades if you estimate the opponents' chances for making 7, 8, 9, 10, or 11 tricks at 9, 25, 55, 10, and 1 percent, respectively.

50   On two tests 20 job applicants scored as follows. Are the average
        scores significantly different? Use a .05 level of significance.
        Interpret your results.

Applicant	Test 1	Test 2
1	40	35
2	59	43
3	66	88
4	79	95
5	20	23
6	41	64
7	54	61
8	55	53
9	45	47
10	31	37
11	76	87
12	45	46
13	20	10
14	89	76
15	76	86
16	35	49
17	72	64
18	57	48
19	51	75
20	63	67

Chapter 15

TIME SERIES ANALYSIS

15.1 THE INGREDIENTS OF TIME SERIES ANALYSIS

A time series is a series of values of a variable at successive points in time or for successive intervals of time. Variables observed at specific points in time are *stock variables*. Thus, we might have year-end data on the value of a firm's capital equipment, month-end data on the number of housing units under construction, and end-of-week data on outstanding currency. By contrast, variables measured over a period of time are *flow variables*. Thus, we can have a yearly series of expenditures for automobiles, a monthly series on the amount of rainfall in New Orleans, a weekly series on the retail sales of a department store, a daily series on the number of calls to a fire station, and so on. Stock variables can be measured at any moment in time. Height is a stock variable. It can be found at any moment of time. Inventory is a stock variable. It can be counted at any moment of time. Growth is a flow variable. It can be measured for a day, a week, a month, or a year, but it is always measured over a period of time. Sales is a flow variable. It is measured over a period of time.

    The series in which we will be most interested concern economic data regarding the national economy as a whole (net investment, gross

Stock
variables
versus flow
variables

production) or pertaining to a particular industry (poultry production, new orders for steel) or even a particular company (passenger miles produced by an airline, hours of overtime in a factory). However, everyone can easily make his own time series, for example, the number of eggs used in the household per week, or the amount spent on lunch each day.

"All that is past is prologue": The past behavior of various time series may tell us something about the future. This is the reason for analyzing a time series. The analysis usually begins by decomposing— breaking down—the time series into various components, *trend, cycle, seasonal,* and *irregular components.* Given these four components, the time series is either reconstructed by adding them (the additive model) *or* by multiplying them (the multiplicative model), which will be explained as we proceed. In actual fact, of course, we start with the one observed time series and decompose it into the four series above. We will, by contrast, begin with the four component series, and then construct the actual time series. In this section, we will discuss the four components in some depth.

Trend

The *trend* gives the long-run direction of the series. It can be derived from yearly data, or from lengthy series of monthly data. The most common shapes are illustrated in Figure 15.1. The straight line corresponds to the trend in which there is a constant amount of increase from period to period. As a first approximation, or over a limited span of time, such a straight-line trend is often appropriate. However, trends in which the *percentage* of increase remains constant are met more often than those in which the *amount* of increase is constant. A trend line of constant percentage growth is illustrated in Figure 15.1*b*. In such a case, the logarithm of the trend will increase by constant amounts. To obtain the trend line we simply convert the actual data to their logarithms (see Section 15.4).

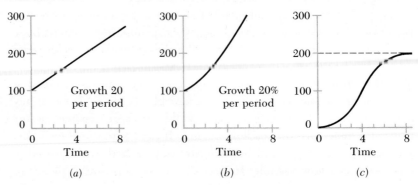

Figure 15.1 Typical trend patterns.

Figure 15.1*c* shows a natural growth curve which is often used as a model for forecasting how new products will permeate the market. The percentage of households owning a color television set as time proceeds may grow according to a curve of this general "stretched-S" shape. The curve is characterized by two parameters. These parameters can be estimated from data in much the same way as the intercept α and the slope β can be estimated when we fit a straight line to a scatter of points.

The *cycle* or business cycle is a historical phenomenon of nearly all   Cycle
economic series in unregulated industrialized societies. Cycles vary greatly in length and severity. The cause for these cycles is a topic of much research and speculation. It is evident that there is no single cause and that different factors have been at work in different cycles, which explains their individual character, although it does not explain their regularity. Differences between net investments and net savings during the same time interval, monetary factors, major inventions (automobiles, computers), changes in inventories, and psychological factors all contribute to the explanation. It is unlikely that business cycles as we know them will continue in the future with their past regularity and severity, in view of our increased knowledge of the mechanism of the economy and the increased powers of governments to regulate, and thus mitigate, cycles.

Seasonal fluctuations ("seasonals") result from both periodicity in   Seasonal
climate and from variations induced by man. Agricultural and sea crops obviously have pronounced seasonal characteristics, as do sales of air conditioners and skis. These are due to changes in climate. Examples of man-made seasonal variations are the introduction of new models in the fall, which leads to regular cycles in automobile production and sales, and Christmas gift buying, which leads to high retail sales in December. The seasonal is usually computed for months or quarters. In addition to these regular patterns of variation within a calendar year, there are many industries with regularly recurring weekly patterns—retail sales are low on Wednesday mornings and high on Saturdays—or even daily patterns—the consumption of electricity is higher during working hours and early evening. The last phenomenon may lead to peak hour pricing (telephones) or peak day pricing and slack day pricing (airline tickets).

Finally, there are *irregular* fluctuations, which are the result of such   Irregular
factors as extreme weather, a strike, an accident, a rise in interest rates, a political election, or a solar eclipse. The irregular component is usually assumed to average to zero and to be completely random in nature, that is, without any systematic component.

EXERCISES

15.1   Two cities have the same population p at the end of 1960. In
       1961, both populations increase by the same amount a. During
       the rest of the decade, the population in city I increases by the
       same amount a each year, and the population in city II increases
       by the same percentage, $[(a + p)/p] \times 100$ percent, each year.
       At the end of 1969, which city has the higher population?

15.2   Is production a stock or a flow variable? Is inventory a stock or
       a flow variable? Is price a stock or a flow variable? Is profit a
       stock or a flow variable?

15.3   Discuss some of the problems in obtaining and comparing time
       series of profits for large banks.

15.2   THE ADDITIVE MODEL

In the additive model the values of the trend, the cycle, the seasonal,
and the irregular components are added. Under the assumption that we
have the true values for the four component series, their total will give
the true value for the series. In our example we have assumed a straight-line
trend, increasing by an amount 1 each month from the starting value of
400. The cycle has a period of 4 years exactly, and has a low of -143
and a high of 133. The sum of the deviations over a complete cycle is
exactly zero. The seasonal is below average during the winter months and
the late summer, and is only really high in December. The pattern is typical
of the sales of retail stores. Again, the sum of the deviations during a
complete year is zero. The irregular component is found by random
drawings from a distribution which assumes the values -9, -8, ...,
0, 1, ..., 9 equally often. They were generated with the help of a table
of random digits.

   All numerical data are summarized in Table 15.1. In July of year 3,
the trend value is 431, the cycle has a strong positive influence of 102,
the seasonal is 20 above the average of 0, and the irregular term is -3.
The value of the series in July of year 3 is

$$431 + 102 + 20 - 3 = 550$$

Figure 15.2 gives these results graphically. The value in July of year 3
is 550, as seen above. The figure shows the four component series and
the actual series. The total of the four components equals the actual value;

TABLE 15.1 EXAMPLE OF ADDITIVE TIME SERIES

Year	Month	Trend	+	Cycle	+	Seasonal	+	Irregular	=	Actual series
1	J	401		−137		−100		5		169
	F	402		−126		−150		1		127
	M	403		−114		− 50		−4		235
	A	404		−101		20		−9		314
	M	405		− 87		20		5		343
	J	406		− 72		20		−9		345
	J	407		− 56		20		6		377
	A	408		− 39		− 20		−3		346
	S	409		− 21		− 40		0		348
	O	410		− 4		30		6		442
	N	411		12		20		−3		440
	D	412		27		230		5		674
2	J	413		41		−100		−3		351
	F	414		54		−150		−8		310
	M	415		66		− 50		3		434
	A	416		77		20		4		517
	M	417		87		20		−1		523
	J	418		96		20		1		535
	J	419		104		20		6		549
	A	420		111		− 20		−1		510
	S	421		117		− 40		5		503
	O	422		122		30		0		574
	N	423		126		20		−2		567
	D	424		129		230		−6		777
3	J	425		131		−100		1		457
	F	426		132		−150		−5		403
	M	427		133		− 50		9		519
	A	428		130		20		1		579
	M	429		125		20		−3		571
	J	430		116		20		−3		563
	J	431		102		20		−3		550
	A	432		82		− 20		−9		485
	S	433		57		− 40		−2		448
	O	434		27		30		2		493
	N	435		− 1		20		−7		447
	D	436		− 27		230		7		646

TABLE 15.1   (Cont'd)

Year	Month	Trend	+	Cycle	+	Seasonal	+	Irregular	=	Actual series
4	J	437		− 51		− 100		− 9		277
	F	438		− 73		− 150		1		216
	M	439		− 93		− 50		− 4		292
	A	440		− 109		20		6		357
	M	441		− 121		20		9		349
	J	442		− 129		20		− 6		327
	J	443		− 135		20		7		335
	A	444		− 139		− 20		5		290
	S	445		− 141		− 40		− 2		262
	O	446		− 142		30		− 3		331
	N	447		− 143		20		− 9		315
	D	448		− 143		230		9		544
5	J	449		− 137		− 100		0		212
	F	450		− 126		− 150		− 7		167
	M	451		− 114		− 50		8		295
	A	452		− 101		20		9		380
	M	453		− 87		20		5		391
	J	454		− 72		20		4		406
	J	455		− 56		20		3		422
	A	456		− 39		− 20		7		404
	S	457		− 21		− 40		4		400
	O	458		− 4		30		− 9		475
	N	459		12		20		− 5		486
	D	460		27		230		4		721
6	J	461		41		− 100		8		410
	F	462		54		− 150		− 3		363
	M	463		66		− 50		− 1		478
	A	464		77		20		0		561
	M	465		87		20		− 7		565
	J	466		96		20		− 7		575
	J	467		104		20		5		596
	A	468		111		− 20		2		561
	S	469		117		− 40		− 8		538
	O	470		122		30		− 9		613
	N	471		126		20		9		626
	D	472		129		230		0		831

TABLE 15.1 (Cont'd)

Year	Month	Trend	+	Cycle	+	Seasonal	+	Irregular	=	Actual series
7	J	473		131		−100		−2		502
	F	474		132		−150		−8		448
	M	475		133		−50		−4		554
	A	476		130		20		8		634
	M	477		125		20		7		629
	J	478		116		20		−5		609
	J	479		102		20		0		601
	A	480		82		−20		7		549
	S	481		57		−40		−2		496
	O	482		27		30		7		546
	N	483		−1		20		−8		494
	D	484		−27		230		3		690
8	J	485		−51		−100		8		342
	F	486		−73		−150		1		264
	M	487		−93		−50		−8		336
	A	488		−109		20		−4		395
	M	489		−121		20		−1		387
	J	490		−129		20		9		390
	J	491		−135		20		2		378
	A	492		−139		−20		−3		330
	S	493		−141		−40		4		316
	O	494		−142		30		−8		374
	N	495		−143		20		0		372
	D	496		−143		230		−5		578

that is,

$$T + C + S + I = A$$

EXERCISES

15.4   In the additive model, does the irregular term sum to zero over a period of 1 year, or 4 years, or 8 years, or only at unpredictable points by luck or accident? Determine the expected value and the variance of the sum of the irregular terms over a period of 1 year, given that each year the distrurbance is equally likely to be anywhere from −9 to +9.

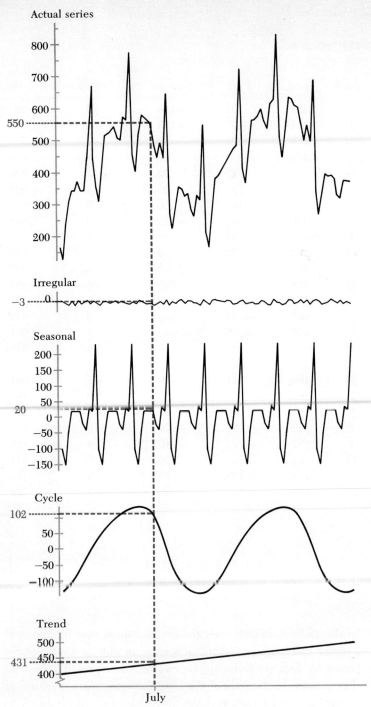

Figure 15.2 Components of a time series: the additive model.

15.5   Predict the value of the additive time series given in Table 15.1 in May of year 9. Spell out the assumptions which underlie this prediction. Would you care to make a prediction for May in year 99?

15.6   Does the distribution of the irregular term, equally likely to be anywhere from -9 to $+9$, seem reasonable? What would be an alternative possibility?

15.3   THE MULTIPLICATIVE MODEL

In a multiplicative time series a typical monthly value is given by

Actual value A = trend value $T \times$ cyclical factor C

$\qquad \times$ seasonal factor $S \times$ irregular factor I

Numerically, this might be

$$A = 348 \times 120\% \times 110\% \times 98\%$$

where   Trend = 348
  Cyclical factor = 120% = 1.20
  Seasonal factor = 110% = 1.10
  Irregular factor = 98% = .98

The factors are traditionally expressed as percentages. The actual value will be

$$348 \times 1.20 \times 1.10 \times .98 = 450.17$$

which is the result of trend and the other three factors combined.

In our example of the multiplicative model we have assumed that the trend increases by 2 percent each month. In January of the first year, the trend is 200, and 1 month later it will be $200 + .02(200) = 204$. In May of the fifth year the trend value has increased to nearly 560, and in the next month, June, the trend value will be $560 + .02(560) = 571.2$. In December of the eighth year the trend value has grown to 1,312. If the increase had been constant at 4 units per month—the size of the first change—instead of 2 percent per month, then the trend value after 8 years would equal only 584.

The cycle again is assumed to have a period of 4 years; the low is 80 percent, the high is 120 percent, and the average over one complete cycle is 100 percent. The seasonal has a low of 85 percent and a high of 113 percent. It averages out to 100 percent over one complete year. The irregular component is drawn from a normal distribution with a 68 percent probability of falling between 99 and 101 percent and a 95 percent probability of falling between 98 and 102 percent.

The complete numerical data are given in Table 15.2, and we here reproduce only 2 months—November and December of the third year.

Trend	Cycle, %	Seasonal, %	Irregular, %	Actual series
392.08	119	105	101.3	496.3
399.92	120	113	98.6	534.7

By November, the trend has reached a value of 392.08, so in December it will be $392.08 + .02(392.08) = 399.92$. In November the cycle is 119, the seasonal 105, and the irregular happens to be 101.3; the value of the series is therefore

$$392.08 \times 119\% \times 105\% \times 101.3\%$$
$$= 392.08 \times 1.19 \times 1.05 \times 1.013 = 496.3$$

Similarly, in December we have

$$399.92 \times 1.20 \times 1.13 \times .986 = 534.7$$

The results are graphically displayed in Figure 15.3.

Obviously, it is perfectly possible to have a time series with a *multiplicative seasonal* but an *additive irregular component*. If we assume that there is no cycle, such a series is then composed as

Hybrid
models

$$T \times S + I = A$$

In this special case the seasonal would be expressed *as a percentage of the trend* and the irregular component as a specific number. For example, the trend at a given period may be 300, the seasonal 103 percent, and the irregular component -8. The value in that period will be 301. All other mixtures of additive and multiplicative factors are conceivable, but usually one works with the straight additive or straight multiplicative model.

TABLE 15.2 EXAMPLE OF MULTIPLICATIVE TIME SERIES

Year	Month	Trend	Cycle, %	Seasonal, %	Irregular, %	Actual series
1	J	200	98	105	100.5	206.8
	F	204	95	107	100.1	207.6
	M	208.08	92	103	101.5	200.1
	A	212.24	90	101	101.0	194.9
	M	216.49	88	98	101.4	189.3
	J	220.81	86	95	100.9	182.0
	J	225.23	85	90	101.2	174.4
	A	229.73	84	85	98.5	161.6
	S	234.32	83	97	99.3	187.3
	O	239.01	82	101	101.3	200.5
	N	243.79	81	105	99.5	206.3
	D	248.67	80	113	98.6	221.7
2	J	253.64	81	105	99.0	213.6
	F	258.71	82	107	100.0	227.0
	M	263.88	83	103	101.4	228.7
	A	269.16	84	101	98.2	224.2
	M	274.54	85	98	99.9	228.5
	J	280.03	86	95	98.7	225.8
	J	285.63	88	90	101.0	228.5
	A	291.34	90	85	100.3	223.5
	S	297.17	92	97	98.2	260.4
	O	303.11	95	101	98.8	287.3
	N	309.17	98	105	100.7	319.1
	D	315.35	100	113	99.6	354.9
3	J	321.65	102	105	101.4	349.3
	F	328.08	105	107	100.2	369.3
	M	334.64	108	103	100.1	372.6
	A	341.33	110	101	102.3	387.9
	M	348.16	112	98	100.0	382.1
	J	355.12	114	95	98.9	380.4
	J	362.22	115	90	99.2	371.9
	A	369.46	116	85	99.6	362.8
	S	376.85	117	97	99.5	425.5
	O	384.39	118	101	100.3	459.5
	N	392.08	119	105	101.3	496.3
	D	399.92	120	113	98.6	534.7

TABLE 15.2 (Cont'd)

Year	Month	Trend	Cycle, %	Seasonal, %	Irregular, %	Actual series
4	J	407.91	119	105	100.1	510.2
	F	414.07	118	107	97.5	509.7
	M	424.39	117	103	99.6	509.4
	A	432.88	116	101	99.5	504.6
	M	441.54	115	98	99.4	494.6
	J	450.37	114	95	99.5	485.3
	J	459.37	112	90	99.0	458.4
	A	468.58	110	85	99.5	435.9
	S	477.95	108	97	100.7	504.2
	O	487.51	105	101	100.3	518.6
	N	497.26	102	105	101.7	541.6
	D	507.21	100	113	98.5	564.6
5	J	517.35	98	105	99.1	527.6
	F	527.70	95	107	98.8	530.0
	M	538.25	92	103	99.7	508.5
	A	549.01	90	101	99.6	497.1
	M	559.99	88	98	101.8	491.6
	J	571.19	86	95	100.5	469.0
	J	582.61	85	90	97.9	436.3
	A	594.26	84	85	98.0	415.8
	S	606.15	83	97	101.2	493.9
	O	618.27	82	101	98.5	504.4
	N	630.64	81	105	100.4	538.5
	D	643.25	80	113	99.7	580.0
6	J	656.12	81	105	100.2	559.1
	F	669.24	82	107	100.3	589.0
	M	682.62	83	103	100.6	587.1
	A	696.27	84	101	99.7	588.9
	M	710.20	85	98	97.9	579.2
	J	724.40	86	95	100.0	591.8
	J	738.89	88	90	98.4	575.8
	A	753.67	90	85	99.7	574.8
	S	768.74	92	97	99.9	685.3
	O	784.11	95	101	103.0	774.9
	N	799.79	98	105	101.2	832.9
	D	815.79	100	113	99.9	920.9

TABLE 15.2 (Cont'd)

Year	Month	Trend	Cycle, %	Seasonal, %	Irregular, %	Actual series
7	J	832.11	102	105	102.5	913.5
	F	848.75	105	107	99.5	948.8
	M	865.73	108	103	99.4	957.3
	A	883.04	110	101	101.3	993.8
	M	900.70	112	98	99.9	987.6
	J	918.71	114	95	99.4	989.0
	J	937.08	115	90	100.0	969.9
	A	955.82	116	85	99.8	940.6
	S	974.94	117	97	98.4	1,088.8
	O	994.44	118	101	100.4	1,189.9
	N	1,014.32	119	105	99.7	1,263.6
	D	1,034.62	120	113	101.4	1,422.6
8	J	1,055.31	119	105	99.1	1,306.7
	F	1,076.42	118	107	100.0	1,359.1
	M	1,097.95	117	103	99.1	1,311.2
	A	1,119.91	116	101	101.2	1,327.8
	M	1,142.31	115	98	98.6	1,269.4
	J	1,165.16	114	98	99.0	1,288.7
	J	1,188.46	112	90	100.7	1,206.4
	A	1,212.23	110	85	100.7	1,141.4
	S	1,236.47	108	97	98.4	1,274.6
	O	1,261.20	105	101	101.1	1,352.2
	N	1,286.42	102	105	101.2	1,394.3
	D	1,312.15	100	113	98.1	1,454.6

EXERCISES

15.7 Determine the expected value and the variance of the sum of the irregular factors over 1 year, if they are normally distributed with an expected value of 100 percent and a standard deviation of 1 percent.

15.8 Do a cyclical factor of 80 percent and a seasonal factor of 120 percent offset one another? If not, how should the factors relate to be offsetting?

15.9 Predict the value of the series in May of year 9.

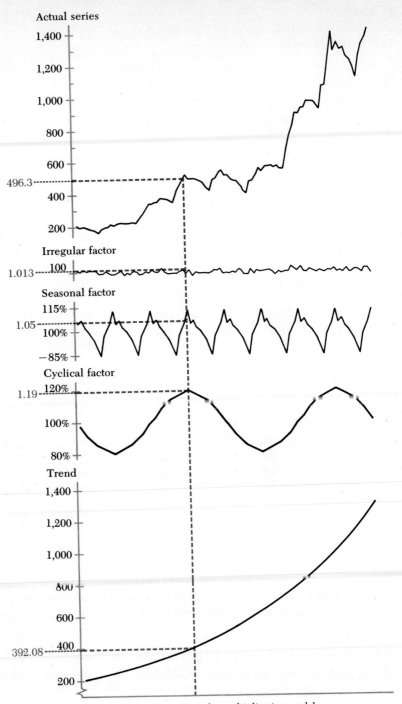

Figure 15.3 Components of a time series: the multiplicative model.

15.4 THE TREND

It is obviously easier, given the appropriate ingredients, to bake a cake than it is, given a cake, to reproduce the flour, butter, sugar, and eggs that went into making it. Similarly, it is obviously easier, given the trend, cycle, seasonal, and irregular components, to determine the values of the time series than it is, given the time series, to reproduce its individual components. In the kitchen the relatively easy baking of the cake is the issue; in our analysis the vastly more complicated untangling of the time series is the problem. A glance back at Figures 15.2 and 15.3 will show how a relatively complicated series is built up from very simple ingredients. However, the world gives us the series, and it is the components which we must find.

As a first step in analyzing the series we will isolate the trend. This can be done by finding an appropriate equation and fitting it by least squares. The values of the series are the dependent variable y, and the independent variable (time) x. We will give an example, assuming a series of 25 quarterly data—beginning the first quarter of some year and ending the same quarter 6 years later. The data are given in Table 15.3.

TABLE 15.3   25 QUARTERLY DATA ON A VARIABLE y

Year and quarter		Time period x	Actual value y	Year and quarter		Time period x	Actual value y
1	I	1	10	4	I	13	15
	II	2	13		II	14	19
	III	3	14		III	15	21
	IV	4	12		IV	16	18
2	I	5	12	5	I	17	15
	II	6	14		II	18	22
	III	7	15		III	19	23
	IV	8	13		IV	20	20
3	I	9	13	6	I	21	20
	II	10	15		II	22	21
	III	11	18		III	23	25
	IV	12	14		IV	24	21
				7	I	25	22

Straight-line
trend

  If we plot these data, measuring 25 equal steps in time along the
horizontal axis (as in Figure 15.4), we get a clear impression of a rising
trend. We will fit a straight-line trend to the actual values, which implies
constant increments over time. Hence we regress the y values on the x
values of Table 15.3. This is done in Table 15.4. The first four columns
of this table are routine. They enable us to determine the slope coefficient
$b = \frac{1}{2}$ and the constant term $a = 10\frac{1}{2}$. In the fifth column we have given
the trend line values, which are drawn in red in Figure 15.4.

$$y_t = a + bx = 10\frac{1}{2} + \frac{1}{2}x$$

Column 6 gives the computed deviations between the actual y values and
these trend values, which are also illustrated in Figure 15.4 for $x = 11$.
From the trend here we conclude that its value increases by $\frac{1}{2}$ unit each
quarter, hence 2 units per year, and, if the trend persists—a big *if* indeed—20 units a decade. Such a long-range extrapolation of the trend,
based on information covering only 7 years, is most dangerous. Over so
long a period many unforeseen events which will have a bearing on the
trend will occur. The trend line is drawn in Figure 15.4.

  From a series as short as this one it is difficult to perceive from the
plotted data whether the trend is one of constant increments or one of

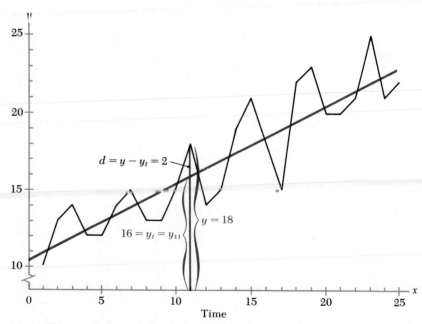

Figure 15.4 Straight-line trend with constant increment per period.

TABLE 15.4 DETERMINATION OF STRAIGHT-LINE TREND WITH CONSTANT INCREMENT PER PERIOD

(1) Actual value y	(2) Time x	(3) xy	(4) x^2	(5) Trend line $y_t = 10\frac{1}{2} + \frac{1}{2}x$	(6) Deviations $d = y - y_t$
10	1	10	1	11	-1
13	2	26	4	$11\frac{1}{2}$	$1\frac{1}{2}$
14	3	42	9	12	2
12	4	48	16	$12\frac{1}{2}$	$-\frac{1}{2}$
12	5	60	25	13	-1
14	6	84	36	$13\frac{1}{2}$	$\frac{1}{2}$
15	7	105	49	14	1
13	8	104	64	$14\frac{1}{2}$	$-1\frac{1}{2}$
13	9	117	81	15	-2
15	10	150	100	$15\frac{1}{2}$	$-\frac{1}{2}$
18	11	198	121	16	2
14	12	168	144	$16\frac{1}{2}$	$-2\frac{1}{2}$
15	13	195	169	17	-2
19	14	266	196	$17\frac{1}{2}$	$1\frac{1}{2}$
21	15	315	225	18	3
18	16	288	256	$18\frac{1}{2}$	$-\frac{1}{2}$
15	17	255	289	19	-4
22	18	396	324	$19\frac{1}{2}$	$2\frac{1}{2}$
23	19	437	361	20	3
20	20	400	400	$20\frac{1}{2}$	$-\frac{1}{2}$
20	21	420	441	21	-1
21	22	462	484	$21\frac{1}{2}$	$-\frac{1}{2}$
25	23	575	529	22	3
21	24	504	576	$22\frac{1}{2}$	$-1\frac{1}{2}$
22	25	550	625	23	-1
425	325	6,175	5,525		0

$\bar{y} = 17 \qquad \bar{x} = 13$

$$b = \frac{6,175 - 25 \times 13 \times 17}{5,525 - 25 \times 13^2} = \frac{6,175 - 5,525}{5,525 - 4,225} = \frac{650}{1,300} = \frac{1}{2}$$

$a = 17 - \frac{1}{2} \times 13 = 10\frac{1}{2}$

Trend line $= y_t = 10\frac{1}{2} + \frac{1}{2}t$

Constant
percentage
growth trend

constant percentage growth. A glance back at Figure 15.3 will show that over small ranges a constant percentage growth trend very closely resembles a straight line. In this example either trend line can be defended. Therefore we will now fit a curve of constant percentage growth through the data of Table 15.3.

To see how this can be done, reconsider the trend values in Table 15.2. We have for the initial trend value 200. For the next value we have 200×1.02, for the next $200(1.02)^2$, for the next $200(1.02)^3$, and so on. The equation of the function which relates these trend values y_t to the value of time x is, therefore,

$$y_t = 200(1.02)^x$$

where the initial value is 200, and the growth rate is 2 percent. For an arbitrary initial value s and an arbitrary growth rate r, we have

$$y_t = s \times r^x$$

We have to determine the s and r values in this equation from the y and x values in Table 15.3. We want to do this by least squares, so the sum of squared differences between the y values in Table 15.3 and the trend values $y_t = s \times r^x$ is minimized. Taking the logarithm of each side of the last equation and using the rules for manipulating expressions involving logarithms, we find

$$\log y_t = \log (s \times r^x) = \log s + \log (r^x) = \log s + x \log r$$

Hence

$$\log y_t = \log s + x \log r$$

This expression we recognize as a straight line, with x as the independent variable and $\log y_t$ as the dependent variable. The intercept $\log s$ and the slope $\log r$ are found by using the values of x and y in Table 15.3 and regressing $\log y$ on x.

The computations are given in Table 15.5. The first column gives the observations on y, and the second transforms these to the logarithms (base 10) of y. The third gives x. Log s and log r are determined by the standard least-squares procedure. We transform back to r and s, and find $r = 1.0306$ and $s = 11.17$. Therefore the trend values are given by

$$y_t = 11.17 \times 1.0306^x$$

The trend value increases by 3.06 percent each period. For example

TABLE 15.5 DETERMINATION OF STRAIGHT-LINE TREND WITH CONSTANT PERCENTAGE GROWTH PER PERIOD

(1)	(1')	(2)	(3)	(4)	(5)	(6)
Actual value		Time	$(1') \times (2)$		Trend line	Deviation
y	$\log y$	x	$x (\log y)$	x^2	y_t	$d = y_t - y$
10	1.0000	1	1.0000	1	11.5118	1.5118
13	1.1139	2	2.2278	4	11.8641	-1.1359
14	1.1461	3	3.4383	9	12.2271	-1.7729
12	1.0792	4	4.3168	16	12.6013	.6013
12	1.0792	5	5.3960	25	12.9869	.9869
14	1.1461	6	6.8766	36	13.3843	$-$ .6157
15	1.1761	7	8.2327	49	13.7939	-1.2061
13	1.1139	8	8.9112	64	14.2199	1.2199
13	1.1139	9	10.0251	81	14.6550	1.6550
15	1.1761	10	11.7610	100	15.1034	.1034
18	1.2553	11	13.8083	121	15.5656	-2.4344
14	1.1461	12	13.7532	144	16.0419	2.0419
15	1.1761	13	15.2893	169	16.5328	1.5328
19	1.2788	14	17.9032	196	17.0387	-1.9613
21	1.3222	15	19.8330	225	17.5601	-3.4399
18	1.2553	16	20.0848	256	18.0974	.0974
15	1.1761	17	19.9937	289	18.6512	3.6512
22	1.3424	18	24.1632	324	19.2219	-2.7781
23	1.3617	19	25.8723	361	19.8101	-3.1899
20	1.3010	20	26.0200	400	20.4163	.4163
20	1.3010	21	27.3210	441	21.0410	1.0410
21	1.3222	22	29.0884	484	21.6849	.6849
25	1.3979	23	32.1517	529	22.3485	-2.6515
21	1.3222	24	31.7328	576	23.0324	2.0324
22	1.3424	25	33.5600	625	23.7372	1.7372
	30.4452	325	412.7604	5,525		

$$\overline{\log y} = 1.2178 \qquad \bar{x} = 13$$

$$\log r = \frac{412.7604 - 25 \times 13 \times 1.2178}{5,525 - 25 \times 13^2} = \frac{412.7604 - 395.7876}{5,525 - 4,225}$$

$$= \frac{16.9728}{1,300} = .013056 \qquad r = 1.0306$$

$$\log s = 1.2178 - 13 \times .013056 = 1.0481 \qquad s = 11.17$$

$$\text{Trend line} = y_t = 11.17 \, (1.0306)^x$$

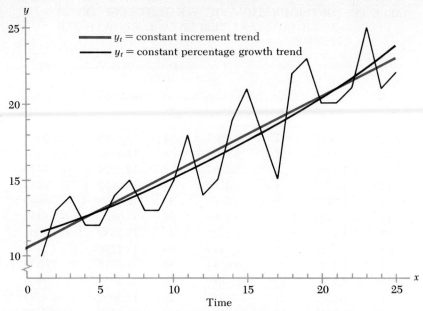

Figure 15.5 Straight-line trend with constant percentage growth per period.

**TABLE 15.6   DETERMINATION OF STRAIGHT-LINE TREND,
                        AFTER SUMMING QUARTERLY DATA TO YEARLY DATA**

(1) *Actual value during year* y	(2) *Year* x	(3) xy	(4) x^2	(5) *Trend line* $y_t = 39 + 8x$	(6) *Deviation* $d = y - y_t$
49	1	49	1	47	2
54	2	108	4	55	−1
60	3	180	9	63	−3
73	4	292	16	71	2
80	5	400	25	79	1
87	6	522	36	87	0
403	21	1,551	91		1

(not quite zero
due to rounding)

$$\bar{y} = 67\tfrac{1}{6} \qquad \bar{x} = 3\tfrac{1}{2}$$

$$b = \frac{1,551 - 6 \times 3\tfrac{1}{2} \times 67\tfrac{1}{6}}{91 - 6 \times 3\tfrac{1}{2} \times 3\tfrac{1}{2}} = \frac{1,551 - 1,410.5}{91 - 73.5} = \frac{140.5}{17.5} \approx 8$$

$$a = 67\tfrac{1}{6} - 8 \times 3\tfrac{1}{2} \approx 39$$

Trend line $= y_t = 39 + 8x$

$$y_5 = 11.17 \times 1.0306^5 = 12.987$$
$$y_6 = 11.17 \times 1.0306^6 = 13.384$$

We see that $y_6 = 1.0306y_5$. A decade hence (40 periods hence) the trend value will be 37.30, *if* the growth rate persists.

Figure 15.5 shows both trends. The fits to the known y values are about equally good. If we extrapolate the trends, their paths will diverge. Before long the constant percentage growth curve will rise much faster. For predictive purposes it makes a great difference which curve we use. Reason and judgment must guide the choice.

We will end this section by showing how we might save a lot of the computation by aggregating the *quarterly* data to *yearly* data, and then determining the trend. The total sales during the 6 years for which observations are available are 49, 54, 60, 73, 80, and 87, for an average of $67\frac{1}{6}$. The computations in Table 15.6 give the straight-line trend fit $y_t = 39 + 8x$. We conclude that the *yearly increment* is 8, which corresponds to a *quarterly increase* of $\frac{1}{2}$. This can be seen as follows:

Trend found by aggregating data

Quarter	Year 1	Year 2
I	10	12
II	$10\frac{1}{2}$	$12\frac{1}{2}$
III	11	13
IV	$11\frac{1}{2}$	$13\frac{1}{2}$
	43	51

A rise of $\frac{1}{2}$ per quarter will make each corresponding quarter 1 year later 2 larger, and since there are four quarters in a year, the yearly total will be 8 larger. In general, to get quarterly increases from yearly ones, divide by $4^2 = 16$, and to get monthly increases from yearly ones divide by $12^2 = 144$. This aggregating procedure to yearly data saves a lot of work, and will give substantially the same results.

EXERCISES

15.10   On January 1, 1970, a grandson receives $1,000. Each subsequent year on January 1 he receives $1,000 more than the previous year. A granddaughter receives $300 on January 1, 1970; she receives $300 more than the previous time every *half* year. At the end of the decade, which child has received more?

15.11   Fit a straight-line trend to the following quarterly data:

Period	Value	Period	Value	Period	Value	Period	Value
1	52	7	43	13	63	19	59
2	58	8	54	14	72	20	70
3	40	9	65	15	56	21	77
4	49	10	70	16	61	22	82
5	57	11	49	17	69	23	60
6	61	12	56	18	77	24	74

15.12   Fit a constant percentage growth trend through the data in Exercise 15.11.

15.5   THE SEASONAL

We will assume that the time series given in Table 15.3 contains, apart from a trend, only a seasonal and an irregular term. The data, as pictured in Figure 15.3, support the contention that there is little, if any, cyclical influence. In this section we will discuss several methods of isolating the seasonal.

All methods of determining seasonals are based on comparing actual figures y with trend figures y_t. Different answers are obtained because different trend figures can be used, as we saw in Section 15.4, *or* because different methods of comparison between y and y_t are used, *or* because slightly different correction and computation methods can be used. As a first example, let us determine the seasonal given the data of Table 15.3 and the trend line $y_t = 10\frac{1}{2} + \frac{1}{2}x$. In Table 15.4, Column 6, the deviations $d = y - y_t$ are determined. These are reproduced in Table 15.7.

Additive
seasonal

An *additive seasonal* is determined by using these absolute deviations $d = y - y_t$.

In the first quarter the actual values are consistently *below* the trend, by amounts 1, 1, 2, 2, 4, 1, and 1, for an average of $1\frac{5}{7}$. In the second quarter they are usually *above* the trend, an average of $\frac{5}{6}$. In the third quarter the values are an average $2\frac{2}{6}$ *above* the trend, and in the fourth, they are $1\frac{1}{6}$ *below* the trend. A straightforward approach is to consider the seasonal as $-1\frac{5}{7}$, $+\frac{5}{6}$, $+2\frac{2}{6}$, $-1\frac{1}{6}$.

These four values should sum to 0, but they sum to $\frac{2}{7}$. We correct by subtracting $\frac{1}{14}$ from each of the four values of the seasonal. The corrected seasonal values, in decimal form, are -1.786, .762, 2.262,

TABLE 15.7 **DEVIATIONS BETWEEN** y **AND** $y_t = 10\frac{1}{2} + \frac{1}{2}x$, **ORDERED BY QUARTER**

Year	Quarter			
	I	II	III	IV
1	-1	$1\frac{1}{2}$	2	$-\frac{1}{2}$
2	-1	$\frac{1}{2}$	1	$-1\frac{1}{2}$
3	-2	$-\frac{1}{2}$	2	$-2\frac{1}{2}$
4	-2	$1\frac{1}{2}$	3	$-\frac{1}{2}$
5	-4	$2\frac{1}{2}$	3	$-\frac{1}{2}$
6	-1	$-\frac{1}{2}$	3	$-1\frac{1}{2}$
7	-1			
	-12	5	14	-7
Average	$-\frac{12}{7} = -1\frac{5}{7}$	$\frac{5}{6}$	$\frac{14}{6} = 2\frac{2}{6}$	$-\frac{7}{6} = -1\frac{1}{6}$
Correction	$-\frac{1}{14}$	$-\frac{1}{14}$	$-\frac{1}{14}$	$-\frac{1}{14}$
Seasonal	-1.786	$.762$	2.262	-1.238 (sum 0)

-1.238. Using the additive model without cycle, we have

$$T + S + I = A$$

Since we now have the trend, the seasonal, and the actual value, the irregular component is implicitly determined. Table 15.8 gives the results.

There are two major variations on the computational procedure used for Table 15.7. One is to take the median rather than the average of the deviations. The argument is that the seasonal ought to be in some sense "normal" or "representative," and an average is often unduly influenced by high peaks or deep troughs, generated perhaps by abnormal situations—an extra cold winter, a political development, a major strike, and so on. As an alternative to taking the median, we sometimes delete the highest and lowest value(s) in each quarter, and compute the average of the remaining, presumably "normal" figures. They are corrected to sum to zero.

The analysis of time series is an art rather than a science, and the individuality of the series may make one method preferable to another in given, concrete, situations. In the specific example considered here, only the -4 in the first quarter of the fifth year stands out, and if there are special circumstances to explain it, this observation might be deleted from the analysis. However, we must proceed rather carefully whenever we look at the data first and only later decide to find reasons to omit

TABLE 15.8   DECOMPOSITION OF ACTUAL SERIES INTO TREND, SEASONAL, AND IRREGULAR, *ADDITIVE MODEL*

Trend†	Seasonal‡	Irregular§	Actual value‖
11	−1.786	.786	10
11.5	.762	.738	13
12	2.262	− .262	14
12.5	−1.238	.738	12
13	−1.786	.786	12
13.5	.762	− .262	14
14	2.262	−1.262	15
14.5	−1.238	− .262	13
15	−1.786	− .214	13
15.5	.762	−1.262	15
16	2.262	− .262	18
16.5	−1.238	−1.262	14
17	−1.786	− .214	15
17.5	.762	.738	19
18	2.262	.738	21
18.5	−1.238	.738	18
19	−1.786	−2.214	15
19.5	.762	1.738	22
20	2.262	.738	23
20.5	−1.238	.738	20
21	−1.786	.786	20
21.5	.762	−1.262	21
22	2.262	.738	25
22.5	−1.238	− .262	21
23	−1.786	.786	22

† Column 5, Table 15.4.
‡ Table 15.7.
§ (Actual − Trend − Seasonal).
‖ Given, see Table 15.3.

them. It is much more honest and safe to look at history *first* and omit, on that basis alone, observations strongly influenced by nonrepetitive factors such as war, strike, flood, etc. We should omit a priori rather than a posteriori.

Multiplicative
seasonal

We move on from the additive seasonal to discuss the *multiplicative seasonal*. To break the monotony, we will determine the multiplicative seasonal by using the trend which gives a constant percentage growth, as determined in Table 15.5. Again, we begin by comparing the actual figures with the trend figures, but in the multiplicative method we express the actual figures as a percentage of the trend. This has been done in Table 15.9.

As before, we proceed by averaging the percentage-of-trend figures for quarters I, II, III, and IV. As we see from Table 15.9, in the first quarter the actual values are 86.9, 92.4, . . . , 94.3 percent of the trend,

TABLE 15.9 DETERMINATION OF ACTUAL VALUE AS A PERCENTAGE OF TREND $y_t = 11.17 \ (1.0306)^x$

	(1)	(2)	(3)	(4)		(1)	(2)	(3)	(4)
				$\frac{A}{T} \times 100$					$\frac{A}{T} \times 100$
	Time x	Actual y	Trend y_t	"Percentage of trend"		Time x	Actual y	Trend y_t	"Percentage of trend"
I	1	10	11.51	86.9	I	13	15	16.53	90.7
II	2	13	11.86	109.6	II	14	19	17.04	111.5
III	3	14	12.23	114.5	III	15	21	17.56	119.6
IV	4	12	12.60	95.2	IV	16	18	18.10	99.4
I	5	12	12.99	92.4	I	17	15	18.65	80.4
II	6	14	13.38	104.6	II	18	22	19.22	114.5
III	7	15	13.79	108.8	III	19	23	19.81	116.1
IV	8	13	14.22	91.4	IV	20	20	20.42	97.9
I	9	13	14.65	88.7	I	21	20	21.04	95.1
II	10	15	15.10	99.3	II	22	21	21.68	96.9
III	11	18	15.57	115.6	III	23	25	22.35	111.9
IV	12	14	16.04	87.3	IV	24	21	23.03	91.2
					I	25	22	23.34	94.3

Seasonal I: $\dfrac{86.9 + 92.4 + 88.7 + 90.7 + 80.4 + 95.1 + 94.3}{7} = 89.8$

Seasonal II: $\dfrac{109.6 + 104.6 + 99.3 + 111.5 + 114.5 + 96.9}{6} = 106.1$

Seasonal III: $\dfrac{114.5 + 108.8 + 115.6 + 119.6 + 116.1 + 111.9}{6} = 114.4$

Seasonal IV: $\dfrac{95.2 + 91.4 + 87.3 + 99.4 + 97.9 + 91.2}{6} = \dfrac{93.7}{404.0}$

We force the sum to be 400 by subtracting 1 from each. The resulting seasonal factors are 88.8, 105.1, 113.4, and 92.7.

for an average of 89.8 percent. The second quarter gives an average of 106.1 percent, which is obtained by adding the percentages 109.6, 104.6, ..., 96.9 and dividing by 6. For the third quarter, we find 114.4 percent, and for the last, 93.7 percent. Roughly the seasonal is, therefore, 89.8, 106.1, 114.4, and 93.7 percent of the trend. These sum to 404.0. They should sum to 400, so they average to 100. Subtracting 1 from each gives 88.8, 105.1, 113.4, and 92.7 percent. The trend and seasonal are now

TABLE 15.10   DECOMPOSITION OF ACTUAL SERIES INTO
              TREND, SEASONAL, AND IRREGULAR,
              MULTIPLICATIVE MODEL

Trend†	Seasonal‡	Irregular§	Actual values¶
11.51	88.8	97.8	10
11.86	105.1	104.3	13
12.23	113.4	100.9	14
12.60	92.7	102.7	12
12.99	88.8	104.0	12
13.38	105.1	99.6	14
13.79	113.4	95.9	15
14.22	92.7	98.6	13
14.65	88.8	100.0	13
15.10	105.1	94.5	15
15.57	113.4	101.9	18
16.04	92.7	94.1	14
16.53	88.8	102.2	15
17.04	105.1	106.1	19
17.56	113.4	105.5	21
18.10	92.7	107.3	18
18.65	88.8	90.6	15
19.22	105.1	108.9	22
19.81	113.4	102.4	23
20.42	92.7	105.6	20
21.04	88.8	107.0	20
21.68	105.1	92.2	21
22.35	113.4	98.6	25
23.03	92.7	98.4	21
23.74	88.8	104.4	22

† Column 5, Table 15.5.
‡ Table 15.9.
§ Actual ÷ (Trend × Seasonal).
¶ Given, see Table 15.3.

known, and in the absence of the cycle we can determine

$$T \times S \times I = A$$

The results are given in Table 15.10.

As in the case of an additive model, the median value is occasionally used in place of the average. Alternatively, we omit the highest and lowest observations for each quarter, and average the remaining ones. Using the data of Table 15.9, we would omit for the first quarter the values 80.4 and 95.1 to get

$$\frac{86.9 + 92.4 + 88.7 + 90.7 + 94.3}{5} = 90.6$$

For the second, third, and fourth quarter we find 106.2, 114.5, and 93.9. Corrected to sum to 400 these are 89.3, 104.9, 113.2, and 92.6. In this example the differences are minute.

Once the seasonal has been found, the actual values can be *deseasonalized,* or adjusted for seasonal variation. For example, the actual value in the first quarter is 10. We know that in the first quarter the actual values are 88.8 percent of what they would have been without seasonal variation. Therefore, in the first quarter, the deseasonalized value is $10/.888 = 11.3$, In the second quarter, the actual value is 13. The corresponding deseasonalized value is, therefore, $13/1.051 = 12.4$. Table 15.11 gives the deseasonalized series. The fluctuations that remain in this series are the result of the trend, a possible cyclical factor, and irregular fluctuations. In practice, most of the time series reported for quarters or months in government publications are deseasonalized.

Deseasonalized series

Exhibit 4 of Appendix A can at this stage be read with profit.

EXERCISES

15.13   Consider the constant percentage growth trend found in Exercise 15.12, and using the actual figures of Exercise 15.11, determine an additive seasonal.

15.14   Consider the straight-line trend found in Exercise 15.11, and determine:
(*a*) Additive seasonal
(*b*) Multiplicative seasonal

15.15   Deseasonalize the values in Exercise 15.11 using the additive seasonal found in Exercise 15.14.

TABLE 15.11   DESEASONALIZED SERIES

(1)	(2)	(3)
		Deseasonalized series
Actual values	*Seasonal*	$(1) \times \dfrac{100}{(2)}$
10	88.8	11.26
13	105.1	12.37
14	113.4	12.35
12	92.7	12.94
12	88.8	13.51
14	105.1	13.32
15	113.4	13.23
13	92.7	14.02
13	88.8	14.64
15	105.1	14.27
18	113.4	15.87
14	92.7	15.10
15	88.8	16.89
19	105.1	18.08
21	113.4	18.52
18	92.7	19.42
15	88.8	16.89
22	105.1	20.93
23	113.4	20.28
20	92.7	21.57
20	88.8	22.52
21	105.1	19.98
25	113.4	22.05
21	92.7	22.65
22	88.8	24.77

15.6   MOVING AVERAGES—THE SEASONAL AND THE CYCLICAL

In the previous two sections we analyzed 25 quarterly values. We first determined a trend, in two alternative ways—straight line and constant percentage. We next computed the seasonal, also in two alternative ways—additive and multiplicative. In both the additive and multiplicative methods we needed the trend figures before the seasonal could be determined, as is evident from Tables 15.7 and 15.9.

Another procedure exists that can be used to determine the seasonal, that is, the method of *moving averages*. In this method we do not need previously computed trends. The method is also useful for isolating a cyclical component, if one is present. Table 15.12 shows the initial

Moving average

TABLE 15.12 FIRST STEPS TO DETERMINE MULTIPLICATIVE SEASONAL WITH MOVING AVERAGES

(1) Year and quarter	(2) Actual value	(3) Four-period moving average	(4) Centered	(5) $\frac{(2)}{(4)} \times 100$
1 I	10			
II	13			
		$12\frac{1}{4}$		
III	14		$12\frac{1}{2}$	112.0
		$12\frac{3}{4}$		
IV	12		$12\frac{7}{8}$	93.2
		13		
2 I	12		$13\frac{1}{8}$	91.4
		$13\frac{1}{4}$		
II	14		$13\frac{3}{8}$	104.7
		$13\frac{1}{2}$		
III	15		$13\frac{5}{8}$	110.1
		$13\frac{3}{4}$		
IV	13		$13\frac{7}{8}$	93.7
		14		
3 I	13		$14\frac{3}{8}$	90.4
		$14\frac{3}{4}$		
II	15		$14\frac{7}{8}$	106.2
		15		
III	18		$15\frac{1}{4}$	118.0
		$15\frac{1}{2}$		
IV	14		16	87.5
		$16\frac{1}{2}$		
4 I	15		$16\frac{7}{8}$	88.9
		$17\frac{1}{4}$		
II	19		$17\frac{3}{4}$	107.0
		$18\frac{1}{4}$		
III	21		$18\frac{1}{4}$	115.1
		$18\frac{1}{4}$		
IV	18		$18\frac{5}{8}$	96.6
		19		
5 I	15		$19\frac{1}{4}$	77.9
		$19\frac{1}{2}$		
II	22		$19\frac{3}{4}$	111.4
		20		
III	23		$20\frac{5}{8}$	111.5
		$21\frac{1}{4}$		
IV	20		$21\frac{1}{8}$	94.7
		21		
6 I	20		$21\frac{1}{4}$	94.1
		$21\frac{1}{2}$		
II	21		$21\frac{5}{8}$	97.1
		$21\frac{3}{4}$		
III	25		22	113.6
		$22\frac{1}{4}$		
IV	21			
7 I	22			

calculations required to determine the multiplicative seasonal by the moving average procedure.

The first column of Table 15.12 gives the time period, and the second column gives the actual values. The third column shows the four-period moving averages. We use four periods, since that covers one year. For monthly figures, we would use a 12-period moving average. The sum of the first four quarters is $10 + 13 + 14 + 12 = 49$, and the average is $\frac{49}{4} = 12\frac{1}{4}$. Next, delete the first observation (10) and add the fifth (12). This gives the sum of the last three quarters of the first year and the first quarter of the second, 51. The average is $\frac{51}{4} = 12\frac{3}{4}$. The next term in the series of moving averages is 13, that is, $14 + 12 + 12 + 14$ divided by 4.

The values so obtained are written down halfway between the *first* and the *last* figures on which the average is based. The $17\frac{1}{4}$ between the first and second quarter of year 4 is the average of 14, 15, 19, and 21. Because there is an even number of quarters, these numbers seem to float between the lines. The same would be true of monthly figures, since 12 is also an even number. The remedy is to center them by taking the average of two successive numbers in the series of moving averages. This has been done in Column 4. Finally, in Column 5, the actual values in Column 2 are expressed as a percentage of the centered moving averages in Column 4.

The first value in the fifth column, 112, means that in the third quarter of year 1 the actual value was 112 percent of the four-period moving average. The values in successive third quarters are 112, 110.1, 118, 115.1, 111.5, and 113.6. The unadjusted seasonal is taken to be the average of these values, or 113.4. In Table 15.13, the computations have been systematically recorded. The analogies between Tables 15.7, 15.9, and 15.13 are obvious. The unadjusted seasonals are 88.5, 105.3, 113.4, and 93.1. They sum to 400.3. We adjust the sum to 400 by subtracting .1 from the three highest. The adjusted seasonals are then 88.5, 105.2, 113.3, and 93.0. In the previous section we found by a different method adjusted multiplicative seasonals of 88.8, 105.1, 113.4, and 92.7. The differences are insignificant.

In Figure 15.6 we have plotted the actual observations and the four-period moving averages, as well as the trends—constant amounts and constant percentages—determined by the least-squares method of Section 15.4. Such a picture is quite suggestive for the purpose of spotting a cycle. Whenever the moving average is alternately below and above the trend line for long successive stretches, a cycle is suggested. In this case a small cyclical effect may be at work, with the downswing in the years 2 and

**TABLE 15.13 DETERMINATION OF MULTIPLICATIVE
SEASONAL FROM TABLE 15.12, COLUMN 5**

Year	Quarter			
	I	*II*	*III*	*IV*
1			112.0	93.2
2	91.4	104.7	110.1	93.7
3	90.4	106.2	118.0	87.5
4	88.9	107.0	115.1	96.6
5	77.9	111.4	111.5	94.7
6	94.1	97.1	113.6	
7				
Average	88.5	105.3	113.4	93.1 (sum 400.3)
Corrected	88.5	105.2	113.3	93.0 (sum 400)

3 and the upswing in years 4 and 5. Knowledge of the economy beyond the information implicit in the time series may be useful to verify our suspicions.

In view of the unique character of a cycle, its numerical specification is more arbitrary than that of a seasonal. As an example, let us try to determine a reasonable multiplicative cycle, given a straight-line trend.

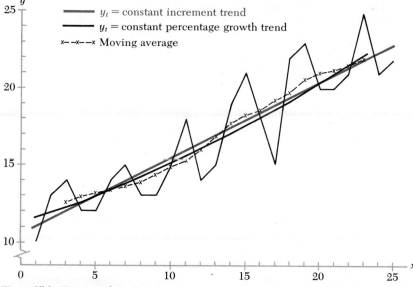

Figure 15.6 Four-period moving average.

We use the moving average values together with the trend. The four-period moving average represents essentially trend and cyclical factors. By calculating it for four periods, we removed seasonal variation, which is, by its nature, exactly four periods in length. The irregular component, which is small in one period and averages 0, will be insignificant in the moving average.

The first step in determining the cycle is to compare each trend value with the corresponding four-period moving average by expressing the moving average as a percentage of the trend. For the trend we again use $y_t = 10\frac{1}{2} + \frac{1}{2}x$ derived above in Table 15.4. We begin with the third period, where the trend equals $10\frac{1}{2} + \frac{1}{2} \times 3 = 12$, because the moving average has only observations from the third period on. The moving averages are taken from Table 15.12. Their comparison is made in Table 15.14.

The cyclical pattern can now be gauged "by eye," keeping the following three criteria in mind: (1) it should be reasonably close to the actual pattern; (2) it should smooth over evident irregularities; and (3) it should average to 100 over one complete cycle. In this example the cycle might be given the values 104, 102, 100, 99, 98, 97, 96, 96, 96, 97, 99, 101, 102, 102, 103, 104, 104, 103, 102, 101, 100, or so. We

TABLE 15.14   DETERMINATION OF CYCLE BY COMPARING TREND WITH MOVING AVERAGES

(1) Time	(2) Trend	(3) Moving average	(4) $\frac{(3)}{(2)} \times 100$	(1) Time	(2) Trend	(3) Moving average	(4) $\frac{(3)}{(2)} \times 100$
1	·			13	17	$16\frac{7}{8}$	99.3
2	·			14	$17\frac{1}{2}$	$17\frac{3}{4}$	101.4
3	12	$12\frac{1}{2}$	104.2	15	18	$18\frac{1}{4}$	101.4
4	$12\frac{1}{2}$	$12\frac{7}{8}$	103.0	16	$18\frac{1}{2}$	$18\frac{5}{8}$	100.7
5	13	$13\frac{1}{8}$	101.0	17	19	$19\frac{1}{4}$	101.3
6	$13\frac{1}{2}$	$13\frac{3}{8}$	99.1	18	$19\frac{1}{2}$	$19\frac{3}{4}$	101.3
7	14	$13\frac{5}{8}$	97.3	19	20	$20\frac{5}{8}$	103.1
8	$14\frac{1}{2}$	$13\frac{7}{8}$	95.7	20	$20\frac{1}{2}$	$21\frac{1}{8}$	103.0
9	15	$14\frac{3}{8}$	95.8	21	21	$21\frac{1}{4}$	101.2
10	$15\frac{1}{2}$	$14\frac{7}{8}$	96.0	22	$21\frac{1}{2}$	$21\frac{5}{8}$	100.6
11	16	$15\frac{1}{4}$	95.3	23	22	22	100
12	$16\frac{1}{2}$	16	97.0	24	·		
				25	·		

conclude that if there is a cycle, it is a mild one, and the period is about 4 years.

The primary goal of time series analysis is to help predict the future. The trend and the seasonal are very useful and moderately reliable instruments for this purpose. The cycle is too irregular and erratic to be successfully analyzed by these simple mathematical methods. For this reason we have given it a subordinate position in the theoretical analysis. In practice, the cycle is of great importance in short-run business forecasting. The forecasting problem is approached with a range of techniques varying from highly sophisticated, computer-based analysis to very personalized, subjective analysis.

EXERCISES

15.16   Determine the four-period moving average of the values in Exercise 15.11.

15.17   Using the constant percentage growth trend found in Exercise 15.12, determine the possibly present cyclical influence.

15.7   FORECASTING WITH TIME SERIES

An international airline must make a short-term, 12 to 18 months, forecast of demand to determine the number of flights to be scheduled. It must make a long-term forecast, 3 to 10 years, to program the purchase of new aircraft. A thorough analysis of this problem would include, but not be limited to, an analysis of the historical data on the number of international air travelers. For short-term forecasts all four factors need to be analyzed and included in the forecasts. For a long-term forecast the trend is the primary concern. The number of passengers, in thousands (quarterly, 1949–1960), are given in Table 15.15 and illustrated in Figure 15.7.

A pronounced seasonal effect and a strong upward trend are evident in Figure 15.7. To form a better idea about the nature of the trend, we sum the data to yearly totals and plot them. The results are shown in Table 15.16 and Figure 15.8.

There appears to be a tendency for the yearly increase to grow as time proceeds, and so we opt for a trend with constant percentage growth, which we fit to the points in Figure 15.8. The necessary computations are reproduced in Table 15.17, which is similar to Table 15.5. We find

TABLE 15.15   NUMBER OF INTERNATIONAL AIR TRAVELERS, THOUSANDS PER QUARTER

Year and quarter	Value y	Year and quarter	Value y	Year and quarter	Value y
1 I	362	5 I	628	9 I	972
II	385	II	707	II	1,125
III	432	III	773	III	1,336
IV	341	IV	592	IV	988
2 I	382	6 I	636	10 I	1,020
II	409	II	725	II	1,146
III	498	III	854	III	1,400
IV	387	IV	661	IV	1,006
3 I	473	7 I	742	11 I	1,108
II	513	II	854	II	1,288
III	582	III	1,023	III	1,570
IV	474	IV	789	IV	1,174
4 I	544	8 I	878	12 I	1,227
II	582	II	1,005	II	1,468
III	681	III	1,173	III	1,736
IV	557	IV	883	IV	1,283

$r = 1.129$ and $s = 1,404$. The conclusion is that the total grows by nearly 13 percent each year.

A yearly increase of 12.9 percent corresponds quite closely to a quarterly increase of 3.08 percent. The yearly value 1,585, obtained for the first year with the trend fitted through yearly data, corresponds to a constant term of about 367 when the fit is made to quarterly data. The trend line expressed in quarterly terms is

$$y_t = 367 \times 1.0308^x$$

For the first 12 years x takes the values 1 through 48.

The next problem is to determine the seasonal. This will be done with moving averages, which will also help us spot cycle effects. The moving average is computed in Table 15.18 and illustrated in Figure 15.7. Table 15.19 is derived from Column 5 of Table 15.18 without difficulty. The unadjusted seasonal is 93.3, 102.4, 116.6, 87.2. The adjusted seasonal is 93.4, 102.5, 116.8, and 87.3. Notice, however, that during the

Number of
travelers

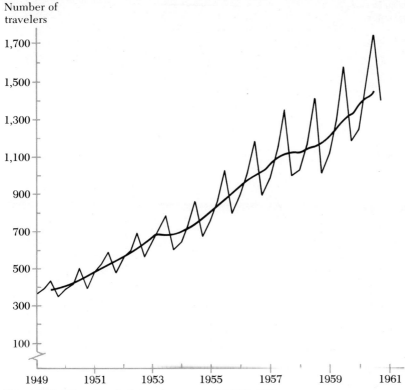

Figure 15.7 International air travelers, quarterly, 1949–1960.

last 4 years the summer peak and the winter trough are more pronounced, and we think this may persist. The values 90.4, 102.3, 120.8, and 87.0 are the unadjusted seasonal values *as computed from the last four observations* in each quarter only. Adjusted, these are 90.3, 102.2, 120.6, and 86.9. For predictive purposes, this seasonal may be the more relevant.

To form an idea about the cyclical effect, we refer back to Figure

**TABLE 15.16   NUMBER OF INTERNATIONAL AIR TRAVELERS,
THOUSANDS PER YEAR**

Year	Value	Year	Value	Year	Value
1	1,520	5	2,700	9	4,421
2	1,676	6	2,876	10	4,572
3	2,042	7	3,408	11	5,140
4	2,364	8	3,939	12	5,714

Number of
travelers

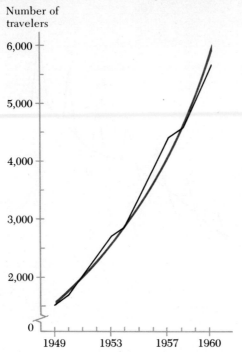

Figure 15.8 Trend of number of international air
travelers annually, 1949–1960.

15.8, in which we compare the actual yearly figures with the trend. No
clear cyclical influence is evident. For predictive purposes, the cycle can
be disregarded. Our prediction for the first quarter of year 13, the 49th
quarter, will be given by

$$90.3 \text{ percent of } 367 \times 103.08^{49} = 1,469$$

The trend is 367×103.08^{49}, and the seasonal is 90.5 percent in the
first quarter of a year. For the other quarters of year 13 the values are

$$102.2 \text{ percent of } 367 \times 103.08^{50} = 1,712$$
$$120.6 \text{ percent of } 367 \times 103.08^{51} = 2,071$$
$$86.9 \text{ percent of } 367 \times 103.08^{52} = 1,552$$

The total sales during year 13 are predicted at 6,804. These are point
estimates for quarterly sales. We prefer interval estimates. As we see from
Table 15.19, the entries in each column, for each quarter, fluctuate. The
stable factor in each column is the seasonal, which we express numerically

as 90.3, 102.2, 120.6, and 86.9. The fluctuation in a column is due to the irregular and cyclical factors, which are not yet allowed for in our estimates. After examining the figures in Table 15.19, we conclude that an allowance of 2 percent for cyclical and irregular should be made. We thus get interval estimates as follows:

First period: $1,469 \pm .02(1469) = 1,440$ to $1,498$
Second period: $1,712 \pm .02(1712) = 1,678$ to $1,746$
Third period: $2,071 \pm .02(2071) = 2,030$ to $2,112$
Fourth period: $1,552 \pm .02(1552) = 1,521$ to $1,583$

TABLE 15.17 DETERMINATION OF CONSTANT PERCENTAGE GROWTH TREND TO YEARLY DATA OF INTERNATIONAL AIR TRAVELERS ($\log y_t = \log s + x \log r$)

(1) Actual value y	(1') $\log y$	(2) Time x	(3) $(1') \times (2)$ $x(\log y)$	(4) x^2
1,520	3.1818	1	3.1818	1
1,676	3.2243	2	6.4486	4
2,042	3.3101	3	9.9303	9
2,364	3.3737	4	13.4948	16
2,700	3.4314	5	17.1570	25
2,876	3.4588	6	20.7528	36
3,408	3.5325	7	24.7275	49
3,939	3.5954	8	28.7632	64
4,421	3.6455	9	32.8095	81
4,572	3.6601	10	36.6010	100
5,140	3.7110	11	40.8210	121
5,714	3.7569	12	45.0828	144
	41.8815	78	279.7703	650

$$\overline{\log y} = 3.4901 \qquad \bar{x} = 6\tfrac{1}{2}$$

$$\log r = \frac{279.7703 - 12 \times 6\tfrac{1}{2} \times 3.4901}{650 - 12 \times 6\tfrac{1}{2} \times 6\tfrac{1}{2}} = \frac{279.7703 - 272.2278}{650 - 507}$$

$$= \frac{7.5425}{143} = .05274 \qquad r = 1.129$$

$\log s = 3.4901 - 6\tfrac{1}{2} \times .05274 = 3.1473 \qquad s = 1,404$
Trend line $= y_t = 1,404(1.129)^x$, or $\log y_t = 3.1473 + .05274x$

**TABLE 15.18   FIRST STEPS TO DETERMINE MULTIPLICATIVE
SEASONAL WITH MOVING AVERAGES**

(1)	(2)	(3)	(4)	(5)
Year and quarter	Value	Moving average	Centered	$\dfrac{(2)}{(4)} \times 100$
1 I	362			
II	385			
		380		
III	432		$382\frac{1}{2}$	112.9
		385		
IV	341		388	87.9
		391		
2 I	382		$399\frac{1}{4}$	95.7
		$407\frac{1}{2}$		
II	409		$413\frac{1}{4}$	99.0
		419		
III	498		$430\frac{3}{4}$	115.7
		$441\frac{3}{4}$		
IV	387		$454\frac{3}{4}$	85.1
		$467\frac{3}{4}$		
3 I	473		$478\frac{1}{4}$	98.9
		$488\frac{3}{4}$		
II	513		$499\frac{5}{8}$	102.7
		$510\frac{1}{2}$		
III	582		$519\frac{3}{8}$	112.1
		$528\frac{1}{4}$		
IV	474		$536\frac{7}{8}$	88.3
		$545\frac{1}{2}$		
4 I	544		$557\frac{7}{8}$	97.5
		$570\frac{1}{4}$		
II	582		$580\frac{5}{8}$	100.1
		591		
III	681		$601\frac{1}{2}$	113.2
		612		
IV	557		$627\frac{5}{8}$	88.7
		$643\frac{1}{4}$		
5 I	628		$654\frac{3}{4}$	95.9
		$666\frac{1}{4}$		
II	707		$670\frac{5}{8}$	105.4
		675		
III	773		$674\frac{7}{8}$	114.5
		$674\frac{3}{4}$		
IV	592		677	87.4
		$679\frac{1}{4}$		
6 I	627		$689\frac{3}{8}$	91.0
		$699\frac{1}{2}$		
II	725		$708\frac{1}{8}$	102.4
		$716\frac{3}{4}$		
III	854		$731\frac{1}{4}$	116.8
		$745\frac{1}{2}$		
IV	661		$761\frac{5}{8}$	86.8
		$777\frac{3}{4}$		
7 I	742		$798\frac{7}{8}$	92.9
		820		
II	854		836	102.2
		852		
III	1,023		869	117.7
		886		
IV	789		$904\frac{7}{8}$	87.2
		$923\frac{3}{4}$		

TABLE 15.18 (Cont'd)

(1) Year and quarter		(2) Value	(3) Moving average	(4) Centered	(5) $\frac{(2)}{(4)} \times 100$
8	I	878		$942\frac{1}{2}$	93.2
			$961\frac{1}{4}$		
	II	1,005		973	103.3
			$984\frac{3}{4}$		
	III	1,173		$996\frac{1}{2}$	117.7
			$1,008\frac{1}{4}$		
	IV	883		$1,023\frac{1}{4}$	86.3
			$1,038\frac{1}{4}$		
9	I	972		$1,058\frac{5}{8}$	91.8
			1,079		
	II	1,125		$1,092\frac{1}{8}$	103.0
			$1,105\frac{1}{4}$		
	III	1,336		$1,111\frac{1}{4}$	120.2
			$1,117\frac{1}{4}$		
	IV	988		$1,119\frac{7}{8}$	88.2
			$1,122\frac{1}{2}$		
10	I	1,020		$1,130\frac{1}{2}$	90.2
			$1,138\frac{1}{2}$		
	II	1,146		$1,140\frac{3}{4}$	100.5
			1,143		
	III	1,400		1,154	121.3
			1,165		
	IV	1,006		$1,182\frac{3}{4}$	85.1
			$1,200\frac{1}{2}$		
11	I	1,108		$1,221\frac{3}{4}$	90.7
			1,243		
	II	1,288		1,264	101.9
			1,285		
	III	1,570		$1,299\frac{7}{8}$	120.8
			$1,314\frac{3}{4}$		
	IV	1,174		$1,337\frac{1}{4}$	87.8
			$1,359\frac{3}{4}$		
12	I	1,227		$1,380\frac{1}{2}$	88.9
			$1,401\frac{1}{4}$		
	II	1,468		$1,414\frac{7}{8}$	103.8
			$1,428\frac{1}{2}$		
	III	1,736			
	IV	1,283			

In fact, the values were reconstructed by the authors as 1,420, 1,650, 2,050, and 1,560. This reconstruction was needed because Hawaii and Alaska, previously counted as international, were considered internal as of 1961. Changes in measurement or definition present a recurring problem when working with time series data.

For a long-run prediction we extrapolate the trend. From Table 15.17 we see that the trend equation for annual values is

$$y_t = 1,404(1.129)^x$$

where x takes the values 1 through 12 for 1949 to 1960. In 1970, when x is 22,

$$y_t = 1,404(1.129)^{22} = 20,264$$

TABLE 15.19   DETERMINATION OF MULTIPLICATIVE SEASONAL FROM TABLE 15.18, COLUMN 5

Year	Quarter			
	I	II	III	IV
1			112.9	87.9
2	95.7	99.0	115.7	85.1
3	98.9	102.7	112.1	88.3
4	97.5	102.1	113.2	88.7
5	95.9	105.4	114.5	87.4
6	91.0	102.4	116.8	86.8
7	92.9	102.2	117.7	87.2
8	93.2	103.3	117.7	86.3
9	91.8	103.0	120.2	88.2
10	90.2	100.5	121.3	85.1
11	90.7	101.9	120.8	87.8
12	88.9	103.8		
Average	93.3	102.4	116.6	87.2
Average based on years 9–12	90.4	102.3	120.8	87.0 (sum 400.5)
Corrected	90.3	102.2	120.6	86.9 (sum 400)

In fact, the value was around 21,600. During the decade the arrival of jet planes and popularity of charters allowed for price decreases, which made the long-run estimate too low.

This prompts us to end with a word of caution. Prediction of the future is a dangerous pastime. Prediction based only on a single historical series is extremely dangerous. Other variables, related to the one in question, ought to be taken explicitly into account. In this instance, what happened to the price of international air travel? To the prices of competing modes of travel? An analysis incorporating these variables is called an *econometric analysis,* and when the chips are down, and the question is whether to order 10 or 20 new airplanes, such an econometric analysis is called for. Today, forecasting is frequently done with econometric methods rather than time series analysis. An econometric model permits us to incorporate in a forecast allowances for anticipated changes in quantitative variables such as air fares. Even so, the results are often unreliable because there are many factors of a qualitative and unpredictable nature influencing the future. In our example these include the impact of supersonic transports and the widespread use of charters. Because such innovations are always a possibility, judgment must temper the use of any forecast.

Answers to Exercises

15.1   At the end of 1960, the population in city I is p. At the end of 1961 it is $p + a$. At the end of 1962 it is $p + a + a = p + 2a$. At the end of 1969 it is $p + 9a$. At the end of 1960, the population in city II is p. At the end of 1961 it is $p[(a + p)/p]$. At the end of 1962 it is

$$\left[p \left(\frac{a + p}{p} \right) \right] \left(\frac{a + p}{p} \right) = p \left(\frac{a + p}{p} \right)^2$$

At the end of 1969 it is

$$p \left(\frac{a + p}{p} \right)^9 = p \left(1 + \frac{a}{p} \right)^9 = p \left(1 + 9 \frac{a}{p} + 36 \frac{a^2}{p^2} + \cdots \right)$$

$$= p + 9a + 36 \frac{a^2}{p} + \cdots$$

which is definitely larger than $p + 9a$. Numerically, if $p = 100{,}000$ and $p + a = 105{,}000$, the population in city I will be 145,000 at the end of 1969, and in city II it will be 155,133.

15.2   Production is a flow variable (60 units in 1 week). Inventory is a stock variable (the inventory *now* is, for example, 27 units; the time dimension does not enter). Price is a stock variable (27 cents per dozen *now*, for example; time is irrelevant). Profit is a flow variable ($115,430 in 1 year).

15.3   Profit measurement is difficult. Judgment must be used in deciding: How to depreciate? What reserves should be formed in view of the risks? It is even more difficult to split up profits into profits in 1972, profits in 1973, etc. Inevitably, some arbitrary decisions will have to be made. If different banks use different accounting procedures or different ways of allocating profits to time periods, comparisons are dangerous.

15.4   The irregular terms will only add to zero at unpredictable times by luck or accident. In Table 15.1, the irregular term is, by accident, exactly zero at the end of year 1. At the end of April in year 5 the sum of all irregular terms is again precisely zero. The expected value of each irregular term is zero, and the expected value of the sum of 12 irregular terms is therefore also zero. The variance is equal to $\frac{1}{19}(-9)^2 + \frac{1}{19}(-8)^2 + \cdots + \frac{1}{19}(9)^2 = 30$. Since all irregular terms are independent, the variance of the sum of 12 irregular terms is the sum of the variances; hence it equals $12 \times 30 = 360$. The standard deviation is $\sqrt{360} = 19$. We would expect the sum of the irregulars over any year to be between -38 and $+38$. In Table 15.1 they were 0, -2, 4, 23, -11, 3, -5.

15.5   *If* the trend continues to move upward at 1 per period and *if* the seasonal will repeat itself precisely, and *if* the cyclical will repeat itself precisely, the value will be

$$501 - 87 + 20 + i = 434 + i$$

The i will be -9 to $+9$ with equal probability. The interval prediction is from 425 to 443 (with perfect confidence given the assumptions). A point estimate is 434, since the expected value of the irregular is zero. A 91-year prediction is ill-advised.

15.6   Assuming that the irregular term results from many small factors, each contributing a little bit, a normal distribution would be more realistic. Furthermore, as time proceeds and the trend rises, the relative importance of the irregular becomes less and less, and this also is not always realistic.

15.7   The expected value will be 1,200 percent. The sum of the variances is 12 percent; the standard deviation of the sum is therefore $\sqrt{12} \approx 3\frac{1}{2}$ percent. In over 99 percent of the years the sum of the irregular factors will fluctuate between 1,190 and 1,210 percent—the average irregular factor will be between 99.1 and 100.9 percent. In our example the factors were 1,203.8; 1,195.8; 1,201.4; 1,195.3; 1,195.2; 1,200.8; 1,201.7; 1,197.2; five of these are within 1 standard deviation, and the other three are within 2 standard deviations.

15.8   No, for $T \times .80 \times 1.20 = .96T$. In general, factors below 100 have more "pulling power" than factors above 100 by the same amount. If the factors are each other's *reciprocal*, they offset one another. For example, a factor of 80 percent $= .8$ is offset by a factor $\frac{1}{.8} = 1.25$ or 125 percent.

15.9 If the cyclical influence and the seasonal influence are repetitive, a point estimate is

$$1,448.72 \times .88 \times .98 = 1,249.38$$

There is a 95 percent probability that, under these assumptions, actual value will be between $.98(1,249.38)$ and $1.02(1,249.38)$, or $1,224.39$ and $1,274.37$.

15.10 The grandson receives \$1,000 in 1970, and each year \$1,000 more, for a total of \$1,000 + \$2,000 + $\cdots$ + \$10,000 = \$55,000 in the decade. The granddaughter receives \$300 + \$600 = \$900 in 1970, and each year \$1,200 more than the previous year. In total she receives \$900 + \$2,100 + \$3,300 + $\cdots$ + \$11,700 = \$63,000.

In general, an amount A more each $\frac{1}{n}$th year gives $n^2 A$ more each year. An amount of \$300 more each $\frac{1}{2}$ year gives $2^2 \times \$300 = \$1,200$ more each year.

15.11

y	x	xy	x^2	y	x	xy	x^2
52	1	52	1	63	13	819	169
58	2	116	4	72	14	1,008	190
40	3	120	9	56	15	840	225
49	4	196	16	61	16	976	256
57	5	285	25	69	17	1,173	289
61	6	366	36	77	18	1,386	324
43	7	301	49	59	19	1,121	361
54	8	432	64	70	20	1,400	400
65	9	585	81	77	21	1,617	441
70	10	700	100	82	22	1,804	484
49	11	539	121	60	23	1,380	529
56	12	672	144	74	24	1,776	576
				1,474	300	19,664	4,900

$$\bar{y} = 61\tfrac{10}{24} \qquad \bar{x} = 12\tfrac{1}{2}$$

$$b = \frac{19,664 - 24 \times 61\tfrac{10}{24} \times 12\tfrac{1}{2}}{4,900 - 24 \times 12\tfrac{1}{2} \times 12\tfrac{1}{2}}$$

$$= \frac{19,664 - 18,425}{4,900 - 3,750} = \frac{1,239}{1,150} = 1.08$$

$$a = 61\tfrac{10}{24} - 1.08 \times 12\tfrac{1}{2} = 61\tfrac{10}{24} - 13\tfrac{12}{24} = 47\tfrac{11}{12}$$

Trend line $= y_t = 47\tfrac{11}{12} + 1.08x$

15.12

$log\ y$	x	$(log\ y)x$	x^2	$log\ y$	x	$(log\ y)x$	x^2
1.7160	1	1.7160	1	1.7993	13	23.3909	169
1.7634	2	3.5268	4	1.8573	14	26.0022	196
1.6021	3	4.8063	9	1.7482	15	26.2230	225
1.6902	4	6.7608	16	1.7853	16	28.5648	256
1.7559	5	8.7795	25	1.8388	17	31.2596	289
1.7853	6	10.7118	36	1.8865	18	33.9570	324
1.6335	7	11.4345	49	1.7709	19	33.6471	361
1.7324	8	13.8592	64	1.8451	20	36.9020	400
1.8129	9	16.3161	81	1.8865	21	39.6165	441
1.8451	10	18.4510	100	1.9138	22	42.1036	484
1.6902	11	18.5922	121	1.7782	23	40.8986	529
1.7482	12	20.9784	144	1.8692	24	44.8608	576
				42.7543	300	543.3587	4,900

$$\overline{log\ y} = 1.7814 \qquad \bar{x} = 12\tfrac{1}{2}$$

$$log\ r = \frac{543.3587 - 24(1.7814)(12\tfrac{1}{2})}{4,900 - 24(12\tfrac{1}{2})(12\tfrac{1}{2})} = \frac{543.3587 - 534.4288}{4,900 - 3,750}$$

$$= \frac{8.9299}{1,150} = .007765 \qquad r = 1.018$$

$$log\ s = 1.7814 - .007765(12\tfrac{1}{2}) = 1.6843 \qquad s = 48.35$$

Trend line $= y_t = 48.35(1.018)^x$

15.13

y	$y_t = 48.35(1.018)^x$	$d = y - y_t$	y	$y_t = 48.35(1.018)^x$	$d = y - y_t$
52	49.22	2.78	63	60.89	2.11
58	50.10	7.90	72	61.98	10.02
40	50.99	-10.99	56	63.09	-7.09
49	51.91	-2.91	61	64.22	-3.22
57	52.84	4.16	69	65.37	3.63
61	53.78	7.22	77	66.54	10.46
43	54.74	-11.74	59	67.73	-8.73
54	55.72	-1.72	70	68.94	1.06
65	56.72	8.28	77	70.18	6.82
70	57.74	12.26	82	71.43	10.57
49	58.77	-9.77	60	72.71	-12.71
56	59.82	-3.82	74	74.01	$-.01$

	Quarter I	Quarter II	Quarter III	Quarter IV	
	2.78	7.90	−10.99	− 2.91	
	4.16	7.22	−11.74	− 1.72	
	8.28	12.26	− 9.77	− 3.82	
	2.11	10.02	− 7.09	− 3.22	
	3.63	10.46	− 8.73	1.06	
	6.82	10.57	−12.71	− .01	
	27.78	58.43	−61.03	−10.62	
	+ 4.630	+ 9.738	−10.172	− 1.770	(sum 2.426)
	− .606	− .607	− .606	− .607	
Seasonal	+ 4.024	+ 9.131	−10.778	− 2.377	(sum 0)

15.14

x	y	$y_t = 47\frac{11}{12} + 1.08x$	$d = y - y_t$	$\dfrac{y}{y_t}(100)$
1	52	49.00	3.00	106.12
2	58	50.08	7.92	115.81
3	40	51.16	−11.16	78.19
4	49	52.24	− 3.24	93.80
5	57	53.32	3.68	106.90
6	61	54.40	6.60	112.13
7	43	55.48	−12.48	77.51
8	54	56.56	− 2.56	95.47
9	65	57.64	7.36	112.77
10	70	58.72	11.28	119.21
11	49	59.80	−10.80	81.94
12	56	60.88	− 4.88	91.98
13	63	61.96	1.04	101.68
14	72	63.04	8.96	114.21
15	56	64.12	− 8.12	87.34
16	61	65.20	− 4.20	93.56
17	69	66.28	2.72	104.10
18	77	67.36	9.64	114.31
19	59	68.44	− 9.44	86.21
20	70	69.52	.48	100.69
21	77	70.60	6.40	109.07
22	82	71.68	10.32	114.40
23	60	72.76	−12.76	82.46
24	74	73.84	.16	100.22

(*a*) The additive seasonal uses the *d* figures:

Quarter I	Quarter II	Quarter III	Quarter IV	
3.00	7.92	−11.16	−3.24	
3.68	6.60	−12.48	−2.56	
7.36	11.28	−10.80	−4.88	
1.04	8.96	− 8.12	−4.20	
2.72	9.64	− 9.44	.48	
6.40	10.32	−12.76	.16	
4.03	9.12	−10.79	−2.37	(sum −.01)
0	0	.01	0	
4.03	9.12	−10.78	−2.37	(sum 0)

(*b*) The multiplicative seasonal uses the $(y/y_t)(100)$ figures:

Quarter I	Quarter II	Quarter III	Quarter IV	
106.12	115.81	78.19	93.80	
106.90	112.13	77.51	95.47	
112.77	119.21	81.94	91.98	
101.68	114.21	87.34	93.56	
104.10	114.31	86.21	100.69	
109.07	114.40	82.16	100.22	
106.77	115.01	82.28	95.95	(sum 400.01)
106.77	115.00	82.28	95.95	(sum 400)

15.15   The additive seasonal found in Exercise 15.14 is 4.03, 9.12,
        −10.78, −2.37. Hence, the value 52 in the first quarter is 4.03
        higher on account of the seasonal, and the deseasonalized value
        is 52 − 4.03 = 47.97. Proceeding in this way, we find:

Period	Deseasonalized value	Period	Deseasonalized value	Period	Deseasonalized value
1	52 − 4.03 = 47.97	9	65 − 4.03 = 60.97	17	69 − 4.03 = 64.97
2	58 − 9.12 = 48.88	10	70 − 9.12 = 60.88	18	77 − 9.12 = 67.88
3	40 + 10.78 = 50.78	11	49 + 10.78 = 59.78	19	59 + 10.78 = 69.78
4	49 + 2.37 = 51.37	12	56 + 2.37 = 58.37	20	70 + 2.37 = 72.37
5	57 − 4.03 = 52.97	13	63 − 4.03 = 58.97	21	77 − 4.03 = 72.97
6	61 − 9.12 = 51.88	14	72 − 9.12 = 62.88	22	82 − 9.12 = 72.88
7	43 + 10.78 = 53.78	15	56 + 10.78 = 66.78	23	60 + 10.78 = 70.78
8	54 + 2.37 = 56.37	16	61 + 2.37 = 63.37	24	74 + 2.37 = 76.37

15.16

y	Four-period moving average	Moving average
52		
58		
	$49\frac{3}{4}$	
40		$50\frac{3}{8}$
	51	
49		$51\frac{3}{8}$
	$51\frac{3}{4}$	
57		$52\frac{1}{8}$
	$52\frac{1}{2}$	
61		$53\frac{1}{8}$
	$53\frac{3}{4}$	
43		$54\frac{3}{4}$
	$55\frac{3}{4}$	
54		$56\frac{7}{8}$
	58	
65		$58\frac{3}{4}$
	$59\frac{1}{2}$	
70		$59\frac{3}{4}$
	60	
49		$59\frac{3}{4}$
	$59\frac{1}{2}$	
56		$59\frac{3}{4}$
	60	
63		$60\frac{7}{8}$
	$61\frac{3}{4}$	
72		$62\frac{3}{8}$
	63	
56		$63\frac{3}{4}$
	$64\frac{1}{2}$	
61		$65\frac{1}{8}$
	$65\frac{3}{4}$	
69		$66\frac{1}{8}$
	$66\frac{1}{2}$	
77		$67\frac{5}{8}$
	$68\frac{3}{4}$	
59		$69\frac{3}{4}$
	$70\frac{3}{4}$	
70		$71\frac{3}{8}$
	72	
77		$72\frac{1}{8}$
	$72\frac{1}{4}$	
82		$72\frac{3}{4}$
	$73\frac{1}{4}$	
60		
74		

15.17 We compare the values of the moving averages with the corresponding trend figures. The trend values are given explicitly in the answer to Exercise 15.13. We begin in period 3; we end in period 22.

x	$y_t = 48.35(1.018)^x$	Moving average	Moving average as % of trend
3	50.99	50.375	98.79
4	51.91	51.375	98.96
5	52.84	52.125	98.65
6	53.78	53.125	98.78
7	54.74	54.750	100.02
8	55.72	56.875	102.07
9	56.72	58.750	103.58
10	57.74	59.750	103.48
11	58.77	59.750	101.67
12	59.82	59.750	99.88
13	60.89	60.875	99.98
14	61.98	62.375	100.64
15	63.09	63.750	101.05
16	64.22	65.125	101.25
17	65.37	66.125	101.15
18	66.54	67.625	101.63
19	67.73	69.750	102.98
20	68.94	71.375	103.53
21	70.18	72.125	102.77
22	71.43	72.750	101.84

No regular cyclical influence can be inferred from these figures.

Chapter 16

INDEX NUMBERS

16.1 INTRODUCTION AND HISTORY

Index numbers are widely used in business and economics to express comparisons and for measuring change. The *base* of an index is the period in time, typically a month or year, used as a basis for the comparison, that is, the period from which change is measured. Each period in time can be compared with the base by calculating the value of the index for that period. For example, the index of automobile production in June 1972, was 108. Since the base for this index is the average monthly level of automobile production during 1967, the index tells us that automobile production in June 1972, was 108 percent of the average monthly level of automobile production during 1967. The index number is the ratio

Base of an index

$$\frac{\text{Value in current period}}{\text{Value in base period}} \times 100$$

The base of an index number, followed by "= 100," is written in parentheses after the number. For example, the medical care price index for June 1972 was 132 (1967 = 100). In words, the cost of medical care in June 1972 was 32 percent above the average monthly cost during 1967. The medical care price index is one component of the *Consumer Price*

Index, which expresses changes in the prices of a whole range of goods and services purchased by consumers. Price indexes will be emphasized in this chapter, since they illustrate the major problems in index number construction and interpretation. There are important indexes in use which are not price indexes, such as the Federal Reserve Board's *Index of Industrial Production.* There will be some discussion of these in later sections.

Carli's index

Historically, the first index number was constructed in 1764 to compare the Italian price level in 1750 with the price level in 1500. Carli, the statistical pioneer who took on this task, limited his index to oil, grain, and wine, probably because records of prices for the two years were available only for these basic items. Fortunately, these three commodities are quite appropriate, for a large proportion of the budget was spent on them, and they are relatively free of changes in style and quality.

The concept of an index number was embodied in a law passed in Massachusetts in 1780. The purpose of the law was to protect lenders against changes in the purchasing power of money. The law stated that a package consisting of five bushels of corn, $68\frac{4}{7}$ pounds of beef, 10 pounds of sheep's wool, and 16 pounds of sole leather cost 130 pounds in current prices. If a citizen borrowed 26 pounds, to be repaid 5 years later, and this package of corn, beef, wool, and leather happened to cost 155 pounds at that time, he was required to pay back not 26, but $26 \times \frac{155}{130} = 31$ pounds! Thus, the lender was protected against inflation, and by symmetry, the borrower against deflation. The provision in modern day wage contracts relating the level of wages to the consumer price index has a long history.

Indexes in current use

The oldest index published continuously for the United States is the *Wholesale Price Index,* which is calculated monthly by the Bureau of Labor Statistics. The series is available from 1890 to the present. The Bureau of Labor Statistics also compiles the monthly *Consumer Price Index* (CPI), a continuing series begun in 1913. These indexes are available in the *Survey of Current Business.* The Board of Governors of the Federal Reserve System has published its monthly *Index of Industrial Production* since the early 1920s. This is an index of physical activity in the economy, showing the current level of activity relative to the level which prevailed in the base period. It is published in the *Federal Reserve Bulletin.* The indexes are currently on a 1967 base.

Index numbers facilitate comparisons

16.2   THE PURPOSE OF AN INDEX NUMBER

The purpose of an index number is to facilitate comparisons. When only a single price or quantity is concerned—the price of a pint of oil or the quantity of salt produced in Siberia—the calculation is elementary and the meaning clear. Thus, if Carli had wished to compare the price of a pint of oil in 1750 with the price of a pint of oil in 1500, his index number would have been simply the ratio of the two prices. In the same way, an index of Siberian salt production would compare current production with production in the base period.

In many situations, the comparison includes not a single price but the prices of a group of products. The result is referred to as a *composite* index. We have composite indexes of construction material prices, prices paid by farmers, prices received by farmers, and so forth. Even Carli, in his primitive attempt at an index number, used the prices of three goods. Currently, the CPI is based on the prices of about 400 items.

Composite index

Using Carli's commodities with hypothetical prices expressed in dollars and cents for convenience, let us explore some of the problems in constructing a composite index. Table 16.1 shows the prices prevailing in 1500 and several possible sets of prices that Carli might have encountered in 1750. Initially, let us assume that he found the 1750 prices as shown in Column 2. A look at the data shows that the 1750 price for each commodity is $2\frac{1}{2}$ times the 1500 price. Obviously, then, we can agree that the price index in 1750, using 1500 as a base, is 250. In 1750, each of the prices individually, and the three prices collectively, are 250 percent of the 1500 price.

If the prices shown in Column 3 prevailed in 1750, the situation becomes a bit cloudy. Each price has increased, but not by the same percentage. The 1750 prices are 200, 175, and 225 percent of the prices in 1500. Clearly, the index for the three prices combined should fall somewhere between 175 and 225, but where? The index number is supposed to give the answer. (As we will see later, more than one index number can be constructed from the same data.)

Finally, suppose that Column 4 represents the prices prevailing in 1750. Not only have the individual prices not changed by the same

TABLE 16.1   PRICES OF BASIC COMMODITIES,
1500 AND 1750, DOLLARS

	1500	1750		
	(1)	(2)	(3)	(4)
Oil (quart)	.10	.25	.20	.40
Grain (bushel)	.40	1.00	.70	.20
Wine (gallon)	.20	.50	.45	.30

percentage, but they have not all moved in the same direction. Grain declined in price, while oil and wine increased. The percentage changes from 1500 to 1750 are 300 percent, *minus* 50 percent and 50 percent, respectively. Even in this complex set of circumstances, an index number value can be found which can be said to represent a comparison of the price level in 1750 with the price level in 1500.

It should be obvious that this third index number, found by using Column 4 prices, is, in some sense, less representative than the one found by using the prices in Column 3. In turn, the latter would be less representative than the index number found by using the prices in Column 2. As with any measure of central tendency, the greater the dispersion of the individual items represented, the less the measure—in this case the index number—can be interpreted as a representative value for the individual items.

Diverging price movements

Changing the scene to modern days, it is still true that prices of commodities do change at different rates, and sometimes in different directions. This is a consequence of changes in tastes and technology, as well as a host of other factors that affect either the demand or the supply of the product. For example, consider the following data on the wholesale prices of goods in June 1972 compared with the average wholesale price during 1967:

Item	Fluctuation, %
Tobacco products	17.5
Leather and leather products	30.9
Metals and metal products	23.6
Textile products and apparel	13.6
Processed foods	19.6
Lumber and wood products	44.2
Furniture and household durables	11.2
Chemicals and chemical goods	4.9
Farm products	24.0
Rubber and plastic products	8.9

It is of interest to notice that these changes themselves are composite indexes. For example, between September 1971 and September 1972 the processed foods went up in price, as a group, by 6.3 percent. This composite included the following price changes:

Item	Fluctuation, %
Meats, poultry, and fish	12.1
Processed fruits and vegetables	3.8
Dairy products	3.1
Animal fats and oils	−7.2
Crude vegetable oils	−25.7

The selection of the items to be included in an index is a basic problem. In a consumer price index we would like to include all those commodities which together make up the bulk of the normal household budget. We will devote Section 16.3 to a somewhat more extensive discussion of this problem. In Section 16.4 we will discuss the problems associated with an appropriate weighting of the price changes. It is intuitively clear that a 10 percent price rise in tomato catsup is less serious than a 10 percent rise in the price of milk. In Section 16.5 we will devote some attention to the problem of the appropriate choice of the base period, and in Section 16.6 we will come to grips with the major problem, which is determining index number formulas.

16.3 SELECTION OF ITEMS FOR AN INDEX

The items included in an index should be determined by the purpose for which the index is constructed. Suppose a state legislature is considering a proposal to make the amount paid monthly to retired state employees vary depending on the behavior of prices. The goods and services bought by these retired persons are not the same as the goods and services bought by families represented in the CPI, mainly because of their age. The retired employees do not buy work clothes, scuba diving equipment, or baby food. They do buy hearing aids, bifocals, and false teeth.

Items should be representative

Ideally, once the purpose of an index has been defined, research should be undertaken to determine the items which should be included. The Bureau of Labor Statistics conducted surveys of consumer expenditures in 66 cities during 1960 and 1961. In these cities 4,860 spending units (families and single persons) completed 76-page questionnaires giving detailed information on their spending habits. The 400 items actually included in the CPI were chosen to represent 1,800 different items reported in the surveys. The probability of an item's being included in the index increased as the relative importance of the item in the average budget increased.

In calculating the index, it is necessary to provide information about each item included in the index. For example, if fresh cut flowers are included in a price index, some definition must be established and price data gathered for the base and current periods. To restrict the number of items while preserving the usefulness of the index, some items may be used as representatives of a larger group, for example, canned peaches as representative of all canned fruits. Occasionally one item is substituted for another—for example, canned pears for canned peaches—if the item formerly used ceases to represent the group satisfactorily.

Great care is taken to define items in successive periods, so the CPI is affected only by changes in prices. Consumer goods change over a short

Quality problem

period of time in a variety of ways—quality of materials, quality of workmanship, packaging, credit or guarantee terms, serviceability, and so forth. One only needs to think of cars to realize the problems this includes. A 1974 car, with all safety features built in, is not the same as a 1970, let alone a 1960 or a 1940, car. One must use judgment to separate price changes from actual changes in the product which would justify a higher price because of improved quality. The CPI is not influenced when it is determined that a change in the price tag of an item reflects a qualitative change in the item bought, a change that is worth the difference in price.

Despite the greatest care, the practical difficulties in constructing a CPI are quite substantial. One must select cities, stores within cities, commodities, methods for measuring prices (do 1-day "specials" count?), and finally weights—to which we turn now.

16.4 DETERMINATION OF WEIGHTS FOR AN INDEX

Weighting pattern should be representative

Just as the items which should be included in an index are determined by the purpose of the index, the weighting pattern, showing the relative importance of the items, should depend on the purpose of the index. In its deliberations on the use of an index number to adjust the pension that will be paid retired state employees, the legislature should use an index which is based on the prices of the items bought by these retired employees, weighted appropriately to reflect their pattern of spending. They spend a greater share of their budget on drugs and medical care and a smaller share on home furnishings and education, compared with the general population.

Consumer surveys

The weighting pattern used in the CPI is based on surveys of the spending patterns of urban wage earner and clerical worker families.

Results of four surveys which have been made are shown in Table 16.2. They reveal the changing pattern of consumer spending over a period of 50 years. The figures are shown for five broad categories of items: food (white bread, sliced bacon, tomatoes, coffee, etc.); housing (home purchase, furniture, appliances, fuel, etc.); apparel (suits, shoes, coats, handkerchiefs, etc.); transportation (new cars, gasoline, taxi fares, etc.); and other goods and services (medical care, tobacco and alcoholic products, recreation, education, and personal care). Each item bought by a consumer is in one and only one category. Savings and taxes are excluded. The relative importance of food in the budget has declined over the past 50 years. Transportation and other goods and services have increased. Keep in mind, however, that 22 percent of income in 1963 is more—in absolute terms— than 40 percent of income in 1917–1919. It is not true that expenditures on food have declined, but only that the percentage of income spent on food has declined.

Table 16.2 shows the weighting pattern used for the CPI at the "major group" level. Each of the 400 individual items in the index has its own weight. If changes in the price index are to reflect only price changes, the weighting pattern employed should be stable through time so that no mingling of price changes and quantity changes blurs the meaning of the index. However, in practice the list of particular items included in the index and the weights given these items are changed occasionally. Great care is taken to ensure that this is done without injuring the validity of the index as a measure of price change alone. Once in a decade a nationwide survey of spending habits is made resulting in a major overhaul of the weighting pattern and the list of items included.

Need for stable weights

TABLE 16.2   PERCENTAGE DISTRIBUTION OF CONSUMER SPENDING BY MAJOR CATEGORY OF CONSUMPTION FOR VARIOUS YEARS, UNITED STATES URBAN WAGE EARNER AND CLERICAL WORKER FAMILIES

	1917–1919	*1934–1936*	*1952*	*1963*
Food	40	33	30	22
Housing	27	32	33	33
Apparel	18	11	9	11
Transportation	3	8	11	14
Other goods and services	12	16	17	20
	100	100	100	100

The weights for an index can be expressed in a variety of ways. The number of units of each commodity bought might be used, as in Carli's index. It is more usual and more appropriate to use the percentage of spending, as is done in the CPI. In the *Index of Industrial Production,* changes in the quantity of output in each industry are weighted by their percentage of the total value added in the industrial sector of the economy. Value added in an industry is the difference between the value of output at market prices and the cost of purchased materials and services embodied in that output.

16.5 SELECTION OF A BASE PERIOD

Reference
base period

The *reference base period* of an index is the point, or interval, in time with which the current period is compared. Carli was interested in comparing the price level in 1750 with the price level in 1500 and designed his index so that the base was 1500. Thus, the value he derived for 1750 expressed the 1750 price level in terms of the 1500 price level. His index for 1500 was 100. Any index number equals, or averages, 100 in the reference base period.

Base should
be recent
period

It is desirable to have an index based on a fairly recent period, since comparisons with a familiar set of circumstances are more helpful than comparisons with vaguely remembered conditions. For this reason, the Office of Management and Budget has encouraged all federal government agencies to use the same base period and has moved this base period forward in time approximately once every 10 years. Most government indexes are on a 1967 base.

Base should
be a normal
period

The reference base period for an index should be a normal period. "Normal" means a time in which relationships among key economic variables were not disrupted by war, depression, rapid inflation, national disasters, strikes, etc. This is obviously a desirable goal, since the values of the index will then compare other periods with a stable state of economic affairs.

It is particularly important to be aware of the conditions in the base period when two or more indexes are used in analysis. For example, in discussing the movement of corporate profits and the level of wages in general manufacturing over a period of several decades, two indexes might be used, both having the same base year. Management might argue that the indexes currently show profits up 20 percent and wages up 35 percent, implying that maladjustment had occurred and the shareholders are entitled to larger profits before any further wage increases are forthcoming. Representatives of labor might counter with the argument that the relationship between wages and profits in the base year did not represent a situation which was fair to labor and therefore should not be perpetuated through the maintenance of the two indexes at the same level. It might be that profits were at a cyclical peak in the base year while wages were lagging during the cyclical upswing. If so, the fact that the two indexes both were 100 in the base year does not mean that the relationship between profits and wages in that year was normal and should be maintained.

The weights used in an index may represent a period different from the reference base. For example, in the 1960s the CPI was on the reference base 1957–1959, while the weighting pattern reflected the pattern of consumption in spending units headed by urban wage earners and clerical workers during 1960 and 1961. *The weight base* for the CPI was, therefore, the period 1960–1961, whereas the *reference base* was the period 1957–1959.

Weight base versus reference base

16.6 INDEX NUMBER FORMULAS

The two best known index formulas are the *Laspeyres* index and the *Paasche* index. In slightly different ways both answer the question, "How much does a package of commodities cost today, compared with the cost of that same package in the reference base year?" The essential difference between the Laspeyres index and the Paasche index is in the "package of commodities." The Laspeyres index is obtained when we take the package actually bought in the weight base period. The Paasche index results when we take the package bought in the current period.

Laspeyres index

Let us first, in words, discuss the idea underlying the Laspeyres index. Suppose a consumer bought three haircuts and five neckties in the base period, for a total cost of

$$3 \times \$2.00 + 5 \times \$1.50 = \$13.50 \,(=100)$$

Apparently, the price of a haircut in the base period was $2.00, and the price of a necktie $1.50. Next, suppose in the current period the price of a haircut is $3.00 and the price of a necktie is $1.00. In the current period three haircuts and five neckties cost

$$3 \times \$3.00 + 5 \times \$1.00 = \$14.00$$

The index for the current period is therefore ($14.00/$13.50) × 100 = 104. This is the Laspeyres price index, which is obtained by comparing the current cost of the base period package with its base period cost.

The Paasche price index is obtained by computing what today's package would have cost in the base year. Suppose that, in the new price situation, the consumer buys only two haircuts and seven neckties (since haircuts have increased in price and neckties have decreased). The total price of today's package in the base year would have been

$$2 \times \$2.00 + 7 \times \$1.50 = \$14.50 \, (= 100)$$

The cost in the current period of that package is

$$2 \times \$3.00 + 7 \times \$1.00 = \$13.00$$

The Paasche price index is therefore $(\$13.00/\$14.50) \times 100 = 90$.

If the composition of the package in the base period and the current period is the same, the Laspeyres index and the Paasche index give the same numerical value. In almost all other cases, the Laspeyres index will be greater than the Paasche index. The reason for this is as follows. Let us go back to the base year situation where three haircuts were bought at $2.00 each and five neckties at $1.50 each for a total cost of $13.50. This *same* package would cost $14.00 in the new situation, but the trouble is that in the new situation one will *not buy this same package*. Instead, one is likely to buy more neckties (which decreased in price) and fewer haircuts (which increased in price). The Laspeyres price index overestimates the damage done to the consumer by the price changes, since it neglects the consumer's ability to react to the changes by altering the amounts of the products he buys. By a similar argument, the Paasche index underestimates the value of the price index. Let us now consider a slightly more elaborate example in more abstract notation.

We will calculate a "students' clothing price index." The items to be included will represent the types of clothing bought by male undergraduate students on campuses of colleges and universities in the United States. We will keep the list short: shirts, socks, slacks, and shoes. The index will be calculated for 1973, using 1960 as a base. All price and quantity information will be given for a single campus. The following symbols will be used:

$$p_{0i} = \text{the price of item } i \text{ in the base period}$$
$$p_{1i} = \text{the price of item } i \text{ in the current period}$$
$$q_{0i} = \text{the quantity of item } i \text{ in the base period}$$
$$q_{1i} = \text{the quantity of item } i \text{ in the current period}$$
$$n = \text{the number of items in the index}$$

In our example, $n = 4$ and i will be 1 for shirt, 2 for socks, 3 for slacks, and 4 for shoes. The first subscript on the p and q is 0 if it relates to the base year 1960 and 1 if it relates to the current year 1973. The relevant price and quantity data are presented in Table 16.3.

Using the information given in Table 16.3, we first compute the Laspeyres index. We recall that this index is the ratio between the cost of buying the base package in the current period and the cost of buying the same package in the base period. In formula, therefore,

$$\text{Laspeyres index} = \frac{p_{11}q_{01} + p_{12}q_{02} + \cdots + p_{1n}q_{0n}}{p_{01}q_{01} + p_{02}q_{02} + \cdots + p_{0n}q_{0n}} \times 100 \text{ percent}$$

$$= \frac{\Sigma p_{1i}q_{0i}}{\Sigma p_{0i}q_{0i}} \times 100 \text{ percent}$$

We will use the compact sum notation throughout. In the Laspeyres index the numerator is the total cost of the package bought in the base period at current prices, and the denominator is the cost of the same package q_0's at the base prices. Table 16.4 shows the calculation of the Laspeyres index of students' clothing prices. The value of the Laspeyres index for 1973 is $282/$206 = 137 percent, or 137 (1960 = 100). We see that the cost of buying 6 shirts, 10 pairs of socks, 5 pairs of slacks, and 3 pairs of shoes in 1973 is 137 percent of the cost in 1960.

The Paasche index expresses the ratio between the cost of buying the current package in the current period and the cost of buying the same package in the base period. In formula, therefore,

$$\text{Paasche index} = \frac{\Sigma p_{1i}q_{1i}}{\Sigma p_{0i}q_{1i}} \times 100 \text{ percent}$$

TABLE 16.3   BASIC PRICE AND QUANTITY DATA FOR STUDENTS' CLOTHING PRICE INDEX, 1960 AND 1973

Item	i	p_{0i}	q_{0i}	p_{1i}	q_{1i}
Shirt	1	$ 8.00	6	$10.00	8
Socks (pair)	2	1.00	10	2.00	5
Slacks (pair)	3	20.00	5	26.00	7
Shoes (pair)	4	16.00	3	24.00	2
		$45.00		$62.00	

TABLE 16.4   COMPUTATION OF LASPEYRES INDEX FOR
STUDENTS' CLOTHING PRICES

Item	i	p_{0i}	q_{0i}	p_{1i}	$p_{0i}q_{0i}$	$p_{1i}q_{0i}$
Shirt	1	$ 8.00	6	$10.00	$ 48	$ 60
Socks (pair)	2	1.00	10	2.00	10	20
Slacks (pair)	3	20.00	5	26.00	100	130
Shoes (pair)	4	16.00	3	24.00	48	72
					$206	$282

where the numerator is the total cost of the package bought in the current
period at current prices, and the denominator is the cost of the same
package q_1's at the base prices.

Table 16.5 shows the calculation of a Paasche index of students'
clothing prices. We see that the index for 1973 is $320/$241 = 133
percent, or 133 (1960 = 100). This means that the cost of buying eight
shirts, five pairs of socks, seven pairs of slacks, and two pairs of shoes
in 1973 is 133 percent of the cost in 1960.

Why do these two formulas give different results when the prices
used in both calculations are identical? The answer lies of course in the
different weighting patterns used. Despite student affluence, which probably accounts for the increased quantity of shirts and slacks purchased in
1973, compared with the quantity in 1960, there has been a remarkable
decline in the purchase of socks and shoes. The cost of buying the 1960
wardrobe rose more during the 13 years than the cost of buying the 1973
wardrobe. Over the 13 years students have increased the relative importance of shirts and slacks, which rose less in price than socks and shoes.

Clearly, if the index is to measure only price changes, a constant
weighting pattern must be used. For practical reasons it is preferable to
use the weighting pattern from the reference base year or a year fairly

TABLE 16.5   CALCULATION OF PAASCHE INDEX FOR STUDENTS'
CLOTHING PRICES

Item	i	p_{0i}	p_{1i}	q_{1i}	$p_{0i}q_{1i}$	$p_{1i}q_{1i}$
Shirt	1	$ 8.00	$10.00	8	$ 64	$ 80
Socks (pair)	2	1.00	2.00	5	5	10
Slacks (pair)	3	20.00	26.00	7	140	182
Shoes (pair)	4	16.00	24.00	2	32	48
					$241	$320

close to the reference base year. Current period weights are inconvenient, since they require the regular collection of new data on consumption patterns, which is expensive and time consuming. In practice we use the Laspeyres index and not the Paasche index.

It is interesting to observe that the Laspeyres price index can be written as a weighted average of the price indexes of the individual commodities. By an appropriate choice of weights, the Laspeyres index equals

$$\frac{\Sigma w_i(p_{1i}/p_{0i})}{\Sigma w_i}$$

The ratios p_{11}/p_{01}, p_{12}/p_{02}, ... are commonly called the *price relatives*. If we choose as weight for the kth price relative the amount spent on the kth commodity in the base year, the Laspeyres price index results:

$$\frac{\Sigma p_{0i}q_{0i}(p_{1i}/p_{0i})}{\Sigma p_{0i}q_{0i}} = \frac{\Sigma p_{1i}q_{0i}}{\Sigma p_{0i}q_{0i}}$$

Price relatives

Occasionally, in particular when we are concerned with historical data, no data are available to establish a pattern of weights. In this case, the individual price relatives are used to calculate

$$\sqrt[n]{\frac{p_{11}}{p_{01}} \frac{p_{12}}{p_{02}} \cdots \frac{p_{1n}}{p_{0n}}}$$

This index is the *unweighted geometric average of relatives*. Table 16.6 shows the calculation of the unweighted geometric average of the price-

Unweighted geometric average of relatives

TABLE 16.6 COMPUTATION OF THE UNWEIGHTED GEOMETRIC AVERAGE OF PRICE RELATIVES FOR STUDENTS' CLOTHING PRICES

Item	i	p_{0i}	p_{1i}	$\dfrac{p_{1i}}{p_{0i}}$
Shirt	1	$ 8.00	$10.00	1.25
Socks (pair)	2	1.00	2.00	2.00
Slacks (pair)	3	20.00	26.00	1.30
Shoes (pair)	4	16.00	24.00	1.50

relatives index of students' clothing prices. We see that the index for 1973 is

$$\sqrt[4]{1.25 \times 2.00 \times 1.30 \times 1.50} = 1.49 \qquad \text{or } 149 \text{ percent}$$

This index cannot be given a simple, intuitive interpretation; however, it has the merit of meeting the time reversal test.

Time reversal test The *time reversal test* is met by any index number formula which yields the reciprocal of the original number when data for the base and current periods are interchanged. If the time reversal test is met by an index, we can use the reciprocal of the index as the correct value of the index for the base period, with the current period index equal to 100. For an individual item, the price relative p_{1i}/p_{0i} meets this criterion. If we interchange the current and base year prices we have the reciprocal p_{0i}/p_{1i}. For example, Table 16.6 shows that in 1973 the price of a shirt was 125 percent, or $\frac{5}{4}$ of the price in 1960. Therefore, the price of a shirt in 1960 was 80 percent, or $\frac{4}{5}$ of the price in 1973. It is obviously desirable that a composite index have the same property.

One of the few virtues of the unweighted geometric average of relatives is that the time reversal test is met. If we consider the price data for students' clothing in 1960 and 1973, the index of 1973 (base 1960) equals 149 percent, and the index of 1960 (base 1973) equals 67 percent. The indexes are each other's reciprocal.

On the other hand, the unweighted arithmetic average of relatives for 1973 is

$$\tfrac{1}{4}(\tfrac{5}{4} + \tfrac{1}{.5} + \tfrac{13}{10} + \tfrac{12}{8}) = 1.51 \qquad 151 \ (1960 = 100)$$

The unweighted arithmetic average of relatives for 1960 is

$$\tfrac{1}{4}(\tfrac{4}{5} + \tfrac{.5}{1} + \tfrac{10}{13} + \tfrac{8}{12}) = .685 \qquad 68.5 \ (1973 = 100)$$

Since $(1.51 \times .685) \neq 1$, the unweighted arithmetic average of relatives fails to meet the time reversal test. This is the reason we prefer the unweighted geometric average over the unweighted arithmetic average.

Strictly speaking, the Laspeyres index and the Paasche index do not meet the time reversal test. If, when the time reference is reversed, the weights are changed so that they refer to the new base or the new current period, it is unlikely that the result will be precisely the reciprocal of the original number, although in practice it is often very close.

With the variety of index number formulas available, one may well ask whether there is a "best" formula. It is generally agreed that a weighted price index is preferable to an unweighted price index. The use of weights assures that the index will be affected by the relative importance of the items in the index. Of the weighted indexes the Laspeyres is preferred over the Paasche for practical reasons.

At the very end of Section 16.3 we quickly enumerated a number of difficulties which loom large in actually determining the CPI. There are a large number of decisions to be made, "Which cities, stores, commodities, prices, weights shall we use?" A comforting thought is that one is essentially interested in *changes* in the CPI from period to period, not in the truly correct absolute level of the CPI. For a proper idea of changes from period to period the method gives workable results.

EXERCISES

16.1 In an article headed Stable Prices during Year, referring to 1961, the *Survey of Current Business* noted the following: There were "price declines of some importance during the year in the fuel, rubber, and chemical product groups," "Used car prices increased substantially through most of 1961," "Price reductions were marked in electrical machinery," and "A strengthening of equipment prices toward the end of the year was evident mainly under the influence of the rising prices of agricultural machinery." Comment on the title of the article.

16.2 You are given the following information about the typical family in a community:

	1967		1973	
Item	Price	Units/week	Price	Units/week
Bread, loaf	.25	3	.40	2
Milk, quart	.20	10	.30	8
Ground beef, pound	.75	3	1.25	4
Tomato soup, can	.15	4	.20	3
Eggs, dozen	.50	3	.70	5
Carrots, bunch	.15	1	.20	2

(a) Construct the Laspeyres and Paasche indexes for 1973 using 1967 as a base.

(b) Do the same for 1967 with 1973 as a base.

(c) What does each index number mean, specifically?

16.3   (*a*) Using the information given in Exercise 16.2, calculate the
index for 1973 with 1967 as the base with the weighted
arithmetic average of price relatives. Take the weights equal
to the value of expenditures on each of the goods during the
base year. Show that we get the Laspeyres index already
calculated for these data.

(*b*) Use as weights $p_{0i}q_{1i}$, that is, current quantities times base
prices. Show that the Paasche index results.

16.4   Do the Laspeyres and Paasche indexes calculated in Exercise 16.2
satisfy the time reversal test?

16.5   The Daily Spot Market Price Index measures change in the price
level of 22 basic commodities such as steel scrap, cotton, lard,
hogs, and cottonseed oil. The index is an unweighted geometric
average of price relatives. Does this index meet the time reversal
test?

16.7   INDEX NUMBER SERIES

We have seen that an index number is a numerical value expressing a
comparison between one period of time (current) and another period of
time (base). By careful selection of items and a weighting pattern, we can
combine price and quantity data, using one of several available formulas,
into a measure comparing the current with the base period. A succession
of index numbers for a series of months or years forms an index.

Fixed base
versus chain
index

The index just described is a *fixed-base index,* since each number
relates a particular period to the reference base for the series. Column 1
of Table 16.7 shows the monthly sales in a department store during 1972
and 1973. We select September 1972 as the reference base for an index
of the value of sales, shown in Column 2. Each term shows sales in a
particular month expressed as a percentage of sales in September 1972.
The index for the value of sales in October 1973 is 138, because $\frac{1,100}{800}$
$\times$ 100 = 138 percent, or 138 (September 1972 = 100).

For certain purposes it is more useful to construct a *chain index,*
in which each number expresses the comparison between a particular
period and the preceding period. In such an index the base for each term
is different, since it is the preceding week, month, or year. The terms

Link relatives

in this index are called *link relatives.* Measures of business activity are
often expressed in link relatives, which give the user a good measure of
current performance compared with performance in the most recent similar
period.

TABLE 16.7 MONTHLY SALES OF ARGUS DEPARTMENT STORE, 1972 AND 1973

Year	Month	*(1)* Sales *($000)*	*(2)* Fixed base index *(September 1972 = 100)*	*(3)* Chain index
1972	J	400	50	
	F	330	41	82
	M	500	62	151
	A	750	94	150
	M	800	100	107
	J	700	88	88
	J	650	81	93
	A	600	75	92
	S	800	100	133
	O	900	112	112
	N	1,200	150	133
	D	1,500	188	125
1973	J	500	62	33
	F	400	50	80
	M	550	69	138
	A	800	100	145
	M	900	113	112
	J	750	94	83
	J	700	88	93
	A	870	109	124
	S	1,000	125	115
	O	1,100	138	110
	N	1,400	175	127
	D	1,800	225	129

Column 3 of the table shows the link relatives of the sales in Column 1. Each term in Column 3 is the corresponding term in Column 1 divided by the preceding term in Column 1. The same result is found by using the values of the fixed-base index in Column 2. The link relative for September 1972, 133, shows that sales in September 1972 were 133 percent of sales in August 1972, $\frac{800}{600} = 1.33$. The link relative for January 1972 cannot be determined because no sales figure for December 1971 is available.

Just as the chain index can be found from the fixed-base index, the fixed-base index can be found from the chain index. For instance, imagine that we know nothing about the sales of the Argus department store except the chain index in Column 3. We will establish a fixed base from this chain index, with September 1972 = 100. Since Column 3 shows that sales in October 1972 were 112 percent of September 1972 sales, the fixed-base index for October must be 112. Similarly, the link relative for November 1972 shows that sales were 133 percent of sales in October 1972. In the fixed-base index, October sales are represented by the entry 112. November sales must be represented by an entry equal to 133 percent of 112, or 149. By a similar multiplication of the fixed-base index for the preceding month by the link relative for the current month, entries may be determined for Column 2 from Column 3. What is the value of the fixed-base index for August 1972? We know that September sales were 133 percent of August sales, and we are representing September sales in the index by 100. Therefore August sales $\times$ 1.33 = 100, or August sales = $\frac{100}{1.33}$ = 75. Thus, we see that the fixed-base index for months preceding September 1972 is found by dividing the link relative for the following month into the fixed-base index for the following month. The value of the index in July 1972 is $\frac{75}{.92}$ = 82.

Comparisons
over longer
period of
time with
link relatives

The link relatives shown in Column 3 express the sales in each month as a percentage of the sales in the preceding month. A series of monthly data frequently shows an important pattern of seasonal variation. It is clear from inspection of Column 1 or Column 2 that the series reaches an outstanding peak in December with a secondary, much smaller peak in May. It is reasonable that management would want to compare sales in any month with the sales in the corresponding month of the preceding year and thereby remove the distortion caused by seasonal variations in comparisons of successive months. January 1973 sales are 125 percent of January 1972 sales. Management can take encouragement from the fact that having allowed for the seasonally poor showing of sales in January of any year, January 1973 is certainly an improvement over January 1972. A series of link relatives comparing periods one year apart is a convenient "deseasonalizing" device.

Shifting the
base of a
fixed-base
index

For ease of comparison it is sometimes useful to *shift* the base of a fixed-base index. For example, suppose indexes of consumer prices are available for country A (1956 = 100) and for country B (1966 = 100). To facilitate comparison between the two countries, the index for country A might be shifted to 1966 as a base year. Table 16.8 shows the index for country A in Column 1, with the original base of 1956. In Column 2, each entry in Column 1 is divided by 150 to give the entry for 1966. The price level of 1966 is now represented as 100, the new

**TABLE 16.8   CONSUMER PRICE INDEXES, COUNTRIES
A AND B, 1956–1972**

Year	(1) Country A (1956 = 100)	(2) Country A (1966 = 100)	(3) Country B (1966 = 100)
1956	100	67	82
1958	111	74	85
1960	119	79	87
1962	127	85	91
1964	141	94	96
1966	150	100	100
1968	161	107	107
1970	173	115	112
1972	189	126	117

base of comparison for the price level in every other year. Column 3 shows the price index for country B, with 1966 as a base. Comparison of Columns 2 and 3 shows the difference between the change in price levels prevailing in countries A and B from the 1966 level. The comparison is possible because all figures in both columns are expressed in terms of the common base year, 1966. Comparison of Column 3 with Column 1 shows how misleading the information from the original indexes would have been if they had been compared without readjusting the index for country A to the 1966 base period. Even after the adjustment of the index for country A, it would be improper to conclude that when the indexes of the two countries attain the same value, as in the year 1968, the absolute price levels in the two countries are the same. All we know is that a package of commodities which cost x dollars in country A in 1966 cost $1.26x$ dollars in 1972. We do not know whether the cost of this package in country B in 1966 was less than x dollars, equal to x dollars, or more than x dollars. We do know that, whatever it cost in 1966, it cost 1.17 times as much in 1972.

Another problem which may arise is solved by *splicing* two indexes together to form one continuous index. Suppose we have two indexes as represented in Table 16.9. By splicing these two indexes together we can make one continuous index on the same reference base. Let us choose 1970 as the reference base. The 1965 price level was represented by 120 in the old series and by 90 in the new series. What is the value of the 1960 price level with 1970 as reference base? In the new series we must

Splicing indexes

TABLE 16.9   TWO INDEXES WHICH ARE TO BE SPLICED

Year	Old index (1960 = 100)	New index (1970 = 100)
1955	80	
1960	100	
1965	120	90
1970		100

preserve the same relationship between any pair of years which existed in the old series. Therefore, if X is the value of the new series in 1960,

$$\frac{X}{90} = \frac{100}{120} \qquad \text{or} \qquad X = \frac{90}{120} \times 100 = 75$$

Similarly, the 1955 index is $\frac{90}{120} \times 80 = 60$ (1970 = 100).

Both the shifting of the base in a fixed-base index and the splicing of two indexes are theoretically correct only if the index numbers used meet the time reversal test. Most index numbers in current use do not meet the test exactly. However, the need to perform these calculations is overriding, and the fact that shifting bases or splicing indexes may introduce small errors is usually overlooked. Another, slightly more serious problem arises when two indexes with different weight bases are spliced to form one index. The result is a hybrid index with a common reference base but different weight bases. The situation should be clearly stated, and the user must be careful when comparing terms of the index which embody different weighting patterns.

EXERCISES

16.6   Table 16.12 gives annual values of the Wholesale Price Index (WPI) (1967 = 100) from 1929–1971. The WPI is shown below for selected years (1926 = 100):

Year:	1890	1895	1900	1905	1910	1915	1920	1925	1930
WPI:	56.2	48.8	56.1	60.1	70.4	69.5	154.4	103.5	86.4

(a) Using the available information, set up a series of comparable WPI values (every fifth year) from 1890 to 1970; in other words, splice the index.

(b) What are the deficiencies, if any, of the series you set up in (a)?

16.7   The Bureau of Labor Statistics publishes indexes of consumer prices for 23 large cities. Each index expresses the current price level in the city in terms of a specified base-period price level in the same city. In August 1972 the Seattle index stood at 120 and the Washington, D.C., index at 128 (1967 = 100 in both cities).
(a) What does each index mean separately?
(b) How does the Seattle price level compare with the Washington, D.C., price level in the given month?

16.8   Table 16.12 shows the behavior of three price indexes over a lengthy period.
(a) Why do these indexes have different values for the same year?
(b) What factors do you believe explain the different patterns shown by these indexes during the period covered?

16.8   QUANTITY INDEXES

In the opening section we referred briefly to a little-known index, the index of Siberian salt production. Unlike most of the indexes discussed since this early reference, the index of Siberian salt production is not a price index, but a quantity index. Presumably, there exist records of the tons of salt produced in Siberia monthly. By using a particular month or average month for a period as the base, the current month's production could be expressed as a percentage of the production in the base period to form a simple quantity index.

Composite quantity indexes can be constructed with formulas that are analogous to those introduced above in the discussion of price index numbers. The comments about the selection of items, the weights, and the base all apply to quantity indexes. Depending on the purpose of the quantity index, the items included may represent the items produced by a factory, a firm, or an industry, the items consumed in a particular type of activity such as construction, or the items composing the output of a region or a nation. As noted previously, in a composite quantity index designed to measure productive activity, the appropriate weights are *value added*. By using the value-added weights, activity can be measured simply without double counting. Double counting would arise, for example, if a bushel of grain, the flour made from the grain, and the bread made

Composite quantity indexes

Value added as weights

from the flour were all counted at their full value in the index. The bread value incorporates the flour value and the flour value incorporates the grain value. Instead, only the net productive contributions of the miller and the baker are counted.

We will compute the annual index of production for the Glamour Dress Company. The necessary data are in Table 16.10. The index calculated is a Laspeyres index, written as a weighted average of quantity relatives. The weights are the values added during the base year.

The q_{0i} and q_{1i} entries in Table 16.10 are the number of dozens of each product produced in the indicated years. The p_{0i} are the *dollar values added* per dozen by the productive effort put into the product by the Glamour Dress Company. For example, in 1965 the wholesale price of 12 dresses exceeded the cost of materials and purchased parts (buttons, zippers, etc.) by $50.

The calculations shown below the table yield an index number of 128 (1965 = 100) for 1970, indicating that the company's physical output in 1970 rose 28 percent from the 1965 level. Clearly, this is a quantity index, since only changes in quantity of output influenced the magnitude of the index. We are assuming that the three products shown represent the entire product line of the company, just as the items in a consumer price index represent the entire range of items in the consumer's budget.

In the example, we have used three products to find the index of production for a particular company. The same logic can be applied to

TABLE 16.10   OUTPUT AND VALUE ADDED, GLAMOUR DRESS COMPANY, 1965 AND 1970

		1965		1970			
	i	p_{0i}	q_{0i}	q_{1i}	$\dfrac{q_{1i}}{q_{0i}}$	$p_{0i}q_{0i}$	$\dfrac{q_{1i}}{q_{0i}}p_{0i}q_{0i}$
Dress, dozen	1	$50	1,000	1,200	1.20	$ 50,000	$ 60,000
Coat, dozen	2	75	500	700	1.40	37,500	52,500
Skirt, dozen	3	30	800	1,000	1.25	24,000	30,000
						$111,500	$142,500

$$\text{Index of output} = \frac{\Sigma p_{0i}q_{0i}\,(q_{1i}/q_{0i})}{\Sigma p_{0i}q_{0i}} = \frac{\Sigma p_{0i}q_{1i}}{\Sigma p_{0i}q_{0i}}$$

$$1970 \text{ index of output} = \frac{\$142,500}{\$111,500} = 1.28 = 128 \ (1965 = 100)$$

TABLE 16.11   AVERAGE WEEKLY EARNINGS IN
              MANUFACTURING INDUSTRIES, IN
              CURRENT AND CONSTANT (1967)
              DOLLARS, SELECTED YEARS

Year	Average weekly earnings	Consumer Price Index (1967 = 100)	Average weekly earnings (1967 prices)
1929	$ 24.76	51.3	$ 48.27
1933	16.65	38.8	42.91
1945	44.20	53.9	82.00
1950	58.32	72.1	80.89
1955	75.70	80.2	94.39
1960	89.72	88.7	101.15
1965	107.53	94.5	113.79
1970	133.73	116.3	114.99
1971	142.44	121.3	117.43

find indexes of productive activity in industries and, continuing the aggregation process, for the entire economy. The Federal Reserve Board's *Index of Industrial Production* is the most widely used comprehensive measure of industrial activity. Calculated according to the same formula used in the illustration, it differs only in the much larger number and greater variety of products included.

16.9   DEFLATION OF A VALUE SERIES

Table 16.11 shows the average weekly earnings of workers in manufacturing industries over a period of years. A casual glance at these figures suggests that in 1970 the average earnings were nearly nine times as high as in 1933. However the impression so created is misleading. To see why, we have added the value of the CPI in Column 2. Column 3 is obtained by dividing the entries in Column 1 by the CPI from Column 2. It is clear that the ability of employees in manufacturing industries to buy goods with their weekly paychecks is shown in Column 3 and not in Column 1. Column 1 gives the wages in *current dollars*. They have increased partly because the price level rose during the period covered by the data. Column 3 gives the wages in *constant dollars*. The effect of the prices has been eliminated by dividing by the price index. This process is called *deflating*. The 1971 worker is not even three times as well off as the 1933 employee.

Deflation enables the researcher to control the effect of one variable, price, which is always at work influencing the magnitude of value series such as earnings, sales, and profits. The difficulty encountered most frequently in using the deflation technique is the lack of an appropriate price index to use as the *deflator*. Theoretically, the deflator should reflect the changing price level of exactly that group of goods and services contained in the current value series to be deflated. This requirement was met reasonably well in our example, since the CPI is based on those items bought by urban workers in manufacturing and clerical occupations.

The analyst is not always so fortunate. A study of the economic history of a particular community or state might call for the deflation of a series showing the dollar value of goods shipped annually from manufacturing plants in the area. Quite possibly no appropriate price index would be available to reflect the price level of the particular items produced in the area, properly weighted to reflect the pattern of manufacturing activity there. Or, in another study, the *purchasing power* of the incomes of the residents of a prosperous suburban area might be required. Purchasing power is another way of describing the result of deflating an income series in current prices to produce a series in constant prices, as shown in Column 3 of Table 16.11. For this area, the CPI would not be an appropriate deflator, since it is deliberately designed to measure the changes in the price level of goods and services bought by wage earners and salaried clerical workers in urban areas. In such cases, diligence and ingenuity must be used to find or devise appropriate deflators.

Purchasing power

EXERCISES

16.9   The "parity ratio" used in establishing the support price levels for agricultural commodities under federal programs is the ratio of prices received by farmers to prices paid by farmers. In June 1972, the index of prices received by farmers was 317 (1910–1914 = 100), and the index of prices paid by farmers was 432 (1910–1914 = 100).

(*a*) What was the parity ratio in June 1972?
(*b*) Comment on the logic behind this ratio.
(*c*) What assumption is embodied in the decision to use 1910–1914 as a base for the indexes?

16.10   You are earning $12,000 per year in your job in Chicago. The opportunity arises to earn £5,000 per year doing the same work in Great Britain. A 1960 study showed that an income of $8,000 in the United States yielded purchasing power equivalent to an income of £3,000 in Britain. The CPI for the United States (1967 = 100) was 88.7 in 1960 and is 130 now. The comparable British index (1960 = 100) is now 150. If the only factor influencing your decision is the opportunity to improve the purchasing power of your income, will you make the move? Why?

16.11 The reciprocal of the CPI is referred to as the "purchasing power of the dollar." When the CPI is 125, the purchasing power is $.80. Comment on the statement one often hears, "The dollar is worth only 80 cents."

16.12 The hourly wage rates of workers in several basic industries are related contractually to changes in the CPI. The Bravo Company has a contract calling for a 2-cent increase in the hourly wage of a particular class of employee whenever the CPI increases by 1 point. The hourly wage rate was $2.00 during 1967. In negotiations on a new contract the union asks that the terms be changed to read "a 1 percent increase in the wage for each 1-point increase in the CPI." What is your reaction to this request?

16.10 SUMMARY

Table 16.12 shows four index series for the years from 1929 to 1971. The only index not previously mentioned is the Implicit Price Index, which is more general than the CPI. It attempts to measure the overall price level for all goods and services produced, including government services. Conceptually the index resembles a Paasche index, embodying current period weights. The prices represented in the index are those paid by the final users of each good or service, including individuals, businesses, institutions, and government. The weights are current values, using prevailing market prices.

Implicit price index

The four series each give us an impression of the seriousness of the depression of the early 1930s. From the production index we see the steep increase after the United States entered World War II. The price controls in effect during the war years were effective, but the lid came off the price level in 1946. Prices during 1952–1955 were once again stable. In the 1960s the production index made giant strides upward, but this was unfortunately accompanied by a steady increase in the price level, particularly after 1964.

TABLE 16.12 PRICE AND PRODUCTION INDEXES, 1929–1971

Year	Consumer Price Index (1967 = 100)	Wholesale Price Index (1967 = 100)	Implicit Price Index (1958 = 100)	Industrial Production Index (1967 = 100)
1929	51.3	49.1	50.6	21.6
1930	50.0	44.6	49.3	18.0
1931	45.6	37.6	44.8	14.9
1932	40.9	33.6	40.2	11.6
1933	38.8	34.0	39.3	13.7
1934	40.1	38.6	42.2	15.0
1935	41.1	41.3	42.6	17.3
1936	41.5	41.7	42.7	20.4
1937	43.0	44.5	44.5	22.3
1938	42.2	40.5	43.9	17.6
1939	41.6	39.8	43.2	21.7
1940	42.0	40.5	43.9	25.0
1941	44.1	45.1	47.2	31.6
1942	48.8	50.9	53.0	36.3
1943	51.8	53.3	56.8	44.0
1944	52.7	53.6	58.2	47.4
1945	53.9	54.6	59.7	40.6
1946	58.5	62.3	66.7	35.0
1947	66.9	76.5	74.6	39.4
1948	72.1	82.8	79.6	41.0
1949	71.4	78.7	79.1	38.8
1950	72.1	81.8	80.2	44.9
1951	77.8	91.1	85.6	48.7
1952	79.5	88.6	87.5	50.6
1953	80.1	87.4	88.3	54.8
1954	80.5	87.6	89.6	51.9
1955	80.2	87.8	90.9	58.5
1956	81.4	90.7	94.0	61.1
1957	84.3	93.3	97.5	61.9
1958	86.6	94.6	100.0	57.9
1959	87.3	94.8	101.6	64.8
1960	88.7	94.9	103.3	66.2
1961	89.0	94.5	104.0	66.7
1962	90.6	94.8	105.8	72.2
1963	91.7	94.5	107.2	76.5
1964	92.9	94.7	108.8	81.7
1965	94.5	96.6	110.9	89.2
1966	97.2	99.8	113.9	97.9
1967	100.0	100.0	117.6	100.0
1968	104.2	102.5	122.3	105.7
1969	109.8	106.5	128.2	110.7
1970	116.3	110.4	135.2	106.6
1971	121.3	113.9	141.6	106.8

We want to end this chapter with a warning. The concept of "price level" is an elusive one. In one number, a price index attempts to express the overall change in the level of a collection of prices—each of which has probably changed differently—for a collection of items—each of which has a different and changing importance to each consumer. Despite the difficulties involved, the usefulness of index numbers leads to constant efforts to improve them.

Answers to Exercises

16.1   The quotations suggest that particular groups of prices rose in 1961 and others fell. This variability in behavior occurs because the forces of supply and demand influence prices in particular markets in different ways. The increases in some groups were apparently offset by the decreases in others, however, so that the overall price level remained stable. It may be that the changes referred to in the quotation were the only significant ones during the year and that the vast majority of prices held unchanged.

16.2   (a)

$$\text{Laspeyres} = \frac{\Sigma p_{1i} q_{0i}}{\Sigma p_{0i} q_{0i}} = \frac{(.40)(3) + (.30)(10) + \cdots + (.20)(1)}{(.25)(3) + (.20)(10) + \cdots + (.15)(1)}$$

$$= \frac{11.05}{7.25} = 152.4 \qquad\qquad (1967 = 100)$$

$$\text{Paasche} = \frac{\Sigma p_{1i} q_{1i}}{\Sigma p_{0i} q_{1i}} = \frac{(.40)(2) + (.30)(8) + \cdots + (.20)(2)}{(.25)(2) + (.20)(8) + \cdots + (.15)(2)}$$

$$= \frac{12.70}{8.35} = 152.1 \qquad\qquad (1967 = 100)$$

(b)

$$\text{Laspeyres} = \frac{\Sigma p_{1i} q_{0i}}{\Sigma p_{0i} q_{0i}} = \frac{(.25)(2) + (.20)(8) + \cdots + (.15)(2)}{(.40)(2) + (.30)(8) + \cdots + (.20)(2)}$$

$$= \frac{8.35}{12.70} = 65.7 \qquad\qquad (1973 = 100)$$

$$\text{Paasche} = \frac{\Sigma p_{1i} q_{1i}}{\Sigma p_{0i} q_{1i}} = \frac{(.25)(3) + (.20)(10) + \cdots + (.15)(1)}{(.40)(3) + (.30)(10) + \cdots + (.20)(1)}$$

$$= \frac{7.25}{11.05} = 65.6 \qquad\qquad (1973 = 100)$$

(c) If the quantities of these six items used in 1967 were purchased at 1973 prices, the total cost would be 152.4 percent of the 1967 cost. The total cost of purchasing the quantities of these six items used in 1973, at 1973 prices, would be 152.1 percent of the 1967 cost. If the quantities of these six items used in 1973 were purchased at 1967 prices, the total cost would be 65.7 percent of the 1973 cost. The total cost of purchasing the quantities of these six items used in 1967, at 1967 prices, would be 65.6 percent of the 1973 cost.

16.3   (a) Weighted arithmetic average of price relatives using $p_{0i} q_{0i}$ weights,

$$\frac{\Sigma p_{0i} q_{0i} (p_{1i}/p_{0i})}{\Sigma p_{0i} q_{0i}} = \frac{\frac{.40}{.25}(.25)(3) + \frac{.30}{.20}(.20)(10) + \cdots + \frac{.20}{.15}(.15)(1)}{(.25)(3) + (.20)(10) + \cdots + (.15)(1)}$$

$$= \frac{11.05}{7.25} = 152.4 \qquad\qquad (1967 = 100)$$

(b) Weighted arithmetic average of price relatives using $p_{0i} q_{1i}$ weights,

$$\frac{\Sigma p_{0i} q_{1i} (p_{1i}/p_{0i})}{\Sigma p_{0i} q_{1i}} = \frac{\frac{.40}{.25}(.25)(2) + \frac{.30}{.20}(.20)(8) + \cdots + \frac{.20}{.15}(.15)(2)}{(.25)(2) + (.20)(8) + \cdots + (.15)(2)}$$

$$= \frac{12.70}{8.35} = 152.1 \qquad\qquad (1967 = 100)$$

16.4   They do not meet the test:

$$\text{Laspeyres} = (1.524)(.657) = 1.001 \neq 1$$
$$\text{Paasche} = (1.521)(.656) = .998 \neq 1$$

16.5   Yes!

$$\sqrt[n]{\frac{p_{11}}{p_{01}} \times \cdots \times \frac{p_{1n}}{p_{0n}}} = \frac{1}{\sqrt[n]{p_{01}/p_{11} \times \cdots \times p_{0n}/p_{1n}}}$$

16.6   (a) To find a pre-1930 value on the 1967 base, multiply the value on the 1926 base by $\frac{44.6}{86.4} = .52$. For 1925, $103.5 \times \frac{44.6}{86.4} = 53.8$. The 103.5 is based on $1926 = 100$, while the 53.8 is based on $1967 = 100$.

Year	WPI (1967 = 100)
1890	$56.2 \times .52 = 29.2$
1895	$48.8 \times .52 = 25.4$
1900	$56.1 \times .52 = 29.2$
1905	$60.1 \times .52 = 31.3$
1910	$70.4 \times .52 = 36.6$
1915	$69.5 \times .52 = 36.1$
1920	$154.4 \times .52 = 80.3$
1925	$103.5 \times .52 = 53.8$
1930	$86.4 \times .52 = 44.9$
1935	41.3
1940	40.5
1945	54.6
1950	81.8
1955	87.8
1960	94.9
1965	96.6
1970	110.4

     (b) The pattern of weights used in the old (1926 = 100) series is retained in the values for years between 1890 and 1925, even though the numerical values have been expressed in terms of the new (1967 = 100) base.

16.7   (a) In the given month, prices in Seattle had increased 20 percent above the level of prices in Seattle in the base period. In the given month, prices in Washington, D.C., had increased 28 percent above the level of prices in Washington, D.C., in the base period.

     (b) This question cannot be answered with the information given. We refer to the discussion in Section 16.7.

16.8   (a) Because they measure the movement of prices for different groups of economic goods, and, to the extent that the same goods may appear in two or all three indexes, they are represented by prices prevailing at different points in the chain of distribution, i.e., in different markets, and will have different weights.

(*b*) Primarily, demand and supply changes lead to differences in the behavior of prices of essential consumer goods versus luxuries, consumer goods versus producer goods, and manufactured goods versus commodities. Technical factors such as changes in items, weights, and formulas influence the indexes slightly, although everything possible is done to remove these influences. The Implicit Price Index includes more services than the CPI and has risen faster, since services have increased in price faster than goods.

16.9 (*a*) $\frac{317}{432} = .73$, or 73 percent

(*b*) The ratio reflects the differential effect on farmers of price changes in the markets in which they sell and price changes in the markets in which they buy. The ratio falls when farmers have been adversely affected by the movement of prices; that is, they can buy less than before with the money realized from the sale of a given amount of product (milk, wheat, corn, pigs, etc.).

(*c*) The assumption is that the relationship between prices received by farmers and prices paid by farmers in 1910–1914 should serve as a "norm" or reference base for future comparisons. As a result, market forces influencing either category of prices are seen as disturbances of a "normal" relationship.

16.10 The United States price level has risen to $\frac{130}{88.7} = 146.6$ percent of the level in 1960, so that it now requires $8,000 × 1.466 = $11,728 to buy what could have been bought for $8,000 in 1960. During the same period the British price level has risen to 150 percent of the 1960 level, so that it now requires £3,000 × 1.50 = £4,500 to buy what could have been bought for £3,000 in 1960. Your present salary will buy $12,000/$9,312 × £3,750 = £4,605 worth of goods at present British prices. Therefore, your purchasing power will be greater if you make the move.

16.11 Obviously, $1 is, by definition, equal to 100 cents at any time. When the CPI is 125, a consumer will be able to buy with $1 the quantity of goods and services he could have purchased with 80 cents *in the base period*.

16.12   The terms proposed are more generous than the terms in the present contract. Under the new contract, if the wage is \$3.00 a 1-point increase in the CPI will bring a \$.03 increase in the wage. Under the old contract the increase would have been \$.02. As the current wage rises, the amount of the wage increase for a 1-point increase in the CPI will also rise, which is not the case under the existing contract.

Chapter 17

STATISTICAL METHODS FOR QUALITY ASSURANCE

17.1 INTRODUCTION

In any manufacturing or service activity, many factors contribute to create variability in the characteristics of the end product. Yet, when considering the purchase of that product, the buyer generally places a high value on uniformity and adherence to established standards. A housewife may prefer a particular brand of tomato soup because she is confident that the color, taste, texture, and amount of soup in a can will be nearly identical with past cans. A man will regularly buy the same brand of shaving cream once he has found the one that gives him the best shave, provided that he can count on constant quality in that brand. What is desirable for consumers is imperative for producers. For example, bolts used in scientific equipment should have a specified diameter; to be of any use, they should have a tolerance of perhaps as little as .003 millimeter.

Management realizes that departures from standards of performance will be costly. Continuing effort is devoted to maintaining standards and raising them if technically possible and economically justified. As stated in the "quality policy" of a major electronics manufacturer, "It is the policy of the Company that its products shall be delivered to its customers on schedule and at competitive price, and shall meet all specified and implied standards of performance, reliability, and quality."

How can management know that this specified standard referred to in its quality policy is being attained in practice? At first thought, the best method might appear to be careful inspection of every unit of product. In some cases, however, this is not possible. Destruction of the product may be necessary in order to measure the characteristics important to the consumer. Safety glass must be shattered to measure its strength, and a fuse must be blown to measure its resistance. These products require destructive testing. In some cases, the effort needed to determine the quality of the product, even though it does not destroy it, is so costly that the consumer would be unwilling to pay the price for 100 percent inspection. For either or both of these reasons, *sampling* is almost universally used to control quality of products. Fortunately, experience has taught that the quality of a product after 100 percent inspection is no better, and may be worse than, the quality of the product subjected to inspection by sampling. A smaller amount of inspection allows the selection and training of a small number of skilled inspectors with an understanding of the need to maintain standards by relatively sophisticated techniques and the sense of responsibility to help maintain these standards.

Quality control techniques have combined effectively the basic concepts of sampling and statistical inference with the conditions which characterize industrial purchasing and production processes. In previous years, these techniques were used only in manufacturing, but in recent years they have been applied successfully in accounting, clerical, and service activities.

Throughout the following discussion, three important facts should be borne in mind.

1. *Quality means conformity with standards.* The standards may be set by the maker of the product or by the purchaser. These standards, which may be expressed in terms of averages and variability, percent defective, minimum weight guarantees, number of defects, and so forth, are determined by considerations such as safety, esthetics, competition, human and machine capabilities, and above all, cost.

2. *Care must be exercised in selecting the characteristics of a product or service whose quality is to be maintained.* For example, the United Fruit Company has identified 60 separate, observable characteristics of a banana. Many, but not all these are used for controlling the quality of fresh bananas. Surveys of consumer preferences are taken periodically to determine which of these characteristics are important to the consumer. Without firsthand knowledge of consumer preferences, management might well emphasize

the wrong characteristics of the product. One company, having established careful controls over the color and texture of its tomato juice, could not understand why consumer acceptance of the product was declining. Careful study showed that the saltiness of the juice, which had not been one of the characteristics under control, was responsible for the adverse consumer reaction.

3. *You cannot inspect quality into a product.* The techniques to be described are diagnostic, not remedial. They will show, at least in a probabilistic sense, when a standard is being maintained. When departure from standard is indicated, the sensitiveness of the techniques may make it easier to locate the cause and prescribe the remedy, but the statistical methods by themselves cannot *cause* a process to conform to standards or remedy the trouble when the product departs from standards.

EXERCISES

17.1   If you were a ballpoint pen manufacturer, which characteristics of your product would you subject to statistical methods for quality assurance?

17.2   Can the use of statistical methods for quality assurance guarantee that every unit of product will meet standards? Discuss.

17.3   A consultant urged a manufacturer of auto tires, designed to last an average life of 30,000 miles, to use statistical methods for quality assurance. He claimed the average life of the tire could be increased 5,000 miles by using these methods. Discuss.

17.4   You buy parts from a supplier and incorporate these parts into a product sold to consumers under your brand name. The supplier uses statistical methods to control the process making these parts. To make sure your brand name is not jeopardized by the supplier's poor quality, what would you want to know about the statistical methods he uses?

17.2   CONTROL OF A PROCESS: VARIABLES

We will look first at the statistical methods for assuring the quality of product through *control of the process* by which the product is created. A *process* exists when a particular operation, such as stamping in a stamping plant, is performed in repetitive fashion under conditions believed to be the same for each repetition. If these conditions are maintained, the process may be thought of as the generating source of an infinite population, made up of the output of the process. The filling of a succession of cereal boxes by a machine set up to put the same weight of cereal in each box is another example of a process.

Assuming the other dimensions of the product are similarly controlled, let us investigate the statistical method by which uniformity in the weight of the cereal placed in each box can be maintained. Weight is a measurable and continuous characteristic, so we will outline procedures generally applicable to the control of quality represented by a continuous variable. Let us first assume the producer knows the process mean μ and wants it maintained at the present value. To fix ideas, let us state $\mu = 8$ ounces. Through experience with this machine, and others like it, the producer knows that the amount of cereal placed in each box will vary because of many uncontrollable sources of variation (none large), which yield a predictable overall pattern of variability known as the normal distribution. The standard deviation of this normal distribution is desig-

Process "in control"

nated σ, and we will assume in this illustration that $\sigma = .3$ ounce. The process is *in control* as long as μ and σ remain unchanged, so that every box contains a weight which may be considered a random drawing out of a normal distribution with mean μ ($= 8$ ounces) and standard deviation σ ($= .3$ ounce). Suppose now that we draw a random sample of size n, which gives observations $x_1, x_2, \ldots, x_n$. As we saw in Chapter 9, the average of the sample $\overline{x}$ can be used as an estimate of μ. The $\overline{x}$ value obtained can be considered a random drawing out of a normal distribution with expected value μ and with a standard deviation equal to $\sigma_{\overline{x}} = \sigma/\sqrt{n}$ (at least this will be true as long as the process remains in control). The *control chart* will tell us whether it is.

Control chart

A *control chart* is constructed as follows: The process mean is indicated on the center line μ, as in Figure 17.1. The *upper control limit* (UCL) is $\mu + 3\sigma_{\overline{x}}$, and the *lower control limit* (LCL) is $\mu - 3\sigma_{\overline{x}}$. By drawing horizontal lines $\mu + 3\sigma_{\overline{x}}$ and $\mu - 3\sigma_{\overline{x}}$ on the chart, we are able to see the pattern of variability of the successive sample averages in relation to the control limits. Since the sample averages are normally distributed, the probability is only .003 that an individual $\overline{x}$ will lie above $\mu + 3\sigma_{\overline{x}}$ or below $\mu - 3\sigma_{\overline{x}}$ when the process is in control. By plotting successive observed values of $\overline{x}$ on such a chart, and noting when a value falls outside the control limits we will be alerted to the possibility that the process

Process "out of control"

has "gone out of control."

The process has gone out of control if there has been a change in

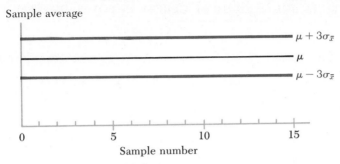

Figure 17.1 Typical control chart.

the process mean from μ to some other value. A sample average falling outside the control limits suggests strongly that the process is out of control, that is, an *assignable cause*, rather than an *unassignable cause* (chance), created the difference. It is the job of someone thoroughly familiar with the process to search out the assignable cause and correct the trouble. Examples of assignable causes would include a change in the machine setting, change in environmental conditions, malfunction of a machine, etc. When a control chart with "$3\sigma_{\bar{x}}$ limits" is used, occasionally the search for an assignable cause will be in vain because the process is *not* out of control. After all, 3 times out of 1,000 the sample average will fall outside the $3\sigma_{\bar{x}}$ limits purely by chance. Narrower limits will lead to more frequent "in vain" searches for assignable causes. In practice the control limits are nearly always put at $\mu \pm 3\sigma_{\bar{x}}$.

Assignable cause

    By contrast, it may happen that the process is out of control, but that—at least initially—the points remain within the control limits. The probability that this will happen for a long period is small, and the more the process is out of control, the smaller the probability.

    If an observed $\bar{x}$ falls outside the control limits, we will obviously look for an assignable cause, but there are other danger signals we can watch for. For example, if seven consecutive sample averages lie above μ, a search for an assignable cause may be warranted, since the probability of such a pattern, if the process is in control, is only $(\frac{1}{2})^7 = \frac{1}{128}$, or less than 1 percent. In addition, the pattern of the successive values of $\bar{x}$ ought to be watched for evidence of persistent increases or decreases.

    So far we have assumed that the producer knew the mean weight μ and the standard deviation σ. In practice these are unknown, and he must rely entirely on the sample evidence to determine whether the process is in control.

TABLE 17.1 WEIGHT OF CEREAL IN BOXES, OUNCES

			Box number					
Sample number	1	2	3	4	5	Sum	Average	Range
1	8.41	7.70	7.90	7.55	7.92	39.48	7.90	.86
2	7.68	8.21	7.58	7.67	8.09	39.23	7.85	.63
3	8.69	7.64	8.16	8.05	8.15	40.69	8.14	1.05
4	7.48	8.17	8.50	7.67	7.66	39.48	7.90	1.02
5	8.38	7 97	8.05	7.98	8.31	40.69	8.14	.41
6	7.48	8.23	8.23	7.74	7.75	39.43	7.89	.75
7	8.29	8.03	8.21	7.57	7.93	40.03	8.01	.72
8	8.00	7.81	8.33	7.95	7.76	39.85	7.97	.57
9	7.90	7.94	8.07	8.02	7.31	39.24	7.85	.76
10	7.52	7.81	7.93	8.14	8.07	39.47	7.89	.62

Table 17.1 shows the individual weights for the five boxes in each of 10 samples. The average of these five observations appears on the control chart. This is more satisfactory than showing each item separately. The reason for this is that the standard deviation of the sample average $\sigma_{\bar{x}} = \sigma/\sqrt{n}$ decreases rapidly as n increases. It is half as large for four observations as it is for one observation, since $\sigma/\sqrt{4} = \frac{1}{2}\sigma$. However, 16 observations are needed to halve the standard deviation once again. When samples are taken frequently, it is desirable to minimize the effort involved. Hence, small samples are commonly used.

Let us return to Table 17.1. The average of sample 1 is

$$\bar{x}_1 = \frac{8.41 + 7.70 + 7.90 + 7.55 + 7.92}{5} = \frac{39.48}{5} = 7.90$$

Similarly, $\bar{x}_2, \ldots, \bar{x}_{10}$ can be computed, and the overall average can be computed by summing all 50 observations and dividing by 50. In our example, the overall average, denoted by $\bar{\bar{x}}$, is

$$\bar{\bar{x}} = \frac{397.59}{50} = 7.95$$

The notation $\bar{\bar{x}}$ suggests that it is the average of averages, which is, in fact, true. We can also compute the overall average from the sample averages

$$\bar{\bar{x}} = \frac{7.90 + 7.85 + \cdots + 7.89}{10} = \frac{79.54}{10} = 7.95$$

For lack of any better information, we consider $\bar{\bar{x}}$ an estimate of the true process mean μ.

Our next problem is to find an estimate for the true σ, the process standard deviation. One *might* proceed by computing the standard deviations from the samples. Thus for the first sample, we would have

$$s_1^2 = \frac{(8.41 - 7.90)^2 + \cdots + (7.92 - 7.90)^2}{4} = \frac{.4230}{4} = .1058$$

Hence $s_1 = .325$.

We can similarly find $s_2^2, \ldots, s_{10}^2$, and we can then take their average as an estimate of σ^2. This, however, is time-consuming and requires fairly involved computations.

Because time is often of the essence and a simple, routine procedure minimizes chances of purely arithmetical mistakes, it is more convenient to use the sample *ranges* to obtain an estimate for σ. The range in each of the 10 samples is given in Table 17.1, and is indicated by $r_1, \ldots, r_{10}$. The average of the ranges is

Use of sample range

$$\bar{r} = \frac{r_1 + \cdots + r_{10}}{10} = \frac{.86 + \cdots + .62}{10} = \frac{7.39}{10} = .74$$

An unbiased estimate for σ can be obtained from $\bar{r}$. This estimate is

$$\frac{\bar{r}}{d_2}$$

where d_2 is a function of the sample size, as shown in Table 17.2. The greater the sample size, the larger d_2 and, hence, the smaller $1/d_2$. This is as we would expect. The standard deviation σ is a specific value, although we do not know what it is. A larger average range value, found when the sample size is larger, must be multiplied by a smaller amount to yield an unbiased estimate of σ.

In our example the sample size is 5, so we will multiply $\bar{r}$ by $1/2.326$ and find as an unbiased estimate for σ

$$\frac{\bar{r}}{d_2} = \frac{.74}{2.326} = .32$$

The control chart for the process mean, called the $\bar{x}$ chart ("x-bar chart") can now be drawn with $\bar{\bar{x}}$ (the estimate for μ) as the center line with upper and lower control limits at

$\bar{x}$ chart

$$\bar{\bar{x}} \pm \frac{3\bar{r}}{d_2\sqrt{n}}$$

TABLE 17.2   FACTORS GIVING UNBIASED ESTIMATE OF σ FROM $\bar{r}$†

Number of observations in subgroup n	*Factor for estimating σ from $\bar{r}$ (multiply $\bar{r}$ by $1/d_2$)* d_2	*Number of observations in subgroup* n	*Factor for estimating σ from $\bar{r}$ (multiply $\bar{r}$ by $1/d_2$)* d_2
2	1.128	22	3.819
3	1.693	23	3.858
4	2.059	24	3.895
5	2.326	25	3.931
6	2.534	30	4.086
7	2.704	35	4.213
8	2.847	40	4.322
9	2.970	45	4.415
10	3.078	50	4.498
11	3.173	55	4.572
12	3.258	60	4.639
13	3.336	65	4.699
14	3.407	70	4.755
15	3.472	75	4.806
16	3.532	80	4.854
17	3.588	85	4.898
18	3.640	90	4.939
19	3.689	95	4.978
20	3.735	100	5.015
21	3.778		

† Adapted by permission from E. L. Grant, "Statistical Quality Control," 3d ed., McGraw-Hill Book Company, New York, 1964.

The upper and lower control limits can be calculated directly from $\bar{r}$ by using the factor

$$A_2 = \frac{3}{d_2\sqrt{n}}$$

for the corresponding n. The values of A_2 are given in the second column of Table 17.3. We have

$$\text{Center line} = \bar{\bar{x}}$$
$$\text{Upper control limit} = \bar{\bar{x}} + A_2\bar{r}$$
$$\text{Lower control limit} = \bar{\bar{x}} - A_2\bar{r}$$

Figure 17.2 shows the $\bar{x}$ chart based on the information in Table 17.1. The control limits are based on the value of A_2 for $n = 5$, which is .58. Further,

$$\text{UCL} = 7.95 + .58(.74) = 8.38$$
$$\text{LCL} = 7.95 - .58(.74) = 7.52$$

Figure 17.2 differs from Figure 17.1 because the center line and control limits are based on $\bar{\bar{x}}$ and $\bar{r}$, rather than the true μ and σ. Incidentally, the values in Table 17.1 are the result of simulating a process

TABLE 17.3 FACTORS FOR DETERMINING CONTROL LIMITS FOR $\bar{x}$ AND r CHARTS†

Number of observations in subgroup n	Factor for $\bar{x}$ chart A_2	Factors for r chart (σ known)		Factors for r chart (σ estimated)	
		LCL D_1	UCL D_2	LCL D_3	UCL D_4
2	1.88	0	3.69	0	3.27
3	1.02	0	4.36	0	2.57
4	.73	0	4.70	0	2.28
5	.58	0	4.92	0	2.11
6	.48	0	5.08	0	2.00
7	.42	.20	5.20	.08	1.92
8	.37	.39	5.31	.14	1.86
9	.34	.55	5.39	.18	1.82
10	.31	.69	5.47	.22	1.78
11	.29	.81	5.53	.26	1.74
12	.27	.92	5.59	.28	1.72
13	.25	1.03	5.65	.31	1.69
14	.24	1.12	5.69	.33	1.67
15	.22	1.21	5.74	.35	1.65
16	.21	1.28	5.78	.36	1.64
17	.20	1.36	5.82	.38	1.62
18	.19	1.43	5.85	.39	1.61
19	.19	1.49	5.89	.40	1.60
20	.18	1.55	5.92	.41	1.59

† Adapted by permission from E. L. Grant, "Statistical Quality Control," 3d ed., McGraw-Hill Book Company, New York, 1964.

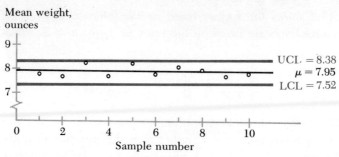

Figure 17.2 $\bar{x}$ chart based on Table 17.1.

yielding a normal distribution with $\mu = 8.00$ and $\sigma = .3$. As you can see, our estimates are close to these parameters.

As stated before, a process can be out of control if either μ or σ changes. The $\bar{x}$ chart is eminently suited to spot changes in μ. If the process mean changes to some value different from μ, it will not be long before points appear on the chart beyond the control limits. It will also help spot increases in σ, but not as fast as an r *chart*, which is especially suited to spot changes in variability quickly. It is advisable to maintain control over variability as well as uniformity.

An r chart is constructed as follows: If the process standard deviation σ is known, the r chart can be established through the use of the factors D_1 and D_2, given in Columns 3 and 4 of Table 17.3, together with d_2, which is given in Table 17.2. We find

r chart,
σ known

$$\text{Center line} = d_2\sigma$$
$$\text{Upper control limit} = D_2\sigma$$
$$\text{Lower control limit} = D_1\sigma$$

r chart,
σ unknown

If the process standard deviation is not known, $\bar{r}$ is used, together with factors D_3 and D_4 (given in Columns 5 and 6 of Table 17.3). We have

$$\text{Center line} = \bar{r}$$
$$\text{Upper control limit} = D_4\bar{r}$$
$$\text{Lower control limit} = D_3\bar{r}$$

Figure 17.3 shows the r chart based on the information in Table 17.1. The control limits are based on the values of D_3 and D_4 for $n = 5$. Due to the small value of n, $D_3 = 0$.

$$\text{UCL} = 2.11(.74) = 1.56$$
$$\text{LCL} = 0(.74) = 0$$

On the control chart for $\bar{x}$, the limits are always symmetrically located around the center line, since the sampling distribution for the mean is symmetric. However, the limits on an r chart are not symmetric, since the sampling distribution of the range is skewed to the right.

At times, only one control limit is established. In making rope, an $\bar{x}$ chart to control breaking strength may have only a lower control limit, since the manufacturer is primarily concerned about the danger of selling rope not as strong as the customer expects it to be. On r charts it is not unusual to see only an upper control limit, since a variability exceeding the standard causes customer dissatisfaction, whereas a variability smaller than the standard can only please the customer.

The control chart cannot be used to determine what μ and σ are acceptable. The manager must establish these values. If the control chart indicates that these values are not being maintained, the process itself must be modified or the design specifications changed. Proper use of control chart techniques can only help to maintain a process in the state prevailing when the control charts were set up. In our illustration, we have assumed that 7.95 and .32 are an acceptable mean and standard deviation for this process. If they are not, the process should be modified.

It is generally advisable to maintain both $\bar{x}$ charts and r charts, since changes in either process mean or the process variability can significantly influence the acceptability of the product. The action called for when the process moves out of control on the r chart is not the same as the action required when the process moves out of control on the $\bar{x}$ chart. Observations outside the control limits on an $\bar{x}$ chart are primarily an indication that something is wrong with the process mean. Observations outside the control limits of an r chart are primarily an indication that something is wrong with the variability.

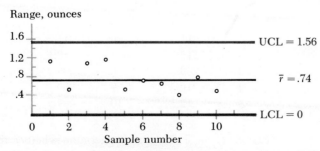

Figure 17.3 r chart based on Table 17.1.

EXERCISES

17.5   A process is designed to yield machined parts known as *spacers* with mean thickness of .8470 inch. Successive samples of size five yield $\bar{x}$ values as follows: .8464, .8465, .8477, .8464, .8473, .8469, .8472, .8482, .8478, .8474, .8465, .8468, .8467, .8472, .8470, .8465, .8470. The mean range $\bar{r}$ in these samples is .0005. Construct an $\bar{x}$ chart, and determine whether this process is in control. What action would you take?

17.6   Answering calls at a switchboard may be thought of as a process. Each call is a unit of product, and the time the caller waits to be answered is a measure of the quality of the service rendered. Five calls, chosen at random, are timed during each hour the board is open. Results for the last 10 hours show (in seconds):

Sample	1	2	3	4	5	6	7	8	9	10
$\bar{x}$	20	34	45	39	26	29	13	34	37	23
r	23	39	14	5	20	17	21	11	40	10

Construct an $\bar{x}$ chart and an r chart, and determine whether this process is in control. What action would you take?

17.7   The maker of baling twine advertises that the product will hold a 200-pound weight without breaking. The twine is manufactured by a process designed to yield a breaking strength with a mean of 210 pounds and a standard deviation of 3 pounds. Nine segments of twine are randomly chosen from each day's production and tested to determine mean breaking strength. The results for a recent sequence of days are as follows (in pounds):

Sample	$\bar{x}$	Sample	$\bar{x}$	Sample	$\bar{x}$
1	211.3	6	211.6	11	208.7
2	210.1	7	210.1	12	209.0
3	209.6	8	209.9	13	208.0
4	210.0	9	209.3	14	208.7
5	212.1	10	209.5	15	209.2

Construct an $\bar{x}$ chart, and determine whether this process is in control. What action would you take?

17.3 CONTROL OF A PROCESS: ATTRIBUTES

As we saw in the preceding section, a process designed to fill boxes with cereal may be controlled by how much cereal is in each box. This characteristic, weight, is a continuous random variable.

In many situations the important characteristic cannot be expressed as a continuous variable; that is, it is either present in the product or it is absent. If it is present, the product is acceptable; if it is absent, the product is not acceptable. Such a characteristic is an *attribute*. Thus, a lamp will burn or it will not, a seed germinates or it does not, a firecracker explodes when lit or it does not. Service functions have similar characteristics. A room clerk gives the bellboy the correct key or he does not, the store bills you for the correct amount or it does not, your secretary files a letter in the correct file folder or she does not. These either/or cases lead to a method of control similar to that in the preceding section, with the binomial distribution, rather than the normal distribution, playing the pivotal role.

To control a process by an attribute, we establish a p chart, where p is the *fraction defective* in the sample. The p chart shows whether the process fraction defective π is being maintained. If π is known and the sample size is n, the p chart has

p chart

$$\text{Center line} = \pi$$

$$\text{Upper control limit} = \pi + 3\sqrt{\frac{\pi(1-\pi)}{n}}$$

$$\text{Lower control limit} = \pi - 3\sqrt{\frac{\pi(1-\pi)}{n}}$$

These values are consistent with our discussion in Section 9.6.

If π is not known, an estimate $\bar{p}$ must be determined from the sample evidence taken from the output of the process. Here, $\bar{p}$ is the ratio of defectives observed in past samples to the total number of observations in these past samples. This value can then be used in place of π in the above formulas.

Figure 17.4 shows a p chart for controlling the quality of operations in a soldering department. The fraction defective represents the ratio of improperly soldered connections to the total connections examined in the sample. Each sample contained 50 connections. The fraction defective $\bar{p}$ in the 750 sampled connections is .20. Thus, in Figure 17.4,

$$\text{Center line} = \bar{p} = .20$$

$$\text{Upper control limit} = \bar{p} + 3\sqrt{\frac{\bar{p}(1 - \bar{p})}{n}} = .3695$$

$$\text{Lower control limit} = \bar{p} - 3\sqrt{\frac{\bar{p}(1 - \bar{p})}{n}} = .0305$$

Clearly, from the level of the value of $\bar{p}$, this is a process in need of study and improvement. However, the chart does show that the workers performed uniformly during the period represented by these samples; that is, there is no evidence that π changed during this period. (We repeat, this does not mean that the value of π which prevails is acceptable to the management.)

In the p chart formulas just given, the control limits are based on the assumption that the normal distribution will be a satisfactory approximation to the binomial distribution for the relevant values of n and π or $\bar{p}$. In light of the small values of both the sample size and the process fraction defective often encountered in quality assurance situations, this assumption may not be fulfilled. If it is not, the exact binomial or the Poisson distribution must be used to determine limits beyond which the sample proportion will seldom fall if the process is in control. Special graphs and tables exist for this purpose.

As we saw in the discussion of the Poisson distribution in Section 7.6, there are occasions when no meaningful interpretation can be given to the notion of "fraction" defective because there is no appropriate value for the denominator, that is, the total number of trials. For example, a

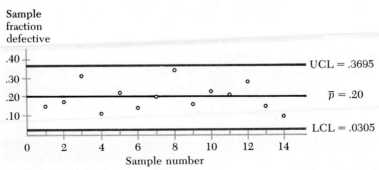

Figure 17.4 p chart for controlling a soldering operation.

manufacturer wishes to control the quality of the fabric woven for use as mattress covering. Examination reveals the number of flaws per square yard. The number of flaws observed is represented by c. The sample size n is undefined and undefinable. Treating the square yard as the unit of product, the number of defects in a succession of randomly chosen non-overlapping square yards can be viewed as the characteristic on which to base the control chart. Such a chart is known as a *c chart*. The process mean number of defects per square yard is estimated from the k sample values of $c_1, \ldots, c_k$, or

c chart

$$\bar{c} = \frac{c_1 + c_2 + \cdots + c_k}{k}$$

The c chart is then established as follows:

$$\text{Center line} = \bar{c}$$
$$\text{Upper control limit} = \bar{c} + 3\sqrt{\bar{c}}$$
$$\text{Lower control limit} = \bar{c} - 3\sqrt{\bar{c}}$$

The variance of a Poisson distribution equals the parameter $\bar{c}$, and hence the standard deviation is $\sqrt{\bar{c}}$. These limits are symmetric, although the relevant distribution is the Poisson, which is not symmetric. This slight error in the limits has proved acceptable in practice.

EXERCISES

17.8   A plastic molding department produces knobs which must fit over a shaft in final assembly. In the final assembly, knobs which do not fit have to be replaced, which is a time-consuming operation. A control chart for the fraction defective is maintained in the molding department, where 100 knobs are checked every 3 hours. The process fraction defective is supposed to be .03. The following numbers of defectives were found in 20 recent samples: 3, 1, 0, 5, 10, 7, 2, 6, 5, 0, 2, 1, 7, 4, 9, 2, 3, 4, 1, 2. Construct the appropriate control chart, and discuss the evidence. What action would you take? (Assume that you can use the normal distribution.)

17.9   The Post Office at Whereareyou, N.M., has one clerk responsible for adding ZIP codes to unzipped mail. To save time, the clerk does this job from memory. His memory is not perfect; in fact, 100 randomly chosen items from each of the last 10 days show the following numbers of incorrectly zipped items per day: 17, 32, 9, 50, 16, 25, 3, 12, 21, 29. Evaluate his performance by means of a control chart. Would you suggest any modification in the "process"? Which and why?

17.10   The enameled outside surface of each Articaire refrigerator is carefully inspected prior to crating. Defects, such as scratches, stains, bubbles, and thin spots, are counted and repaired. The most recent 500 refrigerators inspected revealed $\bar{c} = 2.5$. For the last 10 the numbers of defects were as follows: 3, 0, 2, 9, 4, 2, 1, 3, 7, 1. Construct a c chart. Is the process in control? What action would you recommend?

17.11   A typist has recently been given a new electric typewriter in place of her old manual one. She carefully proofreads each page she types and discovers, about 1 week after the arrival of the new typewriter, that the number of errors on the last 10 consecutive pages has been 6, 8, 3, 6, 4, 9, 3, 1, 0, 0. With joy she announces, "I've got my typing under control again. My aim was to get my average errors per page down to zero and I've done it!" Comment.

17.4   ACCEPTANCE SAMPLING

When shipments, or *lots*, of product are transferred from one firm to another, or from one division of a firm to another, the manager receiving the lot wants to be reasonably sure that it meets whatever standards he has agreed on with the supplier. The supplier has been aware of these standards and presumably has worked to meet them. However, the buyer may still find it desirable to subject the product to further inspection. Certainly the supplier is more likely to adhere to standards when he knows the buyer is inspecting incoming lots.

Acceptance sampling is used to help both the buyer and the seller in this situation. Through appropriate techniques, agreed to by buyer and seller (usually in the contract), the lot is submitted to a test based on sample evidence. The entire lot is then accepted or rejected. Rejected lots may be subjected to 100 percent inspection, with faulty items being replaced by good items. They may be accepted under different contract terms, such as a lower price. In extreme cases they are scrapped.

Lots should be defined so that the items contained in any one lot are homogeneous. The variability among the items in a lot should be caused only by chance. Nonchance factors which might introduce variability, such as differences in plant or process, should be used as the basis for forming different lots.

The acceptance sampling procedures used widely in industry are based on the classification of units of product as defective or nondefective. We assume in this discussion that some way exists in any situation for deciding whether a unit is defective or nondefective. In its simplest form, acceptance sampling requires selecting a random sample of size n from a lot of size N, determining the number of defectives in the sample, and comparing this number with a predetermined value c—the critical value or the *acceptance number*. If the number of defectives is less than or equal to c, the lot is accepted; if the number of defectives is greater than c, the lot is rejected.

Lot size N

Acceptance number c

The theoretical basis for acceptance sampling was given in our earlier discussions of hypothesis testing, and in particular, in Sections 10.4 to 10.6. The terminology used here will differ slightly. Our null hypothesis is that the true percent of defectives is π_0. This is called the *acceptable quality level* (AQL). The alternative hypothesis is that the true percent of defectives is π_1. We will refer to π_1 as the *reject quality level* (RQL). The risk of rejecting a lot with only π_0 percent defective is α, the *producer's risk*. This is equivalent to r_0. The risk of accepting a lot with π_1 percent defective is β, the *consumer's risk*. This is equivalent to r_1. The *sampling plan*, defined by N, n, and c, should be such that the producer's risk and the consumer's risk are limited to α and β. The sampling plan embodies the decision rule.

Acceptable quality level (AQL)

Reject quality level (RQL)

Sampling plan

If π_0, π_1, α, and β are known, a sampling plan can be designed by determining the values of n and c which will yield approximately the required degrees of protection. Methods for computing the sample size and the critical value, or acceptance number, were discussed in Sections 10.4 to 10.6. However, tables exist which enable us to read off n and c without extensive computations. Table 17.4 can be used if the producer's risk α and the consumer's risk β have values of 1, 5, or 10 percent, and π_0 and π_1 are small.

Calculation of n and c

We will discuss how to use this table for the case where $\pi_0 = .75$ percent and $\pi_1 = 3$ percent, $\alpha = .05$ and $\beta = .10$. Thus, if the quality of the batch is so good that only .75 percent is defective, there should be only a 5 percent probability of rejecting the lot. This is the producer's risk α. If, on the other hand, there are in fact 3 percent defectives, the risk of accepting so bad a lot should be only 10 percent. This is the consumer's risk β.

The use of the table proceeds in several steps. First, we look at the

TABLE 17.4   GENERALIZED TABLE OF SINGLE SAMPLING PLANS
FOR $\alpha = .05$, $\beta = .10$†

$\dfrac{\beta_{.10}}{\alpha_{.05}}$	c	$\alpha = 1\%$ $n\pi_{.99}$	$\alpha = 5\%$ $n\pi_{.95}$	$\alpha = 10\%$ $n\pi_{.90}$	$n\pi_{.50}$	$\beta = 10\%$ $n\pi_{.10}$	$\beta = 5\%$ $n\pi_{.05}$	$\beta = 1\%$ $n\pi_{.01}$
45.157	0	.010	.051	.105	.693	2.303	2.996	4.605
10.958	1	.149	.355	.532	1.678	3.890	4.744	6.638
6.506	2	.436	.818	1.102	2.674	5.322	6.296	8.406
4.890	3	.823	1.366	1.745	3.762	6.681	7.754	10.045
4.057	4	1.279	1.970	2.433	4.671	7.994	9.154	11.605
3.549	5	1.785	2.613	3.152	5.670	9.275	10.513	13.108
3.205	6	2.330	3.286	3.895	6.670	10.532	11.842	14.571
2.957	7	2.906	3.981	4.656	7.669	11.771	13.148	16.000
2.768	8	3.507	4.695	5.432	8.669	12.995	14.434	17.403
2.618	9	4.130	5.426	6.221	9.669	14.206	15.705	18.783
2.497	10	4.771	6.169	7.021	10.668	15.407	16.692	20.145
2.397	11	5.428	6.924	7.829	11.668	16.598	18.208	21.490
2.312	12	6.099	7.690	8.646	12.668	17.782	19.442	22.821
2.240	13	6.782	8.464	9.470	13.668	18.958	20.668	24.139
2.177	14	7.477	9.246	10.300	14.668	20.128	21.886	25.446
2.122	15	8.181	10.035	11.135	15.668	21.292	23.098	26.743
2.073	16	8.895	10.831	11.976	16.668	22.452	24.302	28.031
2.029	17	9.616	11.633	12.822	17.668	23.606	25.500	29.310
1.990	18	10.346	12.442	13.672	18.668	24.756	26.692	30.581
1.954	19	11.082	13.254	14.525	19.668	25.902	27.879	31.845
1.922	20	11.825	14.072	15.383	20.668	27.045	29.062	33.103
1.892	21	12.574	14.894	16.244	21.668	28.184	30.241	34.355
1.865	22	13.329	15.719	17.108	22.668	29.320	31.416	35.601
1.840	23	14.088	16.548	17.975	23.668	30.453	32.586	36.841
1.817	24	14.853	17.382	18.844	24.668	31.584	33.752	38.077
1.795	25	15.623	18.218	19.717	25.667	32.711	34.916	39.308
1.707	30	19.532	22.444	24.113	30.667	38.315	40.690	45.401
1.641	35	23.525	26.731	28.556	35.667	43.872	46.404	51.409
1.590	40	27.587	31.066	33.038	40.667	49.390	52.069	57.347
1.548	45	31.704	35.441	37.550	45.667	54.878	57.695	63.231
1.514	50	35.867	39.849	42.089	50.667	60.339	63.287	69.066

† Adapted with permission from the American Society for Quality Control, Inc., Tables for Constructing and for Computing the Operating Characteristics of Single-sampling Plans, J. M. Cameron, "Industrial Quality Control," vol. 9, p. 39, July 1952.

column labeled $\alpha = 5$ percent and the column labeled $\beta = 10$ percent. We divide the corresponding entries in these two columns, the larger by the smaller (for example, $\frac{6.681}{1.366} = 4.890$). These entries are written in the first column of the table. This column can only be used if $\alpha = 5$ percent and $\beta = 10$ percent. For other values, for example, $\alpha = 1$ percent, $\beta = 5$ percent, we would find $\frac{2.996}{.010}$, $\frac{4.744}{.149}$, $\frac{6.296}{.436}$, and so on.

As our second step, we divide the RQL by the AQL, that is, π_1 by π_0. This gives $\pi_1/\pi_0 = \frac{.03}{.0075} = 4$. We now look for the value 4 in the first column, which we just computed under step 1. We find the value 4.057 as the closest value available. Associated with this value, we find in the second column the critical value, in this instance 4.

In the third step we want to find the sample size. We look again at the columns labeled $\alpha = 5$ percent and $\beta = 10$ percent. We have also labeled these $n\pi_{.95}$ and $n\pi_{.10}$, where, in general,

$$\pi_k = \text{proportion defective such that we want to}$$
$$\text{accept the lot with probability } k$$

Therefore, $\pi_{.95}$ is the proportion defective in a batch that we want to accept with 95 percent probability, and this proportion is $\pi_0 = .0075$. Similarly, $\pi_{.10}$ is .03, since if the proportion defective is .03, we want to accept with $\beta = 10$ percent probability. In the row corresponding to the value 4.057 we find the entry 1.970 in the column $n\pi_{.95}$ and 7.994 in the column $n\pi_{.10}$. We now find n by solving the equations

$$n\pi_{.95} = .0075n = 1.970 \qquad \text{or} \qquad n = 262.7$$
$$n\pi_{.10} = .03n \quad = 7.994 \qquad \text{or} \qquad n = 266.5$$

There is a small difference between these values because the value 4.057, which we found in step 2, differs slightly from $\pi_1/\pi_0 = 4$. We choose a value between these limits, $n = 265$. The sampling plan $n = 265$, $c = 4$ will (approximately) satisfy our criteria.

The actual problem is now solved, but it is useful to construct the *operating characteristic (OC) curve* for this sampling plan. *An OC curve shows the probability of accepting a lot as a function of the lot percent defective.* In Table 17.4 in the row corresponding to 4.057 we see the entry 1.279 in the column labeled $n\pi_{.99}$. We know $n = 265$; therefore,

Operating characteristic (OC) curve

$$265\pi_{.99} = 1.279 \qquad \text{or} \qquad \pi_{.99} = .0048$$

In other words, there is a 99 percent probability of accepting the lot if its quality is so good that only .48 percent is defective. Similarly,

$$265\pi_{.95} = 1.970 \quad \text{or} \quad \pi_{.95} = .0074$$
$$265\pi_{.90} = 2.433 \quad \text{or} \quad \pi_{.90} = .0091$$
$$265\pi_{.50} = 4.671 \quad \text{or} \quad \pi_{.50} = .0176$$
$$265\pi_{.10} = 7.994 \quad \text{or} \quad \pi_{.10} = .0301$$
$$265\pi_{.05} = 9.154 \quad \text{or} \quad \pi_{.05} = .0345$$
$$265\pi_{.01} = 11.605 \quad \text{or} \quad \pi_{.01} = .0438$$

If a batch has as many as 4.38 percent defectives, its probability of acceptance—the probability that a sample of size 265 will contain no more than four defectives—is only 1 percent. Table 17.5 summarizes these values, and Figure 17.5 shows the OC curve for our decision rule, that is, $n = 265$, $c = 4$.

The OC curve of a plan shows not only the probability of acceptance of a lot with given percent defective but also the discriminating ability of the plan, that is, the ability of the plan to signal "accept" for 1 percent defective and "reject" for a slightly greater percent defective. For one plan to be more discriminating than another, a larger sample is required. The OC curve of the more discriminating plan will have a steeper slope, reflecting the greater decrease in probability of acceptance for a given increase in lot percent defective.

Stringency

The *stringency* of a sampling plan for lots with π percent defective is shown by the height of the OC curve at π. If lots with π percent defective have a smaller probability of acceptance under plan A than under

TABLE 17.5   OPERATING
             CHARACTERISTIC CURVE
             FOR ACCEPTANCE
             SAMPLING PLAN
             ($n = 265$, $c = 4$)

Lot percent defective	P(acceptance of lot)
.48	.99
.74	.95
.91	.90
1.76	.50
3.01	.10
3.45	.05
4.38	.01

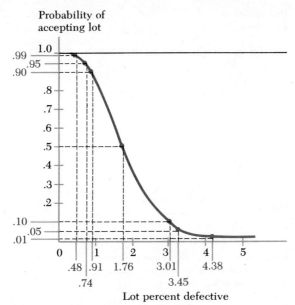

Figure 17.5 Operating characteristic curve for acceptance sampling plan $n = 265$, $c = 4$.

plan B, plan A is more stringent at π. In our example, we set the stringency at .95 for $\pi = .0075$. The plans which provide this stringency for $\pi = .0075$ will vary in their discriminating ability, depending on the sample size n. The larger the n, the steeper the OC curve and the more discriminating power in the plan.

Figure 17.6 shows two OC curves with stringency .95 for $\pi = .05$. Plan A uses a larger sample size than plan B, and therefore has the greater discriminating power.

Figure 17.6 also shows plan C, which has the same discriminating power as plan A but greater stringency than plan A for *every* value of π. Plan C is *uniformly more stringent* than A or B. For two plans with a given n, the plan with the smaller c is uniformly more stringent. For two plans with a given c, the plan with the larger n is uniformly more stringent. In summary, one plan is more stringent than another plan if its OC curve is everywhere below the OC curve of the other plan. A plan has more discriminating power than another if the maximum slope of its OC curve is greater than the maximum slope of the other.

The OC curve for the plan we have derived shows the probability that a lot containing π percent defective will be accepted under the plan.

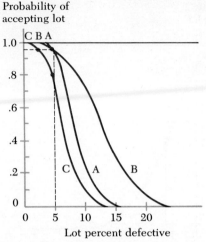

Probability of
accepting lot

Figure 17.6   Three OC curves showing
differences in stringency and discriminating
power of sampling plans.

For each value of π, there is also a probability of rejection. Clearly,
P(rejection) $= 1 - $ P(acceptance). If each rejected lot is subjected to
100 percent inspection and its defective items are replaced by effective
items, it will contain no defectives after inspection. Thus, only lots
originally accepted without 100 percent inspection still contain defective
items after this "rectification" of the lots originally rejected. If lots with
π percent defective are subjected to a sampling plan, including the rectification of rejected lots, the long-run average percent defective in all

**TABLE 17.6   AVERAGE OUTGOING QUALITY
FOR ACCEPTANCE SAMPLING
PLAN** $(n = 265, c = 4)$

(1) Lot percent defective	*(2)* P(*acceptance*)	*(3)* AOQ
.48	.99	.475
.74	.95	.703
.91	.90	.819
1.76	.50	.880
3.01	.10	.301
3.45	.05	.173
4.38	.01	.044

lots is known as the *average outgoing quality* (AOQ) for π. For each plan we can plot the AOQ against π. The maximum value on the curve is labeled the *average outgoing quality limit* (AOQL). This is a significant piece of information, since it shows the worst long-run average quality level the plan will yield, regardless of the quality of the lots fed through the plan. The average quality level actually attained will depend on the values of π in lots submitted under the plan, and this cannot be known ahead of time, although it is a subject worthy of speculation.

Average outgoing quality (AOQ)

Average outgoing quality limit (AOQL)

For lots with π percent defective,

$$AOQ = \pi \cdot P(\text{acceptance}|\pi) + 0 \cdot P(\text{rejection}|\pi)$$

If the lot has π percent defectives, it is either accepted with probability $P(\text{acceptance}|\pi)$ or it is rejected with probability $P(\text{rejection}|\pi)$. If it is rejected, rectification guarantees that the percent defective in the lot will be 0.

Table 17.6 shows the AOQ values for the plan $n = 265$, $c = 4$. The AOQ curve is shown in Figure 17.7. The highest point on this curve, the AOQL, is .93 percent, which is the average outgoing quality when submitted lots contain 1.4 percent defective. Thus no matter what lots are submitted, the average outgoing quality will not be more than .93

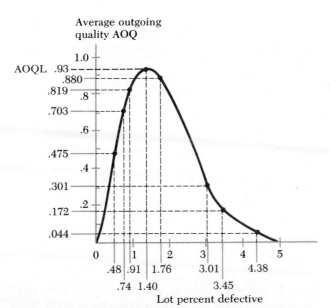

Figure 17.7 Average outgoing quality for acceptance sampling plan $n = 265$, $c = 4$.

percent defective, and it will be below this unless every lot has 1.4 percent defective. In summary, this acceptance plan, including rectification, assures an average of slightly less than 1 percent defective items.

EXERCISES

17.12   Using Table 17.4, find the values of n and c for the single sampling plan which most nearly meets the following requirements:

(a) The probability is .95 that lots with 1 percent defective will be accepted, that is, AQL $\pi_0 = .01$, $\alpha = .05$.

(b) The probability is .10 that lots with 6.5 percent defective will be accepted, that is, RQL $\pi_1 = .065$, $\beta = .10$.

Find and plot the OC curve for this plan. What is the level of quality, i.e., percent of defectives, which has a .50 probability of acceptance?

17.13   In the Department of Defense publication *Military Standard 105D*, a sampling plan is provided for use when $501 < N < 1,200$, and the specified AQL π_0 is 1 percent. This plan is $n = 80$, $c = 2$. Using the Poisson distribution, determine the ordinates of the OC curve for this plan, and plot the curve. Compare the results with those from the preceding exercise.

17.14   Find the AOQ curve for the plan described in the preceding exercise. Plot the curve. What is the AOQL?

17.5   OTHER ACCEPTANCE SAMPLING PLANS

In all our previous sampling plans we established a sample size and a critical value, for example, $n = 265$, $c = 4$. Suppose now that after we have drawn 50 items, we have found 3 defectives. It is tempting to argue that we will waste time and effort by further sampling. The evidence gathered so far strongly suggests the batch is bad and ought to be rejected. It is also possible that we have sampled 200 items and not found a single defective. Can we not stop sampling and accept the lot? Double sampling plans, multiple sampling plans, and sequential sampling plans are designed to enable us to limit the sample size whenever a small sample gives conclusive evidence.

Double
sampling
plans
 In a *double sampling plan*, two sample sizes, n_1 and n_2, are specified. If the first sample of n_1 items contains c_1 or fewer defectives, the lot is accepted. If the first sample contains more than c_1^* defectives, the lot

is rejected. If the number of defectives in the first sample is more than c_1 but not more than $c_1{}^*$, a second sample of n_2 items is chosen. The lot is accepted if the combined sample of $n_1 + n_2$ items contains c_2 or fewer defectives; otherwise it is rejected.

Each double sampling plan has an OC curve showing the probability of acceptance under the plan for each lot percent defective. Figure 17.8 shows the OC curve for the plan $n_1 = 36$, $n_2 = 59$, $c_1 = 0$, $c_1{}^* = 3$, $c_2 = 3$. This plan is designed specifically for lots of 1,000 items. It is implemented as follows: We first draw a sample of size 36, and if it contains $c_1 = 0$ defectives, we accept the lot. If it contains more than $c_1{}^* = 3$ defectives, we reject the lot. If the first sample of size 36 contains 1, 2, or 3 defectives, we draw another sample of size 59. If the total number of defectives in the $36 + 59 = 95$ units is 3 or less we accept the lot; if not, we reject the lot.

Double sampling requires a smaller average number of items selected before a decision is reached. Hence the average sample size under double sampling is never as large as under single sampling—given the same values for the producer's risk α and the consumer's risk β. This should be obvious, for very good or very bad batches have a high probability of being accepted or rejected after the first sample. The reduction in sampling costs often justifies the slightly more complicated sampling procedure. A psychologically appealing reason for double sampling is that many persons

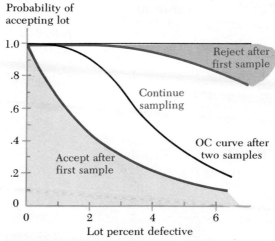

Figure 17.8 The OC curve for the double sampling plan $n_1 = 36$, $n_2 = 59$, $c_1 = 0$, $c_1{}^* = 3$, $c_2 = 3$.

Multiple
sampling
plans

find a plan easier to live with if it gives suspected lots a "second chance." This can be important when introducing a sampling plan.

There is no reason to stop at a double sampling plan. The principle of making a decision if the available evidence is conclusive and delaying it otherwise has led to *multiple sampling plans*. The same OC curve applies to the single plan $n = 125$, $c = 5$, the double plan $n_1 = 80$, $n_2 = 80$, $c_1 = 2$, $c_1^* = 4$, $c_2 = 6$, and the seven-stage plan described in Table 17.7. The table shows that under this seven-stage plan we should continue sampling if, for example, after three samples we find three, four, or five defectives. After seven samples, we must reach a conclusion, for there will be either 9 or fewer defectives, or 10 or more.

The average sample size required when a multiple sampling plan is used is lower than for either a single sample or a double sampling plan with the same OC curve. The advantage is particularly great when the OC curve is relatively steep, since the single sampling plan in that case calls for a relatively large sample to provide the required discriminating power. The advantage is slight when the single sample size is small. In this case, the complexity of administering a double or multiple plan may outweigh the savings from a slightly smaller average sample size.

The average sample size required is at its minimum for any given OC curve when we push the principle of multiple sampling to its limit.

TABLE 17.7   SINGLE-STAGE, DOUBLE-STAGE, AND MULTIPLE-STAGE SAMPLING PLANS WITH THE SAME OC CURVE COMPARED

Sampling plan	Sample number	Individual sample size	Accept	Reject
Single-stage	1	125	5 or less	6 or more
Double-stage	1	80	2 or less	5 or more
	2	80	6 or less	7 or more
Multiple	1	32		4 or more
(seven-stage)	2	32	1 or less	5 or more
	3	32	2 or less	6 or more
	4	32	3 or less	7 or more
	5	32	5 or less	8 or more
	6	32	7 or less	9 or more
	7	32	9 or less	10 or more

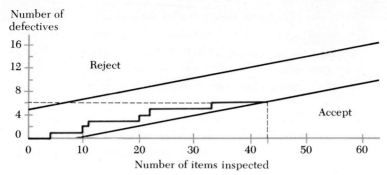

Figure 17.9 Sequential sampling.

This leads to *sequential sampling* where items are inspected one at a time. After each item is classified as defective or not defective, the total number of defectives d is compared with the total number inspected n. If the number of defectives falls above a critical upper limit, the lot is rejected. If the number of defectives falls below a critical lower limit, the lot is accepted. If the number of defectives lies between the limits, another item is inspected.

Sequential sampling

A sequential sampling plan can be found for each combination of values for the producer's risk α, the AQL π_0, the consumer's risk β, and the RQL π_1. Given these values, a graph can be made with two parallel lines forming a narrow band including the origin. An example is given in Figure 17.9.

As long as we stay between the lines, we continue sampling. As soon as we get below the lower line, we accept the lot. As soon as we get above the upper line, we reject the lot. Figure 17.9 illustrates results, showing that after a sample of 43 items we accept the batch.

Theoretically, the sampling might continue forever: we might always be between the lines. In practice, a cutoff point is established at which a decision, one way or the other, must be made. The cutoff point will depend on the cost and time for inspection of an additional item.

Answers to Exercises

17.1   A survey of users might show important characteristics to be ease of removing cap, smoothness of outer surface, assurance pen will write on every occasion, even flow of ink, and uniformity of ink color. Engineers must translate these characteristics into controllable aspects of the manufacturing process such as the percent of impurities in each batch of plastic, temperature of plastic prior to molding, and composition of ink revealed by chemical analysis. Continuing checks on consumer opinions must be made.

17.2   No. Variability will be found in a process, even though statistical methods show that acceptable standards are being maintained. Occasionally, a unit of product will vary beyond the limits set for the standard.

17.3   Use of statistical techniques alone cannot increase the average life. However, dollars saved and knowledge gained partly as the result of using statistical techniques for quality assurance might permit a modification in the process so that a tire with higher average life is produced. This tire is the product of a new process, not the product of the old process subjected to statistical techniques.

17.4   What characteristics of the product is he controlling? At what levels are these characteristics being maintained? What are the details of the sampling techniques in use (sampling method, size, frequency)? What criteria are used to decide when a standard is no longer being met, and what is done about it?

17.5 $$\text{Upper control limit} = \bar{\bar{x}} + A_2\bar{r} = .84703 + .58(.0005)$$
$$= .84732$$
$$\text{Center line} = \bar{\bar{x}} = .84703$$
$$\text{Lower control limit} = \bar{\bar{x}} - A_2\bar{r} = .84703 - .58(.0005)$$
$$= .84674$$

The control chart shows clearly the process is not in control: 4 points are above UCL (.8477, .8482, .8478, .8474), and 6 points are below LCL (.8464, .8465, .8464, .8465, .8467, .8465). The process should be stopped and the conditions investigated to locate assignable causes of excessive variability in the mean. Workers, machines, materials, and the design of the process itself may all require investigation.

17.6   For the $\bar{x}$ chart:

$$\text{Upper control limit} = \bar{\bar{x}} + A_2\bar{r} = 30 + .58(20) = 41.6$$
$$\text{Center line} = \bar{\bar{x}} = 30$$
$$\text{Lower control limit} = \bar{\bar{x}} - A_2\bar{r} = 30 - .58(20) = 18.4$$

For the r chart:

$$\text{Upper control limit} = D_4\bar{r} = 2.11(20) = 42.2$$
$$\text{Center line} = \bar{r} = 20$$
$$\text{Lower control limit} = D_3\bar{r} = 0(20) = 0$$

The process is in control with respect to variability but not with respect to the average. All points lie within the control limits on the r chart. One point, 45, lies above UCL on the $\bar{x}$ chart, and one point, 13, is below LCL. The process should be investigated to locate assignable causes of excessive variability in the mean. (Presumably this is a process which cannot be stopped while the investigation proceeds.) It may be that there is a daily pattern to call volume, so that the "out of control" points represent the peak and trough in the pattern. If so, the process cannot be considered to operate under constant conditions; i.e., the center line on the control chart must be modified to reflect shifts in the process mean.

17.7

$$\text{Upper control limit} = \mu + 3\sigma_{\bar{x}} = 210 + 3\frac{3}{\sqrt{9}} = 213$$

$$\text{Center line} = \mu = 210$$

$$\text{Lower control limit} = \mu - 3\sigma_{\bar{x}} = 210 - 3\frac{3}{\sqrt{9}} = 207$$

No individual $\bar{x}$ value falls outside the control limits. However, eight consecutive points lie below the center line. The probability of this if the process is in control is $(\frac{1}{2})^8 = \frac{1}{256}$. The evidence suggests the process is no longer in control. Investigation for assignable causes is advisable.

17.8

$$\text{Upper control limit} = \pi + 3\sqrt{\frac{\pi(1-\pi)}{n}}$$

$$= .03 + 3\sqrt{\frac{.03(.97)}{100}} = .081$$

$$\text{Center line} = \pi = .03$$

$$\text{Lower control limit} = \pi - 3\sqrt{\frac{\pi(1-\pi)}{n}}$$

$$= .03 - 3\sqrt{\frac{.03(.97)}{100}}$$

$$= -.021 \text{ (that is, 0)}$$

Two individual values of the sample proportion, .10 and .09 (that is, samples with 10 and 9 defectives, respectively), lie above UCL. None lies below LCL, obviously. After the 10 were observed, the process, presumably, was stopped, and an assignable cause may have been found. The values after the 10 reveal no problems, until we reach the 9, where action was taken once again.

17.9
$$\text{Upper control limit} = \bar{p} + 3\sqrt{\frac{\bar{p}(1-\bar{p})}{n}}$$

$$= .214 + 3\sqrt{\frac{.214(.786)}{100}} = .337$$

$$\text{Center line} = \bar{p} = .214$$

$$\text{Lower control limit} = \bar{p} - 3\sqrt{\frac{\bar{p}(1-\bar{p})}{n}}$$

$$= .214 - 3\sqrt{\frac{.214(.786)}{100}} = .091$$

One value, .50, from the day with 50 errors, lies above UCL, and two values, .09 and .03, from the days with 9 and 3 errors, respectively, lie below the LCL. The "process" is not in control. Possible causes appear limited to the volume of mail, the destination patterns in the mail, and, notably, the condition of the clerk. The average error rate $\bar{p}$ is so high it might be best to redesign the process, i.e., tell the clerk to look the ZIP codes up in a book, rather than try to remember them.

17.10
$$\text{Upper control limit} = \bar{c} + 3\sqrt{\bar{c}} = 2.5 + 3\sqrt{2.5} = 7.3$$
$$\text{Center line} = \bar{c} = 2.5$$
$$\text{Lower control limit} = \bar{c} - 3\sqrt{\bar{c}} = 2.5 - 3\sqrt{2.5}$$
$$= -2.3 \text{ (that is, 0)}$$

One point, 9, lies above UCL, and clearly, none lies below LCL. The process was not in control when nine defects were observed. Possibly, an explanation for that extreme value can be made. If not, the process should be studied to locate assignable causes.

17.11 Control chart analysis is not appropriate in this case, since the typist, as she gets used to the new machine, is improving her performance. Thus, the process was not stable during the time the observations were taken.

17.12   Find $\pi_1/\pi_0 = 6.5/1 = 6.5$. Table 17.4 shows $c = 2$ when $\pi_1/\pi_0 = 6.506$. When $c = 2$, then $n\pi_0 = .818$. Therefore, $n(.01) = .818$, or $n = 82$. The plan is $n = 82$, $c = 2$. The equivalent of Table 17.5 is:

(1)	(2)	(3)
		Lot percent defective
Probability of acceptance	$n\pi$	(2) ÷ 82
.99	.436	.0053
.95	.818	.00998
.90	1.102	.0134
.50	2.674	.0326
.10	5.322	.0649
.05	6.296	.0768
.01	8.406	.1025

We conclude that if the true percent of defectives is 3.26 percent, there is a 50–50 chance of accepting the batch. If the batch is so good that only .53 percent is defective, the batch is nearly certain to be accepted, but a batch with 10.2 percent defectives will almost certainly be rejected.

17.13   We accept the batch if there are 0, 1, or 2 defectives in a sample of size 80. If $\pi = .03$, the Poisson parameter is $80 \times .03 = 2.4$, and the probability of 0, 1, or 2 successes is

$$e^{-2.4} \frac{(2.4)^0}{0!} + e^{-2.4} \frac{(2.4)^1}{1!} + e^{-2.4} \frac{(2.4)^2}{2!} = .57$$

Similar computations for a series of values for π give the following results:

π, %	P(accepting lot)	π, %	P(accepting lot)
$\frac{1}{2}$	.99	5	.24
1	.95	6	.14
2	.78	8	.05
3	.57	10	.01
4	.38		

Notice that the resulting OC curve is very similar to the OC curve of Exercise 17.12, which was $n = 82$, $c = 2$. The difference in the sample sizes is slight, so the similarity is not surprising.

17.14

Lot percent defective	AOQ
.005	.0050
.01	.0095
.02	.0157
.03	.01709
.04	.0152
.05	.0119
.06	.0086
.07	.0058
.08	.0037
.09	.0023
.10	.0014

For example, when $\pi = .04$, AOQ = $.04(.38) + 0(.62) = .0152$.

By drawing a smooth line through these points, we see that the maximum AOQL is at about $\pi = .0275$, where the AOQ is .01713, as further computations show.

Chapter 18

DESIGN OF
SAMPLE SURVEYS

18.1   INTRODUCTION

In this chapter our main concern will be the design of samples to obtain
the greatest precision for a given expenditure. A greater precision means
that the interval estimate of a parameter has a smaller width, for the same
confidence level.

We are already familiar with simple random sampling from our
discussion in Section 9.2. Until now we have only used simple random
samples, and you may have the erroneous impression that in every situation
the best sample is a simple random sample. The truth is that under certain
circumstances, a stratified sample or a cluster sample may give more
information than the simple random sample which could be surveyed for
the same cost. Each of these is a type of random sample. *A sample is
random when the probability of selection is known for each element in the
population.*

We will concentrate our discussion on the design of the sample,
although this is only one phase in a survey. The survey begins by specifying the objectives of the survey, the population to be sampled, the data
to be collected, the degree of precision desired, and the methods of
measurement to be used. Following these specifications, the *frame* must

Frame

be constructed. The frame is a list of the individual units in the population from which the sample will be chosen. Once the frame is constructed, the sample must be designed—our present concern—and selected, the questionnaire written and pretested, and the field work organized and carried out. The completed questionnaire will be edited and tabulated, and the data will be analyzed. A report will be prepared that is based on the results, and it is hoped, action will be taken.

Suppose you are asked to design a survey of economic conditions among adults in a nation known as Touristia. In particular we want to know the mean income μ and the proportion of the population employed π. Touristia is a group of islands lying south of Hiltonland and northwest of Sheratonia. The islands have an adult population $N = 5$ million. There is \$10,000 available for the survey, \$6,000 of which is budgeted for the design of the survey, analysis of the data collected, and the publication of the final report. The remaining \$4,000 in the budget allows for 400 interviews at an average cost of \$10.00 per interview. How should we design the sample to obtain the most precise estimate possible within the limits of the budget?

EXERCISES

18.1   Suggest appropriate frames for surveys covering each of the following categories of persons or things (one frame for each category):
(a) Owners of cocker spaniels in Minnesota.
(b) Chevrolet station wagons.
(c) Housing units to be completed within 6 months.
(d) Unemployed bricklayers.
(e) Trees in the United States suffering from Dutch elm disease.

18.2   Suppose you were given the following assignment: "Design a survey to find out what people around here think about flying in commercial supersonic airplanes." What further information would you need before going ahead with the assignment?

18.2 SIMPLE RANDOM SAMPLING RECONSIDERED

The only design available to us at the moment for our survey of Touristia is a simple random sample. We will assume that there is a list of adults which will be used as a frame. If there is no such list, we would have to design our sampling plan in terms of sampling units other than adults, being sure that a list of such units did exist. Most areas are mapped, and urban areas in developed countries are mapped in detail by structures for insurance purposes. These maps make it possible to use sections of land area or individual structures as sampling units.

Throughout the discussion in this chapter we will assume:

1. The population size N is quite large, but finite.
2. The sampling fraction n/N is small, preferably less than 5 percent.

If these assumptions are not met, the formulas we will use should be modified by the inclusion of a *finite population correction*. This would not alter the principles involved nor the interpretation of the conclusions obtained.

Finite population correction

Suppose a simple random sample of 400 adults is chosen in Touristia. Each adult in the sample tells us his 1970 income and whether he is employed. The 1970 income of the ith person in the sample will be denoted by x_i. We will take $y_i = 1$ if the ith adult is employed and $y_i = 0$ if he is not employed. Then

$$\bar{x} = \frac{x_1 + x_2 + \cdots + x_{400}}{400}$$

is an unbiased estimate of μ, and

$$s^2 = \frac{(x_1 - \bar{x})^2 + (x_2 - \bar{x})^2 + \cdots + (x_{400} - \bar{x})^2}{399}$$

is an unbiased estimate of σ^2. Furthermore,

$$\bar{x} \pm k\frac{s}{\sqrt{n}}$$

is a confidence interval for μ, the level of confidence depending on our choice of k.

An unbiased estimate of π is

$$p = \frac{y_1 + y_2 + \cdots + y_{400}}{400}$$

A confidence interval for π, the level of confidence depending on our choice of k, is

$$p \pm k\sqrt{\frac{p(1 - p)}{n}}$$

If the mean income μ is, with given confidence, in the range

$$\bar{x} \pm k\frac{s}{\sqrt{n}}$$

then the total income of Touristian adults will be in the range

Estimates for totals

$$N\left(\bar{x} \pm k\frac{s}{\sqrt{n}}\right) = N\bar{x} \pm Nk\frac{s}{\sqrt{n}}$$

with the same confidence. Similarly if the proportion of adults employed π is, with given confidence, in the range

$$p \pm k\sqrt{\frac{p(1 - p)}{n}}$$

then the number of Touristian adults employed will be in the range

$$N\left[p \pm k\sqrt{\frac{p(1 - p)}{n}}\right] = Np \pm Nk\sqrt{\frac{p(1 - p)}{n}}$$

with the same confidence. It should not be surprising that both the point estimates and the confidence intervals for the totals are N times as large as the point estimates and confidence intervals for μ and π.

When a sample is taken, part of it can be used to make estimates for a subgroup of the population. We may want to estimate the proportion of Touristian male college graduates who are employed. There are 40 male college graduates in the sample, and 350,000 in the nation. The estimate of π', the proportion for this subgroup, must be made by using $n' = 40$ and $N' = 350,000$, in place of the original $n = 400$ and $N = 5,000,000$. If estimates are desired for very small subgroups of the population, it should be recognized that the precision of the estimate drops as n' diminishes, since the confidence interval widens with declining n'. If $\pi' = .8$ in a subgroup for which $n' = 10$, the standard deviation of the estimated proportion in the population will be .063. If $\pi = .8$, with $n = 400$, the standard deviation of the estimated proportion in the population will be .02, which is less than one-third of that in the subgroup.

Estimates for subgroups

Systematic random sampling

The *systematic random sample* is a particularly convenient sample design. The sampling units, listed in the frame, must be numbered serially from 1 through N. If a sample of at least n is needed, we find N/n, and round downward to the nearest integer, which we will call k. The quantity k is designated *the sampling interval*. One unit is chosen at random among $x_1, x_2, \ldots, x_k$. Assume x_7 is chosen ($k \geq 7$); then the systematic random sample consists of $x_7, x_{7+k}, x_{7+2k}, \ldots$. The result is not a simple random sample because the elements chosen are not independent and only k samples of n elements each have any chance of being used. The remaining $C(N,n) - k$ possible samples have zero probability of selection.

If any pattern or ordering exists in the frame, a systematic sample should not be used. For example, you might not know that a file of volunteers in the headquarters of a United Community Fund contains a team captain on every 10th card. If you use a systematic sample with $k = 10$ it will contain either all captains or no captains. Neither is a very desirable result.

Systematic sampling is used when cards are dealt in poker or bridge. Sampling in the United States Census of Population is done systematically by using every 20th, 10th, or 5th person enumerated. A sample of numbers from telephone books can be selected by starting at random among the first k listings and using every kth down the column. Note that this means you will automatically get one unit from a series of k consecutive units, for example, Kelly listings, and three units from $3k$ consecutive units, for example, Smith listings. These results would not be assured by a simple random sample, which could conceivably omit the Smiths and include three Kellys. Thus, systematic sampling has this desirable property in addition to its convenience. We recommend it, so long as you are assured by all possible means that no systematic pattern exists in the frame. In the absence of such a pattern, systematic sampling yields estimates with precision equal to simple random sampling. The formulas for simple random sampling should be used.

EXERCISES

18.3   Assume the simple random sample of 400 Touristian adults has been selected and information gathered by interviewing each sampled person. One question asked how many weeks the respondent worked full-time (35 hours or more) last year. The sample results were $\bar{x} = 30$ and $s = 10.5$.

   (a) Estimate the mean for this variable for all Touristian adults. Make a point estimate and a 95 percent confidence interval.

   (b) Estimate the total weeks worked full-time last year by all Touristian adults. Make a point estimate and a 95 percent confidence interval.

   (c) Give an interpretation for each of your results.

18.4   Refer to the last exercise. The data collected in the interviews
        were analyzed separately for the 170 men and 230 women in the
        simple random sample with these results:

	$\bar{x}$	s
Men	40	2.7
Women	22.6	7.6

(a) Make a 95 percent confidence interval estimate of the mean
    weeks worked for all Touristian men.

(b) Do the same for all Touristian women.

(c) Compare the interval estimate for the mean made in part (a)
    of the last exercise with the estimates made in (a) and (b)
    of this exercise. Why are these intervals of different lengths?

18.5   Refer to Exercise 18.1. Would it be possible to take a systematic
        random sample from each of the frames you suggested? If so,
        would it be safe to treat the resulting sample as a simple random
        sample from the corresponding population? Discuss for each case.

18.6   (a) In a work sampling study, a worker is observed at particular
            instants of time, and the type of activity he is engaged in
            at each instant is recorded. Observations can be by camera,
            TV monitor, or human observer. Would you choose to observe
            him systematically, for example, every 15 minutes? Why?

        (b) The product this worker works on is individually packaged
            and placed in inventory. Inventory is sampled weekly to check
            for spoilage. Would you choose to examine the units system-
            atically, for example, every 50th unit counting left to right,
            bottom to top, and front to back in the storage area? Why?

18.3 THE TRUTH IN TOURISTIA

The objective of this chapter is to show how sample designs other than
the simple random may give greater precision at the same cost. To reach
this objective it is helpful to presume we know the true state of affairs
in Touristia. In particular we know there are $N_M = 2$ million adult men
and $N_W = 3$ million adult women, so that the adult population $N = 5$
million. In calculations we will use $N_M = 2$, $N_W = 3$, and $N = 5$, with

the million omitted. The mean income of the men $\mu_M = \$1,600$, with $\sigma_M = \$406$. Touristian women, by and large, earn less than Touristian men. Their mean income $\mu_W = \$600$, with $\sigma_W = \$300$. The mean income of all Touristian adults is, by using the weighted average concept of Section 5.4,

$$\mu = \frac{N_M \mu_M + N_W \mu_W}{N_M + N_W} = \frac{2 \times \$1,600 + 3 \times \$600}{2 + 3} = \$1,000$$

The variance of the income of all Touristian adults is given by the following formula, which we will not prove:

$$\sigma^2 = \frac{N_M(\mu_M - \mu)^2 + N_W(\mu_W - \mu)^2 + N_M \sigma_M^2 + N_W \sigma_W^2}{N_M + N_W}$$

$$= \frac{2(1,600 - 1,000)^2 + 3(600 - 1,000)^2 + 2(406)^2 + 3(300)^2}{2 + 3}$$

$$= 360,000$$

and the standard deviation $\sigma = \$600$. The variance in the total population therefore depends on the variance in male incomes $(406)^2$ and the variance in female incomes $(300)^2$, both appropriately weighted, and on the variance of the mean income of males and the mean income of females around the population mean, $(1,600 - 1,000)^2$ and $(600 - 1,000)^2$, again appropriately weighted.

From the information we now have, we can verify that in a simple random sample of 400, the confidence interval estimate for the population mean μ is

$$\bar{x} \pm k \frac{600}{\sqrt{400}} = \bar{x} \pm 30k \qquad \text{dollars}$$

This result shows the precision to be expected if a simple random sample is used. In the following sections, we compare this with the precision expected when other types of random sampling are used.

18.4 STRATIFIED RANDOM SAMPLING

Often we know the value of a particular characteristic for each sampling unit in a population. The population can be divided into classes in terms of this known characteristic. We can classify people by age, sex, marital status, or educational attainment. Firms can be grouped according to assets, sales, industry, etc. Such classes are called *strata,* and the creation of strata is *stratification.* We form strata in terms of a known characteristic. We are interested in estimates for a second, unknown characteristic. Stratification according to the known characteristic is helpful if the variability of the unknown characteristic *within* the strata is small and the variability *between* the strata is large. For example, in Touristia the variability of the "unknown" characteristic income is small within the strata defined in terms of the known characteristic sex, but the variability in income between these strata is large.

The critical questions are: (1) According to what known characteristic should we stratify? (2) How should we allocate *n* observations among the strata? (3) How should we handle the observations when we have them? Only a general answer can be given to the first question. *Strata should be defined so the variance of the characteristic under study is smaller within the individual strata than in the population.* We usually do not have any measure of the variability of this unknown characteristic, but experience, logic, or theoretical considerations give us reason to believe a certain known characteristic will give strata with large variability between them and small variability within them. For example, suppose a large food store chain suspects a supplier is not providing the guaranteed average contents of 12 ounces per can of fruit cocktail. The supplier packs and ships from three different canneries in cases marked to show the packing location. The chain should certainly take a sample from inventory stratified according to cannery. Or consider the study of employees' preferences for various types of fringe benefits, such as pensions, medical care, life insurance, sick leave, and vacation. Sex and age of employees were used to stratify the employee group before the sample was chosen. The results showed that preferences varied greatly according to both these characteristics. The stratification was fortunate indeed.

The second question, how to allocate the *n* observations among the strata, will be taken up later in detail. For the time being, assume that we allocate them in proportion to the size of the strata. This is called

proportional allocation. If we allocate a sample of 400 Touristian adults according to sex, we will take 160 males and 240 females in the sample. The proportion, 2 to 3, is the same as the proportion in the population.

How do we handle the data gathered from a sample of n_M males and n_W females in Touristia? This was our third question. First, find the average and the variance of the incomes of the males in the sample $\overline{x}_M$ and s_M^2, and the corresponding values for the females $\overline{x}_W$ and s_W^2. An unbiased estimate of the population mean μ is given by

$$\bar{x}_S = \frac{N_M \bar{x}_M + N_W \bar{x}_W}{N_M + N_W}$$

The subscript S is a reminder that this is based on a stratified sample. The value of $\bar{x}_S$ is a point estimate of μ. To find an interval estimate for μ, we need to estimate the variance of $\bar{x}_S$. Using the results in Section 6.5, this variance can be found as follows:

$$
\begin{aligned}
V\bar{x}_S &= V\left(\frac{N_M}{N}\bar{x}_M + \frac{N_W}{N}\bar{x}_W\right) \\
&= V\left(\frac{N_M}{N}\bar{x}_M\right) + V\left(\frac{N_W}{N}\bar{x}_W\right) \\
&= \left(\frac{N_M}{N}\right)^2 V\bar{x}_M + \left(\frac{N_W}{N}\right)^2 V\bar{x}_W \\
&= \left(\frac{N_M}{N}\right)^2 \frac{\sigma_M^2}{n_M} + \left(\frac{N_W}{N}\right)^2 \frac{\sigma_W^2}{n_W}
\end{aligned}
$$

The variances in the strata σ_M^2 and σ_W^2 are estimated by using the sample results. The estimates are s_M^2 and s_W^2. In the usual situation, before a sample has been taken, $V\bar{x}_S$ cannot be found.

Fortunately, the true variances in the strata are known for Touristia: $\sigma_M^2 = (406)^2$ and $\sigma_W^2 = (300)^2$. Therefore, for proportional allocation

$$V\bar{x}_S = \left(\frac{2}{5}\right)^2 \frac{(406)^2}{160} + \left(\frac{3}{5}\right)^2 \frac{(300)^2}{240} = 300$$

The standard deviation $\sigma_{\bar{x}_S}$ is \$17.32, and the confidence interval estimate for μ is

$$\bar{x}_S \pm k(\$17.32)$$

This is a considerable improvement over the precision obtained with a simple random sample, which yielded a value \$30 for $\sigma_{\bar{x}}$, compared with the \$17.32 for $\sigma_{\bar{x}_S}$.

We can do better. *Optimum allocation* gives the greatest precision obtainable from n observations. It takes account not only of the differences in the size of the strata but of the differences in variability of the unknown characteristic within the strata. Using optimum allocation, the sample sizes in the strata are proportional to *both* the strata standard deviations σ_M

Optimum
allocation

and σ_W *and* the strata sizes $\mathcal{N}_M$ and $\mathcal{N}_W$:

$$\frac{n_M}{n_W} = \frac{\mathcal{N}_M \sigma_M}{\mathcal{N}_W \sigma_W} = \frac{2 \times 406}{3 \times 300} \approx \frac{190}{210}$$

With optimal allocation, a sample of 400 should consist of 190 men and 210 women. Compared with the proportionally allocated sample, the optimally allocated sample contains more men because σ_M is larger than σ_W. Under optimum allocation,

$$V\overline{\mathbf{x}}_S = \left(\frac{2}{5}\right)^2 \frac{(406)^2}{190} + \left(\frac{3}{5}\right)^2 \frac{(300)^2}{210} = 293$$

The standard deviation $\sigma_{\overline{\mathbf{x}}_S}$ is \$17.13, and the confidence interval estimate for μ is

$$\overline{x}_S \pm k(\$17.13)$$

For a variety of reasons interviews may cost more in one stratum than in another. The units in one stratum may require more time to reach, they may have to be paid to induce cooperation, and they may require special assistance, such as the use of an interpreter. Whatever the reason, differences among the unit costs should be considered in allocating a sample, since a dollar will buy more improvement in precision if spent in the right stratum.

By using optimum allocation with different sampling costs in the strata, the sample sizes in the strata are inversely proportional to the square root of the sampling cost:

$$\frac{n_M}{n_W} = \frac{\mathcal{N}_M \sigma_M / \sqrt{C_M}}{\mathcal{N}_W \sigma_W / \sqrt{C_W}}$$

How would our Touristian survey be affected if our budget were held at \$4,000 for interviewing, with the cost of interviewing males \$16 per person and the cost of interviewing females \$9 per person? The ratio would be

$$\frac{n_M}{n_W} = \frac{2(406)/\sqrt{16}}{3(300)/\sqrt{9}} = \frac{19}{28}$$

The total sample n will consist of $[19/(19 + 28)]n$ males and $[28/(19 + 28)]n$ females. With a total budget of \$4,000, n must be such

Different sampling costs in the strata

that

$$\frac{19}{19 + 28}\,n \times \$16 + \frac{28}{19 + 28}\,n \times \$9 = \$4,000$$

This expression gives $n = 338$, which is divided between the strata as follows:

$$n_M = \frac{19}{19 + 28}\,338 = 136$$

$$n_W = \frac{28}{19 + 28}\,338 = 202$$

Under these conditions $\sigma_{\bar{x}_S}$ rises to \$18.83, which reflects the loss in precision due to the decreased sample size. The decrease was brought on by the new, higher cost of sampling men. If there are large differences in costs of sampling in the population, it is very helpful to keep the high cost units in their own stratum when allocating the sample. Setting these units apart acts as a safeguard against spending too much money sampling them.

In practical situations the survey designer rarely knows the σ_M and σ_W values that appear in the formulas we have been using. He must make estimates. As shown by the formulas, he needs only to make estimates of their *relative* sizes, not their *absolute* sizes. In our example, it is not necessary to know σ_M and σ_W for allocation, but only the ratio σ_M/σ_W. He can make judgmental estimates, use values from past surveys of the same population or current surveys of other similar areas, or take a small pilot sample to get estimates. If he has good reason to think the standard deviations vary markedly among the strata, he should use optimum allocation. If he is doubtful that they vary much among strata, he can ignore them and use proportional allocation.

Use of estimated values for strata standard deviations

After the sample has been taken, s_M^2 and s_W^2 should be used for σ_M^2 and σ_W^2 to find the confidence interval estimate for μ by using

$$\bar{x}_S \pm kS\bar{x}_S$$

where

$$S\bar{x}_S = \sqrt{\left(\frac{N_M}{N}\right)^2 \frac{s_M^2}{n_M} + \left(\frac{N_W}{N}\right)^2 \frac{s_W^2}{n_W}}$$

We want to estimate the proportion employed at the time of the survey in Touristia. This proportion can be written as π for the population, π_M and π_W for the strata, and p_M and p_W for the sample proportions.

The estimate of π from a stratified random sample is

Estimation of π from stratified samples

$$p_S = \frac{N_M p_M + N_W p_W}{N_M + N_W}$$

and the variance of $\mathbf{p}_S$ is

$$V\mathbf{p}_S = \left(\frac{N_M}{N}\right)^2 V\mathbf{p}_M + \left(\frac{N_W}{N}\right)^2 V\mathbf{p}_W$$

where

$$V\mathbf{p}_M = \frac{\pi_M(1 - \pi_M)}{n_M} \qquad \text{and} \qquad V\mathbf{p}_W = \frac{\pi_W(1 - \pi_W)}{n_W}$$

The last expressions can be approximated by replacing π_M and π_W with p_M and p_W. The allocation formulas can be used with σ_M and σ_W replaced by $\sqrt{\pi_M(1 - \pi_M)}$ and $\sqrt{\pi_W(1 - \pi_W)}$.

Generalizations to L strata

In general, stratification is not limited to two strata. There may be L strata, among which the sample of n observations must be allocated. The number of observations from the hth stratum is n_h, and

$$n_1 + n_2 + \cdots + n_L = n$$

If we consider stratum sizes, within-stratum variabilities, and sampling costs, we have, summing over i from 1 to L,

$$n_h = n \frac{N_h \sigma_h / \sqrt{C_h}}{\Sigma N_i \sigma_i / \sqrt{C_i}}$$

where

$$n = \text{total cost} \left(\frac{\Sigma N_i \sigma_i / \sqrt{C_i}}{\Sigma N_i \sigma_i \sqrt{C_i}}\right)$$

If the C_h values are different from stratum to stratum by more than trivial amounts, clearly the n_h will be affected. If the C_h are essentially the same, the formula reduces to

$$n_h = n \frac{N_h \sigma_h}{\Sigma N_i \sigma_i}$$

If the σ_h differ from stratum to stratum by more than trivial amounts, clearly the n_h will be affected. If the σ_h are essentially the same, the formula reduces to

$$n_h = n \frac{N_h}{\Sigma N_i} = n \frac{N_h}{N}$$

In other words, we have proportional allocation. If neither the C_h nor the σ_h vary among strata, the proportional allocation is the optimal allocation.

The necessary parameters are estimated from

$$\bar{x}_S = \frac{\Sigma N_i \bar{x}_i}{\Sigma N_i}$$

$$p_S = \frac{\Sigma N_i p_i}{\Sigma N_i}$$

$$V\bar{x}_S = \Sigma \left(\frac{N_i}{N}\right)^2 \frac{s_i^2}{n_i}$$

$$Vp_S = \Sigma \left(\frac{N_i}{N}\right)^2 \frac{p_i(1 - p_i)}{n_i}$$

In all these expressions we sum over i from 1 to L.

EXERCISES

18.7   A company is planning a study of its employees and believes that the key variables to be estimated are closely related to length of employment with the company. Therefore, the random sample of 500 employees will be stratified according to length of employment with the company. Records show the following:

Length of service	h	N_h	σ_h
Under 2 years	1	2,000	.7
2 to 5 years	2	1,000	1.4
Over 5 years	3	1,000	2.8

(a) Allocate the sample by proportional allocation.
(b) Allocate the sample by optimum allocation.
(c) Explain why the results in (a) and (b) differ.

18.8   Refer to Exercise 18.7. A sample was selected which gave these
        results (x = value of holdings of company stock, in dollars):

Length of service	h	x_h	s_h
Under 2 years	1	60	25
2 to 5 years	2	200	60
Over 5 years	3	2,500	300

(a) Assuming proportional allocation was used, find $\bar{x}_S$, the
    estimated average value of company stock owned by all
    employees, and $V\bar{x}_S$, the variance of your estimate.
(b) Assuming optimum allocation was used, find $\bar{x}_S$ and $V\bar{x}_S$.
(c) Compare the values of $\bar{x}_S$ found in (a) and (b), and comment
    on the difference, if any.
(d) Compare the values of $V\bar{x}_S$ found in (a) and (b), and comment
    on the difference, if any.

18.9   Refer to Exercise 18.7. The sample also gave these results
        (x = years of schooling completed):

Length of service	h	$\bar{x}_h$	s_h
Under 2 years	1	13	3
2 to 5 years	2	12	2.5
Over 5 years	3	10	2

(a) Assuming proportional allocation was used, find the estimated
    average years of schooling completed by employees $\bar{x}_S$ and
    the variance of your estimate $V\bar{x}_S$
(b) Assuming optimum allocation was used, find $\bar{x}_S$ and $V\bar{x}_S$.
(c) Compare the values of $V\bar{x}_S$ found in (a) and (b), and comment
    on the difference, if any.
(d) What do the results of this exercise and the preceding exercise
    suggest about stratification in general and optimal allocation
    in particular?

18.10   A survey is being planned to investigate the skills and training
        needs in the area of a city inhabited by low-income families.

Available records make it possible to identify non-English-speaking families. Interviews with these families cost more because more time is needed and a specially trained interviewer is required. The families in the area to be surveyed are divided into strata with the following characteristics:

Primary language	Families	Cost per interview	Standard deviation of family income
English	6,000	$ 9	$500
Not English	4,000	16	800

(a) Allocate a sample of 165 between the strata by proportional allocation.

(b) Do the same by optimal allocation.

(c) If $2,000 is available for interviewing, what is the best way to spend it? In other words, how many interviews should be made in each stratum?

(d) What will $V\bar{x}_S$ be for estimates of average family income under each of these allocations?

(e) What will interviewing cost under each of these allocations?

(f) Compare your findings in (d) and (e), and discuss the implications.

18.11 A distributor's warehouse containing small electrical appliances sustains damage in a hurricane. The distributor decides to open a small number of cartons to inspect the contents for water damage. The storm did more damage on lower floors, so the sample of cartons is stratified by floor. The distribution of the inventory and the sample results are shown in the following table.

Floor	Total	Number of cartons Opened	Contents damaged
1	10,000	60	30
2	12,000	50	15
3	8,000	40	8

(a) Estimate the percentage of all appliances in the warehouse which suffered water damage.

(b) What is Vp_S?

(c) If the appliances have an average retail value of $25, make a 95.45 percent confidence interval estimate of the retail value of damaged appliances.

18.5 RATIO ESTIMATION

We may wish to estimate the population mean μ_y of a characteristic y. It is known that characteristic y is closely correlated with characteristic x, in the sense that there exists a proportional relationship $y_i = \rho x_i$ which has a high coefficient of determination R^2. Although we do not know the value of μ_y, we do know μ_x. If we take a sample of n observations, giving $x_1, x_2, \ldots, x_n$ and $y_1, y_2, \ldots, y_n$, the ratio of the sample means, which is also the ratio of the sample totals

$$r = \frac{\overline{y}}{\overline{x}} = \frac{\Sigma y_i}{\Sigma x_i}$$

is a slightly biased estimate of the ratio of population means

$$\rho = \frac{\mu_y}{\mu_x}$$

The ratio estimate of the population mean μ_y is given by

$$\text{Ratio estimate } \mu_y = r\mu_x$$

The ratio estimate of the population total $N\mu_y$ is given by

$$\text{Ratio estimate } N\mu_y = Nr\mu_x$$

The variance of **r** is given *approximately* by

$$V\mathbf{r} = \frac{\Sigma d_i^2}{n(n-1)\mu_x^2}$$

where $d_i = (y_i - rx_i)$. This shows very clearly that if the y_i/x_i values are equal to r, $V\mathbf{r}$ will be 0. This is rare, of course. However, the more uniform the y_i/x_i values, the smaller the d_i values will be, which will lead to a small value for Vr. The variance of the ratio estimate of μ_y is given by

$$V(\text{ratio estimate } \mu_y) = V(r\mu_x) = \mu_x^2 Vr = \frac{\Sigma d_i^2}{n(n-1)}$$

Variance of
ratio estimate
μ_y

A most ingenious application of ratio estimation was used several years ago in an attempt to take a census in a primitive region. Each tribal chief gave the authorities his estimate of the membership in his tribe. Call this estimate x_i for the ith tribe. The total of the x_i values was far above any reasonable estimate of the total population in the region. A simple random sample of tribes was selected and the members counted carefully by an impartial official. Call his count y_i for the ith tribe. A reliable estimate of the true population of the N tribes in the region was found from $r = \bar{y}/\bar{x}$, a measure of the chiefs' exaggerations. Pride is present in all chiefs, and apparently to the same degree, so y_i/x_i showed little variation among tribes—most fortunate for the statisticians. The population for the region was estimated to be $Nr\mu_x$. Ratio estimation might be used similarly to get a more realistic estimate of the total audience at the stops on a politician's whistlestop campaign trip, with the candidate's press secretary reporting the audience figures.

An illustration from the world of business may be helpful. The manager of marketing for the Jiffy Company wants to estimate the total advance sale of a new product. Sales records give him information on the total sales to each customer last year for a comparable product. This is x_i for the ith customer. The marketing manager observes that y_i/x_i will be rather similar among customers, as shown in Table 18.1. Using the data from Table 18.1, we find

$$r = \frac{\bar{y}}{\bar{x}} = \frac{\frac{5,000}{20}}{\frac{100,000}{20}} = .05$$

The marketing manager knows that the number of customers N is 750 and the average purchase μ_x of the similar product by those stores last year was \$4,500. His ratio estimate of the mean advance sale of the new product to these 750 customers is

$$\text{Ratio estimate } \mu_y = r\mu_x = (.05)(\$4,500) = \$225$$

and his ratio estimate of total advance sales is

$$\text{Ratio estimate } N\mu_y = Nr\mu_x = (750)(.05)(\$4,500) = \$168,750$$

TABLE 18.1 LAST YEAR'S PURCHASES AND ADVANCE ORDERS FOR NEW PRODUCT BY 20 JIFFY COMPANY CUSTOMERS

Customer number	Last year's purchases x_i	Advance orders y_i
1	$ 5,071	$ 325
2	7,230	400
3	1,325	67
4	2,490	105
5	5,170	150
6	9,800	520
7	12,321	705
8	4,750	226
9	6,091	252
10	9,012	397
11	2,748	116
12	5,010	286
13	7,398	296
14	4,111	325
15	2,071	102
16	1,792	31
17	4,620	271
18	4,062	212
19	1,721	68
20	3,207	146
Total	$100,000	$5,000

It is interesting to compare these estimates with those found if we treat the y_i as observations on the y variable in a simple random sample of 20 customers, ignoring the information on last year's purchases. Then

$$\bar{y} = \tfrac{5,000}{20} = \$250$$
$$N\bar{y} = (750)(\$250) = \$187,500$$

The ratio estimates are better because, although we would not realize it if we ignored the information on last year's purchases, our sample contained customers whose purchases averaged more than the population of all customers. The ratio estimate automatically corrects this by including μ_x in the calculation.

A comparison of the formulas and numerical values of the standard deviations of the two estimates is enlightening.

$$S(\text{ratio estimate } \mu_y) = \sqrt{\mu_x^2 Vr} = \sqrt{\frac{\Sigma d_i^2}{n(n-1)}} = \$12.61$$

$$S_{\bar{y}} = \frac{s_y}{\sqrt{n}} = \sqrt{\frac{\Sigma(y_i - \bar{y})^2}{n(n-1)}} = \$37.61$$

The difference is that in the standard deviation of the ratio estimate we use the deviations from the regression line, whereas in the standard deviation of the average we use the deviations from the sample average. In keeping with the concept of the ratio estimate, an individual value of y would be estimated to be r times the value of x associated with it, that is, rx; therefore, the differences $d_i = y_i - rx_i$, for the observations in the sample show the amounts by which such estimates would have been incorrect. We combine these differences to get a measure of the error in ratio estimate μ_y. We estimate the error in $\bar{y}$ in a similar way, except that an individual value of y would be estimated to be simply $\bar{y}$; therefore, the differences $y_i - \bar{y}$ for the observations in the sample show the amounts by which such estimates would have been incorrect.

EXERCISES

18.12 The Argus Chemical Company has developed a new compound which neutralizes the acidic wastes fed into rivers and lakes by certain manufacturing plants. The amount of this compound used by a plant will be closely related to the volume of product produced by the plant, measured in tons. In recent years total annual production in the United States has been 50 million tons, and no change is anticipated. Through special arrangements with the industry, a simple random sample of 15 plants use the compound for a 3-month trial with the results shown in the accompanying table.

(a) What is your estimate of the annual requirement for the compound if all 500 plants in the industry adopt it? Ignore the information on production in the 15 plants as you make this estimate.

Plant number	Tons of product, thousands	Compound, lb
1	22	70
2	29	86
3	17	55
4	20	64
5	31	90
6	26	70
7	19	48
8	24	82
9	27	80
10	19	60
11	25	70
12	30	83
13	12	41
14	18	58
15	35	105

(b) Now make an estimate of the same quantity, utilizing the information on production in the 15 plants. Compare with (a) and comment

(c) Calculate, compare, and comment on the standard deviations of the estimates found in (a) and (b).

18.13   The management of a group of motion picture theaters suggests to a major department store that the store allow its charge customers to patronize the theaters and charge their tickets to their store account. The theaters will pay the store 5 percent of the total value of tickets charged. The store decides to try the idea by authorizing a simple random sample of 25 customers to charge their theater tickets for a 6-month trial period. (The sample is this small for your convenience only.) At the end of the trial the store will estimate annual charges by its 2,500 customers if all are allowed to charge tickets. Assume annual charge sales are $1.5 million. The clerical work resulting from the charging of tickets will cost the store 4 cents per account per month (for all accounts, including those not charging tickets). If the operation at least breaks even, the store will go ahead with the idea. The results of the trial are given in the accompanying table. Should the store authorize all customers to charge tickets at the movie theaters?

Back your answer with statistical reasoning based on the information in the table.

Customer number	Charged during trial	
	Total purchases	Theater tickets
1	$ 60	$11
2	2,100	0
3	10	7
4	300	1
5	200	3
6	50	0
7	40	5
8	550	0
9	20	22
10	0	0
11	40	0
12	320	2
13	10	0
14	60	0
15	70	41
16	900	9
17	150	0
18	0	0
19	10	12
20	10	0
21	0	6
22	100	0
23	60	4
24	40	52
25	1,900	0

18.6 CLUSTER SAMPLING

For reasons of convenience, economy, or just practical necessity a sample design may require the initial selection of sampling units called *clusters*, such as busloads of commuters or file drawers full of customer record cards or villages in Touristia. The bus or the file drawer or the village is referred to as the *primary sampling unit* (psu). Our real interest is in the commuter or the record card or the inhabitant of the village, which

Primary and secondary sampling units

is the *secondary sampling unit*. We sample the primary units only as a way of getting at the secondary units, our true goal.

A sample designed this way is called a *cluster sample*. It is a *single-stage sample* if all the secondary units in the psu's are enumerated. If only a sample of commuters or a sample of inhabitants is studied, we have a *two-stage* design. Theoretically any number of stages can be used. For example, the successive stages could be counties (the psu's), census tracts within counties as the secondary sampling units, blocks within the census tracts as tertiary sampling units, dwellings within the blocks as quaternary sampling units, and finally, the individual(s) within the dwellings as the elementary sampling unit(s). The units at the last stage are always called the *elementary sampling units*.

Cluster sampling is a form of random sampling. At each stage a simple random sample is chosen from the units as defined at that stage. If this rule is observed, it will be possible to calculate the probability of selection of any elementary sampling unit or set of elementary sampling units no matter how many stages there are. Thus, the requirement for random sampling is fulfilled.

Area sampling

When the clusters are geographical areas, as will often be the case in practice, cluster sampling is referred to as *area sampling*. Area sampling utilizes convenient geographic groupings of elementary sampling units to form larger sampling units. The main advantage is economy, resulting from lower expenses for interviewers in moving from one respondent to the next. The number of elementary units included in an area-sample design can be greater than the number in a simple random sample at the same cost. It may, therefore, give results with greater precision. The cost of visiting 400 families scattered all across the island of Touristia is more than the cost of interviewing 500 adults in groups of 20 in 25 different communities.

We will use area sampling in Touristia. Necessary maps and lists must exist if area sampling is to be used. It is quite possible that school districts, police districts, voting districts, or all three, have been mapped and persons listed according to street address in each district. These districts are likely to be fairly homogeneous in terms of the economic and social characteristics of the adult inhabitants. This is the typical situation when area sampling is used. The clusters can be stratified and sampled within strata.

Table 18.2 shows the results obtained in a simple random sample of 25 districts (clusters), with $m_i = 20$ individuals interviewed in each district. Our estimate of the mean income in the population, μ, is a

TABLE 18.2   RESULTS FROM CLUSTER SAMPLE DESIGN
(TOURISTIA ECONOMIC SURVEY)

District (psu) number	Average income of 20 selected adults in district	Standard deviation of average in district
i	$\bar{x}_i$	$\dfrac{s_i}{\sqrt{m_i}}$
1	$1,210	30
2	880	40
3	980	50
4	1,190	60
5	1,140	40
6	840	20
7	930	30
8	1,050	50
9	930	40
10	1,310	70
11	910	40
12	1,060	50
13	860	30
14	810	20
15	710	60
16	1,010	70
17	1,090	60
18	970	30
19	830	50
20	960	40
21	1,040	70
22	1,090	80
23	1,110	50
24	1,180	80
25	1,160	60

weighted average of the sample averages $\bar{x}_i$ found in each district, with weights equal to M_i, the total population in each district. In Touristia all districts have $M_i = 2,000$ inhabitants, so we estimate μ by $\bar{x}_C$, in which the subscript C stands for cluster.

$$\bar{x}_C = \frac{2,000 \times \$1,210 + 2,000 \times \$880 + \cdots + 2,000 \times \$1,160}{2,000 + 2,000 + \cdots + 2,000}$$

$$= \$1,010$$

In general, in a two-stage cluster design with n clusters sampled and $\bar{x}_i$ the average of sample units in the ith cluster,

$$\bar{x}_C = \frac{\Sigma M_i \bar{x}_i}{\Sigma M_i}$$

The variance of $\bar{x}_C$, when all N clusters have the same numbers of elementary sampling units and n/N is below .05, is estimated by

Variance of
$\bar{x}_C$

$$V\bar{x}_C = \frac{\Sigma d_i^2}{n(n-1)} + \frac{1}{Nn} \Sigma \frac{s_i^2}{m_i}$$

where $d_i = \bar{x}_i - \bar{x}_C$.

From Table 18.2, we find $V\bar{x}_C = 854$ and $S\bar{x}_C = \$29.23$, as compared with \$30 for a simple random sample of 400 adults. The precision with our cluster sample is even a little better than with the simple random sample. It is most important to realize we have achieved this at a reduction in interviewing costs, since we send interviewers to 500 persons in 25 compact districts, not to 400 separate locations. Although all the other costs in the survey are the same (or a little greater if related to the number of interviews), the reduction in travel costs is well worth the slightly more complicated design.

EXERCISES

18.14   State whether each of the following is true, false, or ambiguous. Explain your answer in each case. Doubling the number of elements in a sample will cut the variance of the estimated mean in half, provided that the sample is:

(a) A probability sample.
(b) A simple random sample.
(c) A systematic random sample.
(d) A stratified random sample.
(e) An optimally stratified random sample.
(f) A two-stage cluster sample.

18.15   In sampling structures in a city, two alternative proposals have been made:

Plan I: To select a sample consisting of all the structures that lie within a simple random sample of $\frac{1}{1,000}$ of the city blocks

Plan II: To select a simple random sample of $\frac{1}{100}$ of the city blocks and then to select a simple random sample of $\frac{1}{10}$ of the structures within the sample blocks

Complete the following statements, and explain your answers:

(a) The more the structures in a block tend to be alike, the greater the advantage of plan _____ over plan _____ (other things being equal).

(b) The more it costs to reach a block, the greater the advantage of plan _____ over plan _____ (other things being equal).

(c) The greater the length of the interview, the greater the advantage of plan _____ over plan _____ (other things being equal).

18.16   Verify the value of $V\bar{x}_C$ found from Table 18.2.

18.7   SUMMARY

This brief survey of the high spots of sample survey theory has shown the strengths and weaknesses of the principal designs. *The best design is the one that gives greatest precision for a fixed cost or achieves the desired precision at lowest cost.*

Practical considerations generally render the simple random sample inefficient in applications, even though it is conceptually attractive for its simplicity. Greater precision for the same cost can be obtained through stratification, clustering, or both. Ingenuity, knowledge, and experience must be combined to produce the best survey design for each situation.

Answers to Exercises

18.1   (a) List of owners of licensed dogs in the state.

(b) Automobile registration records for all states (available from R. L. Polk Company).

(c) Building permit records for all issuing jurisdictions (available from F. W. Dodge Company).

(d) Records of all state employment services.

(e) No ready-made list exists, but municipal park departments and county forestry or agricultural services might be helpful.

18.2   You would want answers to questions including, but not limited to, these. Are you to study opinions, intentions, knowledge, or all three? Are you to concentrate on potential passengers only or on the general public? What geographic area and time span are to be represented in your results? What use will be made of the results and by whom? What resources are available for the work?

18.3   (a) Point estimate for $\mu = 30$ weeks $(= \bar{x})$. Ninety-five percent confidence interval for $\mu = 30 \pm 1.96(10.5/\sqrt{400}) = 30 \pm 1.03 = 28.97$ to 31.03 weeks.

(b) Point estimate for $N\mu = 150$ million weeks $(= N\bar{x})$. Ninety-five percent confidence interval for $N\mu = 5$ million $[30 \pm 1.96(10.5/\sqrt{400})]$ weeks $= 144.85$ to 155.15 million weeks.

(c) The best estimates available show that the average adult in Touristia worked full time for 30 weeks last year and Touristian adults worked full time a total of 150 million weeks. We can be 95 percent confident that the average adult in Touristia worked full time between 29 and 31 weeks last year and Touristian adults worked full time between 145 and 155 million weeks.

18.4   (a) $40 \pm 1.96(2.7/\sqrt{170}) = 40 \pm .41 = 39.59$ to 40.41 weeks.

(b) $22.6 \pm 1.96(7.6/\sqrt{230}) = 22.6 \pm .98 = 21.62$ to 23.58 weeks.

(c) They differ in length because the values of s and n differ. The length of the interval is directly proportional to s and inversely proportional to $\sqrt{n}$.

18.5   There are no apparent reasons in any of these situations why a systematic random sample could not be treated as a simple random sample. Investigation of the actual frame to be used would be in order to confirm this statement.

18.6   (a) No, because he may become aware of the pattern and see to it that he is productively engaged at the right time. The danger is especially serious if a human observer is used.

(b) Perhaps, depending on how the finished goods are handled after he finishes with them and the process by which they are arranged in inventory. If the 50th unit turns out always to be at the bottom or the back (or any other location) in the storage area, a common factor in the environment may spoil all of them, or conversely, they may be exempt from a factor which induces spoilage elsewhere.

18.7   (a) $n_1 = 500\frac{2,000}{4,000} = 250$ $N = 4,000$

             $n_2 = 500\frac{1,000}{4,000} = 125$ $n = 500$

             $n_3 = 500\frac{1,000}{4,000} = 125$

   (b) $N_1\sigma_1 = 1,400$ $n_1 = 500\frac{1,400}{5,600} = 125$

        $N_2\sigma_2 = 1,400$ $n_2 = 500\frac{1,400}{5,600} = 125$

        $N_3\sigma_3 = 2,800$ $n_3 = 500\frac{2,800}{5,600} = 250$

        $N_1\sigma_1 + N_2\sigma_2 + N_3\sigma_3 = 5,600$

   (c) Only the N_h values affect the results in (a); hence n_1 is twice as large as n_2 and n_3. In (b) the relatively large σ_3 causes a larger sample to be used in stratum 3. The converse is true for stratum 1, where the relatively small σ_1 leads to a smaller sample.

18.8   (a) $\bar{x}_S = \dfrac{2,000(60) + 1,000(200) + 1,000(2,500)}{4,000} = \$705$

$$V\bar{x}_S = \left(\frac{2,000}{4,000}\right)^2\frac{25^2}{250} + \left(\frac{1,000}{4,000}\right)^2\frac{60^2}{125} + \left(\frac{1,000}{4,000}\right)^2\frac{300^2}{125}$$

$$= 47.425$$

   (b) $\bar{x}_S = \dfrac{2,000(60) + 1,000(200) + 1,000(2,500)}{4,000} = \$705$

$$V\bar{x}_S = \left(\frac{2,000}{4,000}\right)^2\frac{25^2}{125} + \left(\frac{1,000}{4,000}\right)^2\frac{60^2}{125} + \left(\frac{1,000}{4,000}\right)^2\frac{300^2}{250}$$

$$= 25.55$$

   (c) There is no difference, since $\bar{x}_S$ does not depend on the sample sizes within the strata.

   (d) $V\bar{x}_S$ under optimum allocation is much smaller. If we compare $S\bar{x}_S$ values, which determine the width of confidence intervals, we find 6.9 under proportional allocation and only 5.05 under optimum allocation. (The finite population correction would have reduced these values to 6.44 and 4.43.)

18.9   (a) $\bar{x}_S = \dfrac{2,000(13) + 1,000(12) + 1,000(10)}{4,000} = 12$ years

$V\bar{x}_S = \left(\dfrac{2,000}{4,000}\right)^2 \dfrac{3^2}{250} + \left(\dfrac{1,000}{4,000}\right)^2 \dfrac{2.5^2}{125} + \left(\dfrac{1,000}{4,000}\right)^2 \dfrac{2^2}{125}$

$= .0141$

(b) $\bar{x}_S = 12$ years

$V\bar{x}_S = \left(\dfrac{2,000}{4,000}\right)^2 \dfrac{3^2}{125} + \left(\dfrac{1,000}{4,000}\right)^2 \dfrac{2.5^2}{125} + \left(\dfrac{1,000}{4,000}\right)^2 \dfrac{2^2}{250}$

$= .0222$

(c) Here, optimum allocation gives the larger $V\bar{x}_S$. This happens because the variability in length of service in each stratum—the variable serving as the basis for the optimum allocation—is negatively correlated with variability in years of schooling, the variable being estimated.

(d) Compared with proportional allocation, the optimum allocation based on variability in years of schooling would have produced relatively more items from stratum 1 and less from stratum 3. The moral of these exercises is, "Select the stratifying variable with great care!"

18.10   (a) $n_1 = 165\dfrac{6,000}{10,000} = 99$ $n_2 = 165\dfrac{4,000}{10,000} = 66$

(b) $n_1 = 165\dfrac{3,000,000}{3,000,000 + 3,200,000} = 80$

$n_2 = 165\dfrac{3,200,000}{3,000,000 + 3,200,000} = 85$

(c) $n = 2,000\dfrac{6,000 \times 500/\sqrt{9} + 4,000 \times 800/\sqrt{16}}{6,000 \times 500\sqrt{9} + 4,000 \times 800\sqrt{16}}$

$= 165$

$n_1 = 165\dfrac{6,000 \times 500/\sqrt{9}}{6,000 \times 500/\sqrt{9} + 4,000 \times 800/\sqrt{16}}$

$= 165\dfrac{1,000,000}{1,000,000 + 800,000} = 92$

$n_2 = 165\dfrac{4,000 \times 800/\sqrt{16}}{6,000 \times 500/\sqrt{9} + 4,000 \times 800/\sqrt{16}}$

$= 165\dfrac{800,000}{1,000,000 + 800,000} = 73$

(d) (1): $V\bar{x}_S = \left(\dfrac{6,000}{10,000}\right)^2 \dfrac{500^2}{99} + \left(\dfrac{4,000}{10,000}\right)^2 \dfrac{800^2}{66} = 2,464$

(2): $V\bar{x}_S = \left(\dfrac{6,000}{10,000}\right)^2 \dfrac{500^2}{80} + \left(\dfrac{4,000}{10,000}\right)^2 \dfrac{800^2}{85} = 2,331$

(3): $V\bar{x}_S = \left(\dfrac{6,000}{10,000}\right)^2 \dfrac{500^2}{92} + \left(\dfrac{4,000}{10,000}\right)^2 \dfrac{800^2}{73} = 2,382$

(e) (1): $C = \$9 \times 99 + \$16 \times 66 = \$1,947$
(2): $C = \$9 \times 80 + \$16 \times 85 = \$2,080$
(3): $C = \$9 \times 92 + \$16 \times 73 = \$1,996$

(f) The optimum allocation of a sample of 165(80,85) gives a greater precision, that is, a smaller $V\bar{x}_S$, than either of the other allocations, but its cost exceeds the available budget for sampling. Proportional allocation (99,66) costs less than the budget amount, but its precision can be improved on by another allocation (92,73) with sampling costs within the budget. The implication is that with differences in the C_h values, the σ_h values and the N_h values should all be taken into account in planning within a fixed sampling budget.

18.11 (a) $p_1 = \frac{30}{60} = .5$ $\qquad p_2 = \frac{15}{50} = .3$ $\qquad p_3 = \frac{8}{40} = .2$

$p_S = \dfrac{10,000(.5) + 12,000(.3) + 8,000(.2)}{10,000 + 12,000 + 8,000} = .34$

(b) $Vp_S = \left(\dfrac{10,000}{30,000}\right)^2 \dfrac{(.5)(1-.5)}{60} + \left(\dfrac{12,000}{30,000}\right)^2 \dfrac{(.3)(.7)}{50}$

$\qquad\qquad + \left(\dfrac{8,000}{30,000}\right)^2 \dfrac{(.2)(.8)}{40} = .0014$

(c) $Sp_S = \sqrt{.0014} = .0375$, and the 95.45 percent confidence interval estimate of π, the true percentage damaged, is $p_S \pm 2Sp_S = .34 \pm 2(.0375) = .2650$ to $.4150$. The corresponding interval estimate of the number damaged is $30,000(.2650)$ to $30,000(.4150)$, or 7,950 to 12,450. The corresponding interval estimate of the retail value of damaged appliances is $\$25(7,950)$ to $\$25(12,450)$, or $\$198,750$ to $\$311,250$.

18.12 (a) Let x_i be the tons of product (in thousands) and y_i the pounds of compound used by the ith plant in 3 months.

$$\bar{y} = \frac{y_1 + \cdots + y_{15}}{15} = \frac{1{,}062}{15}$$

$$= 70.8 \text{ pounds (for 3 months)}$$

Therefore, *at an annual rate,* $\bar{y} = 4 \times 70.8 = 283.2$ pounds. The point estimate of $N\mu_y$ is $N\bar{y} = 500(283.2) = 141{,}600$ pounds.

(*b*) $\bar{x} = \dfrac{x_1 + \cdots + x_{15}}{15} = \dfrac{354}{15} = 23.6$ tons (in thousands)

$$r = \frac{70.8}{23.6} = 3$$

We know total output in the 500 plants is 50 million tons. Therefore, $\mu_x = \frac{50}{500} = .1$ million tons $= 100{,}000$ tons, and ratio estimate $\mu_y = r\mu_x = 3(100{,}000) = 300{,}000$ tons. The point estimate of $N\mu_y$ is $N(\text{ratio estimate } \mu_y) = 500(300{,}000) = 150$ million tons.

(*c*) $\quad V\bar{y} = \dfrac{s_y^2}{n} = \dfrac{(y_1 - \bar{y})^2 + \cdots + (y_n - \bar{y})^2}{n(n-1)}$

$$= \frac{4{,}114.40}{210} = 19.6$$

$$V(r\mu_x) = \frac{d_1^2 + \cdots + d_n^2}{n(n-1)}$$

$$= \frac{(y_1 - rx_1)^2 + \cdots + (y_n - rx_n)^2}{n(n-1)}$$

$$= \frac{428}{210} = 2.038$$

$$S\bar{y} = 4.4 \qquad S(r\mu_x) = 1.43$$

The ratio estimate has a standard deviation less than one third as large as the standard deviation of the estimate based on the y values alone.

18.13   Yes, the store should authorize all customers to charge tickets. If we let x_i be total purchases charged and y_i be tickets charged by the ith customer during the 6-month trial, we have

$$\bar{y} = \frac{y_1 + \cdots + y_{25}}{25} = \frac{\$175}{25} = \$7 \qquad \text{(for 6 months)}$$

and $\bar{y} = 2 \times \$7 = \$14$ per year. The point estimate of $N\mu_y$ is $N\bar{y} = 2{,}500(\$14) = \$35{,}000$.

$$\bar{x} = \frac{x_1 + \cdots + x_{25}}{25} = \frac{7{,}000}{25} = \$280 \qquad \text{(for 6 months)}$$

$$r = \frac{\bar{y}}{\bar{x}} = \frac{\$7}{280} = .025$$

Since total charge sales annually are \$1.5 million to 2,500 customers, $\mu_x = \frac{1{,}500{,}000}{2{,}500} = \$600$ and ratio estimate $\mu_y = r\mu_x = .025(\$600) = \$15$. Inspection of the data suggests there is no relationship between total amount charged and amount of tickets charged. If this is indeed so, the ratio estimate should not be used. Computations give $S_{\bar{y}} \approx \$2.60$ and $S(\textbf{ratio estimate } \boldsymbol{\mu_y}) = \$4.20$, which confirms the initial impression. Estimated annual costs to the store are 2,500 accounts $\times$ 12 months $\times$ \$.04 per account per month $= \$1{,}200$; estimated annual income from ticket sales is 35,000 sales $\times$ .05 $= \$1{,}750$. The store will make $\$1{,}750 - \$1{,}200 = \$550$ annually on ticket sales.

18.14   (*a*) Ambiguous, because the effect depends on which type of probability sample is used.

      (*b*) True, since $V\bar{x} = \sigma^2/n$.

      (*c*) Ambiguous, because unless we can assume the sample is a simple random sample, we do not know how to find $V\bar{x}$.

      (*d*) Ambiguous, since we do not know how the additional sample observations will be distributed among the strata; if each n_h is doubled, $V\bar{x}_S$ will be cut in half.

      (*e*) True, since the allocation of any size sample among the strata is in a proportion determined by the N_h and σ_h. Therefore, doubling n will merely double each n_h.

      (*f*) Ambiguous, since we do not know how the additional sample observations will be distributed among the clusters; if each m_i is doubled, the estimated $V\bar{x}_C$ will be cut in half.

18.15   (*a*) Choose plan II over plan I; that is, use two-stage cluster sampling, since the homogeneity within the blocks makes it preferable to a sample of homes from each of a larger number of blocks.

      (*b*) Choose plan I over plan II, since a smaller number of blocks must be visited, which will keep costs down; bear in mind that everything else (that is, intrablock variability and inter-block variability) is equal.

(c) The length of the interview matters only if the expected number of interviews differs under the two plans. The plan with the smaller expected number of interviews would be preferred for economic reasons. Since each plan yields the same expected number of interviews (assuming one interview per structure), neither plan is preferred.

18.16   The values of $V\bar{x}_C$ and $S\bar{x}_C$ are given in the text.

Chapter 19

NONPARAMETRIC STATISTICS

19.1 INTRODUCTION AND CONFIDENCE INTERVAL FOR THE MEDIAN

In this chapter we will introduce some nonparametric, or distribution-free, statistical techniques. These tests share, in the main, the following characteristics:

1. They do not presuppose any particular distribution. For example, in Section 11.6 on hypothesis testing we discuss as a basic question, "Can we accept the hypothesis that these samples were drawn from populations described by the same *normal* distribution, or should we reject this hypothesis in favor of the conclusion that they come from *normal* distributions with different means?" Analysis of variance was used to answer this question, and it is clear from the formulation that this technique is not distribution-free, but quite specifically designed for normal distributions.

2. They are rather quick and easy to use. They do not require laborious computations, such as those needed to determine standard deviations. In many cases the observations are replaced by their rank order; that is, the n observations are taken to be 1 through n, 1 corresponding to the lowest actual value and n to the highest. It is clearly labor-saving to replace 69.17, 58.28, and 75.52 by 2, 1, and 3, respectively.

Characteristics of nonparametric tests

3. They are not very efficient or "sharp." An interval estimate with 95 percent confidence may be twice as large with the use of nonparametric techniques as with regular, standard methods. Such loss of efficiency is due to the two reasons mentioned above: The tests do not presuppose any specific distribution and hence are much more broadly valid, but this very broadness of validity can only be guaranteed by having wide intervals; and the tests often do not use all the detail, that is, information, in the specific data available, but rather, use groupings or rankings. The price we pay for willfully and wittingly discarding some detailed information is a loss in efficiency.

Confidence interval for median

The problem of determining a confidence interval for the median illustrates these three points. Suppose we have n observations drawn from the same population. The distribution of this population is irrelevant. We will write m for the integer nearest to the value of

$$\frac{n + 1}{2} - \sqrt{n}$$

For $n = 12$ this integer is $m = 3$, because $(12 + 1)/2 - \sqrt{12} = 6.5 - 3.46 = 3.04$. For $n = 32$ the value of m equals 11, because $(32 + 1)/2 - \sqrt{32} = 16.5 - 5.66 = 10.84$. If we now arrange all n observations in order of increasing magnitude, and determine the value of the observation ranked m from the first and m from the last, these two values thus obtained will form a 95 percent confidence interval for the true median.

As an illustration, the $n = 12$ weights given in Table 5.1 are, when arranged in increasing order, 137, 142, 142, 146, 150, 155, 160, 166, 173, 180, 182, 201. Since $m = 3$ when $n = 12$, the 95 percent confidence interval for the median is 142 to 180. This result is valid irrespective of the distribution of the population from which this sample was drawn; it is quick and easy to compute; and the interval itself is quite wide. A 95 percent confidence interval for the true mean, computed by using the techniques of Section 9.4, is roughly from 149 to 173, that is, 161 ± 12.

A fourth property of nonparametric tests is that although the results are easy to use, they are difficult to derive. In this chapter we will give no derivations of the stated results.

EXERCISES

19.1   Determine a 95 percent confidence interval for the median of sugar contents in beets, given the sample of size 25 recorded in Section

9.3. Compare this interval with the 95 percent confidence interval for the mean computed by standard methods.

19.2 SPEARMAN'S RANK CORRELATION AND TESTS FOR DEPENDENCE

If one has n pairs of observations $x_1, y_1; x_2, y_2; \ldots ; x_n, y_n$, then one can check for correlation by computing the correlation coefficient R as in Section 13.3. This computation is fairly laborious, especially if the observations have many digits.

A quick and easy analogous—not identical—computation gives the Spearman rank-correlation coefficient. These computations require, as the name implies, that the actual observations be replaced by their rank. In Table 19.1 we present in the first two columns the actual data of the consumption-income example of Section 13.1. In Columns 3 and 4 we replace these actual data by their rank, giving the value 1 to the lowest value and the value $n = 7$ to the highest value in each series. In Column 5 we record the differences d between the entries in Columns 3 and 4. In Column 6 we square these differences, and we add them at the bottom to get Σd_i^2.

By definition, Spearman's rank-correlation coefficient equals

$$\text{Spearman's } R = 1 - \frac{6\Sigma d_i^2}{n(n^2 - 1)}$$

Spearman's rank-correlation coefficient

TABLE 19.1 COMPUTATION OF Σd_i^2 FOR SPEARMAN TESTS

(1) Income	(2) Consumption	(3) Rank income	(4) Rank consumption	(5) Difference (3) − (4)	(6) Difference²: (5)²
30	27	4	4	0	0
35	30	6	6	0	0
19	18	1	1	0	0
39	32	7	7	0	0
26	19	2	2	0	0
29	29	3	5	−2	4
32	20	5	3	2	4
					$\Sigma d_i^2 = 8$

For the consumption-income example we get the numerical result

$$\text{Spearman's } R = 1 - \frac{6(8)}{7(49 - 1)} = \frac{6}{7}$$

For comparison we mention that the conventionally computed R equals $175/\sqrt{(248)(204)}$, which is very close to $\frac{7}{9}$.

For the example of birth and death dates of American Presidents, discussed in Exercises 13.2, 13.6, and 13.12, we found $R = -.058$. Spearman's R gives in this case $-.072$.

In this day of computers, computational shortcuts are becoming less important. However, computer runs do cost money, and so it may be wise to check whether variables are correlated before turning to the computer with the command "Run, computer, run!" The Spearman rank-correlation test serves this purpose. To test whether two variables are positively correlated, one formulates as the null hypothesis:

Spearman's
rank-
correlation
test

H_0:   These variables are not positively correlated;

against the alternative

H_1:   These variables are positively correlated.

The null hypothesis can be tested at a desired level of significance, say 5 percent, and rejection of H_0 implies acceptance of positive correlation. The test is clearly a one-tail test. It is performed by computing

$$x = \frac{n(n^2 - 1) - 6(\Sigma d_i^2 - 1)}{n(n + 1)\sqrt{n - 1}}$$

If the null hypothesis is true, x is normally distributed with mean zero and standard deviation 1. Therefore, any value of x above 1.645 is significant at the 5 percent (one tail) level. Any value of x above 1.645 leads to rejection of H_0 and acceptance of positive correlation. By specifying a significance level of 5 percent, we run a risk of at most 5 percent that this conclusion is wrong. It will happen 5 percent of the time that wholly uncorrelated variables will give a value for x in excess of 1.645. Values of x over 1.282 are significant at the 10 percent level, and values over 2.326 are significant at the 1 percent level. These values are found from the table of the normal distribution. They are also recorded in Table 10.2 under the column heading "single tail."

If we want to test for negative correlation between two variables, we formulate:

H_0:   These variables are not negatively correlated;

and

H_1:   These variables are negatively correlated.

For this one-tail test we compute

$$x = \frac{n(n^2 - 1) - 6(\Sigma d_i^2 + 1)}{n(n + 1)\sqrt{n - 1}}$$

which differs from the previous expression only by the sign in the last term of the numerator. In this instance values *below* -1.645 are significant at the 5 percent level. The critical region is in the lower tail. If H_0 is rejected, and thus negative correlation is established apart from a small chance of an Error of Type I, the time has come to proceed to the computer. The computer will crank out precise results without great risk of wasting our money.

A two-sided test for existence of correlation is very similar to the one-tail tests, but it will not be spelled out here. If we know so little about two variables that may or may not be correlated that even the direction of correlation, if present, is an open question, then we are clearly out on a "fishing expedition," and it is unwarranted to test at all.

EXERCISES

19.2   Test at the 5 percent level of significance whether the variables x and y are positively correlated:

x	9	11	8	4	5	2
y	12	11	4	8	6	5

19.3   Determine Spearman's rank-correlation coefficient R for:

x	1	1	2	4	3
y	10	8	6	4	2

19.3   THE TEST OF WILCOXON

In Section 10.3 we discussed the problem of whether we could maintain the null hypothesis that two independent samples with observations x_1, $x_2, \ldots, x_m$ and $y_1, y_2, \ldots, y_n$ were drawn from populations with the same mean. The problem we discussed was whether nylon cord was stronger than cotton cord. We tested:

H_0:   These cords are equally strong;

against the alternative

H_1:   The nylon cord is stronger.

This formulation implies a one-tail test, and if H_0 is rejected at the specified level of significance, we conclude that the nylon cord is stronger, as the manufacturer claimed. A fairly sizable amount of computational drudgery is involved in the test. A quicker test is known as the *Wilcoxon,* or *Wilcoxon-Mann-Whitney* test. In this test the test-statistic x is a normally distributed variable with mean zero and variance 1, which can be computed as illustrated in the following example.

A newly developed textile N is claimed to be superior in wear-and-tear characteristics to an old one, coded by the letter L. We want to test:

H_0:   The strength and durability of N and L are equal;

against the alternative

H_1:   The new textile N is superior to old L

at the 10 percent level of significance. The formulation of H_1 implies that we have a one-tail test. Rejection of H_0 leads to the conclusion that the claim of superiority for N can stand.

In the testing laboratory a wooden block is moved up and down over the tightly stretched fabric, and the number of movements before the fabric breaks is recorded. In $m = 10$ tests of the old and $n = 12$ tests of the new fabric the recorded results, ranked in order of magnitude, are as follows:

Old L: 208, 212, 237, 257, 273, 281, 285, 306, 357, 408
New N: 210, 228, 259, 277, 297, 322, 342, 382, 402, 470, 506, 619

Three values are needed for the test of Wilcoxon, of which the first two solely and exclusively depend upon m and n:

$$mn = (10)(12) = 120$$

and

$$\sqrt{\tfrac{1}{3}mn(m + n + 1)} = \sqrt{\tfrac{1}{3}(120)(23)} = \sqrt{920} = 30.3$$

To obtain the third value we need to rank all the observations in order of magnitude, properly identifying their source. In our example the series begins with L, because the lowest value, 208, comes from L. Next we get N, because the next lowest value, 210, comes from N. Proceeding in this way, we find the sequence

L N L N L L N L N L L N L N N L N N L N N N
0   1   2 2   3   4 4   5   7   9

Below the L's we have recorded the *number of* N's *that precede it*—zero for the first L, 1 for the next L, and so on. These values add to $0 + 1 + 2 + 2 + 3 + 4 + 4 + 5 + 7 + 9 = 37$, and this is the third value we need. Let us call this value W, the first letter of Wilcoxon, so that

$$W = 37$$

To test our null hypothesis we compute the value

Wilcoxon
test

$$x = \frac{mn - 2W - 1}{\sqrt{\tfrac{1}{3}mn(m + n + 1)}} = \frac{120 - 74 - 1}{30.3} = 1.48$$

Once again, if the null hypothesis is true, the random variable $\mathbf{x}$ will be normally distributed with mean zero and standard deviation 1. Values of x above 1.282 are thus significant at the 10 percent level in one-tail tests. Our numerical result is significant. Note, however, that it would not have been significant at the 5 percent level, since 1.48 is below 1.645.

To test the hypothesis:

H_0:   These two samples are from populations with the same mean;

against the alternative

H_1:   These two samples are from populations with different means

we need a two-tail test. For this test we compute

$$x = \frac{mn - 2W \pm 1}{\sqrt{\tfrac{1}{3}mn(m + n + 1)}}$$

where the sign of the value 1 is taken so as to minimize the absolute value of the numerator: if $mn > 2W$, we deduct 1; if $mn < 2W$, we add 1. A value of x outside the range -1.645 to $+1.645$ is significant at the 10 percent level. Five percent is in either tail; the critical region consists of two parts.

Use of table for test of Wilcoxon

For $m \leq 10$ and $n \leq 10$, Table 19.2 gives the values of W significant at the 10 percent level for a two-tail test. Values of W at or outside the specified range are significant. If $m = 7$ and $n = 9$ (or vice versa), then values of W at or below 15 and at or above 48 are significant at the 10 percent level in two-tail tests. If we test

H$_0$:   Samples X and Y are drawn from populations with the same mean

against the alternative that they come from populations with different means at the 10 percent level of significance, and if we find 5 values from sample X and 7 values from sample Y arranged in order of magnitude as follows:

X X Y X Y X X Y Y Y Y Y
0 0   1   2 2 $W = 5$

then we can conclude immediately from Table 19.2 that the result is significant; we reject H$_0$. It would have been significant even if W had been 6.

Incidentally, if we had counted the number of X's preceding the Y's,

TABLE 19.2   FOR m AND n AS SPECIFIED, VALUES OF W AT
             THE LIMITS MENTIONED, OR OUTSIDE THOSE
             LIMITS, ARE SIGNIFICANT AT THE 10 PERCENT
             TWO-TAIL LEVEL

n m	3	4	5	6	7	8	9	10
3	0–9	0–12	1–14	2–16	2–19	3–21	4–23	4–26
4		1–15	2–18	3–21	4–24	5–27	6–30	7–33
5			4–21	5–25	6–29	8–32	9–36	11–39
6				7–29	8–34	10–38	12–42	14–46
7					11–38	13–43	15–48	17–53
8						15–49	18–54	20–60
9							21–60	24–66
10								27–73

instead of the number of Y's preceding the X's, we would have found

X X Y X Y X X Y Y Y Y Y
   2   3   5 5 5 5 5 $W = 30$

This value is just as significant as the value $W = 5$. This shows that there is symmetry between the X values and the Y values when we use two-tail tests; we get the same result whichever way we count.

EXERCISES

19.4   Tests for content of particulate matter in air are made independently in two places A and B over a period of time. The higher the count, the more polluted the air. A's counts are 87, 75, 3, 17, 67, 192, 23, 214, 69, and 139. B's counts are 52, 194, 53, 102, 94, 6, 25, 205, 193, 117, 138, 143, 174. Test at the 10 percent level whether B is more polluted than A.

19.5   The values in one sample are 53, 38, 69, 57, 46, 39, 73, 48, 73, 74, 60, and 78. In another sample they are 44, 40, 61, 52, 32, 44, 70, 41, 67, 72, 53, and 72. Test at the 10 percent level the hypothesis that they come from populations with the same mean.

19.6   We want to test whether samples with values 90, 94, 36, and 44 on the one hand, and 53, 39, 6, 24, 33 on the other hand, come from populations with the same mean at the 10 percent level. The alternative is that these samples come from populations with different means.

19.4   WILCOXON SIGNED-RANK TEST

As in Section 10.3, we should carefully distinguish between matched samples and independent samples. For example, in Exercise 19.5 we gave two samples of 12 observations which represent test scores of the same 12 students after and before taking a course (see Exercise 10.10). Student performance differs widely, and this wide variance within each test swamped the difference between the tests themselves. If we match the observations, however, the result is quite significant, as shown in Exercise 10.10.

For such matched samples we should use the *Wilcoxon signed-rank* test. To test

H_0:   The test results are the same

against

H_1:   The after-course test scores were better than the before-
course test scores

at the 5 percent one-tail level we need, once again, three values. Two
of these depend only on n, the number of observations in the samples.
(Since the samples are matched, they have by necessity the same number
of observations.) In this case we have $n = 12$. The two values we need
are

$$\frac{n(n + 1)}{2} = \frac{(12)(13)}{2} = 78$$

and

$$\sqrt{\tfrac{1}{6}n(n + 1)(2n + 1)} = \sqrt{\tfrac{1}{6}(12)(13)(25)} = \sqrt{650} = 25.5$$

To compute the third value, we rank all differences in order of increasing
absolute value, as in Column 4 of Table 19.3. In this table, Column 1

TABLE 19.3   COMPUTATION OF V FOR WILCOXON SIGNED-RANK
TEST

1	2	3	4	5	6
					Ranks of positive
			Ranked	Rank	positive
"After"	"Before"	Difference	difference	order	values
53	44	9		1	
38	40	−2	−2, 2	2	$1\tfrac{1}{2}$
69	61	8	3	3	3
57	52	5		4	
46	32	14	−5, 5	5	$4\tfrac{1}{2}$
39	44	−5		6	
73	70	3	6, 6	7	13
48	41	7		8	
73	67	6	7, 7	9	17
74	72	2	8	10	10
60	53	7	9	11	11
78	72	6	14	12	12
					$V = 72$

gives the after-course test scores, and Column 2 the before-course test scores. In Column 3 their differences are computed and recorded. In Column 4 these differences are ranked in order of increasing absolute value, although the sign is not omitted. Equal observations are ranked on one line. In Column 5 the rank orders are given, from 1 to $n = 12$. In Column 6 the ranks associated with *positive values only* are recorded. The sum of these ranks, 72 in the present example, is the third value we need. We will call it V, and thus we have

$$V = 72$$

We now compute the value

Signed-rank test

$$x = \frac{2V - 1 - n(n + 1)/2}{\sqrt{\frac{1}{6}n(n + 1)(2n + 1)}} = \frac{144 - 1 - 78}{25.5} = 2.55$$

If H_0 is true, the random variable $\mathbf{x}$ computed according to the above formula will be normally distributed with mean zero and standard deviation 1. In a one-tail test, any value of $\mathbf{x}$ over 1.645 is therefore significant at the 5 percent level, and values exceeding 1.960 are significant at the 2.5 percent level.

The same formula can be used to test the hypothesis;

H_0:   These samples come from different distributions with the same mean

against the alternative

H_1:   These samples come from different distributions with different means

provided that we write the numerator as

$$2V \pm 1 - \frac{n(n - 1)}{2}$$

and use the sign, plus or minus, which minimizes the absolute value of the numerator. In such a two-tail test the critical region which is significant at the 10 percent level consists of values of x below -1.645 or above $+1.645$. Table 10.2 can be consulted for a quick review of these values.

If this test is still considered too laborious, a really quick but really dirty (that is, inefficient) test is the *sign test*. If we have matched samples we simply look at the signs of their differences, and we count the number of negative differences. If this number, for the given value of n, is at or

Sign test

TABLE 19.4   FOR n **AS SPECIFIED, A NUMBER OF NEGATIVE SIGNS AT THE LIMITS MENTIONED, OR OUTSIDE THOSE LIMITS, IS SIGNIFICANT IN TWO-TAIL TESTS AT THE STATED LEVEL**

	Level of significance		
n	10 percent	5 percent	1 percent
11	2–9	1–10	0–11
12	2–10	2–10	1–11
13	3–10	2–11	1–12
14	3–11	2–12	1–13
15	3–12	3–12	2–13
16	4–12	3–13	2–14
17	4–13	4–13	2–15
18	5–13	4–14	3–15
19	5–14	4–15	3–16
20	5–15	5–15	3–17
25	7–18	7–18	5–20
30	10–20	9–21	7–23
35	12–23	11–24	9–26
40	14–26	13–27	11–29
45	16–29	15–30	13–32
50	18–32	17–33	15–35
55	20–35	19–36	17–38
60	23–37	21–39	19–41
65	25–40	24–41	21–44
70	27–43	26–44	23–47
75	29–46	28–47	25–50
80	32–48	30–50	28–52
85	34–51	32–53	30–55
90	36–54	35–55	32–58
95	38–57	37–58	34–61
100	41–59	39–61	36–64

outside the range given in Table 19.4, the result is significant at the level stated. For the examination results we have $n = 12$, and the number of negative differences is 2. This is significant at the 10 or 5 percent two-tail level, and at the 5 and 2.5 percent one-tail levels. A similar test can be used for Exercise 1.3 at the very beginning of this book: Two out of forty negative differences is an exceedingly significant result, and it enables us to conclude that it snows more in Buffalo than in Boston.

EXERCISES

19.7   Answer Exercise 14.50, using the Wilcoxon signed-rank test and a 5 percent two-tail level of significance. Also answer this question, using the sign test.

Answers to Exercises

19.1   We have $n = 25$, and therefore $m = (25 + 1)/2 - \sqrt{25} = 13 - 5 = 8$. Ranked in order, the 25 observations are 6.8, 7.2, 7.2, 7.3, 7.4, 7.5, 7.5, 7.6, 7.7, 7.8, 7.9, 8.0, 8.1, 8.2, 8.2, 8.3, 8.5, 8.6, 8.7, 8.7, 8.9, 8.9, 9.0, 9.0, and 9.5. The 95 percent confidence interval for the median is from 7.6 to 8.6, the eighth observations from the first and the last, respectively. The conventional 95 percent confidence interval for the mean is $\bar{x} \pm 2.06s/\sqrt{n} = 8.1 \pm 2.06(.7)/5 = 8.1 \pm 2.06(.14) = 8.1 \pm .29$, or from 7.81 to 8.39. The value 2.06 is read from a table of the t distribution with 24 degrees of freedom at the 5 percent level. The median interval is 1 in width, the mean interval is .58 in width, indicating to some extent the inefficiency of the nonparametric method.

19.2   We have $n = 6$ and $\Sigma d_i^2 = 16$:

x	y	Rank x	Rank y	Difference	(Difference)²
9	12	5	6	−1	1
11	11	6	5	1	1
8	4	4	1	3	9
4	8	2	4	−2	4
5	6	3	3	0	0
2	5	1	2	−1	1
					16

Hence

$$x = \frac{6(36 - 1) - 6(16 - 1)}{(6)(7)\sqrt{5}} = \frac{210 - 90}{93.9} = 1.286$$

This value is not significant at the 5 percent level. It is by the squeakiest of margins significant at the 10 percent level.

19.3

x	y	Rank x	Rank y	Difference	(Difference)²
1	10	$1\frac{1}{2}$	5	$-3\frac{1}{2}$	$12\frac{1}{4}$
1	8	$1\frac{1}{2}$	4	$-2\frac{1}{2}$	$6\frac{1}{4}$
2	6	3	3	0	0
4	4	5	2	3	9
3	2	4	1	3	9
					$36\frac{1}{2}$

$$\text{Spearman's } R = 1 - \frac{6(36\frac{1}{2})}{5(25-1)} = 1 - \frac{219}{120} = -.825$$

19.4 A's counts are, when ranked in order of magnitude, 3, 17, 23, 67, 69, 75, 87, 139, 192, 214, $m = 10$ observations. B's counts in order of magnitude are 6, 25, 52, 53, 94, 102, 117, 138, 143, 174, 193, 194, 205. There are $n = 13$ observations. Ranked in order, identified as to source, we find the sequence:

A B A A B B B A A A A B B B B A B B A B B B A
0   1 1   4 4 4 4   8   10   13

Below the A's we printed the number of B's that precede it. We find for W:

$$W = 0 + 1 + 1 + 4 + 4 + 4 + 4 + 8 + 10 + 13 = 49$$

Hence

$$x = \frac{130 - 98 - 1}{\sqrt{\frac{1}{3}(130)(24)}} = \frac{31}{32.2} = .96$$

This value is not significant at the 10 percent level, since it is less than 1.282.

19.5 In the first sample, we have $m = 12$ observations, in the order 38, 39, 46, 48, 53, 57, 60, 69, 73, 73, 74, 78. In the second sample, we have $n = 12$ observations, in the order 32, 40, 41, 44, 44, 52, 53, 61, 67, 70, 72, 72. If we identify observations from the first sample by A, and those from the second by B, we get the sequence

$$\text{B A A B B B B A A B } \genfrac{}{}{0pt}{}{A}{B} \text{ A A B B A B B B A A A A}$$

$$0 \qquad 2\ 2\ 2\ 2 \qquad 4\ 4\tfrac{1}{2} \qquad 7\ 7 \qquad 8\ 8\ 8$$

Adding the values below the B's gives us $W = 54\tfrac{1}{2}$. Note the two equally ranked observations corresponding to the score 53 which occurs once in each sample. Such a paired ranking counts, rather logically, for $\tfrac{1}{2}$. Since $mn = 144$ exceeds $2W$, we deduct 1 in the numerator of the expression for x, and we get

$$x = \frac{144 - 109 - 1}{\sqrt{\tfrac{1}{3}(144)(25)}} = \frac{34}{34.6} = .98$$

This value is not significant at the 10 percent two-tail level (and therefore also not significant at the 5 percent one-tail level).

19.6   We have $m = 4$ and $n = 5$, and the ranking is

$$n\ n\ n\ m\ n\ m\ n\ m\ m$$
$$0\ 0\ 0\ \ \ 1\ \ \ \ 2 \qquad\qquad W = 3$$

According to Table 19.2 only values at or below 2 and values at or above 18 are significant at the 10 percent two-tail level. The null hypothesis of equal means cannot be rejected.

19.7   We make the following table to compute V:

(1)	(2)	(3)	(4)	(5)	(6)
40	35	5	-1	1	
59	43	16		2	
66	88	-22	$-2, 2$	3	$2\frac{1}{2}$
79	95	-16	-3	4	
20	23	-3	5	5	5
41	64	-23	-6	6	
54	61	-7	-7	7	
55	53	2	8	8	8
45	47	-2	9	9	9
31	37	-6		10	
76	87	-11	$-10, 10$	11	$10\frac{1}{2}$
45	46	-1	-11	12	
20	10	10	13	13	13
89	76	13		14	
76	86	-10	$-14, -14$	15	
35	49	-14		16	
72	64	8	$-16, 16$	17	$16\frac{1}{2}$
97	48	9	-22	18	
51	75	-24	-23	19	
53	67	-14	-24	20	

$$V = 64\frac{1}{2}$$

There are $n = 20$ observations in the matched samples, so we compute

$$x = \frac{129 + 1 - (20)(21)/2}{\sqrt{\frac{1}{6}(20)(21)(41)}} = \frac{129 + 1 - 210}{53.6} = -1.49$$

This value is not in the critical area, which is less than -1.96 or more than $+1.96$ at the 5 percent two-tail level. At the 5 percent level the sign test is not significant. We would need 5 or fewer, or 15 or more, negative signs for significance at the 5 percent level in a two-tail test. We have 13 negative observations. The values 5 and 15 are recorded in Table 19.4.

APPENDIX A

THE USE OF COMPUTERS

Many of the analytic methods discussed in the text call for an unpleasant amount of arithmetic, particularly when the sample size n is large. The examples used have been tailored to keep down the amount of arithmetical work, but the real world is not so kind. Fortunately, we are moving rapidly toward the day when the majority of people who have to do much routine arithmetic will have easy access to a computer. "Remote access terminals" may soon be as plentiful in offices and laboratories as photocopy machines are today.

Advances in computer technology have brought us to the point where the user needs only a slight knowledge of "computerese" to get the answer he wants from the machine. It is not necessary to understand how the computer works or how to program it. Libraries of frequently used programs—sequences of machine operations needed to perform desired analyses—are stored so they can be called by a code name and used whenever needed.

There is not space enough here to discuss and illustrate the variety of statistical analyses that can be made with the help of a computer. We did, however, select six examples from the text, and ran the programs on a computer from a remote access terminal. We shall now give you the procedure and results.

Imagine yourself seated at a remote access terminal. All you see are a typewriter and a telephone. With the telephone, dial the computer. Unless all its lines are busy, you will be connected with the computer. The greeting is a polite "Hello," typed in by you, the user. The machine usually answers with its "slogan of the day," which varies from a comment on the weather to moderately useful information to a rather poor joke. This day (see Exhibit 1) the computer gives us a number to call in case we need assistance. The computer then asks for your user number, which you type in for billing purposes; the typing machine does *not,* however, type out the number, so that it remains secret. If the user number is one that the computer recognizes, it asks for the password; again, the (secret) password is typed in by you but not typed out by the machine.

Next, the computer asks whether you intend to use a program stored in its memory or whether you have written your own program in an appropriate computer language. In our examples, we will use programs from the memory of the computer. Such a library of programs is available and works much the same as a telephone book. So, when the machine asks "new or old" you type "old" (program), and when the machine next asks the program name you type in the library code for the particular program desired. In our first exhibit, we wanted binomial probabilities, so we typed in B.P.D.***.

The computer looks this program up in its memory and types out "ready" when it has been located. You now type "run" to see what happens. The computer types several lines—four in this case—which you carefully read, and it then asks a question. In the first example, we are interested in the probability of getting exactly 32 successes in 47 trials when each trial has a .69 probability of success, in other words $C(47,32)(.69)^{32}(.31)^{15}$. We answer the question by "1," since only one outcome—32—is considered successful. Next the computer asks us to type in n (the number of trials), and f_1, f_2, s_1, and s_2, which were defined by the computer earlier and give the probability of failure and success at any one trial. We type in the answer 47, 31, 100, 69, 100 in the format and order spelled out by the computer. The next question is, "What is R, defined as the number of successes?" We answer 32. The computer types the answer (.122) and, somewhat arrogantly, says, "New problem: How many outcomes are considered successful?" Suppose that we are interested in knowing the probability that 45, 46, 47, 48, or 49 out of 76 trials will be a success if each trial has a .62 probability of success.

```
                    HELLO
FOR USER ASSISTANCE GC-5 SITE 1, PLEASE DIAL 716-854-0242
USER NUMBER-- _____

PASSWORD- _____

NEW OR OLD--OLD
OLD PROBLEM NAME--B.P.D.***

READY.

RUN


THIS PROGRAM CALCULATES BINOMIAL PROBABILITY DISTRIBUTION.
N = NUMBER OF EVENTS.
F1/F2 = PROBABILITY OF A FAILURE.
S1/S2 = PROBABILITY OF A SUCCESS.

HOW MANY DIFFERENT OUTCOMES ARE CONSIDERED SUCCESSFUL? 1

TYPE N, F1, F2, S1, S2 ? 47,31,100,69,100
R = NUMBER OF SUCCESSES.

                                               R = ? 32

P[EXACTLY 32    SUCCESSES] =  .122
                              ------
              P[SUCCESS] =  .122


NEW PROBLEM...
HOW MANY DIFFERENT OUTCOMES ARE CONSIDERED SUCCESSFUL? 5

TYPE N, F1, F2, S1, S2 ? 76,38,100,62,100
R = NUMBER OF SUCCESSES.

                                               R = ? 45
P[EXACTLY 45    SUCCESSES] =  .081             R = ? 46
P[EXACTLY 46    SUCCESSES] =  .09              R = ? 47
P[EXACTLY 47    SUCCESSES] =  .093             R = ? 48
P[EXACTLY 48    SUCCESSES] =  .092             R = ? 49
P[EXACTLY 49    SUCCESSES] =  .086
                              ------
              P[SUCCESS] =  .442


NEW PROBLEM...

STOP.
READY.
```

EXHIBIT 1

Then we answer 5. After we give n, f_1, f_2, s_1, and s_2, the computer asks,

$$R = \text{number of successes} \qquad R = ?$$

We answer 45. The computer types the answer and ends the line with $R = ?$ We answer 46. (The answer $.09 = .090$, since zeroes at the end are omitted.) And so on until we have given the computer the five values of R, ending with 49. The computer then knows these are the five we specified before and adds them all. We are given .442 as the answer.

As the tireless computer automatically starts typing "new problem," we press the S button, and the computer stops and states it is ready for the next challenge. (Until we type "bye" or "goodbye" the telephone line with the computer remains connected.)

```
OLD
OLD PROBLEM NAME--BINOMI***

READY.

RUN


THIS PROGRAM PRINTS A TABLE OF BINOMIAL PROBABILITIES FOR ANY
RANGE OF R [NUMBER OF 'SUCCESSES'], GIVEN P, THE PROBABILITY OF
SUCCESS ON EACH TRIAL, AND N, THE NUMBER OF TRIALS.

N,P =? 21,0.3

GIVE THE LOWER AND UPPER R'S THAT INTEREST YOU? 0,21



N = 21
P = .3
TABLE FOR R = 0      THRU 21


  R             P[@SUCC.=R]      P[@SUCC.<=R]     P[@SUCC.>=R]
  -             -----------      ------------     ------------

  0             5.58546 E-4      5.58546 E-4      1.
  1             5.02691 E-3      5.58546 E-3      .999441
  2             2.15439 E-2      2.71294 E-2      .994415
  3             5.84763 E-2      8.56057 E-2      .972871
  4             .112776          .198381          .914394
  5             .16433           .362712          .801619
  6             .187806          .550518          .637288
  7             .172475          .722993          .449482
  8             .129356          .85235           .277007
  9             8.00777 E-2      .932427          .14765
 10             4.11828 E-2      .97361           6.75728 E-2
 11             1.76498 E-2      .99126           .02639
 12             6.30349 E-3      .99756           8.74017 E-3
 13             1.87027 E-3      .999434          2.43668 E-3
 14             4.58025 E-4      .999892          5.66410 E-4
 15             9.16049 E-5      .999983          1.08385 E-4
 16             1.47222 E-5      .999998          1.67804 E-5
 17             1.85574 E-6      1.               2.05814 E-6
 18             1.76737 E-7      1.               2.02395 E-7
 19             1.19597 E-8      1.               2.56579 E-8
 20             5.12557 E-10     1.               1.36982 E-8
 21             1.04604 E-11     1.               1.31857 E-8


TIME:    2 SECS.
```

EXHIBIT 2

In our next problem (Exhibit 2), we are interested in a complete binomial distribution, with $n = 21$, $\pi = .3$. We might use the previous program, but it is slower and less precise (it only gives three decimal places). We are already connected and without further preliminaries we type "old." The computer asks the name of the program and we type its name, BINOMI***, and ask it to run. The computer types the relevant information, and we answer the questions by telling the computer that $n = 21$, $\pi = .3$, and we want to know the probability for $0, 1, 2, \ldots$, up to 21 successes. The computer types the answers in a table. The symbol E-4 means that the decimal point must be moved four places to the left to get the actual answer. Thus, the value 2.15439 E-2 means .0215439. The computer gives more than we bargained for (as it often does) in the last two columns, where for each value $0, 1, 2, \ldots, 21$ the probability that the number of successes is *equal to or less than* and *equal to or more than* $0, 1, 2, \ldots, 21$ is given. The line

10	4.11828 E-2	.97361	6.75728 E-2

means that the probability of *exactly* 10 successes ($n = 21$, $\pi = .3$) equals .0411828, the probability of *at most* 10 successes is .97361, and the probability of *at least* 10 successes is .0675728. (This last value is equal to $1 - .97361 + .0411828$.)

At the end the computer gives the actual computer operating time required (not including typing time or waiting time), which is of importance in verifying later bills.

In our Exhibit 3 we want the chi-square value of a 2×2 contingency table. The program is called STAT 04***. We ask it to list the program. The first few lines tell us what to do. Before the computer continues to type out the complete program as written, we type stop, since we know enough. The computer then types ready, and we type the data—218, 150, 9, 115—on line 900 as instructed. We then type run. The computer types the answer.

Exhibit 4 illustrates the ability of the computer to save computational effort in deriving a straight-line trend and a seasonal from monthly data, which is a laborious exercise with only an electric desk calculator. The program is in the library TREND 1***. After the computer indicates its readiness, we type list. The computer describes the program and how to use it, and tells us it is ready to give the details of the program. We type stop, and the computer once again tells us it is ready. We type in 4 years of monthly data and tell the computer to run. (At one point we

```
  OLD
OLD PROBLEM NAME-- STAT04***

READY.


LIST

O REM  *   STAT04  *
1     REM  THIS PROGRAM COMPUTES CHI SQUARES FOR 2 BY 2 TABLES
2     REM  THE DATA, WHICH ARE THE FOUR ENTRIES OF THE TABLE
3     REM  IN NORMAL ORDER, CAN BE ENTERED IN DATA STATEMENTS
4     REM  BETWEEN 900 AND 998.



STOP.
READY.

900 DATA 218,150,9,115
RUN


TABLE                               CHI SQUARE

  218             150
  9               115         98.7639



TIME:   1 SECS.
```

EXHIBIT 0

typed 69 where we meant 68, and the correction can be made as shown.) Within a very short time the computer produces the answer. The trend is

$$y_t = 47.2465 + .297764x$$

and the seasonal is given as 1.01815, 1.21226, etc. The forecast for the fifth month in the fifth year is given as 62.5771, which equals

$$(.992847)(47.2465 + .297764 \times 53)$$

A problem of a slightly different nature is exhibited in the next example (Exhibits 5a and 5b). We want to plot points in a scatter. This is time consuming, rather dull work, and we are pleased to be able to farm it out to the computer. The problem name is DTPLOT***. We type run and are faced with the question of whether we want an introduction. Since this is our first experience with this program, we answer yes by typing 1. The computer tells us what it will do for us. Armed with this knowledge, we continue to call the same program—DTPLOT***—as the computer advised in its last line (rerun the program). We then type in the 48 values according to instructions. (Once again we slipped and corrected a 3 to a 4.) We have given a time series (the same as the one used in Exhibit 4) to plot. The computer first asks whether we want the introduction or the plot. By now we want to see the plot, and we answer 0. The computer next types that the horizontal range runs from 35 through 80 and the vertical from 0 to 48 *and spaces automatically to get the fullest possible use of the area*. In other words, the scales as printed out are

```
OLD
OLD PROBLEM NAME--TREND1***

READY.

LIST

0 REM   ***TREND1***
10 REM THIS PROGRAM COMPUTES A SIMPLE LINEAR TREND FORECAST WITH
20 REM SEASONAL ADJUSTMENTS FOR MONTHLY DATA. UP TO NINE YEARS DATA
30 REM BY MONTH CAN BE INPUT. DATA SHOULD BE INPUT FROM LINE 900
40 REM STARTING WITH THE NUMBER OF YEARS(N) OF DATA YOU HAVE AND
50 REM THEN THE MONTHLY DATA, SEQUENTIALLY(12*N).
60 REM THIS WILL ONLY GIVE A GOOD FIT IF THE TREND IS LINEAR.
70 REM THE OUTPUT WILL BE FIRST THE A AND B VALUES FOR THE LINEAR
80 REM TREND OF TYPE Y= A + BX, AND THEN THE FORECASTS FOR THE
90 REM NEXT 12 MONTHS AND THE SEASONAL VALUES.
95 REM SAMPLE DATA IN LINES 900-901.
100 D

STOP.
READY.

900 DATA 4,48,55,60,50,49,40,35,40,60,50,35,60,52,60,61,53,51,42,
901 DATA 40,43,68,52,39,66,55,69←8,70,57,56,44,45,45,75,59,43,72,
902 DATA 60,70,69,63,59,45,40,47,80,63,48,76
RUN


A-VALUE EQUALS 47.2465        B-VALUE EQUALS .297764


PERIOD          FORECAST        SEASONAL FACTOR
   49           62.9592           1.01815
   50           75.3233           1.21226
   51           77.6168           1.24321
   52           65.3341           1.04151
   53           62.5771            .992847
   54           47.7535            .754093
   55           43.8377            .689018
   56           48.7442            .762567
   57           85.2042           1.32678
   58           65.077            1.00868
   59           44.7449            .690353
   60           82.076            1.26053


TIME:    3 SECS.
```

EXHIBIT 4

```
OLD
OLD PROBLEM NAME--DTPLOT***

READY.

RUN


TYPE 1 FOR AN INTRODUCTION OR 0 TO PLOT? 1

****THIS ROUTINE WILL PLOT A MAXIMUM OF 100 POINTS ON THE
SAME SET OF COORDINATE AXES.
****POINTS TO BE PLOTTED ARE ENTERED VIA DATA STATEMENTS
IN THIS FORM:
     XXX   DATA   1, 10, 2, 8, 3, 7, ... ETC.
****THESE STATEMENTS SHOULD BE LABELED FROM 001;
STATEMENT 000 SHOULD CONTAIN THE NUMBER OF POINTS TO BE
PLOTTED [NOT MORE THAN 100].
****THE ROUTINE SORTS AND MERGES ALL ENTRIES IN ORDER OF
INCREASING X VALUES, ALLOWING THE POINTS TO BE ENTERED IN
ANY ORDER.
****A TITLE MAY BE ENTERED BY CODING THE APPROPRIATE
PRINT STATEMENTS IN 5730-5735.
****THE COMPUTER WILL HALT FOLLOWING THIS INTRODUCTION.

TO RECEIVE YOUR FIRST PLOT, ENTER THE NECESSARY DATA
AND PRINT STATEMENTS [PAPER TAPE IS RECOMMENDED] AND
RERUN THE PROGRAM [SKIPPING THIS INTRODUCTION, OF COURSE].


TIME:    2 SECS.


OLD
OLD PROBLEM NAME--DTPLOT***

READY.

000 DATA 48
001 DATA 1,48,2,55,3,60,4,50,5,49,6,40,7,35,8,40,9,60,10,50,11,
002 DATA 35,12,60,13,52,14,60,15,61,16,53,17,51,18,42,19,40,20,
003 DATA 43,21,68,22,52,23,39,24,66,25,55,26,68,27,70,28,57,29,
004 DATA 56,30,44,31,45,32,45,33,75,34,59,35,43,36,72,37,60,38,
005 DATA 70,39,69,40,63,41,59,42,3-45,43,40,44,47,45,80,46,63,
006 DATA 47,48,48,76
RUN


TYPE 1 FOR AN INTRODUCTION OR 0 TO PLOT? 0

HORIZONTAL RANGE 35  [ .9      ] 80
VERTICAL RANGE   1   [ .94     ] 48
```

EXHIBIT 5a

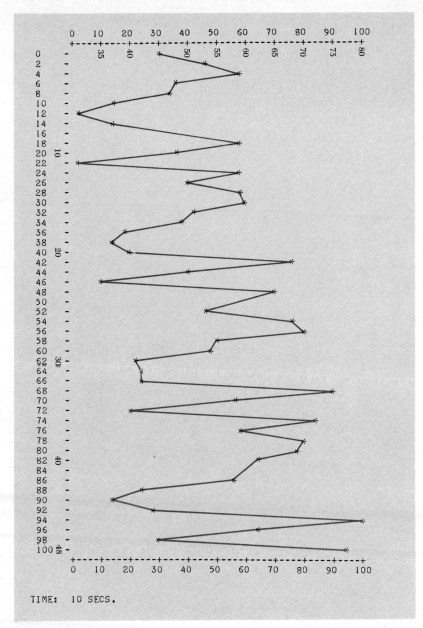

TIME: 10 SECS.

EXHIBIT 5*b*

incorrect, so we have added the relevant scales and connected the points to get a better idea of the regularity and shape of the time series.

In the final example (Exhibit 6) we have used STAT 10*** to run a simple regression, with one independent variable. Our command list gives us the relevant information, and so we type in the data 17, 44, ..., 27, 65 by points, not by series—in lines 901–907. (We might have typed, on line 901, DATA 17, 44, 23, 59, 29, 64, ... etc. which is a little faster

```
OLD
OLD PROBLEM NAME--STAT10***

READY.

LIST

0 REM  *  STAT10  *
1    REM THIS PROGRAM COMPUTES THE SLOPE AND OTHER STATISTICS FOR
2    REM A SIMPLE LINEAR REGRESSION WITH ONE INDEPENDENT
3    REM VARIABLE. DATA STARTING IN LINE 900 ARE N, THE NUMBER
4    REM OF POINTS, THEN THE DATA BY POINT (NOT BY SERIES).
5    REM MAKE SURE THE DATA LINE NUMBERS DO NOT EXCEED 998.
6

STOP.
READY




900 DATA 7
901 DATA 17,44
902 DATA 23,59
903 DATA 29,64
904 DATA 18,49
905 DATA 25,60
906 DATA 16,42
907 DATA 27,65
RUN


NUMBER = 7      SLOPE =  1.7984
MEAN OF X =  22.1429          OF Y =  54.7143
Y-INTERCEPT =  14.8925
SUM-OF-SQUARES TOTAL              21503
               MEAN              20955.6
               SLOPE             520.252
               RESIDUAL          27.1768
STANDARD DEVIATIONS
               X                 5.17179
               Y                 9.55186
               ERROR             2.33138
               Y-BAR             .83188
               SLOPE             .18382
               Y-INTER.          4.1646
F-RATIO FOR SLOPE =  95.7163


TIME:  1 SECS.
```

EXHIBIT 6

to type but not so clear to read.) The computer determines the regression as

$$y = 14.8925 + 1.7984x$$
$$(4.1646) \quad (.18382)$$

It also gives the F ratio (95.7163), which is highly significant. It does not give R^2 explicitly (to our surprise), but we know that

$$R^2 = 1 - \frac{\text{var } d}{\text{var } y} = 1 - \frac{(2.33138)^2}{(9.55186)^2} \approx 1 - \frac{5.4}{91.2} \approx .94$$

It is possible to have the program listed completely and to add some simple instructions which will compute and type out R^2.

These six programs shown here are but a very small fraction of the available programs in the library for this computer. In the area of mathematics the program **DERIV.** gives derivatives of functions, **INVERS** inverts matrices, and **ALG 154** computes characteristic values of symmetric matrices. For finance, programs such as **ANNUITY**, which computes annuities, and **TRUINT**, which computes the true interest rates in installment payments, are useful. The versatility of the library is further illustrated by **EASTER**, which gives the dates of Easter for each year; **J.F.K.**, which prints a portrait of John F. Kennedy; and **TICTAC**, which plays tic-tac-toe. Engineering programs such as **RESIST**, which calculates the current in branches of bridge circuits, and medical programs such as **ISODOS**, which calculates the isodose curves around Ernst radium applicator, are also quite prevalent.

There are different libraries for different computers. All will grow and be perfected as time proceeds.

APPENDIX B

TABLES

Inside the front and back covers there are tables of the areas under one tail of the normal distribution and of squares, square roots, and reciprocals for the values 1 to 100. The tables which follow are:

TABLE 1   5,000 RANDOM DIGITS†

Each digit in Table 1 is randomly selected from the digits 0, 1, 2, 3, 4, 5, 6, 7, 8, and 9.

```
03 99 11 04 61    93 71 61 68 94    66 08 32 46 53    84 60 95 82 32    88 61 81 91 61
38 55 59 55 54    32 88 65 97 80    08 35 56 08 60    29 73 54 77 62    71 29 92 38 53
17 54 67 37 04    92 05 24 62 15    55 12 12 92 81    59 07 60 79 36    27 95 45 89 09
32 64 35 28 61    95 81 90 68 31    00 91 19 89 36    76 35 59 37 79    80 86 30 05 14
69 57 26 87 77    39 51 03 59 05    14 06 04 06 19    29 54 96 96 16    33 56 46 07 80

24 12 26 65 91    27 69 90 64 94    14 84 54 66 72    61 95 87 71 00    90 89 97 57 54
61 19 63 02 31    92 96 26 17 73    41 83 95 53 82    17 26 77 09 43    78 03 87 02 67
30 53 22 17 04    10 27 41 22 02    39 68 52 33 09    10 06 16 88 29    55 98 66 64 85
03 78 89 75 99    75 86 72 07 17    74 41 65 31 66    35 20 83 33 74    87 53 90 88 23
48 22 86 33 79    85 78 34 76 19    53 15 26 74 33    35 66 35 29 72    16 81 86 03 11

60 36 59 46 53    35 07 53 39 49    42 61 42 92 97    01 91 82 83 16    98 95 37 32 31
83 79 94 24 02    56 62 33 44 42    34 99 44 13 74    70 07 11 47 36    09 95 81 80 65
32 96 00 74 05    36 40 98 32 32    99 38 54 16 00    11 13 30 75 86    15 91 70 62 53
19 32 25 38 45    57 62 05 26 06    66 49 76 86 46    78 13 86 65 59    19 64 09 94 13
11 22 09 47 47    07 39 93 74 08    48 50 92 39 29    27 48 24 54 76    85 24 43 51 59

31 75 15 72 60    68 98 00 53 39    15 47 04 83 55    88 65 12 25 96    03 15 21 91 21
88 49 29 93 82    14 45 40 45 04    20 09 49 89 77    74 84 39 34 13    22 10 97 85 08
30 93 44 77 44    07 48 18 38 28    73 78 80 65 33    28 59 72 04 05    94 20 52 03 80
22 88 84 88 93    27 49 99 87 48    60 53 04 51 28    74 02 28 46 17    82 03 71 02 68
78 21 21 69 93    35 90 29 13 86    44 37 21 54 86    65 74 11 40 14    87 48 13 72 20

41 84 98 45 47    46 85 05 23 26    34 67 75 83 00    74 91 06 43 45    19 32 58 15 49
46 35 23 30 49    69 24 89 34 60    45 30 50 75 21    61 31 83 18 55    14 41 37 09 51
11 08 79 62 94    14 01 33 17 92    59 74 76 72 77    76 50 33 45 13    39 66 37 75 41
52 70 10 83 37    56 30 38 73 15    16 03 06 06 40    11 05 49 98 93    02 18 16 81 61
57 15 55 08 98    81 30 44 85 85    68 65 22 73 76    92 85 25 58 66    88 44 80 35 84

20 85 77 31 56    70 28 42 43 26    79 37 59 52 20    01 15 96 32 67    10 62 24 83 91
15 63 38 49 24    90 41 59 36 14    33 52 12 66 65    55 82 34 76 41    86 22 53 17 04
92 69 44 82 97    39 90 40 21 15    59 58 94 90 67    66 82 14 15 75    49 76 70 40 37
77 61 31 90 19    88 15 20 00 80    20 55 49 14 09    96 27 74 82 57    50 81 69 76 16
38 68 83 24 86    45 13 46 35 45    59 40 47 20 59    43 94 75 16 80    43 85 25 96 93

25 16 30 18 89    70 01 41 50 21    41 29 06 73 12    71 85 71 59 57    68 97 11 14 03
65 25 10 76 29    37 23 93 32 95    05 87 00 11 19    92 78 42 63 40    18 47 76 56 22
36 81 54 36 25    18 63 73 75 09    82 44 49 90 05    04 92 17 37 01    14 70 79 39 97
64 39 71 16 92    05 32 78 21 62    20 24 78 17 59    45 19 72 53 32    83 74 52 25 67
04 51 52 56 24    95 09 66 79 46    48 46 08 55 58    15 19 11 87 82    16 93 03 33 61

83 76 16 08 73    43 25 38 41 45    60 83 32 59 83    01 29 14 13 49    20 36 80 71 26
14 38 70 63 45    80 85 40 92 79    43 52 90 63 18    38 38 47 47 61    41 19 63 74 80
51 32 19 22 46    80 08 87 70 74    88 79 95 67 36    00 10 44 94 31    66 91 93 16 78
72 47 20 00 08    80 89 01 80 02    94 81 33 19 00    54 15 58 34 36    35 35 25 41 31
05 46 65 53 06    93 12 81 84 64    74 45 79 05 61    72 84 81 18 34    79 98 26 84 16

39 52 87 24 84    82 47 42 55 93    48 54 53 52 47    18 61 91 36 74    18 61 11 92 41
81 61 61 87 11    53 34 24 42 76    75 12 21 17 24    74 62 77 37 07    58 31 91 59 97
07 58 61 61 20    82 64 12 28 20    92 90 41 31 41    32 39 21 97 63    61 19 96 79 40
90 76 70 42 35    13 57 41 72 00    69 90 26 37 42    78 46 42 25 01    18 62 79 08 72
40 18 82 81 93    29 59 38 86 27    94 97 21 15 98    62 09 53 67 87    00 44 15 89 97

34 41 48 21 57    86 88 75 50 87    19 15 20 00 23    12 30 28 07 83    32 62 46 86 91
63 43 97 53 63    44 98 91 68 22    36 02 40 08 67    76 37 84 16 05    65 96 17 34 88
67 04 90 90 70    93 39 94 55 47    94 45 87 42 84    05 04 14 98 07    20 28 83 40 60
79 49 50 41 46    52 16 29 02 86    54 15 83 42 43    46 97 83 54 82    59 36 29 59 38
91 70 43 05 52    04 73 72 10 31    75 05 19 30 32    47 66 56 43 82    99 78 29 34 78
```

TABLE 1 (Cont'd)

94	01	54	68	74	32	44	44	82	77	59	82	09	61	63	64	65	42	58	43	41	14	54	28	20
74	10	88	82	22	88	57	07	40	15	25	70	49	10	35	01	75	51	47	50	48	96	83	86	03
62	88	08	78	73	95	16	05	92	21	22	30	49	03	14	72	87	71	73	34	39	28	30	41	49
11	74	81	21	02	80	58	04	18	67	17	71	05	96	21	06	55	40	78	50	73	95	07	95	52
17	94	40	56	00	60	47	80	33	43	25	85	25	89	05	57	21	63	96	18	49	85	69	93	26
66	06	74	27	92	95	04	35	26	80	46	78	05	64	87	09	97	15	94	81	37	00	62	21	86
54	24	49	10	30	45	54	77	08	18	59	84	99	61	69	61	45	92	16	47	87	41	71	71	98
30	94	55	75	89	31	73	25	72	60	47	67	00	76	54	46	37	62	53	66	94	74	64	95	80
69	17	03	74	03	86	99	59	03	07	94	30	47	18	03	26	82	50	55	11	12	45	99	13	14
08	34	58	89	75	35	84	18	57	71	08	10	55	99	87	87	11	22	14	76	14	71	37	11	81
27	76	74	35	84	85	30	18	89	77	29	49	06	97	14	73	03	54	12	07	74	69	90	93	10
13	02	51	43	38	54	06	61	52	43	47	72	46	67	33	47	43	14	39	05	31	04	85	66	99
80	21	73	62	92	98	52	52	43	35	24	43	22	48	96	43	27	75	88	74	11	46	61	60	82
10	87	56	20	04	90	39	16	11	05	57	41	10	63	68	53	85	63	07	43	08	67	08	47	41
54	12	75	73	26	26	62	91	90	87	24	47	28	87	79	30	54	02	78	86	61	73	27	54	54
60	31	14	28	24	37	30	14	26	78	45	99	04	32	42	17	37	45	20	03	70	70	77	02	14
49	73	97	14	84	92	00	39	80	86	76	66	87	32	09	59	20	21	19	73	02	90	23	32	50
78	62	65	15	94	16	45	39	46	14	39	01	49	70	66	83	01	20	98	32	25	57	17	76	28
66	69	21	39	86	99	83	70	05	82	81	23	24	49	87	09	50	49	64	12	90	19	37	95	68
44	07	12	80	91	07	36	29	77	03	76	44	74	25	37	98	52	49	78	31	65	70	40	95	14
41	46	88	51	49	49	55	41	79	94	14	92	43	96	50	95	29	40	05	56	70	48	10	69	05
94	55	93	75	59	49	67	85	31	19	70	31	20	56	82	66	98	63	40	99	74	47	42	07	40
41	61	57	03	60	64	11	45	86	60	90	85	06	46	18	80	62	05	17	90	11	43	63	80	72
50	27	39	31	13	41	79	48	68	61	24	78	18	96	83	55	41	18	56	67	77	53	59	98	92
41	39	68	05	04	90	67	00	82	89	40	90	20	50	69	95	08	30	67	83	28	10	25	78	16
25	80	72	42	60	71	52	97	89	20	72	68	20	73	85	90	72	65	71	66	98	88	40	85	83
06	17	09	79	65	88	30	29	80	41	21	44	34	18	08	68	98	48	36	20	89	74	79	88	82
60	80	85	44	44	74	41	28	11	05	01	17	62	88	38	36	42	11	64	89	18	05	95	10	61
80	94	04	48	93	10	40	83	62	22	80	58	27	19	44	92	63	84	03	33	67	05	41	60	67
19	51	69	01	20	46	75	97	16	43	13	17	75	52	92	21	03	68	28	08	77	50	19	74	27
49	38	65	44	80	23	60	42	35	54	21	78	54	11	01	91	17	81	01	74	29	42	09	04	38
06	31	28	89	40	15	99	56	93	21	47	45	86	48	09	98	18	98	18	51	29	65	18	42	15
60	94	20	03	07	11	89	79	26	74	40	40	56	80	32	96	71	75	42	44	10	70	14	13	93
92	32	99	89	32	78	28	44	63	47	71	20	99	20	61	39	44	89	31	36	25	72	20	85	64
77	93	66	35	74	31	38	45	19	24	85	56	12	96	71	58	13	71	78	20	22	75	13	65	18
38	10	17	77	56	11	65	71	38	97	95	88	95	70	67	47	64	81	38	85	70	66	99	34	06
39	64	16	94	57	91	33	92	25	02	92	61	38	97	19	11	94	75	62	03	19	32	42	05	04
84	05	44	04	55	99	39	66	36	80	67	66	76	06	31	69	18	19	68	45	38	52	51	16	00
47	46	80	35	77	57	64	96	32	66	24	70	07	15	94	14	00	42	31	53	69	24	90	57	47
43	32	13	13	70	28	97	72	38	96	76	47	96	85	62	62	34	20	75	89	08	89	90	59	85
64	28	16	18	26	18	55	56	49	37	13	17	33	33	65	78	85	11	61	00	87	06	41	30	75
66	84	77	04	95	32	35	00	29	85	86	71	63	87	46	26	31	37	74	63	55	38	77	26	81
72	46	13	32	30	21	52	95	34	24	92	58	10	22	62	78	43	86	62	76	18	39	67	35	38
21	03	29	10	50	13	05	81	62	18	12	47	05	65	00	15	29	27	61	39	59	52	65	21	13
95	36	26	70	11	06	65	11	61	36	01	01	60	08	57	55	01	85	63	74	35	82	47	17	08
40	71	29	73	80	10	40	45	54	52	34	03	06	07	26	75	21	11	02	71	36	63	36	84	24
58	27	56	17	64	97	58	65	47	16	50	25	94	63	45	87	19	54	60	92	26	78	76	09	39
89	51	41	17	88	68	22	42	34	17	73	95	97	61	45	30	34	24	02	77	11	04	97	20	49
15	47	25	06	69	48	13	93	67	32	46	87	43	70	88	73	46	50	98	19	58	86	93	52	20
12	12	08	61	24	51	24	74	43	02	60	88	35	21	09	21	43	73	67	86	49	22	67	78	37

† Used by permission from "A Million Random Digits with 100,000 Normal Deviates," The Rand Corporation, 1955.

TABLE 2   COMMON LOGARITHMS†

Table 2 gives a table of common logarithms. If the logarithm of x equals y, then $10^y = x$.

The table gives the digits after the decimal point of the logarithm of x. The number before the decimal point of the logarithm of x is one less than the number of digits x has before its decimal point. Thus, the logarithm of 465 equals 2.6675. The 2 results because 465 has three digits (before its decimal point); the .6675 is read from the table in the row labeled 46 and the column labeled 5. The logarithm of 4.65 equals .6675. One may verify that log 7777 = 3.8908. This result is found by interpolation of the numbers in the table which tell us that log 7770 = 3.8904 and log 7780 = 3.8910.

Reading the table backward (looking at an entry in the table and finding what row and column it belongs to), we can derive that if 1.8879 is the logarithm of a certain number, that number will be 77.25, since the number 8879 is between Columns 2 and 3 in row 77. The decimal point in 77.25 is after two digits, since the logarithm was 1.8879. Had the logarithm been .8879, the number would have been 7.725.

N	0	1	2	3	4	5	6	7	8	9
10	0000	0043	0086	0128	0170	0212	0253	0294	0334	0374
11	0414	0453	0492	0531	0569	0607	0645	0682	0719	0755
12	0792	0828	0864	0899	0934	0969	1004	1038	1072	1106
13	1139	1173	1206	1239	1271	1303	1335	1367	1399	1430
14	1461	1492	1523	1553	1584	1614	1644	1673	1703	1732
15	1761	1790	1818	1847	1875	1903	1931	1959	1987	2014
16	2041	2068	2095	2122	2148	2175	2201	2227	2253	2279
17	2304	2330	2355	2380	2405	2430	2455	2480	2504	2529
18	2553	2577	2601	2625	2648	2672	2695	2718	2742	2765
19	2788	2810	2833	2856	2878	2900	2923	2945	2967	2989
20	3010	3032	3054	3075	3096	3118	3139	3160	3181	3201
21	3222	3243	3263	3284	3304	3324	3345	3365	3385	3404
22	3424	3444	3464	3483	3502	3522	3541	3560	3579	3598
23	3617	3636	3655	3674	3692	3711	3729	3747	3766	3784
24	3802	3820	3838	3856	3874	3892	3909	3927	3945	3962
25	3979	3997	4014	4031	4048	4065	4082	4099	4116	4133
26	4150	4166	4183	4200	4216	4232	4249	4265	4281	4298
27	4314	4330	4346	4362	4378	4393	4409	4425	4440	4456
28	4472	4487	4502	4518	4533	4548	4564	4579	4594	4609
29	4624	4639	4654	4669	4683	4698	4713	4728	4742	4757
N	0	1	2	3	4	5	6	7	8	9

TABLE 2 (Cont'd)

N	0	1	2	3	4	5	6	7	8	9
30	4771	4786	4800	4814	4829	4843	4857	4871	4866	4900
31	4914	4928	4942	4955	4969	4983	4997	5011	5024	5038
32	5051	5065	5079	5092	5105	5119	5132	5145	5159	5172
33	5185	5198	5211	5224	5237	5250	5263	5276	5289	5302
34	5315	5328	5340	5353	5366	5378	5391	5403	5416	5428
35	5441	5453	5465	5478	5490	5502	5514	5527	5539	5551
36	5563	5575	5587	5599	5611	5623	5635	5647	5658	5670
37	5682	5694	5705	5717	5729	5740	5752	5763	5775	5786
38	5798	5809	5821	5832	5843	5855	5866	5877	5888	5899
39	5911	5922	5933	5944	5955	5966	5977	5988	5999	6010
40	6021	6031	6042	6053	6064	6075	6085	6096	6107	6117
41	6128	6138	6149	6160	6170	6180	6191	6201	6212	6222
42	6232	6243	6253	6263	6274	6284	6294	6304	6314	6325
43	6335	6345	6355	6365	6375	6385	6395	6405	6415	6425
44	6435	6444	6454	6464	6474	6484	6493	6503	6513	6522
45	6532	6542	6551	6561	6571	6580	6590	6599	6609	6618
46	6628	6637	6646	6656	6665	6675	6684	6693	6702	6712
47	6721	6730	6739	6749	6758	6767	6776	6785	6794	6803
48	6812	6821	6830	6839	6848	6857	6886	6875	6884	6893
49	6902	6911	6920	6920	6937	6946	6955	6964	6972	6981
50	6990	6998	7007	7016	7024	7033	7042	7050	7059	7067
51	7076	7084	7093	7101	7110	7118	7126	7135	7143	7152
52	7160	7168	7177	7185	7193	7202	7210	7218	7226	7235
53	7243	7251	7259	7267	7275	7284	7292	7300	7308	7316
54	7324	7332	7340	7348	7356	7364	7372	7380	7388	7396
55	7404	7412	7419	7427	7435	7443	7451	7459	7466	7474
56	7482	7490	7497	7505	7513	7520	7528	7536	7543	7551
57	7559	7566	7574	7582	7589	7597	7604	7612	7619	7627
58	7634	7642	7649	7657	7664	7672	7679	7686	7694	7701
59	7709	7716	7723	7731	7738	7745	7752	7760	7767	7774
60	7782	7789	7796	7803	7810	7818	7825	7832	7839	7846
61	7853	7860	7868	7875	7882	7889	7896	7903	7910	7917
62	7924	7931	7938	7945	7952	7959	7966	7973	7980	7987
63	7993	8000	8007	8014	8021	8028	8035	8041	8048	8055
64	8062	8069	8075	8082	8089	8096	8102	8109	8116	8122
65	8129	8136	8142	8149	8156	8162	8169	8176	8182	8189
66	8195	8202	8209	8215	8222	8228	8235	8241	8248	8254
67	8261	8267	8274	8280	8287	8293	8299	8306	8312	8319
68	8325	8331	8338	8344	8351	8357	8363	8370	8376	8382
69	8388	8395	8401	8407	8414	8420	8426	8432	8439	8445
N	0	1	2	3	4	5	6	7	8	9

TABLE 2 (Cont'd)

N	0	1	2	3	4	5	6	7	8	9
70	8451	8457	8463	8470	8476	8482	8488	8494	8500	8506
71	8513	8519	8525	8531	8537	8543	8549	8555	8561	8567
72	8573	8579	8585	8591	8597	8603	8609	8615	8621	8627
73	8633	8639	8645	8651	8657	8663	8669	8675	8681	8686
74	8692	8698	8704	8710	8716	8722	8727	8733	8739	8745
75	8751	8756	8762	8768	8774	8779	8785	8791	8797	8802
76	8808	8814	8820	8825	8831	8837	8842	8848	8854	8859
77	8865	8871	8876	8882	8887	8893	8899	8904	8910	8915
78	8921	8927	8932	8938	8943	8949	8954	8960	8965	8971
79	8976	8982	8987	8993	8998	9004	9009	9015	9020	9025
80	9031	9036	9042	9047	9053	9058	9063	9069	9074	9079
81	9085	9090	9096	9101	9106	9112	9117	9122	9128	9133
82	9138	9143	9149	9154	9159	9165	9170	9175	9180	9186
83	9191	9196	9201	9206	9212	9217	9222	9227	9232	9238
84	9243	9248	9253	9258	9263	9269	9274	9279	9284	9289
85	9294	9299	9304	9309	9315	9320	9325	9330	9335	9340
86	9345	9350	9355	9360	9365	9370	9375	9380	9385	9390
87	9395	9400	9405	9410	9415	9420	9425	9430	9435	9440
88	9445	9450	9455	9460	9465	9469	9474	9479	9484	9489
89	9494	9499	9504	9509	9513	9518	9523	9528	9533	9538
90	9542	9547	9552	9557	9562	9566	9571	9576	9581	9586
91	9590	9595	9600	9605	9609	9614	9619	9624	9628	9633
92	9638	9643	9647	9652	9657	9661	9666	9671	9675	9680
93	9685	9689	9694	9699	9703	9708	9713	9717	9722	9727
94	9731	9736	9741	9745	9750	9754	9759	9763	9768	9773
95	9777	9782	9786	9791	9795	9800	9805	9809	9814	9818
96	9823	9827	9832	9836	9841	9845	9850	9854	9859	9663
97	9868	9872	9877	9881	9886	9890	9894	9899	9903	9908
98	9912	9917	9921	9926	9930	9934	9939	9943	9948	9952
99	9956	9961	9965	9969	9974	9978	9983	9987	9991	9996
N	0	1	2	3	4	5	6	7	8	9

† Used by permission from E. L. Grant, "Statistical Quality Control," 3d ed., McGraw-Hill Book Company, New York, 1964.

TABLE 3 BINOMIAL COEFFICIENTS†

Table 3 gives the binomial coefficients, or the triangle of Pascal. Each number is the sum of the one directly above it plus the one above it one column to the left. By symmetry, we can find $C(18,13)$, for we know $C(18,13) = C(18,5) = 8,568$.

N	$C(N,0)$	$C(N,1)$	$C(N,2)$	$C(N,3)$	$C(N,4)$	$C(N,5)$	$C(N,6)$	$C(N,7)$	$C(N,8)$	$C(N,9)$	$C(N,10)$
0	1										
1	1	1									
2	1	2	1								
3	1	3	3	1							
4	1	4	6	4	1						
5	1	5	10	10	5	1					
6	1	6	15	20	15	6	1				
7	1	7	21	35	35	21	7	1			
8	1	8	28	56	70	56	28	8	1		
9	1	9	36	84	126	126	84	36	9	1	
10	1	10	45	120	210	252	210	120	45	10	1
11	1	11	55	165	330	462	462	330	165	55	11
12	1	12	66	220	495	792	924	792	495	220	66
13	1	13	78	286	715	1287	1716	1716	1287	715	286
14	1	14	91	364	1001	2002	3003	3432	3003	2002	1001
15	1	15	105	455	1365	3003	5005	6435	6435	5005	3003
16	1	16	120	560	1820	4368	8008	11440	12870	11440	8008
17	1	17	136	680	2380	6188	12376	19448	24310	24310	19448
18	1	18	153	816	3060	8568	18564	31824	43758	48620	43758
19	1	19	171	969	3876	11628	27132	50388	75582	92378	92378
20	1	20	190	1140	4845	15504	38760	77520	125970	167960	184756

† Used by permission from W. J. Dixon and F. J. Massey, "Introduction to Statistical Analysis," 2d ed., McGraw-Hill Book Company, New York, 1957.

TABLE 4   VALUES OF e^{-x}†

Table 4 gives the values of e^{-x} for many values of x. We can find that
$e^{-1.24} = .28938$.

x	e^{-x} (value)	x	e^{-x} (value)	x	e^{-x} (value)	x	e^{-x} (value)
.00	1.00000	.45	.63763	.90	.40657	1.35	.25924
.01	.99005	.46	.63128	.91	.40252	1.36	.25666
.02	.98020	.47	.62500	.92	.39852	1.37	.25411
.03	.97045	.48	.61878	.93	.39455	1.38	.25158
.04	.96079	.49	.61263	.94	.39063	1.39	.24908
.05	.95123	.50	.60653	.95	.38674	1.40	.24660
.06	.94176	.51	.60050	.96	.38289	1.41	.24414
.07	.93239	.52	.59452	.97	.37908	1.42	.24171
.08	.92312	.53	.58860	.98	.37531	1.43	.23931
.09	.91393	.54	.58275	.99	.37158	1.44	.23693
.10	.90484	.55	.57695	1.00	.36788	1.45	.23457
.11	.89583	.56	.57121	1.01	.36422	1.46	.23224
.12	.88692	.57	.56553	1.02	.36060	1.47	.22993
.13	.87809	.58	.55990	1.03	.35701	1.48	.22764
.14	.86936	.59	.55433	1.04	.35345	1.49	.22537
.15	.86071	.60	.54881	1.05	.34994	1.50	.22313
.16	.85214	.61	.54335	1.06	.34646	1.51	.22091
.17	.84366	.62	.53794	1.07	.34301	1.52	.21871
.18	.83527	.63	.53259	1.08	.33960	1.53	.21654
.19	.82696	.64	.52729	1.09	.33622	1.54	.21438
.20	.81873	.65	.52205	1.10	.33287	1.55	.21225
.21	.81058	.66	.51685	1.11	.32956	1.56	.21014
.22	.80252	.67	.51171	1.12	.32628	1.57	.20805
.23	.79453	.68	.50662	1.13	.32303	1.58	.20598
.24	.78663	.69	.50158	1.14	.31982	1.59	.20393
.25	.77880	.70	.49659	1.15	.31664	1.60	.20190
.26	.77105	.71	.49164	1.16	.31349	1.61	.19989
.27	.76338	.72	.48675	1.17	.31037	1.62	.19790
.28	.75578	.73	.48191	1.18	.30728	1.63	.19593
.29	.74826	.74	.47711	1.19	.30422	1.64	.19398
.30	.74082	.75	.47237	1.20	.30119	1.65	.19205
.31	.73345	.76	.46767	1.21	.29820	1.66	.19014
.32	.72615	.77	.46301	1.22	.29523	1.67	.18825
.33	.71892	.78	.45841	1.23	.29229	1.68	.18637
.34	.71177	.79	.45384	1.24	.28938	1.69	.18452
.35	.70469	.80	.44933	1.25	.28650	1.70	.18268
.36	.69768	.81	.44486	1.26	.28365	1.71	.18087
.37	.69073	.82	.44043	1.27	.28083	1.72	.17907
.38	.68386	.83	.43605	1.28	.27804	1.73	.17728
.39	.67706	.84	.43171	1.29	.27527	1.74	.17552
.40	.67032	.85	.42741	1.30	.27253	1.75	.17377
.41	.66365	.86	.42316	1.31	.26982	1.76	.17204
.42	.65705	.87	.41895	1.32	.26714	1.77	.17033
.43	.65051	.88	.41478	1.33	.26448	1.78	.16864
.44	.64404	.89	.41066	1.34	.26185	1.79	.16696

TABLE 4   (Cont'd)

x	e^{-x} (value)	x	e^{-x} (value)	x	e^{-x} (value)	x	e^{-x} (value)
1.80	.16530	2.25	.10540	2.70	.06721	3.75	.02352
1.81	.16365	2.26	.10435	2.71	.06654	3.80	.02237
1.82	.16203	2.27	.10331	2.72	.06587	3.85	.02128
1.83	.16041	2.28	.10228	2.73	.06522	3.90	.02024
1.84	.15882	2.29	.10127	2.74	.06457	3.95	.01925
1.85	.15724	2.30	.10026	2.75	.06393	4.00	.01832
1.86	.15567	2.31	.09926	2.76	.06329	4.10	.01657
1.87	.15412	2.32	.09827	2.77	.06266	4.20	.01500
1.88	.15259	2.33	.09730	2.78	.06204	4.30	.01357
1.89	.15107	2.34	.09633	2.79	.06142	4.40	.01227
1.90	.14957	2.35	.09537	2.80	.06081	4.50	.01111
1.91	.14808	2.36	.09442	2.81	.06020	4.60	.01005
1.92	.14661	2.37	.09348	2.82	.05961	4.70	.00910
1.93	.14515	2.38	.09255	2.83	.05901	4.80	.00823
1.94	.14370	2.39	.09163	2.84	.05843	4.90	.00745
1.95	.14227	2.40	.09072	2.85	.05784	5.00	.00674
1.96	.14086	2.41	.08982	2.86	.05727	5.10	.00610
1.97	.13946	2.42	.08892	2.87	.05670	5.20	.00552
1.98	.13807	2.43	.08804	2.88	.05613	5.30	.00499
1.99	.13670	2.44	.08716	2.89	.05558	5.40	.00452
2.00	.13534	2.45	.08629	2.90	.05502	5.50	.00409
2.01	.13399	2.46	.08543	2.91	.05448	5.60	.00370
2.02	.13266	2.47	.08458	2.92	.05393	5.70	.00335
2.03	.13134	2.48	.08374	2.93	.05340	5.80	.00303
2.04	.13003	2.49	.08291	2.94	.05287	5.90	.00274
2.05	.12873	2.50	.08208	2.95	.05234	6.00	.00248
2.06	.12745	2.51	.08127	2.96	.05182	6.25	.00193
2.07	.12619	2.52	.08046	2.97	.05130	6.50	.00150
2.08	.12493	2.53	.07966	2.98	.05079	6.75	.00117
2.09	.12369	2.54	.07887	2.99	.05029	7.00	.00091
2.10	.12246	2.55	.07808	3.00	.04979	7.50	.00055
2.11	.12124	2.56	.07730	3.05	.04736	8.00	.00034
2.12	.12003	2.57	.07654	3.10	.04505	8.50	.00020
2.13	.11884	2.58	.07577	3.15	.04285	9.00	.00012
2.14	.11765	2.59	.07502	3.20	.04076	9.50	.00007
2.15	.11648	2.60	.07427	3.25	.03877	10.00	.00005
2.16	.11533	2.61	.07353	3.30	.03688		
2.17	.11418	2.62	.07280	3.35	.03508		
2.18	.11304	2.63	.07208	3.40	.03337		
2.19	.11192	2.64	.07130	3.45	.03175		
2.20	.11080	2.65	.07065	3.50	.03020		
2.21	.10970	2.66	.06995	3.55	.02872		
2.22	.10861	2.67	.06925	3.60	.02732		
2.23	.10753	2.68	.06856	3.65	.02599		
2.24	.10646	2.69	.06788	3.70	.02472		

† Used by permission from E. B. Cox (ed.), "Basic Tables in Business and Economics," McGraw-Hill Book Company, New York, 1967.

TABLE 5 FACTORIALS AND THEIR LOGARITHMS

Table 5 gives the factorials of the numbers 1 through 100, as well as the logarithms of these factorials.

n	$n!$	$\log n!$	n	$n!$	$\log n!$
			50	3.0414×10^{64}	64.48307
1	1.0000	0.00000	51	1.5511×10^{66}	66.19065
2	2.0000	0.30103	52	8.0658×10^{67}	67.90665
3	6.0000	0.77815	53	4.2749×10^{69}	69.63092
4	2.4000×10	1.38021	54	2.3084×10^{71}	71.36332
5	1.2000×10^{2}	2.07918	55	1.2696×10^{73}	73.10368
6	7.2000×10^{2}	2.85733	56	7.1100×10^{74}	74.85187
7	5.0400×10^{3}	3.70243	57	4.0527×10^{76}	76.60774
8	4.0320×10^{4}	4.60552	58	2.3506×10^{78}	78.37117
9	3.6288×10^{5}	5.55976	59	1.3868×10^{80}	80.14202
10	3.6288×10^{6}	6.55976	60	8.3210×10^{81}	81.92017
11	3.9917×10^{7}	7.60116	61	5.0758×10^{83}	83.70550
12	4.7900×10^{8}	8.68034	62	3.1470×10^{85}	85.49790
13	6.2270×10^{9}	9.79428	63	1.9826×10^{87}	87.29724
14	8.7178×10^{10}	10.94041	64	1.2689×10^{89}	89.10342
15	1.3077×10^{12}	12.11650	65	8.2477×10^{90}	90.91633
16	2.0923×10^{13}	13.32062	66	5.4435×10^{92}	92.73587
17	3.5569×10^{14}	14.55107	67	3.6471×10^{94}	94.56195
18	6.4024×10^{15}	15.80634	68	2.4800×10^{96}	96.39446
19	1.2165×10^{17}	17.08509	69	1.7112×10^{98}	98.23331
20	2.4329×10^{18}	18.38612	70	1.1979×10^{100}	100.07841
21	5.1091×10^{19}	19.70834	71	8.5048×10^{101}	101.92966
22	1.1240×10^{21}	21.05077	72	6.1234×10^{103}	103.78700
23	2.5852×10^{22}	22.41249	73	4.4701×10^{105}	105.65032
24	6.2045×10^{23}	23.79271	74	3.3079×10^{107}	107.51955
25	1.5511×10^{25}	25.19065	75	2.4809×10^{109}	109.39461
26	4.0329×10^{26}	26.60562	76	1.8855×10^{111}	111.27543
27	1.0889×10^{28}	28.03698	77	1.4518×10^{113}	113.16192
28	3.0489×10^{29}	29.48414	78	1.1324×10^{115}	115.05401
29	8.8418×10^{30}	30.94654	79	8.9462×10^{116}	116.95164
30	2.6525×10^{32}	32.42366	80	7.1569×10^{118}	118.85473
31	8.2228×10^{33}	33.91502	81	5.7971×10^{120}	120.76321
32	2.6313×10^{35}	35.42017	82	4.7536×10^{122}	122.67703
33	8.6833×10^{36}	36.93869	83	3.9455×10^{124}	124.59610
34	2.9523×10^{38}	38.47016	84	3.3142×10^{126}	126.52038
35	1.0333×10^{40}	40.01423	85	2.8171×10^{128}	128.44980
36	3.7199×10^{41}	41.57054	86	2.4227×10^{130}	130.38420
37	1.3764×10^{43}	43.13874	87	2.1078×10^{132}	132.32382
38	5.2302×10^{44}	44.71852	88	1.8548×10^{134}	134.26830
39	2.0398×10^{46}	46.30959	89	1.6508×10^{136}	136.21769
40	8.1592×10^{47}	47.91165	90	1.4857×10^{138}	138.17194
41	3.3453×10^{49}	49.52443	91	1.3520×10^{140}	140.13098
42	1.4050×10^{51}	51.14768	92	1.2438×10^{142}	142.09477
43	6.0415×10^{52}	52.78115	93	1.1568×10^{144}	144.06325
44	2.6583×10^{54}	54.42460	94	1.0874×10^{146}	146.03638
45	1.1962×10^{56}	56.07781	95	1.0330×10^{148}	148.01410
46	5.5026×10^{57}	57.74057	96	9.9168×10^{149}	149.99637
47	2.5862×10^{59}	59.41267	97	9.6193×10^{151}	151.98314
48	1.2414×10^{61}	61.09391	98	9.4269×10^{153}	153.97437
49	6.0828×10^{62}	62.78410	99	9.3326×10^{155}	155.97000
50	3.0414×10^{64}	64.48307	100	9.3326×10^{157}	157.97000

TABLE 6 PERCENTAGE POINTS FOR χ^2 DISTRIBUTIONS†

Table 6 gives values of a χ^2 distributed variable exceeded with the specified probability, for n degrees of freedom. If u is χ^2 distributed with 19 degrees of freedom, values higher than 30.144 occur less than 5 percent of the time. For large values of n, the variable $x = \sqrt{2u} - \sqrt{2n - 1}$ is normally distributed with mean 0 and variance 1.

				Probability				
n	.99	.95	.90	.50	.10	.05	.01	.001
1	.000157	.00393	.0158	.455	2.706	3.841	6.635	10.827
2	.0201	.103	.211	1.386	4.605	5.991	9.210	13.815
3	.115	.352	.584	2.366	6.251	7.815	11.345	16.266
4	.297	.711	1.064	3.357	7.779	9.488	13.277	18.467
5	.554	1.145	1.610	4.351	9.236	11.070	15.086	20.515
6	.872	1.635	2.204	5.348	10.645	12.592	16.812	22.457
7	1.239	2.167	2.833	6.346	12.017	14.067	18.475	24.322
8	1.646	2.733	3.490	7.344	13.362	15.507	20.090	26.125
9	2.088	3.325	4.168	8.343	14.684	16.919	21.666	27.877
10	2.558	3.940	4.865	9.342	15.987	18.307	23.209	29.588
11	3.053	4.575	5.578	10.341	17.275	19.675	24.725	31.264
12	3.571	5.226	6.304	11.340	18.549	21.026	26.217	32.909
13	4.107	5.892	7.042	12.340	19.812	22.362	27.688	34.528
14	4.660	6.571	7.790	13.339	21.064	23.685	29.141	36.123
15	5.229	7.261	8.547	14.339	22.307	24.996	30.578	37.697
16	5.812	7.962	9.312	15.338	23.542	26.296	32.000	39.252
17	6.408	8.672	10.085	16.338	24.769	27.587	33.409	40.790
18	7.015	9.390	10.865	17.338	25.989	28.869	34.805	42.312
19	7.633	10.117	11.651	18.338	27.204	30.144	36.191	43.820
20	8.260	10.851	12.443	19.337	28.412	31.410	37.566	45.315
21	8.897	11.591	13.240	20.337	29.615	32.671	38.932	46.797
22	9.542	12.338	14.041	21.337	30.813	33.924	40.289	48.268
23	10.196	13.091	14.848	22.337	32.007	35.172	41.638	49.728
24	10.856	13.848	15.659	23.337	33.196	36.415	42.980	51.179
25	11.524	14.611	16.473	24.337	34.382	37.652	44.314	52.620
30	14.953	18.493	20.599	29.336	40.256	43.773	50.892	59.703
40	22.164	26.509	29.051	39.335	51.805	55.759	63.691	73.402
50	29.707	34.764	37.689	49.335	63.167	67.505	76.154	86.661
60	37.485	43.188	46.459	59.335	74.397	79.082	88.379	99.607
70	45.442	51.739	55.329	69.334	85.527	90.531	100.425	112.317

† Table 6 is adapted from Table IV of Fisher and Yates, "Statistical Tables for Biological, Agricultural and Medical Research," published by Oliver & Boyd Ltd., Edinburgh, by permission of the authors and publishers.

TABLE 7a   BINOMIAL PROBABILITIES†

Table 7a gives the binomial probabilities $P(x = k)$ when $x = B(n,\pi)$, for values of n up to 10, and a large number of specific values for π. From it, we can derive $P(x = 4)$ when $x = B(9,\frac{1}{3})$ equals .2048. We can also find the probability of obtaining six successes in eight trials when $\pi = .90$ by arguing that this is the same as the probability of obtaining two failures in eight trials when $\pi = .10$. The answer is .1488. In general,

$$P(x = k) \qquad \text{when} \qquad x = B(n,\pi)$$

equals

$$P(x = n - k) \qquad \text{when} \qquad x = B(n, 1 - \pi)$$

n	k	π .01	.05	.10	.15	.20	.25	.30	$\frac{1}{3}$	.35	.40	.45	.50
2	0	.9801	.9025	.8100	.7225	.6400	.5625	.4900	.4444	.4225	.3600	.3025	.2500
	1	.0198	.0950	.1800	.2550	.3200	.3750	.4200	.4444	.4550	.4800	.4950	.5000
	2	.0001	.0025	.0100	.0225	.0400	.0625	.0900	.1111	.1225	.1600	.2025	.2500
3	0	.9703	.8574	.7290	.6141	.5120	.4219	.3430	.2963	.2746	.2160	.1664	.1250
	1	.0294	.1354	.2430	.3251	.3840	.4219	.4410	.4444	.4436	.4320	.4084	.3750
	2	.0003	.0071	.0270	.0574	.0960	.1406	.1890	.2222	.2389	.2880	.3341	.3750
	3	.0000	.0001	.0010	.0034	.0080	.0156	.0270	.0370	.0429	.0640	.0911	.1250
4	0	.9606	.8145	.6561	.5220	.4096	.3164	.2401	.1975	.1785	.1296	.0915	.0625
	1	.0388	.1715	.2916	.3685	.4096	.4219	.4116	.3951	.3845	.3456	.2995	.2500
	2	.0006	.0135	.0486	.0975	.1536	.2109	.2646	.2963	.3105	.3456	.3675	.3750
	3	.0000	.0005	.0036	.0115	.0256	.0469	.0756	.0988	.1115	.1536	.2005	.2500
	4	.0000	.0000	.0001	.0005	.0016	.0039	.0081	.0123	.0150	.0256	.0410	.0625
5	0	.9510	.7738	.5905	.4437	.3277	.2373	.1681	.1317	.1160	.0778	.0503	.0312
	1	.0480	.2036	.3280	.3915	.4096	.3955	.3602	.3292	.3124	.2592	.2059	.1562
	2	.0010	.0214	.0729	.1382	.2048	.2637	.3087	.3292	.3364	.3456	.3369	.3125
	3	.0000	.0011	.0081	.0244	.0512	.0879	.1323	.1646	.1811	.2304	.2757	.3125
	4	.0000	.0000	.0004	.0022	.0064	.0146	.0284	.0412	.0488	.0768	.1128	.1562
	5	.0000	.0000	.0000	.0001	.0003	.0010	.0024	.0041	.0053	.0102	.0185	.0312
6	0	.9415	.7351	.5314	.3771	.2621	.1780	.1176	.0878	.0754	.0467	.0277	.0156
	1	.0571	.2321	.3543	.3993	.3932	.3560	.3025	.2634	.2437	.1866	.1359	.0938
	2	.0014	.0305	.0984	.1762	.2458	.2966	.3241	.3292	.3280	.3110	.2780	.2344
	3	.0000	.0021	.0146	.0415	.0819	.1318	.1852	.2195	.2355	.2765	.3032	.3125
	4	.0000	.0001	.0012	.0055	.0154	.0330	.0595	.0823	.0951	.1382	.1861	.2344
	5	.0000	.0000	.0001	.0004	.0015	.0044	.0102	.0165	.0205	.0369	.0609	.0938
	6	.0000	.0000	.0000	.0000	.0001	.0002	.0007	.0014	.0018	.0041	.0083	.0156
7	0	.9321	.6983	.4783	.3206	.2097	.1335	.0824	.0585	.0490	.0280	.0152	.0078
	1	.0659	.2573	.3720	.3960	.3670	.3115	.2471	.2048	.1848	.1306	.0872	.0547
	2	.0020	.0406	.1240	.2097	.2753	.3115	.3177	.3073	.2985	.2613	.2140	.1641
	3	.0000	.0036	.0230	.0617	.1147	.1730	.2269	.2561	.2679	.2903	.2918	.2734
	4	.0000	.0002	.0026	.0109	.0287	.0577	.0972	.1280	.1442	.1935	.2388	.2734
	5	.0000	.0000	.0002	.0012	.0043	.0115	.0250	.0384	.0466	.0774	.1172	.1641
	6	.0000	.0000	.0000	.0001	.0004	.0013	.0036	.0064	.0084	.0172	.0320	.0547
	7	.0000	.0000	.0000	.0000	.0000	.0001	.0002	.0005	.0006	.0016	.0037	.0078

TABLE 7a (Cont'd)

n	k	.01	.05	.10	.15	.20	.25	.30	$\frac{1}{3}$	.35	.40	.45	.50
8	0	.9227	.6634	.4305	.2725	.1678	.1001	.0576	.0390	.0319	.0168	.0084	.0039
	1	.0746	.2793	.3826	.3847	.3355	.2670	.1977	.1561	.1373	.0896	.0548	.0312
	2	.0026	.0515	.1488	.2376	.2936	.3115	.2965	.2731	.2587	.2090	.1569	.1094
	3	.0001	.0054	.0331	.0839	.1468	.2076	.2541	.2731	.2786	.2787	.2568	.2188
	4	.0000	.0004	.0046	.0185	.0459	.0865	.1361	.1707	.1875	.2322	.2627	.2734
	5	.0000	.0000	.0004	.0026	.0092	.0231	.0467	.0683	.0808	.1239	.1719	.2188
	6	.0000	.0000	.0000	.0002	.0011	.0038	.0100	.0171	.0217	.0413	.0703	.1094
	7	.0000	.0000	.0000	.0000	.0001	.0004	.0012	.0024	.0033	.0079	.0164	.0312
	8	.0000	.0000	.0000	.0000	.0000	.0000	.0001	.0002	.0002	.0007	.0017	.0039
9	0	.9135	.6302	.3874	.2316	.1342	.0751	.0404	.0260	.0207	.0101	.0046	.0020
	1	.0830	.2985	.3874	.3679	.3020	.2253	.1556	.1171	.1004	.0605	.0339	.0176
	2	.0034	.0629	.1722	.2597	.3020	.3003	.2668	.2341	.2162	.1612	.1110	.0703
	3	.0001	.0077	.0446	.1069	.1762	.2336	.2668	.2731	.2716	.2508	.2119	.1641
	4	.0000	.0006	.0074	.0283	.0661	.1168	.1715	.2048	.2194	.2508	.2600	.2461
	5	.0000	.0000	.0008	.0050	.0165	.0389	.0735	.1024	.1181	.1672	.2128	.2461
	6	.0000	.0000	.0001	.0006	.0028	.0087	.0210	.0341	.0424	.0743	.1160	.1641
	7	.0000	.0000	.0000	.0000	.0003	.0012	.0039	.0073	.0098	.0212	.0407	.0703
	8	.0000	.0000	.0000	.0000	.0000	.0001	.0004	.0009	.0013	.0035	.0083	.0176
	9	.0000	.0000	.0000	.0000	.0000	.0000	.0000	.0001	.0001	.0003	.0008	.0020
10	0	.9044	.5987	.3487	.1969	.1074	.0563	.0282	.0173	.0135	.0060	.0025	.0010
	1	.0914	.3151	.3874	.3474	.2684	.1877	.1211	.0867	.0725	.0403	.0207	.0098
	2	.0042	.0746	.1937	.2759	.3020	.2816	.2335	.1951	.1757	.1209	.0763	.0439
	3	.0001	.0105	.0574	.1298	.2013	.2503	.2668	.2601	.2522	.2150	.1665	.1172
	4	.0000	.0010	.0112	.0401	.0881	.1460	.2001	.2276	.2377	.2508	.2384	.2051
	5	.0000	.0001	.0015	.0085	.0264	.0584	.1029	.1366	.1536	.2007	.2340	.2461
	6	.0000	.0000	.0001	.0012	.0055	.0162	.0368	.0569	.0689	.1115	.1596	.2051
	7	.0000	.0000	.0000	.0001	.0008	.0031	.0090	.0163	.0212	.0425	.0746	.1172
	8	.0000	.0000	.0000	.0000	.0001	.0004	.0014	.0030	.0043	.0106	.0229	.0439
	9	.0000	.0000	.0000	.0000	.0000	.0000	.0001	.0003	.0005	.0016	.0042	.0098
	10	.0000	.0000	.0000	.0000	.0000	.0000	.0000	.0000	.0000	.0001	.0003	.0010

† Used by permission from W. J. Dixon and F. J. Massey, "Introduction to Statistical Analysis," 2d ed., McGraw-Hill Book Company, New York, 1957.

TABLE 7*b*   CUMULATIVE BINOMIAL PROBABILITIES†

Table 7*b* gives the cumulative binomial probabilities $P(x \leq k)$ for selected values of n and π. The probability of obtaining at least 7 successes in 15 trials when $\pi = .40$ equals .78690. The probability of exactly 7 successes is $P(x \leq 7) - P(x \leq 6) = .78690 - .60981 = .17709$.

n	k	$\pi = .10$	$\pi = .20$	$\pi = .25$	$\pi = .30$	$\pi = .40$	$\pi = .50$
5	0	.59049	.32768	.23730	.16807	.07776	.03125
	1	.91854	.73728	.63281	.52822	.33696	.18750
	2	.99144	.94208	.89648	.83692	.68256	.50000
	3	.99954	.99328	.98437	.96922	·91296	.81250
	4	.99999	.99968	.99902	.99757	.98976	.96875
	5	1.00000	1.00000	1.00000	1.00000	1.00000	1.00000 ·
10	0	.34868	.10737	.05631	.02825	.00605	.00098
	1	.73610	.37581	.24403	.14931	.04636	.01074
	2	.92981	.67780	.52559	.38278	.16729	.05469
	3	.98720	.87913	.77588	.64961	.38228	.17187
	4	.99837	.96721	.92187	.84973	.63310	.37695
	5	.99985	.99363	.98027	.95265	.83376	.62305
	6	.99999	.99914	.99649	.98941	.94524	.82812
	7	1.00000	.99992	.99958	.99841	.98771	.94531
	8		1.00000	.99997	.99986	.99832	.98926
	9			1.00000	.99999	.99990	.99902
	10				1.00000	1.00000	1.00000
15	0	.20589	.03518	.01336	.00475	.00047	.00003
	1	.54904	.16713	.08018	.03527	.00517	.00049
	2	.81594	.39802	.23609	.12683	.02711	.00369
	3	.94444	.64816	.46129	.29687	.09050	.01758
	4	.98728	.83577	.68649	.51549	.21728	.05923
	5	.99775	.93895	.85163	.72162	.40322	.15088
	6	.99969	.98194	.94338	.86000	.60981	.30362
	7	.99997	.99576	.98270	.94999	.78690	.50000
	8	1.00000	.99921	.99581	.98476	.90495	.69638
	9		.99989	.99921	.99635	.96617	.84912
	10		.99999	.99988	.99933	.99065	.94077
	11		1.00000	.99999	.99991	.99807	.98242
	12			1.00000	.99999	.99972	.99631
	13				1.00000	.99997	.99951
	14					1.00000	.99997
	15						1.00000

TABLE 7b (Cont'd)

n	k	$\pi = .10$	$\pi = .20$	$\pi = .25$	$\pi = .30$	$\pi = .40$	$\pi = .50$
20	0	.12158	.01153	.00317	.00080	.00004	.00000
	1	.39175	.06918	.02431	.00764	.00052	.00002
	2	.67693	.20608	.09126	.03548	.00361	.00020
	3	.86705	.41145	.22516	.10709	.01596	.00129
	4	.95683	.62965	.41484	.23751	.05095	.00591
	5	.98875	.80421	.61717	.41637	.12560	.02069
	6	.99761	.91331	.78578	.60801	.25001	.05766
	7	.99958	.96786	.89819	.77227	.41589	.13159
	8	.99994	.99002	.95907	.88667	.59560	.25172
	9	.99999	.99741	.98614	.95204	.75534	.41190
	10	1.00000	.99944	.99606	.98286	.87248	.58810
	11		.99990	.99906	.99486	.94347	.74828
	12		.99998	.99982	.99872	.97897	.86841
	13		1.00000	.99997	.99974	.99353	.94234
	14			1.00000	.99996	.99839	.97931
	15				.99999	.99968	.99409
	16				1.00000	.99995	.99871
	17					.99999	.99980
	18					1.00000	.99998
	19						1.00000
25	0	.07179	.00378	.00075	.00013	.00000	.00000
	1	.27121	.02739	.00702	.00157	.00005	.00000
	2	.53709	.09823	.03211	.00896	.00043	.00001
	3	.76359	.23399	.09621	.03324	.00237	.00008
	4	.90201	.42067	.21374	.09047	.00947	.00046
	5	.96660	.61669	.37828	.19349	.02936	.00204
	6	.99052	.78004	.56110	.34065	.07357	.00732
	7	.99774	.89088	.72651	.51185	.15355	.02164
	8	.99954	.95323	.85056	.67693	.27353	.05388
	9	.99992	.98267	.92867	.81056	.42462	.11476
	10	.99999	.99445	.97033	.90220	.58577	.21218
	11	1.00000	.99846	.98027	.95575	.73228	.34502
	12		.99963	.99663	.98253	.84623	.50000
	13		.99992	.99908	.99401	.92220	.65498
	14		.99999	.99979	.99822	.96561	.78782
	15		1.00000	.99996	.99955	.98683	.88524
	16			.99999	.99990	.99567	.94612
	17			1.00000	.99998	.99879	.97836
	18				1.00000	.99972	.99268
	19					.99995	.99796
	20					.99999	.99954
	21					1.00000	.99992
	22						.99999
	23						1.00000

TABLE 7b   (Cont'd)

n	k	$\pi = .10$	$\pi = .20$	$\pi = .25$	$\pi = .30$	$\pi = .40$	$\pi = .50$
50	0	.00515	.00001	.00000	.00000		
	1	.03379	.00019	.00001	.00000		
	2	.11173	.00129	.00009	.00000		
	3	.25029	.00566	.00050	.00003		
	4	.43120	.01850	.00211	.00017		
	5	.61612	.04803	.00705	.00072	.00000	
	6	.77023	.10340	.01939	.00249	.00001	
	7	.87785	.19041	.04526	.00726	.00006	
	8	.94213	.30733	.09160	.01825	.00023	
	9	.97546	.44374	.16368	.04023	.00076	.00000
	10	.99065	.58356	.26220	.07885	.00220	.00001
	11	.99678	.71067	.38162	.13904	.00569	.00005
	12	.99900	.81394	.51099	.22287	.01325	.00015
	13	.99971	.88941	.63704	.32788	.02799	.00047
	14	.99993	.93928	.74808	.44683	.05396	.00130
	15	.99998	.96920	.83692	.56918	.09550	.00330
	16	1.00000	.98556	.90169	.68388	.15609	.00767
	17		.99374	.94488	.78219	.23688	.01642
	18		.99749	.97127	.85944	.33561	.03245
	19		.99907	.98608	.91520	.44648	.05946
	20		.99968	.99374	.95224	.56103	.10132
	21		.99990	.99738	.97491	.67014	.16112
	22		.99997	.99898	.98772	.76602	.23994
	23		.99999	.99963	.99441	.84383	.33591
	24		1.00000	.99988	.99763	.90219	.44386
	25			.99996	.99907	.94266	.55614
	26			.99999	.99966	.96859	.66409
	27			1.00000	.99988	.98397	.76006
	28				.99996	.99238	.83888
	29				.99999	.99664	.89868
	30				1.00000	.99863	.94054
	31					.99948	.96755
	32					.99982	.98358
	33					.99994	.99233
	34					.99998	.99670
	35					1.00000	.99870
	36						.99953
	37						.99985
	38						.99995
	39						.99999
	40						1.00000

† Used by permission from W. C. Guenther, "Concepts of Statistical Inference," McGraw-Hill Book Company, New York, 1965.

TABLE 8 POISSON PROBABILITIES†

Table 8 gives Poisson probabilities for various values of the parameter. If the parameter is 2.6, the probability of obtaining 0, 1, 2, 3, . . . successes is given by .0743, .1931, .2510, .2176, ...

					λ					
x	.1	.2	.3	.4	.5	.6	.7	.8	.9	1.0
0	.9048	.8187	.7408	.6703	.6065	.5488	.4966	.4493	.4066	.3679
1	.0905	.1637	.2222	.2681	.3033	.3293	.3476	.3595	.3659	.3679
2	.0045	.0164	.0333	.0536	.0758	.0988	.1217	.1438	.1647	.1839
3	.0002	.0011	.0033	.0072	.0126	.0198	.0284	.0383	.0494	.0613
4	.0000	.0001	.0002	.0007	.0016	.0030	.0050	.0077	.0111	.0153
5	.0000	.0000	.0000	.0001	.0002	.0004	.0007	.0012	.0020	.0031
6	.0000	.0000	.0000	.0000	.0000	.0000	.0001	.0002	.0003	.0005
7	.0000	.0000	.0000	.0000	.0000	.0000	.0000	.0000	.0000	.0001

					λ					
x	1.1	1.2	1.3	1.4	1.5	1.6	1.7	1.8	1.9	2.0
0	.3329	.3012	.2725	.2466	.2231	.2019	.1827	.1653	.1496	.1353
1	.3662	.3614	.3543	.3452	.3347	.3230	.3106	.2975	.2842	.2707
2	.2014	.2169	.2303	.2417	.2510	.2584	.2640	.2678	.2700	.2707
3	.0738	.0867	.0998	.1128	.1255	.1378	.1496	.1607	.1710	.1804
4	.0203	.0260	.0324	.0395	.0471	.0551	.0636	.0723	.0812	.0902
5	.0045	.0062	.0084	.0111	.0141	.0176	.0216	.0260	.0309	.0361
6	.0008	.0012	.0018	.0026	.0035	.0047	.0061	.0078	.0098	.0120
7	.0001	.0002	.0003	.0005	.0008	.0011	.0015	.0020	.0027	.0034
8	.0000	.0000	.0001	.0001	.0001	.0002	.0003	.0005	.0006	.0009
9	.0000	.0000	.0000	.0000	.0000	.0000	.0001	.0001	.0001	.0002

					λ					
x	2.1	2.2	2.3	2.4	2.5	2.6	2.7	2.8	2.9	3.0
0	.1225	.1108	.1003	.0907	.0821	.0743	.0672	.0608	.0550	.0498
1	.2572	.2438	.2306	.2177	.2052	.1931	.1815	.1703	.1596	.1494
2	.2700	.2681	.2652	.2613	.2565	.2510	.2450	.2384	.2314	.2240
3	.1890	.1966	.2033	.2090	.2138	.2176	.2205	.2225	.2237	.2240
4	.0992	.1082	.1169	.1254	.1336	.1414	.1488	.1557	.1622	.1680
5	.0417	.0476	.0538	.0602	.0668	.0735	.0804	.0872	.0940	.1008
6	.0146	.0174	.0206	.0241	.0278	.0319	.0362	.0407	.0455	.0504
7	.0044	.0055	.0068	.0083	.0099	.0118	.0139	.0163	.0188	.0216
8	.0011	.0015	.0019	.0025	.0031	.0038	.0047	.0057	.0068	.0081
9	.0003	.0004	.0005	.0007	.0009	.0011	.0014	.0018	.0022	.0027
10	.0001	.0001	.0001	.0002	.0002	.0003	.0004	.0005	.0006	.0008
11	.0000	.0000	.0000	.0000	.0000	.0001	.0001	.0001	.0002	.0002
12	.0000	.0000	.0000	.0000	.0000	.0000	.0000	.0000	.0000	.0001

					λ					
x	3.1	3.2	3.3	3.4	3.5	3.6	3.7	3.8	3.9	4.0
0	.0450	.0408	.0369	.0334	.0302	.0273	.0247	.0221	.0202	.0183
1	.1397	.1304	.1217	.1135	.1057	.0984	.0915	.0850	.0789	.0733
2	.2165	.2087	.2008	.1929	.1850	.1771	.1692	.1615	.1539	.1465
3	.2237	.2226	.2209	.2186	.2158	.2125	.2087	.2046	.2001	.1954
4	.1734	.1781	.1823	.1858	.1888	.1912	.1931	.1944	.1951	.1954
5	.1075	.1140	.1203	.1264	.1322	.1377	.1429	.1477	.1522	.1563
6	.0555	.0608	.0662	.0716	.0771	.0826	.0881	.0936	.0989	.1042
7	.0246	.0278	.0312	.0348	.0385	.0425	.0466	.0508	.0551	.0595
8	.0095	.0111	.0129	.0148	.0169	.0191	.0215	.0241	.0269	.0298
9	.0033	.0040	.0047	.0056	.0066	.0076	.0089	.0102	.0116	.0132
10	.0010	.0013	.0016	.0019	.0023	.0028	.0033	.0039	.0045	.0053
11	.0003	.0004	.0005	.0006	.0007	.0009	.0011	.0013	.0016	.0019
12	.0001	.0001	.0001	.0002	.0002	.0003	.0003	.0004	.0005	.0006
13	.0000	.0000	.0000	.0000	.0001	.0001	.0001	.0001	.0002	.0002
14	.0000	.0000	.0000	.0000	.0000	.0000	.0000	.0000	.0000	.0001

TABLE 8 (Cont'd)

x	4.1	4.2	4.3	4.4	4.5	4.6	4.7	4.8	4.9	5.0
					λ					
0	.0166	.0150	.0136	.0123	.0111	.0101	.0091	.0082	.0074	.0067
1	.0679	.0630	.0583	.0540	.0500	.0462	.0427	.0395	.0365	.0337
2	.1393	.1323	.1254	.1188	.1125	.1063	.1005	.0948	.0894	.0842
3	.1904	.1852	.1798	.1743	.1687	.1631	.1574	.1517	.1460	.1404
4	.1951	.1944	.1933	.1917	.1898	.1875	.1849	.1820	.1789	.1755
5	.1600	.1633	.1662	.1687	.1708	.1725	.1738	.1747	.1753	.1755
6	.1093	.1143	.1191	.1237	.1281	.1323	.1362	.1398	.1432	.1462
7	.0640	.0686	.0732	.0778	.0824	.0869	.0914	.0959	.1002	.1044
8	.0328	.0360	.0393	.0428	.0463	.0500	.0537	.0575	.0614	.0653
9	.0150	.0168	.0188	.0209	.0232	.0255	.0280	.0307	.0334	.0363
10	.0061	.0071	.0081	.0092	.0104	.0118	.0132	.0147	.0164	.0181
11	.0023	.0027	.0032	.0037	.0043	.0049	.0056	.0064	.0073	.0082
12	.0008	.0009	.0011	.0014	.0016	.0019	.0022	.0026	.0030	.0034
13	.0002	.0003	.0004	.0005	.0006	.0007	.0008	.0009	.0011	.0013
14	.0001	.0001	.0001	.0001	.0002	.0002	.0003	.0003	.0004	.0005
15	.0000	.0000	.0000	.0000	.0001	.0001	.0001	.0001	.0001	.0002

x	5.1	5.2	5.3	5.4	5.5	5.6	5.7	5.8	5.9	6.0
					λ					
0	.0061	.0055	.0050	.0045	.0041	.0037	.0033	.0030	.0027	.0025
1	.0311	.0287	.0265	.0244	.0225	.0207	.0191	.0176	.0162	.0149
2	.0793	.0746	.0701	.0659	.0618	.0580	.0544	.0509	.0477	.0446
3	.1348	.1293	.1239	.1185	.1133	.1082	.1033	.0985	.0938	.0892
4	.1719	.1681	.1641	.1600	.1558	.1515	.1472	.1428	.1383	.1339
5	.1753	.1748	.1740	.1728	.1714	.1697	.1678	.1656	.1632	.1606
6	.1490	.1515	.1537	.1555	.1571	.1584	.1594	.1601	.1605	.1606
7	.1086	.1125	.1163	.1200	.1234	.1267	.1298	.1326	.1353	.1377
8	.0692	.0731	.0771	.0810	.0849	.0887	.0925	.0962	.0998	.1033
9	.0362	.0423	.0454	.0486	.0519	.0552	.0586	.0602	.0654	.0688
10	.0200	.0220	.0241	.0262	.0285	.0309	.0334	.0359	.0386	.0413
11	.0093	.0104	.0116	.0129	.0143	.0157	.0173	.0190	.0207	.0225
12	.0035	.0045	.0051	.0058	.0065	.0073	.0082	.0092	.0102	.0113
13	.0015	.0104	.0021	.0024	.0028	.0032	.0036	.0041	.0046	.0052
14	.0006	.0007	.0008	.0009	.0011	.0013	.0015	.0017	.0019	.0022
15	.0002	.0002	.0003	.0003	.0004	.0005	.0006	.0007	.0008	.0009
16	.0001	.0001	.0001	.0001	.0001	.0002	.0002	.0002	.0003	.0003
17	.0000	.0000	.0000	.0000	.0000	.0001	.0001	.0001	.0001	.0001

x	6.1	6.2	6.3	6.4	6.5	6.6	6.7	6.8	6.9	7.0
					λ					
0	.0022	.0020	.0018	.0017	.0015	.0014	.0012	.0011	.0010	.0009
1	.0137	.0126	.0116	.0106	.0098	.0090	.0082	.0076	.0070	.0064
2	.0417	.0390	.0364	.0340	.0318	.0296	.0276	.0258	.0240	.0223
3	.0848	.0806	.0765	.0726	.0688	.0652	.0617	.0584	.0552	.0521
4	.1294	.1249	.1205	.1162	.1118	.1076	.1034	.0992	.0952	.0912
5	.1579	.1549	.1519	.1487	.1454	.1420	.1385	.1349	.1314	.1277
6	.1605	.1601	.1595	.1586	.1575	.1562	.1546	.1529	.1511	.1490
7	.1399	.1418	.1435	.1450	.1462	.1472	.1480	.1486	.1489	.1490
8	.1066	.1099	.1130	.1160	.1188	.1215	.1240	.1263	.1284	.1304
9	.0723	.0757	.0791	.0825	.0858	.0891	.0923	.0954	.0985	.1014
10	.0441	.0469	.0498	.0528	.0558	.0588	.0618	.0649	.0679	.0710
11	.0245	.0265	.0285	.0307	.0330	.0353	.0377	.0401	.0426	.0452
12	.0124	.0137	.0150	.0164	.0179	.0194	.0210	.0227	.0245	.0264
13	.0058	.0065	.0073	.0081	.0089	.0098	.0108	.0119	.0130	.0142
14	.0025	.0029	.0033	.0037	.0041	.0046	.0052	.0058	.0064	.0071
15	.0010	.0012	.0014	.0016	.0018	.0020	.0023	.0026	.0029	.0033
16	.0004	.0005	.0005	.0006	.0007	.0008	.0010	.0011	.0013	.0014
17	.0001	.0002	.0002	.0002	.0003	.0003	.0004	.0004	.0005	.0006
18	.0000	.0001	.0001	.0001	.0001	.0001	.0001	.0002	.0002	.0002
19	.0000	.0000	.0000	.0000	.0000	.0000	.0000	.0001	.0001	.0001

TABLE 8 (Cont'd)

					λ					
x	7.1	7.2	7.3	7.4	7.5	7.6	7.7	7.8	7.9	8.0
0	.0008	.0007	.0007	.0006	.0006	.0005	.0005	.0004	.0004	.0003
1	.0059	.0054	.0049	.0045	.0041	.0038	.0035	.0032	.0029	.0027
2	.0208	.0194	.0180	.0167	.0156	.0145	.0134	.0125	.0116	.0107
3	.0492	.0464	.0438	.0413	.0389	.0366	.0345	.0324	.0305	.0286
4	.0874	.0836	.0799	.0764	.0729	.0696	.0663	.0632	.0602	.0573
5	.1241	.1204	.1167	.1130	.1094	.1057	.1021	.0986	.0951	.0916
6	.1468	.1445	.1420	.1394	.1367	.1339	.1311	.1282	.1252	.1221
7	.1489	.1486	.1481	.1474	.1465	.1454	.1442	.1428	.1413	.1396
8	.1321	.1337	.1351	.1363	.1373	.1382	.1388	.1392	.1395	.1396
9	.1042	.1070	.1096	.1121	.1144	.1167	.1187	.1207	.1224	.1241
10	.0740	.0770	.0800	.0829	.0858	.0887	.0914	.0941	.0967	.0993
11	.0478	.0504	.0531	.0558	.0585	.0613	.0640	.0667	.0695	.0722
12	.0283	.0303	.0323	.0344	.0366	.0388	.0411	.0434	.0457	.0481
13	.0154	.0168	.0181	.0196	.0211	.0227	.0243	.0260	.0278	.0296
14	.0078	.0086	.0095	.0104	.0113	.0123	.0134	.0145	.0157	.0169
15	.0037	.0041	.0046	.0051	.0057	.0062	.0069	.0075	.0083	.0090
16	.0016	.0019	.0021	.0024	.0026	.0030	.0033	.0037	.0041	.0045
17	.0007	.0008	.0009	.0010	.0012	.0013	.0015	.0017	.0019	.0021
18	.0003	.0003	.0004	.0004	.0005	.0006	.0006	.0007	.0008	.0009
19	.0001	.0001	.0001	.0002	.0002	.0002	.0003	.0003	.0003	.0004
20	.0000	.0000	.0001	.0001	.0001	.0001	.0001	.0001	.0001	.0002
21	.0000	.0000	.0000	.0000	.0000	.0000	.0000	.0000	.0001	.0001

					λ					
x	8.1	8.2	8.3	8.4	8.5	8.6	8.7	8.8	8.9	9.0
0	.0003	.0003	.0002	.0002	.0002	.0002	.0002	.0002	.0001	.0001
1	.0025	.0023	.0021	.0019	.0017	.0016	.0014	.0013	.0012	.0011
2	.0100	.0092	.0086	.0079	.0074	.0068	.0063	.0058	.0054	.0050
3	.0269	.0252	.0237	.0222	.0208	.0195	.0183	.0171	.0160	.0150
4	.0544	.0517	.0491	.0466	.0443	.0420	.0398	.0377	.0357	.0337
5	.0882	.0849	.0816	.0784	.0752	.0722	.0692	.0663	.0635	.0607
6	.1191	.1160	.1128	.1097	.1066	.1034	.1003	.0972	.0941	.0911
7	.1378	.1358	.1338	.1317	.1294	.1271	.1247	.1222	.1197	.1171
8	.1395	.1392	.1388	.1382	.1375	.1366	.1356	.1344	.1332	.1318
9	.1256	.1269	.1280	.1290	.1299	.1306	.1311	.1315	.1317	.1318
10	.1017	.1040	.1063	.1084	.1104	.1123	.1140	.1157	.1172	.1186
11	.0749	.0776	.0802	.0828	.0853	.0878	.0902	.0925	.0948	.0970
12	.0505	.0530	.0555	.0579	.0604	.0629	.0654	.0679	.0703	.0728
13	.0315	.0334	.0354	.0374	.0395	.0416	.0438	.0459	.0481	.0504
14	.0182	.0196	.0210	.0225	.0240	.0256	.0272	.0289	.0306	.0324
15	.0098	.0107	.0116	.0126	.0136	.0147	.0158	.0169	.0182	.0194
16	.0050	.0055	.0060	.0066	.0072	.0079	.0086	.0093	.0101	.0109
17	.0024	.0026	.0029	.0033	.0036	.0040	.0044	.0048	.0053	.0058
18	.0011	.0012	.0014	.0015	.0017	.0019	.0021	.0024	.0026	.0029
19	.0005	.0005	.0006	.0007	.0008	.0009	.0010	.0011	.0012	.0014
20	.0002	.0002	.0002	.0003	.0003	.0004	.0004	.0005	.0005	.0006
21	.0001	.0001	.0001	.0001	.0001	.0002	.0002	.0002	.0002	.0003
22	.0000	.0000	.0000	.0000	.0001	.0001	.0001	.0001	.0001	.0001

					λ					
x	9.1	9.2	9.3	9.4	9.5	9.6	9.7	9.8	9.9	10
0	.0001	.0001	.0001	.0001	.0001	.0001	.0001	.0001	.0001	.0000
1	.0010	.0009	.0009	.0008	.0007	.0007	.0006	.0005	.0005	.0005
2	.0046	.0043	.0040	.0037	.0034	.0031	.0029	.0027	.0025	.0023
3	.0140	.0131	.0123	.0115	.0107	.0100	.0093	.0087	.0081	.0076
4	.0319	.0302	.0285	.0269	.0254	.0240	.0226	.0213	.0201	.0189
5	.0581	.0555	.0530	.0506	.0483	.0460	.0439	.0418	.0398	.0378
6	.0881	.0851	.0822	.0793	.0764	.0736	.0709	.0682	.0656	.0631
7	.1145	.1118	.1091	.1064	.1037	.1010	.0982	.0955	.0928	.0901
8	.1302	.1286	.1269	.1251	.1232	.1212	.1191	.1170	.1148	.1126
9	.1317	.1315	.1311	.1306	.1300	.1293	.1284	.1274	.1263	.1251

TABLE 8 (Cont'd)

					λ					
x	9.1	9.2	9.3	9.4	9.5	9.6	9.7	9.8	9.9	10
10	.1198	.1210	.1219	.1228	.1235	.1241	.1245	.1249	.1250	.1251
11	.0991	.1012	.1031	.1049	.1067	.1083	.1098	.1112	.1125	.1137
12	.0752	.0776	.0799	.0822	.0844	.0866	.0888	.0908	.0928	.0948
13	.0526	.0549	.0572	.0594	.0617	.0640	.0662	.0685	.0707	.0729
14	.0342	.0361	.0380	.0399	.0419	.0439	.0459	.0479	.0500	.0521
15	.0208	.0221	.0235	.0250	.0265	.0281	.0297	.0313	.0330	.0347
16	.0118	.0127	.0137	.0147	.0157	.0168	.0180	.0192	.0204	.0217
17	.0063	.0069	.0075	.0081	.0088	.0095	.0103	.0111	.0119	.0128
18	.0032	.0035	.0039	.0042	.0046	.0051	.0055	.0060	.0065	.0071
19	.0015	.0017	.0019	.0021	.0023	.0026	.0028	.0031	.0034	.0037
20	.0007	.0008	.0009	.0010	.0011	.0012	.0014	.0015	.0017	.0019
21	.0003	.0003	.0004	.0004	.0005	.0006	.0006	.0007	.0008	.0009
22	.0001	.0001	.0002	.0002	.0002	.0002	.0003	.0003	.0004	.0004
23	.0000	.0001	.0001	.0001	.0001	.0001	.0001	.0001	.0002	.0002
24	.0000	.0000	.0000	.0000	.0000	.0000	.0000	.0001	.0001	.0001

					λ					
x	11	12	13	14	15	16	17	18	19	20
0	.0000	.0000	.0000	.0000	.0000	.0000	.0000	.0000	.0000	.0000
1	.0002	.0001	.0000	.0000	.0000	.0000	.0000	.0000	.0000	.0000
2	.0010	.0004	.0002	.0001	.0000	.0000	.0000	.0000	.0000	.0000
3	.0037	.0018	.0008	.0004	.0002	.0001	.0000	.0000	.0000	.0000
4	.0102	.0053	.0027	.0013	.0006	.0003	.0001	.0001	.0000	.0000
5	.0224	.0127	.0070	.0037	.0019	.0010	.0005	.0002	.0001	.0001
6	.0411	.0255	.0152	.0087	.0048	.0026	.0014	.0007	.0004	.0002
7	.0646	.0437	.0281	.0174	.0104	.0060	.0034	.0018	.0010	.0005
8	.0888	.0655	.0457	.0304	.0194	.0120	.0072	.0042	.0024	.0013
9	.1085	.0874	.0661	.0473	.0324	.0213	.0135	.0083	.0050	.0029
10	.1194	.1048	.0859	.0663	.0486	.0341	.0230	.0150	.0095	.0058
11	.1194	.1144	.1015	.0844	.0663	.0496	.0355	.0245	.0164	.0106
12	.1094	.1144	.1099	.0984	.0829	.0661	.0504	.0368	.0259	.0176
13	.0926	.1056	.1099	.1060	.0956	.0814	.0658	.0509	.0378	.0271
14	.0728	.0905	.1021	.1060	.1024	.0930	.0800	.0655	.0514	.0387
15	.0534	.0724	.0885	.0989	.1024	.0992	.0906	.0786	.0650	.0516
16	.0367	.0543	.0719	.0866	.0960	.0992	.0963	.0884	.0772	.0646
17	.0237	.0383	.0550	.0713	.0847	.0934	.0963	.0936	.0863	.0760
18	.0145	.0256	.0397	.0554	.0706	.0830	.0909	.0936	.0911	.0844
19	.0084	.0161	.0272	.0409	.0557	.0699	.0814	.0887	.0911	.0888
20	.0046	.0097	.0177	.0286	.0418	.0559	.0692	.0798	.0866	.0888
21	.0024	.0055	.0109	.0191	.0299	.0426	.0560	.0684	.0783	.0846
22	.0012	.0030	.0065	.0121	.0204	.0310	.0433	.0560	.0676	.0769
23	.0006	.0016	.0037	.0074	.0133	.0216	.0320	.0438	.0559	.0669
24	.0003	.0008	.0020	.0043	.0083	.0144	.0226	.0328	.0442	.0557
25	.0001	.0004	.0010	.0024	.0050	.0092	.0154	.0237	.0336	.0446
26	.0000	.0002	.0005	.0013	.0029	.0057	.0101	.0164	.0246	.0343
27	.0000	.0001	.0002	.0007	.0016	.0034	.0063	.0109	.0173	.0254
28	.0000	.0000	.0001	.0003	.0009	.0019	.0038	.0070	.0117	.0181
29	.0000	.0000	.0001	.0002	.0004	.0011	.0023	.0044	.0077	.0125
30	.0000	.0000	.0000	.0001	.0002	.0006	.0013	.0026	.0049	.0083
31	.0000	.0000	.0000	.0000	.0001	.0003	.0007	.0015	.0030	.0054
32	.0000	.0000	.0000	.0000	.0001	.0001	.0004	.0009	.0018	.0034
33	.0000	.0000	.0000	.0000	.0000	.0001	.0002	.0005	.0010	.0020
34	.0000	.0000	.0000	.0000	.0000	.0000	.0001	.0002	.0006	.0012
35	.0000	.0000	.0000	.0000	.0000	.0000	.0000	.0001	.0003	.0007
36	.0000	.0000	.0000	.0000	.0000	.0000	.0000	.0001	.0002	.0004
37	.0000	.0000	.0000	.0000	.0000	.0000	.0000	.0000	.0001	.0002
38	.0000	.0000	.0000	.0000	.0000	.0000	.0000	.0000	.0000	.0001
39	.0000	.0000	.0000	.0000	.0000	.0000	.0000	.0000	.0000	.0001

† Used by permission from R. S. Burrington and D. C. May, Jr., "Handbook of Probability and Statistics with Tables," McGraw-Hill Book Company, New York, 1953.

TABLE 9 VALUES OF F EXCEEDED WITH PROBABILITIES OF 5 AND 1 PERCENT†

Table 9 gives values of F exceeded with probabilities 5 and 1 percent (shown in red). The degrees of freedom in the numerator are shown at the top of the table, and the degrees of freedom in the denominator are shown down the side of the table. If there are 5 degrees of freedom in the numerator and 14 in the denominator, the probability is 5 percent that F will exceed 2.96 and 1 percent that F will exceed 4.69.

f_2	f_1 degrees of freedom (for numerator)															f_2
	1	2	3	4	5	6	8	10	12	16	20	30	40	50	100	
1	161	200	216	225	230	234	239	242	244	246	248	250	251	252	253	1
	4,052	4,999	5,403	5,625	5,764	5,859	5,981	6,056	6,106	6,169	6,208	6,258	6,286	6,302	6,334	
2	18.51	19.00	19.16	19.25	19.30	19.33	19.37	19.39	19.41	19.43	19.44	19.46	19.47	19.47	19.49	2
	98.49	99.00	99.17	99.25	99.30	99.33	99.36	99.40	99.42	99.44	99.45	99.47	99.48	99.48	99.49	
3	10.13	9.55	9.28	9.12	9.01	8.94	8.84	8.78	8.74	8.69	8.66	8.62	8.60	8.58	8.56	3
	34.12	30.82	29.46	28.71	28.24	27.91	27.49	27.23	27.05	26.83	26.69	26.50	26.41	26.35	26.23	
4	7.71	6.94	6.59	6.39	6.26	6.16	6.04	5.96	5.91	5.84	5.80	5.74	5.71	5.70	5.66	4
	21.20	18.00	16.69	15.98	15.52	15.21	14.80	14.54	14.37	14.15	14.02	13.83	13.74	13.69	13.57	
5	6.61	5.79	5.41	5.19	5.05	4.95	4.82	4.74	4.68	4.60	4.56	4.50	4.46	4.44	4.40	5
	16.26	13.27	12.06	11.39	10.97	10.67	10.27	10.05	9.89	9.68	9.55	9.38	9.29	9.24	9.13	
6	5.99	5.14	4.76	4.53	4.39	4.28	4.15	4.06	4.00	3.92	3.87	3.81	3.77	3.75	3.71	6
	13.74	10.92	9.78	9.15	8.75	8.47	8.10	7.87	7.72	7.52	7.39	7.23	7.14	7.09	6.99	
7	5.59	4.74	4.35	4.12	3.97	3.87	3.73	3.63	3.57	3.49	3.44	3.38	3.34	3.32	3.28	7
	12.25	9.55	8.45	7.85	7.46	7.19	6.84	6.62	6.47	6.27	6.15	5.98	5.90	5.85	5.75	
8	5.32	4.46	4.07	3.84	3.69	3.58	3.44	3.34	3.28	3.20	3.15	3.08	3.05	3.03	2.98	8
	11.26	8.65	7.59	7.01	6.63	6.37	6.03	5.82	5.67	5.48	5.36	5.20	5.11	5.06	4.96	
9	5.12	4.26	3.86	3.63	3.48	3.37	3.23	3.13	3.07	2.98	2.93	2.86	2.82	2.80	2.76	9
	10.56	8.02	6.99	6.42	6.06	5.80	5.47	5.26	5.11	4.92	4.80	4.64	4.56	4.51	4.41	
10	4.96	4.10	3.71	3.48	3.33	3.22	3.07	2.97	2.91	2.82	2.77	2.70	2.67	2.64	2.59	10
	10.04	7.56	6.55	5.99	5.64	5.39	5.06	4.85	4.71	4.52	4.41	4.25	4.17	4.12	4.01	
11	4.84	3.98	3.59	3.36	3.20	3.09	2.95	2.86	2.79	2.70	2.65	2.57	2.53	2.50	2.45	11
	9.65	7.20	6.22	5.67	5.32	5.07	4.74	4.54	4.40	4.21	4.10	3.94	3.86	3.80	3.70	
12	4.75	3.88	3.49	3.26	3.11	3.00	2.85	2.76	2.69	2.60	2.54	2.46	2.42	2.40	2.35	12
	9.33	6.93	5.95	5.41	5.06	4.82	4.50	4.30	4.16	3.98	3.86	3.70	3.61	3.56	3.46	
13	4.67	3.80	3.41	3.18	3.02	2.92	2.77	2.67	2.60	2.51	2.46	2.38	2.34	2.32	2.26	13
	9.07	6.70	5.74	5.20	4.86	4.62	4.30	4.10	3.96	3.78	3.67	3.51	3.42	3.37	3.27	
14	4.60	3.74	3.34	3.11	2.96	2.85	2.70	2.60	2.53	2.44	2.39	2.31	2.27	2.24	2.19	14
	8.86	6.51	5.56	5.03	4.69	4.46	4.14	3.94	3.80	3.62	3.51	3.34	3.26	3.21	3.11	
15	4.54	3.68	3.29	3.06	2.90	2.79	2.64	2.55	2.48	2.39	2.33	2.25	2.21	2.18	2.12	15
	8.68	6.36	5.42	4.89	4.56	4.32	4.00	3.80	3.67	3.48	3.36	3.20	3.12	3.07	2.97	
16	4.49	3.63	3.24	3.01	2.85	2.74	2.59	2.49	2.42	2.33	2.28	2.20	2.16	2.13	2.07	16
	8.53	6.23	5.29	4.77	4.44	4.20	3.89	3.69	3.55	3.37	3.25	3.10	3.01	2.96	2.86	
17	4.45	3.59	3.20	2.96	2.81	2.70	2.55	2.45	2.38	2.29	2.23	2.15	2.11	2.08	2.02	17
	8.40	6.11	5.18	4.67	4.34	4.10	3.79	3.59	3.45	3.27	3.16	3.00	2.92	2.86	2.76	

TABLE 9   (Cont'd)

f_2	1	2	3	4	5	6	8	10	12	16	20	30	40	50	100	f_2
						f_1 degrees of freeedom (for numerator)										
18	4.41	3.55	3.16	2.93	2.77	2.66	2.51	2.41	2.34	2.25	2.19	2.11	2.07	2.04	1.98	18
	8.28	6.01	5.09	4.58	4.25	4.01	3.71	3.51	3.37	3.19	3.07	2.91	2.83	2.78	2.68	
19	4.38	3.52	3.13	2.90	2.74	2.63	2.48	2.38	2.31	2.21	2.15	2.07	2.02	2.00	1.94	19
	8.18	5.93	5.01	4.50	4.17	3.94	3.63	3.43	3.30	3.12	3.00	2.84	2.76	2.70	2.60	
20	4.35	3.49	3.10	2.87	2.71	2.60	2.45	2.35	2.28	2.18	2.12	2.04	1.99	1.96	1.90	20
	8.10	5.85	4.94	4.43	4.10	3.87	3.56	3.37	3.23	3.05	2.94	2.77	2.69	2.63	2.53	
25	4.24	3.38	2.99	2.76	2.60	2.49	2.34	2.24	2.16	2.06	2.00	1.92	1.87	1.84	1.77	25
	7.77	5.57	4.68	4.18	3.86	3.63	3.32	3.13	2.99	2.81	2.70	2.54	2.45	2.40	2.29	
30	4.17	3.32	2.92	2.69	2.53	2.42	2.27	2.16	2.09	1.99	1.93	1.84	1.79	1.76	1.69	30
	7.56	5.39	4.51	4.02	3.70	3.47	3.17	2.98	2.84	2.66	2.55	2.38	2.29	2.24	2.13	
40	4.08	3.23	2.84	2.61	2.45	2.34	2.18	2.07	2.00	1.90	1.84	1.74	1.69	1.66	1.59	40
	7.31	5.18	4.31	3.83	3.51	3.29	2.99	2.80	2.66	2.49	2.37	2.20	2.11	2.05	1.94	
50	4.03	3.18	2.79	2.56	2.40	2.29	2.13	2.02	1.95	1.85	1.78	1.69	1.63	1.60	1.52	50
	7.17	5.06	4.20	3.72	3.41	3.18	2.88	2.70	2.56	2.39	2.26	2.10	2.00	1.94	1.82	
60	4.00	3.15	2.76	2.52	2.37	2.25	2.10	1.99	1.92	1.81	1.75	1.65	1.59	1.56	1.48	60
	7.08	4.98	4.13	3.65	3.34	3.12	2.82	2.63	2.50	2.32	2.20	2.03	1.93	1.87	1.74	
80	3.96	3.11	2.72	2.48	2.33	2.21	2.05	1.95	1.88	1.77	1.70	1.60	1.54	1.51	1.42	80
	6.96	4.88	4.04	3.56	3.25	3.04	2.74	2.55	2.41	2.24	2.11	1.94	1.84	1.78	1.65	
100	3.94	3.09	2.70	2.46	2.30	2.19	2.03	1.92	1.85	1.75	1.68	1.57	1.51	1.48	1.39	100
	6.90	4.82	3.98	3.51	3.20	2.99	2.69	2.51	2.36	2.19	2.06	1.89	1.79	1.73	1.59	
150	3.91	3.06	2.67	2.43	2.27	2.16	2.00	1.89	1.82	1.71	1.64	1.54	1.47	1.44	1.34	150
	6.81	4.75	3.91	3.44	3.14	2.92	2.62	2.44	2.30	2.12	2.00	1.83	1.72	1.66	1.51	
200	3.89	3.04	2.65	2.41	2.26	2.14	1.98	1.87	1.80	1.69	1.62	1.52	1.45	1.42	1.32	200
	6.76	4.71	3.88	3.41	3.11	2.90	2.60	2.41	2.28	2.09	1.97	1.79	1.69	1.62	1.48	
400	3.86	3.02	2.62	2.39	2.23	2.12	1.96	1.85	1.78	1.67	1.60	1.49	1.42	1.38	1.28	400
	6.70	4.66	3.83	3.36	3.06	2.85	2.55	2.37	2.23	2.04	1.92	1.74	1.64	1.57	1.42	
1000	3.85	3.00	2.61	2.38	2.22	2.10	1.95	1.84	1.76	1.65	1.58	1.47	1.41	1.36	1.26	1000
	6.66	4.62	3.80	3.34	3.04	2.82	2.53	2.34	2.20	2.01	1.89	1.71	1.61	1.54	1.38	
∞	3.84	2.99	2.60	2.37	2.21	2.09	1.94	1.83	1.75	1.64	1.57	1.46	1.40	1.35	1.24	∞
	6.64	4.60	3.78	3.32	3.02	2.80	2.51	2.32	2.18	1.99	1.87	1.69	1.59	1.52	1.36	

† This table is adapted by permission from "Statistical Methods," 6th ed., by George W. Snedecor and William G. Cochran, © 1967 by The Iowa State University Press.

TABLE 10 PERCENTAGE POINTS FOR t DISTRIBUTIONS†

Table 10 gives values of a t-distributed variable exceeded with the specified probability, for n degrees of freedom. If **u** is t-distributed with 19 degrees of freedom, values higher than 1.729 occur less than 5 percent of the time. This is a one-tail probability. Values outside the range -1.729 to 1.729 occur less than 10 percent of the time. (Table 9.3 in the text gives two-tail probabilities.)

	Probability								
n	.60	.70	.80	.90	.95	.975	.990	.995	.999
1	.325	.727	1.376	3.078	6.314	12.71	31.82	63.66	318.3
2	.289	.617	1.061	1.886	2.920	4.303	6.965	9.925	22.33
3	.277	.584	.978	1.638	2.353	3.182	4.541	5.841	10.22
4	.271	.569	.941	1.533	2.132	2.776	3.747	4.604	7.173
5	.267	.559	.920	1.476	2.015	2.571	3.365	4.032	5.893
6	.265	.553	.906	1.440	1.943	2.447	3.143	3.707	5.208
7	.263	.549	.896	1.415	1.895	2.365	2.998	3.499	4.785
8	.262	.546	.889	1.397	1.860	2.306	2.896	3.355	4.501
9	.261	.543	.883	1.383	1.833	2.262	2.821	3.250	4.297
10	.260	.542	.879	1.372	1.812	2.228	2.764	3.169	4.144
11	.260	.540	.876	1.363	1.796	2.201	2.718	3.106	4.025
12	.259	.539	.873	1.356	1.782	2.179	2.681	3.055	3.930
13	.259	.538	.870	1.350	1.771	2.160	2.650	3.012	3.852
14	.258	.537	.868	1.345	1.761	2.145	2.624	2.977	3.787
15	.258	.536	.866	1.341	1.753	2.131	2.602	2.947	3.733
16	.258	.535	.865	1.337	1.746	2.120	2.583	2.921	3.686
17	.257	.534	.863	1.333	1.740	2.110	2.567	2.898	3.646
18	.257	.534	.862	1.330	1.734	2.101	2.552	2.878	3.611
19	.257	.533	.861	1.328	1.729	2.093	2.539	2.861	3.579
20	.257	.533	.860	1.325	1.725	2.086	2.528	2.845	3.552
21	.257	.532	.859	1.323	1.721	2.080	2.518	2.831	3.527
22	.256	.532	.858	1.321	1.717	2.074	2.508	2.819	3.505
23	.256	.532	.858	1.319	1.714	2.069	2.500	2.807	3.485
24	.256	.531	.857	1.318	1.711	2.064	2.492	2.797	3.467
25	.256	.531	.856	1.316	1.708	2.060	2.485	2.787	3.450
26	.256	.531	.856	1.315	1.706	2.056	2.479	2.779	3.435
27	.256	.531	.855	1.314	1.703	2.052	2.473	2.771	3.421
28	.256	.530	.855	1.313	1.701	2.048	2.467	2.763	3.408
29	.256	.530	.854	1.311	1.699	2.045	2.462	2.756	3.396
30	.256	.530	.854	1.310	1.697	2.042	2.457	2.750	3.385
40	.255	.529	.851	1.303	1.684	2.021	2.423	2.704	3.307
60	.254	.527	.848	1.296	1.671	2.000	2.390	2.660	3.232
120	.254	.526	.845	1.289	1.658	1.980	2.358	2.617	3.373
∞	.253	.524	.842	1.282	1.645	1.960	2.326	2.576	3.090

† Adapted from R. A. Fisher and F. Yates, "Statistical Tables for Biological, Agricultural, and Medical Research," Table III, 6th ed., Oliver and Boyd Ltd., Edinburgh, 1963. By permission of the authors and publishers.

TABLE 11   VALUES OF $f(D)$†

Table 11 gives $f(D)$ as a function of D (see Section 12.7 of the text). If $D = 1.62$, we read from the table that $f(D) = .02217$. For $D = 3.76$, we find $f(D) = .0^4 2016$, which is shorthand for $.00002016$.

D	.00	.01	.02	.03	.04	.05	.06	.07	.08	.09
.0	.3989	.3940	.3890	.3841	.3793	.3744	.3697	.3649	.3602	.3556
.1	.3509	.3464	.3418	.3373	.3328	.3284	.3240	.3197	.3154	.3111
.2	.3069	.3027	.2986	.2944	.2904	.2863	.2824	.2784	.2745	.2706
.3	.2668	.2630	.2592	.2555	.2518	.2481	.2445	.2409	.2374	.2339
.4	.2304	.2270	.2236	.2203	.2169	.2137	.2104	.2072	.2040	.2009
.5	.1978	.1947	.1917	.1887	.1857	.1828	.1790	.1771	.1742	.1714
.6	.1687	.1659	.1633	.1606	.1580	.1554	.1528	.1503	.1478	.1453
.7	.1429	.1405	.1381	.1358	.1334	.1312	.1289	.1267	.1245	.1223
.8	.1202	.1181	.1160	.1140	.1120	.1100	.1080	.1061	.1042	.1023
.9	.1004	.09860	.09680	.09503	.09328	.09156	.08986	.08819	.08654	.08491
1.0	.08332	.08174	.08019	.07866	.07716	.07568	.07422	.07279	.07138	.06999
1.1	.06862	.06727	.06595	.06465	.06336	.06210	.06086	.05964	.05844	.05726
1.2	.05610	.05496	.05384	.05274	.05165	.05059	.04954	.04851	.04750	.04650
1.3	.04553	.04457	.04363	.04270	.04179	.04090	.04002	.03916	.03831	.03748
1.4	.03667	.03587	.03508	.03431	.03356	.03281	.03208	.03137	.03067	.02998
1.5	.02931	.02865	.02800	.02736	.02674	.02612	.02552	.02494	.02436	.02380
1.6	.02324	.02270	.02217	.02165	.02114	.02064	.02015	.01967	.01920	.01874
1.7	.01829	.01785	.01742	.01699	.01658	.01617	.01578	.01539	.01501	.01464
1.8	.01428	.01392	.01357	.01323	.01290	.01257	.01226	.01195	.01164	.01134
1.9	.01105	.01077	.01049	.01022	$.0^2 9957$	$.0^2 9698$	$.0^2 9445$	$.0^2 9198$	$.0^2 8957$	$.0^2 8721$
2.0	$.0^2 8491$	$.0^2 8266$	$.0^2 8046$	$.0^2 7832$	$.0^2 7623$	$.0^2 7418$	$.0^2 7219$	$.0^2 7024$	$.0^2 6835$	$.0^2 6649$
2.1	$.0^2 6468$	$.0^2 6292$	$.0^2 6120$	$.0^2 5952$	$.0^2 5788$	$.0^2 5628$	$.0^2 5472$	$.0^2 5320$	$.0^2 5172$	$.0^2 5028$
2.2	$.0^2 4887$	$.0^2 4750$	$.0^2 4616$	$.0^2 4486$	$.0^2 4358$	$.0^2 4235$	$.0^2 4114$	$.0^2 3996$	$.0^2 3882$	$.0^2 3770$
2.3	$.0^2 3662$	$.0^2 3556$	$.0^2 3453$	$.0^2 3352$	$.0^2 3255$	$.0^2 3159$	$.0^2 3067$	$.0^2 2977$	$.0^2 2889$	$.0^2 2804$
2.4	$.0^2 2720$	$.0^2 2640$	$.0^2 2561$	$.0^2 2484$	$.0^2 2410$	$.0^2 2337$	$.0^2 2267$	$.0^2 2199$	$.0^2 2132$	$.0^2 2067$
2.5	$.0^2 2004$	$.0^2 1943$	$.0^2 1883$	$.0^2 1826$	$.0^2 1769$	$.0^2 1715$	$.0^2 1662$	$.0^2 1610$	$.0^2 1560$	$.0^2 1511$
2.6	$.0^2 1464$	$.0^2 1418$	$.0^2 1373$	$.0^2 1330$	$.0^2 1288$	$.0^2 1247$	$.0^2 1207$	$.0^2 1169$	$.0^2 1132$	$.0^2 1095$
2.7	$.0^2 1060$	$.0^2 1026$	$.0^3 9928$	$.0^3 9607$	$.0^3 9295$	$.0^3 8992$	$.0^3 8699$	$.0^3 8414$	$.0^3 8138$	$.0^3 7870$
2.8	$.0^3 7611$	$.0^3 7359$	$.0^3 7115$	$.0^3 6879$	$.0^3 6650$	$.0^3 6428$	$.0^3 6213$	$.0^3 6004$	$.0^3 5802$	$.0^3 5606$
2.9	$.0^3 5417$	$.0^3 5233$	$.0^3 5055$	$.0^3 4883$	$.0^3 4716$	$.0^3 4555$	$.0^3 4398$	$.0^3 4247$	$.0^3 4101$	$.0^3 3959$
3.0	$.0^3 3822$	$.0^3 3689$	$.0^3 3560$	$.0^3 3436$	$.0^3 3316$	$.0^3 3199$	$.0^3 3087$	$.0^3 2978$	$.0^3 2873$	$.0^3 2771$
3.1	$.0^3 2673$	$.0^3 2577$	$.0^3 2485$	$.0^3 2396$	$.0^3 2311$	$.0^3 2227$	$.0^3 2147$	$.0^3 2070$	$.0^3 1995$	$.0^3 1922$
3.2	$.0^3 1852$	$.0^3 1785$	$.0^3 1720$	$.0^3 1657$	$.0^3 1596$	$.0^3 1537$	$.0^3 1480$	$.0^3 1426$	$.0^3 1373$	$.0^3 1322$
3.3	$.0^3 1273$	$.0^3 1225$	$.0^3 1179$	$.0^3 1135$	$.0^3 1093$	$.0^3 1051$	$.0^3 1012$	$.0^4 9734$	$.0^4 9365$	$.0^4 9009$
3.4	$.0^4 8666$	$.0^4 8335$	$.0^4 8016$	$.0^4 7709$	$.0^4 7413$	$.0^4 7127$	$.0^4 6852$	$.0^4 6587$	$.0^4 6331$	$.0^4 6085$
3.5	$.0^4 5848$	$.0^4 5620$	$.0^4 5400$	$.0^4 5188$	$.0^4 4984$	$.0^4 4788$	$.0^4 4599$	$.0^4 4417$	$.0^4 4242$	$.0^4 4073$
3.6	$.0^4 3911$	$.0^4 3755$	$.0^4 3605$	$.0^4 3460$	$.0^4 3321$	$.0^4 3188$	$.0^4 3059$	$.0^4 2935$	$.0^4 2816$	$.0^4 2702$
3.7	$.0^4 2592$	$.0^4 2486$	$.0^4 2385$	$.0^4 2287$	$.0^4 2193$	$.0^4 2103$	$.0^4 2016$	$.0^4 1933$	$.0^4 1853$	$.0^4 1776$
3.8	$.0^4 1702$	$.0^4 1632$	$.0^4 1563$	$.0^4 1498$	$.0^4 1435$	$.0^4 1375$	$.0^4 1317$	$.0^4 1262$	$.0^4 1208$	$.0^4 1157$
3.9	$.0^4 1108$	$.0^4 1061$	$.0^4 1016$	$.0^5 9723$	$.0^5 9307$	$.0^5 8908$	$.0^5 8518$	$.0^5 8158$	$.0^5 7806$	$.0^5 7469$
4.0	$.0^5 7145$	$.0^5 6835$	$.0^5 6538$	$.0^5 6253$	$.0^5 5980$	$.0^5 5718$	$.0^5 5468$	$.0^5 5227$	$.0^5 4997$	$.0^5 4777$
4.1	$.0^5 4566$	$.0^5 4364$	$.0^5 4170$	$.0^5 3985$	$.0^5 3807$	$.0^5 3637$	$.0^5 3475$	$.0^5 3319$	$.0^5 3170$	$.0^5 3027$
4.2	$.0^5 2891$	$.0^5 2760$	$.0^5 2635$	$.0^5 2516$	$.0^5 2402$	$.0^5 2292$	$.0^5 2188$	$.0^5 2088$	$.0^5 1992$	$.0^5 1901$
4.3	$.0^5 1814$	$.0^5 1730$	$.0^5 1650$	$.0^5 1574$	$.0^5 1501$	$.0^5 1431$	$.0^5 1365$	$.0^5 1301$	$.0^5 1241$	$.0^5 1183$
4.4	$.0^5 1127$	$.0^5 1074$	$.0^5 1024$	$.0^6 9756$	$.0^6 9296$	$.0^6 8857$	$.0^6 8437$	$.0^6 8037$	$.0^6 7655$	$.0^6 7290$
4.5	$.0^6 6942$	$.0^6 6610$	$.0^6 6294$	$.0^6 5992$	$.0^6 5704$	$.0^6 5429$	$.0^6 5167$	$.0^6 4917$	$.0^6 4679$	$.0^6 4452$
4.6	$.0^6 4236$	$.0^6 4029$	$.0^6 3833$	$.0^6 3645$	$.0^6 3467$	$.0^6 3297$	$.0^6 3135$	$.0^6 2981$	$.0^6 2834$	$.0^6 2694$
4.7	$.0^6 2560$	$.0^6 2433$	$.0^6 2313$	$.0^6 2197$	$.0^6 2088$	$.0^6 1984$	$.0^6 1884$	$.0^6 1790$	$.0^6 1700$	$.0^6 1615$
4.8	$.0^6 1533$	$.0^6 1456$	$.0^6 1382$	$.0^6 1312$	$.0^6 1246$	$.0^6 1182$	$.0^6 1122$	$.0^6 1065$	$.0^6 1011$	$.0^7 9588$
4.9	$.0^7 9096$	$.0^7 8629$	$.0^7 8185$	$.0^7 7763$	$.0^7 7362$	$.0^7 6982$	$.0^7 6620$	$.0^7 6276$	$.0^7 5950$	$.0^7 5640$

† Reproduced by permission of the copyright holders, The President and Fellows of Harvard College, from Unit Normal Loss Function Tables in Robert Schlaifer, "Introduction to Statistics for Business Decisions," McGraw-Hill Book Company, New York, 1961.

BIBLIOGRAPHY

Probability

Feller, W.: "An Introduction to Probability Theory and Its Applications," vol. 1, 3d ed., John Wiley & Sons, Inc., New York, 1968.

> The classic treatment of probability in discrete sample spaces; the patient reader will be well rewarded, but do not be fooled by the title; this is an "introduction" that says about all there is to say on the subject.

Feller, W.: "An Introduction to Probability Theory and Its Applications," vol. 2, 2d ed., John Wiley & Sons, Inc., New York, 1971.

> Extends the discussion of volume 1 from discrete to continuous sample spaces; requires a knowledge of calculus; another classic for the patient reader.

Mosteller, F., R. E. K. Rourke, and *G. B. Thomas, Jr.:* "Probability with Statistical Applications," 2d ed., Addison Wesley Publishing Company, Inc., Reading, Mass., 1970.

> An outstanding introductory text which covers much of the material on inference in this book, as well as an extended treatment of probability; written at the mathematical level of this book.

General Statistics—Not Requiring Calculus

Blackwell, D.: "Basic Statistics," McGraw-Hill Book Company, New York, 1969.

> An outstanding statistician presents a clear, concise, elementary introduction to statistics, with a Bayesian emphasis.

Dixon, W. J., and *F. J. Massey, Jr.:* "Introduction to Statistical Analysis," 3d ed., McGraw-Hill Book Company, New York, 1969.

> An introductory text with illustrations from many fields of application; written at the mathematical level of this text; good source for nonparametric statistics, with specialized tables.

Guenther, W. C.: "Concepts of Statistical Inference," McGraw-Hill Book Company, New York, 1965.

> Covers the material in Chapters 1 to 13 in slightly greater detail but at the same level of mathematical difficulty; well written.

Moroney, M. J.: "Facts from Figures," 3d ed., Penguin Books, Inc., Baltimore, 1956.

> A fine coverage of basic statistics with emphasis on industrial applications; at the mathematical level of our text, but written with an English flavor; paperback.

Snedecor, G. W., and *W. G. Cochran:* "Statistical Methods," 6th ed., The Iowa State University Press, Ames, Iowa, 1967.

> A standard reference for working statisticians; slanted toward problems in experimental situations; extensive coverage of methods in readable language at the mathematical level of this book.

Yamane, T.: "Statistics, an Introductory Analysis," 2d ed., Harper & Row, Publishers, Incorporated, New York, 1967.

> A very broad coverage of basic general statistical techniques; readable text written at the mathematical level of our text; extends the coverage of this book slightly.

General Statistics—Calculus Required

Freund, J. E.: "Mathematical Statistics," 2d ed., Prentice-Hall, Inc., Englewood Cliffs, N.J., 1971.

> Basic mathematical statistics through analysis of variance; assumes a knowledge of elementary calculus.

Hoel, P. G.: "Introduction to Mathematical Statistics," 4th ed., John Wiley & Sons, New York, 1971.

> A mathematical theory of statistics; assumes knowledge of calculus.

Contingency Tables, Experimental Design, and Variance Analysis

Cochran, W. G., and *G. Cox:* "Experimental Designs," 2d ed., John Wiley & Sons, Inc., New York, 1971.

> The standard reference used by practicing statisticians for techniques of experimental design (how to learn most from an experiment); not mathematically difficult, but demanding great concentration from the novice; a rewarding effort if you perform experiments.

Maxwell, A. E.: "Analyzing Qualitative Data," John Wiley & Sons, Inc., New York, 1961.

Chi-square and other methods for analyzing data in categories, as in contingency tables; rank correlation; attitude measurement; oriented to the behavioral sciences.

Statistical Decision Theory

Schlaifer, R.: "Introduction to Statistics for Business Decisions," McGraw-Hill Book Company, New York, 1961.

Subjective probability, utility theory, and Bayes' theorem are combined in this already classic statement of the modern approach to decision-making; a full treatment of the material in Chapter 12 of our text.

Schlaifer, R.: "Analysis of Decisions under Uncertainty," McGraw-Hill Book Company, New York, 1969.

Extends Schlaifer's work on decision analysis with new emphasis on large-scale problems at the policy-making level.

Schmitt, S.: "Measuring Uncertainty: An Elementary Introduction to Bayesian Statistics," Addison-Wesley Publishing Company, Inc., Reading, Mass., 1969.

Introduction to modern decision theory and enjoyable, too!

Multivariate and Time Series Analysis, Econometrics

Butler, W. F., and *R. A. Kavesh* (eds.): "How Business Economists Forecast," Prentice-Hall, Inc., Englewood Cliffs, N.J., 1966.

A collection of articles by forecasters on tools, techniques, and problems in forecasting in business; readable, practical; not the best source for the statistical theory of forecasting (see Fox or Johnston).

Ferber, R., and *P. J. Verdoorn:* "Research Methods in Economics and Business," The Macmillan Company, New York, 1962.

Gives an overview of research design and the collection and analysis of data; deals with time series analysis and the cross-section approach, forecasting, demand analysis, and economic models; assumes elementary knowledge of economics and statistics.

Fox, K. A.: "Intermediate Economic Statistics," John Wiley & Sons, Inc., New York, 1968.

The statistical methods for economic research—simple and multiple regression analysis, the econometric analysis of single time series, and the construction of economic models; written at the mathematical level of this text, assuming knowledge of basic economics and statistics.

Johnston, J.: "Econometric Methods," 2d ed., McGraw-Hill Book Company, New York, 1972.

A sound treatment of econometrics, assuming knowledge of the material covered in this book, plus calculus and matrix algebra.

Morrison, D. F.: "Multivariate Statistical Methods," McGraw-Hill Book Company, New York, 1967.

The basic techniques for studying the relations among several characteristics of an individual; oriented to behavioral science research, with a mathematical level similar to this book's, but a much more detailed treatment.

Theil, H., J. C. G. Boot, and *T. Kloek:* "Operations Research and Quantitative Economics: An Elementary Introduction," McGraw-Hill Book Company, New York, 1965.

Integrates econometrics, statistics, and operations research with emphasis on basic ideas and results, not mathematics.

Index Numbers

Mudgett, B. D.: "Index Numbers," John Wiley & Sons, Inc., New York, 1951.

The problems in constructing and using index numbers; see more recent government publications for descriptions of current indexes.

U.S. Department of Labor: The Consumer Price Index: History and Techniques, *Bur. Labor Stat., Bull.* 1517, undated.

Describes the CPI with complete detail on items, weights, formulas, and data collection.

Quality Control

Duncan, A. J.: "Quality Control and Industrial Statistics," 3d ed., Richard D. Irwin, Inc., Homewood, Ill., 1965.

A comprehensive coverage of quality control and statistics used in industry; written at the mathematical level of this book.

Grant, E. L.: "Statistical Quality Control," 3d ed., McGraw-Hill Book Company, New York, 1964.

A practical discussion emphasizing control charts and acceptance sampling for the user; written at the mathematical level of this book.

Survey Methods

Cochran, W. G.: "Sampling Techniques," 2d ed., John Wiley & Sons, Inc., New York, 1963.

Sampling theory for use in sample surveys; assumes an understanding of probability theory and differential calculus.

Raj, D.: "The Design of Sample Surveys," McGraw-Hill Book Company, New York, 1972.

A comprehensive treatment at a modest mathematical level; an excellent reference source.

Nonparametric Statistics

Conover, W. J.: "Practical Non-parametric Statistics," John Wiley & Sons, Inc., New York, 1971.

An introductory text and reference book for applied-research workers; covers the important techniques thoroughly.

Noether, G. E.: "Elements of Non-parametric Statistics," John Wiley & Sons, Inc., New York, 1967.

   An introductory, elementary text; good as a starting point for the interested student.

Tables, Dictionaries, and Computers

Burrington, R. S., and *D. C. May, Jr.:* "Handbook of Probability and Statistics with Tables," 2d ed., McGraw-Hill Book Company, New York, 1970.

   A reference for quick summaries of key ideas in mathematical statistics, and a valuable source of tables; not a textbook.

Davis, G. B.: "An Introduction to Electronic Computers," 2d ed., McGraw-Hill Book Company, New York, 1971.

   A general introduction to computers and programming, including treatment of BASIC, FORTRAN, and COBOL.

Kendall, M. G., and *W. Buckland:* "A Dictionary of Statistical Terms," 3d ed., Hafner Publishing Company, Inc., New York, 1971.

   An excellent reference for the meaning of technical terms.

Shelby, S.: "Standard Mathematical Tables," 17th ed., The Chemical Rubber Company, Cleveland, Ohio, 1969.

   A standard source for reference tables.

INDEX

INDEX